C++ Windows NT Programming

SECOND EDITION

Mark Andrews

M&T BOOKS

M&T Books
A Division of MIS:Press, Inc.
A Subsidiary of Henry Holt and Company, Inc.
115 West 18th Street
New York, New York 10011
http://www.mispress.com

Limits of Liability and Disclaimer of Warranty

Library of Congress Cataloging-in-Publication Data

Andrews, Mark.
   C++ Windows NT programming / Mark Andrews. — 2nd ed.
     p.   cm.
   ISBN 1-55851-493-7
   1. C++ (Computer program language) 2. Microsoft Windows NT.
I. Title
QA76.73.C153A486   1996
005.26'2—dc20   96-26234
                                               CIP

10 9 8 7 6 5 4 3 2

Associate Publisher: *Paul Farrell*

Executive Editor: *Cary Sullivan*
Development Editor: *Judy Brief*
Copy Edit Manager: *Shari Chappell*

Production Editor: *Anne Incao*
Technical Editor: *Rex Jaeschke*
Copy Editor: *Betsy Hardinger*

Dedication

To Mother

CONTENTS

CHAPTER SEVEN: MULTITHREADING 367

PREFACE TO THE FIRST EDITION

There are many books about Microsoft Windows, and more and more books are being written about Windows NT. But this is the first programming book to focus on the most important new features of the Win32 operating system: features such as threads, pipes, console windows, network communications, and Windows NT graphics.

This book doesn't waste its pages or your time explaining the standard features of Windows NT that everyone knows about: features such as windows, icons, message-driven programs, and pull-down menus. Books about those subjects abound. Instead, this book deals exclusively with what's new and different about Windows NT: brand-new capabilities such as client-server communications, threading and multithreading, NT-style DLLs, 32-bit graphics, and support for networking protocols such as NetBEUI and TCP/IP. It explains how all these new features work, and it shows how you can use them in C++ applications written especially for Windows NT.

Also, because one line of source code is worth at least a thousand words, this book comes with a diskful of sample applications that show you simply and clearly how you can use the new features of Windows NT in your own programs. Source-code listings of all the sample programs in the book are provided on the bonus disk that is bundled with the volume. And you can use any of the code in the book and on its companion disk in any way you wish.

All the code in the book is written in C++, so you can easily port it to your own C++ Windows NT programs. All the sample programs were written using the Microsoft Visual C++ development system, so you'll need a Visual C++ development system if you want to compile them as they are written. Many code modules that appear in the programs are compiler-independent, and therefore can be compiled using Borland C++ 4.0 or any other C++ compiler that is compatible with Windows NT.

What You Need to Use This Book

You don't need any special hardware to run the example programs on your bonus disk, except what's required to run 32-bit Visual C++ and the Win32 SDK. You should have access to Version 3.1 or later of the Microsoft Windows NT SDK, and I recommend that you have Version 1.0 or later of the 32-bit edition of Microsoft Visual C++.

To make the best possible use of this volume, you should have a basic knowledge of Windows programming and a working knowledge of C++. You don't have to be a Windows guru or a world-class C++ developer to understand the material that's presented; if your Windows programming skills are a bit rusty or your knowledge of C++ is a little weak, that's OK. If you know what people mean when they say that Windows programs are message-based and event-driven, and if you have a general idea of what C++ classes and objects are and how they work, you probably have enough knowledge to follow most of the material in the book. In case you need extra help, a number of books about Windows programming and the C++ language are listed in the Bibliography.

Visual C++ and Windows NT

The example programs in this book were compiled using the Microsoft Visual C++ development system. This was not an easy decision to make; programmers who use Borland C++ outnumber those who use Visual C++, and many consider Version 4.0 of Borland C++ to be superior to Visual C++ in a number of ways. But the Windows interface that shipped with Borland C++ 4.0 didn't work on Windows NT, and that shortcoming made Visual C++ the only logical choice for writing the programs presented in this volume.

That doesn't mean that this book is useless if you have a Borland C++ computer. Much of the sample code written for the book is compiler-independent and can be used in programs that are compiled on any Windows NT–compatible compiler—including Borland 4.0. But the frameworks for most of the programs in the book were built using AppWizard, ClassWizard, and the graphically oriented development tools that come with Visual C++. So, to compile and link the example programs in the form in which they are written, you must have access to a Microsoft Visual C++ development system.

There's much, much more between these covers—far too much for me to explain in the Preface. So just plunge in. I hope you have as much fun reading this book as I had writing it. Happy programming!

Mark Andrews
Santa Clara, CA

Preface to the Second Edition

Windows NT has evolved so much since the first edition of this book was published that the first edition is beginning to look like something from an earlier era. With the introduction of version 4.0, Windows NT has taken on a new look that has left the old Windows 3 user interface behind us forever. And under the hood, Windows NT has been upgraded even more. So I'm very glad M&T Books has decided to publish a second edition of this volume.

The most obvious new feature of Windows NT 4.0 is a slick new desktop-style user interface that has unified the look and feel of Windows NT and Windows 95. This new user interface—just like the Windows 95 UI—sports a taskbar, a Start menu, drag-and-drop capabilities, and much more.

To the casual Windows NT user, the new interface doesn't amount to much more than an interesting facelift that makes Windows NT a little more user-friendly. It simplifies the job of navigating to different applications and opening them, and the new drag-and-drop feature makes file management a little easier. But the average Windows NT user would probably be hard-pressed to point out any more significant improvements than that.

To the observant Windows developer, however, the technological advances reflected in the new Windows NT interface are much more significant. In fact, if you look just beneath the surface of the Windows user interf<None>ace, you can see that it marks the beginning of a new era in Windows program design.

One of the most important new features of the new Windows NT UI is that every new user-interface tool built into it is also available to you for use in your own applications. For example, the Windows NT taskbar is implemented as a common control—

that is, a control that is available not only to the Windows operating system but also to designers of Windows applications. The drag-and-drop capabilities of the icons on the Windows NT desktop are implemented using OLE technology, which is also available for use by Windows application developers. And so on.

One new goal of this book is to show you how you can incorporate the new design features built into the Windows NT desktop into your own applications. Chapter 1, "Introducing Windows NT," new to this second edition, describes all the new kinds of controls and devices that are built into the new Windows NT desktop. It also presents an example program that shows how you can use the new common controls in your own Windows NT programs.

Of course, this book does not limit its focus to the new features that were added to Windows NT with the release of version 4.0. Along with showing you what's new and different, this book explores all the advanced features that have distinguished Windows NT from other versions of Windows all along.

In these pages, you will see how different the Windows NT operating system is from the operating systems of Windows 95, Windows 3.1, and earlier versions of Windows. The chapter that will help you sort all this out is Chapter 2, "Underneath Windows NT." In that chapter, you'll see how Windows NT was designed as a 32-bit operating system from the ground up, whereas Windows 95 is a cross between a 16-bit operating system and a 32-bit operating system. You'll learn what this difference means to Windows 95 and Windows NT programmers, and this insight will help you understand how to write better applications for both operating systems.

In subsequent chapters, this book introduces you to specific features of Windows NT. It's packed with sample code that shows you how you can incorporate each feature into your own Windows NT programs.

The source code for each example program is provided on the companion disk that comes with this volume.

Visual C++ and the MFC Library

To help you tap all the new power that's now built into Windows NT—and into its little cousin, Windows 95—Microsoft has overhauled both Visual C++ and the Microsoft Foundation Class (MFC) library, the two most popular programming tools for Windows developers. In fact, the newest releases of Visual C++ and the MFC library were designed specifically to support the new features of Windows 95 and version 4.0 of Windows NT.

Version 4.0 of MFC library, which some Microsoft executives have called the "new Windows API," has built-in support for all the new user-interface features of

Windows NT 4.0, including common controls, OLE controls, multithreading, new networking capabilities, and much more. In turn, Visual C++ 4.0 is equipped with a number of new tools to support all the new features of MFC 4.0. You'll learn about many of the new features of both Visual C++ 4.0 and MFC 4.0 in Chapter 4, "Programming Windows NT with Visual C++."

One major new feature of the MFC library is complete support for OLE controls—Microsoft's 32-bit successors the to 16-bit VBX controls that have proved to be so popular among Windows 3.1 programmers. To show you how you can take advantage of this new feature and start using OLE controls in your Windows applications, this book presents a new Chapter 5, "OLE Today," which focuses solely on the OLE mechanism and OLE controls. This new chapter presents a sample program that shows how you can use OLE controls in your Windows applications.

What's in This Book

C++ *Windows NT Programming* starts with four introductory chapters. Then it describes and demonstrates features of Windows NT in seven more chapters. The four introductory chapters cover the following topics:

+ Chapter 1, "Introducing Windows NT," explores all the new controls and devices built into the Windows NT 4.0 user interface. Chapter 1 also presents a sample application that shows how to create a Windows common control and incorporate it into a Windows NT application.

+ Chapter 2, "Underneath Windows NT," compares the Windows NT operating system with the operating systems of Windows 95 and earlier versions of Windows. A sample application presented in Chapter 2 shows how to use one of the most important features of Windows NT, the registry, in Windows NT programs.

+ Chapter 3, "The Win32 API," introduces the application programming interface that is encapsulated into the Microsoft Foundation Class library. Sample programs show how you can call functions provided in the Win32 API to write Windows NT applications without relying on the C++ classes supplied in MFC.

+ Chapter 4, "Programming Windows NT with Visual C++," introduces version 4.0 of the MFC library and version 4.1 of Microsoft Visual C++, the release of Visual C++ that was current when this book was written. Several sample programs show how to write simple Windows NT applications using Visual C++ and the MFC library.

The topics covered in Chapters 5 through 11 are as follows:

+ Chapter 5, "OLE Today," introduces OLE controls and OLE (object linking and embedding) technology and presents a sample program showing how you can create and use OLE controls in your own Windows NT applications.

+ Chapter 6, "Processes," explains how Windows NT processes work and demonstrates the use of console windows: DOS-style text windows that come in handy when you want to port a text-based application to Windows NT or when you want to do some special job the easy way, such as testing a snippet of code without having to compile a complete Windows-based application. With console windows, you can also execute MS-DOS programs under Windows NT, and you can communicate with computer systems running character-based operating systems. In Chapter 6, you'll learn how to use console windows in Windows NT applications, and you'll get a chance to compile, link, and execute two sample console applications.

+ Chapter 7, "Multithreading," explains one of the most important new features of Windows NT. Multithreading gives Windows NT applications the power to divide processes into threads that share CPU time in accordance with predetermined thread priorities. This chapter tells you everything you need to know to create multithreaded Windows NT programs. To illustrate the use of threads, the chapter presents several working applications that demonstrate multithreading and the use of thread-scheduling mechanisms such as mutexes, semaphores, and wait events.

+ Chapter 8, "Dynamic Link Libraries," explains and illustrates how DLLs are used in Windows NT. DLLs are an essential ingredient of Windows applications, and Windows NT handles DLLs in new and different ways—some of which have never before been documented. This chapter simplifies the topic of DLLs by dividing Windows NT DLLs into three neat categories and explaining how you can use each variety of DLL in your Windows NT applications.

+ Chapter 9, "Interprocess Communications", explains how Windows NT increases the amount of memory available for applications by using disk caching and file mapping, and how Windows NT enables processes to share data by using anonymous and named pipes. Pipes are communications conduits that carry information from one process to another or from one thread to another, either on the same workstation or over a network. Windows NT supports both anonymous pipes, which connect related processes or threads, and named pipes, which can connect unrelated threads or processes and can work across a network. To illustrate the use of anonymous and named pipes, Chapter 9 presents a simple example program named ANON and a pair of more ambitious example programs named SERVER and CLIENT. The ANON program demonstrates the use of anonymous pipes in a Windows NT program. The CLIENT and SERVER programs work together to show how you can use named pipes for client-server communications, either on a single computer or across a network.

✦ Chapter 10, "Networking Windows NT," demonstrates the use of the Windows NT network API, a software package for writing applications that can set up and maintain communications across a network. This chapter also introduces TCP/IP (the transmission control protocol and internet protocol) and shows how you can write applications that communicate with each other across networks, including local area networks (LANs) and the Internet. The chapter includes a sample program that shows how computers connected across a network can communicate with each other using miniterminals. Another sample program demonstrates how you can connect and disconnect remote disk drives, how you can obtain information about disk drives on remote machines, and more.

✦ Chapter 11, "Windows NT Graphics," explains and demonstrates many of the graphics and animation techniques available in Windows NT. The sample application presented with Chapter 11 demonstrates fast, flicker-free sprite animation in Windows NT. It shows how you can move irregularly shaped bitmaps over complex backgrounds at high speeds. And it does it all with C++ classes that you can implement in your own 32-bit animation programs.

The 11 chapters in *C++ Windows NT Programming* not only explore the features of Windows NT that all professional Windows NT programmers know about, but they also beam some light into many of the murkier corners of Windows NT that are referred to skimpily—if at all—in other volumes about Windows NT programming. By the time you have finished this book and have experimented with the many sample programs that it provides, you'll be well on your way to becoming an expert Windows NT programmer.

Happy programming!

Mark Andrews
Santa Clara, CA

CHAPTER ONE

INTRODUCING WINDOWS NT

Windows NT—the NT stands for "New Technology"—is a whole new breed of operating system. It isn't UNIX, it isn't a successor to Windows 3.1, and it isn't a supercharged version of Windows 95. On the outside, Windows NT looks and feels almost exactly like its younger sibling, Windows 95. But on the inside, where it counts, Windows NT is much more advanced than Windows 3.x or Windows 95.

Windows NT is an industrial-strength operating system that runs not only on small Intel-based personal computers but also on higher-performance workstations such as DEC Alpha and MIPS machines. Windows NT is designed for corporate-sized computer systems that have higher performance requirements than most Windows 95 computer systems. Windows NT runs faster, offers more protection against crashes and data corruption, and offers more advanced networking and more secure communications than Windows 95. It also costs more—and demands more powerful hardware—than Windows 95.

But even though Windows NT was designed mainly for business and industry—and even though it places increased demands on your wallet and your computer system, it is now becoming increasingly popular not only among corporate users but also among private Windows users who want to step up to a more powerful operating environment than Windows 95.

As the prices of memory and processing power have continued to fall, power users of Windows have become interested in learning more about Windows NT. And in the months and years ahead, it is likely that more power users of small-scale operating environments such as Windows 95 will move to Windows NT.

In this book, you'll get a close-up look at many of the powerful new features of Windows NT, including its advanced operating system architecture, its multitasking and multithreading capabilities, its networking mechanisms, its 32-bit graphics features, and much more. You'll also have opportunities to experiment with example programs that show exactly how you can incorporate Windows NT features into your own NT programs.

The Windows NT User Interface

When you start Windows NT (version 4.0 or later), the first thing you see is a sharp new user interface that is a tremendous improvement over the user interface from earlier versions. To the casual Windows NT user, this new interface may look like a simple facelift. It improves the looks of the NT desktop, and it makes Windows NT considerably easier to use. But once the novelty of the new interface wears off, the average Windows NT user probably won't think much more about it.

To the Windows developer, though, the new Windows NT user interface (see Figure 1.1) has a much greater significance—in fact, as you'll see in this chapter, it's the key to many of the new engineering concepts that went into the overall design of Windows NT. Furthermore, if you want your application to qualify for a Microsoft Windows-compatible logo, the engineering principles that went into the design of the new Windows NT interface *must* be reflected from now on in the design of every application you write for both Windows NT and Windows 95. The more you know about the new interface, the better you'll be at writing well-behaved applications for Windows NT and Windows 95.

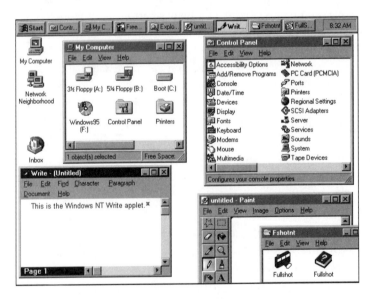

FIGURE 1.1 THE WINDOWS NT USER INTERFACE.

To get an idea of why this is true, let's take a quick look at some of the most important new features that are now built into the Windows NT user interface:

✦ **Drag and drop.** Instead of using the familiar file-and-directory system for disk
I/O, Windows NT now uses a drag-and-drop metaphor that allows the user to
drag files into folders—and to cut, paste, and copy files and folders—using the
mouse. This new feature of Windows NT (and Windows 95) is based on a new
Windows mechanism called OLE, which seems to be popping up everywhere
in the world of Windows these days. Along with making drag-and-drop file
management possible, OLE is also the technology behind many other new
features in Windows NT—features such as in-place editing and OLE controls.
You'll learn more about these new features in this chapter and in later chapters
in this volume.

✦ **Common controls.** Many of the Windows controls used by the Windows NT
interface and other system-software components—such as taskbars, dockable
toolbars, progress-bar controls, and spin controls—are now implemented as
common controls that you can also use in your own Windows NT programs.
This chapter describes these common controls and presents a hands-on sample
program that shows how you can write and implement one useful kind of
common control, a progress bar. The principles that you'll learn when you
write and build this sample program will also provide you with the knowledge
you'll need to write other kinds of common controls.

✦ **Common dialog boxes.** Many of the dialog boxes that have long been used by
the folks who write Windows system software are now also available to
Windows developers in the form of common dialog boxes. These dialog boxes
have sleek new looks, and many of them are easier to use in Windows programs
than ever before. Examples of common dialog boxes include the Load and
Save dialog boxes, the Font and Color dialog boxes, and various kinds of
dialog boxes and property sheets (tabbed dialog boxes) that are used to create,
implement, and use OLE controls.

✦ **Document-centric programming.** With the debut of Windows 95 and
Windows NT 4.0, Windows became what Microsoft engineers call a document-centric operating environment—an environment in which the user can
focus on the job that needs to be done rather than on the specific tool that's
used to do it. In contrast, Windows 3.1 and its predecessors were *application-
centric* environments, requiring users to focus on the applications that created
documents rather than on the documents being created. A document-centric
interface lets the user open an application not only by clicking its icon but also

by merely clicking on the icon of a document that has been created by the application. The document then opens automatically. Of course, the application that created the document opens, too, but with the help of OLE, the creating application and the importing application can now be made to appear in the same window. That new concept is so radical that we're still waiting to see whether it will catch on. What's important is that as a Windows developer, your focus is now supposed to be on the document that is being worked with and not on the application that created it.

Windows NT Workstations and Windows NT Servers

There are two varieties of Windows NT: Windows NT Workstation, which is what this book is about, and Windows NT Server. Windows NT Server is a premium edition of Windows NT that is designed primarily for network administrators; it has special features for managing networks, the workstations that make up networks, and network users.

Windows NT servers can manage networks made up of many different kinds of workstations, including those running Windows NT, Windows 95, Windows 3.1, and even the Macintosh operating system.

Although Windows NT Workstation and Windows NT Server are identical in many ways, the special network-oriented features of the Windows NT Server operating system are not covered in this book. The networking features of the Windows NT Workstation operating system are examined in Chapter 10, "Networking Windows NT."

About This Chapter

Because the Windows NT user interface is so different from the interface used in earlier versions of Windows, this chapter introduces Windows NT by taking a close look at its user interface. I'll look at the elements that make up the Windows NT user interface and explain how they work together. I'll also provide some tricks and tips on how to make your applications take advantage of—and work well under—the Windows NT user interface, which now sets the standards for Windows NT and Windows 95 applications.

The chapter concludes with a pair of hands-on example programs that demonstrate two important new features of Windows NT. The first sample program, PROGBAR, shows how easy it is to create a Windows common control—in this case, a progress-bar control—using Visual C++. Figure 1.2 shows the output of the PROGBAR program.

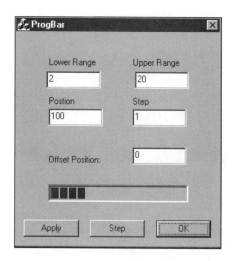

FIGURE 1.2 OUTPUT OF THE **PROGBAR** SAMPLE PROGRAM.

The second sample program in this chapter, REGDEMO, demonstrates the use of the registry, a vital new feature of both Windows NT and Windows 95. The registry has replaced the **CONFIG.SYS** and **AUTOEXEC.BAT** files that were used in earlier versions of Windows. Moreover, unless you write system software at Microsoft, the registry has also replaced the **WIN.INI** and **SYSTEM.INI** files. (Those two files still exist in Windows NT but are now strictly off-limits to ordinary Windows applications.)

The REGDEMO sample program is a simple registry browser that shows you the structure of the registry and lets you poke around in the registry to learn a little about how it works. REGDEMO is a prerequisite for a more ambitious registry-related program, TEXTCHNG, which is presented in Chapter 2. TEXTCHNG shows you exactly how to use the registry in a Windows NT program.

Figure 1.3 shows the output of the TEXTCHNG program.

FIGURE 1.3 OUTPUT OF THE TEXTCHNG SAMPLE PROGRAM.

Developing Windows 95 Applications under Windows NT

The new Windows NT desktop has many useful and impressive new features, such as a taskbar and special icons for opening the contents of your computer. Because of its new window design, you can place an icon representing either an application or a document inside each window's title bar. Because the Windows 95 user interface also has all these features, it's easy to develop programs under Windows NT that work equally well under Windows 95. Windows NT is an ideal environment for developing Windows 95 applications.

Behind the Windows NT Desktop

When Microsoft introduced Windows NT, Windows 95 had not made its debut, so the earliest versions of Windows NT were not equipped with the impressive new user-interface features that would later be introduced in Windows 95. The user interface of Windows NT 1.0—and of every subsequent version through version 3.51—looked and worked just like the user interface of NT's immediate predecessor, Windows 3.1.

Not until the unveiling of Windows NT 4.0—the version that was current when this book was written—did the Windows NT user interface get the facelift that would give it a look and feel as up-to-date as that of Windows 95.

The updated Windows NT desktop does not rely on separate Program Manager and File Manager programs as did earlier versions of Windows. Instead, Windows NT has combined the old Windows 3.1 Program Manager and File Manager into a unified desktop that contains both application icons and folder (or directory) icons. When you double-click a folder icon, Windows NT opens a window that displays the contents of the folder.

THE DOCUMENT-CENTRIC PROGRAMMING MODEL

If you want to create applications that work seamlessly with the new and improved Windows NT and Windows 95 desktop and take advantage of its new features, it may help to know more about the concepts that the designers had in mind when they created the user-interface features that these two operating systems now share.

As I mentioned in the introduction to this chapter, one important new user-interface concept is the document-centric model. As an alternative to the application-centric programming model, the document-centric user-interface model focuses on documents rather than on applications. Because Windows NT uses a document-centric interface, the Windows 95 user can open a document on the NT desktop by simply double-clicking on the document's icon. You no longer have to open an application before you open a document that it has created.

That change lets the Windows NT user focus attention on the document that he or she is creating instead of having to be concerned with the intricacies of operating the application that is being used to create the document. Microsoft engineers say that they came up with the document-centric design concept after extensive tests showed that users were more concerned with the documents they were creating than with the applications being used to create the documents.

THE OLE MECHANISM

The document-centric design of Windows NT is based on OLE, an increasingly important technology in the world of Windows programming. When you create a document using an application that supports OLE, you do not have to launch the application that created your document every time you want to look at your handiwork. Instead, you can open your document—and even edit it—inside any other OLE application.

What's OLE?

When Microsoft introduced OLE, its name was an acronym for *object linking and embedding*. The main purpose of OLE was to embed objects inside other objects—for example, to place a Paintbrush bitmap inside a Microsoft Word document so that users could edit the bitmap without leaving Word. Today, OLE is still used for object linking and embedding, but it is also used for many other purposes—for example, to create OLE controls, which are the topic of Chapter 5, "OLE Today." Because OLE can be used for so many things, OLE is no longer considered an abbreviation of "object linking and embedding." Now, OLE just means OLE.

The OLE mechanism also lets you drag documents from the folders that contain them and drop them into other containers. The OLE *containers* in which you drop documents can be other folders or even applications. One special container on the Windows NT desktop is the Recycle Bin, where you can drag things you want to discard.

One important OLE-related feature that has been added to Windows NT is full support for OLE controls, the 32-bit successors to the VBX controls supported by Windows 3.1. With OLE controls, you can develop reusable components that you can import into any OLE-compatible 16-bit or 32-bit application. To make it still easier to import components into programs that support OLE, Visual C++ provides a graphical component-warehouse tool called the Component Gallery. You'll learn more about OLE controls in Chapter 5.

THE OBJECT METAPHOR

To develop a document-centric model for future Windows products, Microsoft engineers have focused on what the company calls the *object metaphor*—the same metaphor that has been used in the development of object-oriented languages such as C++.

The object metaphor, which encapsulates functions and data into objects in object-oriented languages such as C++, works nicely in a windows-oriented operating system. It is natural and convenient to treat Windows-style user-interface devices, such as menus, icons, and dialog boxes, as objects. When you view a Windows user-interface device as an object, it is easy to extend that view and treat the device as a container of other objects.

CONTAINMENT

Viewing an object as a container of other objects is such an important concept in modern Windows design that Microsoft engineers have given it a name: *containment*. Containment makes it possible to drag icons that represent documents across the Windows NT desktop and drop them into other icons that represent folders or applications. Containment is also what makes it possible, in applications that support OLE, to open documents without having to open the applications that created them.

PROPERTIES, METHODS, AND EVENTS

Computer users naturally understand properties of objects, Microsoft says, because all tangible objects have attributes such as weight, color, and size. Because tangible objects have these kinds of qualities, or *properties*, people can hold them, manipulate them, and use them.

When you treat objects on a computer desktop as though they were tangible objects, it isn't difficult to convince users that these objects can be treated just like real objects. Desktop objects, like real-world objects, have properties such as color, size, and location on the desktop. Furthermore, desktop objects can be programmed to serve in different kinds of roles, such as being containers for other objects.

Because user-interface objects can interact with other objects, there are operations— or, in object terminology, *methods*—that you can place in programs to describe interactions with objects. In a Windows program that deals with user-interface objects such as OLE objects, methods are procedures that work the same way that member functions work in C++. They are called methods to distinguish them from ordinary C or C++ functions.

You can also program desktop objects to respond to *events* such as mouse clicks. And finally, you can program desktop objects to generate events of their own, or *fire* events, when certain conditions arise.

Property Sheets

In the world of document-centric Windows programming, the attributes, or properties, of user-interface objects can change dynamically as the user manipulates the objects. For example, the name of each folder and document displayed on the Windows NT desktop is a property. To change the name of a displayed folder or a document, all you have to do is to select the document's name (beneath or beside its icon) and type in a new name. The name property of the selected file or folder then changes to the name you have typed in.

Although properties made their initial public appearance on the Windows NT desktop, you can also use properties in your own Windows NT applications. In fact, OLE controls and other kinds of OLE objects come with built-in sets of properties. You'll learn more about the properties of OLE controls and other kinds of OLE objects in Chapter 5, "OLE Today."

When an object has properties, you can change them by right-clicking the mouse over the object's icon. For example, if you right-click any OLE-aware icon on the Windows NT desktop, a menu resembling the one shown in Figure 1.4 pops up.

FIGURE 1.4 OPENING A POP-UP MENU ON THE WINDOWS NT DESKTOP.

Property Pages

When a desktop object's pop-up menu appears, you can select the property you want to change by choosing the **Properties** menu item. Windows then displays a dialog box called a *property sheet*. In Microsoft Windows terminology, a property sheet is a dialog box that contains a set of tabbed dialog boxes called *property pages*. A property page, in modern Windows jargon, is a tabbed dialog-box page that lists the properties of an object. With the controls displayed in a property-page dialog box, you can change the properties of whatever object is associated with the property page.

For example, when the Microsoft SQL Server relational database is installed on your computer system, you can display the pop-up menu shown in Figure 1.4 by clicking the **SQL Server** icon on the Windows NT desktop. Then, when you can choose **Properties**, Windows displays the SQL Object Manager Properties dialog box (Figure 1.5). You can then edit properties associated with your SQL Server application.

Version 4.0 of the Microsoft Foundation Class (MFC) library, which was introduced with Windows NT 4.0, provides C++ classes that make it easy for you to equip OLE objects with property sheets. Users of your applications can then easily change the properties of objects you use in your applications. You'll learn more about property sheets and how to use them in your applications in Chapter 5, "OLE Today."

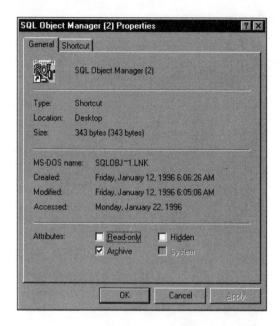

FIGURE 1.5 THE SQL OBJECT MANAGER PROPERTIES DIALOG BOX.

Pop-Up Menus and Contextual Commands

The commands that appear in a Windows NT pop-up menu are called *contextual commands*—commands that are related to the object over which the user right-clicks. By using pop-up menus, the user of your application can obtain quick access to menu commands. You can use this same feature in your own Windows NT applications.

Keep your pop-up menus as simple as possible. They should not be long lists of rarely used menu items, but should instead provide the user with access to frequently used commands that are directly related to the object over which the menus pop up.

When you implement pop-up menus, remember that they should always pop up when the user releases the mouse button and not when the button goes down. If you display pop-up menus only when a right-button-up message is dispatched, your application will a follow a consistent model that is compatible with Windows NT drag-and-drop commands.

Characteristics of Property Sheets

A property sheet is a special kind of dialog box that is designed to present a list of an object's properties. Figure 1.6 is a typical property sheet for a Windows NT application. (The property sheet shown is the one Microsoft provides for the Visual C++ 4.0 compiler.)

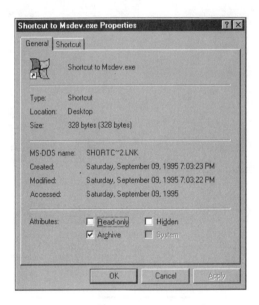

FIGURE 1.6 A PROPERTY SHEET.

Generally, a property sheet is implemented as a modeless dialog box so that the user can make multiple changes in an object's properties without facing the annoyance of a dialog box that keeps disappearing.

Using Property Sheets and Property Pages

A property sheet can be equipped with any number of tabbed property pages for showing different categories of properties, and it can offer controls such as drop-down lists for moving up and down hierarchies of properties. A property sheet is usually equipped with the kinds of *transaction buttons* seen in most dialog boxes: a standard row of buttons with labels such as **OK, Cancel,** and **Apply,** as shown in Figure 1.6.

The MFC library supplies two C++ classes—CPropertyPage and CPropertySheet—that you can use to implement property pages in your applications. Property pages and property sheets are covered in more detail in Chapter 5, "OLE Today."

New Gadgets and User-Interface Devices

With the double-barreled release of Visual C++ 4.0 and MFC 4.0, Microsoft introduced a host of new classes and member functions that you can use to equip your applications with all the new kinds of user-interface devices found in the new Windows NT and Windows 95 desktop.

New controls now available for use by Windows NT and Windows 95 developers include the following:

✦ *Docking toolbars*, which can be glued to the edges of a window or torn off and used as floating tool palettes (Figure 1.7).

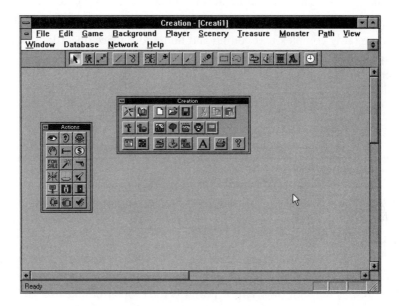

FIGURE 1.7 DOCKING TOOLBARS.

✦ *Status bars*, which can be placed at the bottom of windows to provide the user with important messages and notification of events.

✦ A *tree-view control*, which creates a hierarchical view for navigating through various icons. Tree views are often used in browser-style applications such as the Explorer and can also be used to display hierarchical views such as outlines.

✦ A *list-view control*, which can display lists of graphics objects such as icons.

✦ A *column heading control,* which can be used to place column titles at heads of lists. The column heading control supports automatic resizing and can trap events, including user events, so that you can reformat list boxes when necessary.

✦ A *slide control* with a pointer that you can move back and forth (or up and down) to move to a specific location in an object—for example, to a particular frame in a video sequence or to a particular part of a waveform sound.

✦ A *progress-bar control* that you can use to track the progress of time-consuming operations. Windows programmers have been designing their own slide controls for years. Now they no longer have to.

✦ *Property sheets* that can be used to construct tabbed dialog boxes.

✦ *Tab controls* that can be used to equip dialog boxes and other objects with tabs.

✦ A *rich text box* that supports RTF (rich text format) files, multiple fonts and some fairly complex text-editing and find-and-replace operations. The WordPad application, which you can activate from the desktop, uses the rich text box control. Now this control is available for you to use in your own applications.

These and other new controls introduced in MFC 4.0 are described in more detail later in this chapter and in Chapter 4, "Programming Windows NT with Visual C++."

Docking Toolbars

Although a toolbar class was available in earlier versions of MFC, the toolbar class introduced in MFC 4.0 has many new features that make it more powerful and easier to use than earlier MFC toolbars.

Along with its docking feature, this new toolbar supports button-wrapping (automatic adjustments in the numbers of a button's columns and rows, depending on how the user resizes the window). This feature lets the toolbar double as a palette window. You'll learn more about docking toolbars and how to use them in Chapter 4.

The Windows NT toolbar control also supports *tool tips*—small text windows that pop up as the mouse moves over toolbar buttons to inform the user of each button's functionality, (see Figure 1.8). You can customize the tool tips displayed by a toolbar, or you can let the system automatically provide default tool tips, which display the name of each button.

FIGURE 1.8 A TOOL TIP.

Common Controls and Common Dialog Boxes

Many of the new controls introduced in version 4.0 of the MFC library are common controls that can dramatically reduce the effort required to develop Windows NT applications. These are Windows controls are used by the Windows NT system and are available to developers for use in their own Windows NT applications.

Common controls offer many benefits. Because they are prewritten, they save time in development. Because they are fully tested and debugged, they also save time in the debugging stage of program development. And because they have the same look and feel as the controls used in the Windows interface, they provide an overall look of consistency in Windows applications.

Examples of common controls introduced in MFC 4.0 include the tree-view control, the list-view control, and the progress-bar control. You'll learn how to create a progress-bar control when you build the PROGBAR sample program later in this chapter.

COMMON DIALOG BOXES

Version 4.0 of the MFC library also introduced a number of new classes and member functions for creating and manipulating common dialog boxes. Common dialog boxes, like common controls, were designed for the Windows operating system but have now been made available to all developers of Windows applications.

With the release of MFC 4.0, Microsoft updated the looks of all the common dialog boxes used in earlier versions of Windows and also added some new dialog boxes. Common dialog boxes that you can now create and manipulate using MFC classes include a new Find and Replace dialog box, a newPage Setup dialog box, a new Font dialog box, and a new Color dialog box.

The Open common dialog box looks like the one shown in Figure 1.9.

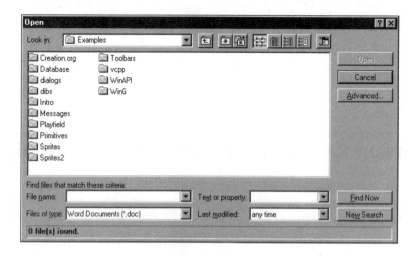

FIGURE 1.9 THE OPEN COMMON DIALOG BOX.

In the new and improved user interface that was introduced with Windows NT 4.0, common dialog boxes that display file and folder icons have a look similar to that of the system's Open window and other windows. They work in a similar fashion.

In the Win32 API, common controls are implemented a dynamic link library (DLL) called the common control DLL, or common control library. The common control library is supplied with version 3.51 and later of Windows NT as well as with Windows 95. You can't use common controls in programs that run under earlier versions of Windows.

Common controls should be distinguished from OLE controls, Microsoft's 32-bit successors to the VBX controls used in earlier versions of Windows. OLE controls are covered in Chapter 5, "OLE Today."

If you want to use common controls in a Windows API–style application, you must make sure that your program loads the common control DLL supplied in the Win32 API. In a non–Visual C++ application, the way to do that is to call the Win32 function `InitCommonControls`. Then you can create a common control at any time by calling the Win32 function `CreateWindowEx`.

When you write a Visual C++ application using the AppWizard framework (see Chapter 4, "Programming Windows NT with Visual C++"), you don't have to worry about any of that. Every common control used in Windows is encapsulated in a class in the MFC library, and when you write an AppWizard program, AppWizard makes sure that your application has all the functionality it needs to use common controls.

In the MFC library, common controls can be divided into five categories:

✦ **List-related controls,** which help you create and manage lists

✦ **Utility controls,** which provide user-interface functionalities that are often used in Windows 95 programs

✦ **Control-bar objects,** which you can use to create toolbars, status bars, and objects to support them

✦ **Property pages,** tabbed dialog boxes that can be used to display and set the properties of objects

✦ **Editing controls,** which can create text-editing windows that support the RTF rich text format.

Table 1.1 lists and describes the kinds of common controls implemented in MFC.

TABLE 1.1 COMMON CONTROLS.

MFC Class	Description	Kind of Control
CToolbar	Base class for creating and managing toolbar controls.	Control bar
CToolbarCtrl	Displays a toolbar control.	Control bar
CToolTipCtrl	Displays tiny tool-tip windows when the mouse passes over toolbar buttons.	Control bar
CStatusBar	Base class for creating and managing status bars.	Control bar
CStatusBarCtrl	Displays a status-bar control.	Control bar
CPropertyPage	Creates and manages a property-page (tabbed) dialog box.	Property page
CPropertySheet	Creates and manages a tabbed panel in a property-page dialog box.	Property page
CTabCtrl	Displays a tab control like those used in property-page dialog boxes.	Property page
CProgressCtrl	Displays a progress control.	Utility
CSpinButtonCtrl	Displays a spin-button control.	Utility
CSliderCtrl	Displays a slider control.	Utility

continued

TABLE 1.1 CONTINUED

CAnimateCtrl	Displays a control that can play AVI video files (without sound).	Utility
CHotKeyCtrl	Displays a dialog box that lets the user create hot keys (keystroke shortcuts).	Utility
CListCtrl	Encapsulates the functionality of a list view control, whichdisplays a collection of items. Each item is represented by an icon (or a user-defined image) and a label.	List-related
CTreeCtrl	Displays a hierarchical list of items, such as headings in a document, entries in an index, or files and directories on a disk.	List-related
CImageList	A tool for storing and displaying graphics images (such as icons) that can be used alongside the names of items in lists.	List-related
CDragListBox	Constructs list boxes with items that can be dragged and dropped.	List-related
CHeaderCtrl	Displays windows that can be used as column headings in lists and tables.	List-related

COMMON CONTROL MEMBER FUNCTIONS

Once you have created a common control, you can get and set its attributes and manipulate it in other ways by calling member functions of its MFC class. For example, progress-bar controls have the following attributes:

✦ **SetRange** sets the minimum and maximum ranges for a progress-bar control and redraws the bar if necessary to reflect the bar's new ranges.

✦ **SetPos** sets a progress bar's current position and redraws the bar if necessary to reflect the new position.

✦ **OffsetPos** advances the current position of a progress-bar control by a specified increment and redraws the bar to reflect the new position.

✦ **SetStep** specifies the step increment for a progress-bar control.

✦ **StepIt** advances the position of a progress-bar control by the bar's step increment and redraws the bar to reflect its new position.

Two of the most important attributes of a progress-bar are its *range* and its *current position*. The range property usually represents the entire duration of the operation that the progress bar is monitoring. A progress bar's current position property—along with the text displayed inside the progress bar, if any—gives the user an idea of how much longer it will take to complete the operation.

COMMON CONTROL I/O

Common controls are implemented as child windows. These child windows are used with their parent windows to perform input and output (I/O) tasks. A common control uses the Windows callback mechanism to send its parent window *notification messages* when the user of an application takes an action that affects the control. The application can then determine how it should respond to the user's action.

Common controls respond to user actions in two ways. Slider controls, sometimes called track bars, fire WM_HSCROLL messages when they detect user actions. All other common controls respond to user actions by dispatching WM_NOTIFY messages. When a common control sends a WM_NOTIFY message to its parent window, the common control identifies itself and provides its parent window with a notification code that specifies what kind of action the user has taken.

Because common controls are windows, an application can send messages to common controls as well as receive messages from them. For example, an application can find out what font a control is using by sending a WM_GETFONT message or can set a label or a caption used by a control by sending a WM_SETTEXT message. Also, there are many control-specific messages, functions, and macros that applications can use to manage various kinds of special features of individual controls.

PROGRESS-BAR CONTROLS

One example of a control-bar object is a progress-bar control, which indicates the progress of time-consuming operations. When you copied this book's accompanying disk onto your hard disk, a progress bar displayed the progress of the operation.

A progress bar usually takes the form of a long horizontal or vertical rectangle that gradually fills with color as an operation progresses. However, progress bars can also appear in other kinds of locations—for example, inside a taskbar control, as shown in Figure 1.10.

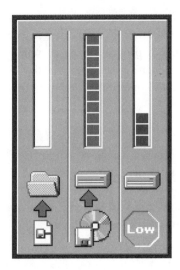

FIGURE 1.10 PROGRESS-BAR CONTROLS.

Displaying Text in Progress-Bar Controls

Text is often displayed inside a progress bar. This text, if used, typically is a number expressed as a percentage. This number generally decrements to zero as the operation progresses.

When you ran the Setup program that installs this book's sample programs, you saw how the text in a progress bar works. The Installer's progress bar contains a number that starts at 100% and decrements to zero as the installation proceeds. That convention is used in many Installer programs.

A progress-bar control, like all common controls provided in MFC 4.0, can be created in two ways: interactively (using the Developer Studio's dialog box editor) and programmatically (using MFC member functions).

To create a common control programmatically, you must instantiate an object of the appropriate class. For example, to create a progress-bar control, you instantiate an object of the `CProgressCtrl` class. You first call the `CProgressBar` constructor and then call the `CProgressBar::Create` member function.

In a Visual C++ program, the easiest way to implement a common control is to create it interactively using the Developer Studio dialog box editor. You can then use the ClassWizard utility to create member variables that are associated with the control and to link those variables to the rest of your application. The PROGBAR program presented in the next section shows how to create a common control using the Developer Studio method.

Example: Creating a Progress-Bar Control

To create a common control programmatically, you instantiate an object of the appropriate class—for example, to create a progress-bar control, you instantiate an object of the CProgressCtrl class. You first call the CProgressBar constructor and then call the CProgressBar::Create member function. Once you have created a common control, you get and set its attributes and manipulate it in other ways by calling member functions of its MFC class.

Before you start examining the PROGBAR program's source code, you may want to build the program, execute it, and experiment with it to see exactly how a progress bar works.

CREATING A PROGRESS-BAR CONTROL STEP BY STEP

Now that you know how common controls work, you're ready to try your hand at creating one. To create a common control like the one implemented in the PROGBAR sample program on the accompanying disk, these are the general steps to follow:

1. Start Developer Studio if it isn't already started.

2. Use AppWizard to generate a dialog-based application—one that displays a dialog box when it starts and is not equipped with any other windows. To create a dialog-based application, do this:

   ✦ Choose Developer Studio's **File|New** menu item.

   ✦ When the New dialog box opens, choose the **Project Workspace** item from the New list box.

   ✦ When AppWizard starts (Figure 1.11), navigate to an empty directory using the Location edit box and then select the **MFC AppWizard** item from the Type list box.

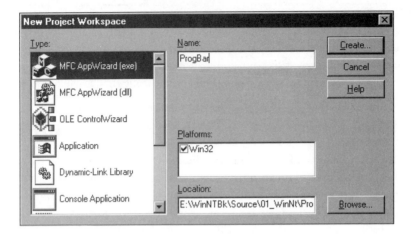

FIGURE 1.11 CREATING AN APPLICATION WITH APPWIZARD.

♦ Type the word **ProgBar** in the Name edit box, as shown in Figure 1.11.

♦ Start the process of creating a new application by clicking **Create**.

♦ When the MFC AppWizard - Step 1 dialog box opens, select the radio button labeled **Dialog based**, as shown in Figure 1.12.

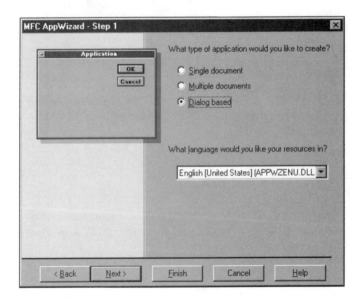

FIGURE 1.12 CREATING A DIALOG-BASED PROGRAM.

In this exercise, you'll be creating an ordinary control—and not an OLE control—so you won't have to choose any of the OLE options that AppWizard offers when you generate the framework for your application.

3. When AppWizard prompts you for the names of the files for your project, name your program's dialog box files **ProgDlg.cpp** and **ProgDlg.h**. (Although Windows NT and Visual C++ 4.x accept long file names, many DOS-based utilities, such as file-compression programs, choke on long file names. I think it's a good idea to use file names no more than 11 characters long whenever that's possible.)

4. Finish creating PROGBAR by clicking the **Finish** button.

5. You're now ready to create a progress-bar control for the dialog box that the PROGBAR application displays. Open the dialog box editor by clicking the resource tab (the one labeled with a tiny bitmap) under the left-hand panel in Developer Studio's editor window. Then open the dialog box folder in the ProgBar resources list box and double-click the small dialog box icon labeled IDD_PROGBAR_DIALOG. Developer Studio responds by opening its dialog box editor (Figure 1.13).

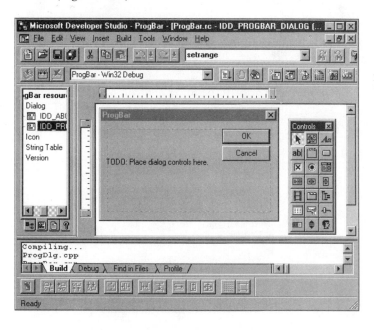

FIGURE 1.13 THE DEVELOPER STUDIO DIALOG BOX EDITOR.

6. Check to see whether a Controls toolbar like the one shown in Figure 1.13 is visible (it may have a different shape; the Controls toolbar is user-realizable). If you don't see a Controls toolbar, open one by choosing the **View|Toolbars** menu item and then checking the **Controls** check box.

7. Select the button that represents the control you went to create. In this case, that is the progress-bar button shown in Figure 1.14. Then click the mouse inside the dialog box template (shown earlier in Figure 1.13) by clicking the mouse inside the dialog box.

FIGURE 1.14 THE PROGRESS-BAR TOOLBAR BUTTON.

When you have created your new progress-bar control, Developer Studio automatically names it IDC_PROGRESS1. If you like, you can confirm that by double-clicking the mouse inside your dialog box template and checking the ID list box inside the Progress dialog box that is then displayed.

8. When you have created the progress-bar control, you can drag the control around and resize it to suit the needs of your application. For example, to place a progress-bar control in the center of a dialog box, simply drag it there. Then extend the length of your dialog box by dragging its bottom edge down with the mouse, and add all the other controls shown in Figure 1.15.

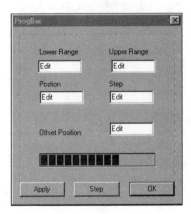

FIGURE 1.15 ADDING CONTROLS TO A DIALOG BOX TEMPLATE.

9. Double-click each edit control you have created and assign it a more intuitive name when its property sheet appears. For example, when the property sheet for the edit box labeled Lower Range appears, change its ID from IDC_EDIT*n* to IDC_EDIT_LOWRANGE, as shown in Figure 1.16. Name the rest of the edit controls, in turn, IDC_EDIT_HIGHRANGE, IDC_EDIT_POSITION, IDC_EDIT_STEP, and IDC_EDIT_OFFSETPOS. Name your Apply and Step buttons ID_APPLY and ID_STEP. The only progress-bar control in your dialog box is named IDC_PROGRESS1. There's no need to improve that designation, so leave it as it is.

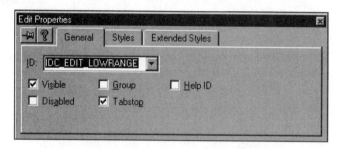

FIGURE 1.16 CHANGING AN EDIT CONTROL'S ID.

TRYING OUT THE **PROGBAR** PROGRAM

When you have completed the preceding exercise, test your application at its current stage of development by executing Developer Studio's **Build|Execute** menu command. At this point, the dialog box displayed by your PROGBAR program has an empty progress bar, as shown in Figure 1.17. That's because you haven't yet set any member variables. Later, you'll get a chance to complete the PROGBAR application and execute it in its finished form.

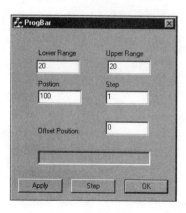

FIGURE 1.17 THE PROGBAR APPLICATION, PHASE 1.

Associating Member Variables with Dialog Box Controls

When AppWizard generates a dialog-based application, AppWizard automatically creates a C++ class for the application's dialog box. When you created the PROGBAR program in the previous exercise, AppWizard named this class `CProgBarDlg` and implemented it in a pair of source files named **PROGDLG.CPP** and **PROGDL.H**.

PROGBARDLG.CPP   *PROGBARDLG.H*

In the next exercise, you'll create several member variables that you can use to manage the progress-bar control inside the PROGBAR dialog box. When you finish this exercise, your progress-bar control will be connected to the other controls in the PROGBAR dialog box, and you'll be able to use those controls to change the appearance of your progress-bar control.

To create a member variable that will be associated with your progress-bar control, follow these steps:

1. With the Visual C++ dialog box editor still open, choose the **View/ClassWizard** menu item.

2. When the ClassWizard property sheet comes into focus, make sure that the name of your new progress control (IDC_PROGRESS1) is highlighted inside the Control IDs text box (Figure 1.18). Then click the **Member Variables** tab.

Object

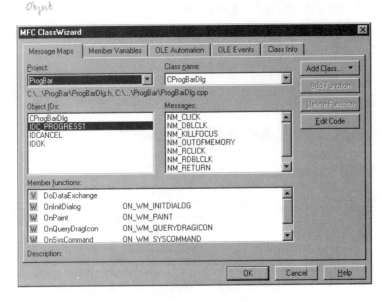

FIGURE 1.18 ADDING A MEMBER VARIABLE, STEP 1.

3.   Click the **Add Variable** button.

4.   When the Add Member Variable dialog box (Figure 1.19) appears, make sure that the word **Control** appears in the Category list box and that the class name CButton ||? appears inside the Variable type list box. Then add a member variable named m_progCtrl to your application by typing **m_progCtrl** in the text box labeled Member variable name.

5.   Assign your progress-bar control the variable name m_progCtrl by typing **m_progCtrl** in the list box labeled Member variable name, as show in Figure 1.19.

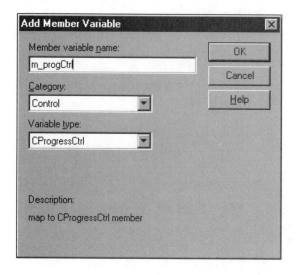

FIGURE 1.19 ADDING A MEMBER VARIABLE, STEP 2.

6.   Close the Add Member Variable dialog box by clicking **OK**.

7.   Repeat Steps 4 through 6 to create member variables for the edit controls and the **Apply** and **Step** buttons in your dialog box. Use the names shown in Figure 1.19. Make each member variable an int data type by selecting the word **int** in the Variable type edit box in the Add Member Variable dialog box each time you create a new member variable.

8.   When the ClassWizard property sheet reclaims the focus, refer to the Control IDs text box and notice that the member variables you have created are now associated with the interactive controls in your dialog box. When everything is in order, close the ClassWizard property sheet by clicking **OK**.

You have now finished designing the dialog box that will be used in the PROGBAR application. You're ready to start writing the code that will be needed to add functionality to your dialog box, your progress-bar control, and its associated dialog box controls.

THE DoDataExchange MEMBER FUNCTION

From Developer Studio, open **PROGDLG.CPP**, the source file that implements your application's dialog box. Locate a member function named `CProgBarDlg::DoDataExchange`, and notice that ClassWizard has placed one statement inside that function for each interactive control you have placed inside your dialog box. Each of those statements calls a macro that is defined by the system. Notice that each macro call contains not only the name of each control inside your application's dialog box, but also the name of the member variable that you associated with that control in the previous exercise.

```
void CProgBarDlg::DoDataExchange(CDataExchange* pDX)
{
    CDialog::DoDataExchange(pDX);
    //{{AFX_DATA_MAP(CProgBarDlg)
    DDX_Control(pDX, ID_STEP, m_btnStep);
    DDX_Control(pDX, ID_APPLY, m_btnApply);
    DDX_Control(pDX, IDC_PROGRESS1, m_progCtrl);
    DDX_Text(pDX, IDC_EDIT_HIGHRANGE, m_highRange);
    DDX_Text(pDX, IDC_EDIT_LOWRANGE, m_lowRange);
    DDX_Text(pDX, IDC_EDIT_OFFSETPOS, m_offsetPos);
    DDX_Text(pDX, IDC_EDIT_POSITION, m_position);
    DDX_Text(pDX, IDC_EDIT_STEP, m_step);
    //}}AFX_DATA_MAP
}
```

Every time you create a dialog box with Developer Studio, the code that implements the dialog box contains a `DoDataExchange` member function. The program that implements the dialog box can then use `DoDataExchange` to associate member variables with dialog box controls. All this happens automatically, however; when you create a dialog box, you'll rarely have an occasion to examine its `DoDataExchange` very closely. You'll generally work at a higher level, working only with the actual member variables that are referred to inside `DoDataExchange`.

As long as you're looking at a `DoDataExchange` member function anyway, however, you might want to notice that each member-variable name that you created in steps 4 through 6 appears in a separate statement inside the `DoDataExchange` function, alongside its corresponding dialog-control ID. Once you have noticed that, you can forget about the intricacies of how `DoDataExchange` works and concentrate instead on how to work with the member variables it refers to.

A Warning

When ClassWizard places text inside a `DoDataExchange` member function, the data is always placed inside a block of text called a *data map*. A data map always begins with the line

```
//{{AFX_DATA_MAP(CProgBarDlg)
```

and ends with the line

```
//}}AFX_DATA_MAP
```

Generally speaking, you should never modify the automatically generated code that appears between these two lines in a data map. If you do, it can confuse ClassWizard and result various kinds of bizarre error messages.

The DDX Mechanism

In a Visual C++ application, the `DoDataExchange` member function is the heart of a mechanism named *dialog data exchange* (DDX). You'll learn more about DDX later in this chapter in the section headed "Retrieving Dialog Box Data with the DDX Mechanism." For the moment, it's sufficient to know that DDX is the mechanism that Visual C++ uses to pass information back and forth between dialog box controls and member variables defined in an application.

To use DDX, an application calls an MFC member function named `CWnd::UpdateData`. (Dialog boxes are descended from the `CWnd` class, so dialog box classes can override the `UpdateData` member function.) `UpdateData` does its work by calling `DoDataExchange`, which in turn calls an appropriate system macro. It is this macro that does the work of moving data between member variables and dialog box controls.

When you call UpdateData, you pass it one Boolean parameter: a TRUE value to pass a value from a member function to its associated dialog box control, or a FALSE value to pass a value from a dialog box control to its associated member variable.

Calling UpdateData

By making a single UpdateData(TRUE) call, an application moves the values of all the controls inside a dialog box into the member functions that are associated with those controls. By calling UpdateData(FALSE), an application copies data in the opposite direction—from all the member functions inside a dialog box into all the controls that are associated with those member functions.

Those capabilities, as interesting as they are, would have no value in an application without a method for determining when UpdateData should be called and whether a TRUE parameter or a FALSE parameter should be passed to it. In PROGBAR, as you will see momentarily, UpdateData(TRUE) is called whenever the program needs to send data to the application's progress-bar control, and UpdateData(FALSE) is called whenever data needs to be collected from the program's edit controls.

MESSAGE HANDLING IN VISUAL C++ PROGRAMS

User events are so important in Windows programs that they are covered extensively in two of the chapters in this book: Chapter 3, "The Win32 API," and Chapter 4, "Programming Windows NT with Visual C++." In the paragraphs that follow, you'll get a brief introduction to user events and see how they are detected and used in the PROGBAR application. A more detailed examination of user events will have to wait until Chapter 3.

User Events and Message Maps

Here's the world's shortest explanation of Windows events: In Windows, each time the user of an application generates an event by taking an action such as pressing a key or clicking the mouse, the operating system detects the event and dispatches a message to the application that's currently being executed. The application then determines how to handle the event.

In Visual C++ applications generated by AppWizard, events are detected and passed to their proper destinations using a mechanism called a *message map*. AppWizard automatically creates a message map and places it in your source code in much the same way that it creates the data maps that you learned about earlier in this section. A message map created by AppWizard resembles a data map—and message maps and data maps are created and used in similar ways.

When you used AppWizard to create PROGBAR, AppWizard automatically created a message map and placed it in **PROGDLG.CPP.** At this point in its development, the PROGBAR program's message map looks like this:

```
BEGIN_MESSAGE_MAP(CProgBarDlg, CDialog)
    //{{AFX_MSG_MAP(CProgBarDlg)
    ON_WM_SYSCOMMAND()
    ON_WM_PAINT()
    ON_WM_PAINT()
    ON_BN_CLICKED(ID_APPLY, OnApply)
    ON_BN_CLICKED(ID_STEP, OnStep)
    //}}AFX_MSG_MAP
END_MESSAGE_MAP()
```

You'll learn exactly how message maps work in Chapters 3 and 4. At this point, it's sufficient to know that when NT detects a user event and notifies a Visual C++ application by sending it a message, the application handles the message by routing it through a message map. The message map then handles the message by passing it to a special kind of function called a *message handler.*

Message Maps and Message Handlers

The message map shown in the preceding code fragment is designed to handle five different Windows messages. Three of the messages—ON_WM_SYSCOMMAND, ON_WM_PAINT, and ON_WM_PAINT—are handled automatically by the system and will examined in later chapters. In this chapter, we're interested only in the last two messages shown in the preceding example:

```
ON_BN_CLICKED(ID_APPLY, OnApply)
ON_BN_CLICKED(ID_STEP, OnStep)
```

In Windows, ON_BN_CLICKED is sent to an application when the user clicks the mouse button. As an illustration of how this process works, examine the two statements shown in the preceding code fragment. The first statement is executed when the user clicks the

Apply button, and the second statement is executed when the user clicks the **Step** button. As you can see, a mouse click inside the **Apply** button causes a message handler named OnApply to be called, and a mouse click inside the **Step** button causes a message handler named OnStep to be called.

In PROGBAR, as you'll see momentarily, the **Step** and **Apply** message handlers are used to control the size of the colored bar inside the program's progress-bar control. When the user clicks **Step**, the program calls its OnStep message handler, and the progress bar advances one step. (You determine the size of the bar's steps by setting the dialog box's Steps edit control.) When the user clicks **Apply**, the program calls its OnApply message handler, which reads the contents of all the application's edit controls and sets the appearance of the progress bar accordingly.

In a Visual C++ program generated by AppWizard, it's easy to construct the message maps that perform all this magic. You just use ClassWizard, as you'll learn in an upcoming exercise before you finish this chapter.

CREATING MESSAGE MAPS AND MESSAGE HANDLERS

Now that you understand how message maps work in Visual C++ programs, you're ready to do two things:

✦ Construct a message map that accepts messages dispatched by the system and passes them to message handlers.

✦ Write a set of message handlers that change the contents of the program's controls in accordance with user input.

To perform these two operations, follow these steps:

1. Open the ClassWizard property sheet.
2. Tab to the Message Maps property page, if necessary.
3. In the list boxes labeled **Object IDs** and **Messages**, select the **ID_APPLY** and **BN_CLICKED** entries, as shown in Figure 1.20.

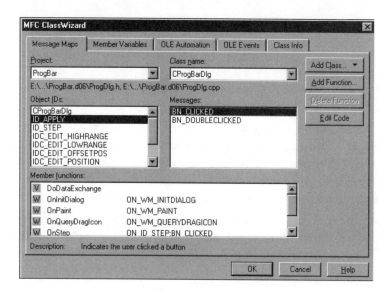

FIGURE 1.20 CREATING AN ONAPPLY MESSAGE HANDLER.

4. When ClassWizard displays a dialog box suggesting that your new message handler be named `OnApply`, click **OK**.

5. Click the **Add Function** button.

6. Select the **ID_STEP** and **BN_CLICKED** entries in the Object IDs and Message list boxes.

7. Click **Add Function** and accept ClassWizard's offer to name this new message handler `OnStep`.

8. Close ClassWizard by clicking **Edit Code**.

9. The **PROGDLG.CPP** source file is displayed in Developer Studio's C++ editor, and the editor is automatically scrolled to the following function:

```
void CProgBarDlg::OnStep()
{
    // TODO: Add your control notification handler code here
}
```

This function, named OnStep, is a message handler that ClassWizard automatically added to your code when you clicked **Add Function** in step 6. At the same time, ClassWizard added the following entry to the PROGBAR program's message map:

```
ON_BN_CLICKED(ID_STEP, OnStep)
```

In the PROGBAR program, the OnStep member function and the OnStep message-map entry work together. When the user clicks the application's **Step** button, NT dispatches an ON_BN_CLICKED message to the application. The program's message-map entry receives the message and passes it to the OnStep member function that ClassWizard has inserted in the program.

10. Unfortunately, ClassWizard doesn't know what you want your application to do when the user clicks the **Step** button, so you must edit ClassWizard's OnStep message-handler function to read as follows:

```
void CProgBarDlg::OnStep()
{
    // Move the progress bar one step.
    m_progCtrl.StepIt();
}
```

When you have made that change, your application's progress bar advances one step forward each time the user clicks the program's **Step** button.

11. In steps 2 and 3, when you added an OnApply message handler to the PROGBAR program, ClassWizard automatically inserted the following line in the program's message map:

```
ON_BN_CLICKED(ID_APPLY, OnApply)
```

At the same time, ClassWizard added an OnApply message handler to **PROGDLG. CPP**. Now find the OnApply member function and add some functionality to it by editing it to read as follows:

```
void CProgBarDlg::OnApply()
{
    // Copy data from controls to variables,
    // and then set the progress-bar control.
    UpdateData(TRUE);
    m_progCtrl.SetRange(m_lowRange, m_highRange);
    m_progCtrl.SetPos(m_position);
```

```
        m_progCtrl.SetStep(m_step);
        m_progCtrl.OffsetPos(m_offsetPos);
}
```

12. Now, when you build your application and a user opens it, a click of the **Apply** button will execute the preceding `OnApply` member function. As you can see, `OnApply` calls `UpdateData` to copy the contents of your dialog box's edit controls into their corresponding member variables. Then the `OnApply` message handler uses the new values of those variables to call a series of functions that set the attributes of the application's progress bar. As each attribute is set, the Visual C++ application framework constructed by AppWizard automatically updates the appearance of the progress bar as its attributes change.

INITIALIZING THE VALUES OF DIALOG BOX CONTROLS

Once a data map and a message map have been constructed for an AppWizard application, the two maps can be used together to transfer information between dialog box controls and their corresponding member variables.

If you like, you can set initial values for the controls in a dialog box before the dialog box is displayed. In PROGBAR, the values that appear in the application's edit boxes are initialized to default values before the dialog box opens. Consequently, when the program starts, its dialog box looks like the one shown in Figure 1.21.

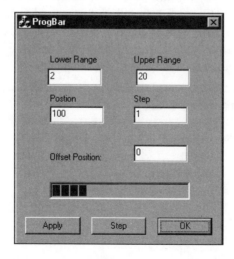

FIGURE 1.21 THE PROGBAR PROGRAM'S INITIAL DISPLAY.

Initializing the Values of Edit Controls

In the PROGBAR program, the constructor of the `ProgBar` dialog box object uses a special block of code called an AFX_DATA_INIT block to initialize the values of the dialog box's edit controls:

```
CProgBarDlg::CProgBarDlg(CWnd* pParent /*=NULL*/)
    : CDialog(CProgBarDlg::IDD, pParent)
{
    //{{AFX_DATA_INIT(CProgBarDlg)
    m_highRange = 20;
    m_lowRange = 2;
    m_offsetPos = 0;
    m_position = 100;
    m_step = 1;
    //}}AFX_DATA_INIT
    // Note that LoadIcon does not require a subsequent DestroyIcon in Win32
    m_hIcon = AfxGetApp()->LoadIcon(IDR_MAINFRAME);
}
```

The AFX_DATA_INT code block that you see in the preceding constructor was created automatically by AppWizard when AppWizard generated the PROGBAR application framework. The member variables that you see inside the code block are the same member variables that you created earlier in this chapter, in the section titled "Associating Member Variables with Dialog Box Controls." Recall that you used ClassWizard to create these variables and to associate them with dialog box controls. When you closed ClassWizard, the names of your variables were automatically placed in the AFX_DATA_INT code block shown in the preceding code fragment.

Another Warning (Sort Of)

When AppWizard creates an AFX_DATA_INIT code block, the code block always begins with the line

```
//{{AFX_DATA_INIT(CProgBarDlg)
```

and ends with the line

```
//}}AFX_DATA_INIT
```

Under most circumstances, you should avoid modifying the automatically generated code that appears between these two lines, in the same way that you avoid modifying the data that appears between the `//{{AFX_DATA_MAP` and `//}}AFX_DATA_INIT` delimiters in a data map. But there is one situation in which it is perfectly fine to modify the information inside an AFX_DATA_INIT code block. That situation arises when you want to initialize the values of controls inside a dialog box. You do that by substituting an initialization value for the zero value that AppWizard assigns to each member variable by default. For example, in PROGBAR, the initial value of the `m_highRange` member variable is set to 20 in the following statement:

```
m_highRange = 20;
```

Initializing Attributes of Common Controls

Common controls, unlike ordinary Windows controls, have multiple attributes that applications can initialize and modify. Moreover, common controls are supplied with member variables that can be used to get and set their attributes.

For example, these are the window style attributes you can place in the `dwStyle` parameter when you create any common control:

✦ **WS_CHILD.** Creates a child window. Set by default when you create a common control; all common controls are child windows.

✦ **WS_VISIBLE.** Creates a control that is initially visible.

✦ **WS_DISABLED.** Creates a control that is initially disabled.

✦ **WS_GROUP.** Specifies the first control of a group of controls in which the user can move from one control to the next with the arrow keys. All controls defined with the WS_GROUP style after the first control belong to the same group. The next control with the WS_GROUP style ends the style group and starts the next group (one group ends where the next begins).

✦ **WS_TABSTOP.** Specifies one of any number of controls through which the user can move by using the **Tab** key. The **Tab** key moves the user to the next control specified by the WS_TABSTOP style.

Many common controls also have member functions for getting and setting various other kinds of attributes and for manipulating the control in various ways. For example, when you have created a list control using the `CListCtrl` class, you can get and set items in the list by calling `GetItem` and `SetItem`; search for an item in the list by setting up a loop that calls `GetNextItem`; and get or replace the text of an item by calling `GetItemText` or `SetItemText`.

Other common controls have member functions for getting and setting other attributes. For example, PROGBAR executes the following statements to set up the initial attributes of the program's progress-bar control:

```
m_progCtrl.SetRange(0, 100);
m_progCtrl.SetPos(2);
m_progCtrl.SetStep(1);
m_progCtrl.OffsetPos(20);
```

These four statements call four separate member functions that are supplied by MFC. The four functions are member functions of an MFC class named `CProgressCtrl`. You may recall that the `m_progCtrl` member variable used in PROGBAR is an object of the `CProgressCtrl` class. (To refresh your memory, see "Associating Member Variables with Dialog Box Controls" earlier in this chapter.) As a member of the `CProgressCtrl` class, the `m_progCtrl` member variable can execute these four functions:

✦ **CProgressCtrl::SetRange** sets the starting and ending ranges of a progress-bar control.

✦ **CProgressCtrl::SetRange** sets the current size of the colored bar inside a progress-bar control.

✦ **CProgressCtrl::SetStep** sets the distance that the progress bar advances each time it receives a signal to advance.

✦ **CProgressCtrl::OffsetPos** advances the current position of a progress-bar control by a specified increment and redraws the bar to reflect the new position.

In PROGBAR, these four member functions are implemented inside a member function named `OnInitDialog`, which you can find in **PROGDLG.CPP**. In a Visual C++ program built on an AppWizard framework, `OnInitDialog` is always called automatically between the time a dialog box is initialized and the time it is displayed. That's why the dialog box displayed by PROGBAR looks like the one shown in Figure 1.21 when it is first displayed.

INITIALIZING THE CONTROLS IN THE PROGBAR PROGRAM

In the preceding section, you saw how an application can initialize the values of the controls in a dialog box. Now you can use what you've learned to initialize the PROGBAR dialog box controls. Follow these steps:

1. Find the `CProgBarDlg` constructor in **PROGDLG.CPP** and update its contents to read as follows:

```
CProgBarDlg::CProgBarDlg(CWnd* pParent /*=NULL*/)
    : CDialog(CProgBarDlg::IDD, pParent)
{
    //{{AFX_DATA_INIT(CProgBarDlg)
    m_highRange = 20;
    m_lowRange = 2;
    m_offsetPos = 0;
    m_position = 100;
    m_step = 1;
    //}}AFX_DATA_INIT
    // Note that LoadIcon does not require a subsequent DestroyIcon
    in Win32
    m_hIcon = AfxGetApp()->LoadIcon(IDR_MAINFRAME);
}
```

2. Find the `OnInitDialog` member function in **PROGDLG.CPP** and insert the following lines just above the function's `return` statement:

```
m_progCtrl.SetRange(0, 100);
m_progCtrl.SetPos(2);
m_progCtrl.SetStep(1);
m_progCtrl.OffsetPos(20);
```

When you have finished that operation, the program's `OnInitDialog` member function reads as follows:

```
BOOL CProgBarDlg::OnInitDialog()
{
    CDialog::OnInitDialog();

    // Add "About..." menu item to system menu.

    // IDM_ABOUTBOX must be in the system command range.
    ASSERT((IDM_ABOUTBOX & 0xFFF0) == IDM_ABOUTBOX);
    ASSERT(IDM_ABOUTBOX < 0xF000);

    CMenu* pSysMenu = GetSystemMenu(FALSE);
```

```
CString strAboutMenu;
strAboutMenu.LoadString(IDS_ABOUTBOX);
if (!strAboutMenu.IsEmpty())
{
      pSysMenu->AppendMenu(MF_SEPARATOR);
      pSysMenu->AppendMenu(MF_STRING, IDM_ABOUTBOX,
      strAboutMenu);
}

// Set the icon for this dialog.  The framework does this
automatically
//  when the application's main window is not a dialog
SetIcon(m_hIcon, TRUE);            // Set big icon
SetIcon(m_hIcon, FALSE);            // Set small icon

m_progCtrl.SetRange(0, 100);
m_progCtrl.SetPos(2);
m_progCtrl.SetStep(1);
m_progCtrl.OffsetPos(20);

return TRUE;  // return TRUE  unless you set the focus to a control
}
```

BUILDING AND RUNNING THE PROGBAR PROGRAM

When you have initialized the ProgBar dialog box's member functions by following the steps shown in the previous section, the PROGBAR application is ready to build and execute. Build the program by choosing the **Build|Build** menu item and then execute it by choosing **Build|Run**.

When the program starts, experiment with it by changing the values in its text boxes and then clicking the **Apply** and **Step** buttons. Each time you click the **Step** button, the program's progress bar advances one step. When you modify the values of the program's edit boxes and then click the **Apply** button, the changes you have entered in the edit boxes are transferred to the progress-bar control, and its appearance is modified accordingly. To close the dialog box, click **OK**.

Now that you've created and implemented a progress-bar control, you know the basic steps involved in creating and implementing any common control. As you saw in Table 1.1, there are now plenty of common controls to choose from. Have fun!

Other Kinds of User-Interface Devices

Along with its new common controls and its new common dialog boxes, MFC 4.0 introduced a number of other new classes that can be used to create and manipulate other kinds of user-interface devices such as icons, taskbars, and title bars.

Icons have a more important role in the Windows NT interface than they had under previous versions of Windows. Icons are no longer merely representations of minimized windows. In Windows NT, an icon is a representation of an object that can be manipulated by the user and can cause operations to be performed on the associated object.

NEW VARIETIES OF WINDOWS ICONS

Another important change is that a single icon size is no longer sufficient in Windows NT. In addition to the standard 32-pixel by 32-pixel icon that is familiar to Windows 3.x users, Windows NT supports a 16-pixel by 16-pixel icon that can appear both in desktop windows (when you click the **Small Icon** menu item) and inside the title bars of windows. (For more about Windows title bars, see "Title Bars" later in this section.) In addition, Windows NT supports a giant-size 48-pixel by 48-pixel icon designed for high-resolution screen displays.

Because Windows NT uses icons of different sizes in different ways, it is no longer enough for you to provide a single icon for each application you create; now you should also design icons for each kind of document that each application creates. That's because Windows NT users must be able to differentiate between data objects and application objects when both kinds of objects can appear on the desktop.

Using Icons in Title Bars

In Windows 3.1, almost all icons had a standard size of 32 by 32 pixels. Because version 4 of the MFC library supports Windows NT 4.0–style user-interface devices, applications developed under Windows NT now support the use of smaller icons—specifically, 16-by-16 icons—that can be placed inside the title bars of windows. When a Windows NT 4.0–style window is associated with an object—usually an application or a document—a 16-by-16 version of the object's icon appears in the upper-left corner of the window's title bar (Figure 1.22).

FIGURE 1.22 A TITLE-BAR ICON.

It's important to remember that since the introduction of Windows NT 4.0, the icon shown in a window's title bar is not always an application icon. When the user opens a window that displays a document (or data file), the icon that appears in the window's title bar is usually associated with the displayed document and not with the application that created the document.

There are exceptions to this rule. For example, the Windows NT 4.0 desktop calculator application has no data file, so the icon that appears in the calculator window's title bar is the application's icon.

Different Windows, Different Icons

When a Windows 95 user opens a multiple document interface (MDI) application, it is now possible for the title bars of different windows associated with the application to display different icons at the same time. For example, some windows might be associated with data files opened by the application, and they might display document icons. Other windows might be associated with the application itself and might display application icons.

Still another kind of icon that can appear in a title bar is a *tool icon*—an icon that does not represent an application or a data file but instead attempts to represent what an application does. For example, when you open the Windows NT Explorer application, the icon you see in the Explorer window's title bar (Figure 1.23) shows a magnifying desk in front of a folder—a graphic representation of one of the Explorer's main functions, which is to browse through the contents of folders.

FIGURE 1.23 THE EXPLORER ICON.

TITLE BARS

Because some windows are associated with data files and others are associated with applications, the formatting of the text in title bars also changed significantly with the release of Windows NT 4.0. Now the text in a window's title may be the name of a document, the name of a folder, or the name of an application. Figure 1.24 shows the three different kinds of titles. The top title bar contains the name of a folder, the middle bar contains the name of an application, and the bottom bar contains the name of a file.

FIGURE 1.24 ICONS AND TEXT IN TITLE BARS.

Figure 1.24 illustrates a useful rule to remember about text in new-style Windows NT title bars: In the title bar of a Windows 95 window, the icon that is displayed should match the first entry that appears in the title bar's text. If a data-file icon appears in a title bar, the first name that appears in the title bar's text should be the name of that data file. Similarly, if an application's icon appears in the title bar, the first name in the title bar's text should be the name of the application.

Title-Bar Pop-Up Menus

Another new feature of Windows NT is that a window no longer has a System/Control menu—a device that all standard documents had under Windows 3.1. The System/Control menu, as Windows 3.1 veterans may recall, popped up when you pressed **Alt+Spacebar** while a window was active. With the System/Control menu, you could perform such actions as moving, sizing, or closing a window.

Since the release of Windows NT 4.0, what used to be called the System/Control menu is now simply called a pop-up menu for the window being displayed. Microsoft would like you to forget about it, so it no longer has the dignity of a particular name. To activate a window's pop-up menu, you can still press **Alt+Spacebar**, and the menu that pops up still offers the same functionality (Figure 1.25).

FIGURE 1.25 A POP-UP MENU FOR A WINDOW.

The reason Microsoft would like you to forget about the menu shown in Figure 1.25 is that it's a holdover from the past; Windows NT supports the menu mainly for backward compatibility with earlier versions of Windows. The menu represents a window—and not an application, a document, or a tool—so it is not considered a useful part of the Windows NT system because it does not fit in well with the document-centered model. So you should just let it remain there and not try to do anything special with it in your Windows NT applications.

Instead of being concerned with this kind of pop-up menu, Microsoft suggests that you provide your application's windows with a Windows 95–style pop-up menu that opens when the user right-clicks the title-bar icon. You should not think of a new-style window pop-up menu as being directly associated with the window being displayed. Instead, you should see it as being associated with the *object* that's represented by the window being displayed.

For example, when you click the **Network Neighborhood** icon on the Windows NT desktop, the pop-up menu that now appears is the one shown in Figure 1.26. This pop-up menu is associated with networking properties, and not with any particular window. Generally, this is the kind of menu that should come up when the user right-clicks a desktop icon that opens a window.

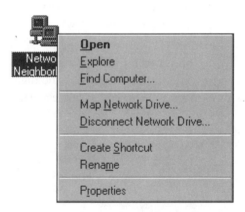

FIGURE 1.26 A POP-UP MENU ASSOCIATED WITH AN OBJECT.

Title-Bar Buttons

The UI makeover that accompanied the release of Windows NT 4.0 brought about some changes in the conventions for the buttons that appear in window title bars. In primary application windows, the minimize and maximize buttons have been updated to provide what Microsoft considers a clearer representation of these operations (Figure 1.27). A close box—a welcome addition to a window when a dialog box lacks a **Close** button—has been added to the right-hand end of Windows NT title bars.

FIGURE 1.27 IMPROVED TITLE-BAR BUTTONS IN WINDOWS NT.

MDI Applications in Windows NT

When the new Windows 95 and Windows NT interface was in the testing stage, one question that software designers often asked Microsoft designers was, "Can I still do MDI?" Officially, the answer is yes—but it sounds very much like a qualified yes when you question Microsoft officials closely about MDI.

In Windows NT, as in earlier versions of Windows, an MDI application supports the use of multiple windows—a main frame window and as many child windows as an application requires. An SDI or *single document interface*, application supports only a single window.

WINDOWS TASKBARS

The Windows taskbar, another user-interface device that made its first appearance on the Windows 95 desktop, is also available to applications written for Windows NT. For the Windows user, the taskbar is a home base for starting programs, switching between applications, quitting programs, and obtaining general information about desktop objects.

To see what a Windows taskbar looks like, you need only examine the bottom edge of the new Windows NT desktop. There you will see a taskbar like the one shown in Figure 1.28. The Windows NT taskbar displays buttons that tell the user which objects are currently open on the desktop.

FIGURE 1.28 THE WINDOWS NT TASKBAR.

The Windows NT taskbar has several properties you can set by choosing the **Start|Settings|Taskbar** menu item. For example, if you check the **Auto hide** button in the taskbar's property sheet, Windows NT makes the taskbar invisible until the mouse touches the bottom edge of the desktop window. Then the taskbar pops up and becomes visible. You can use the taskbar's auto hide feature to increase the size of the client area of the Windows NT desktop window.

The taskbar makes it easy for the user to navigate from one application to another and from one kind of window to another in multiple-window applications. It can even eliminate the need for the MDI programming model in Windows applications.

Opening Documents without Opening Applications

As Windows programmers move toward the document-centric programming model, one of the most important differences is a change in the methods that can be used to open documents. In Windows, documents must be opened within the applications that were used to create them. In applications developed for use under Windows 95 and version 4.0 and later of Windows NT, users should be able to open any document from the desktop by double-clicking on its icon. The document should open by itself without forcing the originating application to open first.

Letting documents open by themselves is the OLE way of doing things, and in case you don't know it, Microsoft has decreed that OLE is the only way to go in Windows programming. As you'll see in Chapter 5, "OLE Today," OLE allows the user to insert an object into a container without opening the application that created the object. Instead, the object simply merges itself into the interface of the existing container.

Similarly, the new Windows NT user interface lets you right-click anywhere on the desktop and choose an item from the menu that pops up. Windows then automatically executes the menu option you have chosen. If the chosen menu item is connected to a particular application, Windows need not open that application to execute the menu option.

Here's how this operation works: To create a new text document from the Windows NT desktop without opening any text-editing application, simply right-click anywhere on the desktop, choose **New** from the menu that pops up, and then choose **Text Document** from the hierarchical menu that appears beside the **New** item (Figure 1.29).

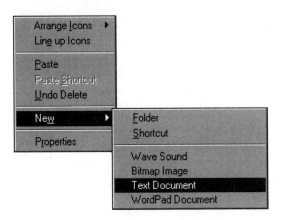

FIGURE 1.29 OPENING A POP-UP MENU ON THE WINDOWS NT DESKTOP.

A new **Notepad** icon then appears on the desktop in the location you have chosen. (Notepad is a simple text-editing application provided by the desktop.)

When you double-click the **Notepad** icon, a new Notepad window opens (Figure 1.30). But the Notepad application never actually opens—at least, not in the way that ordinary Windows applications used to open—and you are spared both the inconvenience and the overhead that would be required to open the Notepad application in the conventional way.

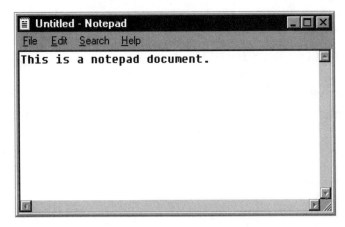

FIGURE 1.30 A NOTEPAD DOCUMENT.

Transfer Operations in Windows NT

Transfer operations are one of the most important interactive capabilities of the new document-centric model for Windows programming. In post–Windows 3.1 applications, a transfer operation is a procedure that can be broken down into three basic operations: moving, copying, or linking an object.

All commonly used editing procedures are transfer operations, and some procedures that are not normally considered editing operations can also be viewed as transfer operations. For example, printing is, in a sense, a copying operation, so it can be considered a transfer operation. Sending mail is usually either a moving or a copying operation depending on how it is set up in an application, so it, too, can be categorized as a transfer operation.

The document-centric Windows design supports transfer operations in two different ways:

✦ Through the *Command model*—the cut-and-paste model that has long been familiar to users of Windows applications.

✦ Through the *direct manipulation model*—a new Windows 95 and Windows NT term that refers to the dragging and dropping of objects. Dragging and dropping has been available in the Windows shell since the days of Windows 3.1 and has been expanded into an important transfer-operation model.

CUTTING AND PASTING OBJECTS

In the Windows 3.1 era, data was transferred from one application to another in Windows using the familiar **Cut/Copy/Paste** menu commands. In Windows NT, **Cut/Copy/Paste** has become a universal paradigm for moving objects around.

In an application that supports OLE (see Chapter 5, "OLE Today"), the user can select a data object, move to the desktop, and paste the object on the desktop. The object then becomes what Windows developers call a *scrap object*. Alternatively, a Windows 95 application can *link* an object to the desktop or place it in a particular folder or any other kind of file container that the Windows operating environment supports.

As a result, the **Cut/Copy/Paste** paradigm no longer supports transfer operations only between applications. Now it has been made universal across applications and even within the Windows shell. This means that there's now only one command model that users need to know to perform transfer operations.

Dragging and Dropping Objects

Another transfer-operation technique that's important to support in Windows is the direct manipulation model, in which an object can be dragged from one location to another. One of the most common examples of a direct-manipulation *drag-and-drop* operation is the act of dragging a document into a folder on the Windows NT desktop (Figure 1.31).

FIGURE 1.31 DRAGGING AND DROPPING AN OBJECT IN WINDOWS NT.

You can also implement this kind of drag-and-drop functionality in your own applications. The trick is to learn to use OLE, which is examined in more detail in Chapter 5, "OLE Today."

The Windows NT Registry

One tool that has taken on major new importance in Windows NT (and in Windows 95) is the system registry. The registry is important in 32-bit Windows programming because it has replaced **CONFIG.SYS** and **AUTOEXEC.BAT** in both Windows NT and Windows 95 and has also replaced **WIN.INI** and **SYSTEM.INI** in nonsystem software.

Because Windows NT is a stand-alone operating system that does not use MS-DOS or even contain any DOS code, Windows NT does not execute a DOS-style **CONFIG.SYS** file or an **AUTOEXEC.BAT** file each time it starts up. So you cannot provide a Windows NT application with configuration or initialization data at startup time by placing that data in a **CONFIG.SYS** or **AUTOEXEC.BAT** file. Instead, you must place any initialization or configuration information that your application (or the user's system) requires in the registry.

In nonsystem software, the registry has also replaced the old text-based **WIN.INI** and **SYSTEM.INI** files. They still exist in Windows NT, but unless you design system software for Microsoft, **WIN.INI** and **SYSTEM.INI** are now strictly off-limits to your Windows applications.

In this section, you'll see how you can configure the registry for an individual Windows NT user or an individual NT workstation using the REGEDIT editor. You'll also have an opportunity to build the REGDEMO sample program, which shows you the architecture of the registry and lets you examine some of its features. Figure 1.32 shows the output of the REGDEMO program.

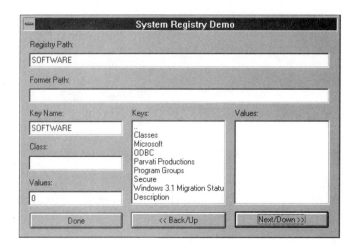

FIGURE 1.32 OUTPUT OF THE **REGDEMO** PROGRAM.

INTRODUCING THE REGISTRY

The registry is designed to be used as a repository for various kinds of important data, including:

- ✦ Information about the configuration of the user's Windows NT workstation.

- ✦ Hardware and software preferences that have been set by the current user.

- ✦ Information about applications that have been installed on the system currently being used, including the file name extensions used by various applications, the directory structure that each application uses for file storage, and even corporate information about the manufacturer of each application, such as the manufacturer's name, the product name, and the application's version number.

✦ Command lines that can be used to open various applications from DOS-style console windows or from the Windows NT desktop's **Start|Run** menu item.

✦ Uninstall information that allows the user to uninstall registered applications easily, safely, and without interfering with other software on the system.

Unfortunately, it is not quite as easy to store information in the registry as it is to stuff data into a **WIN.INI** or SYSTEM.INI file. The registry is a binary file and not a DOS-style text file, so you can't just open the registry in an ordinary text editor and edit it. Instead, you must either use the REGEDIT registry-editing tool (which you'll learn more about later in this section) or access the registry programmatically using functions provided in the MFC library or the Windows API.

KEYS, SUBKEYS, AND VALUES

The registry, like **WIN.INI** and **SYSTEM.INI,** is divided into sections that can be used to store different kinds of data. In the registry, these sections are called *keys*. Each key can be further divided into multiple levels of *subkeys*. The last subkey in the chain can contain individual data elements called *values*.

The top-level keys in the registry are called *root* keys. The registry contains the following root keys:

✦ The HKEY_CLASSES_ROOT key contains, among other things, the file name extensions used by all currently registered applications.

✦ The HKEY_CURRENT_USER key contains data about the current user.

✦ The HKEY_LOCAL_MACHINE key contains information about the system currently being used.

✦ The HKEY_USERS key contains all currently loaded user profiles, including the one maintained in the HKEY_CURRENT_USER key.

You'll learn more details about these keys later in this section.

WHAT IS THE REGISTRY?

If you've ever poked around in the **WIN.INI** file used in Windows 3.x programs, you may recall that it is usually divided into blocks that contain different kinds of data. Figure 1.33 shows a fragment of a typical **WIN.INI** file. Notice that the part of the file that's shown contains three section headings: windows, Desktop, and Intl.

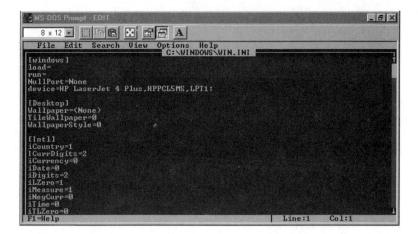

FIGURE 1.33 A SECTION OF DATA IN A WIN.INI FILE.

Although the illustration doesn't show it very clearly, there are two levels of section headings in a **WIN.INI** file: one level known as *branches* and another level known as *leaves*. In Figure 1.33, the section headings labeled windows, Desktop, and Intl are branch headings, and the data entries that appear under each heading are leaf headings. Together, these two levels of headings can be used to construct a data structure known as a *tree*.

In Windows NT, registry data is arranged in a slightly more complex tree structure. In the Windows NT registry tree, each branch can be subdivided into subbranches, and each subbranch can be divided into still more subbranches. The branches and data elements (or leaves) have specific names:

✦ Branches at the root level are called *keys*.

✦ Subbranches are called *subkeys*.

✦ Data elements, or leaves, are called *values*.

Thus, in the Windows NT registry, a value is a data element that can be nested inside multiple levels of keys and subkeys.

Registry Keys

Each key in the registry, like each section heading in a **WIN.INI** file, is used as a container for a different kind of information. Windows NT recognizes four predefined keys that can contain standard kinds of configuration information. (All four of these predefined keys, and two others, are recognized by Windows 95; see box, "The Windows NT and Windows 95 Registries," later in this section.)

Here are four predefined keys recognized by Windows NT and the kinds of information they can contain:

✦ HKEY_CLASSES_ROOT: Contains OLE information and information about the relationships that exist among different kinds of files that are currently registered by the user's system. When an application is designed to create special DOS-style file name extension (a three-letter extension preceded by a dot), you can register that extension by placing it in the HKEY_CLASSES_ROOT key. Other kinds of special files, such as those used by Microsoft Access and Microsoft Excel, are automatically registered in the HKEY_CLASSES_ROOT key category.

✦ HKEY_CURRENT_USER: Contains a user profile of the user who is currently logged on. This information includes environment variables set by the current user and the user's personal program groups, desktop settings, network connections, printers, and application preferences.

✦ HKEY_LOCAL_MACHINE: Contains information about the local workstation currently in use, including startup control data and hardware and operating system data. Hardware information stored in the HKEY_LOCAL_MACHINE key includes data about the local workstation's bus types, the system's memory, and device drivers used by the system.

✦ HKEY_USERS: Contains all currently loaded user profiles, including the one maintained in the HKEY_CURRENT_USER key. The HKEY_CURRENT_USER key is always a subkey of the HKEY_USERS key and is always the default profile. On a server, the HKEY_USERS key does not maintain profiles of users who access the server remotely. Instead, their profiles are loaded into the registries of their own local computers.

Keys and Handles

You may wonder why the names of registry keys begin with the characters HKEY_. The convention is designed to show software developers that key names are handles that can be used in programs. (In Windows, a *handle* is a value that is used to identify a resource uniquely so that a program can access it. Handles are widely used in Windows programming; if you don't know what they are, you might want to read a good book on Windows programming, such as *Programming Windows 3.1*, by Charles Petzold, or one of the other Windows programming books listed in the Bibliography.

Subkeys

Each key in the registry can contain any number of subkeys. Figure 1.34 shows the four predefined keys recognized by Windows NT along with a set of subkeys that have been defined for the HKEY_LOCAL_MACHINE key. (The window shown is the output window of a registry editor named REGEDIT, which is provided with Windows NT. To learn more about REGEDIT, see "The REGEDIT Editor" later in this chapter.)

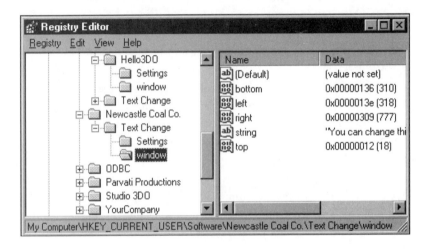

FIGURE 1.34 THE REGEDIT EDITOR.

Adding Keys to the Registry

At any time you like, you can add extra keys to the four predefined keys recognized by Windows NT. You can also define custom keys, either interactively (by using the REGEDIT editor) or programmatically (by calling Windows API functions from within applications). By calling the Windows API's registry functions, Windows applications can define their own custom keys and can add them to the user's registry.

Registering Resources

You can use the registry to store an application's resources as well as information about its associated data. It is especially important to record your application's icons in the registry. Then the system can display your program's icons properly on the Windows NT desktop and can use them in a neat and consistent way when the user is executing your application.

You can also register other kinds of resources that your application uses. Registered resources can include bitmaps, menus, and multimedia resources such as video clips and sounds. The system can help you manage your program's resources while it is running.

There are several ways to provide your applications with resources that the registry recognizes. You can embed them in your application's executable (**.EXE**) file or in your application's resource (**.RES**) file. You can store icons in icon files (**.ICO**), in Windows metafiles (**.WMF**), or as device-dependent or device-independent bitmap (**.BMP**) files. The system can create icons using any of these file types as long as you register your icons and their file types properly with the registry.

Icon Madness

Although the REGEDIT editor uses folder and document icons to represent keys, subkeys, and values in the registry, it is important to note that registry keys and subkeys are not really folders and that registry values are not really files. Keys and subkeys represent memory locations in which Windows stores particular categories of registry information, and values represent the data stored in those locations.

It would be better, perhaps, if Microsoft had designed a new set of icons for keys, subkeys, and values instead of borrowing existing icons from the Windows Explorer. But REGEDIT is designed the way it is designed, so you might as well get used to it. Just be aware that REGEDIT's icons are misleading.

WHY USE THE REGISTRY?

Windows NT does not configure applications or store application-specific information in **CONFIG.SYS** and **AUTOEXEC.BAT**. Instead, Windows NT stores this information in the registry.

Equally important, the registry manages various kinds of interactions between Windows NT applications and the Windows NT system. Overall, the registry is so important in the world of Windows NT and Windows 95 programming that applications must support the use of the registry to qualify for Microsoft's Windows NT logo.

Even if earning an NT-compatible logo is not your goal for every application you write, there are many other reasons to become familiar with the registry. Because the days of **CONFIG.SYS** and **AUTOEXEC.BAT** are numbered, you should not develop any Windows applications that use these files. Instead, you should learn how to use the registry for storing all the configuration and initialization information that your applications require.

By using the registry, you can automate the way Windows NT handles your applications and their documents and data when the user takes certain actions that Windows NT supports. For example, when you register a Windows NT application, you can place DOS-style file name extensions in the registry's HKEY_CLASSES_ROOT key to provide the user's system with information about the kinds of documents your application may create. The user of your application can then open any document that your program has created by double-clicking on the document's desktop icon without having to open your application.

Repairing the Registry

Understanding the registry can also help you solve various kinds of problems that may arise while you're using Windows NT. For example, well-behaved Windows NT programs are supposed to be equipped with uninstall applications that can gracefully delete registered programs and their data from the user's system by removing all traces of registered programs and data from the registry. But disk crashes and other kinds of accidents can erase portions of registered applications and data and leave other portions behind, so it's sometimes helpful to know how to use the REGEDIT editor and other tools to clear leftover files from the registry.

Customizing the Registry

One important feature of the registry is that it can initialize the same computer system in different ways for individual users of the same workstation. For example, if several people use the same Windows NT workstation, the registry can configure the workstation differently for each user.

System administrators can also use the registry to configure different workstations connected across a network. Such workstations can be configured in different ways depending on what kind of job each one performs. The registry can also recognize an individual user (for example, the system administrator) who may log on from time to time on different machines. By recognizing a user's logon name and password, the registry can set up a correct profile for the user no matter which workstation he or she uses to log on.

Applications can use the registry as a long-term storage area for any kind of information that they need to keep on file when the user's system is not running. For example, you can use the registry to store information about user preferences such as screen colors, screen wallpaper, and screen savers. When you have stored such preferences in the registry, they are activated as soon as the user starts your application.

If you store this kind of information in the registry, you should make sure that your storage needs aren't too great. Storing too much information in the registry can make it grow much larger than it should be and can slow the whole system. If your application needs to store large amounts of information—for example, a database of system users and their E-mail addresses—you shouldn't even think about storing that data in the registry. Instead, you should create your own database file on a disk and store the information there.

A program that uses the registry must register itself on the user's system at installation time and must store any startup information that it needs—such as communications passwords, fonts, and information about the kinds of files it generates—in the registry.

Storing Type Information in the Registry

One benefit of storing information in binary form in the registry is that you can store many different kinds of configuration data in registry files. For example, the registry is a good place to store the type of data that your application creates and uses. (In Windows NT terminology, *type* is what determines the way the user differentiates one object from another thing in the interface.)

When you store information about your application's type in the registry, Windows NT can execute your application when the user double-clicks the icon of a document your application has created. If you don't register your application's type, your application is more of a clunker; Windows NT assigns generic icons to your program's documents, because the system has no way to associate them with any stored icons.

A more important consideration is that if you don't register your program's type, Windows does not have the information it needs to open a document automatically when the user clicks on the document's icon. Instead, the system displays an error-message dialog box or (in Windows 95) an Open With dialog box like the one shown in Figure 1.35. The Open With dialog box prompts the user to type in the name of the application that created the document.

FIGURE 1.35 THE OPEN WITH DIALOG BOX.

When you want to register the types associated with your application and its documents, all you have to do is to record their file name extensions in the registry. (In Windows NT, as in MS-DOS, a file name extension is a three-letter extension following a dot.) Windows NT can then find your application and open it when the user clicks on an appropriate document icon.

Extending the Registry

Another useful feature of the registry is its extensibility. You can add commands to the registry for your files and for other file types that are in the system. For example, suppose you write a special piece of code to modify files created by a particular application. Because the registry is extensible, you can associate your applications and the documents they create with pop-up menu commands that are easily accessible to the Windows NT user. Using registry functions provided by the Windows Software Development Kit (SDK), you can add menu commands to the pop-up menu that appears each time the user right-clicks on a document created by your application. You can then write code that executes each time the user chooses the pop-up menu command that you have provided.

You can also write code that provides property pages for objects associated with applications you have registered. If you wish, you can create specific properties for the objects and store those properties in the registry. Then you can place information about those properties on a property sheet associated with your application. When you have done that, the Windows NT user can display your property sheet by right-clicking on a document associated with your application and then choosing **Properties** from the document's pop-up menu. When the document's property sheet opens, the user can change its properties using whatever property-sheet items you have provided.

The Windows NT and Windows 95 Registries

Although both Windows NT and Windows 95 support the use of a system registry, there are some significant differences between the Windows NT registry and the Windows 95 registry. Here are three differences:

+ Windows 95 has no built-in security features, so the HKEY_LOCAL_MACHINE key has no SECURITY subkey. The Windows API functions `RegGetSecurityKey` and `RegSetSecurityKey`, which are available in Windows NT, are not available in Windows 95. These two functions do nothing in Windows 95; they don't even protect your data. Consequently, you can't rely on security settings managed by the registry in programs that can be run under both Windows NT and Windows 95.

+ Windows NT supports the use of *volatile* registry keys, which are purged from the registry automatically when the system shuts down, and *nonvolatile* keys, which are not. In Windows NT, you can make a key volatile or nonvolatile by setting a volatility attribute when you call the API function `RegCreateKey`. Windows 95 ignores this volatility setting.

+ Both Windows NT and Windows 95 support the four standard registry keys HKEY_CLASSES_ROOT, HKEY_CURRENT_USER, HKEY_LOCAL_MACHINE, and HKEY_CURRENT_USER. In addition, Windows 95 supports two keys that Windows NT does not recognize: HKEY_CURRENT_CONFIG and HKEY_DYN_DATA. In Windows 95, the HKEY_CURRENT_CONFIG key is used to store hardware profile information that supports the Windows 95 Plug and Play mechanism. The HKEY_DYN_DATA key is used to store information that supports Windows 95–specific virtual device drivers, or VxDs. (For more about virtual device drivers, see Chapter 2, "Underneath Windows NT.")

EDITING REGISTRY DATA

Because registry information is stored in binary form rather than in text form, you can't make or edit entries in the registry using an ordinary text editor. Even if you could, you shouldn't, because Microsoft makes no guarantees about the exact location of registry information in memory or how it is stored. But Microsoft does supply a number of mechanisms for creating, removing, and editing registry data.

Here are techniques for placing information in the registry:

+ The Win32 application programming interface (API) provided with Microsoft Visual C++ provides a number of registry-related functions to help you build registry support into your applications. For example, you can place information in the registry by calling the `RegCreateKey` or `RegSetValue` function, and you can retrieve information stored in the registry by calling functions such as `RegEnumKeyEx`, `RegEnumValue`, or `RegQueryInfoKey`. The example program presented in this chapter (see "Example Program: Exploring the Registry") shows how you can use these functions and other registry-related functions in your Windows NT programs.

+ When you need to store registry information about a computer, a user, or a group of computers connected across a network, you can view and edit your system's registry interactively using the REGEDIT editor, which is supplied with Windows NT. (For more details, see "The REGEDIT Editor.")

+ When you are ready to ship a Windows application, you can make it a self-registering program by including an installer that registers it properly. For your application to qualify for a Microsoft Windows–compatible logo, you must make the program self-registering and you must also provide an uninstall utility. One easy way to create an installer and an uninstaller is to use a commercial registry-compatible installation generator. One such generator is InstallShield, which is provided (in an introductory version) with Microsoft Visual C++. Using InstallShield, you can register your applications and their resources with the user's Windows NT system at install time. InstallShield can automatically equip your application with both an installer and an uninstall utility.

THE REGEDIT EDITOR

To help developers and power users manage information stored in the registry, Microsoft ships a special editor called REGEDIT with Windows NT. REGEDIT is not designed for casual Windows NT users, so it is not documented in entry-level user manuals, and you won't find a REGEDIT icon on the Windows NT desktop. To access the registry, you must open a DOS-style console window from the Windows NT Start menu and then enter the command line

REGEDIT

Windows NT responds by opening the REGEDIT window (Figure 1.36).

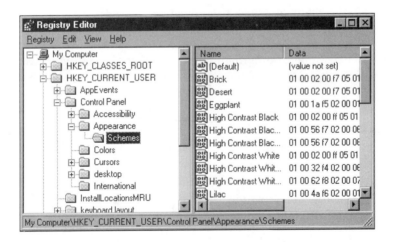

FIGURE 1.36 THE REGEDIT WINDOW.

When REGEDIT starts, it opens a graphical user interface (GUI) editor that you can use to examine and experiment with your system's registry. The REGEDIT editor displays registry information in a two-panel window. The left panel contains a directory-like tree structure that you can use to view the keys and subkeys currently in use by your system's registry. The right panel contains a list of file icons that represent values stored in the registry.

The registered objects displayed in the right panel are called *value entries*, or simply values. When you select a subkey icon in the left panel by clicking the mouse, any value entries it contains appear in the right panel. In Figure 1.36, a subkey icon named **Schemes** is selected in the left panel, and a list of font information that the Scheme subkey contains is displayed in the right panel.

IMPORTANT REGISTRY KEYS

To understand how application information is stored in the registry, it helps to recognize the most important keys and to understand how they are used. The following paragraphs examine some of these registry keys. When you create an installer for an application using a commercial installer generator such as InstallShield, you can make use of the keys described in this section using scripting techniques that are explained in the documentation that comes with the installer generator.

The Application Information Key

One important registry key is the *application information* key, which identifies your application by its name, its version number, and the name of your company. The general format of the application key is

```
[HKEY_LOCAL_MACHINE]\Software\Company\Product\Version
```

For example, the following is the application information key entry for version 1.0 of an application called Creation manufactured by a company named The Game Lab:

```
[HKEY_LOCAL_MACHINE]\Software\TheGameLab\Creation\1.0
```

The Uninstall Information Key

Another critical key is the *uninstall information* key. This key stores information that lets Windows users remove your program and all its data from their systems easily and safely.

Uninstall information, when it exists, is stored in an application-specific key under the general key:

```
[HKEY_LOCAL_MACHINE]\Software\Microsoft\Windows\
CurrentVersion\Uninstall
```

In the following example, the key `SampleAppV3` identifies the location of two values. The `[DisplayName]` value is the name that appears in the Add/Remove Programs applet in the Windows NT Control Panel. The `[UninstallString]` value identifies the exact locations and names of the uninstall executable file and the log file containing uninstall data.

```
[HKEY_LOCAL_MACHINE]\Software\Microsoft\Windows\
CurrentVersion\Uninstall\SampleAppV3
[DisplayName]= Sample App
[UninstallString] =    C:\WINDOWS\deinst.exe

    C:\ProgramFiles\Company\SampleApp\Deinslog.1
```

The Per Application Paths Information Key

The *per application paths information* key stores path information that enables Windows NT to find your application's executable files. In Windows NT, path information is stored in the registry under an application-specific key located under the general key:

```
[HKEY_LOCAL_MACHINE]\Software\Microsoft\Windows\
CurrentVersion\App Paths
```

The following example is a per application paths key entry that shows the `[Path]` and `[Default]` values stored under an application-specific key named `designer.exe`:

```
[HKEY_LOCAL_MACHINE]\Software\Microsoft\Windows\
CurrentVersion\App Paths\designer.exe

[Path] = C:\Program Files\Company\SampleApp\PROGRAM;
    C:\Program Files\Company\SampleApp\System

[Default] = C:\Program Files\Company\SampleApp\PROGRAM\designer.exe
```

Example Program: Exploring the Registry

The example program REGDEMO, in this chapter's directory on the accompanying disk, is a simple program you can experiment with to see how the registry works in Windows NT. REGDEMO, like the PROGBAR sample program presented earlier in this chapter, is a dialog-based application that was created using AppWizard.

REGDEMO introduces you to the registry and lets you cruise around in it, but it is not intended to teach you how to use the registry in your own programs. In Chapter 2, "Underneath Windows NT," you'll get a chance to examine a more ambitious sample program, named TEXTCHNG, that shows how you can use the registry in your own applications.

To create a dialog-based program, follow these steps:

1. Select **File\New** from the Developer Studio menu and then create a new project by selecting **Project Workspace** in the New dialog box. Click the **OK** button.

2. When the New Project Workspace dialog box opens, choose **MFC AppWizard (exe)** from the Type list box.

3. Type a name for your project in the Name edit box.

4. Close the New Project Workspace dialog box by clicking **Create**.

5. When the AppWizard window (Figure 1.37) opens, select the radio button labeled **Dialog based**.

From Step 4 on, follow the normal procedures for creating a Visual C++ project.

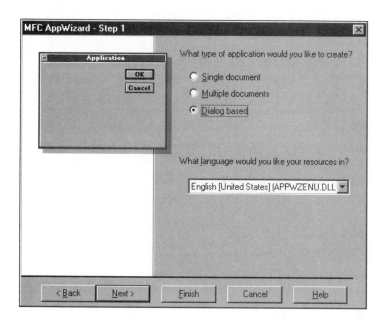

FIGURE 1.37 CREATING A DIALOG-BASED APPLICATION.

FEATURES OF THE **REGDEMO** PROGRAM

REGDEMO is a Visual C++ adaptation of the example program named MONKEY that is provided with Visual C++. The MONKEY program is written in C and not in Visual C++, and it seems outdated because it uses old-fashioned, Windows 3.1–style controls. In contrast, REGDEMO was written using version 4.0 of Visual C++ and updates the MONKEY program by using many of the advanced features of Visual C++.

REGDEMO also has a neater and more intuitive user interface than its C-language predecessor. The buttons labeled **Back/Up** and **Next/Down**, which display information in the program's two list boxes, are placed directly under the list boxes they're associated with and are provided with arrows that show the two directions in which data is moved.

More important, both buttons are implemented as C++ classes so that they can be equipped with member functions that give the designer more control over their functionality. For example, the **Back/Up** button is disabled when it is not functional; the button grays out when you reach the root level of the registry's keys and can't back up any farther. This design is more user-friendly than the MONKEY program's solution, which is to display a dialog box that pops up and chastens you for clicking the **Back** button when it isn't functional.

RETRIEVING DIALOG BOX DATA WITH THE **DDX** MECHANISM

Instead of using complicated callbacks to access the information in dialog-box controls—a headache until Visual C++ made things easier—the new member functions added to REGDEMO use the Visual C++ dialog data exchange system for passing the values of variables between dialog-box controls and program functions. Some of the original callbacks in the MONKEY program have not been updated to use the DDX mechanism. They work fine just the way they are, so there was no reason to change them. Leaving these callbacks in the program demonstrates an important fact about Visual C++: You can make Windows API calls from a Visual C++ program just as you always could. So when you port a non-Visual C++ application to Visual C++, you need update only the API calls that need updating; you need not spend the time or energy it would take to update all of them.

To use the Visual C++ DDX system, all you have to do is to create member variables for your dialog box controls using ClassWizard. Then call the MFC member function UpdateData to transfer information between your dialog box's controls and their corresponding member variables.

If you call UpdateData with a FALSE parameter, the function copies data from all member variables associated with a dialog box's controls to their corresponding controls.

The same function, called with a TRUE parameter, copies data the other way: from all controls associated with member variables to their corresponding variables.

It's difficult to remember that UpdateData(FALSE) copies data from variables to controls, whereas UpdateData(TRUE) copies data in the opposite direction. In **DLGDEMO.H**, file, I have provided these two #define directives to make things easier to remember:

```
#define VAR2CTRL FALSE
#define CTRL2VAR TRUE
```

With these two definitions in place, it's easy to remember that in the following function in **DLGDEMO.CPP**, the REGDEMO program copies into a text box a string that the user has selected from a list box into a text box:

```
UpdateData(.i.CTRL2VAR definition;CTRL2VAR);
m_ideName = m_lbStr1;
UpdateData(.i.VAR2CTRL definition;VAR2CTRL);
```

In the first line of the preceding code fragment, the UpdateData function is called to copy the data from all dialog-box controls associated with member variables into their corresponding data members. The second line copies the contents of a member variable named m_lbStr1, which is associated with a list-box entry, into another member variable named m_ideName, which is associated with a text-box string. The third line calls UpdateData again, this time to copy the contents of all member variables associated with dialog-box controls into their corresponding controls.

To make the preceding code fragments work properly, you must use ClassWizard to associate the m_ideName and m_lbStr1 variables with the appropriate dialog-box controls. For more information about how ClassWizard can be used to create member variables and associate them with controls, see Chapter 4, "Programming Windows NT with Visual C++."

HOW THE REGDEMO PROGRAM WORKS

Using the REGDEMO application, you can navigate the branches of the registry tree and observe as the program displays the data values of individual keys.

REGDEMO is a simple program that lets you poke around in the registry and get an idea of how it works. In Chapter 2, "Underneath Windows NT," you'll get a chance to create a sample program that actually makes changes in the registry and uses them to configure attributes of a program at load time.

When you start REGDEMO, it displays a dialog box that contains a pair of list boxes and a number of other dialog box controls. The list box on the left, labeled Keys, always displays the child keys of the current key. The list box on the right, labeled Values, displays values stored in the selected key—provided that the local key has any values. When the program starts, the Keys list box contains four entries, representing the four key handles that are predefined in both Windows NT and Windows 95: HKEY_LOCAL_MACHINE, HKEY_CURRENT_USER, HKEY_USERS, and HKEY_CLASSES_ROOT.

If you select any of these four entries and click the **Next/Down** button, the name of the selected key appears in the Key Name text box and the program calls a helper member function named `EnumerateLevel`. The `EnumerateLevel` function calls the Win32 function `RegOpenKey` to open a handle to a registry key and then calls another member helper function, `QueryKey`. The `QueryKey` function then calls the Win32 function `RegQueryInfoKey` to obtain registry information about the selected key. All this happens in **DLGDEMO.CPP**, which is provided in this chapter's folder on the accompanying disk.

When you select the name of a key in the Keys list box and then click **Next/Down**, the names of the children of the selected key replace the entries in the Keys list box. For example, if you select HKEY_LOCAL_MACHINE, the name HKEY_LOCAL_MACHINE appears in the Key Name text box and the children of the HKEY_LOCAL_MACHINE key—HARDWARE, SECURITY, SOFTWARE, and SYSTEM—appear in the Keys list box. To move deeper into the tree, double-click another child key. You can back out of the registry by clicking **Back/Up**.

If the currently selected key is associated with any values, the names of these values are listed in the Values list box when you click **Next/Down**. If the current key is not associated with any values, nothing is displayed in the Values list box and a zero appears in the Values text box.

If the current key is associated with a class type, the key's class appears in the Class text box.

SOURCE CODE OF THE REGDEMO PROGRAM

Listing 1.1 is **REGDEM.CPP,** file, which implements the dialog box portion of REGDEMO. The objects and member functions in the listing are defined in **REGDEM.H.**

LISTING 1.1 USING THE REGISTRY.

```
// dlgdemo.cpp : implementation file
//

#include "stdafx.h"
```

```
#include "RegDem.h"
#include "dlgdemo.h"
#include "BtnBack.h"
#include "BtnNext.h"

#ifdef _DEBUG
#undef THIS_FILE
static char BASED_CODE THIS_FILE[] = __FILE__;
#endif

#define _UNICODE

/////////////////////////////////////////////////////////////////////////
// CDlgDemo dialog

CDlgDemo::CDlgDemo(CWnd* pParent /*=NULL*/)
    : CDialog(CDlgDemo::IDD, pParent)
{
    //{{AFX_DATA_INIT(CDlgDemo)
    m_ideACL = _T("");
    m_ideClass = _T("");
    m_ideName = _T("");
    m_lbStr1 = _T("");
    m_lbStr2 = _T("");
    m_ideTextOut = _T("");
    //}}AFX_DATA_INIT
    m_pStrList = NULL;
    m_btnBack = NULL;
}

CDlgDemo::~CDlgDemo()
{
    ASSERT_VALID(m_pStrList);
    delete m_pStrList;
    ASSERT_VALID(m_btnBack);
    delete m_btnBack;
}

void CDlgDemo::DoDataExchange(CDataExchange* pDX)
{
```

```
      CDialog::DoDataExchange(pDX);
      //{{AFX_DATA_MAP(CDlgDemo)
      DDX_Text(pDX, IDE_ACL, m_ideACL);
      DDV_MaxChars(pDX, m_ideACL, 128);
      DDX_Text(pDX, IDE_CLASS, m_ideClass);
      DDV_MaxChars(pDX, m_ideClass, 128);
      DDX_Text(pDX, IDE_NAME, m_ideName);
      DDV_MaxChars(pDX, m_ideName, 128);
      DDX_LBString(pDX, IDL_LISTBOX, m_lbStr1);
      DDX_LBString(pDX, IDL_LISTBOX2, m_lbStr2);
      DDX_Text(pDX, IDE_TEXTOUT, m_ideTextOut);
      DDV_MaxChars(pDX, m_ideTextOut, 128);
      //}}AFX_DATA_MAP
}

BEGIN_MESSAGE_MAP(CDlgDemo, CDialog)
      //{{AFX_MSG_MAP(CDlgDemo)
      ON_BN_CLICKED(IDB_BACK, OnIDBBack)
      ON_BN_CLICKED(IDB_NEXT, OnIDBNext)
      ON_LBN_DBLCLK(IDL_LISTBOX, OnDblclkListbox)
      ON_LBN_DBLCLK(IDL_LISTBOX2, OnDblclkListbox2)
      //}}AFX_MSG_MAP
END_MESSAGE_MAP()

//////////////////////////////////////////////////////////////////////////
// App-specific member functions.
// Override CDialog::OnInitDialog();

BOOL CDlgDemo::OnInitDialog()
{
    m_pStrList = new CStringList;

    // Rectangle coordinates for 'Back' button.
    RECT btnBackRect = { 166,266,310,290 };

    // Construct 'Back' button.
    m_btnBack = new CBtnBack;

    // Create 'Back' button.
    BOOL bRetVal = m_btnBack->Create("<< Back/Up", BS_PUSHBUTTON | WS_VISIBLE
```

```
         | WS_CHILD, btnBackRect, this, IDB_BACK);

    // Make 'Back' button's font match this dialog's font.
    CFont *thisDlgFont = new CFont;
    thisDlgFont = GetFont();
    m_btnBack->SetFont(thisDlgFont);

    // When program starts, m_btnBack button is disabled
    // because we're at Level 0 and can't back up any
    // further.
    m_btnBack->EnableWindow(FALSE);

    // Fill in the 'Keys' list box with its initial values.
    ListBox1().AddString("HKEY_LOCAL_MACHINE");
    ListBox1().AddString("HKEY_CURRENT_USER");
    ListBox1().AddString("HKEY_USERS");
    ListBox1().AddString("HKEY_CLASSES_ROOT");

    m_hKeyRoot = 0;    // Initialize m_hKeyRoot.
    m_regPath = ""; // Registry path.
    m_fullBranches = TRUE; // Initialize m_fullBranches (see

    // dlgdemo.h for details).

    return TRUE;
}

//////////////////////////////////////////////////////////////////////
// CDlgDemo message handlers

// This function executes when the user clicks the 'Next' button.
void CDlgDemo::OnIDBNext()
{
    // Get the index number of the item the user has selected
    // in the 'Keys' list box.
    int index = ListBox1().GetCurSel();

  // We're no longer at Level 0, so enable the 'Back' list box.
    m_btnBack->EnableWindow(TRUE);

    // Prompt user for a selection if there is none.
```

```
    if (index == LB_ERR) {
        MessageBox("Please select an item in the left-hand list box.");
        // m_btnBack->EnableWindow(FALSE);
        return;
    }

    // If list-box item 0 is selected, user wants to move
    // back (up), so execute OnIDBBack (below).
    if (index = 0 && m_hKeyRoot) {
        OnIDBBack();
        return;
    }

    // Copy user's list-box selection into the Name text box...
    UpdateData(CTRL2VAR);
    m_ideName = m_lbStr1;

    // ... and clear both list boxes.
    ListBox1().ResetContent();
    ListBox2().ResetContent();

    // The EnumerateLevel() member function is defined later
    // in this file.
    char *sTemp = m_ideName.GetBuffer(128);
    char *sTemp2 = m_regPath.GetBuffer(128);
    EnumerateLevel(sTemp, sTemp2, &m_hKeyRoot);

    // Add the new path to the string list
    m_pStrList->AddTail(m_regPath);
    UpdateData(VAR2CTRL);
}

// This function executes when the user clicks the 'Back' button.
void CDlgDemo::OnIDBBack()
{
    HWND hDlg = m_hWnd;
    CString s;
    int index;
    char NameLBSelect[256];
    CString regPath = m_regPath;
```

```
// Get the item the user has selected in the 'Keys' list box.
ListBox1().GetText(256, NameLBSelect);

// If !m_hRootKey, we're already at the top level.
// So we'll inform the user and then return. (Actually,
// this should never happen in this version of the
// program because the 'Back' button should be disabled
// at this point. But I'm leaving this 'if' statement in,
// just to make sure everything is working properly.)
if (!m_hKeyRoot) {
    MessageBox ("Top Level; you can't back up any further.",
    "RegDemo Application", MB_OK);
    return;
}

//For all remaining cases, clear the list boxes.
ListBox1().ResetContent();
ListBox2().ResetContent();

// If hRootKey has a value, but the pathname is blank,
// then we must be one level deep. So we'll reset to
// Level 0.

if (strlen(m_regPath) == 0) {
    m_ideName = "";
    UpdateData(VAR2CTRL);
    ListBox1().AddString("HKEY_LOCAL_MACHINE");
    ListBox1().AddString("HKEY_CURRENT_USER");
    ListBox1().AddString("HKEY_USERS");
    ListBox1().AddString("HKEY_CLASSES_ROOT");

    // We're back at Level 0, so disable the 'Back' button.
    m_btnBack->EnableWindow(FALSE);

    m_hKeyRoot = 0;    // Initialize m_hKeyRoot.
    return;
}

// Just two cases left: Either (a) the path has only one
// key name in it, and there's no backslash character in that
```

```
// name, or (b) there is more than one key name in the path
// and there is at least one backslash in the name.
// If this is case (a), we will fool EnumerateLevel
// into thinking we have picked one of the predefined keys.
// Then EnumerateLevel will re-enumerate the child key's
// parent key, taking us back to Level 0. If this is case (b),
// we will retrieve the last key name from m_pStrList and
// then call EnumerateLevel.

// First we check to see if (a) the path has only one
// key name in it, and there is no backslash in that name.
// If so, we will fool EnumerateLevel into thinking we have
// picked one of the pre-defined keys. Then EnumerateLevel
// will re-enumerate the child key's parent key, taking us
// back to Level 0. .

// If there is no backslash, m_regPath.Find
// returns -1.
if ((index = m_regPath.Find('\\')) == -1) {
    m_regPath = "";
    switch ((DWORD)m_hKeyRoot) {
        case (DWORD)HKEY_LOCAL_MACHINE:
            strcpy (NameLBSelect, "HKEY_LOCAL_MACHINE");
            break;
        case (DWORD)HKEY_USERS:
            strcpy (NameLBSelect, "HKEY_USERS");
            break;
        case (DWORD)HKEY_CURRENT_USER:
            strcpy (NameLBSelect, "HKEY_CURRENT_USER");
            break;
        case (DWORD)HKEY_CLASSES_ROOT:
            strcpy (NameLBSelect, "HKEY_CLASSES_ROOT");
            break;
    }

    ::SetDlgItemText (hDlg, IDE_NAME, NameLBSelect);
    m_hKeyRoot = 0;
    EnumerateLevel (NameLBSelect, m_regPath.GetBuffer(256),
        &m_hKeyRoot);
```

```
        // We're at Level 0, so clear the string list.
        m_pStrList->RemoveAll();

    } else {

        // This must be case (b) (see preceding comment),
        // so we can retrieve the last key named from
        // the string list and then re-enumerate the
        // resulting level.

        // First, copy user's list-box selection into the
        // m_ideName variable.
        // (The old way was:
        //     ::SetDlgItemText (hDlg, IDE_NAME, NameLBSelect);)
        m_ideName = NameLBSelect;
        UpdateData(VAR2CTRL);

        // If the string list isn't empty, retrieve the
        // last item from the string list. This will be
        // our new key selection.
        CString tempStr;
        if (!m_pStrList->IsEmpty()) {
            tempStr = m_pStrList->GetTail();
            // We've now retrieved the last item in the string
            // list, so discard it.
            m_pStrList->RemoveTail();

        } else {

            // The following was for debugging only.
            // MessageBox("The string list is empty!");

        }

        // Enumerate level for new key string.
        char *s = tempStr.GetBuffer(128);
        m_regPath = tempStr;
        EnumerateLevel (NameLBSelect, s, &m_hKeyRoot);
    }
}
```

```
void CDlgDemo::OnDblclkListbox()
{
    // TODO: Add your control notification handler code here
    // Decided not to do this; see the original MONKEY program.
}

void CDlgDemo::OnDblclkListbox2()
{
    // TODO: Add your control notification handler code here
    // Decided not to do this; see the original MONKEY program.
}

// The EnumerateLevel() Function
//
// The following function gets a valid key handle (either to
// determine if the one sent to the function was one of the
// six pre-defined keys, or to open a key specified by the
// path), and to pass that key handle along to QueryKey().
//
// To enumerate the children of a key, you must have
// an open handle to it. Four top-level keys of the
// registry are predefined and open for use:
// HKEY_LOCAL_MACHINE, HKEY_USERS, HKEY_CURRENT_USER,
// and HKEY_CLASSES_ROOT. These keys can be used to call
// RegEnumKey as is, but to RegEnumKey on any of the
// children of these you must first have an open key
// handle to the child.
//
// If hKeyRoot != 0, assume that you are lower than the
// first level of the Registry and that the user is trying
// to enumerate one of the children. First calculate
// the name of the child, and then use RegOpenKey to
// get an open handle.
//
// If hKeyRoot == 0, assume that you are at the top level
// of the Registry, and set the hKey to be enumerated
// to be one of the 4 predefined values, the specific
// one indicated by the ListBox selection.
//
```

```
void CDlgDemo::EnumerateLevel (/* HWND hDlg, */
    LPTSTR NameLBSelect,
    LPTSTR RegPath, HKEY *hKeyRoot)
{
    HKEY hKey;
  UINT retCode;
  CHAR  Buf[255];
    if (*hKeyRoot) {
        // If RegPath is not NULL, you must add a backslash to the
        // path name before appending the next-level child name.
        if (strcmp (RegPath, "") != 0)
            strcat (RegPath, "\\");
        // Add the next-level child name.
        strcat (RegPath, NameLBSelect);
        // Call RegOpenKeyEx() with the new registry path
        // to get an open handle to the child key you want to
        // enumerate.
        retCode = RegOpenKeyEx (*hKeyRoot, RegPath, 0,
            KEY_ENUMERATE_SUB_KEYS | KEY_EXECUTE |
            KEY_QUERY_VALUE, &hKey);
        if (retCode != ERROR_SUCCESS) {
            if (retCode == ERROR_ACCESS_DENIED)
                wsprintf (Buf,
                "Error: Can't open key, probably for security reasons.");
            else
                wsprintf (Buf,
                    "Error: Can't open key, RegOpenKey = %d, Line = %d",
                    retCode, __LINE__);
            MessageBox (Buf, "", MB_OK);

            // PostMessage (hDlg, WM_COMMAND, IDB_BACK, 0);
            OnIDBBack();

            return;
        }
    } else {
        // Set the *hKeyRoot handle based
        // on the text taken from the ListBox.
```

```
        if (strcmp (NameLBSelect, "HKEY_CLASSES_ROOT") == 0)
            *hKeyRoot = HKEY_CLASSES_ROOT;
        if (strcmp (NameLBSelect, "HKEY_USERS") == 0)
            *hKeyRoot = HKEY_USERS;
        if (strcmp (NameLBSelect, "HKEY_LOCAL_MACHINE") == 0)
            *hKeyRoot = HKEY_LOCAL_MACHINE;
        if (strcmp (NameLBSelect, "HKEY_CURRENT_USER") == 0)
            *hKeyRoot = HKEY_CURRENT_USER;
        hKey = *hKeyRoot;    // hKey is used in RegEnumKey().
    } //end if/else *hKeyRoot
    QueryKey (/* hDlg, */ hKey);
    RegCloseKey (hKey);  // Close the key handle.
    m_ideTextOut = m_regPath;
    UpdateData(VAR2CTRL);
}


// The QueryKey() Function
//
// This function displays the key's children (subkeys
// and the names of the Values associated with them.
// This function calls RegEnumKey, RegEnumValue, and
// RegQueryInfoKey.
//

void CDlgDemo::QueryKey (/* HWND hDlg, */ HKEY hKey)
{
    HWND hDlg = m_hWnd;


    CHAR    KeyName[MAX_PATH];
    CHAR    ClassName[MAX_PATH] = "";  // Buffer for class name.
    DWORD   dwcClassLen = MAX_PATH;   // Length of class string.
    DWORD   dwcSubKeys;          // Number of sub keys.
    DWORD   dwcMaxSubKey;        // Longest sub key size.
    DWORD   dwcMaxClass;         // Longest class string.
    DWORD   dwcValues;           // Number of values for this key.
    DWORD   dwcMaxValueName;     // Longest Value name.
    DWORD   dwcMaxValueData;     // Longest Value data.
    DWORD   dwcSecDesc;          // Security descriptor.
    FILETIME ftLastWriteTime;    // Last write time.
```

```
DWORD i;
DWORD retCode;
DWORD j;
DWORD retValue;
CHAR ValueName[MAX_VALUE_NAME];
DWORD dwcValueName = MAX_VALUE_NAME;
CHAR Buf[255];

// Get Class name and Value count.
RegQueryInfoKey (hKey, // Key handle.
    ClassName,      // Buffer for class name.
    &dwcClassLen,   // Length of class string.
    NULL,        // Reserved.
    &dwcSubKeys,    // Number of subkeys.
    &dwcMaxSubKey,   // Longest subkey size.
    &dwcMaxClass,   // Longest class string.
    &dwcValues,     // Number of values for this key.
    &dwcMaxValueName, // Longest Value name.
    &dwcMaxValueData, // Longest Value data.
    &dwcSecDesc,     // Security descriptor.
    &ftLastWriteTime); // Last write time.
::SetDlgItemText (hDlg, IDE_CLASS, ClassName);
::SetDlgItemInt (hDlg, IDE_CVALUES, dwcValues, FALSE);
::SendMessage (::GetDlgItem (hDlg, IDL_LISTBOX),
    LB_ADDSTRING, 0, (LONG)"..");

// Loop until RegEnumKey fails. Then get the name of
// each child and place it in the list box.
// Enumerate the Child Keys.
SetCursor (LoadCursor (NULL, IDC_WAIT));
for (i=0, retCode = ERROR_SUCCESS; retCode ==
    ERROR_SUCCESS; i++) {
    retCode = RegEnumKey (hKey, i,
        KeyName, MAX_PATH);
    if (retCode == (DWORD)ERROR_SUCCESS)
        ::SendMessage (::GetDlgItem(hDlg, IDL_LISTBOX),
        LB_ADDSTRING, 0, (LONG)KeyName);
    }

    SetCursor (LoadCursor (NULL, IDC_ARROW));
```

```
        // Enumerate the Key Values
        SetCursor (LoadCursor (NULL, IDC_WAIT));
        if (dwcValues)
            for (j = 0, retValue = ERROR_SUCCESS;
                j < dwcValues; j++) {
                dwcValueName = MAX_VALUE_NAME;
                ValueName[0] = '\0';
                retValue = RegEnumValue (hKey, j, ValueName,
                    &dwcValueName,
                    NULL,
                    NULL,        //&dwType,
                    NULL,        //&bData,
                    NULL);       //&bcData);
                if (retValue != (DWORD)ERROR_SUCCESS &&
                    retValue != ERROR_INSUFFICIENT_BUFFER) {
                    wsprintf (Buf,
                "Line:%d 0 based index = %d, retValue = %d, ValueLen = %d",
                        __LINE__, j, retValue, dwcValueName);
                    ::MessageBox (hDlg, Buf, "Debug", MB_OK);
                }
                Buf[0] = '\0';
                if (!strlen(ValueName))
                    strcpy (ValueName, "<NO NAME>");
                wsprintf (Buf, "%d) %s ", j, ValueName);
                ::SendMessage (::GetDlgItem (hDlg, IDL_LISTBOX2),
            LB_ADDSTRING, 0, (LONG)Buf);
                // We're at the top level, so disable the 'Next' button.
                // m_btnNext->EnableWindow(FALSE);

            } // end for(;;)
    SetCursor (LoadCursor (NULL, IDC_ARROW));registry
    }
```

Summary

This chapter explores the technology behind the Windows NT interface and explains how you can use some of the features of the interface in your Windows NT applications. Many of the topics introduced in this chapter are covered in more detail in later chapters.

By mastering and using the Windows interface features introduced in this chapter—including the two sample programs it presents, REGDEMO and PROGBAR—you can start building better Windows interfaces right now. Here are some examples:

✦ Your Windows NT applications should use contextual interfaces such as pop-up menus, properties and property sheets, and contextual help interfaces.

✦ When a window displays a data file or a document type, the name of the displayed object should usually appear in the title bar.

✦ Create icons not only for your applications but also for your data files—and register your icons (and other application resources) with the registry.

✦ Consider writing applications that support the single-instance model—that is, let the user open only one instance of your application at a time.

✦ Support OLE. This is one of the most important tips for Windows programmers. If you understand OLE, you understand the future of Windows, and can support the new OLE-related features built into Windows NT and future versions of Windows.

✦ Microsoft does not exactly frown on the continued use of MDI, but suggests that you consider alternatives to make your applications more document-centric. For some of these alternatives, see section titled "Opening Documents without Opening Applications."

✦ To enhance and streamline your Windows NT applications, consider using some of the interface gadgets and controls that are used in the Windows NT interface and are made available in the MFC library. These gadgets and controls include common dialog boxes, pop-up menus, and many new controls, such as toolbars, status bars, tree views, and rich text controls.

✦ Learn to use the registry. You must know how to use the registry to create well-behaved applications for Windows NT.

CHAPTER TWO

UNDERNEATH WINDOWS NT

Long ago, in the era of MS-DOS and Windows 3.1, it was essential for Windows programmers to be on intimate terms with the internal intricacies of the Windows operating environment. Essentially, the folks who designed Windows 3.x had to cram the capabilities of a 32-bit CPU into a 16-bit operating system, and the result was something like Dr. Samuel Johnson's description of a dog walking on its hind legs: the wonder was not that it was done well, but that it was done at all.

Because Windows 3.x was cobbled together from 16-bit and 32-bit parts, developers had to understand all kinds of memory-management concepts, such as segmented addresses, code and data segments, and various "memory models" that varied from application to application, depending on how much memory the program was designed to use. Today, with the advent of Windows NT and Windows 95, that's all behind us forever, and we don't have to make our Windows applications walk on their hind legs anymore. Now Windows has a real, live 32-bit memory map that has eliminated the need for such contrivances as segment:offset addresses, near and far pointers, and small, medium, large, and huge memory models. And C++, with its `new` and `delete` operators, has almost completely automated memory management in Windows programs written in Visual C++.

So now can we all sit back, forget about memory management, and never again have to be concerned about how Windows performs all its memory management? As if.

As so often happens in the world of computer programming, the solving of one set of problems has brought along with it the introduction of many more. As you read this chapter, you may find yourself wondering whether the dark days of DOS were so grim after all. We may not have segment:offset addressing to kick around any more, but we do have a host of new complexities, such as multithreading, client-server networking, and interprocess communications, to name just a few.

My aim in writing this book was to demystify all these new and potentially intimidating features of Windows NT. In these pages, you'll find whole chapters on multithreading, networking, and interprocess communications, as well as chapters on Visual C++, OLE, a new breed of Windows NT–style dynamic link libraries, and the fundamentals of Windows NT graphics.

This chapter is an overall introduction to many important topics that are covered in more detail in later chapters. In this chapter, you'll get a chance to take a peek under the hood of the Windows NT operating system and examine its parts in considerable detail. You'll also get an opportunity to see how all those parts work together. By the time you finish this chapter, you'll be ready to move to other chapters that examine each part of Windows NT IN more detail.

A number of topics are introduced in this chapter:

✦ The Windows NT operating system model

✦ Windows NT subsystems

✦ Windows NT's client-server design

✦ The Windows NT I/O subsystem

✦ The Windows NT executive

✦ Processes and threads, which are covered in more detail in Chapter 6, "Processes"

✦ Virtual memory and file mapping, which are examined in more detail in Chapter 9, "Interprocess Communications"

✦ The virtual DOS machine, which emulates MS-DOS in Windows NT

✦ Windows NT security

The Windows NT registry, which was introduced in Chapter 1, is covered in more detail in this chapter.

Using the Registry: A Sample Program

The registry, as you learned in Chapter 1, is an important Windows mechanism that replaces the **CONFIG.SYS** and **AUTOEXEC.BAT** files that MS-DOS and Windows programs used before the advent of Windows NT and Windows 95. The registry also replaces the **WIN.INI** and **SYSTEM.INI** files that were used in Windows 3.x programs. (**WINI.INI** and

SYSTEM.INI still exist in Windows NT and Windows 95, but they are now reserved for use by the operating system and are off-limits to ordinary applications.)

At the end of this chapter, you'll get a chance to experiment with a sample program that will give you some valuable hands-on experience using the registry. This sample program, TEXTCHNG, shows how a Windows NT application can use the registry. TEXTCHNG shows how an application can call Windows API functions to do the following:

+ Retrieve information from the registry at startup time.

+ Write new information to the registry when the user quits.

+ Retrieve the newest information from the registry the next time the program starts up, and display it in a window.

Once you know how to do all those things programmatically in a Windows NT application, you'll be ready to start using the registry in your own applications. And that's an important thing to learn—not only because you don't have **CONFIG.SYS** and **AUTOEXEC.BAT** to kick around any more, but also because Microsoft won't award your application a Windows-compatible logo unless it uses the registry properly.

Introducing the Windows NT Operating System

The Windows NT operating system shows what a great job system engineers can do when the boss pulls out all the stops, there's plenty of 20/20 hindsight to rely on, and the whole team is freed from most of the restrictions that have traditionally made small-computer operating systems difficult to design.

When the designers of Windows NT went to work, those were the enviable conditions that they were given to toil under. The Windows NT design team did not have to face the memory restrictions, backward-compatibility requirements, or budget limitations that had been (and were still being) encountered by the developers of less ambitious Windows programming environments such as Windows 3.1 and Windows 95. From the outset, Windows NT was envisioned as a high-end, high-performance operating system that would appeal to large, high-budget corporate customers and would compete with UNIX and other older, networked, multiuser operating systems widely used in business and industry.

To make Windows NT competitive with traditional commercial-style operating systems, Microsoft borrowed features from many sources—not only small-computer operating environments such as MS-DOS and Windows 3.1 but also multiuser client-server systems such as UNIX and even multiprocessor computer systems such as the multi-80486 systems manufactured by NCR.

Windows NT broke new ground in many areas. It was the first Windows operating system with a flat 32-bit address space, the first to support multithreading, the first to support client-server networking, the first to be equipped with built-in security features, and the first to be designed with support for open systems in mind.

Because of its many advanced capabilities and because many of its features are derived from different origins, Windows NT offers a unique set of programming challenges to developers of Windows software. Because Windows NT has the same look and feel as that of Windows 95, you can use the two operating systems interchangeably without knowing much about their differences or similarities. But if you want to learn how to write Windows NT applications, it helps to be familiar with the architecture of Windows NT and the structure of its operating system.

This chapter describes the most important new features of Windows NT and shows how they are incorporated into the operating system. The chapter is divided into two main parts. The first part describes the Window NT operating system, and the second part describes how all the components of the operating system fit together.

As noted in Chapter 1, the Windows NT 4.0 user interface looks and works almost exactly like the user interface that was originally designed for Windows 95. Under the hood, however, Windows NT and Windows 95 are built on two very different operating systems. Windows 95 was designed to be as compact and as backward-compatible as possible with Windows 3.1, so it is implemented as a kind of hybrid operating system made up of 16-bit code and 32-bit code. In contrast, Windows NT is a pure 32-bit operating system that does not rely on MS-DOS and does not contain any 16-bit code.

Because Microsoft engineers pulled out all the stops (or most of them, anyway) when they designed the Windows NT operating system, Windows NT runs faster, offers more protection against crashes and data corruption, and has more advanced memory-management, file-management, and networking capabilities than earlier versions of Windows. To support its added capabilities, Windows NT has special features, including:

✦ **Support for preemptive multitasking and multithreading.** Windows NT can run multiple applications simultaneously by assigning each application a separate slice of CPU time. This capability, known as *preemptive multitasking*, was not available in Windows 3.1 or its predecessors. Along with preemptive multitasking, Windows NT supports a related mechanism called *multithreading*. The NT operating system manages multithreading automatically by allocating a portion of processor time to each currently active process in accordance with predetermined task priorities and by providing mechanisms such as mutexes and semaphores to help applications synchronize thread use. Multitasking and multithreading are covered in detail in Chapter 7, "Multithreading."

✦ **Network support.** Windows NT is the first Windows system to support client-server networking (see Chapter 10, "Networking Windows NT"). Moreover, Windows NT networks support an advanced client-server network mechanism called *distributed computing.* By making remote procedure calls (RPCs) to applications running on remote computers, a Windows NT workstation can execute programs and processes that are not resident locally but reside instead on host machines. This capability can increase the computing power of workstations connected over a network by providing each local workstation with multiprocessor capabilities, even though each individual workstation may have only a single CPU.

✦ **Support for open systems.** Windows NT supports network communications—not only the kind of peer-to-peer communications available in Windows for Workgroups and the Microsoft LAN Manager but also real information-superhighway-style networking that supports the use of client-server communications and popular communications protocols such as TCP/IP.

✦ **Security.** The security features of Windows NT have earned a C2 security rating from the U.S. government. A logon system protects data owned by individual users as well as data owned by the system administrator, and the design of the system protects the integrity of data stored in memory.

✦ **Reliability.** In Windows NT, every 32-bit application stored in memory has its own private address space and cannot modify memory that lies outside that address space. Consequently, an application cannot overwrite operating system code or data and cannot corrupt areas of memory that are controlled by other applications or the operating system.

In the remainder of this chapter, all these features will be examined in more detail. In subsequent chapters, you'll learn how to incorporate them into your own Windows NT programs.

The NT Operating System Model

The Windows NT operating system is a hybrid of two classic operating system models: one known as the layered model, the other known as the client-server model.

In a *layered* operating system, the procedures that make up the operating system's code are isolated from one another. They are grouped by functionality and arranged in layers.

The only code that a module in any layer can call is the code in the layer below it. The layered operating system model is illustrated in Figure 2.1.

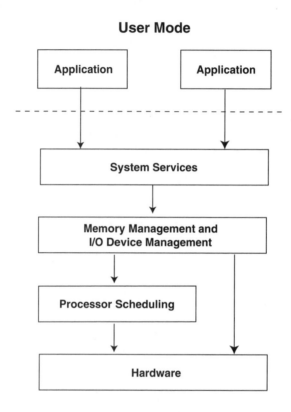

FIGURE 2.1 ARCHITECTURE OF A LAYERED OPERATING SYSTEM.

In a layered operating system, as Figure 2.1 illustrates, the procedures that make up the operating system's code cannot call each other freely. Each module contains a set of functions that other modules can call, but code in any layer can call only code in a lower layer.

When an application program is added to this mix, the only code that it can call is code in the top layer of the diagram shown in Figure 2.1: the *system services* layer. This restriction prevents application programs from accessing operating system code that is too delicate or dangerous to be touched by user-written applications.

Because each code module has access only to the code in layers below it, the system as a whole receives a measure of protection from individual code modules that might otherwise wield dangerous power. An added advantage of layered operating systems is that their modular design makes them especially easy to upgrade and maintain. Finally, layered operating systems are easier to debug than some other kinds of systems. Code at lower levels in the stack can be debugged first, and code in other levels can be debugged in succession until the entire system is operating properly.

In a *client-server* operating system, tasks are divided into processes. Each process implements a set of *services*, such as memory services, file services, and communications services. Each service is associated with a module called a *server*, which runs in user mode, along with any application programs that are running on the system. Figure 2.2 is a diagram of a client-server OS model.

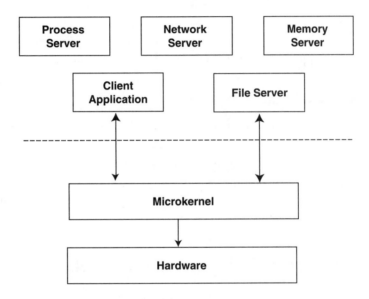

FIGURE 2.2 ARCHITECTURE OF A CLIENT-SERVER OPERATING SYSTEM.

Your Serve

The client-server structure of the Windows NT operating system should not be confused with client-server networking, which is conceptually similar but implemented differently. Client-server networking is described in Chapter 10, "Networking Windows NT."

KERNELS AND MICROKERNELS

In a typical operating system built on the client-server model, only one module runs in kernel mode. That module is called a *microkernel*. When an application needs to access a service—for example, the memory-management service—the application requests the service by sending a message to the microkernel. The microkernel relays the message to the appropriate server, which performs the operation and then notifies the server that the operation is complete. The microkernel then sends a message back to the application informing it of the result of the operation.

The primary advantage of using a client-server operating system is that each component in the system is small and self-contained. Each server runs in a separate user-mode process (see "Processes and Threads" later in this chapter), so it is possible for a server to fail—and even to be restarted—without crashing the system or corrupting any of its data. Another advantage is that different servers can run on different microprocessors (in a multiprocessor computer) or even on separate computers across a net.

VARIETIES OF CLIENT-SERVER SYSTEMS

Client-server operating systems come in many flavors. In some systems the microkernel performs many tasks, and in other systems it performs only a few.

Figure 2.2 is a simplified diagram of a client-server operating system. The microkernel is represented as nothing more than a message-passing module. In practice, it often performs other tasks, such as thread scheduling, managing virtual memory, and controlling device drivers.

The Windows NT Operating-System

The Windows NT operating system, shown in part in Figure 2.3, has features of both the layered operating system model and the client-server model. Overall, the Windows NT operating system works more like a client-server system than a layered system. But the kernel-mode portion of the NT system contains some elements of a layered system. These elements include the lower part of the kernel-mode portion, which contains the kernel itself and a module called the *hardware abstraction layer*, or HAL.

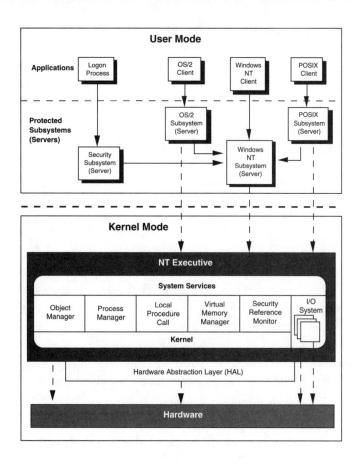

FIGURE 2.3 THE WINDOWS NT OPERATING SYSTEM.

User Mode and Kernel Mode

Notice that in Figure 2.3, a heavy line separates the application-program level in the diagram from all the levels below. The layer above that line—the application-program level—is labeled *User Mode*. The layer below the line, where the operating-system modules appear, is labeled *Kernel Mode*.

This division reflects the fact that the Windows NT operating system, like most operating systems, divides the code that it is executing into two different categories, or *modes*. Windows NT runs its system code in privileged-process mode, which has access to computer hardware and system data. Applications run in a nonprivileged mode.

Most of the components that make up the kernel-mode portion of Windows NT are grouped in a larger package called the *NT executive*. The components that make up the NT executive perform system tasks such as virtual memory management, resource management, input-output (I/O) operations, file management, and management of network drivers, inter-process communications, and portions of the Windows NT security system. The components grouped under the umbrella of the NT executive interact through a set of carefully specified internal routines.

The Windows NT kernel performs low-level operating system functions similar to those that are usually performed by the microkernel in client-server operating systems—for example, thread scheduling, interrupt and exception dispatching, and multiprocessor synchronization. The NT kernel also includes a set of routines and resources that other components of the executive use to implement higher-level tasks.

Below the kernel is HAL, which isolates the kernel and the rest of the NT executive from the platform-specific hardware on which Windows NT runs. HAL is the component most responsible for making Windows NT compatible with multiple hardware systems.

HAL, incidentally, is implemented as a *dynamic link library* (DLL). DLLs—libraries that are bound at run time to the routines that call them—are the topic of Chapter 8.

The Windows NT user-mode module is examined more closely in the next section. For more details about the kernel-mode module, see "The Kernel Mode" later in this chapter.

The User-Mode Module

The user-mode module of the NT operating system contains the components that perform most of the tasks ordinarily associated with an operating system. Windows NT applications run in user mode, as clients. Application programming interfaces (APIs) that interface with applications also run in user mode, but as servers. These servers are sometimes called *protected subsystems*. Figure 2.4 illustrates this arrangement.

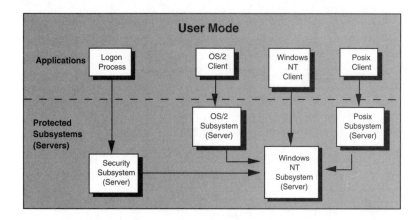

FIGURE 2.4 THE WINDOWS NT USER-MODE MODULE.

Application Programming Interfaces

An *API* is a set of libraries or interfaces that enable an application to use the language in which it is written to access the functionality of lower-level modules—such as operating systems, graphical user interfaces (GUIs), and communications protocols. There are many kinds of applications, so there are many kinds of APIs.

In Figure 2.3, the code layer labeled *System Services* can be referred to as an API. In a larger sense, the Windows NT system itself, the overall interface between application programs and the Windows NT operating system, is an API. In fact, the Windows NT system, the giant software package that is the topic of the five-volume *Microsoft Win32 Programmer's Reference*, is often referred to as "the Win32 API."

The servers in the bottom half of Figure 2.4 are labeled *protected subsystems*. Each server works a separate process, and the memory used by each process is isolated from the memory used by other processes. This isolation protects the memory space used by each process from potentially dangerous infringement by activities of other processes.

Because the protected subsystems in the user-mode module do not automatically share memory, they communicate by passing messages, as shown in Figure 2.5. The solid lines in Figure 2.5 represent paths that messages can take between clients and servers or between servers.

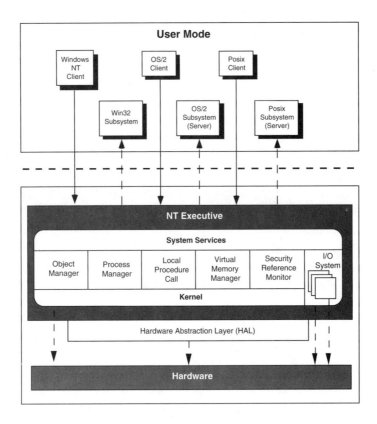

FIGURE 2.5 CLIENTS AND SERVERS ON THE WINDOWS NT OPERATING SYSTEM.

All messages dispatched by protected subsystems pass through the NT executive, as suggested by the dotted lines that end with arrows. The NT executive is an operating system engine capable of supporting any number of server processes. The servers act as the NT executive's user and programming interfaces and provide execution environments for various types of applications.

Each protected subsystem acts as a server by providing an API that programs can call. When an application—or another server—needs to call an API routine that a server provides, a message is sent to the server that implements the API routine. The message is sent via the NT executive's *local procedure call* (LPC) facility, a message-passing mechanism that resides in the operating system's system services module. The server executes the API routine and returns the result to the application process by sending another LPC. This process is illustrated in Figure 2.5.

Local and Remote Procedure Calls

The LPC system that NT servers use to communicate with the executive is adapted from the RPC that is used when workstations need to access functions provided by a server on distributed computing systems.

The RPC technique is a classic method for calling code that resides on a remote machine across a network. A calling program on one machine bundles the parameters required by the function and sends them in a packet across the network to a second machine, where the remote procedure performs the reverse procedure on the packet. The remote procedure unpacks the call parameters, executes the function, and sends the reply packet to the calling machine.

THE WINDOWS NT SUBSYSTEM

The Win32 API includes protected subsystems for the POSIX, OS/2, 16-bit Windows, and MS-DOS environments. But the most important protected subsystem is the Windows NT subsystem, a kind of superserver that makes the 32-bit Windows API available to application programs.

The Windows NT environment subsystem supplies Windows NT's graphical user interface and controls all user input and all application output. The other subsystems receive user input and display output through the Windows NT subsystem. They can be loaded into memory as needed, with several subsystems in operation at a time if desired.

ENVIRONMENT SUBSYSTEMS AND INTEGRAL SUBSYSTEMS

Windows NT has two kinds of protected subsystems: environment subsystems and integral subsystems. An *environment subsystem* is a user-mode server that provides an API specific to an operating system. An *integral subsystem* is a server that provides an interface between the operating system and important facilities such as network services.

The environment subsystems provide Windows NT with the ability to run particular operating system environments such as Windows NT, 16-bit Windows, DOS, POSIX, and OS/2. Windows NT runs these environment subsystems simultaneously. That's what makes it possible for the Windows NT system to run applications written for other environments, such as 16-bit Windows and MS-DOS, alongside applications written specifically for the Win32 API.

THE WINDOWS NT ENVIRONMENT SUBSYSTEM

The Windows NT environment subsystem provides the Windows NT user interface. The subsystem controls the video display, the keyboard, the mouse, and other input devices attached to the local computer. Implementing the Win32 API, it is also a server for Win32 applications.

The Windows NT subsystem does not control the execution of non-Win32 applications; it does not manage 16-bit Windows applications, DOS applications, or POSIX applications. If the user launches an application that the Windows NT subsystem does not recognize as a 32-bit Windows program, the subsystem determines what type of application it is and then calls another subsystem to run the application.

Each of the environment subsystems supplies an API that its client applications use. For example, the Windows NT subsystem provides 32-bit Windows API routines, but the OS/2 subsystem supplies OS/2 API routines.

Running DOS Applications and 16-Bit Windows Programs

Windows NT runs MS-DOS applications and Windows 3.x applications by emulating the DOS and Windows 3.x environments. Windows NT performs this emulation using an environment subsystem called a *virtual DOS machine* (VDM). The Windows NT VDM emulates a complete MS-DOS environment.

Each MS-DOS application or 16-bit Windows application running under Windows NT executes within the context of a separate VDM process. Thus, multiple VDM processes can be running at the same time. This is a unique feature of VDM processes; other kinds of environment subsystem processes can run only one at a time. (For more details on VDM processes, see "The Virtual DOS Machine" later in this chapter.)

All You Can See Is Windows NT

A Windows NT environment subsystem can support many client applications. Each subsystem keeps track of its clients and maintains any global information that all the client applications share. Although several subsystems and VDMs might be running on a Windows NT system at any given time, the Windows NT subsystem is the only environment subsystem that ever makes itself visible to the user. To the user, it appears that Windows is running all the applications.

Managing Video Output

The Windows NT subsystem handles all video output, so the other environment subsystems must direct the video output of their applications to the Windows NT subsystem. The VDM running 16-bit Windows applications translates the applications' output calls into Win32 calls and sends them a message to the Windows NT subsystem for display.

The OS/2 and POSIX subsystems, as well as any VDMs running MS-DOS applications, direct their applications' character-mode output to the Windows NT subsystem. The Windows NT subsystem displays that output in a character-mode console window. Console windows are covered in Chapter 6, "Processes."

THE SECURITY SUBSYSTEM

In addition to the Windows NT subsystem and the other NT environmental subsystems, the user-mode module contains several other protected subsystems that fall into the category of integral subsystems. These integral subsystems perform various operating system functions. One important integral subsystem is the security subsystem.

The Windows NT environment subsystems are sometimes referred to as protected subsystems because they are isolated from one another and are thus protected from one another. One protected subsystem, the security subsystem, manages the security protection that is in effect on the local computer on which it is running. The security subsystem keeps track of which user accounts have special privileges and which system resources are to be audited for user access. As shown in Figure 2.6, it also determines whether audit alarms or audit messages should be generated when protected resources are accessed. And it maintains a database of information about user accounts, including account names, passwords, any groups the user belongs to for security purposes, and any special privileges the user owns. The security subsystem also accepts user logon information and initiates logon authentication.

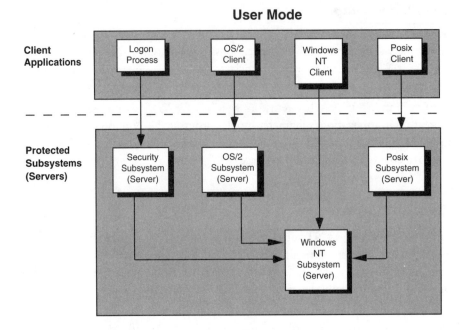

FIGURE 2.6 THE WINDOWS NT SECURITY SUBSYSTEM.

NETWORK-RELATED SERVERS

Several software components related to networking are implemented as integral sub-systems. Two of the most important network-related integral subsystems—often referred to as services—are the workstation service and the server service. Each of these services is a user-mode process that implements an API to access and manage a pair of network-related utilities called the network redirector and the network server. The *network redirector* and the *network server* are shown in Figure 2.7.

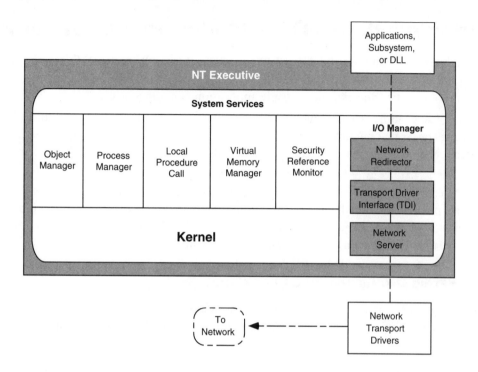

FIGURE 2.7 THE NETWORK REDIRECTOR AND NETWORK SERVER.

The network redirector sends (redirects) I/O requests across a network when the file or device to be accessed is not local but is connected to the local machine through a network. A server on the remote machine receives the network redirector's requests.

Both the network redirector and the network server are implemented as file system drivers—that is, as part of the NT I/O system. For more information about them, see "The I/O System" later in this chapter.

Using Windows NT on Multiprocessor Systems

As explained in "Processes and Threads" later in this chapter, Windows NT uses programming entities called *threads* to divide CPU time among processes, making it possible for the system to prioritize and execute multiple applications simultaneously.

On a single-processor computer system, the use of multiple threads, or multithreading, makes it appear that multiple threads are executing at the same time. On a single-processor system, this is only an illusion. Actually, the threads are carrying out their tasks sequentially in separate slices of CPU time allocated by the system.

When Windows NT is running on a multiprocessor computer, such as the multi-80486 systems manufactured by NCR, it is not an illusion that Windows NT is executing multiple threads simultaneously. On a multiprocessor machine, Windows NT actually executes multiple threads at the same time, running each thread on an individual CPU.

SYMMETRIC AND ASYMMETRIC PROCESSING

Operating systems that run on computers with multiple processes fall into two categories: Some systems support *symmetric multiprocessing*, or SMP, whereas others support *asymmetric processing*, or ASMP.

Asymmetric Multiprocessing

When a multiprocessor operating system uses asymmetric processing, it typically isolates the operating system from user-written code by executing operating system code on one processor while other processors run only application code. Because an asymmetric processing operating system runs operating system code on a single processor, it is not extraordinarily difficult to develop an ASMP operating system; all you have to do is to make a relatively small number of improvements to an existing single-processor operating system.

An ASMP operating system works well on an asymmetric hardware platform, such as a processor with an attached coprocessor or two processors that don't share all available memory. The problem is that it is difficult to make ASMP operating systems portable. Hardware from different vendors (and even different versions of hardware from the same vendor) often varies in its specifications and its degree of asymmetry. Either the hardware vendors must target their hardware for specific operating systems, or the operating system must be substantially rewritten for each hardware platform.

Figure 2.8 illustrates the operation of an ASMP operating system.

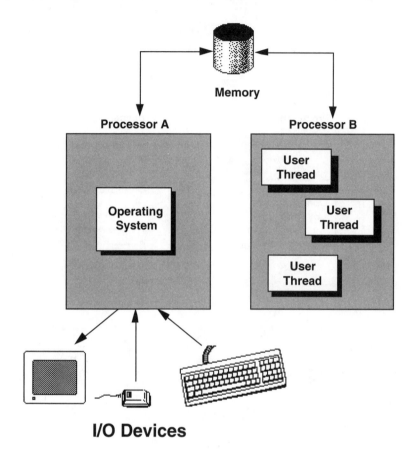

FIGURE 2.8 ASYMMETRIC MULTIPROCESSING SYSTEM.

Symmetric Processing

An SMP system, unlike an ASMP system, allows the operating system to run on any free processor—or even on all processors simultaneously. When Windows NT runs on a multiprocessor computer, it runs as an SMP system.

The SMP approach, shown in Figure 2.9, is more efficient in a multiple-processor system because the operating system is not restricted to using just one processor. When an operating system runs only on a single processor, the system can tax that processor to its limit, slowing it to a crawl while other processors remain idle.

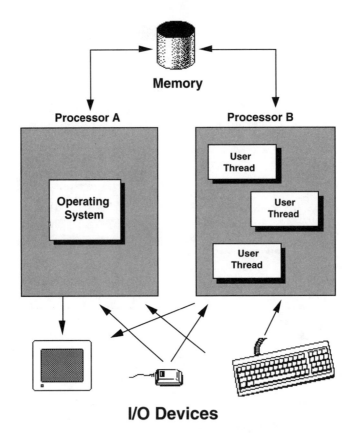

I/O Devices

FIGURE 2.9 SYMMETRIC MULTIPROCESSING SYSTEM.

This extra work decreases the efficiency of the overall system. In contrast, in an SMP system, if the operating system needs extra CPU power, it can obtain it from an idle processor.

In addition to increasing efficiency, an SMP system can reduce system downtime because the operating system code can switch to other processors if one processor fails.

The SMP approach has one more advantage: Because symmetric hardware is implemented similarly from vendor to vendor, it is easier to create a portable SMP operating system.

The Kernel Mode

Figure 2.10 shows how the kernel-mode portion of the NT operating system can be broken down into more modules. These modules include a file systems module, a cache manager, device drivers, and network drivers.

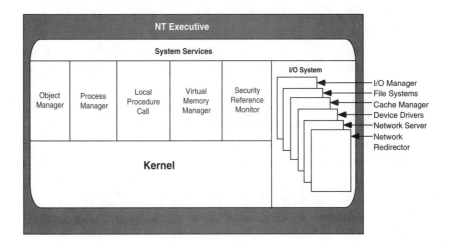

FIGURE 2.10 COMPONENTS OF THE I/O SYSTEM.

THE I/O SYSTEM

Figure 2.10 illustrates a group of subcomponents responsible for processing input from and delivering output to a variety of devices. These subcomponents are as follows:

+ *The I/O manager*: Implements device-independent I/O facilities and establishes a model for NT executive input-output.

+ *File systems:* These are managed by Windows NT drivers that receive file-oriented input-output requests and translate them into I/O requests bound for a particular device.

+ *The cache manager:* Stores the most recently read disk information in system memory. This capability improves the performance of file-based I/O. The cache manager uses the paging facility of the virtual memory manager (VMM) to write modifications to a disk in the background and automatically.

+ *Device drivers:* Low-level drivers that directly manipulate hardware to write output to or retrieve input from a physical device or network.

+ *The network redirector and the network server:* File system drivers that, respectively, transmit remote I/O requests to a machine on the network and receive such requests.

THE NT EXECUTIVE

The heart of the kernel-mode module is the NT executive. The NT executive, although it has a user interface, is a complete operating system in its own right. It is made up of several components, each of which implements two sets of functions. One set, known as system services, can be called by environment subsystems and other executive components. The other set is made up of internal routines, which are available only to components within the executive. The components that make up the NT executive are shown in Figure 2.11.

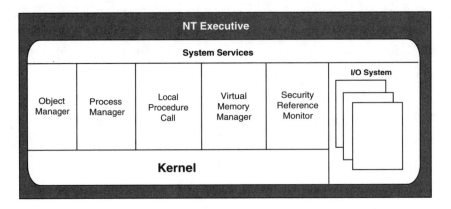

FIGURE 2.11 COMPONENTS OF THE NT EXECUTIVE.

Although the NT executive provides system services that work like APIs, the executive is fundamentally different from the environment subsystems. For example, it does not run continually in a process of its own. Instead, it runs in the context of an existing process by taking over an executing thread when important system events occur. For instance, when a thread calls a system service and is trapped by the processor or when an external device interrupts the processor, the NT kernel assumes control of the thread that is currently running. The kernel calls the appropriate system code to handle the event, executes it, and then returns control to the code that was executing before the interruption occurred.

The components of the NT executive are isolated from one another and maintain independence from one another, each creating and manipulating the system data structures it requires. Because interfaces between components are carefully controlled, it is possible to remove a component from the operating system and replace it with one that operates differently. As long as the new version implements all the system services and internal interfaces correctly, the operating system runs as before. Maintaining the operating system is also an easier task because the NT executive components interact in predictable ways.

Table 2.1 lists and describes the components of the NT executive.

TABLE 2.1 COMPONENTS OF THE NT EXECUTIVE.

Component	Task
Kernel	Schedules threads for execution, responds to interrupts and exceptions, synchronizes the activities of multiple processors, and supplies a set of elemental objects and interfaces that the rest of the NT executive uses to implement higher-level objects.
Object manager	Creates, manages, and deletes NT executive objects (abstract data types that are used to represent operating system resources).
Process manager	Creates and terminates processes and threads. The process manager also suspends and resumes the execution of threads and stores and retrieves information about NT processes and threads.
I/O system	A group of components responsible for processing input from and delivering output to a variety of devices.
Hardware abstraction layer (HAL)	A dynamic link library that interfaces the NT executive with the hardware platform on which Windows NT is running. HAL hides hardware-dependent details such as I/O interfaces, interrupt controllers, and multiprocessor communication mechanisms. Instead of accessing the platform hardware directly, components of the NT executive maintain maximum portability by calling HAL routines when they need platform-dependent information.
Local procedure call (LPC) facility	Passes messages between a client process and a server process on the same computer. LPC is a flexible, optimized version of remote procedure call (RPC), an industry-standard communication facility for client and server processes across a network.
Virtual memory (VM) manager	Implements virtual memory, a memory management system that provides a large, private address space for each process and protects each process's address space from other processes. When memory usage is too high, the VM manager transfers selected memory contents to disk and reloads the contents when they are used again—a practice known as *paging*.
Security reference monitor	Enforces security on the local computer; guards operating system resources, performing run-time object protection and auditing.

NT NATIVE SERVICES

The services provided by individual components of the NT executive are called *NT native services*. The Windows NT environment subsystems implement their API routines by calling NT native services. For example, the virtual manager (see "Virtual Memory" later in this chapter) supplies memory allocation and deallocation services to the environment subsystems. Similarly, the process manager provides services to create and terminate processes and threads.

NT native services are low-level services that are used primarily by protected subsystems, DLLs, and NT executive components. Applications that run on Windows NT do not ordinarily access NT native services. Instead, NT applications access APIs such as the Win32 API or the APIs supplied by environment subsystems for MS-DOS, 16-bit Windows, POSIX, or OS/2.

Processes and Threads

In Windows NT, a *process* is an executing instance of an application. A process—roughly equivalent to a *task* in pre-NT versions of Windows—consists of code loaded from an executable file, along with global and static variables. A process can own resources such as dynamic memory allocations and threads. These resources are created during the life of a process and are destroyed when the process terminates.

A thread is a unit of execution in an application. Every thread is associated with a sequence of CPU instructions, a set of CPU registers, and a stack. In a Windows 3.x application, a task has only one thread of execution. This thread of execution is usually controlled by an event loop in the application's `WinMain` function. So a Windows 3.x application has only one code path.

In Windows NT, a process can have multiple threads, and threads can create other threads. The Windows NT kernel uses a service called a *scheduler* to apportion CPU time to each executing thread. On a multiprocessor computer system, each processor can execute a separate thread.

When a Windows NT process is created, the system automatically creates one thread for the process. This thread is known as the process's *primary thread*. A primary thread can create additional threads, and each additional thread has the power to create even more threads.

Virtual Memory

Windows NT is equipped with a disk-caching system that can automatically move data between memory and a hard disk, giving applications much more *virtual memory* than the amount of physical memory that is available. This virtual memory is managed by the virtual memory manager.

The VMM provides each executing process with access to four gigabytes of virtual-memory address space by caching files to and from disk. Within the 4 GB of virtual memory locations that Windows NT allocates to each process residing in RAM, the Windows NT operating system reserves the upper 2 GB of virtual memory for itself. The lower 2 GB of virtual memory space in the block is allocated to the process.

This arrangement supplies each process with much more memory than any application is likely to need using today's technology or in the foreseeable future.

Figure 2.12 shows how the VMM implements virtual memory. In the diagram, two Windows NT processes are running on a computer that has 32 megabytes of physical memory. The virtual memory manager has allocated four gigabytes of virtual address space to each process. To each process, it appears that 4 GB of memory is available.

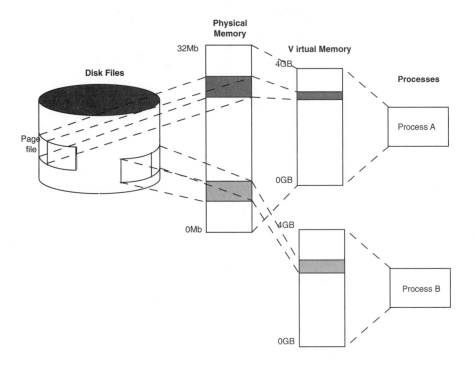

FIGURE 2.12 HOW WINDOWS NT MANAGES VIRTUAL MEMORY.

Figure 2.13 shows how Windows NT allocates virtual memory to processes.

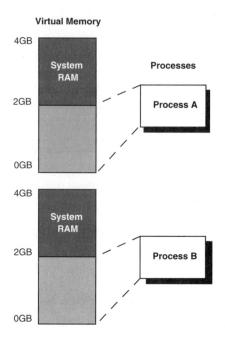

FIGURE 2.13 HOW PROCESSES USE VIRTUAL MEMORY.

As Figure 2.13 illustrates, the lowest 2 GB of memory (0x00 to 0x7FFFFFFF) is available to the user, and the highest 2 GB of memory (0x80000000 to 0xFFFFFFFF) is reserved for the kernel.

PAGE FAULTS

When a process is created, the Windows NT executive maps an executable file stored on disk into the process's 4 GB of virtual address space. A virtual address descriptor is created, but no bytes are initially read from the disk into RAM. Instead, physical pages are allocated only when an attempt is made to access a particular location in the file.

When an application attempts to access a location in an executable that has been mapped into a process's address space, the virtual memory manager searches for the location in RAM. If the page containing the address being accessed has not yet been read into memory, the CPU raises a *page fault* exception. When a page fault occurs, the page that contains the address being accessed is loaded into memory.

When a page that has been swapped into memory is no longer needed, the operating system relinquishes control of the page on behalf of the process that owns it, freeing the memory for use by another process.

PAGE FILES

The VMM performs its disk-caching operations by using disk files called page files to swap files between hard disks and RAM. On disks and in RAM, memory is divided into *pages*: units of memory whose sizes depend on the host computer. For example, computers equipped with Pentium processors have a page size of four kilobytes, whereas DEC Alpha computers have a page size of 8 KB.

The Windows NT kernel manages memory by swapping pages of physical memory to and from a page file that is kept on disk. When a page of information is moved from a disk into physical memory or from physical memory to a page file on a disk, the kernel updates page maps that are maintained by all processes affected by the move. When the kernel needs space in physical memory, it moves the least recently used pages of physical memory to a page file. Manipulation of physical memory by the kernel is transparent to applications, which operate only in their virtual address spaces.

Paging data to disk frees physical memory so that applications and the NT system can use it for other purposes. When a thread accesses a virtual address that has been paged to disk, the VMM loads the information back into memory from disk. When a computer's physical memory fills up, the VMM transfers, or pages, some of the memory contents to disk.

THE SYSTEM PAGE FILE

In addition to the page files that are associated with executing processes, the operating system maintains a page file of its own. This page file is known as the *system page file*.

When information needed by a process is moved from a disk into memory, executable code is paged into one part of RAM and data is paged into another part. Specifically, executable code is moved into the process's page file, but data used by the process is moved into the system page file. In this way, data that a process pages into memory can be shared by other processes.

Figure 2.14 illustrates how Windows NT stores information in the system page file and in the page files owned by individual processes.

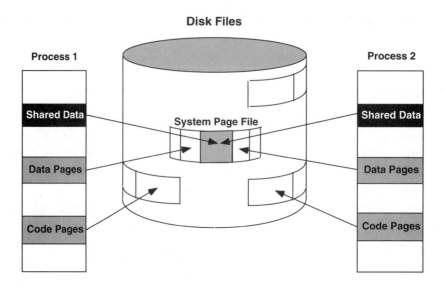

FIGURE 2.14 THE SYSTEM PAGE FILE AND PAGE FILES OWNED BY PROCESSES.

HOW PROCESSES SHARE DATA STORED IN MEMORY

When data from a process is stored in the system page file, other processes cannot access the data directly. The strict security restrictions imposed by Windows NT make that impossible.

However, Windows NT provides an indirect mechanism that processes can use to share data. This mechanism is called a *prototype page table entry* (PPTE). PPTEs are controlled by the system, so they are a safe mechanism for letting processes share data. Before data owned by a process can be shared by another process, the process that owns the data must grant access to the requesting process. If access is granted, it is controlled by the operating system.

Figure 2.15 shows how processes share data in Windows NT. When a page of data has been moved into memory, its address is stored in a block of memory called a *page table*. Each address stored in a page table is called a *page table entry*, or PTE.

When a process grants another process access to a page whose address is stored in a page table, the operating system creates a PTTE. In this PTTE, the system stores a reference to the table to which access has been granted. The process that has been granted permission to the page can then access the page through the page's PTTE.

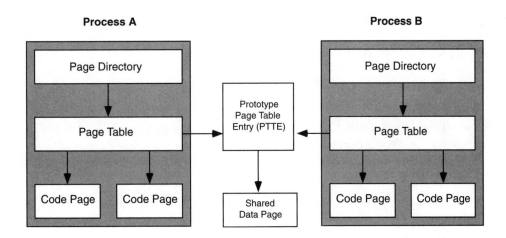

FIGURE 2.15 ACCESSING DATA USING PTTEs.

VIRTUAL MEMORY AND NON-WIN32 APPLICATIONS

One challenge faced by the VMM is to take care of application programs that were not designed to run in a flat, 32-bit memory environment. To run applications written for Windows, MS-DOS, POSIX, or OS/2, the VMM must provide an operating system environment that behaves like those environments when required. The challenge is to allow all these types of applications to run without being rewritten and without infringing on one another's memory spaces.

To meet this challenge, the Windows NT environment subsystems that serve non-Win32 applications provide the programs with a view of memory that corresponds to what the applications expect. Underneath the environment subsystems, the NT executive has its own memory structure, which the environment subsystems access by calling NT native services.

The native NT memory architecture is, as you've seen, a virtual memory system based on 32-bit addresses in a flat (linear) address space. The virtual address space that is available to a process is the set of addresses that is available for the process's threads to use.

When Windows NT is running, the VMM—with some help from the host hardware—translates, or *maps*, the virtual addresses of the processes that are running into physical addresses. By controlling memory mapping, the operating system can ensure that individual processes don't corrupt one another's memory or overwrite the operating system.

Windows NT File Systems

Windows NT supports the following file systems:

+ The file allocation table (FAT) file system used by Windows 3.x and MS-DOS.
+ The high-performance file system (HPFS) supported by OS/2.
+ The NT file system (NTFS), introduced with the premiere of Windows NT.

NTFS extends the capabilities present in both the FAT file system and the HPFS. NTFS has the following new features:

+ File system recovery that allows for quick restoration of data stored on disk after a system failure.
+ The ability to handle extremely large storage media ranging up to 17 billion gigabytes.
+ Security features, including execute-only files.
+ The removal of the FAT file system's 11-character length restriction on names (eight characters plus a three-character extension). In NTFS, as in HPFS, names of files and directories can be as many as 254 characters long.
+ Support for Unicode file names and mirroring.

On a Windows NT computer system, each disk volume or disk partition can be formatted for a different file system, but only one file system can be used in an individual partition.

The first time a file function accesses a volume, and whenever a volume is placed in a floppy-disk drive, Windows examines the volume to determine which file system must be used to access the files on the volume. Through a device driver that supports the appropriate file system, Windows NT then manages all I/O that accesses that volume. If an error occurs, the device driver returns control to the operating system, which then passes control to the application currently being executed.

CREATING AND OPENING FILES

An application can create a new file or open an existing file by calling the Win32 function CreateFile. The CreateFile expects its calling function to specify the name of the file and to tell CreateFile whether it intends to read from the file, write to the file, or do both.

The application must also tell CreateFile what to do if a file with the specified name already exists. For example, an application can tell CreateFile to create a file with the specified name whether or not a file with that name exists. If this is the case, CreateFile creates the file if it does not exist, and overwrites the file if it does exist.

When an application calls CreateFile, the application can also provide the function with information about file sharing. The application creating the file can give other users read access, write access, both read and write access, or no access at all. But when two processes have the same file open at the same time, each process has a different handle.

For purposes of file sharing, the Windows NT operating system assigns a unique identifier, called a *file handle*, to each file that is opened or created. An application can use the file's handle in parameters to functions that read from the file, write to the file, or obtain information about it. A file's handle is valid until the file is closed.

An application can close files when they are no longer needed by calling the Win32 function CloseHandle. If a file is open when an application terminates, Windows NT closes it automatically.

The DeleteFile function deletes a file if the file is closed. If the file is not closed, DeleteFile returns an error.

In Windows NT, file-related functions such as CreateFile and DeleteFile can be used not only with files but also with file-like objects. For example, file-related functions can open and close objects called *pipes*, which are used in Windows NT programs to exchange data between threads running in different processes. Pipes are discussed in Chapter 9, "Interprocess Communications."

FILE MAPPING AND FILE I/O

Windows NT can copy a file's contents into a process's virtual address space. This procedure is called *file mapping*.

When the contents of a file are copied into virtual memory, the copy of the file that is stored in virtual memory is called a *file view*. The internal structure used by the operating system to maintain the copy of the file stored in virtual memory is called a *file-mapping object*.

A Windows NT process maps a file to virtual memory by calling the CreateFile-Mapping function and passing the function a name. CreateFileMapping responds by creating a file-mapping object with the specified name. Other processes can then pass the name of the object to either CreateFileMapping or OpenFileMapping to obtain a handle to the mapped object.

File mapping is examined in much more detail in Chapter 9, "Interprocess Communications." In Chapter 9, you'll find two sample programs that show you how to implement file mapping in your Windows NT applications.

Sharing Files

When a file is mapped into virtual memory, a process can create an identical file view in its own virtual address space by creating its own file view of the first process's file-mapping object. This arrangement enables the processes to share data. Any process that has the name or a handle of a file-mapping object can create a file view.

If two or more processes need to share a file, one process can open the file for exclusive access by using the CreateFile function. CreateFileMapping can then use the handle returned by CreateFile to create a file-mapping object. Processes that have the name of the file-mapping object or a handle to the object can share the file's data.

The handle of a file that is being shared in this fashion should stay open until there are no more processes sharing the file. This technique prevents nonsharing processes from reading from or writing to the file.

The Virtual DOS Machine

Windows NT does not run under MS-DOS. Instead, DOS applications run within the context of a virtual DOS machine. A VDM is a Win32 application that emulates a computer running DOS. Architecturally, a VDM is similar to an enhanced-mode MS-DOS operating system running on a virtual 80x86-based computer. However, a VDM has an address-space layout like the memory map shown in Figure 2.16.

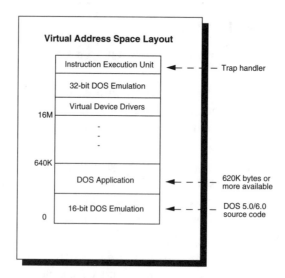

FIGURE 2.16 THE VIRTUAL DOS MACHINE.

As Figure 2.16 illustrates, all code below 16 MB in the virtual DOS machine is based on 16-bit segmented addresses. Code above the 16-MB boundary is written in the Windows NT format using 32-bit flat addresses.

The 32-bit portion of the VDM's address space includes a collection of virtual device drivers and 32-bit DOS emulation code that does not vary across processor architectures. The instruction execution unit is written in processor-dependent code. On the Intel Pentium microprocessor, the instruction execution unit acts as a trap handler, capturing instructions that cause hardware traps and transferring control to the code, such as the virtual device drivers, that handles them. On MIPS processors, this code is an instruction emulator, that converts Pentium instructions to MIPS instructions.

The VDM's virtual device drivers act as a layer between DOS applications and the hardware attached to the host (Windows NT) computer. The VDM environment provides virtual device drivers for standard PC devices, including the mouse, keyboard, printer, communications (COM) ports, and so on.

HOW THE VDM WORKS

The 32-bit code above the 16-MB boundary handles DOS I/O operations by trapping them and then calling either Win32 APIs or native NT system services to carry out the I/O. For example, the 32-bit code processes communications port requests by opening the COM device driver and sending it *I/O control codes* (IOCTLs). To update the video, a thread within the VDM process periodically examines the video RAM where the DOS application is writing and calls Win32 API functions to update the screen pixels that have changed.

Because VDMs are user-mode processes, they are completely pageable. This means that NT's virtual memory manager loads into physical memory only the portions of MS-DOS code that an application uses, as the application uses them. The VDM also temporarily transfers application code to disk when the system's memory supply is low.

HOW THE VDM HANDLES WIN3.x PROGRAMS

The 16-bit Windows environment provided by Windows NT is a hybrid application that runs within the address space of a VDM process. It calls Win32 API functions to do most of its work, but occasionally it also calls NT services. Windows NT programmers often refer to the 16-bit Windows environment as WOW, short for (16-bit) Windows on Windows NT.

The layout that the VDM uses for DOS and 16-bit Windows environments—one DOS application per VDM, and all 16-bit Windows applications in a single VDM—is similar to the way enhanced-mode DOS Windows uses DOS on virtual 8086 machines. In fact, the Intel version of Windows uses the virtual 8086 mode of the 80386 and 80486 processors in its VDMs. The most important difference is that under Windows 3.x, the operating system resides in the same address space where applications live. Windows NT, in contrast, places DOS and the 16-bit Windows environment in user-mode processes. This system protects the NT executive from problems that can occur in those environments, because they can access NT only by calling system services.

Graphical Device Interfaces

One component of the Windows 3.x operating system—the graphical device interface (GDI)—is completely rewritten for Windows NT. The GDI component handles all graphics operations under Windows, and it has been significantly updated for Windows NT. (GDI is described in more detail in Chapter 3, "The Win32 API.")

In updating the GDI component, Windows NT designers replaced large chunks of assembly language code with portable C++ code and redesigned the component's internal structure and content to support some of the advanced features of Windows NT.

New features of the Win32 GDI include built-in support for following:

+ Bezier curves, which give users of drawing packages more control over the curves they draw

+ Paths, which let users create arbitrarily shaped objects using sequences of drawing commands

+ Object transformations, which give users the ability to map the contents of one coordinate space into another

+ Correlation, a way to easily determine whether one object or region overlaps another

The Windows NT GDI is also equipped with a new device driver interface. This interface gives the GDI drivers, which are responsible for creating device-specific images and sending them to output devices, a finer degree of control over graphics operations.

To accomplish this feat, Win32 tailors its output to each GDI driver to match the kind of operations that the driver understands. For example, if a particular driver understands how to handle Bezier curves, the GDI can pass complete Bezier curves to the driver. If a driver doesn't understand Bezier curves, the GDI breaks the curve into simple line segments before sending it to the driver.

In addition, GDI has incorporated new support for creating bitmap images. This means that device drivers—particularly video and printer drivers—can use bitmaps provided by the GDI instead of having to write their own.

Graphics are covered in more detail in Chapter 11, "Windows NT Graphics."

Security

The U.S. government has established precise specifications for the security of computer systems, extending from level A (the most stringent) to level D (the least stringent). The Windows NT system complies with what its designers decided was an appropriate security standard: the government's C2 security specification.

The C2 level of security does not require the encryption of computer data, but it does permit the creator of a file or a directory to determine who can see it, who can change it. Logging mechanisms detect when the data is accessed and by whom.

The security features built into Windows NT protect both the NT operating system and its applications from ill-behaved applications and malicious attacks.

How Windows NT Security Works

From the Windows NT user's point of view, the first indication that NT has a security system comes when a message requesting a logon appears on the screen. The requirement to log on prevents careless or malicious users from accidentally or intentionally corrupting or destroying data.

There are two ways to gain access to Windows NT: through an interactive logon or by logging on over a network connection. The security subsystem ensures that any user who tries to access Windows NT has been granted logon authority by a system administrator. In most cases, "authority" means that an entry exists for the user in Windows NT's *security account manager* (SAM), a database containing user names, passwords, and other security information. Windows NT is flexible in the number and types of external logon devices it can support.

Logon can be requested directly—through a local workstation keyboard—or from a server over a network. In both cases, a local process must intercede and make sure that the access is legitimate. The network server process does this job for network logons. For interactive logons, a Windows NT process waits for you to press **Ctrl-Alt-Del** and then prompts the user for logon information.

Windows NT requires two kinds of information to verify that a user is authorized to log on: identification information and authentication information. The identification information is the user's account name; the authentication information is the user's password. An account name can be almost anything that the user and his or her network administrator agree on: a nickname, a company name, or even the number of an ATM card. (But think twice if your network administrator asks you for a copy of that!)

Once the security subsystem receives a user's identification and authentication information, the subsystem verifies both entries using an authentication package. If a user enters a password that matches the password currently recorded for the user in a security database, the system returns an ID number, a list group, and any alias IDs that are currently associated with the user's account.

The Windows NT security subsystem then retrieves from a local policy database any additional information it may need about the user from a local policy database, including any network privileges that the user has been granted. Finally, the security subsystem constructs a security token to represent the user and passes a handle to that token to the logon process a handle to that token. When all that is done, the user is successfully logged on.

From the software developer's point of view, the Windows NT security system operates without much programming effort. Every application launched under Windows NT automatically receives the security protection—and is subject to the security restrictions—built into the Windows NT operating system.

OBJECT-ORIENTED SECURITY

To attain the government C2 security rating, the creators of Windows NT designed the security system using ideas borrowed from object-oriented programming. In the area of security, the most important goal of the objects-oriented approach is to provide security protection for system resources that applications can share.

Using the same object-oriented approach followed in other areas of the operating system's design, the creators of Windows NT encapsulated shared resources as objects and applied security restrictions to those objects. These shared-resource objects include not only files but also user interface resources such as windows.

Here's how the system works: The first time an application tries to access a shared object, the Windows NT subsystem verifies its right to do so. If the security check succeeds, the Windows NT subsystem allows the application to proceed. If access is not granted, an error message is generated and the application is not allowed to use the object.

The Windows NT subsystem implements object security on a number of shared objects, including window objects, menu objects, files, processes, threads, and synchronization objects.

HOW WINDOWS NT ENFORCES SECURITY

In Windows NT, all named objects and some unnamed objects can be given security protection. Every securable object has an identifier called a *security descriptor*. This descriptor contains information about the owner of the object. To keep track of secured objects, the Windows NT operating system maintains an *access-control list* (ACL) that identifies all users and groups that are granted or denied access to the object.

An ACL contains an entry for each user, global group, local group, or alias that is granted or denied access to each secured object. The entries in an access-control list are called *access-control entries*, or ACEs.

When a Windows NT user logs on, the system assigns the user an access token containing identifiers that represent the user and any groups to which the user belongs. Subsequently, every process associated with that user is supplied with a copy of the user's access token.

When a process attempts to use any object in the system, the system compares the security attributes listed in the user's access token with the ACEs in the object's ACL. The system compares the user's access token with each ACE until access is granted or denied or until there are no more ACEs to check.

If multiple ACEs apply to a token, the access rights granted by each ACE accumulate. For example, if one ACE grants read access to a group in an access token and another ACE grants write access to a user who is a member of the group, the user is granted both read and write access to the object when the access check is complete.

HOW NT SECURITY CAN AFFECT PRE-NT CODE

The security features built into Windows NT have certain unavoidable effects on some existing Windows 3.x applications. For example, an application cannot create its own global window class; only the window classes that are predefined by the Windows NT system are global.

Under DOS and Windows, an application can install its own window procedures for predefined window classes. Applications cannot do that under Windows NT, because it would leave the system open to security risks; for example, a program running on a workstation might take over the standard edit control and secretly spy on everything you typed into an edit control.

Security is also a consideration in the method that was developed for the Win32 API to handle 16-bit Windows applications. Under Windows 3.x, all applications loaded into memory at any given time share a single, global address space. This system, as Windows programmers know all too well, gives any application in memory the power to corrupt or crash other applications or even to crash the Windows operating system. This is not an acceptable feature for the Windows NT operating system to inherit—not only because of its obvious effects on the system's behavior, but also because Windows NT meets the government's C2 security rating, which does not allow applications to infringe upon each other's memory space or to invade areas of memory that belong to the operating system.

To protect applications from one another, and to protect the operating system from applications, Windows NT places all 16-bit applications that are loaded into memory in their own special confined area. Within this reserved memory area, Windows 3.x applications have the power to crash or corrupt other 16-bit Windows applications, but they cannot endanger memory that is used by the operating system or by any 32-bit application.

Example: Using the Registry

Now that you know how the Windows NT operating system works, it's time to revisit the Windows NT registry and see how it's used in commercial-quality Windows NT and Windows 95 applications. The registry as noted several times in this chapter and in Chapter 1, has replaced **CONFIG.SYS** and **AUTOEXEC.BAT** in both Windows NT and Windows 95 and has also replaced **WIN.INI** and **SYSTEM.INI** in nonsystem software.

The registry is a binary file (not a DOS-style text file) that can be used as a repository for various kinds of important data. The registry, like **WIN.INI** and **SYSTEM.INI**, is divided into sections called *keys*. Each key can be further divided into multiple levels of *subkeys*. The last subkey in the chain can contain individual data elements called *values*.

The top-level keys in the registry are called *root keys*. The Windows NT registry contains the following root keys:

+ The HKEY_CLASSES_ROOT key contains, among other things, the file name extensions used by all currently registered applications.

✦ The HKEY_CURRENT_USER key contains data about the current user.

✦ The HKEY_LOCAL_MACHINE contains information about the system currently being used.

✦ The HKEY_USERS key contains all currently loaded user profiles, including the one maintained in the HKEY_CURRENT_USER key.

Because the registry is a binary file, it's a little more difficult to use than **CONFIG.SYS,** **AUTOEXEC.BAT,** and other DOS-style text files. You can't just open the registry in an ordinary text editor and edit it as if it were a DOS-style file. To manage the registry, you must either use a special registry editor named REGEDIT—which is singularly un-user-friendly and is almost completely undocumented outside these pages—or access it programmatically by calling special registry-related functions that are supplied in the MFC library and the Win32 API.

INTRODUCING THE **TEXTCHNG** PROGRAM

In Chapter 1, "Introducing Windows NT," you had a chance to get acquainted with the REGEDIT utility. You also had a chance to cruise the registry using an example program named REGDEMO. But Chapter 1 didn't explain how to access the registry from a Windows NT program—and that's what you'll have do if you want to write Windows NT or Windows 95 programs that qualify for a Microsoft Windows–compatible logo, because such programs use the registry.

In this section, we'll take a look at a sample program that calls MFC and Win32 API functions to register itself with the Windows NT system and to use the registry as a storage facility for important data. The program is called TEXTCHNG, and you can find it—along with all the other sample programs presented in this book—on the accompanying disk.

When the TEXTCHNG application starts, it retrieves two pieces of information from the registry: a CString object and a CRect object that defines the current size and position of the program's main window. TEXTCHNG then opens its main window and displays the string it has retrieved inside the window's client area. The program's output is shown in Figure 2.17.

FIGURE 2.17 OUTPUT OF THE TEXTCHNG PROGRAM.

When TEXTCHNG has started and has displayed its main window, you can resize the window and move around the screen with the mouse in the same way you move and resize windows in any standard Windows application. You can also edit the string by choosing the **Change Text** item from the Windows menu and then typing a new string in a dialog box titled Text Change Operation (Figure 2.18). When you close the Text Change Operation dialog box, the string you have typed in replaces the original string in the program's main window.

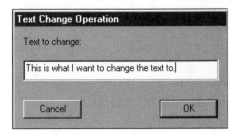

FIGURE 2.18 EDITING THE TEXTCHNG STRING.

All these capabilities are interesting enough, but they aren't what we're focusing on in this chapter. In Chapters 3 and 4, you'll learn a number of different ways to display windows on the screen and to display text strings that are neatly centered inside windows. But that is not what we're concentrating on in this section. At the moment, we're more interested in a peculiar capability that the TEXTCHNG application possesses: an ability to remember information when it shuts down and to recall that information when it starts again. The secret of this capability lies in—you guessed it—the registry.

To see how TEXTCHNG handles persistent information, start the program and change the message displayed in its main window. Then resize the program's window, move it to some other spot on the screen, and quit the program.

Then start the program again. You'll see that TEXTCHNG has remembered the new message that you supplied and now displays that message in place of its original message in its main window. Also notice that the program has remembered the new size and location of its main window and has used its resized and relocated window to create its new screen display.

If you have written 16-bit Windows programs, you may know that they can perform such tricks by storing information in .INI-style text files and then retrieving that information the next time they start. In Windows NT and Windows 95, Microsoft strongly advises developers not to use .INI files for this purpose (or for any other purpose). Instead, Windows developers are now encouraged to use the registry.

How the TEXTCHNG Program Works

When you start the TEXTCHNG program, it calls two registry-related MFC member functions: `SetRegistryKey` and `LoadStdProfileSettings`. To see what these two functions do, follow these steps:

1. Open Developer Studio if it isn't already open.
2. Navigate to the copy of the TEXTCHNG project that you have installed on your hard disk.
3. From the Developer Studio editor, open the **TEXTCHNG.CPP** file.
4. Scroll to a member function named `CWinApp::InitInstance`.

5. Locate these two statements:

```
SetRegistryKey("Newcastle Coal Co.");
LoadStdProfileSettings();
```

In this code fragment, the second statement is a call to the MFC member function `CWinApp::LoadStdProfileSettings`, which loads appropriate registry settings into memory on behalf of the currently executing application. The `LoadStdProfileSettings` member function requires a longer explanation, which is provided under the next heading.

The *SetRegistryKey* Member Function

One of the first functions executed by a Visual C++ application is an MFC member function named `CWinApp::InitInstance`. Every Windows NT application is an object of the `CWinApp` type—and, as you might guess from its name, `CWinApp::InitInstance` is the MFC member function that initializes an instance of a Windows NT application at startup time.

Because `InitInstance` is one of the first functions that executes when a Windows NT application starts, TEXTCHNG makes its first registry-related call from inside `InitInstance`:

```
SetRegistryKey("Newcastle Coal Co.");
```

`SetRegistryKey` is a `CWinApp` member function that causes an application's configuration and initialization settings to be stored in the registry. `SetRegistryKey` takes one parameter: a pointer to a string that is usually the name of a company.

The first time `SetRegistryKey` is called in a particular application to register a particular company's name, that name is stored in the registry. For example, when TEXTCHNG executes the preceding `SetRegistryKey` statement, the name of a company called Newcastle Code Co. is placed in the registry. When you exit Windows NT, any company name that you have registered with a call to `SetRegistryKey` is stored to disk, along with everything else in the registry. Later, when you restart Windows NT, you can use the REGEDIT editor to confirm that the company name you have registered by calling `SetRegistryKey` has been placed in the registry.

As an illustration of how this works, execute TEXTCHNG and then quit Windows NT. Then restart Windows NT and launch REGEDIT by choosing the Windows NT desktop's **Start|Run** command. When the REGEDIT window appears, open the HKEY_CURRENT_USER key (Figure 2.19). You can see that the name of the Newcastle Coal Co. has been placed in the HKEY_CURRENT_USER section of the registry.

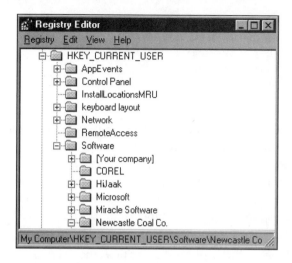

FIGURE 2.19 CONFIRMING A REGISTRY ENTRY.

The GetProfileString Statement

The next registry-related member function called by TEXTCHNG is CWinApp::Get-ProfileString. GetProfileString is called in a member function named CChngTextDoc::OnNewDocument, which you can find in **CHNGTEXTDOC.CPP**. OnNewDocument is an MFC member function that the Visual C++ framework calls automatically each time a program opens a new document. Listing 2.1 is the CChngTextDoc::OnNewDocument member function.

LISTING 2.1 THE ONNEWDOCUMENT MEMBER FUNCTION

```
BOOL CChngTextDoc::OnNewDocument()
{
    if (!CDocument::OnNewDocument())
        return FALSE;

    // TODO: add reinitialization code here
    // (SDI documents will reuse this document)
    SetMessageString("You can change this message.");

    CWinApp *theApp = AfxGetApp();
    CString theString;
```

```
theString = theApp->GetProfileString("window", "string",
    "You can change this message.");
SetMessageString(theString);

return TRUE;
}
```

GetProfileString is an MFC member function that an application can use to access a string stored in the registry. This function takes four parameters, all of them pointers to strings. In TEXTCHNG, the first two string pointers passed to GetProfileString are the names of a pair of nested subkeys. The second subkey is always nested inside the first subkey. In Listing 2.1, these two subkeys are named window and string. When GetProfileString is called, this pair of subkeys may or may not contain the string value that is being sought.

When TEXTCHNG is executed for the first time, the window and string subkeys are created, if they do not already exist, and are entered in the registry under the company name that was registered earlier with a call to SetRegistryKey. Later, when TEXTCHNG is executed again, it is a certainty that the window and string subkeys already exist, so they are searched for in the string being sought when GetProfileString is called again.

The third argument to GetProfileString is a string pointer that GetProfileString returns if it can't find a string under the window and string subkeys. If it can find a string under the window and string subkeys, it returns that string and discards the hard-coded string that has been passed to it as a parameter.

TESTING IT OUT

All this may sound complicated, but when you see firsthand how it works, it gets much simpler. To get a feel for it, execute TEXTCHNG and then quit both TEXTCHNG and Windows NT. Then you can restart Windows NT and use REGEDIT to confirm that a pair of subkeys named window and string have indeed been created and stored in the registry.

When Windows NT boots up, open REGEDIT and double-click the **HKEY_CURRENT_ USER** icon, the **Software** icon, and the **Newcastle Coal Co.** icon. Finally, double-click the **window** icon to open the window subkey.

You'll see that the left pane of the REGEDIT window resembles the screen shot shown in Figure 2.19. The window subkey is nested inside the Text Change application's subkey, which is nested inside the Newcastle Coal Co. subkey. The string value that has been stored under this key sequence—"You can change this message"—is visible in the right pane of the REGEDIT window.

STORING WINDOW COORDINATES IN THE REGISTRY

If you examine Figure 2.20 closely, you'll also see that four hexadecimal values are stored under the Text Change application's `window` subkey. These four values—`bottom`, `left`, `right`, and `top`—are the coordinates of the TEXTCHNG application's main window. TEXTCHNG stores the coordinates of its main window in these four values before it shuts down so that it can restore the size and location of its main window the next time the program starts again. It's easy to store numeric values in the registry, and you'll learn how it's done before you finish this chapter. First, though, let's take a look at another function that's used in Listing 2.1: the `SetMessageString` function.

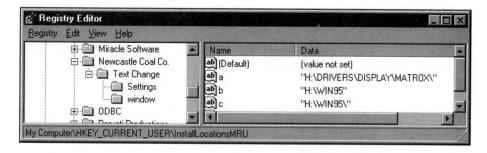

FIGURE 2.20 KEYS, SUBKEYS, AND VALUES STORED IN THE REGISTRY.

THE SETMESSAGESTRING STATEMENT

`SetMessageString` is not an MFC member function; it's a homemade member that was created for the TEXTCHNG program. All it does is set a member variable named `m_messageString` to a specified value:

```
void CChngTextDoc::SetMessageString( CString str )
{
     m_ m_messageString = str;
}
```

In Listing 2.1, `SetMessageString` is called twice. This is the first call:

```
SetMessageString("You can change this message.");
```

When the preceding statement calls `SetMessageString`, the `SetMessageString` member function sets the `m_messageString` member variable to a string that reads, "You can change this message." That, as you have seen, is the default string that TEXTCHNG displays when it first starts and keeps displaying until you choose **Windows|Change Text** and type in a different string.

The second call to `SetMessageString` in Listing 2.1 occurs in this code fragment:

```
theString = theApp->GetProfileString("window", "string",
     "You can change this message.");
SetMessageString(theString);
```

In the preceding code fragment, `GetProfileString` is called just before a call to `SetMessageString`. The `GetProfileString` member function that is called in the first statement creates the `window` and `string` substrings if they aren't already created. If both subkeys exist, `GetProfileString` checks the `string` subkey to see whether it holds a string. If it does, `GetProfileString` returns the string stored in the `string` subkey. If `GetProfileString` can't find a string in the `string` subkey, `GetProfileString` returns the TEXTCHNG program's default string: "You can change this message."

When `GetProfileString` returns, the string that it returns is stored in a local variable named `theString`. Then `SetMessageString` is called to set the `m_messageString` member variable to the string that has been returned by `SetMessageString`.

To modify the string that TEXTCHNG displays, the user of the program chooses the **Windows|Change Text** menu item and then enters a new string in a dialog box titled Text Change Operation. The Text Change Operation dialog box is opened by a `DoModal` member function that is called from the following message handler:

```
void CChngTextDoc::OnViewChangetext()
{
    // TODO: Add your command handler code here
    CChangeTextDlg dlg;

    if (dlg.DoModal() == IDOK) {
        SetMessageString( dlg.m_messageStr );
        UpdateAllViews( NULL );
    }

}
```

The preceding function opens the Text Change Operation dialog box and calls SetMessageString to set the CChngTextDoc::m_messageString member variable to whatever string has been typed in by the user. Then a member function named UpdateAllViews is called to update the program's window so that it will display the new string.

When the user quits the TEXTCHNG program, the MFC framework calls a member function named OnCloseDocument. As you can see in the following code fragment, OnCloseDocument does two important things. First, it calls GetMessageString, which retrieves the string that's currently stored in the m_messageString member variable.

Then OnCloseDocument calls an MFC member function named WriteProfileString, which writes the string that has just been retrieved by m_messageString into the string subkey in the registry. Those operations ensure that the m_messageString value most recently typed in by the user is the string that's stored in the registry just before TEXTCHNG closes down.

```
void CChngTextDoc::OnCloseDocument()
{
    CWinApp *theApp = AfxGetApp();
    CString theString;

    theString = GetMessageString();
    theApp->WriteProfileString("window", "string", theString);

    CDocument::OnCloseDocument();
}
```

From that point on, TEXTCHNG displays the user's new message in its main window. The new message is then stored in the registry and remains persistent—no matter how many times the program quits and restarts—until the user changes it again.

STORING NUMBERS IN THE REGISTRY

Now that you know how strings are stored in the registry, you won't have any trouble understanding how numeric data is stored, because the procedure is almost the same. TEXTCHNG stores four numeric values—specifically, the coordinates of its main window—in the window subkey, along with the message that is displayed in the window. Figure 2.21 shows the bottom, left, right, and top coordinates that are kept in the registry.

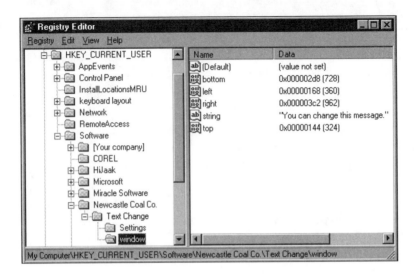

FIGURE 2.21 STORING NUMERIC VALUES IN THE REGISTRY.

The code that retrieves window coordinates from the registry appears in the TEXTCHNG application's **MAINFRM.CPP** file, which implements the program's main window. The window coordinates are retrieved from a message handler named OnCreate, which creates the program's main window.

The following statements in the OnCreate message handler make a set of four calls to a CWinApp member function named GetProfileInt, which works just like GetProfileString. If GetProfileInt can find four window coordinates stored in the registry, it transfers them to a local CRect structure named theRect. If GetProfileInt can't find a set of window coordinates in the registry, it sets theRect to a set of default coordinates. It then uses whichever set of coordinates is available to display the TEXTCHNG program's main window.

```
theRect.left = theApp->GetProfileInt("window", "left", 20);
theRect.right = theApp->GetProfileInt("window", "rightv, 300);
theRect.top = theApp->GetProfileInt("window", "top", 20);
theRect.bottom = theApp->GetProfileInt("window", "bottom", 200);

this->MoveWindow(&theRect);"
```

The code that stores window coordinates in the registry just before TEXTCHNG shuts down is also similar to the code that saves the newest string to the registry. This is the member function—also in **MAINFRM.CPP**—that saves window coordinates to the registry:

```
void CMainFrame::OnClose()
{
    CRect theRect;

    this->GetWindowRect(&theRect);
    CWinApp *theApp = AfxGetApp();

    theApp->WriteProfileInt("window", "left", theRect.left);
    theApp->WriteProfileInt("window", "right", theRect.right);
    theApp->WriteProfileInt("window", "top", theRect.top);
    theApp->WriteProfileInt("window", "bottom", theRect.bottom);

    CFrameWnd::OnClose();
}
```

This is a straightforward block of code that you probably won't have any trouble understanding by now. It simply makes four calls to a `CWinApp` member function named `WriteProfileInt`, which copies each current coordinate of the TEXTCHNG program's main window into the registry.

Summary

This chapter describes the new features of Windows NT and shows how they were combined to create the Windows NT operating system. Topics covered in this chapter include support for open systems, support for multithreading, support for networking, and the security and reliability of the Windows NT operating system.

In Chapter 3, "The Win32 API," you'll learn how the Win32 Application Programming Interface implements the features of Windows NT described in this chapter. You'll also see how the Microsoft Visual C++ software development system and the MFC library make it easy for you to use the new features of Windows NT in your own 32-bit Windows programs.

CHAPTER THREE

THE WIN32 API

Back in the era of Windows 3.1, before Visual C++ was even a gleam in Bill Gates's eye, Windows programmers developed their applications using a giant library of C-language functions called the Windows API. When Microsoft developed Windows NT—the first 32-bit Windows operating system—operating system engineers rewrote the entire Windows API in 32-bit code, and Microsoft named the result the Win32 API. Today, even though most Windows programmers do most of their work in C++ and use higher-level development environments—such as Microsoft Visual C++ and Borland C++—it is still important for Windows developers to know something about the operation of the Win32 API.

Why? Because all popular C++ compilers, including Microsoft C++ and Borland C++, still do most of their work by calling functions that are implemented in the Win32 API. For example, the Visual C++ compiler accesses the Win32 API using the enormous C++ class library, MFC. The MFC library, in turn, performs most of its tasks by calling C-language functions that are implemented in the Win32 API. (You'll learn much more about the MFC library in Chapter 4, "Programming Windows NT with Visual C++".)

This chapter does not focus on the MFC library; instead, its purpose is to introduce the Windows API and to familiarize you with the architecture of a simple Windows NT program. To demonstrate how the Windows API works, I'll present a short API-style sample program named HELLOWIN. The HELLOWIN program creates and displays a window by calling C-language functions implemented in the Win32 API. In Chapter 4, you'll learn how to create and build a similar program by using classes and member functions implemented in the MFC library. Then, in later chapters, you'll learn how to write more-complex MFC programs for Windows NT.

What Is the Windows API?

The Windows API is a set of functions and data structures that form the foundation of all Windows software development systems. There are two versions of the Windows API: the original 16-bit Windows API—sometimes referred to as the Win16 API—and the 32-bit Win32 API. You can write programs for Windows NT using either API. But applications that call functions in the Win16 API execute as 16-bit applications under Windows NT, whereas applications that rely on the Win32 API run as native 32-bit Windows NT programs.

The Win32 API is a superset of the Win16 API, so the Win32 API contains 32-bit versions of all the Windows functions that are familiar to Windows 3.x programmers. In addition, the Win32 API provides many new functions that the Win16 API does not support. Examples include functions to create and manage all the new features and user-interface controls that were added to Windows with the introduction of Windows 95—features such as taskbars, docking toolbars, support for object linking and embedding (OLE), desktop drag-and-drop support, and much more. All these new features have been encapsulated into MFC and OWL classes and member functions, and you'll learn much more about them in later chapters.

The Win32 API also contains several other categories of functions that were not available in the Win16 API. For example, Win32 offers new sets of functions that support 32-bit memory management, 32-bit file management, 32-bit multithreading, and 32-bit network communications. In addition, many capabilities of the original Win16 API have been improved and updated in the Win32 API. Many of these features can be found in the categories of window management, message handling, and graphics.

HELLO, WINDOWS; HELLO, WORLD

If you're a C programmer, you probably recognize the application that's reprinted in its entirety in Listing 3.1. It's a copy of the first sample C-language program ever written: the "Hello, world" program that appeared in Chapter 1 of Brian Kernighan and Dennis Ritchie's classic 1978 text, *The C Programming Language*. (The programs aren't strictly identical. The line `#include <stdio.h>` didn't show up until the book's second edition.) It's presented here not because it is a Windows API program, but because it isn't. Later, you'll see what the "Hello, world" program looks like when it is converted into a Windows application that does its work by calling functions implemented in the Windows API.

LISTING 3.1 THE "HELLO, WORLD" PROGRAM.

```
/* hello.c */
```

```
#include <stdio.h>

main()
{
    printf("Hello, world\n");
}
```

The "Hello, world" program, although short, is a complete C-language application. Because C is an almost perfect subset of C++, you can compile "Hello, world" as a C++ program, so you could say that "Hello, world" is a fully functional C++ program, too.

Figure 3.1 shows the output of the original "Hello, world" program in a Windows NT console window. (*Console* windows are text windows that Windows NT provides for command-line operations and character displays. Console windows are covered in Chapter 6, "Processes.")

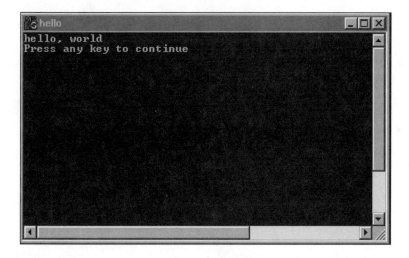

FIGURE 3.1   OUTPUT OF THE ORIGINAL "HELLO, WORLD" PROGRAM.

Console Applications

Because the original "Hello, world" program is a text-based application, it is compiled for this chapter as a Visual C++ console application. In the Visual C++ programming environment, a console application is a text-based program that executes in a console window when it is executed under Windows 95 or Windows NT. Other text-based programs in this book are also compiled as console programs.

When you write a Visual C++ 4.0 application using the automatic application-generator utility AppWizard, you can compile the program as a console application by choosing **Console** in the AppWizard list box shown in Figure 3.2. Then AppWizard automatically creates a DOS-style application that can be executed in a console window. (You'll learn more about how to generate a Visual C++ program using AppWizard in Chapter 4, "Programming Windows NT with Visual C++.")

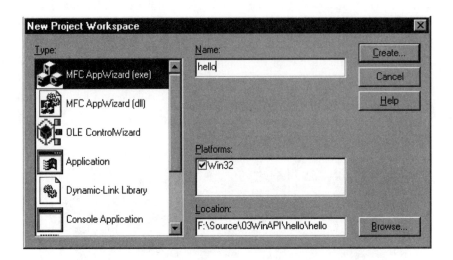

FIGURE 3.2 CHOOSING AN APPLICATION TYPE WITH APPWIZARD.

ANATOMY OF THE ORIGINAL "HELLO, WORLD" PROGRAM

If you're familiar with the history of C, you can see right away how the "Hello, world" program works. It has just one function, `main`. This `main` function contains a single statement that invokes, or calls, a function named `printf`:

```
printf("Hello, world\n");
```

The `printf` routine then works some magic that prints the line

```
Hello, world
```

on your computer monitor.

A Windows NT "Hello, world" Program

Now that you know all about the original version of "Hello, world," forget it. That isn't the way a Windows program works at all. Listing 3.2 is an example of a simple Windows NT program that prints "Hello, world" in a window. HELLOWIN is in this chapter's folder on the accompanying disk. HELLOWIN doesn't contain any code that's specific to either 16-bit or 32-bit applications, so it can be compiled as either a 16-bit program or a 32-bit program.

Listing 3.2 The HELLOWIN program.

```
// HELLOWIN: A Windows API "Hello, world" Program

#include <windows.h>
long FAR PASCAL WndProc(HWND hwnd, UINT message, UINT wParam, LONG lParam)
{
    HDC             hdc;
    PAINTSTRUCT     ps;
    RECT            rect;
    HPEN            hpen, hpenOld;

    switch(message) {

    case WM_PAINT :
        hdc = BeginPaint(hwnd, &ps);
        GetClientRect(hwnd, &rect);

        GetClientRect(hwnd, &rect);
        hpen = CreatePen(PS_SOLID, 6, RGB(255, 0, 0));

        hpenOld = SelectObject(hdc, hpen);

        Rectangle(hdc, rect.left + 10, rect.top + 10,
            rect.right - 10, rect.bottom - 10);

        DrawText(hdc, "Hello, world", -1, &rect,
            DT_SINGLELINE | DT_CENTER | DT_VCENTER);
            return 0;

        SelectObject(hdc, hpenOld);
        DeleteObject(hpen);
```

```
            EndPaint(hwnd, &ps);

        case WM_DESTROY :
                PostQuitMessage(0);
                return 0;
            }
    return DefWindowProc(hwnd, message, wParam, lParam);
}

int PASCAL WinMain(HANDLE hInstance, HANDLE hPrevInstance, LPSTR lpszCmdParam,
int nCmdShow)
{
    static char szAppName[] = "HelloWin";
    HWND        hwnd;
    MSG         msg;
    WNDCLASS    wndclass;
    if(!hPrevInstance) {
        wndclass.style = CS_HREDRAW | CS_VREDRAW;
            wndclass.lpfnWndProc   = WndProc;
            wndclass.cbClsExtra    = 0;
            wndclass.cbWndExtra    = 0;
            wndclass.hInstance     = hInstance;
            wndclass.hIcon         = LoadIcon(NULL,
                IDI_APPLICATION);
             wndclass.hCursor      = LoadCursor(NULL,
                IDC_ARROW);
            wndclass.hbrBackground =
                GetStockObject(WHITE_BRUSH);
            wndclass.lpszMenuName  = NULL;
            wndclass.lpszClassName = szAppName;
            RegisterClass(&wndclass);
    }

    hwnd = CreateWindow(szAppName,   // window class name
        "HelloWin Program",          //window caption
        WS_OVERLAPPEDWINDOW,   // window style
        CW_USEDEFAULT,         // initial x position
        CW_USEDEFAULT,         // initial y position
        CW_USEDEFAULT,         // initial x size
        CW_USEDEFAULT,         // initial y size
```

```
        NULL,                       // parent window handle
        NULL,                       // window menu handle
        hInstance,                  // program instance handle
        NULL);                      // creation parameters
    ShowWindow(hwnd, nCmdShow);
    UpdateWindow(hwnd);
    while(GetMessage(&msg, NULL, 0, 0)) {
        TranslateMessage(&msg);
        DispatchMessage(&msg);
    }
    return msg.wParam;
}
```

Although HELLOWIN is a C++ application, it does its work by calling C-language functions implemented in the Windows API. It is important to note that the program does not use the MFC library. You'll learn how to write programs that use MFC in Chapter 4, "Programming Windows NT with Visual C++."

The version in Listing 3.2 is considerably more complicated than the original "Hello, world" program. The reason for its increased complexity is that many extra things are required to create and open a window. We'll examine most of these extra features as we move through this chapter. Figure 3.3 shows the output of the HELLOWIN program.

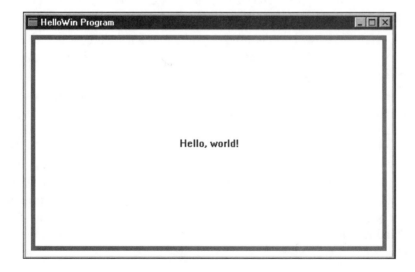

FIGURE 3.3 OUTPUT OF THE WINDOWS API "HELLO, WORLD" PROGRAM.

Events and Messages in Windows Programs

Some texts say that the most significant difference between a text-based program and a Windows-based program is that a text-based program is *proactive*, whereas a Windows-based program is *reactive*. When a user executes a text-based program, the application prompts the user for input and then waits for the user to do something, such as press a key or click a mouse. When the user responds to the program's prompt, the application responds appropriately and then prompts the user to do something else. This process continues until the program ends.

Windows-based programs handle user input in a completely different way. A Windows application spends most of its time in what is sometimes called a *main loop*, waiting for various kinds of user-generated events, such as mouse clicks, mouse movements, key presses, or the choosing of menu items.

MESSAGES AND MESSAGE HANDLERS

In a Windows program, when the user takes an action that triggers an event, the event generates a hardware interrupt that causes Windows to send a *message* to the application. In Windows, a message is nothing more than a function that is dispatched, along with information that describes the kind of event that has taken place, to an application. For example, when the user presses the left mouse button, Windows dispatches a WM_LBUTTONDOWN message. When the user types a character, Windows dispatches a WM_CHAR message. When the user or the program closes a window, Windows issues a WM_CLOSE message.

Events originated by the system can also cause messages to be generated. For instance, a WM_CREATE message is generated when a window is being created, and a WM_DESTROY message is dispatched when a window is about to be destroyed.

Messages that are sent to an application window when the user selects a menu item are called *command messages*. An application can also define its own messages, which are known as *user messages*. In applications that are written using the Windows API, messages are customarily dispatched from a `switch` statement that calls functions known as *message handlers*. When an API-style Windows program is executed, it executes this `switch` statement over and over, monitoring user input and executing the appropriate message handlers as events of various kinds are detected. You saw how the Windows messaging system works in the HELLOWIN example program presented earlier in this chapter. Because Windows programs work this way, the Windows environment is often referred to as an *event-based*, *message-driven* operating system.

Figure 3.4 shows how events and messages work in a Windows program.

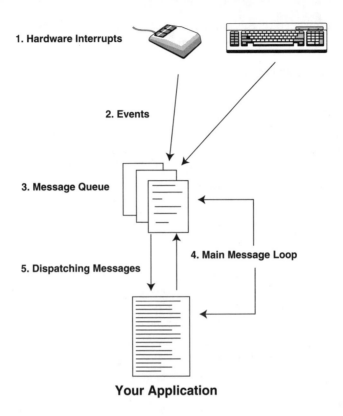

1. Hardware Interrupts

2. Events

3. Message Queue

4. Main Message Loop

5. Dispatching Messages

Your Application

FIGURE 3.4 HOW EVENTS AND MESSAGES WORK IN A WINDOWS PROGRAM.

MESSAGES ORIGINATED BY THE SYSTEM

Although most Windows events are triggered by user actions, Windows itself can also originate and dispatch messages. For example, if Windows detects that the background of a window needs erasing, the system passes that information to the currently active application. Then the application can respond to the information in whatever way it considers appropriate.

It is important to remember that in Windows, a message is simply a procedure that Windows sends to an application each time Windows detects an event. Along with each message, Windows passes the current application a set of parameters specifying the kind of event that has been generated. The application can use that information to determine what to do about the event. To get a sense of how this messaging system works, it helps to have some knowledge of the architecture of a typical Windows API program. Let's take a closer look at how a Windows program is constructed.

THE WINMAIN FUNCTION

The main message loop in a Windows program is usually found in a function named WinMain. In a Windows application, WinMain takes the place of the main function in a text-based C or C++ program. WinMain is always the first function that is executed when the application starts. When the WinMain function terminates, the program ends. WinMain is declared in a header file named **WINDOWS.H,** where the Windows operating system declares all Windows functions. This is the syntax of the WinMain function:

```
int WinMain(HANDLE hInstance, HANDLE hPrevInstance, LPSTR lpszCmdParam,
int nCmdShow)
```

If you are familiar with the way the WinMain function works in Windows 3.x applications, you may be surprised to learn that it works differently in Windows NT. In Windows NT, just as in Windows 3.x, WinMain takes four parameters. But Windows NT and Windows 3.x treat these four parameters differently. In Windows 3.x, the parameters passed to WinMain have the following meanings:

✦   hInstance: A handle to the current instance of the executing application.

✦   hPrevInstance: A handle to the previous instance of the executing application.

✦   lpszCmdParam: A pointer to a command line that can be called to start the application.

✦   nCmdShow: A constant or a set of constants (separated by bitwise OR ("|") symbols) that can be used to specify the window's size, its coordinates, and other attributes that specify how it is displayed. To obtain a list of all the constants that can be used in this parameter, consult your compiler's on-line help files.

In a Windows 3.x application, when the WinMain call terminates normally, it returns the return value of another Windows API function named PostQuitMessage. Windows then sends the application a WM_QUIT message. Then, if the application is written correctly, it exits the message loop in its main function and returns control to Windows. When something goes wrong in a 16-bit Windows program and the application's call to WinMain is not successful, WinMain terminates before it enters the message loop and returns NULL.

The WinMain function has the same syntax in Windows NT that it has in Windows 3.1. But every WinMain parameter except one—lpszCmdLine—has a different meaning in

Windows NT. For example, in pre-NT versions of Windows, the hModule parameter of WinMain specifies the module database for an .EXE or .DLL file. (Dynamic link libraries are object-code libraries that can be dynamically linked to applications at run time; for details, see Chapter 8, "Dynamic Link Libraries.") Even if multiple instances of an application are running, there is only one module database for the application. This means that a single hModule value is shared by all instances of the application.

This arrangement makes sense in 16-bit versions of Windows. Only one instance of a given DLL can be loaded under Win16, so there is only one hModule value for each loaded DLL.

THE hINSTANCE PARAMETER

In 16-bit versions of Windows, each running instance of a task also receives its own hInstance value, which identifies the default data segment for the task. For example, if four instances of the task are running, there are four hInstance values, one for each instance. In Windows NT, there is no distinction between the hModule parameter of a process and its hInstance values; they are exactly the same. When the documentation for a Win16 API states that an hModule value is required, you can pass an hInstance value—and vice versa—if you are programming for Windows NT.

When a Win32 process calls a WinMain function, the value that is passed to the function in the hInstance parameter is a base address that specifies the point where the .EXE file is mapped into the process's address space. By default, an .EXE file is mapped into a process's address space starting at 0x00010000. (You can change this default by using the /BASE:address linker switch.) Thus, the default hInstance variable for an .EXE file is 0x10000. This means that the hInstance value for all running processes is the same— specifically, 0x10000.

A corollary is that a process cannot load a resource—for example, a dialog-box template—from the resource file of another process that is currently executing. Even in Windows 3.x, this is not generally a wise thing to do—and in Windows NT, it is not possible. In Windows NT, when you make a call to an API function that expects an hInstance value, the Win32 system interprets the call to mean that you are requesting information from an .EXE or a .DLL mapped into your own process's address space at the address specified by hInstance.

DLL ENTRY POINTS IN WINDOWS NT

The Win32 system also provides every dynamic link library with its own hInstance value, which, again, is identical to the DLL's hModule value under Windows NT.

In Windows NT—as you'll see in Chapter 8, "Dynamic Link Libraries"—DLL entry points look different. Unlike Windows 3.x programs, Windows 95 and Windows NT applications call one function, DllMain, for both initialization and termination of DLLs. DllMain also makes calls on both a per-process and a per-thread basis, so several initialization calls can be made if a process is multithreaded. The function is optional; if you don't provide it in source code, the compiler links its own version, which does nothing but return TRUE.

DllMain uses the WINAPI convention and three parameters. The following code shows the header line in a DllMain definition:

```
BOOL WINAPI DllMain (HANDLE hInst, ULONG ul_reason_for_call, LPVOID lpReserved)
```

The DllMain function returns TRUE (1) to indicate success. If the function returns zero during per-process initialization, the system cancels the process.

THE HPREVINSTANCE PARAMETER

In a 16-bit Windows-based application, the WinMain function's hPrevInstance parameter specifies the instance handle to another instance of the same task. If no other instance of the task is running, a NULL value is passed in the hPrevInstance parameter. Applications frequently examine this value for two purposes:

✦ To determine whether another instance of the same task is already running and, if it is, to terminate the instance that has just been invoked.

✦ To determine whether window classes need to be registered. (When you write an application using the Windows API, your program must *register* each kind of window that it uses by calling an API function named RegisterClass; you'll learn more about RegisterClass under the heading "Registering Window Classes" later in this chapter.)

Window Classes

In Windows programs, a *window class* is different from a C++ class; it merely means a type of window. A Windows application can use many different types of windows, and, as you will see later in this chapter, you must register a window class before you can use a particular type of window in an application.

In a 16-bit Windows application, a module can call the RegisterClass function to register a particular window class only once. This class is then shared by all instances of the application. If a second instance attempts to register the same window class a second time, the call to RegisterClass fails.

In Windows NT, each instance of an application must register its own window classes, because different instances of the same application do not share window classes. Therefore, in a Win32 application, a NULL value is always passed in the hPrevInstance parameter to WinMain. This characteristic can simplify the porting of Win16 applications to Win32. If a 16-bit application examines hPrevInstance when it registers a window class and finds a NULL value, all instances of the application discover that hPrevInstance is NULL and automatically re-register their window classes.

THE LPSZCMDLINE PARAMETER

The lpszCmdLine parameter of the WinMain function is the only one that has the same meaning in Windows 3.x and Windows NT. The lpszCmdLine parameter points to a string containing the command line that is passed to the application to start it.

THE NCMDSHOW PARAMETER

The nCmdShow parameter, the last parameter to WinMain, is usually SW_SHOWNOR-MAL or SW_SHOWMINNOACTIVE in applications written for Windows 3.x. In Windows NT, the value of nCmdShow is always SW_SHOWDEFAULT.

In Windows NT, when an application displays a window that has been created using SW_SHOWDEFAULT, Windows NT examines the nCmdShow member of the window's STARTUPINFO structure to find out what process owns the window. Win32 then uses this value to determine how the window should be displayed.

HOW WINDOWS HANDLES WINDOWS HANDLES

In Windows, a *handle* is a data type that is used in much the same way that pointers are used in text-based operating systems. Unlike a pointer, a handle does not point to an actual memory address. Instead, a handle points to a private list or table of addresses that Windows maintains.

In a Windows NT program, the WinMain function takes two handles as parameters: a handle to the current instance of the executing application, and a handle to any previous instance of the application that may exist. Notice the two occurrences of HANDLE in the following syntax example:

```
int PASCAL WinMain(HANDLE hInstance, HANDLE hPrevInstance, LPSTR lpszCmdParam,
int nCmdShow)
```

Many Windows API functions return handles, and many others take handles as parameters. In your Windows applications, you need only use handles in the same way you would use any other data type. Because Windows dereferences handles automatically whenever it needs to, the use of handles becomes almost second nature to Windows programmers.

To get a handle (pardon the pun) on how `WinMain` works in a Windows NT program, it helps to know something about how handles work. In Windows, handles are tools that applications use to access Windows objects, in much the same way that pointers are used to access C++ objects in non-Windows C++ programs.

What is the difference between a pointer and a handle? The main difference is that a pointer always holds a hard-coded memory address, whereas a handle can access an object that has been moved from one memory location by Windows. No matter where an object resides in memory, a Windows program can always access the object using a handle, because handles are always created and kept up-to-date by Windows.

Why do Windows programs use handles instead of pointers? Because the Windows memory manager often moves objects around from one memory location to another—to eliminate gaps in memory, for example—without notifying applications that the addresses of the juggled objects have been changed. If Windows applications used pointers to keep track of Windows objects, Windows programs would be constantly locking, unlocking, and dereferencing pointers, and that would be a big headache. Windows handles make such chores unnecessary.

When Windows moves an object created by the system from one memory location to another, the Windows memory manager automatically arranges everything so that the object's handle is still valid. In Windows applications, many different kinds of objects are designed to be accessed through handles. There are so many such objects that they have a special name: Windows objects.

Windows objects are not the same thing as C++ objects; windows objects have nothing to do with C++ or object-oriented programming. In Windows terminology, Windows objects are merely objects that can be accessed via handles; they can be (and are) used in C-language Windows programs as well as Windows programs written in C++.

Because Windows NT does everything that is required to keep track of the handles that it maintains, you never have to dereference them. Except for this difference, handles can be used to access objects in Windows programs in the same way that pointers are used to access objects in non-Windows programs.

EVENT LOOPS AND MESSAGE PUMPS

In a Windows API program, the `WinMain` function usually contains a main *event loop* that repeatedly checks for messages and takes the required actions. This main event loop is sometimes referred to as a *message pump*. Figure 3.5 shows how a message pump works in a Windows program.

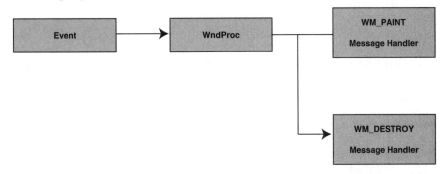

FIGURE 3.5 A MESSAGE PUMP.

In the HELLOWIN example program presented earlier (Listing 3.2), the `WinMain` function creates and displays a window and then executes this message pump:

```
while(GetMessage(&msg, NULL, 0, 0)) {
    TranslateMessage(&msg);
    DispatchMessage(&msg);
}
```

HELLOWIN's message pump is built on a `while` statement that calls a Windows API function named `GetMessage`. The `while` statement calls `GetMessage` over and over until `GetMessage` returns `NULL`. Then the loop ends, and HELLOWIN moves to its next function—generally, a function that terminates the program.

What does `GetMessage` do in this example? Answer: It retrieves messages dispatched by Windows. `GetMessage` is called using this format:

```
GetMessage(&msg, NULL, 0, 0);
```

`GetMessage` takes four parameters. The first parameter, `&msg`, is the address of a C-language `struct` called MSG. The Windows API defines the MSG `struct` using the following `typedef`:

```
typedef struct tag MSG {
```

```
HWND    hwnd;
UINT    message;
WPARAM wParam;
LPARAM lParam;
DWORD time;
POINT pt;
} MSG;
```

In the Win32 API, a MSG `struct` is defined as a structure that `GetMessage` uses to retrieve information about Windows messages. In its `hwnd` and `message` fields, the MSG `struct` identifies the message being referred to and the window that the message affects.

The `wParam` and `lParam` fields in a MSG `struct` are used to store information about the kind of event the message refers to and the source of the event. For instance, if the event is caused by keyboard input, the MSG `struct`'s `wParam` and `lParam` fields identify the key being pressed and also reveal whether a command key was being pressed at the same time. When an application calls `GetMessage` and passes it the address of a MSG structure, `GetMessage` responds by placing essential information about the event it is retrieving in the MSG structure that you have provided. Your application can then use that information to respond to the event.

Refer to the message pump that calls `GetMessage` in Listing 3.2, and you'll see that the `msg` parameter is accessed not only by `GetMessage` but also by two other Windows API functions: `TranslateMessage` and `DispatchMessage`. `TranslateMessage` translates virtual key messages—keyboard messages that use special keys such as **Shift** and **Ctrl**—into ordinary character messages. `DispatchMessage` dispatches messages to a special kind of procedure called a *window procedure:* a function that handles the messages that are detected and retrieved by `GetMessage`. Window procedures are described later in this section.

MESSAGE PUMPS AND MESSAGE QUEUES

When Windows NT originates an event or detects that a user-originated event has taken place, it dispatches a message to the currently executing application by placing the message in a queue that belongs to the application. This queue is often referred to as a *message queue*. In a Windows program, messages that are waiting in the message queue are retrieved by `GetMessage`. When a Windows application is being executed, its message pump repeatedly calls `GetMessage`. Each time `GetMessage` executes, it checks the application's message queue to see whether any messages have been received from the system.

Whenever an application receives a message from Windows, `GetMessage` retrieves the message—together with any information that has been passed along with the message in its parameters—from the application's message queue. The application then calls `DispatchMessage` to dispatch the message to Windows. Windows responds by performing whatever system operations the message may require. Then Windows dispatches the specified message to a window procedure.

WINDOW PROCEDURES

A window procedure can be found in every Windows program. One unusual feature of a window procedure is that it is always implemented in an application's source code but is always called by the Windows operating system and never by the user's code. The main job of a window procedure is to handle messages that Windows dispatches to an application in response to the program's calls to `DispatchMessage`. Figure 3.6 shows how a window procedure works in a Windows application.

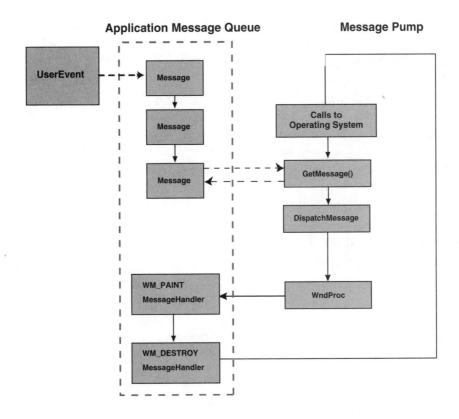

FIGURE 3.6 DIAGRAM OF A WINDOW PROCEDURE.

By convention, a window procedure is called `WndProc`, or something similar. (`WndProc` is the name of the window procedure used in the HELLOWIN program.) You do not have to give a window procedure any particular name, but you are required to tell Windows the name of your window procedure. Window procedures must be written using a predetermined syntax that demands certain kinds of parameters.

If an application displays different kinds of windows, each kind of window (or each *window class*) can have a separate window procedure. To handle the messages it receives, a window procedure generally executes a `switch` statement that checks the parameters of those messages and then passes them to message handlers. These message handlers finally handle the messages that are dispatched in a Windows program.

MESSAGES AND MESSAGE HANDLERS

When a Windows program calls `DispatchMessage`, Windows responds by calling the application's window procedure. To let the application's window procedure know what kind of event has occurred, Windows places information about the event in the parameters that it passes to the window procedure. The window procedure examines the parameters and, if possible, calls the appropriate message handler.

Windows applications typically have various kinds of message handlers that are designed to handle particular kinds of messages. Some of these message handlers are handled internally by Windows, but you must write others yourself. For example, your application may handle a right mouse-button click differently than another application might handle the same kind of event. The way your application handles a double-click is determined by your application's own right-mouse-button-click message handler.

EXAMPLE OF A WINDOW PROCEDURE

The code fragment shown in Listing 3.3 is an example of a message-handling `switch` statement. This statement appears in the window procedure used in the HELLOWIN example program shown in Listing 3.2.

LISTING 3.3 A SWITCH STATEMENT FOR HANDLING WINDOWS MESSAGES.

```
switch(message) {

    case WM_PAINT :
        hdc = BeginPaint(hwnd, &ps);
        GetClientRect(hwnd, &rect);
```

```
        GetClientRect(hwnd, &rect);
        hpen = CreatePen(PS_SOLID, 6, RGB(255, 0, 0));

        hpenOld = SelectObject(hdc, hpen);

        Rectangle(hdc, rect.left + 10, rect.top + 10,
            rect.right - 10, rect.bottom - 10);

        DrawText(hdc, "Hello, world", -1, &rect,
            DT_SINGLELINE | DT_CENTER | DT_VCENTER);

        SelectObject(hdc, hpenOld);
        DeleteObject(hpen);
        EndPaint(hwnd, &ps);
        return 0;

    case WM_DESTROY :
        PostQuitMessage(0);
        return 0;
    }
```

An Easier Way: Use MFC

When you write a Windows application using the C-language functions implemented in the Windows API, you are responsible for writing most of the code that receives event messages from Windows and calls the appropriate message handlers. You must also write the message handlers that implement the responses that are appropriate to each event.

As you'll see in Chapter 4, "Programming Windows NT with Visual C++," it doesn't take nearly that much work to create message-handling mechanisms for an MFC application. You can create most kinds of message handlers by simply opening a ClassWizard dialog box and selecting the kind of message handler you want to create. ClassWizard generates your message handler automatically. You'll see how this works in Chapter 4 and in subsequent chapters.

At the moment, though, we're focusing on a traditional API-style Windows program. In that kind of program, you must write all your own message handlers.

HANDLING MESSAGES WITH *SWITCH* STATEMENTS

When a Windows program executes a switch statement such as the one shown in Listing 3.3, each case clause in the switch statement tests a variable named message, a parameter that the window procedure has received from Windows. It is a message ID that identifies the kind of message that Window has dispatched. The `switch` statement tests the message ID parameter and then uses two `case` clauses to invoke the appropriate message handlers.

If none of the message handlers called by the `switch` statement can handle the message, the Windows API function `DefWindowProc` is called to send the message back to Windows. (`DefWindowProc` is called in the last line of the preceding code fragment.) Windows handles the message by executing a set of default procedures that take care of unhandled messages.

That WM_ Prefix

The `switch` statement shown in Listing 3.3 has only two `case` clauses: a WM_PAINT clause that is executed each time the window associated with the window procedure needs to be redrawn, and a WM_DESTROY clause that is executed whenever the window needs to be destroyed.

The WM_PAINT and WM_DESTROY messages begin with the prefix WM_ because they are *Windows messages*—messages that are not triggered by user events but are generated by Windows. As you will see in later chapters, user-generated events have different kinds of prefixes. For example, Windows dispatches a message that begins with the word ON_COMMAND whenever the user of an application triggers a message by choosing a menu command. The Windows-based HELLOWIN program shown in Listing 3.2 does not check for user events, because it does not have a user interface; all it does is print the greeting "Hello, world" in a window. In later chapters, you'll learn how to write message handlers for user-triggered messages.

In the "Hello, world" program, the WM_PAINT clause in the message that the window procedure receives from Windows executes a message handler that prints "Hello, world." The WM_DESTROY message handler calls a Windows API function named `PostQuitMessage`, which informs Windows that the application is ready to terminate. When an application posts a message to Windows by calling `PostQuitMessage`, Windows performs all the housekeeping to let the application exit from its main message loop and return control to Windows.

ANATOMY OF A WINDOW PROCEDURE

Whatever you name your window procedure (the HELLOWIN program uses `WndProc`), this is the syntax you must use to define it:

```
long FAR PASCAL WndProc(HWND hwnd, UINT message, UINT wParam, LONG lParam)
```

It's easy to provide a window procedure with a name; place the name in a designated field inside the Windows API WNDCLASS `struct`, which is designed to provide Windows with information about windows before they are created. In addition to the field that identifies the window procedure associated with a window, the WNDCLASS `struct` has a number of other fields that hold information about a window you are planning to create.

CREATING AND USING MESSAGE PUMPS

The Windows-based HELLOWIN program presented in Listing 3.2 has a `WinMain` function that works in the conventional way. The primary responsibility of `WinMain` is to call three other API functions: `GetMessage`, `TranslateMessage`, and `DispatchMessage`. In a traditional API-style program, these three functions are called in a message pump:

```
while (GetMessage(&msg, NULL, 0, 0)) {
    if ((hwndDlgModeless == NULL ||
            !IsDialogMessage(hwndDlgModeless, &msg)) &&
            !TranslateAccelerator(hwnd, haccl, &msg)) {
        TranslateMessage(&msg);
        DispatchMessage(&msg);
    }
}
```

REGISTERING WINDOW CLASSES

A Windows NT application can use as many different window classes as it needs. Before you can create a window that belongs to a particular class, you must register the window's class by calling the API's `RegisterClass` function. As you have seen, a Windows application registers each of its window classes by creating a WNDCLASS `struct` and then calling the API function `RegisterWindow`. The parameters passed to `RegisterWindow` provide Windows with the information that it requires about the different kinds of classes used by the application.

The WNDCLASS structure is defined as follows in **WINDOWS.H**:

```
typedef struct tagWNDCLASS {
    UINT        style;
    WNDPROC     lpfnWndProc;
    int         cbClsExtra;
    int         cbWndExtra;
```

```
HINSTANCE hInstance;
HICON     hIcon;
HCURSOR   hCursor;
HBRUSH    hbrBackground;
LPCSTR    lpszMenuName;
LPCSTR    lpszClassName;
} WNDCLASS;
```

The WNDCLASS struct contains the attributes of a particular window class. To register a window class, you must first create a WNDCLASS structure that describes the attributes of that class; then you call RegisterWindow to register the class of window that your WNDCLASS structure describes. Only then can you create a window of that class.

When an application calls RegisterClass to register a window's class, the program passes to RegisterClass the address of the appropriate WNDCLASS structure. The operating system then registers a window class that has the requested attributes, and Windows gives this new class the name that the application has specified.

Before you call RegisterClass to register a window, you must fill in the fields of the WNDCLASS structure using a set of properties to specify the attributes of the window class. For example, you must place the name of the window procedure in the WNDCLASS structure's lpfnWndProc field. You also define the window's style in the WNDCLASS structure's style field using style constants that are defined by the Windows API.

Calling the *RegisterClass* Function

The HELLOWIN example program shows how a Windows API program can register a window class. In HELLOWIN, the following statement (which appears in the WinMain function) constructs a WNDCLASS struct and registers a window class named szAppName:

```
if(!hPrevInstance) {
        wndclass.style        = CS_HREDRAW | CS_VREDRAW;
        wndclass.lpfnWndProc  = WndProc;
        wndclass.cbClsExtra   = 0;
        wndclass.cbWndExtra   = 0;
        wndclass.hInstance    = hInstance;
        wndclass.hIcon        = LoadIcon(NULL,
            IDI_APPLICATION);
```

```
wndclass.hCursor        = LoadCursor(NULL, IDC_ARROW);
wndclass.hbrBackground  = GetStockObject(WHITE_BRUSH);
wndclass.lpszMenuName   = NULL;
wndclass.lpszClassName  = szAppName;

RegisterClass(&wndclass);
}
```

Notice that the address passed to `RegisterClass` is the address of a WNDCLASS structure named `wndclass`. The `hInstance` variable is tested to see whether a previous instance of HELLOWIN is running. If a previous instance is running, a window like the one being described has already been registered, and there is no need to register the same class of window again.

For another example of registering a window class, see the heading "Creating and Displaying a Window." In the example described under that heading, the class name `szAppName` is used to create a window of the class that has been registered by calling `RegisterClass`.

Window Styles

In the call to `RegisterClass` in the preceding example, two predefined constants are used to set the style of the window used in HELLOWIN:

```
wndclass.style = CS_HREDRAW | CS_VREDRAW;
```

In the preceding statement, two style constants—CS_HREDRAW and CS_VREDRAW—are used to set two style attributes of the window to be created. When you set the CS_HREDRAW constant, windows that belong to the class you are creating are redrawn whenever their horizontal size changes. Similarly, CS_VREDRAW causes a window to be redrawn whenever its vertical size changes. In HELLOWIN, specifying CS_HREDRAW and CS_VREDRAW constants ensures that the application's window is redrawn each time its size changes. That action automatically centers the "Hello, world" greeting inside the window.

CS_HREDRAW and CS_VREDRAW are not the only style constants that are available in Windows. There are many other style attributes that you can use when you register window classes. For a complete list, see Books Online or refer to your compiler's on-line help files.

Loading Application Resources with *RegisterClass*

The Win32 API provides a number of functions that you can use to set window-class attributes in RegisterClass statements. For example, the RegisterClass statement used in HELLOWIN calls the Windows API functions LoadIcon and LoadCursor to fill in the hIcon and hCursor fields of the window class that is being registered:

```
wndclass.hIcon =      LoadIcon(NULL, IDI_APPLICATION);
wndclass.hCursor =      LoadCursor(NULL, IDC_ARROW);
```

Creating and Displaying Windows

When you create a window class in a Windows NT application, you call the Win32 API functions CreateWindow and ShowWindow to create a window of the class you have specified and to display the window on the screen. Then you call UpdateWindow whenever your window needs to be redrawn.

CreateWindow can create an overlapped window, a pop-up window, or a child window, depending on the parameters you pass to it. When you call CreateWindow, you specify the class, the title, the style, and (optionally) the initial position and size of the window you are creating. You also specify the new window's parent (if there is one) and the new window's menu.

SYNTAX OF THE CREATEWINDOW FUNCTION

This is the syntax of the CreateWindow function:

```
HWND CreateWindow(LPCTSTR lpszClassName, LPCTSTR lpszWindowName, DWORD dwStyle,
int x, int y, int nWidth, int nHeight, HWND hwndParent, MENU hmenu, HANDLE hinst,
LPVOID lpvParam)
```

Table 3.1 lists and describes the parameters expected by the CreateWindow function.

TABLE 3.1 PARAMETERS EXPECTED BY THE CREATEWINDOW FUNCTION.

Parameter	Description
lpszClassName	The address of the name of a registered window class—in this case, the szAppName class, which is the window class used by the HELLOWIN program. The szAppName class was registered earlier in the WinMain function by a call to the RegisterClass.
lpszWindowName	A pointer to a string that specifies the name of the window being created.

dwStyle	A constant or a set of constants (separated by "|" symbols) that can be used to specify various attributes of a window. You can obtain a list of all the constants that can be used in this parameter by looking up the WinMain entry under the Developer Studio's Help menu item.
x	The horizontal position of the window being created.
y	The vertical position of the window being created.
nWidth	The width of the window being created.
nHeight	The height of the window being created.
hwndParent	The handle of the parent window of the window being created (if there is a parent window).
hmenu	The meaning of this parameter depends on the style of the window being created. For overlapped or pop-up windows, hmenu identifies the menu to be used with the window. If the default menu for the window's class is to be used, this value can be NULL. For child windows, hmenu is an integer value that identifies the child window. For more details, see the CreateWindow entry in your on-line help files.
hinst	The handle of the current application instance.
lpvParam	A pointer to a value that is passed to the window through the CREATESTRUCT structure referenced by the lParam parameter of the WM_CREATE message. If an application is calling CreateWindow to create a multiple-document interface client window, lpvParam must point to a CLIENTCREATESTRUCT structure.

CALLING CREATEWINDOW, SHOWWINDOW, AND UPDATEWINDOW

In the WinMain function of HELLOWIN, the following block of code calls CreateWindow, ShowWindow, and UpdateWindow:

```
hwnd = CreateWindow(szAppName,  // window class name
    "Hello Program",        //window caption
    WS_OVERLAPPEDWINDOW,    // window style
    CW_USEDEFAULT,          // initial x position
    CW_USEDEFAULT,          // initial y position
    CW_USEDEFAULT,          // initial x size
    CW_USEDEFAULT,          // initial y size
    NULL,                   // parent window handle
    NULL,                   // window menu handle
    hInstance,              // program instance handle
    NULL);                  // creation parameters
ShowWindow(hwnd, nCmdShow);
```

ShowWindow displays the windows specified in its hwnd parameter using the style specified in nCmdShow. For a list of styles that can be passed to ShowWindow, refer to your compiler's on-line help files.

The UpdateWindow command draws the window specified in its hwnd parameter. It is used after the call to ShowWindow to draw the window used in the HELLOWIN program.

How Windows NT Manages Windows

There are two kinds of Windows NT processes: console processes and Windows processes. *Console processes*, described in Chapter 6 ("Processes"), use text-based windows that are created by Windows NT. *Windows processes* create their own windows. When a 16-bit Windows process is running under Windows NT, the Windows NT operating system displays screen windows that look and feel just like Win16 windows.

THE WIN32 WINDOWS HIERARCHY

When Windows NT boots up, the NT operating system creates a desktop window that is sized to cover the entire screen display area. All other windows are displayed on top of the desktop window. Consequently, the desktop window is at the top of the windows hierarchy, just as in Windows 3.x.

When a window creates another window, the new window is called a *child window*, and the window that does the creating is called a *parent window*. As Windows programmers know, windows that descend from child windows are *descendant windows* of both that child window and the child's parent window. In Windows NT, as in earlier, 16-bit versions of Windows, every window that can be placed on the desktop can be traced back to the desktop window through child window lists. The order in which windows are displayed when they become active is determined by a display order called the *Z order*. When a window is created or becomes active, the window manager places it at the top of the Z order. The newly created or newly activated window appears on top of all other windows on the screen display.

Windows NT adds one new level to the window hierarchy used in Windows 3.x. Every computer that runs Windows NT has a WindowStation object, which provides the first level of security for a Windows NT workstation.

When Windows NT is initialized, the WindowStation object displays a desktop window that did not exist in Windows 3.x. This desktop window displays a modal dialog box that prompts the user to type **Ctrl+Alt+Delete** and then log on. The desktop window created by the `WindowStation` object stays on the screen until the user is properly logged on. Only then does the `WindowStation` object relinquish control of the desktop and allow the main Win32 desktop window to be displayed.

Windows NT also defines two new window types that are not part of the standard window hierarchy: *foreground windows* and *background windows*. The foreground window is the window in which the user is currently working. All other windows are background windows. Normally, it is not necessary for an application to find out whether a given window is a foreground window or a background window or to change this information; under most circumstances, the user should make that decision. However, in case an application needs to obtain or provide this information, it can call the Win32 function `SetForegroundWindow` or `GetForegroundWindow`.

WINDOW STYLES

In addition to the main frame window, applications can create windows that have many different styles. In Windows NT, as in Windows 95 and Windows 3.x, you can create pop-up windows, windows with and without captions, windows with and without scrollbars, and so on.

An application determines a window's style by passing a style parameter to the `CreateWindow` or `CreateWindowEx` function that creates the window. You'll learn more about how these functions work later in this chapter.

Multithreading

As mentioned in Chapter 2, "Underneath Windows NT," preemptive multitasking is an important new feature of Windows NT. Windows 95 also supports preemptive multitasking.

In preemptive multitasking, an operating system carves up a CPU's processing time into individual slices and then allocates each slice to a particular task. In a preemptive multitasking environment, an operating system can assign a priority to each task and then schedule processing time so that each thread (see Chapter 7, "Windows NT Thread Management") receives its fair share of CPU time without infringing on the time allocated to other processes. Thus, the operating system makes sure that multiple processes are executed simultaneously as efficiently as possible. Multithreading is the technique that Windows NT uses to implement preemptive multitasking.

PROCESSES AND THREADS

To understand how multithreading works in Windows NT, it helps to have a general understanding of how processes and threads work in 32-bit Windows programs. In a 32-bit Windows environment such as Windows NT or Windows 95, a process is an executable object-code module that can run independently as a program. In other words, a process is a program or task that has been loaded into memory and is ready for execution. In pre-NT versions of Windows, a task was the smallest Windows code entity that could receive CPU time. In Windows NT, however, the smallest entity that can receive CPU time is a thread. A process can contain multiple threads and can also create other processes.

When a process is created under Windows NT, the operating system allocates the process its own 4-GB virtual address space. All threads that belong to a process share its address space. (Windows NT memory is described in more detail in Chapter 9, "File and Memory Management.") When a process starts up, it has a single thread called a primary thread. Later, other independently executing threads can be created. A thread can execute any part of a process's code, including a part currently being executed by another thread. Because all threads of a process share the process's virtual address space, they can access the process's global variables and system resources.

The threads that run in a multithreaded environment can belong to a single process or to multiple processes. A multithreaded process consists of the code, data, and other system resources that are accessible to the process's threads. In Windows NT, multiple threads often work better than do routines that rely on software timers, because a thread, unlike a procedure controlled by a timer, has its own private slice of CPU time. Also, once a thread is set up, it can operate transparently, independently, and without any further effort on the part of the process that created the thread.

HOW NON-PREEMPTIVE MULTITASKING WORKS

In an operating environment that uses *non-preemptive multitasking*—such as Windows 3.x—multithreading is not supported. This means that one process cannot make way for a high-priority task using the sophisticated task scheduling and CPU time-sharing that a preemptive multitasking system requires. Consequently, the Win16 API does not support preemptive multitasking. But applications that use the Win32 API support preemptive multitasking, as do the C++ encapsulations of the Win32 API, such as the MFC and OWL C++ libraries.

Because the Win16 API does not support preemptive multitasking, 16-bit programs that rely on the Win16 API must perform all their message-handling operations using a single user-input event queue. Under most circumstances, that one queue holds all input from the user until the executing application removes the events from the queue.

The GetMessage and PeekMessage Functions

The Win16 API implements non-preemptive multitasking by requiring applications to call `GetMessage` or `PeekMessage` to process a message, and by requiring applications to process input from the user along with messages that result from non-user events. When a 16-bit Windows program executes a `GetMessage` or `PeekMessage` function, Windows performs any needed task-switching. In a 16-bit Windows operating environment, only one application can execute at any given time. The active application is always the last one that has issued a `GetMessage` or `PeekMessage`. All other applications must wait until the function returns.

This kind of message handling—as you know if you've ever tried printing in the background under Windows 3.x—does not make for a very robust multitasking system. If one application has a long or complex task to perform, the whole system can grind to a halt. Such tasks include printing, reading database records, repaginating, saving or reading a file, and other kinds of operations.

Some 16-bit Windows applications address this problem by placing long processes in `PeekMessage` loops. An application calls `PeekMessage` repeatedly, scheduling other activities while the long process continues to run. That is a lot of trouble for an application to go through to process messages, and it is not the kind of job that an application should be required to do. Message handling should be the responsibility of the operating system and not of applications running on the system. And that's the way it is in Windows NT.

Input Processing in Windows NT

Windows NT solves the multitasking problem in a much better way—by using preemptive multitasking. When a process is created in Windows NT, the system also creates a high-priority thread called a *raw input thread*. As long as a process is alive, its raw input thread remains active to process the user's keyboard and mouse input.

When a process has started, it can create other threads. Every thread that is created can create still more threads. Even if an input queue is created, the thread that obtains it does not have to use it. But that is no problem, because an input queue does not create any overhead by merely being allocated. When a 32-bit program running under Windows NT detects a user event, the event is placed in the system queue, and the raw input thread immediately transfers the event to the thread input queue for which the input is intended.

Earlier sections of the chapter explain how functions provided in the Windows NT SDK handle events and messages. Chapter 4, "Programming Windows NT with Visual C++," explains and demonstrates how you can incorporate the message-handling features of Windows NT into your own applications.

CREATING THREADS AND PROCESSES

In Windows NT, a process can create another process by calling `CreateProcess`. A process terminates when all its threads terminate—typically, when its primary thread terminates. When `CreateProcess` is called, it runs an executable file. When all the threads in a process terminate, the process terminates.

The `CreateProcess` function takes 10 parameters, including the name of an executable file to launch, any command-line arguments that are to be passed to the executable, and a flag that specifies the security attributes of the process being created. Other parameters determine whether the new process can inherit handles to objects, whether the new process should notify its creating process, and what scheduling priority the new process should have.

Two of the parameters passed to `CreateProcess` are pointers to structures: a STARTUPINFO structure and a PROCESS_INFORMATION structure. If the process being created has a main window, the STARTUPINFO structure specifies properties of the window, such as its size, screen location, and style. Unlike the STARTUPINFO structure, the PROCESS_INFORMATION structure is empty when `CreateProcess` is called. `CreateProcess` fills the fields in PROCESS_INFORMATION with information about the new process and the process's primary thread. This information includes a handle to the new process, a handle to the process's primary thread, and ID numbers that can be used to identify the new process and its primary thread.

To create a thread, a process calls the Win32 function `CreateThread` (or, alternatively, `CreateRemoteThread`, which can create a thread that does not belong to the calling process). Parameters expected by `CreateThread` or `CreateRemoteThread` include a pointer to a function to execute, a stack size (because every thread has its own stack), and a SECURITY_ATTRIBUTES structure, which establishes security protection for the new thread. You can also specify whether you want the thread to start as soon as it is created or to start at a future time.

SYNCHRONIZING THREADS

An application can control the execution of threads by creating *synchronization objects* called mutexes, semaphores, and event objects. A *mutex* is an object that prevents a thread from running while another thread is executing. A *semaphore* limits the instances of a thread that can be executed at the same time. An *event object* prevents a thread from executing until a specified event takes place.

A process can terminate a thread by calling `ExitThread`. For a more detailed examination of threads and processes as well as a set of example programs that show how threads and processes work, see Chapter 7, "Multithreading."

Windows NT provides a service called a *scheduler* that schedules the operation of threads. The scheduler allocates CPU time to each thread in accordance with predetermined thread priorities. Thread priorities can be set by the Windows NT system or by the code in your own applications. To schedule thread operations, an application uses synchronization objects. The scheduler schedules all threads available to run. Blocking a thread—having it wait for synchronization—removes it from the scheduler's list.

Another new feature of the Win32 window manager is related to multithreading. In Windows NT, all windows that descend from a common parent share the same input queue. Under most circumstances, this means that windows behave the same way in Windows NT and in Windows 3.x. In Windows NT, however, it is possible for a process to spawn threads and for those threads to create windows that do not descend from a common parent and therefore do not share the same input queue. Under these circumstances, the Z order of windows displayed on the screen may not be the same as it would be in a nonthreaded environment. If this situation arises, there are at least three corrective measures you can take:

+ Modify the way your application handles threading.

+ Call `PeekMessage` or `GetMessage` to detect window-related messages, and then change your application's window-related procedures manually.

+ Change your expectations about what the Z order of windows should be when your application is running.

In addition to these thread-related changes, the Win32 API contains two new functions that support threading. To enumerate each window in a window hierarchy and to call an application-supplied callback function for each window in the hierarchy, you call the `EnumChildWindows` function. To obtain a handle to a specified thread's desktop window, you call `GetThreadDesktop`.

Windows NT Graphics

Since the advent of Windows NT and Windows 95, hardware and software manufacturers have developed many new graphics-related products for Windows users and developers. So far, these new products included the following:

+ OpenGL, a 3-D graphics package for Windows NT and Windows 95.

+ WinG, a new software package from Microsoft that makes it possible to develop high-speed action games for both Windows 3.1 and Windows NT.

✦ The Windows Game SDK, which combines ultra-fast software routines with direct access to video hardware, making it possible to design even faster games. The Windows Game SDK also provides direct access to game controllers, sound cards, hardware-based 3-D graphics engines, and the networking features built into Windows NT and Windows 95.

Despite all these new developments, most Windows NT graphics continue to rely on two operating system software mechanisms that have been around since the earliest days of Windows: *device contexts*, or DCs, and *graphical device interface* objects, or GDI objects. In Windows, a device context is something you draw *on*, and a GDI object is something you draw *with*. DC objects and GDI objects can seem complicated at first glance, but, once you learn how they work, they lose most of their mystery.

How DC Objects and GDI Objects Work

One easy way to distinguish DC objects from GDI objects is to view a device context as a drawing surface, such as a canvas or a piece of paper, and to view a GDI object as a drawing implement, such as a brush or a pen. Figure 3.7 is a fanciful illustration that shows how an artist might work if real-world drawing surfaces were called device contexts and drawing implements were referred to as GDI objects.

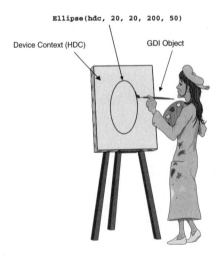

FIGURE 3.7 DEVICE CONTEXTS AND GDI OBJECTS.

Artists use different kinds of drawing implements to paint or draw images on different kinds of surfaces. For example, an artist creating a oil painting typically uses a brush;

on a different kind of drawing surface, such as a drawing tablet, the artist might use other kinds of drawing implements, such as pencils or charcoal.

Similarly, Windows makes different kinds of GDI objects available for different kinds of drawing operations—or for similar kinds of drawing or painting operations on different kinds of surfaces. In a Windows application, for example, you can draw a line in a window by declaring the window to be a device context and then requesting that the Windows API object provide you with a GDI pen object. Then you can use the pen object to draw as many lines as you like inside the device context that is your window. Alternatively, you can declare a printed page to be a device context and then ask Windows to provide you with a font that can be used as a GDI object. You can use the font object to print text on the device context that you have declared to be a printed page.

Sometimes an artist might use two different varieties of the same implement to draw or paint images on different kinds of surfaces. For example, an artist working in oils might apply paint to a canvas using a stiff-bristled brush, and a watercolor artist might use a softer brush to apply watercolors to a paper surface. In the same way, Windows allows Windows artists to use slightly different kinds of GDI objects to draw images to different kinds of output devices. For example, to fill an area of a window with a color or pattern, you can select the window as your device context and then request a brush-type GDI object from Windows. Windows responds by providing you with a brush that is suitable for drawing into a window. You can then call a Windows API drawing function—for example, the `Rectangle` function, which draws rectangles— and Windows responds by filling a rectangle with the color or pattern you have selected.

In contrast, if you need a brush-type GDI object to fill an area of a printed page with a color or pattern, you select a printer driver as your device context and then ask Windows for a brush. Because you have chosen a printer driver as your DC, Windows automatically responds by handing you a GDI brush that is designed for drawing colors or patterns on a printed page. Then, when you call `Rectangle`, Windows responds by executing code to fill a rectangle with color or a pattern on a printed page.

In other words, when an application has obtained both a DC object handle and a GDI object handle from Windows, the application can use the GDI object to draw whatever kind of image it needs to draw in the device context that it has selected. Later in this section, you'll learn exactly how applications do that.

ACCESSING DEVICE CONTEXTS AND GDI OBJECTS

Windows API programs access both DC objects and GDI objects using various kinds of handles. To perform a graphics operation in a Windows application, you must set up a device context using a type of handle defined as an HDC handle, and then you must create a GDI handle for a specific kind of graphics device.

A Windows application can access any kind of device context using an HDC handle. But the Windows API does not define a generic GDI handle; instead, it provides many different kinds of GDI objects. For example, there is an HBRUSH handle for brushes (which fill areas with color or patterns), an HPEN handle for pens (which can be used to draw lines), and an HBITMAP handle for bitmaps (which you learned about in Chapter 1, "Introducing Window NT").

In Chapter 4, when you start writing Windows applications using the Microsoft Foundation Class library, you'll learn how to access DC and GDI objects using C++ classes and member functions. But we're discussing Windows API programs at the moment, so we'll focus on accessing DC and GDI objects using handles.

GDI FUNCTIONS

Along with a large collection of GDI objects, the Windows API also provides many kinds of GDI functions that you can use to draw images using various kinds of GDI objects. Recall, for example, Rectangle, which you use to draw the outline of a rectangle in a window or on a printed page. Other GDI functions include Ellipse (for drawing ellipses), DrawText (for drawing text), BitBlt (for transferring and copying bitmaps), and many, many more. The DrawText function is described in more detail later in this chapter, and you'll learn more about BitBlt and other GDI functions in later chapters.

To use Rectangle, you first obtain a device context to draw into; then you obtain an HPEN handle—a handle to a pen-type GDI object. Then you can draw a rectangle into the device context by calling the Rectangle function:

```
Rectangle(hdc, 100, 100, 200, 200);
```

If you execute the preceding statement while you are using a window as a device context, the statement draws a rectangle whose four corners lie at the following screen coordinates :

- ✦ Upper-left corner: $x = 100$, $y = 100$
- ✦ Lower-right corner: $x = 200$, $y = 200$

Later in this chapter, you'll get a chance to experiment with three sample programs that show how DC handles and GDI handles are used in Windows programs.

WHY USE DCS AND GDI OBJECTS?

To developers of graphics programs, DC objects and GDI objects and functions are essential parts of Windows, because they simplify the job of interfacing Windows applications with the many different kinds of graphics devices that Windows supports. If Windows didn't provide applications with GDI objects and DC objects, every Windows program would have to supply an enormous number of routines and a massive amount of device-context data to support many varieties of video cards, printers, and other kinds of graphics devices. Fortunately, the Windows GDI and DC mechanisms supply all that code automatically, so, unless you happen to write software for a hardware company, you never have to worry about diving into the Windows device driver kit (DDK) and writing a device driver. If you're an ordinary games programmer, you need only learn how to use the GDI and DC tools that Windows provides for you. Then you can write one-size-fits-all programs that will automatically work correctly with any Windows-compatible graphics device.

Understanding Device Contexts

From an operating system point of view, a DC is a Windows object that accepts drawing commands from Windows applications and translates those commands into lower-level instructions that are then issued directly to a particular device driver. In other words, a device context is an object that interfaces your application with a particular kind of graphics output device such as a printer or a video card.

DCs simplify graphics operations because they permit applications to perform drawing routines without having to be concerned about which output device will display or print the images. Instead, an application can simply obtain a handle to a device context and then draw to that DC. The main benefit of using DCs is that every DC recognizes exactly the same set of drawing commands. For example, when a Windows application uses a DC to draw a rectangle, all the program has to do is to create a device context and then call `Rectangle`. If everything goes well, Windows then draws a rectangle to the graphics device currently in use. It doesn't matter whether the device is a video card, which creates images by displaying dots on a screen, or a laser printer, which draws shapes at such high resolutions that a rectangle appears to be made up of four smooth, straight lines. It also doesn't matter whether the device displays images in color or in black and white. The DC provided by the Windows API takes care of all that. All your application has to do is to make a `Rectangle` call.

From a more technical point of view, the device context that is associated with a particular drawing operation converts an application's drawing commands into lower-level device-driver commands and then dispatches them to a device driver. The device driver then sends the device context's commands to the appropriate output device, which does the job of displaying the desired object in a window or printing it on a page.

Understanding GDI Objects

Windows implements each GDI object as a collection of data and supporting routines that are designed to perform a specific set of drawing operations within a particular device context. For example, the Windows API function `Rectangle`—which, as you have seen, can be used to draw a rectangle in a window or on a printed page—is a GDI function that is used with pen-type GDI objects. To draw an ellipse, you use `Ellipse`, which is also used with pen-type GDI objects. To draw text, you set up a font-type GDI object by creating an HFONT handle and then call `DrawText`. And so on.

The Windows API provides many other kinds of GDI functions. There are GDI functions to draw brush lines, to draw bitmaps, to draw many kinds of shapes and fill them with colors or patterns, to draw text in various ways, and so on. This chapter's HELLOWIN program uses `DrawText` to print text on the screen.

DRAWING AN IMAGE STEP BY STEP

The specific steps that are used to draw an image can vary from application to application, depending on the requirements of the program. The drawing operation used in this chapter's sample programs is fairly typical. In HELLOWIN, these are the steps that are used to print the three lines of text in the program's title window:

1. The program calls the Windows API function `BeginPaint`. When you want to draw into a window in a Windows API program, you must always call `BeginPaint` before you start drawing, and you must call `EndPaint` when you're finished. `BeginPaint` prepares a specified window for painting and fills a PAINTSTRUCT data structure with information about the painting. `EndPaint` performs essential cleanup operations.

   `BeginPaint` takes two parameters: the handle of the window where the painting is to take place, and the address of a PAINTSTRUCT. HELLOWIN doesn't use the information stored in the PAINTSTRUCT that is passed to `BeginPaint`; for details about PAINTSTRUCT, see the on-line help.

2. The program obtains a handle to a device context. There are a number of Windows functions you can call to obtain a DC handle. HELLOWIN obtains a DC handle when it issues the `BeginPaint` call:

   ```
   hdc = BeginPaint(hwnd, &ps);
   ```

3. Call the Windows API function GetClientRect to obtain a handle to the client area of the window. The client area is the area inside all the window's decorations and controls—that is, the area where drawing takes place. This is the GetClientRect call from HELLOWIN:

```
GetClientRect(hwnd, &rect);
```

4. When the measurements of the active window's client rectangle have been obtained, the program obtains a handle to a specific kind of GDI object, such as a pen or a brush. The GDI object used by HELLOWIN is a pen, which is created in this statement:

```
hpen = CreatePen(PS_SOLID, 6, RGB(0, 0, 255));
```

CreatePen takes three parameters: a pen-style parameter, a width parameter, and a color parameter. In HELLOWIN, the parameters passed to CreatePen are PS_SOLID, which creates a solid pen; the integer 6, which creates a pen that is six pixels wide; and the macro RGB(0, 0, 255), which creates a blue pen. The RGB macro takes three parameters: the intensity of the color red, the intensity of the color green, and the intensity of the color blue. Intensities range from 0 to 255 and can be mixed and matched. HELLOWIN passes the parameters 0, 0, 255 to the RGB macro, so the result is a pure blue rectangle.

5. Before drawing can take place in a Windows program, the application calls a function that associates a particular DC with the specific GDI object that is about to be used. This step is often referred to as *selecting* a GDI object *into* a device context. In HELLOWIN, the following statement selects a pen object into the variable hdc (the handle of the DC object obtained in Step 1):

```
hpenOld = SelectObject(hdc, hpen);
```

SelectObject returns a handle to a GDI object. This handle can then be stowed away for safekeeping during the drawing operation. The handle returned by SelectObject is kept because it may already be in use by a previously selected GDI object. In that case, the handle can be restored with another call to SelectObject as soon as it is no longer needed by the drawing operation. The handle is then once again freed for use by the object that originally owned it. In Step 7, you'll see how SelectObject can be used to restore a handle to its original owner.

6. The program performs its drawing operation. In HELLOWIN, Rectangle is called to draw a blue border around the application's window:

```
Rectangle(hdc, rect.left + 10, rect.top + 10, rect.right - 10,
rect.bottom - 10);
```

7. HELLOWIN makes a call to `DrawText` to print "Hello, world" inside the window. `DrawText` does not require the specific use of a GDI object, but it does take five other parameters: the handle of the window into which text is to be printed; the address of the string to be printed; the length of the string (or the number –1, which allows the string to be computed automatically); a pointer to the window's client rectangle; and a set of text-drawing flags.

```
DrawText(hdc, "Hello, world", -1, &rect, DT_SINGLELINE |
    DT_CENTER | DT_VCENTER);
```

8. When drawing is complete, the program restores the DC handle used by `Rectangle` to its original owner by making another call to `SelectObject`:

```
SelectObject(hdc, hpenOld);
```

9. The program frees the DC object that was obtained by calling `BeginPaint` in Step 2:

```
DeleteObject(hpen);
```

10. The program calls `EndPaint` to terminate its painting operation:

```
EndPaint(hwnd, &ps);
```

The preceding steps—with program-specific variations—are used in all drawing operations in Windows API programs. In Visual C++ programs that use the MFC library, the steps are similar. In Chapter 4, "Programming Windows NT with Visual C++," you'll learn how to perform drawing operations in MFC applications.

Example 1: The HELLOWIN Program

This chapter's example program, a Windows API program named HELLOWIN, demonstrates how DC and GDI objects work in a simple Windows NT application. The program also shows how `WinMain` and `WndProc` work. When you execute HELLOWIN, it opens a window that contains the familiar "Hello, world" greeting neatly centered inside a colored border in the window's client area (see Figure 3.8).

FIGURE 3.8 OUTPUT OF THE HELLOWIN PROGRAM.

BUILDING THE HELLOWIN PROGRAM STEP BY STEP

To build the HELLOWIN program shown in Listing 3.2 using Developer Studio, follow these steps. (If you don't quite understand how they work, don't worry; they are explained in more detail in Chapter 4, "Programming Windows NT with Visual C++.")

1. Choose Developer Studio's **File|New** menu item. Developer Studio opens a dialog box named New (Figure 3.9).

2. Select **Project Workspace** in the New list box and click **OK**. Developer studio then opens another dialog box labeled New Project Workspace.

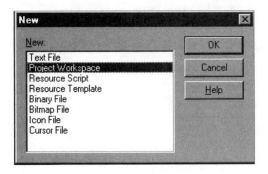

FIGURE 3.9 THE NEW DIALOG BOX.

3. Browse to a directory in which you can create a new project.

4. Select the **Application** icon in the Type list box.

5. Type a name for your project in the **Name** edit box.

6. Close the New Project Workspace dialog box by clicking the **Create** button.

7. AppWizard displays a series of dialog boxes where you can select various attributes for the new project. For the sake of simplicity in this introductory exercise, accept the default attributes in each dialog box, and move to the next dialog box by clicking **Next.** When the final dialog box (the one titled "Step 6 of 6") appears, close it by clicking **Finish.**

8. AppWizard displays a dialog box named New Project Information. Read the information in it and then create your new project by clicking **OK.**

9. When AppWizard has finished creating your project, you'll need to provide Developer Studio with the source code that implements your application. Start the process of opening a new text-file window by choosing **File|New.**

10. When the New dialog box opens, select **Text File** from the New list box and close the New dialog box by clicking **OK.**

11. Developer Studio now opens a new text window containing a flashing cursor. Type in the source code presented in Listing 3.2. If you don't want to do all that typing, you can use the Developer Studio editor's cut-and-paste capabilities. Copy the listing from this chapter's folder on the accompanying disk and paste it into your text window. (Developer Studio uses standard cut-and-paste features like those used by Microsoft Word and other editors that conform to Microsoft's user-interface guidelines; if you aren't familiar with the way they work, you can read about them by using the Visual C++ on-line help feature, which is described in Chapter 4.)

12. When you have finished typing or copying the source file, use **File|Save As** to save it using the file name **HELLOWIN.CPP.** Make sure that you save the file in the project directory that you created in Step 2.

13. Add **HELLOWIN.CPP** to the project by choosing the **Files into Project** item from the Insert menu.

14. Build your project by choosing **Build** from the Build menu.

15. Execute your project from Developer Studio by choosing the **Build|Execute** menu item.

DRAWING TEXT IN A WINDOW

When you execute HELLOWIN, the following case clause is executed to redraw the application's main window whenever a WM_PAINT message is received:

```
HDC          hdc;
HPEN         hpen, hpenOld;
PAINTSTRUCT ps;
RECT         rect;

switch(message) {
    case WM_PAINT :
            hdc = BeginPaint(hwnd, &ps);
            GetClientRect(hwnd, &rect);
            hpen = CreatePen(PS_SOLID, 6, RGB(0, 0, 255));
            hpenOld = SelectObject(hdc, hpen);
            Rectangle(hdc, rect.left + 10,
                           rect.top + 10,
                           rect.right - 10,
                           rect.bottom - 10);

            DrawText(hdc, "Hello, world", -1, &rect,
                           DT_SINGLELINE | DT_CENTER | DT_VCENTER);

            SelectObject(hdc, hpenOld);
            DeleteObject(hpen);
            EndPaint(hwnd, &ps);
            return 0;
/* . . . */
```

Summary

This chapter explains how the Win32 API implements the new features built into Windows NT. In Chapter 4, "Programming Windows NT with Visual C++," you'll see how Visual C++ makes it easier for you to use the functions provided by the Win32 API in your own Windows NT programs.

CHAPTER FOUR

PROGRAMMING WINDOWS NT WITH VISUAL C++

In Chapter 3, "The Win32 API," you learned how to write Windows NT programs the hard way—by making direct calls to functions implemented in the Windows API. In this chapter, you'll find the going a little easier. It focuses on writing Windows NT programs using Microsoft Visual C++, the most popular software development package for Windows programmers.

Visual C++ and the Microsoft Foundation Class (MFC) library make it easier for you to use the functions implemented in the Win32 Windows API, and in this chapter you'll see why. Topics covered in this chapter include:

- ✦ Developer Studio, the Visual C++ programming environment. Developer Studio provides you with a compiler, a linker, a C++ editor, a resource editor, a source-code browser, and the Visual C++ wizards—a set of graphics-based interactive tools designed to help you create and build Windows programs.

- ✦ MFC, a mammoth C++ class library that Microsoft supplies with Visual C++. Closely integrated with Visual C++, MFC is so inextricably tied to the Windows API (described in Chapter 3) that Microsoft executives have now started referring to MFC as the "new Windows API." This chapter gives you a close-up look at classes and member functions that make up the MFC library and shows you how you can use them in your Windows NT programs.

✦   A large collection of Visual C++ programming techniques—many of them difficult to track down in other texts—that you're sure to find helpful when you start writing Windows NT programs.

This Chapter's Example Programs

To illustrate the topics covered in this chapter, four example programs are provided on the accompanying disk:

✦   SDIAPP is a single-document interface (SDI) application generated by AppWizard. For more information on AppWizard, see "Creating a Project with AppWizard" later in this chapter.

✦   MDIAPP is a multiple document interface (MDI) application generated by AppWizard. In addition to showing how AppWizard generates an MDI framework, the MDIAPP program demonstrates a technique for changing the size of a main frame window in a Visual C++ application. This technique is explained in "Customizing Windows" later in this chapter.

✦   JUSTENUF is an SDI application without the default document-view interface that AppWizard creates. The document-view architecture of Visual C++ programs is described in "Documents and Views."

✦   SLIMMDI is an MDI application designed without documents or views.

New Features of Visual C++

Microsoft Visual C++ is a graphically oriented software development system for creating and building Windows programs. Visual C++ was initially released as a 16-bit development package designed to be used with Windows 3.0. Later, a 32-bit version was released for use with Windows NT. When this book was written, the current version of Visual C++ was version 4.1, a release designed to be used with Windows NT and Windows 95.

DEVELOPER STUDIO

The Visual C++ 4.0 development system is built around a set of programming tools called Developer Studio. By selecting items from the Developer Studio menu, you can run the Visual C++ compiler, the Visual C++ linker, and the other tools. Figure 4.1 shows the Developer Studio editor's main screen display.

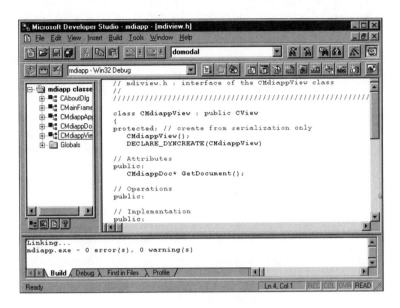

FIGURE 4.1 DEVELOPER STUDIO.

The Developer Studio tools are more tightly integrated into Visual C++ than those provided with earlier versions. For example, both the App Studio resource-management tool and the Control Developer's Kit (CDK) are no longer add-on tools. Their functionalities are now built right into Developer Studio.

As you will see in Chapter 5, "OLE Today," Visual C++ and MFC now provide full support for OLE controls without any add-ons, and a set of resource editors in the Developer Studio package has replaced the App Studio application that came with earlier versions of Visual C++.

COMPONENT GALLERY

One of the most important new features of Visual C++ is Component Gallery, a new tool that lets you use predesigned custom components in Visual C++ projects. The introduction of Component Gallery marks an important milestone in the evolution of Windows programming, because Component Gallery brings Windows developers one step closer to the elusive goal of object-oriented programming: real code reusability.

With Component Gallery, you can create reusable software components that can be stored in a central repository and then imported into different applications as needed. When you have an object that you want to tuck away for future use, the Component

Gallery utility stores your object in the form of a component: a special kind of dynamic link library (DLL) that is portable across different operating systems and even across applications and processes written in different computer languages. Once you have exported a component into Component Gallery, you can use the component whenever you like, in whatever application you like, and for any purpose you choose.

Many different kinds of components can be stored, including dialog boxes, dialog-box controls, C++ classes created with ClassWizard, and custom-designed software objects such as OLE controls. (OLE controls, the 32-bit successors to VBX controls, are introduced in Chapter 5, "OLE Today.")

There are three main reasons you might want to use Component Gallery during the development of a project:

✦ To add OLE controls or other components to a project.

✦ To remove OLE controls or other components from Component Gallery. In this case, you need not open a project.

✦ To make OLE controls or other components available to other developers.

As you increase the number of components stored in your computer's Component Gallery, the amount of reusable C++ code at your disposal inevitably starts to grow. Eventually, you may find that you have many different kinds of components at your disposal, all instantly available to you and to any other developers you choose at the click of a button or a menu item.

In Chapter 5, you'll see exactly how Component Gallery works. You'll get an opportunity to create an OLE control and store it in Component Gallery. Then you'll import an OLE component from Component Gallery and incorporate it into a Windows NT program.

OTHER NEW FEATURES OF VISUAL C++

Visual C++ got a major overhaul with the release of version 4.0, and it has many impressive new features. These are some of the most important ones:

✦ **New resource editors.** The old Visual C++ resource-generator program, App Studio, has been replaced by a set of graphics editors that you can open by tabbing to Developer Studio's Build page and double-clicking your application's resource (**.RC**) icon. The dialog-box resource editor introduced with Visual C++ 4.0 is described in more detail later in this chapter, as are other resource editors that were used to create the example programs in this chapter and later chapters.

✦ **Support for OLE controls and OLE control containers.** This long-awaited new feature lets you turn almost any object in an application into an OLE control container. In pre-4.0 versions of Visual C++, you could create OLE controls, but there was no way to use them in your applications because you couldn't create OLE containers. Now you can create both controls and containers easily, so you can finally use OLE controls in your applications. OLE controls are covered in much more detail in Chapter 5, "OLE Today."

✦ **MFC extensions** let you add your own extensions to the MFC library. The MFC extensions that support OLE controls include the `COleControl` class and a host of new tools for developing OLE controls.

✦ **Custom AppWizards,** another powerful feature introduced with MFC 4.0, let you design customized AppWizards that work just like the Microsoft AppWizard that comes with Visual C++.

Other new features of Visual C++ 4.0 include support for all the new user-interface devices on the Windows NT and Windows 95 desktop and support for all the new Windows NT and Windows 95 common controls and common dialog boxes.

Familiar Features of Visual C++

Although many new capabilities have been added to Visual C++, many features haven't changed. Here are some familiar features of the Visual C++ development package:

✦ **AppWizard:** An application generator that can generate a fully functioning Visual C++ application at the click of a menu command. When you choose the **AppWizard** command from Developer Studio's Project menu, AppWizard automatically generates a fully commented set of source files for a bare-bones Windows application. You can then add source code to expand AppWizard's source files into the application you want to create.

✦ **ClassWizard:** A utility that can create Visual C++ classes and can automatically incorporate them into the source code of the program being edited. ClassWizard can create classes for dialog boxes, documents and views (described later in this chapter), and other kinds of objects that are often used in Visual C++ programs. When you create a class with ClassWizard, ClassWizard automatically generates a source file that implements the class and a header file that defines the class. These files are then added automatically to the program being developed.

✦ **The Visual C++ debugger**: A built-in debugger that can be launched from the Developer Studio menu bar. With this debugger, you can insert and manipulate breakpoints, step through a program, skip into and out of functions, and perform all the other standard features of a source-file debugger without leaving Developer Studio.

✦ **The Visual C++ source browser**: A built-in C++ browser, also selectable from the Developer Studio menu bar. This tool displays the classes and objects in your application in a hierarchy tree that you can edit interactively.

✦ **Visual C++ on-line help**: Developer Studio has an on-line help utility that gives you menu access to a set of C/C++, Windows API, and Visual C++ manuals.

Developer Studio, like many other development environments, groups all the files that are needed to compile an application into a *project*: a collection of all the user-supplied source files, library files, and resource files that are needed to build a working Windows program. Projects simplify program development by giving you an easy way to keep track of the files and libraries you need. Projects also streamline the build process; they speed software development by recompiling only those files that have changed since the program's last compilation or build. There are two ways to create a project with Developer Studio: with AppWizard or without it.

CREATING A PROJECT WITH APPWIZARD

When you develop a Visual C++ program, AppWizard can write most routine Windows code for you, leaving you free to concentrate on the functionality of your application. To create a new project using Developer Studio, choose **File|New**. Developer Studio then displays a dialog box labeled New (Figure 4.2).

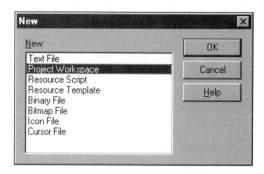

FIGURE 4.2 THE NEW DIALOG BOX.

Selecting a Path for a Project

To start a new project, select **Project Workspace** from the New list box. Developer Studio opens a dialog box titled New Project Workspace (Figure 4.3).

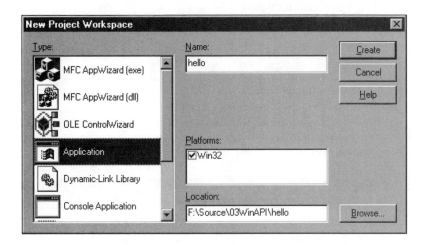

FIGURE 4.3 THE NEW PROJECT WORKSPACE DIALOG BOX.

In the New Project Workspace dialog box, you can select a folder for the project by browsing to the folder of your choice. Click the **Browse** button, type a name for your new project in the Name text box, and select the kind of project you want to create.

Specifying an Application Type

By selecting an item from the Type list box, you can create an AppWizard application, a dynamic link library (see Chapter 8), a console application (see Chapter 6), or even a special kind of wizard dialog box that can then be used to generate OLE controls. (OLE controls are covered in Chapter 5, "OLE Today.")

When you have specified the kind of application, library, or wizard you want to develop, you can create your new project by clicking **Create**. If the **AppWizard** item is selected when you click **Create**, Developer Studio opens a series of AppWizard dialog boxes (Figure 4.4) that you can use to specify a set of attributes for your application. For example, the first AppWizard dialog box lets you choose a language for your application and specify whether you want to develop an SDI or an MDI application.

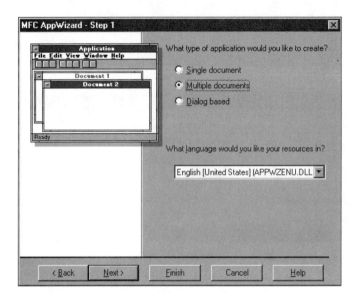

FIGURE 4.4 THE FIRST APPWIZARD DIALOG BOX.

If you choose to develop an application without using AppWizard, Developer Studio creates an empty project that you can then populate with your own source files.

MDI and SDI Applications

A Windows application that has just one window (the main window) is an SDI application. An application that has multiple windows is an MDI application. When you use AppWizard to generate an application, you can specify whether you want to build an SDI application or an MDI application (for details, see "What AppWizard Creates" later in this section). In versions of Visual C++ before version 4.0, most commercial-quality programs were MDI applications. With the double-barreled release of Visual C++ 4.0 and MFC 4.0, Microsoft began suggesting that application developers move back to the SDI format when possible. The reason: The application taskbar displayed on the Windows 95 and Windows NT desktop now makes it easy for users to switch from one document window to another, so the complexity that the MDI format adds to a Windows application is no longer necessary. To replace the MDI format, Microsoft suggests several alternatives. For details, see my Windows 95 book for Windows 3.1 programmers, *Migrating to Windows 95*, which is listed in the Bibliography.

Specifying Names for Files and Classes

The last dialog box that AppWizard displays lets you specify names for the classes and files in your project. When you make those choices and click **Finish**, AppWizard generates your new project.

Although AppWizard offers you a list of default names for the files and classes in your project, the names it generates for the classes and files used by documents and views are sometimes not very intuitive. For example, if you compile a project named JUSTENUF, AppWizard names your view files **JUSTENVW.CPP** and **JUSTENVW.H**—a pair of names that can be improved upon.

To preview the names proposed by AppWizard and to modify those names if you don't like them, just edit the suggested class names that appear in AppWizard's edit controls. For example, you can shorten AppWizard's proposed names from **JUSTENUFVIEW.CPP** and **JUSTENUFVIEW.H** to **JUSTVIEW.CPP** and **JUSTVIEW.H**, as shown in Figure 4.5.

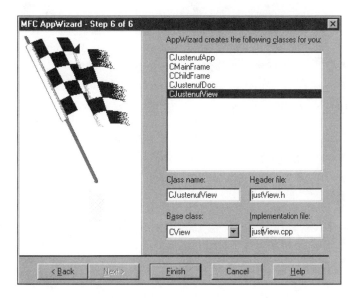

FIGURE 4.5 CHOOSING NAMES FOR FILES AND CLASSES.

How AppWizard Works

In a Visual C++ program, every application is implemented as an *application object* derived from the MFC class `CWinApp`. When AppWizard creates an application, it creates an application object for the program. When AppWizard generates the source code for a C++ program, it instantiates the program's application object in a source file that contains the following:

+ An empty constructor for the program's application class.

+ A member function named `InitInstance`, which initializes the program's application object. `InitInstance` is a member function of the MFC class `CWinApp`. Every Visual C++ application is built around an object of the `CWinApp` class.

+ The `CWinApp` application object around which the program is built.

+ A *message map* that binds (connects) system and user messages to the program's application object. (See "How Messages Are Processed in Visual C++" later in this chapter.)

AppWizard places these four elements in a .**CPP** file with the same name as the project being created. (For more information about how they work together, see "Visual C++ Programming" later in this chapter.) The file that contains these elements is the application's main source file. It always includes a header (.**H**) file, also created by AppWizard, that has the same name as the project being created. For example, if AppWizard creates a project named APROJECT, the .**CPP** file that instantiates the project's application object is named **APROJECT.CPP**, and the program's header file is named **APROJECT.H**.

AppWizard also generates a number of other files, some of which have names that are based on the name of the project. For example, when AppWizard creates a project, it always creates a file with a name written in the form **xxxxDOC.CPP** and another file written in the form **xxxxVIEW.CPP** or **xxxxxVW.CPP**, depending on the length of the project's name. The DOC file implements a *document object*, and the VIEW or VW file creates a *view object*; for details about document and view objects, see "Documents and Views" later in this chapter.

What AppWizard Creates

An application generated by AppWizard is a program skeleton with a working menu, a main window (with menu items for creating and managing child windows, if your program is an MDI application), a toolbar, a set of document and view classes, and all the C++ code that's needed to combine these components into a rudimentary but fully functioning program. An AppWizard application has a menu bar equipped with a standard set of file commands. It also has an About box and a main frame window. If it is an MDI application, it can create child windows that open when the user selects **New** or **Open** from the File menu. At first glance, that's about all an AppWizard application can do when it is first created. However, in the source files that AppWizard creates, there's a wealth of code that can easily be expanded to do much more.

When AppWizard generates a bare-bones application—sometimes referred to as an *application framework*—application framework, the framework contains many member functions that are also frameworks. By adding whatever custom source code your program requires, you can expand the bare-bones member functions generated by AppWizard into robust functions that load and save files, link data with document windows, and much more. Using Developer Studio's resource editors (described later in this chapter), you can create all the user-interface objects that your application requires: menus, dialog boxes, bitmaps, icons, tables of often-used strings, and accelerator keys.

Files in an AppWizard Project

A project generated by AppWizard contains a number of source files, including an application file, a document file, and a view file. Table 4.1 lists and describes the source files that AppWizard created when it generated MDIAPP. Notice that the names of the document files (**xxxxxDOC**) and view files (**xxxxVIEW**) in the following paragraphs are not default names generated by AppWizard; they have been modified using the technique described in "Specifying Names for Files and Classes" earlier in this chapter.

TABLE 4.1 FILES IN AN APPWIZARD PROJECT.

File Name	Description
MDIAPP.MAK	When AppWizard creates an application framework, it automatically generates a makefile that ends with the extension .**MAK**. A makefile is a special kind of text file that creates programs by running the Visual C++ compiler and linker. A makefile is also generated when you create a new Visual C++ application without AppWizard's help. Makefiles generated by AppWizard are compatible with the Visual C++ compiler. They are also compatible with the Microsoft NMAKE utility, which compiles and links Windows programs from a command line.
MDIAPP.CPP	When AppWizard generates a set of source files for an application, the application's main source file receives the same name as the project along with a .CPP extension. The **PROJECTNAME.CPP** file instantiates the program's application object and contains the program's `InitInstance` member function.
MDIAPP.H	This is the MDIAPP program's main header file. It includes **RESOURCE.H,** the header file for the application's resources. It also declares the program's application class.

continued

TABLE 4.1 CONTINUED

MDIAPP.RC	This is a text file that App Studio uses to create the application's resources. It contains definitions of the icons, bitmaps, and cursors that are stored in a special subdirectory named RES. When you edit resources with App Studio, it modifies this file.
MDIAPP.ICO	This icon file, stored in the application's RES subdirectory, is used to create the application's icon. The icon is defined in the resource file **MDIAPP.RC**.
MDIAPP.RC2	This resource file, also stored in the RES subdirectory, contains resources that are not created by App Studio. Initially, this file contains a VERSIONINFO resource that you can customize for your application. You can also place in this file other resources that are not created with the Developer Studio's resource editors.
MDIAPP.DEF	This module definition file contains information that must be provided by applications designed to run under Windows. It defines important parameters of the application, such as the name and description of the application and the size of the initial local heap. The default entries in this file are typical for applications that use MFC. You can edit this file to modify your application's default stack size.
MDIAPP.CLW	This file contains information used by ClassWizard to edit existing classes or add new classes. ClassWizard also uses this file to store information needed to generate and edit message maps and dialog data maps and to generate prototype member functions. (For more about message maps, see the "Message Maps" section later in this chapter.)
MAINFRM.CPP	This source file implements the CMainFrame class, which provides a framework-based application with its main frame window. CMainFrame is not an MFC class but is created by AppWizard when your application's framework is generated. The CMainFrame class, derived from the MFC class CMDIFrameWnd, controls all features of your application's main frame window.
MAINFRM.H	This header file contains the definition of the CMainFrame class.
TOOLBAR.BMP	This bitmap file is used to create tiled images for the toolbar. The initial toolbar and status bar are constructed in the CMainFrame class. To add more toolbar buttons, you can edit this bitmap.
MDIDOC.CPP	This source file implements the application's document class by instantiating an object derived from the CDocument class. (A CDocument object is one in which an application's data can be stored. For more about document objects, see "Documents and Views" later in this chapter.) You can edit your application's document implementation file to add customized data and to implment file serialization (the automatic saving and loading of files).

MDIDOC.H	This is the header file for the **MDIDOC.CPP** source file. It defines the application's document class.
MDIVIEW.CPP	This source file contains the application's view object, an object derived from the `CView` class. A `CView` object is one that can be used to view data stored in an object of the `CDocument` class. The `CView` class is derived from the `CWnd` class, which provides all document windows used in Windows programs. For more about view objects, see "Documents and Views" later in this chapter.
MDIVIEW.H	This header file defines the application's view class.
MDIDOC.ICO	This icon file is stored in the application's RES subdirectory. It creates the icon used by MDI child windows. The icon is defined in the resource file **MDIAPP.RC.** You can edit it using App Studio.
STDAFX.CPP	AppWizard uses this file to build a precompiled header (.PCH) file named **STDAFX.PCH,** and a precompiled types (.PCT) file named **STDAFX.PCT.** These files are needed to compile a file using precompiled headers, which can significantly speed compilation.
STDAFX.H	This is the header file for the **STDAFX.CPP** source file described above.
RESOURCE.H	This header file defines the application's resources. App Studio refers to this file when it creates or modifies resources and updates the file if necessary.

CREATING A PROGRAM WITHOUT APPWIZARD

You don't have to use AppWizard to create a Visual C++ program. Under some circumstances, you might find it more convenient to ignore AppWizard and create the program's source files from scratch. For example, you don't need AppWizard to create a console application (see Chapter 6, "Processes") or to import an application from another development environment.

The easiest way to create a project without using AppWizard is to open a Visual C++ project that has already been built, modify it to suit your needs, and then recompile it as a new project. Another technique is to choose **Application** or **Console Application** from the Type list box in the New Project Workspace dialog box described earlier in this chapter.

Two of the example programs in this chapter were compiled without the assistance of AppWizard. The SDI application **JUSTENUF** and the MDI application **SLIMMDI** have one feature in common: Both were created without the document-view architecture that AppWizard automatically incorporates into every application it generates. For more information on the document-view architecture and for an explanation of why it is used in some programs and not in others, see "Documents and Views" later in this chapter. Because **JUSTENUF** and **SLIMMDI** lack the document-view structure, it was easier to develop them from scratch than to let AppWizard create them and then remove the unneeded elements.

SETTING COMPILER AND LINKER OPTIONS

When you have created a project, you can set all the compiler and linker options by choosing the **Build|Settings** command from the Developer Studio menu. Developer Studio then opens a Project Settings property sheet (Microsoft's term for a multitabbed dialog box) like the one shown in Figure 4.6. This property sheet, and the property pages (nested dialog boxes) that it contains, automatically implements most of the options that used to be executed from command lines in the days of text-based compilers.

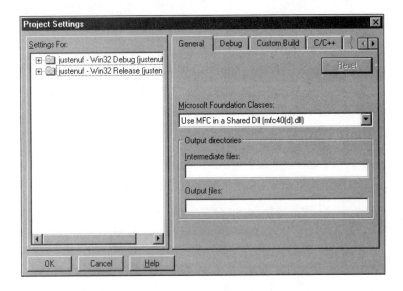

FIGURE 4.6 THE PROJECT SETTINGS PROPERTY SHEET.

When the Project Settings property sheet opens, you can set compiler and linker options for a Visual C++ project by following the steps listed in the paragraphs that follow.

To set compiler options for your project, follow these steps:

1. Click the **C/C++** tab in the Project Options dialog box. The C/C++ property page then opens (Figure 4.7) .

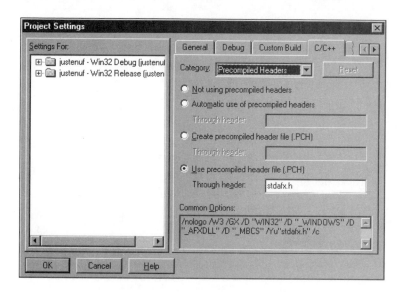

FIGURE 4.7 THE C/C++ PROPERTY PAGE.

2. Open the list box labeled **Category**. Notice that each time you select a different item from the Category list box, the C/C++ property page displays a different set of options. For example, if you choose the **Precompiled Headers** item, Developer Studio displays the C/C++ property page shown in Figure 4.7. It's beyond the scope of this chapter to describe the many compiler options that you can set using the C/C++ property page. But now that you know how the property pages work, you can get all the additional help you need by clicking the **Help** button while the property page is open.

To set linker options for your project, click the **Link** tab while the Project Settings property sheet is open. When the Link property page (Figure 4.8) opens, follow these steps to familiarize yourself with the operation of the Project Options dialog box:

1. Select a few different items from the list box labeled **Category** and note the changes in the contents of the Link property page. To link simple Visual C++ applications, the Link settings that Developer Studio assigns by default usually work fine. Later, when you start linking Visual C++ applications, you may be modifying some of these options.

2. To close the Project Settings property sheet without taking any action, click **Cancel**.

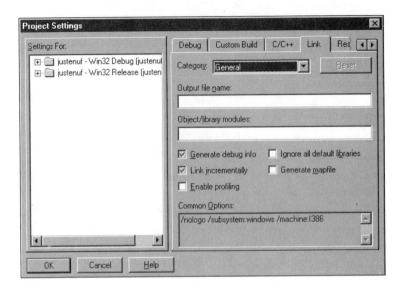

FIGURE 4.8 THE LINK PROPERTY PAGE.

BUILDING A VISUAL C++ APPLICATION

When you have created a Visual C++ application—with or without AppWizard—you can build your program (compile and link it) without leaving Developer Studio. Alternatively, you can compile your program, or an individual source file, without doing any linking. To build a program, choose **Build** or **Rebuild All** from Developer Studio's Build menu. To compile a program without linking it, choose the **Compile** command from the Build menu. The **Build** command builds a program by recompiling only those files that have changed since the last build. To build a program by compiling all relevant files, select **Rebuild All**.

The Visual C++ compiler is integrated with Developer Studio, so you can run the compiler without leaving the Developer Studio editor. In fact, the compiler runs invisibly in the background, so you can switch to other applications—even leave the Developer Studio environment—while the compiler hums along, merrily compiling your application in the background. When compilation is finished, Developer Studio sounds a beep, and you can return to the editor to see whether your program has compiled successfully.

While the compiler is working, it displays a running summary of its progress in an output window. Error and warning messages are displayed while problems and potential trouble spots are detected. If your compiler encounters an internal bug, it stops with an error message.

The Visual C++ compiler can compile both C and C++ programs. It determines a file's language by checking the file name extensions of your source files. It compiles .C source files as C-language files and compiles .CPP files into C++ object files.

CLASSWIZARD

ClassWizard is the interface between Developer Studio and the MFC library. More specifically, ClassWizard is a class browser that can create C++ classes and member variables, and automatically incorporate them into your Visual C++ projects. With ClassWizard, you can link your program's message handlers with documents, windows, menus, dialog boxes, and other entities that are implemented as C++ objects in your program.

From an operating system point of view, ClassWizard is an executable implemented as a DLL. To open ClassWizard, choose the **ClassWizard** item from Developer Studio's View menu. Developer Studio displays the Class Wizard property sheet shown in Figure 4.9.

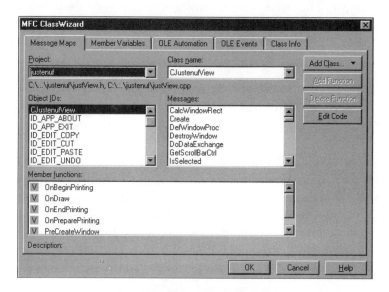

FIGURE 4.9 THE MESSAGEMAPS PROPERTY PAGE.

When the ClassWizard property sheet appears, you can:

+ Create new C++ classes that encapsulate objects such as dialog boxes, menus, icons, bitmaps, accelerator keys, and strings.

+ Create source files and header files that define and implement these new classes.

+ Connect, or bind, member functions of these new classes with system messages and user messages. For example, you can bind objects such as menu items and dialog controls to message-handler functions.

+ Generate code that automatically retrieves text and data from dialog-box controls and transfers data from member functions to dialog-box controls.

When ClassWizard creates a new class, it automatically generates the implementation and header files to implement the new class and automatically includes the new files in your project. However, if you need to access your new class's header file from other source files in your project, you must place #include directives in the files that require access.

When you use ClassWizard to perform class bindings, ClassWizard automatically writes all its work to disk. You don't have to do anything special to save the class bindings and function templates that ClassWizard creates—unless you do some file editing, as you will when you fill in a function template that ClassWizard has created.

THE DEVELOPER STUDIO RESOURCE EDITORS

App Studio, the old Visual C++ resource-management tool, has been replaced by something better: a new set of interactive resource editors. When you want to edit a resource, you simply open the Visual C++ resource editor. You can open the resource editor by clicking the resource tab just below the left-hand panel of the Developer Studio window.

The resource icon is the one that depicts a cactus in the desert. The other small icons that are lined up with the resource icon represent classes, source files, and help files. The *classes* icon opens a list box that shows the classes used in your applications. The *files* icon opens a list box that list your application's source files. With a little experimentation, it's easy to figure out how these three work. All three are shown in Figure 4.10.

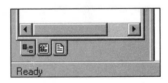

FIGURE 4.10 THE DEVELOPER STUDIO'S FILE-SELECTOR AND CLASS-SELECTOR ICONS.

What Are Resources?

Every Windows program contains one or more files that create resources—special objects such as menus, dialog boxes, and icons that the program requires. Resources are written in a special language called a *resource-definition language* and are stored in an .RC file. When an .RC file is placed in an application's project, the application can access the resources when they are needed at run time. When you create an application with the tools supplied in the Developer Studio, AppWizard places the definitions of the program's resources in the application's .RC file.

The resources defined in a program's resource-definition file are compiled into object-code modules with file names that have various extensions, such as .ICO (for an icon resource), .BMP (for a bitmap resource), and .RC2 (for resources such as menus and dialog boxes that you create for your applications). When you execute your application, your program manages these resources dynamically, loading them when they are needed and unloading them when they are no longer required.

When you click the bitmap tab, Developer Studio opens its bitmap editor (Figure 4.11).

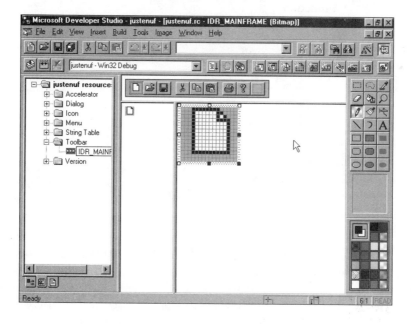

FIGURE 4.11   THE DEVELOPER STUDIO BITMAP EDITOR.

USING THE VISUAL C++ RESOURCE EDITORS

Every well-behaved Visual C++ application has a resource folder like the one shown in the list box in Figure 4.11. When you click the resource tab, Developer Studio opens your application's resource folder and displays subfolders that contain various kinds of resources. You can open any subfolder by double-clicking the appropriate icon displayed inside the resource property page. For example, in Figure 4.12, the Dialog folder icon has been opened, revealing that it contains one resource: an About box template.

When you have opened a resource subfolder and have found a resource you want to edit, you can open the appropriate resource editor by simply double-clicking it. For example, if you double-click the **About box** icon shown in Figure 4.11, Developer Studio opens its dialog-box editor, as illustrated in Figure 4.12.

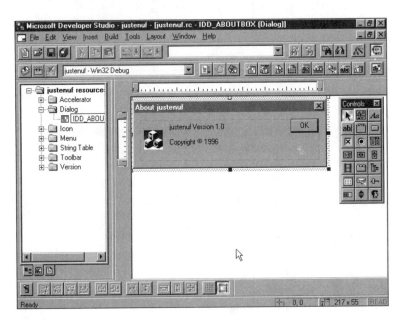

FIGURE 4.12 THE DEVELOPER STUDIO DIALOG-BOX EDITOR, WITH AN ABOUT BOX DISPLAYED.

If you want to create a new resource instead of editing an existing one, you can choose Developer Studio's **Insert|Resource** menu item. Developer Studio opens a dialog box named Insert Resource, which contains a list from which you can pick the kind of resource you want to create. Developer Studio then opens the appropriate resource editor. For example, if you select **Dialog** in the Insert Resource dialog box, Developer Studio displays a dialog box that enables you to open the Visual C++ dialog-box editor. When the dialog-box editor opens, it displays a default dialog box, as shown in Figure 4.13. When this dialog box appears, you can edit it to suit your preferences and the needs of your application.

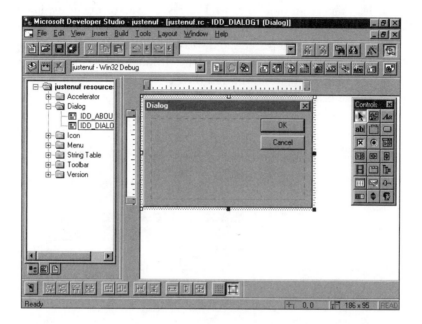

FIGURE 4.13 THE INSERT RESOURCE DIALOG BOX.

OTHER FEATURES OF THE RESOURCE EDITORS

With the resource editors, you can create, edit, and import 10 kinds of resources. (To see a list, open the Insert Resource dialog box described in the preceding paragraphs.) Developer Studio can also import resources from other applications. To import a resource, open the Insert Resource dialog box and click the **Import** button. Browse to the folder that contains the resource you want to import and import it into your project.

When you import a resource, Developer Studio places it in your project's resource (**.RC**) file. A Visual C++ project that is created using Developer Studio has one **.RC** file, which is usually generated by AppWizard. AppWizard automatically incorporates the file into your project and connects the file with any header files that it needs access to.

Resources created or edited with App Studio are stored in text files with the extension **.RC**. When App Studio has made entries in an **.RC** file, editing the file outside App Studio is not recommended, because it can adversely affect your application's compilation.

ON-LINE HELP

Whether you're a novice or a seasoned developer, you'll probably need to consult Developer Studio's on-line help files from time to time. The easiest way to obtain on-line help is to click the **Help** tab: the question-mark tab that appears at the bottom of the left pane in the Developer Studio window. Developer Studio displays the contents of its on-line help in the form of small book icons, as shown in Figure 4.14. To obtain the kind of help you need, double-click on the appropriate icon. You can then browse through various levels of help files until you find the help you're looking for. You can also open Developer Studio's help files by choosing an item from the Help menu.

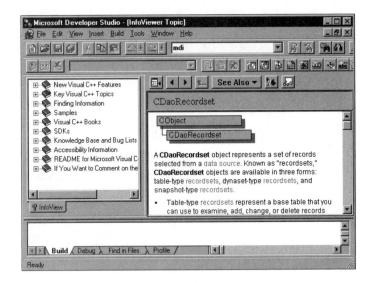

FIGURE 4.14 USING ON-LINE HELP.

The MFC Library

The MFC library is a mammoth collection of C++ classes designed to simplify the development of Windows-based programs. As Windows programmers have moved from C to C++, and to Visual C++ in particular, the MFC library has become more important in the world of Windows programming. One reason is that MFC is a fast and efficient C++ encapsulation of the C-language functions implemented in the Windows API. Microsoft engineers and evangelists say that the MFC library owes its speed and efficiency to the fact that its core is the code that implements the Windows API. In other words, Microsoft execs explain, the MFC library has been designed to serve as a "thin veneer" over the Windows API.

Because MFC 4.0 is so closely integrated with the Windows API—and with Windows NT and Windows 95—it has come a long way toward becoming a new Windows API. With one notable exception, all the major manufacturers of Windows-compatible C++ compilers—Symantec, Watcom, and MetaWare—have licensed the MFC library from Microsoft and include it in the compiler packages they sell. The one holdout is Borland, Microsoft's old rival in the compiler business. But with the introduction of Borland C++ 5.0, even Borland reluctantly climbed halfway onto the MFC bandwagon by announcing that its compiler would henceforth be MFC-compatible. With the release of Borland C++ 5.0, Borland didn't go so far as to license MFC from Microsoft but announced that if you have obtained the MFC library from another source—for example, from Microsoft—you can use the Borland C++ compiler to write and build MFC programs.

The MFC library contains string classes, collection classes, time classes, and much more. Almost all classes in the library are descended from the master class CObject. The CObject class provides all its descendants with important capabilities, including the capability to serialize files—that is, to store them on disk and read them from disk automatically.

Some of the classes and member functions encapsulate the functionality of the Windows API. Other classes encapsulate application concepts used in Visual C++, such as documents, views, and architectural models that represent complete Visual C++ applications. Still other classes encapsulate OLE features and data-access functionality.

Altogether, the classes provided in the MFC library help to simplify the writing of Windows applications, because they make it possible to use C++ programming tools—and a vast number of prewritten and pretested C++ classes—to write programs for Windows 95 and Windows NT.

MFC Naming Conventions

By convention, the names of MFC classes begin with a capital C followed by a capital letter. So if you create classes that are not derived from MFC classes, as I have in several chapters in this volume, you should make sure that they begin with some other letter. If you derive a class from an MFC class, however, you should follow the standard MFC naming convention and start the name of your homemade class with a capital C.

THE MFC LIBRARY AND THE WIN32 API

The parameters that Visual C++ programs pass to MFC member functions are similar to the parameters that are expected by corresponding Windows API functions, with certain fairly consistent exceptions. For example, in an MFC member function, the this pointer of the MFC object for which the function is called often serves the same purpose an object handle serves in a Windows API function. For this reason, an MFC member function often takes one less argument than its corresponding Windows API function. Usually, the missing parameter is an object handle, which an MFC object never requires because it has its own `this` pointer.

MFC classes can be divided into two general categories: those that predate MFC 4.0 and those that were released concurrently with MFC 4.0 or later. This division makes sense, because MFC 4.0 is the first version of the MFC library to support all the new features of Windows 95 and version 4.0 of Windows NT. MFC 4.0 is also the first version of the MFC library to be made available in a 32-bit version only.

The following are the classes that the MFC library contained before the introduction of MFC 4.0: the root class, the general-purpose classes, the application architecture classes, the window classes, the OLE classes, and the ODBC classes. In the paragraphs that follow, each of these categories of classes is described under a separate heading.

CObject: The Root Class

In MFC, `CObject` is designated as the **root class** of most other classes. The `CObject` class is described in more detail later in this chapter.

The General-Purpose Classes

Five MFC classes fall into the category of general-purpose classes (see Figure 4.15). The five subcategories of general-purpose classes are the file classes, the collection classes, the diagnostic classes, the exception classes, and the miscellaneous support classes:

+ The **file classes** are used to write functions for input/output processing. You won't use these classes very much if you let the Visual C++ foundation mechanism handle file I/O for you. The four MFC file classes are `CFile`, `CMemFile`, `CStdioFile`, and `CArchive`. They encapsulate functions that handle disk-file storage, files stored in memory, file I/O operations, and file archiving.

+ The **collection classes** are designed for handling aggregates of data such as arrays, lists, string lists, and collections of mapped data. These classes, all derived directly from `CObject`, include `CObArray` and `CObList` (for C++ objects), `CStringList` (for strings), and various kinds of mapping objects such as `CMapPtrToWord`, `CMapWordToOb`, and `CMapStringToPtr`.

+ The **diagnostic classes** help you debug your application. The diagnostic classes are `CDumpContext`, `CMemoryState`, and `CRuntimeClass`.

+ The **exception classes** provide a set of exception-handling mechanisms that are described in the Visual C++ *Class Library Reference*. The base class in this group is `CException`. Other exception classes include `CArchiveException` (for archives), CFileException (a file-oriented group), and CMemoryException (for out-of-memory exceptions).

✦ The **miscellaneous support classes** encapsulate strings, drawing coordinates, and time and date information. This group includes the classes CPoint, CSize, CRect, CString, CTime, and CTimeSpan. CRect, CPoint, and CString are used in several of the example programs in this book.

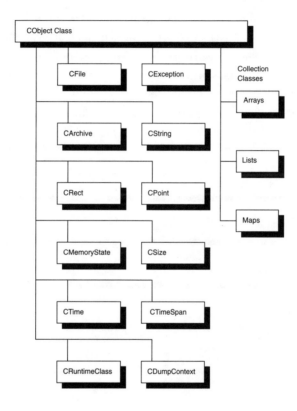

FIGURE 4.15 GENERAL-PURPOSE CLASSES.

The Application Architecture Classes

The application architecture classes contribute to the architecture of a framework application. Application classes, diagrammed in Figure 4.16, can be further divided into three groups: the Windows application classes, the command-related classes, and the document classes:

✦ There is only one **Windows application** class: CWinApp. Every framework-based Visual C++ program is an instantiation of the CWinApp class. Consequently, every Visual C++ application built with the MFC framework has one and only one application object, and this object is always an instance of the CWinApp class.

✦ The **command-related classes,** and their child classes, provide objects that encapsulate messages to windows. There are two command-related classes. CCmdTarget serves as the base class for all classes of objects that can receive and respond to messages. The other class in this category, CCmdUI, provides objects that can be used to update user-interface objects such as menu items and toolbar buttons.

✦ The **document classes** are related to documents and, indirectly, to views (there is a separate CView class). CDocTemplate is the base class for document templates, which are described in "Documents and Views" later in this chapter. Other classes in the document group include CDocument (the base class for application-specific documents); CSingleDocTemplate, used to create SDI applications; and CMultiDocTemplate, used to create MDI applications.

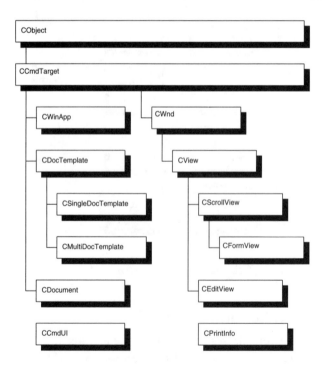

FIGURE 4.16 APPLICATION ARCHITECTURE CLASSES.

The Window Classes

All MFC classes that create window objects fall into a category called the window classes. They are derived from CWnd, the largest class in the MFC library. The MFC window classes include CFrameWnd, the base class for the main frame window of SDI applications; CMDIFrameWnd, the base class for the main frame window of MDI applications; and CMDIChildWnd, the base class for document windows in MDI applications. There are six subcategories of window classes: dialog classes, view classes, control classes, device-context classes, drawing object classes, and a menu class.

- **Dialog classes.** These classes—the base class CDialog and its descendants—encapsulate the implementations of dialog boxes. Descendants of CDialog include CDataExchange, which collects and provides initialization and validation information for dialog boxes; and several classes that provide standard dialog boxes for common operations. Standard dialog classes include CFileDialog, CPrintDialog, CFontDialog, CColorDialog, and CFindReplaceDialog, which provides a standard dialog for search-and-replace file operations.

- **View classes.** Objects created from view classes draw the client areas of frame windows and provide input and output for information stored in documents. View classes include CView, CScrollView, CEditView, and CFormView. CScrollView is the base class for application-specific views. CFormView, a kind of cross between a document window and a dialog box, provides the user interface for the sample programs in Chapter 10, "Networking Windows NT," and Chapter 11, "Windows NT Graphics."

- **Control classes.** These classes encapsulate the functionality of standard dialog-box controls. They include CStatic (for static controls), CEdit (for edit controls), CButton (for dialog-box buttons), and the rest.

- **Device context classes.** The base class in this group is the CDC class, which encapsulates the graphics objects that are known as HDC objects in C-language programs. Other classes in the device context group include CClientDC, CPaintDC, CWindowDC, and CMetafileDC. Chapter 11, "Windows NT Graphics," explains and illustrates the use of the CDC class.

- **Drawing object classes.** These classes encapsulate handle-based GDI objects. They are designed to be used with CDC objects. Figure 4.17 shows the MFC device context and drawing object classes.

- **The menu class.** There is one MFC menu class: CMenu. It encapsulates the functionality of both pull-down and pop-up menus.

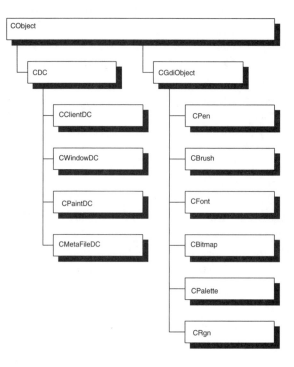

FIGURE 4.17 GRAPHICS CLASSES.

The OLE Classes

The **OLE (object linking and embedding) classes** were added to the MFC library with the introduction of MFC 3.0. OLE provides MFC programs with many kinds of useful capabilities. For example, OLE supports OLE controls (see Chapter 5, "OLE Today"). OLE also lets users create and edit *compound documents*—documents that can contain data created or modified by multiple applications. When a user changes the information stored in a document, the change is automatically recognized (and can be immediately displayed) by other OLE-aware applications.

The ODBC Classes

ODBC (open database connectivity) classes were also added to the MFC library with the introduction of MFC 3.0. Applications with ODBC connectivity objects can support the SQL database language and can access databases from many major vendors, including Microsoft SQL Server, Oracle, Informix, and Ingres. To access a third-party database, you need a special driver. Many drivers already exist, and others are becoming available.

THE NEWEST MFC CLASSES

Many new classes were added to the MFC library with the release of version 4.0. Here are some examples:

+ Classes supporting **common controls.** Common controls are a group of new Windows controls (to be distinguished from OLE controls) that support the new user-interface features of Windows 95 and Windows NT 4.0. These new controls are called common controls because they are used by the system as well as by applications and are useful in many kinds of programs. New or enhanced common controls added to MFC 4.0 include dockable toolbar controls; spin-button, progress-bar, and slider-bar controls; and many more.

+ Classes designed to support the **common dialog boxes** that are used by the Windows NT and Windows 95 shell and are also available for use by Windows developers. The new common dialog boxes made available in MFC 4.0 include a new Windows 95-style Open File dialog box and a new Page Setup dialog box that replaces the old Print Setup dialog box used by previous versions of Windows.

+ New classes for creating and managing tabbed dialog boxes, or **property sheets.** The ClassWizard dialog box is an example of a property sheet. Each tab in a property sheet opens a dialog box within a dialog box, called a **property page.**

+ Classes for creating and managing **OLE control property pages**: A special collection of property sheets that are designed for getting, setting, and viewing the properties of OLE controls.

+ New support for **OLE,** including full support for OLE control containers. With the OLE classes in the MFC library, you can make your application an OLE visual editing container, an OLE visual editing server, or both. You can also add OLE automation to your application so that other applications can use objects from your application or even drive it remotely. (The OLE-related features of the MFC library are covered in more detail in Chapter 5, "OLE Today.")

+ Increased MFC support for **networking,** including two new classes that support Windows sockets. (For more about Windows sockets, see Chapter 10, "Networking Windows NT.")

+ Enhanced MFC support for **multithreading,** including new synchronization classes for creating mutexes, semaphores, and event objects. (See Chapter 7, "Multithreading," for more details.)

+ An expanded set of new database classes, called the **DAO classes,** that simplify the writing of data-aware applications. Using the MFC library's new DAO classes, you can speed access to database applications such as Microsoft Access and Microsoft FoxPro by connecting MFC applications directly to the database engines that drive them. Along with its new DAO classes, MFC continues to support remote databases using an ODBC mechanism.

+ New classes designed specifically to support other new features of Windows NT and Windows 95, including classes that support the registry.

CWND: THE BASE CLASS FOR WINDOWS

The CWnd class is the base class for all window classes in MFC. Classes derived from CWnd include CFrameWnd, the base class for the main frame window of SDI applications; CMDIFrameWnd, the base class for the main frame window of MDI applications; and CMDIChildWnd, the base class for document windows in MDI applications.

By encapsulating all window functions in a very large Windows class and then incorporating that class into MFC in a new and different way, the designers of MFC created a system for managing windows that is very different from the way windows work in traditional C-language Windows applications and the way they work in framework-based MFC programs. The main difference lies in the way windows handle messages. In a traditional C-language Windows program, messages are dispatched to windows from a master switch statement that runs the program's main loop. In a framework-based Visual C++ program, the application's main loop is managed by the Visual C++ framework, so a different system is used for handling window messages. This system is described in "Message Maps" later in this chapter.

THE CCMDTARGET CLASS

CCmdTarget is an important MFC class that has become even more important with the release of MFC 4.0. CCmdTarget is the base class for all classes of MFC objects that can receive and respond to messages. CCmdTarget has always been important because it implements message maps—the mechanisms through which functions in Visual C++ applications communicate with one another by sending and receiving messages. (You'll read more about message maps in the section titled "Message Maps" later in this chapter.) CCmdTarget is even more important since the release of MFC 4.0, because it also implements *dispatch maps.* In MFC 4.0, dispatch maps are used by OLE controls, the 32-bit successors to VBX controls. Windows NT and Windows 95 did not fully support OLE controls until

Visual C++ 4.0 made its debut. You'll learn more about OLE controls in Chapter 5, "OLE Today."

Dispatch Maps

In Visual C++ programs that use OLE controls, dispatch maps work much like the message maps that connect Windows messages with their message handlers. You may recall from Chapter 4, "Programming Windows NT with Visual C++," that when a Windows event takes place in a framework-based Visual C++ application, Windows dispatches a WM_COMMAND or WM_NOTIFY to the application. In a Visual C++ program, the application then passes the message to an appropriate member by using a message map. The function to which a message is mapped in this way is often referred to as a *handler function*.

In OLE-aware applications, objects of the CCmdTarget class are equipped to provide not only message maps but also dispatch maps, which OLE-automation objects (including OLE controls) use in a similar fashion. Here's how a dispatch works in a program that uses OLE controls: When the program creates an OLE control or adds an existing control to a project, the control automatically creates a dispatch map and inserts it into the application's source code. A dispatch map bears a strong resemblance to a message map. It looks like this:

```
BEGIN_DISPATCH_MAP(COleCtrlCtrl, COleControl)
    //{{AFX_DISPATCH_MAP(COleCtrlCtrl)
    // NOTE - ClassWizard will add and remove dispatch
    // map entries
    // DO NOT EDIT what you see in these blocks of
    // generated code !
    //}}AFX_DISPATCH_MAP
    DISP_FUNCTION_ID(COleCtrlCtrl, "AboutBox",
        DISPID_ABOUTBOX, AboutBox, VT_EMPTY, VTS_NONE)
END_DISPATCH_MAP()
```

When a dispatch map has been inserted into an OLE control's source file, the application using the control can refer to the dispatch map when it needs to locate the properties or methods of an OLE control. Once a dispatch map has been created, OLE uses it to define the properties and methods for the OLE objects referred to in the dispatch map. Each time a program defines a new property or method for an OLE object, a macro defining that property or method is inserted into the application's dispatch map. When an OLE object with a particular property is needed, the application can use a dispatch map to track down a CCmdTarget object that implements that property.

The CWnd class is derived from the CCmdTarget class. Another important class—the COleControl class, which supplies most of the functionality used by OLE controls—is derived from CWnd. You'll learn more about COleControl and how it works in Chapter 5, "OLE Today."

THE COBJECT CLASS

All the classes in the Microsoft Foundation Class library are derived from the CObject class. You can also derive your own objects from CObject, gaining benefits such as support for serialization, the availability of C++ class information at run time, and retrieval of diagnostic information during debugging. The only overhead that a derived class adds to your application is a total of four virtual functions and a single CRuntimeClass object (CRuntimeClass objects are described in "Dynamically Created Objects" later in this chapter.)

Although CObject contains many useful member functions, MFC programs usually override some of them to handle specific needs of user-defined classes. For example, the Dump function defined by CObject is usually overridden to provide class-specific debugging operations. You can override Dump to print information about an object during debugging. Similarly, you can override AssertValid during debugging to test your assumptions about the validity of an object's internal state. You can accomplish the same goal by invoking an MFC macro named ASSERT_VALID. This macro is described later in this chapter.

Serialization

When you derive an object from CObject, the Visual C++ framework provides your object with the ability to read and write file information about that object automatically. The process of writing or reading an object automatically to or from a storage medium, such as a disk file, is called *serialization*. When your Visual C++ application supports serialization, AppWizard automatically provides the application with a File menu that implements serialization. A user can load a file by selecting **Open** from the application's File menu and can save a file by selecting **Save** or **Save As** from the File menu.

When you use the MFC serialization tool, you don't have to write all the code for those operations. Instead, you give AppWizard a few hints about the kinds of loading and saving capabilities you want, and AppWizard writes most of the code for you. By taking advantage of these serialization capabilities, you can often transfer a file or any other serializable object to disk with a single line of code. Even a collection of serializable objects, such as a list, can be serialized simply, conveniently, and with a small amount of code.

Dynamically Created Objects

One big advantage of objects derived from the CObject class is that they can be dynamically created, or created at run time. Dynamically created objects are often used when, for example, a program serializes an object. The MFC library's DECLARE_DYNCREATE and IMPLEMENT_DYNCREATE macros let you dynamically create objects that are derived from CObject.

Objects are dynamically created by the CreateObject member function of a class named CRuntimeClass. The DECLARE_DYNCREATE and IMPLEMENT_DYNCREATE macros override CreateObject. To create an object dynamically, you must call the DECLARE_DYNCREATE macro in the declaration of the CObject that you want to create, and you must call IMPLEMENT_DYNCREATE when you implement objects of the class. The document, view, and frame classes that typically make up a Windows application should support dynamic creation, because, as you'll see in later classes, the MFC framework often needs to create those classes dynamically.

Formats of the DYNCREATE Macros

The syntax of the DECLARE_DYNCREATE macro is as follows:

```
DECLARE_DYNCREATE(className)
```

where className is the name of the class that is to have serialization capability. Here is the syntax of the IMPLEMENT_DYNCREATE macro:

```
IMPLEMENT_DYNCREATE(className, baseClassName)
```

where className is the name of the class being serialized and baseClassName is the name of that class's base class.

The DYNAMIC Macros

The DECLARE_DYNAMIC and IMPLEMENT_DYNAMIC macros let you access information about classes dynamically (at run time). The ability to determine the class of an object at run time can come in handy when you have function arguments that need extra type checking or when you must write special-purpose code based on the class of an object.

When you derive a class from CObject, and call the DECLARE_DYNAMIC and IMPLEMENT_DYNAMIC macros from the appropriate spots in your program, you can use member functions to access, at run time, the name of the class and the classes above it in the derivation hierarchy.

You can also retrieve class information for any CObject-derived class that is declared in your program. This information allows you to cast a generic CObject pointer safely to a derived-class pointer. For example, suppose that in a Windows-based program, you want to process the child windows in a frame window. In this case, you can use the frame window's GetWindow member function to return a generic CWnd pointer for each child window.

Any class derived from CObject can supply you with run-time information about itself and its base class, provided that you invoke the DECLARE_DYNAMIC macro from the class's header file and call the IMPLEMENT_DYNAMIC macro from the class's implementation file. These two macros add code to your class to enable dynamic run-time information.

Formats of the DYNAMIC Macros

The syntax of the DECLARE_DYNAMIC macro is as follows:

```
DECLARE_DYNAMIC(className)
```

where className is the name of the class that is to have serialization capability. Here is the syntax of the IMPLEMENT_DYNAMIC macro:

```
IMPLEMENT_DYNAMIC(className, baseClassName)
```

where className is the name of the class being serialized and baseClassName is the name of that class's base class.

Caution

....

The IMPLEMENT_DYNAMIC macro should be evaluated only one time during any one compilation. This means that you should not use IMPLEMENT_DYNAMIC in an interface file that can be included in more than one file. The safest policy is to make sure that you always put IMPLEMENT_DYNAMIC in the implementation file (.**CPP**) for the class it's associated with.

How the DYNAMIC Macros Work

When you have placed calls to the DECLARE_DYNAMIC and IMPLEMENT_DYNAMIC macros in a program and you have derived a class from CObject, you can call the RUNTIME_CLASS macro and the CObject::IsKindOf function at run time to obtain information about your CObject subclass. With the RUNTIME_CLASS macro and the CObject::IsKindOf function, you can determine the exact class of an object at run time, and you can find out what base class it was derived from.

The RUNTIME_CLASS macro works by extracting the runtime class information for the specified class derived from CObject. The macro returns an object of the class CRuntimeClass. A CRuntimeClass structure has member variables that contain the name of the class, the size of the object, the schema number, the object's base class, and other information, all of which you can access directly. CRuntimeClass is defined in the header file **AFX.H**.

You can also use the IsKindOf member function of class CObject to determine whether an object belongs to a specified class. For more information on the RUNTIME_CLASS macro and the IsKindOf member function, see the Visual C++ *Class Library User's Guide*.

THE CARCHIVE CLASS

CArchive is an MFC library class that provides a context for reading and writing object data to and from a disk file. It is the class that makes serialization possible. CArchive overloads the insertion and extraction operators (<< and >>) to write and read object data to and from the storage media.

Although an archive uses the same overloaded operators as the general-purpose C++ I/O stream objects such as cin and cout, it's important to note that a CArchive object is different from an I/O stream. An archive object works much like an input/output stream but handles binary data. Like a binary I/O stream, an archive is associated with a file and permits the buffered writing and reading of data back and forth between the file and persistent (usually disk) storage. An archive processes binary object data in much the same way that a stream processes text data, in an efficient, non-redundant format.

Before you create a CArchive object, you must create a CFile object. (The MFC CFile class provides objects that are designed to support file I/O operations.) Also, you must ensure that the archive's load/store status is compatible with the file's open mode; if you want to load an archive into memory, the file object that it's associated with must be opened for reading. If you want to store an archive, the target file must be opened for writing. A file can be associated with only one active archive.

When you have constructed a CArchive object, you can attach it to an object of class CFile (or a class derived from CFile) that represents an open file. You must specify whether you want to use the archive for loading or for storing information. Then you can use the archive for the purpose you have specified.

CArchive objects can serialize primitive data types, such as words, longs, and binary types, and can also serialize objects that are derived from the CObject-derived classes designed for serialization. A serializable class must have a Serialize member function and must call the DECLARE_SERIAL and IMPLEMENT_SERIAL macros, as described earlier in this chapter. The Serialize function takes one argument: the CArchive object in which serialized data is stored.

By using the MFC serialization macros to read and write data, you can ensure that all the contents of the base-class portion of your object are correctly serialized. If the base class is itself a derived class, the DECLARE_SERIAL and IMPLEMENT_SERIAL macros also call the Serialize function for the base class that is being serialized. Thus, Serialize is called for all classes in the hierarchy above the class that is being serialized.

DIAGNOSTIC AIDS

The MFC library supplies many classes, functions, and macros that help you debug your MFC programs. Debugging aids range from features that track memory allocations to assertion testing (described under the next heading), which causes your program to abort and print an error message when problems are encountered. Microsoft's proprietary debugging aids supplement the C++-style exception-handling mechanisms that were added to Visual C++ with the introduction of Visual C++ 2.0.

Diagnostic aids provided by MFC include the ASSERT and ASSERT_VALID macros, which test the validity of objects and the validity of assumptions that you make in your program.

THE ASSERT MACRO

ASSERT can help you test code when you're writing and debugging an MFC program. Examine the source code of the example programs in this book, and you'll see ASSERT many times.

ASSERT evaluates a specified expression and returns a Boolean value. If the expression evaluates to FALSE, the macro prints a diagnostic message and aborts the program (not very gracefully, alas!). If the expression evaluates to TRUE, ASSERT takes no action. When Windows is running, ASSERT displays its messages in a pop-up dialog box.

When you use ASSERT in a program, the Visual C++ compiler uses the macro only during debugging. When you compile the release version of your program, the compiler does not evaluate ASSERT expressions and therefore does not interrupt the program if they evaluate to FALSE. If you want the program to abort if a tested expression evaluates to TRUE, use the VERIFY macro instead of ASSERT. Then the release version of your program will behave just like the debugging versions.

The syntax of the ASSERT macro is as follows:

```
ASSERT(booleanExpression)
```

where booleanExpression is an expression (which can include pointer values) that evaluates to TRUE or FALSE. If the result of the evaluation is zero (FALSE), the macro prints a diagnostic message and aborts the program. If the result is nonzero (TRUE), ASSERT takes no action.

When ASSERT detects an error or an expression evaluates to FALSE, the Visual C++ compiler generates an error message written in this format:

```
assertion failed in file <name> in line <number>
```

where name is the name of the source file and num is the line number of the assertion that failed in the source file.

THE ASSERT_VALID MACRO

ASSERT_VALID is another MFC macro that can help you test code when you're writing and debugging a program. You can use ASSERT_VALID to check the validity of any object derived from CObject. ASSERT_VALID can also evaluate expressions to determine whether assumptions in your program are valid. ASSERT_VALID, like ASSERT, is used extensively in the example programs in this book.

ASSERT_VALID calls a CObject member function named AssertValid. You can customize the AssertValid function by overriding it in your own class definitions. When you have overridden AssertValid, you can call the ASSERT_VALID macro to test your assumptions about the validity of an object's internal state. When you pass an object's pointer to ASSERT_VALID, the macro checks the validity of the pointer and then calls your overridden AssertValid function. If the pointer is not valid or fails any tests that you have supplied in AssertValid, the ASSERT_VALID macro displays a diagnostic message. In the Windows environment, ASSERT_VALID displays its messages in a pop-up dialog box.

You can use ASSERT_VALID to make any kind of test of an object. For example, ASSERT_VALID can test the validity of data that an object contains or can check to see that an object is placed in the correct position in a list.

You call the ASSERT_VALID macro using this syntax:

```
ASSERT_VALID(object)
```

where object is an object of a class derived from CObject.

The following code fragment, for example, checks the validity of a CDocument pointer returned by the GetDocument function:

```
m_pDoc = (CClientDoc*)GetDocument();
ASSERT_VALID(m_pDoc);
```

TIME-RELATED CLASSES

The MFC library supplies two time-related classes: CTime and CTimeSpan. A CTime object represents a specific time and date. A CTimeSpan object represents a time interval.

A CTime object encapsulates a time and date represented as a time_t data type, a data type standardized with an ANSI specification. A CTime object can represent any absolute date and time between Jan. 1, 1900, and Dec. 31, 2036.

The CTime class has run-time member functions that can convert between 24-hour time and a.m. and p.m. time, and between the Julian and Gregorian calendars. Other member functions can convert a time_t value to integers that represent years, months, days, hours, minutes, and seconds. The CTime class contains overloaded insertion and extraction operators for archiving and for diagnostic dumping.

The Win32 function CTime::GetCurrentTime is called to obtain the current time. CTime::Format is then called to construct a CString that contains the date and time expressed in a specified format. This is the function in which these two calls are made:

```
CString CClientDoc::SetStartTime()
{
    CTime theTime = CTime::GetCurrentTime();
    CString m_timeStr = theTime.Format("%A, %b %d, %Y, %I:%M %p");
    return m_timeStr;
}
```

The CTime::Format function uses the same time-formatting function as the C-language function strftime uses.

The CTimeSpan class can represent time intervals. If one CTime object is subtracted from another, the result is a CTimeSpan object. You can add CTimeSpan objects to CTime objects, and you can subtract CTimeSpan objects from CTime objects. A CTimeSpan value is limited to the range of plus or minus approximately 68 years.

Visual C++ Programming

To program effectively in Visual C++, it helps to have a basic understanding of how the Visual C++ development system handles the following:

+ Applications and instances
+ Windows

+ Events and messages
+ Documents and views

In this section, each of these topics is covered under a separate heading.

APPLICATIONS AND INSTANCES

When AppWizard generates a project for an application, the application's main source file has the same name as the project, with a .**CPP** file name extension. For example, if a project is named CREATION, its main source file is **CREATION.CPP**. The main source file of an application always includes one (and only one) object derived from the MFC class CWinApp. This object is called an application object. Every Visual C++ application generated by AppWizard is built on an application object.

In a framework-based Visual C++ application, the MFC member function InitInstance initializes a program's application object. A Visual C++ program is built around this C++ object in much the same way that a Windows API program is built around an HINSTANCE object. InitInstance is a member function of the CWinApp class. AppWizard always creates an InitInstance function when it generates an application framework, but most applications override this default InitInstance function to add customized processing. The program calls InitInstance from its WinMain function. (In a framework-based Visual C++ program, AppWizard generates the WinMain function. You'll find more information about how the WinMain function works in Visual C++ later in this chapter.) InitInstance performs the following tasks:

+ It opens one of two things: a document specified by the program or the user, or a new, empty document.

+ It loads standard file options from an .**INI** file, including the names of the most recently used files.

+ It registers one or more *document templates* (not C++ templates) that create and manage documents, views, and frame windows. (Document templates are described in more detail later in this chapter.)

When AppWizard generates an MDI application, InitInstance also creates a main frame window.

MESSAGE MAPS

A Windows message generated in response to an event is often referred to as an *event message*. In Windows NT, various kinds of objects—such as documents, views, windows, and even your application (which is an object itself)—have built-in capabilities for handling event messages. Every object that is designed to handle messages has a member function that is known as a message handler function or, more succinctly, as a message handler. Each time Windows generates an event message in a Windows application, a message handler passes the incoming message from one object to another in a carefully orchestrated sequence, until Windows finds an object that can handle the message. The object then carries out the instructions contained in the message, and the program continues.

How Messages Are Processed in Visual C++

When you execute a Visual C++ program with a framework generated by AppWizard, the application processes messages differently from the way they are processed in traditional C-language Windows programs. When an object in a framework-based Visual C++ program receives a command, the object determines whether it can handle the command by checking a message map, an object-oriented alternative to the `switch` statement used in traditional Windows programs to handle messages sent to a window.

Message maps work in a Visual C++ program in the following way: When the application detects that a message is to be handled by a window, it does not execute a `switch` statement. Instead, the application refers to a message map. Every entry in a message map connects, or binds, a particular message to a particular member function. When the application finds a message-map entry that corresponds to the message being processed, the application executes the appropriate member function. The mechanism that makes this possible is designed to work much like the virtual-function mechanism of C++ but in a more efficient way that requires less internal storage.

How Message Maps Are Created

When AppWizard generates a framework for a Visual C++ program, AppWizard automatically creates all the message maps that the framework needs. Each message map is implemented in the source file that implements a class and is defined in the header file that defines the same class. In this way, during the generation of the framework, every class that can be a target of a message is equipped automatically with a message map.

When you add source code to an AppWizard framework to implement your application's functionality, you can add extra entries to your application's message maps. Under most circumstances, you don't have to write any code to do that; with Developer Studio's ClassWizard utility, you can add entries to message maps and bind them to member functions automatically.

Message Maps and Message-Map Definitions

In a Visual C++ program, every class with objects that can receive messages has a message map. A message map contains an entry for each message that the target class can handle. When an object receives a message, it checks to see whether the message matches any of the kinds of messages that its message map says it can handle. If the command matches an entry in the message map, Windows NT calls the specified member function of the target class to handle the incoming message.

When you create a source file for a class using ClassWizard, it places the class's message map in the source-code file that implements the member functions. A message map is easy to spot in a .**CPP** file because it is always bracketed by the macros BEGIN_MESSAGE_MAP and END_MESSAGE_MAP. Here's an example:

```
BEGIN_MESSAGE_MAP(CNewprojView, CView)
    //{{AFX_MSG_MAP(CNewprojView)
    ON_WM_PAINT()
    //}}AFX_MSG_MAP
END_MESSAGE_MAP()
```

This message map contains one message: ON_WM_PAINT. When an object of the class that implements the message map receives an ON_WM_PAINT message, the message map sends the message to a specific member function. To locate the member function, the message map uses a *message-map definition*.

For every message map that appears in a source file, there is a message-map definition in a corresponding header file. A message-map definition stands out because it is bracketed by the symbols //{{ and }}// and includes one or more message-handler definitions preceded by the keyword afx_msg. A message-map definition also includes the macro name DECLARE_ MESSAGE_MAP. By convention, this macro appears at the end of the definition. This is a definition of the message map shown in the previous example:

```
class CAWnd : public CAParentWndClass {
{
protected:
    //{{AFX_MSG(CAWnd)
    afx_msg void OnPaint();
    //}}AFX_MSG
DECLARE MESSAGE MAP()
};
```

Every function name corresponds to a message and is preceded by `afx_msg`. Each function name starts with the letters `On` (as in the name `OnPaint` shown in the preceding example). These two letters are followed by the name of the Windows message in the corresponding message map, with the letters `WM` removed and only the first letter of each word capitalized.

In a message-map definition, parameters that are passed to each function always appear in the same order: `wParam`, followed first by `LOWORD(lParam)` and then by `HIWORD(lParam)`. Unused parameters are not passed. Any handles that are encapsulated in MFC classes are converted to pointers to the appropriate MFC objects.

Command Messages

Command messages are generated by menus and accelerator keys. In a message map, command messages are handled by the `ON_COMMAND` macro, which accepts two parameters: a command ID and a member function. The macro has this form:

```
ON_COMMAND(commandID, memberFunction)
```

The `ON_COMMAND` macro handles a message if both the `WM_COMMAND` parameter and the `wParam` passed to the macro match the command ID and function name of an available member function. When you write a member function that is to be handled by the `ON_COMMAND` macro, the member function must take no parameters and must return `void`.

Following is an example of a message map that contains command-message handlers:

```
BEGIN_MESSAGE_MAP(CNewprojView, CView)
    //{{AFX_MSG_MAP(CNewprojView)
    ON_COMMAND(ID_HELLO_DISPLAY, OnHelloDisplay)
    //}}AFX_MSG_MAP
    // Standard printing commands
    ON_COMMAND(ID_FILE_PRINT, CView::OnFilePrint)
    ON_COMMAND(ID_FILE_PRINT_PREVIEW, CView::OnFilePrintPreview)
END_MESSAGE_MAP()
```

This example has three command-message handlers. The first handler was generated by AppWizard; you can tell that because it is bracketed by the symbols //{{ and //}}. This handler detects command messages that are dispatched when an application-defined message named ID_HELLO_DISPLAY is dispatched. When the handler detects an ID_HELLO_DISPLAY message, it calls a member function named `OnHelloDisplay`.

The other two message handlers shown in the example send printing and print-preview messages to the appropriate member functions.

Creating Message Maps with ClassWizard

When you write a Windows application using Developer Studio, you can use ClassWizard to create your application's message maps. When ClassWizard creates a Visual C++ class, it can associate a member function of any class that it creates with a resource such as a menu item, a dialog box, or a dialog-box control. ClassWizard can also bind message-map entries to member functions at the time it creates a class, or it can perform the operation later, when new menu and dialog-box commands are being created and new messages are being bound to member functions.

When a class in a Visual C++ application has been equipped with a message map, ClassWizard updates the message map automatically each time a new message is added. Each time you use ClassWizard to generate a new message handler, ClassWizard updates the appropriate message map automatically, making all necessary changes in the class's header file as well as in the source code that implements the member functions.

For a working example of how message maps work in a Visual C++ application, see the example program presented in Chapter 11, "Windows NT Networking." That program contains many application-defined message maps and message handlers.

When ClassWizard Needs Help

One warning: If you use ClassWizard to delete a command binding that has been created for a class, ClassWizard removes the class's message-map entry but does not remove the message handler function associated with the message. Neither does it remove any other references that you have made to the message handler in your other code. If such items exist, you must delete them manually.

ClassWizard and the Visual C++ Resource Editors

One of ClassWizard's most powerful features is the ability to create classes for dialog boxes and views that you design using Developer Studio's resource editors. To create a class that implements the functionality of a dialog box or a view, simply create the dialog box or view using the appropriate Developer Studio resource editor, and then launch ClassWizard from the App Studio menu. You can encapsulate the functionality of your dialog box or view into a class by clicking the **Add Class** button in the ClassWizard browser window.

Where Angels Fear to Tread

The lines that appear between the //{{ and //}} symbols in the preceding example identify functions that have been generated by AppWizard or ClassWizard. You should never write or change any text that appears between these symbols unless you know exactly what you're doing. If you disturb this generated code and the Visual C++ compiler does not understand your code when it starts binding messages to functions, your program may not compile.

VISUAL C++ WINDOW MANAGEMENT

AppWizard can create MDI or SDI applications. Both kinds of applications are message-based and event-driven. When a user runs a Windows-based application, the program continually polls for events—which can be originated by the system or by the user—while cycling through a message loop controlled by a `while` statement. Such events include not only keyboard and mouse actions initiated by the user but also other kinds of occurrences, such as interrupts, that can take place during the running of the program.

Each time the user moves the mouse, clicks a mouse button, or presses a key, Windows dispatches a message to the part of the program that controls the window where the action has taken place. Messages are also dispatched by applications and by Windows NT. Every time a message is dispatched, the procedure that receives the message takes an appropriate action. In some cases—for example, when the system originates an event—the message that is generated is handled by the system. In other cases—for example, when the user chooses a menu command provided by an application—the application handles the message.

MFC and the *WndProc* Function

In a traditional Windows API (non–Visual C++) Windows application, a `WndProc` function processes the program's main message loop. In a Windows API application, every window class (not to confused with a C++ class) has a window procedure, and every window created with that class uses that same window procedure to respond to messages. A Windows API application tells Windows where to find a window's `WndProc` function by placing the address of the `WndProc` in the window's WNDCLASS structure when the window is registered. To register the window, the application calls the Windows API function `RegisterClass`, usually from its `WinMain` function. For more information about `WinMain`, see the next section.

When the WNDCLASS structure has the address of the `WndProc` function, the system sends messages to the `WndProc` as they are received, passing information about each message in parameters to the `WndProc`. The `WndProc` carries out an appropriate action for each message, usually by running the parameters through a `switch` statement.

In a Visual C++ application, none of this work is necessary; the Visual C++ framework takes care of registering window classes and handles the creating and calling of the application's `WndProc` function. To register the windows that a Visual C++ application requires, the application's framework assigns a predetermined windowX class (not a C++ class) to each type of window that the application uses. For example, all view windows share the same window class. If you wish, you can change the sizes, locations, and styles of the windows that the framework creates for your application. Techniques for doing this are outlined in "Customizing Windows" at the end of this chapter.

Typically, a framework-based Visual C++ application has one `WndProc` function that it uses for all view windows—that is, for windows managed automatically by the framework. AppWizard does not place this `WndProc` function in your application's source code but instead implements it in one of several hidden files that the Visual C++ compiler incorporates into your application at compile time. The source code for the Visual C++ framework's `WndProc` function is in **WINCORE.CPP**, which the Visual C++ installer places in your \MSVCNT\SRC directory. When a Windows message is generated in a Visual C++ application, the application's framework processes the message by calling the application's `WndProc` function. The `WndProc` function, with the help of the Visual C++ message-map system (see "How Messages Are Processed in Visual C++" earlier in this chapter), responds to the message by calling the appropriate member function.

MODIFYING THE FRAMEWORK'S WINDOW OPERATIONS

Microsoft asserts that the default window-management procedures provided by Visual C++ can handle most kinds of window operations. However, I have found that the framework's off-the-rack window-handling features often need extra help. For example, you must modify the framework's default behavior to create a main window that fills the screen, to create a pop-up window, or to create a child window of a specific (nondefault) size.

There are several methods you can use to create windows with custom-tailored styles and sizes. For example, you can customize the size of your application's main frame window by modifying a variable that is passed to the `ShowWindow` function. This technique is described in "The ShowWindow Function" later in this chapter. If your application uses child windows, you can also modify their sizes and styles, as explained in "Customizing Windows" later in this chapter.

The WinMain Function

A Visual C++ program, like any other Windows program, always has a main function named `WinMain`. However, when you let AppWizard generate your application's framework, you don't have to write the `WinMain` function yourself; it is supplied by the application framework and is called automatically at the appropriate time when the application starts. The framework calls `WinMain` from a function implemented in a source file named **WINMAIN.CPP**, which resides in your \MSVCNT\MFC\SRC directory (it is placed there when you install Visual C++). The Visual C++ linker links your application with the `WinMain` function when you build your application.

In a Visual C++ application, as in any other kind of Windows application, `WinMain` performs standard services, such as registering window classes and executing a `while` loop that gathers and processes messages. In a framework-generated Visual C++ application, `WinMain` also creates a view to display the application's main window and a document that stores the data to be displayed in the view. Finally, `WinMain` executes the user-written code that provides your application with its individual functionality. When it's time for your application to terminate, `WinMain` calls a member function of the application object named `ExitInstance`.

By Any Other Name

Every Windows NT program has an entry-point function that creates a main window, and that function is conventionally named `WinMain`. But Windows NT, unlike Windows 3.x, does not require an application to name its entry-point function `WinMain`. You can give your application's entry-point function any valid name. As long as you also give it the right syntax and an APIENTRY tag, it will do the same job that it would do if you named it `WinMain`.

When a Windows 3.x application is launched, the system launches the program's `WinMain` function. `WinMain` then performs a number of standard tasks, such as registering the main window's class and then creating the main window. In a Windows 3.x application, `WinMain` registers the main window's class by calling the Windows API function `RegisterClass`, and it creates the main window by calling `CreateWindow` or `CreateWindowEx`.

Ordinarily, a Visual C++ application does not have to call `RegisterClass`, `CreateWindow`, or `CreateWindowEx` to create its main frame window. If an application's main window has no special requirements, these calls are taken care of by the Visual C++ framework. If your application's main frame window has special requirements—

for example, if you want to customize the window's size, location, or style—you can create a custom main frame window. Some techniques for doing this are outlined in "Customizing Windows" later in this chapter.

The ShowWindow Function

Windows NT does not automatically display an application's main window when the window has been created; an application must call the Windows API function ShowWindow to display its main window on the screen. In a traditional Windows API application, WinMain typically calls ShowWindow immediately after creating the main window. However, in a framework-based Visual C++ program, the framework calls a member function named CWnd::ShowWindow from the **MAINFRAME.CPP** file generated by AppWizard. (CWnd is the MFC library's base class for creating windows; see the section "The MFC Library" earlier in this chapter.)

In the example program MDIAPP, this code sequence in **MDIAPP.CPP** calls the CWnd:: ShowWindow member function:

```
pMainFrame->ShowWindow(m_nCmdShow);
```

In a Visual C++ program, as the preceding example shows, CWnd::ShowWindow takes only one parameter: the member variable m_nCmdShow, which specifies the initial size, location, and style of the window. CWnd::ShowWindow, unlike ShowWindow, does not require a window handle to be passed as a parameter. That's because the window that is being created is always the window referenced by the this pointer.

Normally, the minimize/maximize flag passed to CWnd::ShowWindow can be set to any of the constants beginning with the SW_ prefix that are defined in the Windows header files. However, when CWnd::ShowWindow is called to display an application's main window for the first time, Microsoft advises you to set the flag to SW_SHOWDEFAULT. This flag tells Windows to display the window as directed by the program that launched the application—for example, the Program Manager **Run** command. In a Visual C++ application with a framework generated by AppWizard, the framework makes the initial call to ShowWindow using the SW_SHOWDEFAULT parameter.

Creating Windows in Visual C++

A traditional Windows API (non-Visual C++) application creates its main window by calling the Win32 function CreateWindow (or, alternatively, the CreateWindowEx function, which has one extra parameter for specifying a window's style). Parameters that are passed to the CreateWindow or CreateWindowEx function define attributes of the window that is created. MFC provides two member functions that correspond to the Windows API functions CreateWindow and CreateWindowEx. The CWnd::Create and CWnd::CreateEx functions are member functions of the CWnd class.

Although CWnd::Create and CWnd::CreateEx are available to any Visual C++ program, a well-behaved Visual C++ application does not ordinarily call either of these functions to create its main frame window or its child windows. Instead, it relies on the Visual C++ framework to handle the creation and management of windows. However, when a Visual C++ program needs to create a window with a special size, a special design, or a special set of behaviors, the program can create a customized window by calling CWnd::Create and CWnd::CreateEx and passing special parameters to these functions. For more information about modifying windows in Visual C++ programs, see "Customizing Windows" later in this chapter.

Using Windows in Multithreaded Applications

In a Windows NT application, every process can support multiple threads of execution (see Chapter 7, "Multithreading"), and each thread can create windows. When a window is active, it is displayed in the foreground and is called the foreground window. Similarly, the thread that created the window is called the *foreground thread*. All other threads are referred to as *background threads*, and the windows created by background threads are called background windows. In a multithreaded Windows NT program, each thread has a priority level that determines the amount of CPU time that thread receives. Although an application can set the priority level of its threads, the foreground thread normally has a higher priority level and receives more CPU time than the background threads. This means that it can respond to system events and user events more rapidly.

A multithreaded application can call the Win32 function EnumThreadWindows to enumerate the functions created by a particular thread. The GetWindowThreadProcessId function can be called to obtain an identifier of the thread that created a particular window. The sample code listed at the end of Chapter 7 shows how EnumThreadWindows can be used in a Windows NT program.

Destroying Windows in Windows API Programs

Generally speaking, an application is responsible for destroying all the windows it creates. A Windows API program destroys windows by calling the Win32 function DestroyWindow. The operating system hides the window if it is visible and then removes from memory any internal data that is associated with the window. This operation invalidates the window's handle so that it can no longer be used by the application.

When DestroyWindow is called to eliminate a window, a WM_DESTROY message is sent first to the window and then to its child and descendant windows. In this way, all descendants of the window being terminated are also destroyed.

Destroying Windows in Visual C++ Programs

When you write an application using the Visual C++ framework, it takes less effort to destroy window. Every frame window has a default message handler named OnClose that can be overridden using ClassWizard. When the user closes a frame window, the window's default OnClose handler calls the member function DestroyWindow, along with various other functions. You can override DestroyWindow to perform any additional operations that your application requires.

You should not yield to the temptation to destroy a frame window simply by using the delete operator. That isn't good enough, because delete does not destroy objects created by windows or perform other essential housekeeping operations. Instead, always use the OnClose handler to call DestroyWindow.

DOCUMENTS AND VIEWS

A Visual C++ application with a ClassWizard-generated framework is built around a pair of objects called a document and a view. A *document* is an object that manages the data used by an application. A *view* is an object that manages the display of that data on the screen. Thus, documents and views are closely linked in Visual C++ programs.

Documents are powerful objects that can read files from a disk or save files to a disk automatically. When a window contains text or graphics data that can be updated by the user and stored on a disk, it is often convenient to display that data using a view. A view object is the user's window into the data stored in a document. A view object determines how the user sees the data in the program's document object, and the view lets the user interact with that data.

Document objects are derived from the MFC class CDocument. View objects are derived from CView. Figure 4.18 shows how documents and views work together in a Visual C++ application.

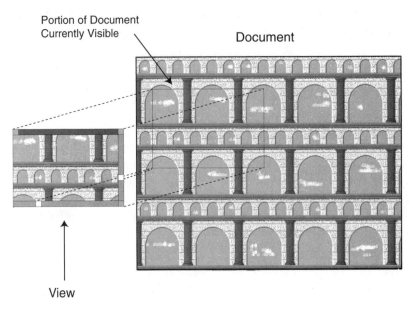

Portion of Document
Currently Visible

Document

View

FIGURE 4.18 DOCUMENTS AND VIEWS.

Typically, a Visual C++ program creates a document object when the user of an application selects **New** from the program's File menu. As soon as the document is created, a view that is associated with the document is displayed on the screen. When the user wants to open an existing document, the user chooses **Open** from the program's File menu. The document opens, and information that the document contains is displayed in a view. When the user selects **Save** or **Save As** from the File menu, a typical application saves the information that is stored in the currently active document and displayed in the currently active view.

The example programs SDIAPP and MDIAPP show how document-view structure can be used in a Visual C++ application. The example programs JUSTENUF and SLIMMDI demonstrate ways to create Visual C++ programs without using AppWizard's document-view structure. For more information on applications that do not use the document-view architecture, see "Visual C++ Programs without Documents or Views" later in this section.

Many applications can show the data in documents by using more than one view. When an application has multiple views, it can display information in multiple formats. If you need a view that scrolls, you can derive a view object from the MFC class CScrollView instead of from CView. If your view has a user interface that is laid out in a way that is tailored for entering data—such as in a database—you can create a form-like screen display by deriving a view object from a class named CFormView. The THRDDEMO program presented in Chapter 7, "Multithreading," displays its data in a CFormView object.

Drawing in Windows and Views

Visual C++ applications usually display text and graphics without making direct calls to CWnd functions. Instead, a Visual C++ program ordinarily writes to a view object. This view displays data and accepts user input to edit or select the data.

When the information in a view changes, a document object that is associated with the view object stores the data that is displayed in the view.

A Windows API (non-Visual C++) application generally draws in windows by calling the Windows API function BeginPaint, which starts a drawing in a window. EndPaint is called when the drawing is finished. In a Visual C++ program that draws in views, the drawing process is slightly different. MFC provides an OnPaint member function for drawing in windows and an OnDraw member function for drawing in views.

The SLIMMDI example program, in this chapter's directory on the accompanying disk, is not constructed using the standard Visual C++ document-view architecture, so it draws in windows rather than in views. In this code sequence, SLIMMDI calls OnPaint to print a text message in a child window:

```
void CChildFrame::OnPaint()
{
    CString s = "Where's Doc? Where's the view?";
    CPaintDC dc(this);
    CRect rect;
    GetClientRect(rect);
    dc.SetTextAlign(TA_BASELINE | TA_CENTER);
    dc.SetBkMode(TRANSPARENT);
    dc.TextOut(rect.right / 2, rect.bottom / 2, s);
}
```

The MDIAPP example program is designed using windows and views. In the following code fragment, MDIAPP prints a message in a view by calling OnDraw:

```
void CMdiappView::OnDraw(CDC *pDC)
{
    CMdiappDoc* pDoc = GetDocument();
    // TODO: add draw code here
    CString s = "A program with a view.";
    CRect rect;
    GetClientRect(rect);
    pDC->SetTextAlign(TA_BASELINE | TA_CENTER);
```

```
    pDC->SetBkMode(TRANSPARENT);
    pDC->TextOut(rect.right / 2, rect.bottom / 2, s);
}
```

The member functions shown in both examples do their drawing with a CPaintDC object—that is, a DC object designed for painting. For more information on device contexts and other topics related to Visual C++ graphics, see Chapter 11, "Windows NT Graphics."

Document Templates

A framework-based Visual C++ program manages documents using a document template, which creates and manages all open documents of one type. For example, if an application supports both spreadsheets and text documents, the application needs a document template for each kind of document.

When Is a Template Not a Template?

A Visual C++ document template is not the same thing as the C++-style template structure used in Visual C++. A Visual C++ document template is a structure that manages documents in a Visual C++ program. C++-style template structures are used to group classes.

When a document template is created for a category of documents, the document template handles the creation of all documents in that category and manages the views and frame window that are associated with them. You can create a set of document templates by calling the Windows API function AddDocumentTemplate or the MFC member function CWinApp::AddDocTemplate. When you generate a framework for an application with AppWizard, AppWizard creates a set of document templates for you by calling CWinApp::AddDocTemplate. AppWizard places this call in the InitInstance function in the program's main source file. You can also write your own document templates if your application has special kinds of windows.

A document template contains pointers to the CRunTimeClass objects for an application's document, view, and frame window classes. To obtain a pointer to a CRuntimeClass object, an application must call the RUNTIME_CLASS macro.

The following AddDocTemplate function appears in the MDIAPP program's Init-Instance function, in the file **MDIAPP.CPP**:

```
AddDocTemplate(new CMultiDocTemplate(IDR_NEWPROTYPE,
    RUNTIME_CLASS(CMdiappDoc),
    RUNTIME_CLASS(CMDIChildWnd), // standard MDI child frame
    RUNTIME_CLASS(CMdiappView)));
```

Applications that support multiple kinds of documents can be equipped with multiple document templates. The MFC library has a `CSingleDocTemplate` class that manages documents used in SDI applications, and a `CMultiDocTemplate` class that manages documents used in MDI applications.

Visual C++ Programs without Documents or Views

When AppWizard generates the framework for a Visual C++ application, it automatically creates a view and a document for each window in the application (with the exception of the main window in an MDI application). If you want to generate an application framework using AppWizard but your program doesn't require a document-view architecture, you can modify the files created by AppWizard to eliminate the document-view structure and employ a typical window structure instead. That can eliminate unnecessary code from your application.

The JUSTENUF application, in this chapter's directory on the accompanying disk, is an example of a Visual C++ application generated by AppWizard that has been edited this way. These are some of the differences between JUSTENUF and a document-view application created by AppWizard:

+ JUSTENUF has no source file for implementing a document object and no header file for defining one.

+ The JUSTENUF application's **MAINFRM.CPP** file has no `OnCreate` function. Instead, the constructor of the program's `CMainFrame` object creates a window by calling the `Create` member function.

+ Because JUSTENUF has no document object and no view object, its `InitInstance` member function does not call the `AddDocTemplate` function.

+ The program's **MAINFRM.CPP** file contains no `IMPLEMENT_DYNCREATE` macro.

+ The program's **MAINFRM.H** file contains no `DECLARE_DYNCREATE` macro.

CUSTOMIZING WINDOWS

When AppWizard generates a framework for an application, the utility's default behavior is to give the program a main frame window that covers about two-thirds of the screen. This window can show up in various locations, depending on where it was the last time you closed your application.

When a main frame window has a child window, the Visual C++ framework gives the child window a default size that is somewhat smaller than the size of its parent window.

By default, the upper-left corner of this child window is placed in the upper-left corner of the client area of its parent window.

The MFC library does not provide any easy way to change the default sizes or placements of child or parent windows. However, there are some tips and tricks that you can use to control the sizes, locations, and styles of your application's windows.

Changing Attributes of Windows

One way to modify the characteristics of a window is to use the CWnd member function GetWindowPlacement, which returns a structure containing a specified window's size and location. You obtain a window's properties by calling GetWindowPlacement and then call the CWnd member function SetWindowPlacement to modify those properties. Then call ShowWindow to apply the changes to your window.

In the Client program presented in Chapter 9, "Interprocess Communications," a code sequence in **MAINFRM.CPP** calls GetWindowPlacement to set the size of the program's main frame window to half the screen's size—exactly the size needed to accommodate the CFormView object used to draw the window. This code sequence, which appears in the program's OnCreate function, reads as follows:

```
// Adjust main frame window's size and placement
ShowWindow(SW_SHOWMAXIMIZED);
GetWindowPlacement(&wpl);
wpl.rcNormalPosition.top = 0;
wpl.rcNormalPosition.left = 0;
wpl.rcNormalPosition.right =
wpl.rcNormalPosition.right / 2;
wpl.rcNormalPosition.bottom =
wpl.rcNormalPosition.bottom + 76;
SetWindowPlacement(&wpl);
ShowWindow(SW_SHOWNORMAL);
```

Changing the Value of m_nCmdShow

If your program is an MDI application, an alternative way to change the size of the program's main frame window is to change the value of its m_nCmdShow variable. The m_nCmdShow variable is a member variable of the CWinApp class, the class from which application objects are created. It corresponds to the nCmdShow variable that Windows passes to WinMain. When an application starts, m_nCmdShow holds a default value that determines the size, location, and style of the main frame window.

When AppWizard generates a framework for a Visual C++ application, InitInstance initializes the application's main frame window by calling CWnd::ShowWindow. When this call is made, the value of m_nCmdShow is passed as an argument to CWnd::ShowWindow.

The MDIAPP application, one of the example programs presented with this chapter, has been modified to display a screen-size main frame window. Originally, when AppWizard generated the program's **MDIAPP.CPP** file, this code sequence called ShowWindow:

```
// create main MDI frame window
CMainFrame *pMainFrame = new CMainFrame;
if (!pmainFrame->LoadFrame(IDR_MAINFRAME))
    return FALSE;
pMainFrame->ShowWindow(m_CmdShow);
pMainFrame->UpdateWindow();
m_pMainWnd = pMainFrame;
```

When MDIAPP was compiled using this code sequence, the result was an application with a default main frame window that covered about two-thirds of the screen when displayed on a standard-size monitor.

In the version of MDIAPP that is provided on the accompanying disk, this code sequence has been slightly modified. Only one line of code has been added, but the result is code that displays a screen-size main frame window. The edited version looks like this:

```
// create main MDI frame window
CMainFrame *pMainFrame = new CMainFrame;
if (!pmainFrame->LoadFrame(IDR_MAINFRAME))
    return FALSE;
m_nCmdShow = m_nCmdShow | SW_SHOWMAXIMIZED;
pMainFrame->ShowWindow(m_CmdShow);
pMainFrame->UpdateWindow();
m_pMainWnd = pMainFrame;
```

The line that has been added is

```
m_nCmdShow = m_nCmdShow | SW_SHOWMAXIMIZED;
```

This line of code uses the C++ OR operator (|) to combine the contents of m_nCmdShow with the constant SW_SHOWMAXIMIZED. The result is a main frame window that covers the entire screen.

Calling the PreCreateWindow Function

Still another way to modify the size of a window in a Visual C++ application is to override the CWnd member function PreCreateWindow. This technique is a little more complicated than the one just described, but it is also more versatile. It works in MDI and SDI applications, and it works with child windows as well as with main frame windows. The PreCreateWindow function gives applications access to a window-creation process that is normally carried out internally. When AppWizard generates an application framework, the framework calls PreCreateWindow just before it creates the window. By modifying a CREATESTRUCT structure that is passed to the PreCreateWindow function, your application can change the attributes that are used to create the window.

To change the window attributes in an SDI application, override PreCreateWindow in the source file that creates the program's main frame window. For example, this code sequence reduces the size of a main frame window to one-third of the screen's size and then centers the window:

```
BOOL CMainFrame::PreCreateWindow(CREATESTRUCT& cs)
{
    cs.cx = ::GetSystemMetrics(SM CXSCREEN) / 3;
    cs.cy = ::GetSystemMetrics(SM CYSCREEN) / 3;
    cs.x = ((cs.cx * 3) - cs.cx) / 2;
    cs.y = ((cs.cy * 3) - cs.cy) / 2;
    return CFrameWnd::PreCreateWindow(cs);
}
```

With a little more work, you can use PreCreateWindow to customize child windows in MDI applications. To change the style of an MDI child window, you must derive a new class from CMDIChildWnd. Then you must search through your application and replace all references to CMDIChildWnd with references to your new class. That is usually not as difficult as it sounds, because a typical application contains only one reference to CMDIChildWnd. You can find that reference in the application's InitInstance member function.

To change the attributes of an MDI application's child windows, you override the PreCreateWindow function in the source file that instantiates CMDIChildWnd. For example, in the Creation program presented in Chapter 11, "Windows NT Graphics," this code sequence appears in the **ANIMWND.CPP** source file:

```
BOOL CAnimWnd::PreCreateWindow(CREATESTRUCT& cs)
{
```

```
    const char *animWndClass = AfxRegisterWndClass(CS_NOCLOSE
    |CS_BYTEALIGNCLIENT | CS_HREDRAW | CS_DBLCLKS);
    cs.cy = ::GetSystemMetrics(SM CXSCREEN) * .18;
    cs.y = 0;
    cs.cx = ::GetSystemMetrics(SM CXSCREEN) * .82;
    cs.cx = ::GetSystemMetrics(SM CYSCREEN) * .62;
    return CFrameWnd::PreCreateWindow(cs);
}
```

This code creates a client window whose characteristics include the constant CS_BYTE-ALIGNCLIENT. This constant causes the window that is being created to be aligned on a byte boundary—a configuration that speeds drawing inside the window. The code also sets other characteristics of the window and sets the window's size.

To support this modification, several other changes have been made in the Creation program. First, a new class named CAnimWnd has been derived from CMDIChildWnd. CAnimWnd is implemented in **ANIMWND.CPP** and is defined in **ANIMWND.H.**The first line of the definition reads as follows:

```
class CAnimWnd : public CMDIChildWnd
```

Next, in the Creation program's InitInstance function—which appears in **CREATION. CPP**—the parameter list of the AddDocTemplate function has been modified. In a standard Visual C++ AddDocTemplate function, the parameter of the second RUNTIME_C LASS macro passed to the CMultiDocTemplate function is CMDIChildWnd. However, in the Creation program's AddDocTemplate function, the second RUNTIME_CLASS parameter is CAnimWnd, the name of the new class that has been derived from CMDIChildWnd:

```
AddDocTemplate(new CMultiDocTemplate(IDR_MDIAPPTYPE,
    RUNTIME_CLASS(CMdiappDoc),
    RUNTIME_CLASS(CAnimWnd),
    RUNTIME_CLASS(CMdiAppView)));
```

Finally, the PreCreateWindow function that has been implemented in **ANIMWND.CPP** is defined in **ANIMWND.H**:

```
BOOL PreCreateWindow(CREATESTRUCT& cs);
```

As a result of these changes, the AnimWnd window in the Creation program is byte-aligned, and its size and location are customized.

Summary

This chapter is the last of four introductory chapters. Its aim is to wrap up the book's introductory material, so it covers much territory. It describes the components of Developer Studio—the GUI programming interface that comes with Visual C++—and it explains how to use Developer Studio to create and edit Visual C++ programs. The chapter provides an overview of the MFC library and reveals some tips and tricks that you might find useful when you start writing your own Visual C++ applications.

Now your introduction to Windows NT and Visual C++ is complete, and you're ready to move to topics that are more challenging—and more fun. In Chapter 5, "OLE Today," you'll learn how to create OLE controls and how to use them in your Windows NT applications.

CHAPTER FIVE

OLE Today

OLE (originally an acronym for "object linking and embedding") is one of the most powerful tools available in the world of Windows programming, but it intimidates many otherwise stalwart Windows developers because it has gained a reputation for being mysterious and difficult to understand. Like many other Windows mechanisms, though, OLE becomes less mysterious as soon as you learn more about it. Once you understand what OLE was designed to do and gain a general understanding of how it does the jobs it was designed for, you'll find that you don't have to master every single OLE intricacy before you can start using it in your Windows applications.

The trick is to keep it simple in the beginning. If you're new to OLE, start with something easy. For example, use the Visual C++ ControlWizard to create an OLE control and place it in a dialog box. When your OLE control works, you can move gradually to more-complex implementations, such as embedding one OLE object in another and then editing the object in a client application by using in-place activation. By using this step-by-step approach, you can learn all you need to know about OLE without too many tears and without having to wade through a library of theoretical books before you start getting hands-on experience writing OLE programs.

About This Chapter

Because OLE is such a broad and multifaceted topic, many thick books have been written about it (some of the better ones are listed in the Bibliography). This chapter doesn't attempt to explain all the intricacies of OLE that you'll find in those hefty books. Instead, its goal is to give you a head start on the long journey toward mastering OLE. I'll provide simple explanations of a few complicated topics and then presenting a relatively simple example program that shows you how to use OLE controls in your Windows applications.

This chapter keeps the subject of OLE as simple as possible by using a step-by-step approach. The chapter begins with an overall description of what OLE can do and presents the various components of OLE. Sample programs demonstrate some of the things OLE can do and gives you valuable hands-on experience in working with a well-designed OLE application.

The sample program that shows you how all the components of OLE work together is named FASTDRAW. By experimenting with FASTDRAW, you can learn about OLE by seeing how it's done instead of just listening to someone tell you how to do it.

FASTDRAW shows how applications can use OLE to import objects that have been created using other applications. The user of the imported application can edit the imported object from the importing program without having to open the application that created it. FASTDRAW also shows off some of the graphics capabilities of Visual C++ and Windows NT. With FASTDRAW, you can draw straight lines, curved lines, and closed shapes such as ellipses, rectangles, and polygons. You can fill closed figures with colors, and you can drag, cut, paste, and edit shapes drawn in windows. Figure 5.1 shows the output of the FASTDRAW program.

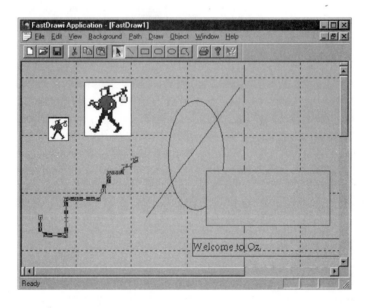

FIGURE 5.1 OUTPUT OF THE FASTDRAW PROGRAM.

The two example programs presented at the end of the chapter are named COMPGAL and OLEDEMO. COMPGAL demonstrates the use of Component Gallery, a Visual C++ tool that makes OLE components available to Visual C++ applications. OLEDEMO zeros in on OLE controls. With the help of a step-by-step tutorial, OLEDEMO shows you how to place an existing OLE control in a dialog box so that you can use it in an application. (Later, you'll learn how to create your own customized OLE controls and use them in your applications.)

When you work through the OLEDEMO tutorial, you'll design an OLE control and place it in a dialog box. When you click the control, you'll fire an event that makes the control change its appearance each time you click it. With each click of the mouse, a picture inside the control will change from a happy face to a sad face and back again. Figure 5.2 shows the output of the OLEDEMO program.

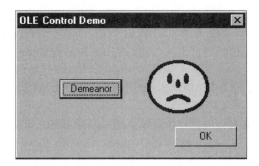

FIGURE 5.2 OUTPUT OF THE OLEDEMO PROGRAM.

The Purpose of OLE

One question that may be on your mind at this point is, What's OLE for? Why did Microsoft go to the trouble of creating and designing OLE?

OLE is such a massive package, with so many parts that do so many different things, that it's difficult to pin down exactly what OLE is. Many large books and many long chapters have attempted to describe OLE, and most of them make for difficult reading. I'll outline some of the most important features of OLE along with a short description of how each feature came into being and what it is designed to do.

When Microsoft engineers started thinking about OLE, an old Windows platform was nearing obsolescence and a new one was emerging. Windows 3.1, which was built around a 16-bit operating environment, was about to be succeeded by Windows NT, the first 32-bit Windows operating system. Applications running under either operating system could share code with other programs written for the same operating system using dynamic link libraries, or DLLs (the topic of Chapter 8), but 16-bit programs written for Windows 3.1 could not easily share code with 32-bit programs written for Windows NT using ordinary DLLs. A new kind of DLL had to be devised for this purpose, and it turned out to be OLE.

The development of OLE also solved a perennial problem faced by software designers: the problem of versioning. As new versions of applications are released and as new versions of DLLs that are used with those applications are developed, the versions of applications and the DLLs they rely on can get out of sync, causing coding nightmares. So OLE *interfaces* (the mechanisms that make OLE possible) are designed with built-in features for keeping version numbers straight throughout a product's lifetime. OLE interfaces are examined in detail in the section titled "OLE Interfaces" later in this chapter.

The Windows NT and Windows 95 operating systems are based in part on a client-server operating system model. This design simplifies many kinds of advanced capabilities of operating systems, such as remote file access, remote procedure calls, and client-workstation communications across computer networks. Because OLE is also based on a client-server model, it fits seamlessly with the client-server features and capabilities of both Windows NT and Windows 95.

The most important reason that OLE was designed is that it had to be. In the standard Microsoft reference on OLE—*Inside OLE* (published by Microsoft Press; see Bibliography)— author Kraig Brockschmidt likens the invention of OLE components (the basic building blocks of OLE) to the invention of the integrated circuit. OLE was developed, he explains, because the time finally came when enough pieces of software were available to do almost any job but they couldn't do a big job effectively because no way existed to connect them all. Today, for the first time, OLE technology gives developers a way to connect all those pieces of software in almost any fashion, regardless of what kinds of computer systems they were developed on, what kinds of operating systems they are running on, what computer language they were written in, or how the computers sharing them are linked.

An OLE Glossary

Because OLE is based on a client-server model, an application or process that wants to use a piece of software that's being made available by another application or process is called a *client*, and the provider of the software is called a *server*. The software being shared is called a *component*. Components are OLE *objects* that follow certain standards and specifications that enable them to be shared by different applications and processes. These standards and specifications are prescribed by an OLE protocol that is called the *component object model*, (COM).

Here are some additional important OLE-related terms along with details about the terms defined in the preceding paragraph:

+ **Object linking and embedding.** Two different methods that applications and processes use to share OLE components. For example, an OLE server might be requested to make available a graph produced by a spreadsheet to a word processing document being executed on a client workstation. If the client obtains the graph using object linking, the graph can be displayed inside the client's word processing document, but the client is given only indirect access to the graph (through a pointer), and the client cannot modify the graph. In contrast, if the graph is made available to the client using object embedding, the graph is actually embedded in the client's word processing document (sometimes called a *container document*) and can be modified by the client using a technique called in-place activation (see next item). You'll see how object embedding works in the FAST-DRAW sample program presented later in this chapter.

+ **In-place activation.** The mechanism that allows an OLE client to edit an embedded component made available by an OLE server. When a component is embedded in a container application using in-place activation, the interface of the container application often changes to take on some of the features of the application that created the embedded item. For example, OLE might add certain items to the container application's menu bar to provide editing commands that aren't ordinarily available within the container application but are available in the originating application. You'll see how in-place activation works in the demonstration application CLIDEMO, provided later in this chapter.

+ **Components.** Reusable OLE objects that OLE servers can make available in binary form to OLE clients. Because components adhere to a binary standard (the COM standard), they can be shared by clients running on any kind of computer and written in almost any computer language. Examples of OLE components include OLE controls, MFC classes, dialog boxes, sound clips, spreadsheets, and bitmaps. To make components easy to use and easy to copy from one application to another, Visual C++ provides a utility called the Component Gallery, which is described in more detail in the "Component Gallery" section later in this chapter.

+ **OLE interfaces.** When a client issues a request for access to an OLE object, the client must issue its request indirectly through this OLE mechanism. OLE interfaces are the glue that make it possible for OLE clients to access code and components that are made available by clients that may be running on different machines or different operating systems and may be written in different languages. All OLE interfaces have names that begin with the letter *I*, in the same way that names of MFC classes begin with the letter *C*. Examples of OLE interfaces are `IOleObject`, `IUnknown`, and `IDispatch`. The standards for designing and using OLE interfaces are prescribed by OLE's component object model. For more details on OLE interfaces, see the section headed "OLE Interfaces" later in this chapter.

✦ **OLE automation.** OLE technology that's different from object linking and embedding. OLE automation lets you can write software in any OLE-compatible language (C++, for example) and execute it from a program written in another language (Visual Basic perhaps, or maybe one of those special-purpose languages that have been invented to write applications for Microsoft Access or Excel). When you use OLE automation to execute procedures that reside in one program from an entirely different program, the client that executes the code is known as an *automation client* or *automation controller*, and the application that contains the code is called an *automation server* or *automation component*. OLE controls, which are described later in this list, are implemented using OLE automation.

✦ **Persistence of objects.** In OLE, objects that can save and load themselves from disk automatically without any particular effort on the part of the user. OLE objects can have persistent properties which are also saved and loaded automatically, along with the objects they belong to.

✦ **OLE controls.** Microsoft's 32-bit successors to the 16-bit VBX controls that were once popular among Windows 3.1 programmers. OLE controls can do everything that VBX controls used to do and much, much more. You can even use OLE controls in Web pages on the Internet. You learn how OLE controls work, and how to use them in your applications, later in this chapter.

Using OLE

In this section, you'll learn how to tap the power of OLE in your own Windows NT applications. First, you'll learn about three methods that you can use to implement OLE in your Windows programs. Then you'll get an opportunity to build a simple OLE-aware application. By examining this program and experimenting with it, you'll get a valuable firsthand look at how OLE-friendly programs created by AppWizard differ from the ordinary AppWizard programs we've been dealing with in previous chapters. Then we'll be ready resume our discussion of the features and capabilities of OLE.

THREE WAYS TO USE OLE

There are three ways to create OLE components and incorporate them into Windows NT applications. The first technique is to use the raw OLE function calls that are provided in the OLE libraries that Microsoft provides with the MFC library and Visual C++.

The second method is to instantiate an OLE object using the OLE-related classes and member functions that are provided in MFC.

The third method—and the easiest one by far—is to create OLE-aware applications using AppWizard and then use the interactive OLE-related tools provided in the Visual C++ compiler package to incorporate OLE controls and other kinds of OLE components into your applications.

Using the OLE API

The Visual C++ compiler package comes with a set of object-code libraries that contain all the tools you need to implement OLE objects and OLE components. All the low-level libraries that come with Visual C++ have names that begin with the word OLE, such as **OLE32.LIB** and **OLEAUT32.LIB.**

To use the OLE libraries, which I refer to generically as the OLE API, all you have to do is to link your application to them at build time. Then, if you know how to make your application OLE-aware and how to call the functions in the OLE libraries, you can build all the OLE functionality you like into your Windows programs without accessing any of the OLE-related MFC classes and member functions.

Although that's the most difficult way to use OLE, it was the only way until OLE-related classes and member functions started finding their way into the MFC library. Today, you can incorporate OLE into your applications much more easily by taking advantage of the help you can get from MFC and from the interactive OLE tools built into the Visual C++ compiler.

Occasionally, however, you might run across a situation in which some OLE capability that you need has not yet been incorporated into MFC. You may find that you must bypass MFC and access one of the OLE libraries directly. If that ever happens, it may be helpful for you to know how to call an OLE API function directly without relying on MFC.

Once you become familiar with how OLE works, you may also find that you can bypass MFC and make direct calls to OLE API functions when you want to design leaner and meaner OLE objects that lack some of the overhead—for example, interfaces that you may not need—that MFC builds into OLE objects by default.

You'll learn much more about the OLE API in the section headed "The OLE API" later in this chapter.

An Easier Way: Using the MFC Library

An easier way to use OLE is to take advantage of the OLE-related MFC member functions. To make an MFC application OLE-aware, you need only derive the program's document class from the `COleDocument` or `COleLinkingDoc` base class instead of from the familiar `CDocument` class; then you add some macros and other embellishments to make your application work with OLE. Then you link your program with the OLE libraries it requires when you build your application.

For more information about the MFC OLE classes, see "OLE and the MFC Library" later in this chapter.

The Easiest Way: Using AppWizard

The third method of using OLE—the AppWizard method—is the quickest and easiest way to write Visual C++ programs using OLE. To create an OLE-aware application using AppWizard, you simply select the appropriate radio button in the step 3 dialog box, as shown in Figure 5.3. Then follow the steps outlined in the next section, "Example: The MINIOLE Program."

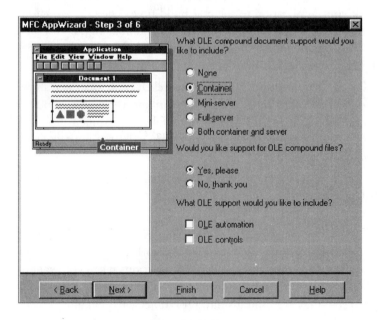

FIGURE 5.3 BUILDING AN OLE APPLICATION.

EXAMPLE: THE **MINIOLE** PROGRAM

In this section, you'll get a chance to build a program named MINIOLE, which demonstrates how AppWizard creates an OLE-friendly program and lets you take a look at the extra files, classes, and member functions that AppWizard creates to make an MFC application OLE-compatible.

When AppWizard opens the dialog box shown in Figure 5.3, these are the choices you can make by selecting one of the "just say yes" radio buttons that AppWizard displays:

✦ **None** (default option). Select this option if you do not want OLE support.

✦ **Container.** Select this option if you want your application to be a container for linked and embedded objects. A container is an application that can incorporate embedded or linked items into its own documents.

✦ **Mini-server.** This option gives your application the ability to create and manage compound document objects. Note that mini-servers cannot run stand-alone and they support only embedded items.

✦ **Full-server.** Choose this option if you want your application to have the ability to create and manage compound document objects. A server is an application that can create OLE items for use by container applications. Full servers are applications that can run stand-alone and support both linked and embedded items.

✦ **Both container and server.** This option creates an application that is both a container and a server.

✦ **Yes, please.** Select this option to serialize your OLE container application's documents using the OLE compound-file format. The compound-file format stores a document that contains one or more OLE objects to one file and still allows access to the files of the individual OLE objects.

✦ **No, thank you.** If you select this option, AppWizard creates an application that does not serialize your OLE container application's documents using the OLE compound-file format.

The two radio buttons at the bottom of the dialog box shown in Figure 5.3 can be used to create applications that use OLE automation and OLE controls. OLE automation allows your application to call functions from programs written in other languages, such as Visual Basic, and allows programs written in other languages to call functions that are implemented in your program.

✦ **OLE automation.** Select this option if you want your application to be accessible to OLE automation clients, such as Microsoft Excel. For more information about OLE automation, see "OLE Automation and OLE Controls" section later in this chapter.

✦ **OLE controls.** Choose this option if you want your application to use OLE controls which are described in "OLE Controls" near this end of this chapter. If you do not choose this option at installation time but change your mind later, you must add a call to `AfxEnableControlContainer` to your application's `InitInstance` member function to make your program compatible with OLE controls.

Although Windows implements OLE controls using OLE automation technology, you don't have to select **OLE automation** in the dialog box shown in Figure 5.3 to use OLE controls in your application; selecting **OLE controls** is sufficient.

Building the MINIOLE Program

You can find the MINIOLE program in this chapter's folder on the accompanying disk. To build your own copy of the program, compile and link it in the same way you would build any other AppWizard program. Select the **Container** radio button when AppWizard opens the dialog box shown in Figure 5.3. Then complete the build process and execute the program.

Architecture of the MINIOLE Program

When you use AppWizard to build an OLE container application, AppWizard creates one extra source file that is not generated for ordinary non-OLE applications. This extra file, named **CNTRITEM.CPP** in the MINIOLE project, is shown in Listing 5.1.

LISTING 5.1 THE CNTRITEM.CPP FILE.

```
// CntrItem.cpp : implementation of the CMiniOLECntrItem class
//

#include "stdafx.h"
#include "MiniOLE.h"

#include "OLEDoc.h"
#include "OLEView.h"
#include "CntrItem.h"

#ifdef _DEBUG
#define new DEBUG_NEW
```

```
#undef THIS_FILE
static char THIS_FILE[] = __FILE__;
#endif

/////////////////////////////////////////////////////////////////////////////
// CMiniOLECntrItem implementation

IMPLEMENT_SERIAL(CMiniOLECntrItem, COleClientItem, 0)

CMiniOLECntrItem::CMiniOLECntrItem(CMiniOLEDoc* pContainer)
    : COleClientItem(pContainer)
{
    // TODO: add one-time construction code here

}

CMiniOLECntrItem::~CMiniOLECntrItem()
{
    // TODO: add cleanup code here

}

void CMiniOLECntrItem::OnChange(OLE_NOTIFICATION nCode, DWORD dwParam)
{
    ASSERT_VALID(this);

    COleClientItem::OnChange(nCode, dwParam);

    // When an item is being edited (either in-place or fully open)
    //  it sends OnChange notifications for changes in the state of the
    //  item or visual appearance of its content.

    // TODO: invalidate the item by calling UpdateAllViews
    //  (with hints appropriate to your application)

    GetDocument()->UpdateAllViews(NULL);
    // for now just update ALL views/no hints
}

BOOL CMiniOLECntrItem::OnChangeItemPosition(const CRect& rectPos)
{
    ASSERT_VALID(this);
```

```
        // During in-place activation CMiniOLECntrItem::OnChangeItemPosition
        //  is called by the server to change the position of the in-place
        //  window.  Usually, this is a result of the data in the server
        //  document changing such that the extent has changed or as a result
        //  of in-place resizing.
        //
        // The default here is to call the base class, which will call
        //  COleClientItem::SetItemRects to move the item
        //  to the new position.

        if (!COleClientItem::OnChangeItemPosition(rectPos))
            return FALSE;

        // TODO: update any cache you may have of the item's rectangle/extent

        return TRUE;
}


void CMiniOLECntrItem::OnGetItemPosition(CRect& rPosition)
{
        ASSERT_VALID(this);

        // During in-place activation, CMiniOLECntrItem::OnGetItemPosition
        //  will be called to determine the location of this item.  The default
        //  implementation created from AppWizard simply returns a hard-coded
        //  rectangle.  Usually, this rectangle would reflect the current
        //  position of the item relative to the view used for activation.
        //  You can obtain the view by calling CMiniOLECntrItem::GetActiveView.

        // TODO: return correct rectangle (in pixels) in rPosition

        rPosition.SetRect(10, 10, 210, 210);
}


void CMiniOLECntrItem::OnActivate()
{
    // Allow only one in-place activated item per frame
    CMiniOLEView* pView = GetActiveView();
    ASSERT_VALID(pView);
```

```
    COleClientItem* pItem = GetDocument()->GetInPlaceActiveItem(pView);
    if (pItem != NULL && pItem != this)
        pItem->Close();

    COleClientItem::OnActivate();
}

void CMiniOLECntrItem::OnDeactivateUI(BOOL bUndoable)
{
    COleClientItem::OnDeactivateUI(bUndoable);

    // Hide the object if it is not an outside-in object
    DWORD dwMisc = 0;
    m_lpObject->GetMiscStatus(GetDrawAspect(), &dwMisc);
    if (dwMisc & OLEMISC_INSIDEOUT)
        DoVerb(OLEIVERB_HIDE, NULL);
}

void CMiniOLECntrItem::Serialize(CArchive& ar)
{
    ASSERT_VALID(this);

    // Call base class first to read in COleClientItem data.
    // Since this sets up the m_pDocument pointer returned from
    //   CMiniOLECntrItem::GetDocument, it is a good idea to call
    //   the base class Serialize first.
    COleClientItem::Serialize(ar);

    // now store/retrieve data specific to CMiniOLECntrItem
    if (ar.IsStoring())
    {
    // TODO: add storing code here
    }
    else
    {
    // TODO: add loading code here
    }
}
```

```
//////////////////////////////////////////////////////////////////////////
// CMiniOLECntrItem diagnostics

#ifdef _DEBUG
void CMiniOLECntrItem::AssertValid() const

{

    COleClientItem::AssertValid();

}


void CMiniOLECntrItem::Dump(CDumpContext& dc) const
{
    COleClientItem::Dump(dc);
}
#endif
```

```
//////////////////////////////////////////////////////////////////////////
```

As you can see, **CNTRITEM.CPP** implements a special OLE class named CMiniOLECntrItem. This class manages a number of OLE-related functionalities of the MINIOLE program using OLE-related member functions such as OnChange, OnChangeItemPosition, and OnGetItemPostion. The comments in Listing 5.1 provide brief descriptions of some of these member functions.

Because MINIOLE is OLE-aware, there are extra features in its InitInstance member function, which is implemented in **MINIOLE.CPP**. Part of the program's InitInstance member function appears in Listing 5.2.

LISTING 5.2 PART OF THE MINIOLE PROGRAM'S *INITINSTANCE* MEMBER FUNCTION.

```
BOOL CMiniOLEApp::InitInstance()
{
    // Initialize OLE libraries
    if (!AfxOleInit())
    {
        AfxMessageBox(IDP_OLE_INIT_FAILED);
        return FALSE;
    }
// . . .
```

One special feature of the MINIOLE program's `InitInstance` member function is that it initializes the OLE libraries provided with Visual C++:

```
if (!AfxOleInit()) // . . .
```

You can detect another special feature of an OLE application if you open **OLEDOC.H**, where the MINIOLE program's document class is defined. In an OLE container application, the program's document class is derived from the MFC `COleDocument` class instead of from the `CDocument` class used for non-OLE applications. In **MINIOLE**, the application's document class is defined as follows in **OLEDOC.H**:

```
class CMiniOLEDoc : public COleDocument
{
protected: // create from serialization only
    CMiniOLEDoc();
    DECLARE_DYNCREATE(CMiniOLEDoc)

// Attributes
public:
// . . .
```

Running the **MINIOLE** Program

When you have created and built the MINIOLE program, you can demonstrate its object embedding and in-place editing capabilities by choosing **Insert New Object** from the program's Edit menu (Figure 5.4). AppWizard then opens a dialog box titled Insert Object (Figure 5.5).

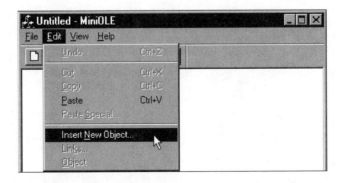

FIGURE 5.4 INSERTING AN OBJECT INTO AN OLE DOCUMENT.

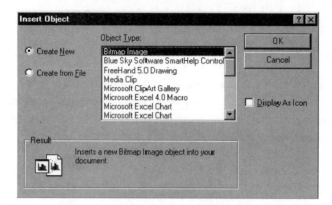

FIGURE 5.5 THE INSERT OBJECT DIALOG BOX.

When the Insert Object dialog box opens, you can examine the capabilities of the MINIOLE program by following these steps:

1. Select **Create from File** and use **Browse** to navigate to a bitmap file named **JEREMY.BMP**, which you can find in the same folder where MINIOLE is stored. When you have found the **JEREMY.BMP** file, open it. MINIOLE then uses object embedding to display the **JEREMY.BMP** file in its document window, as shown in Figure 5.6.

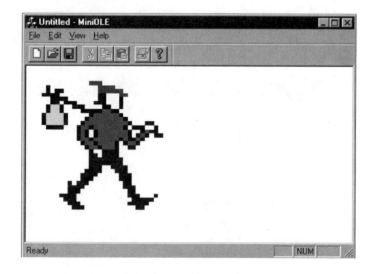

FIGURE 5.6 EMBEDDING A DOCUMENT IN AN OLE CONTAINER.

2. Select **Edit|Bitmap Object** and choose the Edit pop-up menu. MINIOLE then opens the Windows Paint applet (or an alternate default drawing program, if you have one installed), as shown in Figure 5.7. Then you can edit the bitmap you have displayed using in-place editing.

3. When you have finished editing **JEREMY.BMP** , you can save it in its new form if you like. Then you can close **JEREMY.BMP** but leave the MINIOLE program open by choosing the **File|New** menu item.

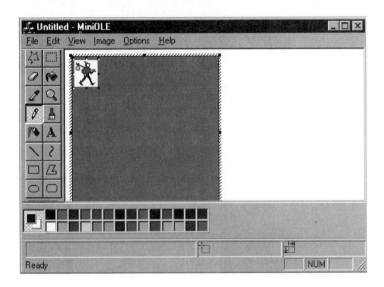

FIGURE 5.7 OPENING A PAINTING PROGRAM TO EDIT A BITMAP.

MINIOLE is a bare-bones application that approaches the limits of its capabilities by displaying a bitmap and letting you edit and save it. FASTDRAW is a much more ambitious application that demonstrates many more features of OLE.

OLE and the Component Object Model

All the different parts that make up OLE have one thing in common: They rely on COM, a set of standards and specifications. The COM standard, implemented in a set of functions called the COM API, is much like a communications protocol; it lays down a set of rules that allow OLE-aware applications and processes to call functions that reside in other applications or processes.

The component object model derives its name from the fact that it defines a model that applications can use to create and manage *component objects*—that is, reusable OLE objects containing data and procedures that can be accessed in binary form from remote applications and processes. To use the component object model, applications and processes must issue their requests for access in accordance with the standards and specifications defined in the COM API.

OLE and the COM standard are so closely related that the two terms are often used interchangeably. However, their meanings are subtly different. Strictly speaking, OLE is a collection of functions, objects, and interfaces that comply with the COM standard. Although they overlap in many areas, OLE and the COM standard are implemented in different APIs.

COMPARING VISUAL C++ WITH OLE

The component object model and the OLE API encompass such a complex collection of features and capabilities that it is hard to paint one picture that takes everything in. But if you're familiar with Visual C++ and the MFC library (and at this point in this book, you surely must be), I think I can give you some idea of what OLE and the COM standard are all about by briefly describing some of the similarities and differences between Visual C++ and OLE.

This comparison has validity because Visual C++ and OLE have three major goals in common. They use object-oriented techniques to help programmers do these three things:

+ Write reusable code.
+ Share code across different platforms and different operating systems.
+ Protect data from being inadvertently modified by functions that access it from outside the function in which it is defined.

To shed light on how the COM standard and OLE accomplish these three goals, we'll take a look at some of the most important similarities and differences between the OLE approach to object-oriented programming and the approach used in Visual C++ and MFC:

+ *Similarity*: OLE, like C++, is object-oriented. C++ objects are structures that have member variables and member functions. OLE objects also have member variables, which are called *properties*, and member functions, which are called *methods*.

✦ *Difference*: To create a C++ program, you generally write it using C++ source code and then build it using a compiler and a linker that is specific to a single language (C++), a particular kind of computer, and a particular operating system. In contrast, COM is a *binary standard* that is language-independent, machine-independent, and even independent of operating systems. When an application creates an OLE object that adheres to the COM standard (as all OLE objects do), the fact that COM is a binary standard makes it possible for other applications to access that object from any Windows-compatible language, from any Windows-compatible computer, and from any Windows-compatible operating system.

✦ *Difference*: In a C++ program, an object can make a direct call to any member function of any other object, provided that the object that owns the member function is in the calling function's scope and has declared the function to be public (or protected, if the calling function is in a derived class). In OLE, the only way that an object can access a member function of another object is to use an interface to set up a communications channel with the object that owns the function. An OLE interface is a language-specific mechanism that applications must use to access OLE objects. OLE objects are not directly accessible to applications at a source-code level, because they are binary objects. But OLE interfaces are accessible to source code on one side and to object code on the other. So they can be used to interface programs written in C++ or other languages with binary OLE objects. For more information about OLE interfaces, see "OLE Interfaces" later in this chapter.

✦ *Similarity*: Visual C++ programs can instantiate objects from classes implemented in MFC. As you know, MFC classes have names that begin with the letter *C* followed by another capital letter. In the same way, OLE interfaces have names that begin with the letter *I* followed by a capital letter.

✦ *Similarity*: Most MFC classes are derived from a common base class named `CObject`. In a slightly similar but not identical fashion, all OLE interfaces have access to a base OLE interface named `IUnknown`.

✦ *Difference*: In C++, derived classes inherit behaviors from base classes. OLE objects do not directly inherit behaviors from other classes but can be assigned object behaviors through mechanisms that are available through interfaces. The internal mechanisms of interfaces are complex and beyond the scope of this chapter. I refer you to *Inside OLE* or other OLE-specific books listed in the Bibliography.

◆ *Similarity*: Although OLE doesn't use inheritance, OLE interfaces that you create using Visual C++ are implemented as C++ classes and consequently can use inheritance, just as other kinds of C++ classes can. But the OLE objects that you access through such interfaces do not support C++-style inheritance. This characteristic of interfaces seems confusing at first, but once you start getting a feel for OLE objects and OLE interfaces, things clear up.

◆ *Similarity*: Both C++ and OLE use mechanisms called *v-tables*. In C++, v-tables are used to call virtual functions. When you call a virtual function in C++ using a pointer to a base class, the base class passes the call to a derived class; the results of your call then vary depending on which derived function executes the function. C++ implements this feature by allowing virtual functions to be called using a v-table (Figure 5.8). When you call a virtual function using a v-table, pointers stored in the v-table route the function to the appropriate derived class.

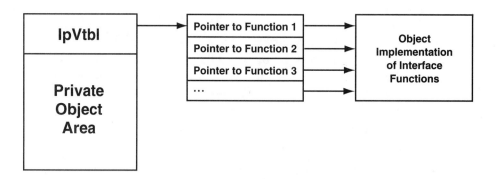

FIGURE 5.8 A V-TABLE.

In OLE, interfaces access OLE objects using a mechanism that works much like the v-table shown in Figure 5.8. The access table that OLE interfaces provide is introduced in the section titled "C++ V-Tables and OLE Interfaces" later in this chapter.

SIMILARITIES BETWEEN OLE AND MFC

Now that we've compared OLE with Visual C++, let's take a look at some comparisons between OLE and MFC. OLE interfaces have a number of things in common with MFC classes in addition to the way they are named. These are some of the similarities between the COM standard and the MFC library:

✦ At the source-code level, there is a similarity between the syntax of C++ member functions and the syntax of the methods used by OLE objects. In C++ source code, you can access OLE methods using the same operators that are used to access C++ member functions: the arrow operator (->), the dot operator (.), and the scope resolution operator. For example, `IUnknown::Release` is an OLE method that releases a pointer to an OLE interface when the pointer is no longer needed. (`IUnkown` is an OLE interface that provides clients with pointers to other interfaces; for details, see "C++ V-Tables and OLE Interfaces" in this chapter.)

✦ When you have instantiated an OLE interface, OLE clients can use your interface to set and get the properties of OLE objects using the objects' methods in much the same way that an MFC application gets and sets member variables of objects using `Get` and `Set` member functions.

✦ You can use OLE methods to manipulate OLE interfaces in many other ways, just as you can use member functions to manipulate objects instantiated from C++ classes in C++ applications.

Although you can do all those things by using OLE interfaces, the need to access OLE interfaces directly is an exercise whose importance is diminishing in the world of MFC programming. That's because more and more OLE functionalities are being encapsulated into OLE-related classes in the MFC library. You'll learn more about how MFC encapsulates OLE functionality in "OLE and the MFC Library" later in this chapter.

OLE Clients and OLE Servers

I mentioned earlier that OLE is designed along client-server lines. To make an OLE object available to clients, you need both an OLE client and an OLE object provider, or server. When a client needs access to an OLE object, the client sends a request to a server. The client always makes its request indirectly, through an OLE interface, because that's the only way a client can access an OLE object. When a client's request is granted, the server uses an interface to grant the requested OLE access.

Figure 5.9 shows how clients and servers communicate through interfaces using OLE technology.

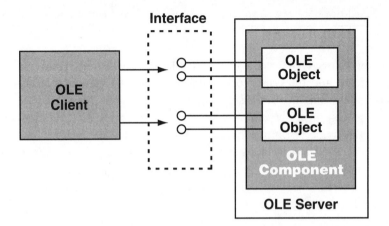

FIGURE 5.9 HOW CLIENTS AND SERVERS COMMUNICATE THROUGH OLE INTERFACES.

By convention, OLE interfaces are represented as small open circles at the ends of straight lines. These circles are modeled after the small circles in electronics diagrams that represent plug-in jacks. This representation is used to show that when an OLE client needs to access an OLE object through an interface, the client must plug into that interface. To extend the electronics analogy, before a client can use an interface that plugs into an object, the client must have a plug that fits—it must be equipped with code that is compatible with the methods that the object defines.

When a client is granted access to an OLE object through an OLE interface, the client receives a pointer to the interface. Then the client can safely use the binary OLE object on the other side of the interface without needing to know any details of how the object is implemented. This is how OLE implements data encapsulation—the safeguarding of data from unwanted modification by outside functions. When a client obtains access to an OLE object through an interface, details of the object's implementation are not provided to the client. The client has no need for them and no business knowing anything about them, because OLE guarantees that objects accessed using OLE interfaces always behave the same way. That's one way the OLE system simplifies code reuse and code sharing.

A CONTRACT WITH OLE

Because OLE interfaces provide clients with transparent but safe remote access to OLE objects, an OLE interface is sometimes said to have a *contract* with each of its clients.

This contract defines what an OLE interface does and does not provide to its clients. An OLE interface always honors its contracts with clients even if the client is running on a different operating system, is written in a different computer language, or is implemented in a version of an application that the interface has never encountered.

By defining interfaces as contracts between objects and their clients, the COM standard offers a solution for a thorny versioning problem that has long plagued software developers. The COM strategy for handling this problem is based on the way OLE implements an object-oriented mechanism called polymorphism: the ability of different objects to handle the same instruction in different ways, eliminating the need for an application to issue different sets of instructions to each object. For more details on how polymorphism is handled in OLE, see "How OLE Implements Polymorphism" later in this chapter.

The exact way in which OLE smoothes out versioning problems is another specialized feature of OLE that is beyond the scope of this chapter. It's sufficient to say that in C++, OLE interfaces are implemented as DLLs designed to deal with difficult problems regarding versioning, licensing, and registration. If you're interested in such issues, you should get a copy of *Inside OLE* or another good book that deals with OLE in more detail.

I can say, though, that because OLE handles versioning as transparently as it handles code sharing, software vendors can use OLE to mix and match different versions of applications and their supporting libraries in a way that was never before possible. If a software manufacturer markets applications and libraries that are OLE-aware and conform to the COM standard, the manufacturer can ensure that old and new versions of applications and libraries work together by simply leaving old versions of libraries in place when new libraries are developed and added to applications. Then, even when old and new versions of applications are running simultaneously on an individual computer or on a network, they can safely use OLE to share their code and libraries. OLE will handle all potential versioning conflicts safely and transparently.

MARSHALING

When a client requests access to an OLE object, the component object model makes the object accessible to the client using a process called *marshaling*, a term that is often used in OLE to describe the passing of function calls and parameters across process boundaries. Because a COM object's code can execute in a process space that is not the one in which it resides, COM handles the translation of calling conventions when the object and the routine using the object are written in different languages. The COM library also handles the conversion between 16-bit and 32-bit parameters when the object and the routine using the object are running in different process spaces.

For example, if a COM object is executing in a 32-bit process space, the COM object might treat data types such as UINT as 32-bit values. The user of the object might be running in a 16-bit process space and might attempt to call a function in the object by passing a 16-bit UINT as a parameter. The COM library, which sits between the two processes, has the responsibility of marshaling the 16-bit UINT into a 32-bit UINT that can be processed by the function that receives the parameter.

Other types, such as pointers and memory handles, are handled in a similar fashion by the COM library. The library makes sure that when an OLE object and the user of an object communicate, each sees the other in terms of its own process space.

OLE Interfaces

Figure 5.10 shows how interfaces work in OLE-aware applications. When a client needs to access an OLE object through an interface, the client must plug into that interface. To extend the electronics analogy, before a client can use a jack (an interface) that plugs into an object, the client must have a plug that fits—it must have code that is compatible with the methods that the object defines.

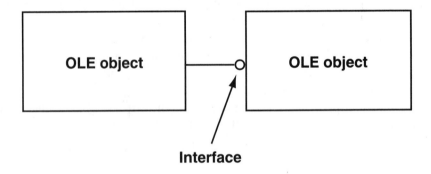

FIGURE 5.10 OLE INTERFACES.

C++ V-TABLES AND OLE INTERFACES

Figure 5.10 also shows how OLE implements data encapsulation—that is, how it protects the methods defined inside OLE objects from being inadvertently changed by other objects.

If you're an intermediate to advanced C++ programmer, you may recognize the similarity between the interface diagram shown in Figure 5.10 and the diagram of a v-table (you saw one such diagram in Figure 5.8 earlier in this chapter.) The interface shown in Figure 5.10 looks like a v-table because, essentially, it *is* one. When an OLE interface is created, it is implemented as an array of pointers to methods defined by the object. Any application that has access to such an array—generally through a pointer that lets the application access the top of the array—can call the methods in the corresponding interface.

The resemblance between a C++ v-table and the OLE interface access table is not coincidental; both mechanisms are designed to implement polymorphism, so it's hardly an accident that they look and work very much alike. Moreover, this similarity makes it convenient for C++ programmers to create OLE objects using C++. The design also makes it easy for C++ programmers to see that when they derive a C++ object class from an OLE interface definition, they can typecast the object's this pointer into an OLE interface pointer.

Another important characteristic of OLE-interface access tables is that they let multiple clients access OLE objects at the same time. OLE interfaces also make it possible for 16-bit and 32-bit objects and applications to communicate with each other. Finally, interfaces make it possible for users of your application to drag a document created with one application into a document created by another application, and to edit the document on the spot, without starting the application that created the document.

HOW OLE IMPLEMENTS POLYMORPHISM

In C++, v-tables are used to implement polymorphism (the ability of different objects to handle the same instruction in different ways), eliminating the need for an application to issue different sets of instructions to each object. Briefly, this is how polymorphism works in C++: When you call a virtual member function of a base class using a pointer, your application can wind up executing a different version of the function that is defined by a derived class. For example, suppose your application defines a base class named CEmployee and a derived class named COffshoreEmployee. Also suppose that your program contains two versions of a virtual member function called PrintAddress: a base class function named CEmployee::PrintAddress and a derived class version named COffshoreEmployee::PrintAddress.

Now suppose that your application creates pointer to the CEmployee class (not the COffshoreEmployee class) and names the pointer pEmployee. And finally, suppose your application calls CEmployee::PrintAddress (not COffshore-Employee::PrintAddress) by executing a pair of statements like this:

```
CEmployee pEmployee = new CEmployee;
pEmployee->PrintAddress();
```

Now the big question: Which version of `PrintAddress` executes—the `CEmployee::`
`PrintAddress` version or the `COffshoreEmployee::PrintAddress` version?

The answer depends on whether `PrintAddress` is virtual. If `PrintAddress` is
declared to be a virtual function, the code we are looking at calls the base class version
(`CEmployee::PrintAddress`). If `PrintAddress` is not a virtual function, the result is
just the opposite: The `COffshoreEmployee::PrintAddress` function (the derived class's
version of the function) is called.

V-TABLES AND THE IUNKNOWN INTERFACE

If you understand how polymorphism works in C, you also understand how it works in
OLE. Because OLE interface access tables are similar to virtual function v-tables, they
work in a similar way. In fact, OLE interfaces are even more miraculous objects than
C++ v-tables are. When an OLE client uses an OLE interface to call a method defined
by an OLE object and if more than one version of the method is available, the OLE
interface that the client is using can carry on a conversation with the client to determine
which version of the method to use.

To initiate this conversation, OLE uses the important OLE interface `IUnknown`.
`IUnknown` is the base OLE interface in much the same way that `CObject` is the base
class for most MFC classes. `IUnknown` is so important that it is implemented as part of
every interface. That's because part of its job is to provide clients with pointers to other
interfaces.

To obtain a pointer to an OLE interface, you call the `IUnknown` method
`QueryInterface`, which returns pointers to interfaces that a given object supports.
Every time a client obtains a new copy of a pointer to a given OLE object, the client
should call the `IUnknown::AddRef` method, which increments a count to keep track of
pointers that have been obtained for OLE objects. When you no longer need to use an
interface pointer, you should call the pointer you have been using.

The OLE API I

OLE is defined and implemented in a set of libraries with names that begin with **OLE**,
such as **OLE32.LIB** and **OLEAUT32.LIB**. All the object-code libraries that implement
OLE functionality are supplied with MFC and Visual C++. **OLE32.LIB** and the other
OLE libraries that come with Visual C++—which I collectively refer to as the OLE API—
are similar to the Windows API in some ways and similar to C++ class library in others.

The functions implemented in the OLE API work closely with those implemented in the COM API, which was described earlier in the section titled "The Component Object Model." Both the OLE API and the COM API are similar to the Windows API. They are made up of raw function calls that work much like the C-language functions implemented in the Windows API. (See Chapter 3, "The Win32 API.") You can access OLE objects from programs written in any Windows-compatible language (such as C or Visual Basic), in the same way that pre-C++ programmers used to call the C-language Windows functions implemented in the Windows API.

One of the most important differences between the OLE API and the Windows API functions is that the OLE API, unlike the Windows API, offers full object-oriented functionality. In this respect, the OLE API has more in common with the object-oriented MFC library than with the non-object-oriented Windows API.

You should not confuse **OLE32.LIB** and Microsoft's other OLE libraries with OLE type libraries, which are customized libraries of OLE information that you can create yourself. OLE type libraries, which are customized libraries of OLE information that you can create yourself. OLE type libraries contain information that let you work with OLE objects without having to know much about their structures. It is beyond the scope of this chapter to go into any more detail about OLE type libraries, but they are thoroughly documented in the on-line help files that come with the Visual C++ compiler.

Table 5.1 lists some of the most important OLE interfaces and briefly explains how they are used in OLE-aware programs.

TABLE 5.1 NAMES AND DESCRIPTIONS OF OLE INTERFACES

Interface	Description
IOleObject	The principal interface for providing embedded objects with the basic functionality that they need to communicate with their containers.
IUnknown	Provides pointers to other interfaces (see "C++ V-Tables and OLE Interfaces" earlier in this chapter).
IClassFactory	Provides two methods (CoGetClassObject and CoCreateInstance) for creating OLE objects.
IConnectionPoint	Creates *connection points*, which allow clients to connect to OLE objects.

continued

TABLE 5.1 CONTINUED

IMarshal	Marshals OLE objects that do not provide their own implementations. (Marshaling is a mechanism that lets a client in one process call functions implemented in another process or to access remote objects running on other machines.)
IMoniker	Contains methods that allow you to use a moniker object, which contains information that uniquely identifies a COM object.
IOleControl	An interface for OLE control objects, which are described in the "OLE Controls" section of this chapter.
IOleControlSite	A container that supports the embedding of OLE controls and implements a site object to manage each control.
IPersist	The base interface for a set of three other persistence-related interfaces. Persistence interfaces are used to access persistent objects (objects that can serialize themselves to a storage, stream, or file). The three other persistence-related objects are IPersistStorage, IPersistStream, and IPersistFile.
IPropertyPage	An interface for managing a property page in a property sheet.

Many other OLE interfaces are introduced and described in other sections of this chapter.

OLE and the MFC Library

Now that you understand the basic principles of OLE, it's time to take a look at how the functionality of the OLE API has been encapsulated into the OLE-related classes and functions provided in MFC. MFC contains OLE classes and member functions that support most of the features offered by OLE, including OLE containers, OLE servers, OLE drag and drop features, OLE automation, OLE file-management features, and OLE controls.

This section examines the OLE-related MFC classes. Figure 5.11 shows the OLE hierarchy in the MFC library, and the tables that follow list and describe the interfaces that are provided in the OLE API.

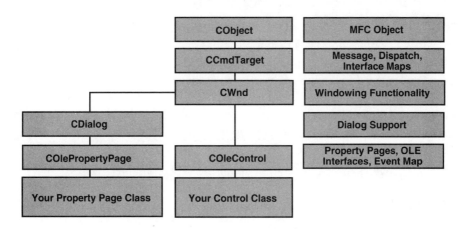

FIGURE 5.11 THE OLE HIERARCHY IN THE MFC LIBRARY.

GENERAL-PURPOSE OLE CLASSES

The MFC library provides four kinds of classes that do not fall into any specific category but are widely used in connection with OLE. Table 5.2 lists and describes these general-purpose OLE classes.

TABLE 5.2 GENERAL-PURPOSE OLE INTERFACES.

Class	Description
COleObjectFactory	Used to create items when requested from other OLE containers. This class serves as the base class for more specific types of factories, including COleTemplateServer.
COleMessageFilter	Used to manage concurrency with OLE lightweight remote procedure calls (LRPC).
COleStreamFile	Uses the OLE IStream interface to provide CFile access to compound files. This class (derived from CFile) enables MFC serialization to use OLE structured storage.
CRectTracker	Used to create rectangles that facilitate the moving, resizing, and reorientation of in-place OLE objects. You can create editing and object-moving and object-sizing rectangles that can be equipped with many kinds of special features, such as dotted or hatched outlines, hatched interiors, and resizing handles.

OLE Container Classes

MFC provides a number of classes that applications can use to create OLE containers. For example, the COleLinkingDoc and COleDocument classes can be used to manage collections of COleClientItem objects. The document classes in OLE-aware applications are not derived from CDocument, but from either from COleLinkingDoc or COleDocument, depending on whether you want support for links to objects embedded in your document. You can use a COleClientItem object to represent each OLE item in your document that is embedded from another document or is a link to another document.

Table 5.3 provides more information about the OLE container classes.

TABLE 5.3 OLE CONTAINER CLASSES.

Class	Description
COleDocument	Used for OLE compound document implementation as well as basic container support. Serves as a container for classes derived from CDocItem. This class can be used as the base class for container documents and is the base class for COleServerDoc.
COleLinkingDoc	A class derived from COleDocument that provides the infrastructure for linking. You should derive the document classes for your container applications from this class instead of from COleDocument if you want them to support links to embedded objects.
CRichEditDoc	Maintains the list of OLE client items that are in the rich edit control. Used with CRichEditView and CRichEditCntrItem.
CDocItem	Abstract base class of COleClientItem and COleServerItem. Objects of classes derived from CDocItem represent parts of documents.
COleClientItem	A client item class that represents the client's side of the connection to an embedded or linked OLE item. Derive your client items from this class.
CRichEditCntrItem	Provides client-side access to an OLE item stored in a rich edit control when used with CRichEditView and CRichEditDoc.
COleException	An exception resulting from a failure in OLE processing. This class is used by both containers and servers.

OLE Server Classes

MFC contains one collection of classes that are used exclusively by server applications. In OLE, server documents are derived from COleServerDoc rather than from

CDocument, COleLinkingDoc, or COleDocument. However, COleServerDoc is derived from COleLinkingDoc, so server documents can also be containers that support linking.

Another OLE server class is COleServerItem, which can be used to instantiate a document or portion of a document that can be linked to or embedded in another document.

COleIPFrameWnd and COleResizeBar are OLE server classes that support in-place editing of an object when the object is in a container. Another OLE server class, COleTemplateServer, supports the creation of OLE-aware document-view pairs so that OLE objects from one application can be dropped into another application and edited there.

Table 5.4 lists and describes the OLE server classes.

TABLE 5.4 OLE SERVER CLASSES.

Class	Description
COleServerDoc	The base class for server application document classes. COleServerDoc objects provide most of the support for OLE servers through interactions with COleServerItem objects. Visual editing capability is provided using the class library's document-view architecture.
CDocItem	Abstract base class for COleClientItem and COleServerItem. Objects of classes derived from CDocItem represent parts of documents.
COleServerItem	Used to instantiate the OLE interface to COleServerDoc items. A server document usually has one COleServerDoc object, which represents the embedded part of a document. In servers that support links to parts of documents, there can be many COleServerItem objects, each of which represents a link to a portion of the document.
COleIPFrameWnd	Provides the frame window for a view when a server document is being edited in place.
COleResizeBar	Provides the standard user interface for in-place resizing. Objects of this class are always used in conjunction with COleIPFrameWnd objects.
COleTemplateServer	Used to create documents using the framework's document-view architecture. A COleTemplateServer object delegates most of its work to an associated CDocTemplate object.
COleException	An exception resulting from a failure in OLE processing. This class is used by both containers and servers.

OLE DRAG-AND-DROP DATA-TRANSFER CLASSES

MFC contains a special group of classes that can be used to create objects used in OLE data transfers. These classes, called the OLE drag-and-drop transfer classes, allow data to be transferred between applications by using the Clipboard or through drag and drop. They are listed and described in Table 5.5.

TABLE 5.5 OLE DRAG-AND-DROP TRANSFER CLASSES.

Class	Description
COleDropSource	Controls the drag-and-drop operation from start to finish. This class determines when the drag operation starts and when it ends. It also displays cursor feedback during the operation.
COleDataSource	Instantiates objects that are used when an application provides data for a data transfer. COleDataSource could be viewed as an object-oriented Clipboard object.
COleDropTarget	Instantiates objects used as targets of drag-and-drop operations. A COleDropTarget object corresponds to a window on screen. It determines whether to accept any data dropped onto it and implements the actual drop operation.
COleDataObject	An object instantiated from the COleDataObject class can be used as the receiver side to COleDataSource. COleDataObject objects provide access to the data stored by a COleDataSource object.

OLE COMMON DIALOG BOX CLASSES

Several classes in the MFC library can help the user of your application perform common OLE tasks by implementing a number of standard OLE dialog boxes. These classes, known as the OLE common dialog box classes, also provide a consistent user interface for OLE functionality. Table 5.6 lists and describes the OLE common dialog box classes that are provided in MFC.

TABLE 5.6 OLE COMMON DIALOG BOX CLASSES.

Class	Description
COleDialog	Base class used by MFC to contain common implementations for all OLE dialog boxes. All dialog box classes in the user interface category are derived from this base class. COleDialog cannot be used directly.
COleInsertDialog	Displays the Insert Object dialog box, the standard user interface for inserting new OLE linked or embedded items.
COlePasteSpecialDialog	Displays the Paste Special dialog box, the standard user interface for implementing the **Edit Paste Special** command.
COleLinksDialog	Displays the Edit Links dialog box, the standard user interface for modifying information about linked items.
COleChangeIconDialog	Displays the Change Icon dialog box, the standard user interface for changing the icon associated with an OLE embedded or linked item.
COleConvertDialog	Displays the Convert dialog box, the standard user interface for converting OLE items from one type to another.
COlePropertiesDialog	Encapsulates the Windows common OLE Properties dialog box. Common OLE Properties dialog boxes provide an easy way to display and modify the properties of an OLE document item in a manner consistent with Windows standards.
COleUpdateDialog	Displays the Update dialog box, the standard user interface for updating all links in a document. The dialog box contains a progress indicator for the update procedure.
COleChangeSourceDialog	Displays the Change Source dialog box, the standard user interface for changing the destination or source of a link.
COleBusyDialog	Displays the Server Busy and Server Not Responding dialog boxes, the standard user interface for handling calls to busy applications. Usually displayed automatically by the COleMessageFilter implementation.

OLE Automation Classes

The OLE automation classes in MFC are used to instantiate objects that support OLE automation clients (applications that control other applications). The OLE automation classes do not support OLE automation servers (applications that can be controlled by other applications). OLE automation servers are supported by dispatch maps, which are described in the section headed "Dispatch Maps" later in this chapter.

Table 5.7 lists and describes the OLE automation classes.

Table 5.7 OLE automation OLE classes.

Class	Description
COleDispatchDriver	Instantiates objects that are used to call automation servers from automation clients. ClassWizard uses this class to create type-safe classes for automation servers that provide a type library.
COleDispatchException	An exception resulting from an error during OLE automation. OLE automation exceptions are thrown by automation servers and caught by automation clients.

OLE Control Classes

The OLE control classes are the classes you'll use most often when you create and implement OLE controls. The COleControlModule class is the OLE control equivalent to the CWinApp class used in Windows applications. Each module you create using COleControlModule implements one or more OLE controls. In turn, each control is instantiated from a COleControl object. OLE controls communicate with their containers using CConnectionPoint objects.

The CPictureHolder and CFontHolder classes encapsulate OLE interfaces for pictures and fonts used in OLE controls, and the COlePropertyPage and CPropExchange classes help you implement property pages and property persistence for your control.

Table 5.8 lists and describes the OLE control classes. The "OLE Controls" section of this chapter shows how you can create and use OLE controls in your Windows applications.

TABLE 5.8 OLE CONTROL CLASSES.

Class	Description
COleControlModule	The OLE control module equivalent of the CWinApp class. Classes derived from COleControlModule are used to develop objects used as OLE control module objects. It provides member functions for initializing your OLE control's module.
COleControl	The main class used for creating OLE controls. The COleControl class, derived from the CWnd class, inherits all the functionality of a Windows window object plus additional functionality specific to OLE, such as event firing and the ability to support methods and properties. So objects derived from COleControl are used to create an OLE control.
CConnectionPoint	Implements a special type of interface, called a connection point, used to communicate with other OLE objects. A connection point is an outgoing interface that initiates actions on other objects, such as firing events and change notifications.
CPictureHolder	Encapsulates the functionality of a Windows picture object and the IPicture OLE interface; used to implement the custom Picture property of an OLE control.
CFontHolder	Encapsulates the functionality of a Windows font object and the IFont OLE interface; used to implement the stock Font property of an OLE control.
COlePropertyPage	Objects instantiated from COlePropertyPage display the properties of an OLE control in a property-page dialog box.
CPropExchange	Supports the implementation of property persistence for your OLE controls. Analogous to CDataExchange for dialog boxes.

Example: The FASTDRAW Program

FASTDRAW, one of this chapter's example programs, shows how you can use OLE to implement object embedding in Windows NT programs. FASTDRAW shows how you can embed an object created by one application in a document created by another application and then edit the imported document on the spot, without going through the trouble of opening the application that was used to create it.

To demonstrate some of the features of OLE, FASTDRAW is equipped with a set of features that make it qualify as an *OLE container*. An OLE container, sometimes referred to as an OLE client, is an object that can import other objects for in-place visual editing.

To see how FASTDRAW uses object embedding and in-place editing, open the program and choose **Insert New Object** from the Edit menu. FASTDRAW displays the Insert Object dialog box (Figure 5.12), which you can use to link any OLE object with FASTDRAW, or to embed any OLE object inside the FASTDRAW window you have opened.

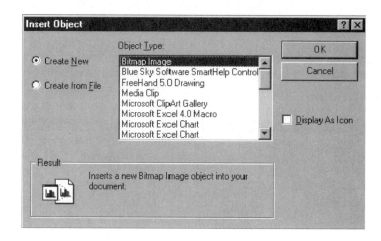

FIGURE 5.12 THE FASTDRAW PROGRAM'S INSERT OBJECT DIALOG BOX.

About FASTDRAW

FASTDRAW is based on two sample Microsoft programs that you can find in the Samples folder on the Visual C++ CD-ROM. One of those programs is SCRIBBLE, a simple drawing application that Microsoft uses extensively in its Visual C++ tutorials. The other program is DRAWCLI, which was designed to illustrate the use of OLE but also demonstrates many line-drawing and shape-drawing techniques that are often used in graphics programs.

The FASTDRAW program also shows the features you must incorporate into an application to qualify the program for Microsoft's "Windows-compatible" logo. To learn more about that feature, read the README file in the DRAWCLI project's folder, which can be found inside the Sample folder on the Visual C++ CD-ROM.

Still another feature of FASTDRAW is that it shows how to write a program that complies with all the requirements to earn a Windows-compatible logo. For more information on this topic, see the README file in the FASTDRAW folder on the accompanying disk.

ARCHITECTURE OF THE **FASTDRAW** PROGRAM

FASTDRAW is a Visual C++ program written with AppWizard, so it has the standard document-view architecture that is common to MFC framework applications. It also contains some extra files that are used for special purposes. For more information about those, see the section "Extra Files in the FASTDRAW Program" later in this chapter.

Because FASTDRAW is compiled as an OLE client, the program's document class, CDrawDoc, is derived from COleDocument instead of from CDocument.x

CDrawDoc is equipped with several special menu commands that are provided by COleDocument. These menu commands, used only by OLE containers, are **Edit Paste**, **Paste Link**, and **Links**. By experimenting with FASTDRAW, you can see how these menu commands work in an OLE client application.

The FASTDRAW program's view-object class, CDrawView, is derived from the MFC CScrollView class. Most of the program's graphics features, which do not rely on OLE, are implemented in CDrawView.

HOW **FASTDRAW** WORKS

FASTDRAW creates its Insert Object dialog box using the MFC COleInsertDialog class, the standard user interface for accessing new or existing OLE components and placing them in windows using either object linking or object embedding. The Insert Object dialog box is a common Windows dialog box, so you can also use it in your own Windows NT applications.

When the Insert Object dialog box opens, you can either create a new OLE object for linking and embedding or import an existing object from a file. You can even navigate to a directory that contains the object you want to retrieve by clicking **Browse**.

IMPORTING **OLE** OBJECTS

It's beyond the scope of this chapter to present a detailed description of object linking and embedding and to explain all the intricacies of how in-place activation works. But by experimenting with FASTDRAW and examining its source code, you can get enough hands-on experience to see how the mechanism works. If you're interested in learning more about object embedding and in-place editing, you can refer to Books Online and some of the books in the Bibliography that cover the whole topic of OLE in more detail.

Figure 5.13 shows the FASTDRAW main window when the user has opened a new OLE-aware document—in this case, a Microsoft Word document—for editing inside the FASTDRAW document window. Notice that the decorations around the FASTDRAW window, including the window's menu bar, modified themselves to take on the look of a Microsoft Word document. But the client area of the window has not changed; it still displays the grid lines shown previously in Figure 5.12.

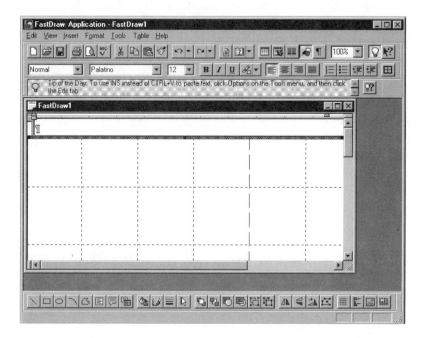

FIGURE 5.13   CREATING A WORD PROCESSING DOCUMENT IN AN OLE CLIENT WINDOW.

Figure 5.14 shows what happens when the user types a line inside the program's embedded word processing window and then deactivates Microsoft Word. The user can the restore the focus to the FASTDRAW window by clicking the mouse in an area of the client window that lies outside the Word window. Notice that the Microsoft Word menu items and gad gets have now disappeared and have been replaced by the original FASTDRAW gadgetry. But the Word document that has been created and embedded in the window is still there. The sizing handles that appear when you select show that it has now become just another object inside the FASTDRAW window.

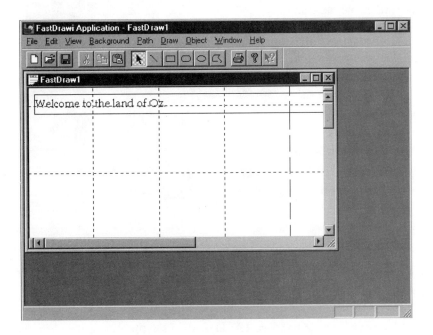

FIGURE 5.14 RETURNING THE FOCUS TO THE FASTDRAW WINDOW.

SIZING HANDLES AND THE CRECTTRACKER CLASS

FASTDRAW lets you fill closed shapes with any color you like, and it equips all the shapes it draws with sizing handles (little black squares) that you can use not only to size shapes but also to select them for cutting, copying, and pasting. You can also use the handles of any shape to drag the shape around. Figure 5.15 shows how sizing handles can be placed around objects in FASTDRAW.

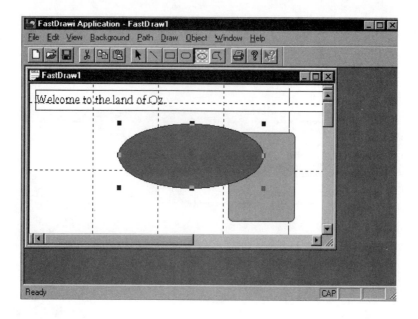

FIGURE 5.15 SIZING HANDLES.

The FASTDRAW program's sizing handles put on their best show when you create or select a polygon. By grabbing a polygon handle with the mouse and dragging it around, you can dramatically modify the polygon by changing the lengths and positions of its sides.

To implement its sizing handles, FASTDRAW uses the CRectTracker MFC class. You can read more about CRectTracker and examine other sample programs that show how it's used by consulting the on-line help files that came with your Visual C++ compiler.

USING THE FASTDRAW PROGRAM

Figure 5.16 shows a FASTDRAW window after some shapes have been drawn in it and some embedded bitmaps have been imported into it for editing. FASTDRAW can save and load drawings that have been created by other applications and can perform various other kinds of OLE magic. For example, try playing around with the pop-up menus you can display by right-clicking the mouse; you can use those menus to open property pages for viewing and changing the properties of the OLE objects used in the program.

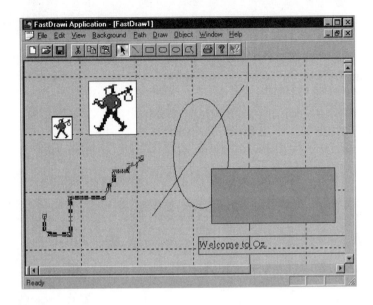

FIGURE 5.16 DRAWING SHAPES AND EDITING BITMAPS.

To draw objects using FASTDRAW, you choose items from the program's Draw, Object, and View menus. To see how the program draws lines using the CDC class's LineTo and MoveTo member functions, choose the **Draw|Line** menu item.

NON-OLE FEATURES OF THE **FASTDRAW** PROGRAM

Along with introducing you to object embedding and in-place activation, FASTDRAW demonstrates a number of graphics features provided by Visual C++ and Windows NT. By choosing commands from the program's Draw menu, you can draw the standard shapes that are ordinarily provided in drawing programs: lines, rectangles, round-cornered rectangles, ellipses, and polygons. To draw lines and shapes, FASTDRAW calls member functions of C++ classes implemented in MFC.

When you have drawn a shape using FASTDRAW, you can select the shape by either double-clicking the mouse over it or choosing **Draw|Select**. You can then cut or copy the shape or drag it around in a window. When you have finished a drawing, you can save it to disk. You can load saved drawings into memory, modify them, and save them in their new forms.

You can set and change the colors of objects you create with FASTDRAW, and you can change the background color of any drawing. When you choose the **Background\ Color** menu item, FASTDRAW displays the MFC common color dialog box, a useful color picker that you can easily incorporate into your own Windows NT applications.

FASTDRAW can display gridlines in its window, as shown in Figure 5.17. You can make these lines visible or invisible by toggling **View\Grid Lines**, and you can change the color of the window's background by choosing **Background\Color**.

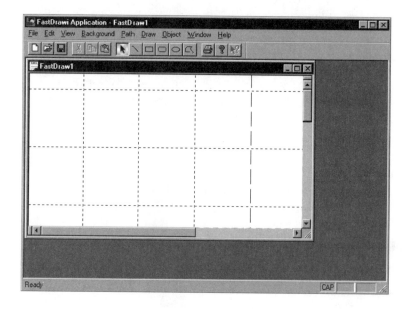

FIGURE 5.17 GRIDLINES.

EXTRA FILES IN THE **FASTDRAW** PROGRAM

Along with its standard MFC framework files FASTDRAW contains some extra files that are used for special purposes. Some of them implement dialog boxes and features of OLE, and you can study them at your leisure. Here are the additional files that we are more immediately interested in:

+ **DRAWTOOL.H** and **DRAWTOOL.CPP**, which define and implement classes of tools that can draw figures in windows. Classes implemented in **DRAWTOOL.CPP** include `CRectTool`, `CLineTool`, and classes for all the other shapes that FAST-DRAW can draw.

✦ **DRAWOBJ.H** and **DRAWOBJ.CPP**, which draw figures on the screen using the drawing-tool classes defined and implemented in **DRAWTOOL.H** and **DRAWTOOL.CPP**.

DRAWTOOL.CPP contains a set of message-handling functions that determine which drawing tools should be used when the user chooses menu items, clicks mouse buttons, or moves the mouse. Initially, such events are trapped by a message map in **DRAWVW.CPP**, the file that implements the program's `CView`-derived class. Each time a message is received, it is passed in the usual way to a message handler that is implemented in **DRAWVW.CPP**. But in FASTDRAW, the message handlers in **DRAWVW.CPP** don't do much; they merely decide what kind of drawing tool can handle each message and then hand off the message to the appropriate drawing tool defined in **DRAWTOOL.CPP**.

FASTDRAW's `CDrawObj` class, implemented in **DRAWOBJ.CPP**, is a base class for objects that are used to draw lines and closed shapes in the program's document window. `CDrawObj` does not rely on OLE. It handles the hit testing, the moving, and the resizing of shapes. All the shapes managed by the program are derived from two classes: `CDrawRect` and `CDrawPoly`.

A class named `CDrawOleObj`, which is derived from CDrawObj, relies on the program's OLE container functionality. `CDrawOleObj` is used to instantiate OLE embedded objects. When `CDrawOleObj` is used to draw an imported OLE object, it delegates the drawing to a `CDrawItem` object (described below). The `CDrawItem` class, derived from another OLE-specific class named `COleClientItem`, handles all the OLE-specific behavior for OLE embedded objects.

FASTDRAW uses `CDrawRect` to create rectangles, rounded rectangles, ellipses, and lines. The `CDrawPoly` class is used to draw polygons. Both classes are independent of the FASTDRAW program's OLE container functionality.

When one of the program's drawing tools receives a message, it analyzes the message and determines how it should be handled. Then it passes the message to a member function that can perform the appropriate action. For example, if the user presses the left mouse button inside a rectangle, a round rectangle, or an ellipse, FASTDRAW executes a message-handling member function named `CRectTool::OnLButtonDown` that is implemented in **DRAWTOOL.CPP**.

The `CRectTool::OnLButtonDown` member function contains a `switch` statement that sets a member variable named `pObj->m_nShape` to match whatever drawing tool the user has chosen at the time drawing begins. If the user has chosen the

Draw|Rectangle menu item before starting to draw, CRectTool::OnLButtonDown sets a member variable named m_nShape (an object of the CObjDraw class) to the value of a constant named rectangle. But if the user has chosen **Draw|Ellipse** when drawing begins, CRectTool::OnLButtonDown sets m_nShape to the value of ellipse.

What happens next depends on whether the user has pressed the left mouse button inside or outside an object of the type of object that has been chosen. If the user chooses **Draw|Rectangle** and then presses the mouse button inside a rectangle object, FAST-DRAW selects the object in which the mouse has been clicked (an action that includes drawing sizing handles around the object) and then tracks OnMouseMove events. Then, each time an OnMouseMove event is detected, the program moves the selected object.

If the user chooses **Draw|Rectangle** and then presses the mouse button *outside* a rectangle object, FASTDRAW creates a new rectangle object, adds it to a list of objects currently displayed in the active window, and then waits for OnMouseMove events. Then, each time an OnMouseMove event is detected, the program changes the size of the new rectangle that the user is drawing. In this scenario, when an OnLButtonUp event occurs, the drawing of a new rectangle is complete.

OLE Controls

When Microsoft introduced version 4.0 of the MFC library, the most valued new feature was full support of OLE controls and OLE control containers. Microsoft had spent months proclaiming that OLE controls would soon be introduced as the 32-bit successors to VBX controls, which had been immensely popular in 16-bit Windows programming but had never been very easy to incorporate into 32-bit applications.

MFC 4.0, with its support of both OLE controls and OLE control containers, finally provided the solution to that problem. Now there are companies devoted solely to marketing OLE controls, in the same way that many vendors specialized in producing VBX controls in the days of Windows 3.1.

WHAT ARE OLE CONTROLS?

More than just 32-bit successors to VBX controls, OLE controls are much more powerful and are much better suited for use in C++ programs. An OLE control, like a VBX control, is a Windows custom control that you can easily incorporate into any application. An OLE control is usually, but not always, a visual element such as a button or a list box. When an OLE control is visible, it is often indistinguishable from an ordinary Windows custom control such as a list box or a group of radio buttons.

It is possible to implement an entire application, such as Microsoft Excel, as an OLE control. It would be a hefty OLE control, but it could be done. More often, an OLE control is a visible object that can interact with the user and can also display values in specific ways—for example, in the form of a pie chart.

The code that implements an OLE control resides in a dynamic link library (DLLs are covered in much more detail in Chapter 8, "Dynamic Link Libraries"). By convention, an OLE control file has the extension .OCX. Typically, an OLE control container uses as many .OCX files as it needs to communicate with its OLE controls, and each OLE control uses the OLE run-time DLL. (See "The OLE Control Run-Time DLLs" later in this chapter.)

Figure 5.18 shows how different kinds of files work together to implement OLE controls.

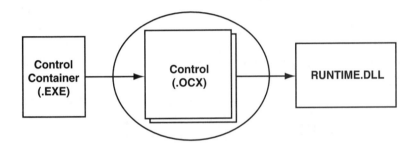

FIGURE 5.18 OLE CONTROL FILES.

OLE controls can be used a wide variety of 16-bit and 32-bit platforms. They can be used on RISC, Power PC, MIPS, and Intel systems, and the list keeps growing. So you can create an OLE control using one operating systems and then just recompile it for use in other systems.

OLE AUTOMATION AND OLE CONTROLS

OLE automation lets software packages make their features and capabilities available to other applications or processes. Most important to Windows NT programmers, OLE automation is the part of OLE that is used to create and manage OLE controls. Later in this chapter, you'll learn how to create your own OLE controls and incorporate them into your Windows NT applications.

You can also use OLE automation to do the following:

✦ Create applications and programming tools that expose objects.

◆ Create and manipulate objects exposed in one application from another application.

◆ Create tools that access and manipulate objects. These tools can include embedded macro languages, external programming tools, object browsers, and compilers.

When an application uses OLE automation to make member functions or member variables available to other applications, it is said to be *exposing* those features. The objects that an application or programming tool exposes using OLE automation are called *OLE automation objects*. Applications and programming tools that access those objects are called *OLE automation controllers*.

The core of OLE automation is the IDispatch interface. Through IDispatch, an OLE automation controller invokes methods and properties that are made available by OLE automation servers. To access an automation object using the OLE API, a client calls an IDispatch method named IDispatch::Invoke, the workhorse of OLE automation. In fact, an OLE automation object is defined as an OLE object that can be accessed by calling IDispatch::Invoke.

This chapter does not present any example programs that show how to use OLE by making direct calls to functions implemented in the OLE API. That's because the focus of the chapter is on creating OLE-aware applications using Visual C++ and MFC. OLE API examples would make the chapter more difficult to understand and probably would not be of much use to most readers. For more information on implementing OLE automation without using MFC, refer to *Inside OLE* or to one of the other books on OLE listed in the Bibliography.

CAPABILITIES AND FEATURES OF OLE CONTROLS

OLE controls share several important features with all OLE automation components. These features include methods, properties, event firing, persistence, and portability. This section describes each of these properties of OLE controls.

Methods and Properties

Methods are the OLE control equivalents of C++ member functions, and *properties* are the OLE control equivalents of C++ member variables. When you create an OLE control, you have the option of equipping it with property pages that the user can open to set and get the control properties. Property pages were introduced in Chapter 1, "Introducing Windows NT."

An OLE control can have four kinds of properties:

+ A *stock property* is a standard property whose semantics are predefined. When you implement a stock property, what you get is its predefined implementation, which is built in. When ControlWizard creates an OLE control, it implements the control's stock properties.

+ A *custom property* is one for which you determine the name, the parameter types, and the return value. You also determine what it actually does.

+ An ambient *property* belongs not to an OLE control but to the *client site* where the control is embedded. (A client is the part of a window or dialog box in which a control is placed; see "OLE Control Containers and Container Sites" later in this chapter.) A control's client site, like the control itself, can be equipped with properties, such as a font or a color. When you embed an OLE control in a client site that has properties, the client site's properties become ambient properties of the control and the control can access those properties.

+ An *extended property* is a property that an OLE control appears to own but that is actually a property of the control's container. Properties of a control that determine the position of the control in a window—such as left, right, and tab position—are often maintained by a control's container instead of by the control. So it is sometimes convenient to implement those kinds of properties as extended properties owned by the container but used by the control.

Event Firing

OLE controls have the ability to notify their containers when they detect important user events such as mouse clicks and data input. When an OLE control notifies its container that such an event has taken place, the control is said to be *firing an event*. Along with detecting user events, OLE controls can implement stock events, such as `Click`, or custom events that may be unique to a particular control.

Persistent Storage

In MFC terminology, a persistent object is one that can be automatically loaded from disk and saved to disk using the MFC serialization mechanism. In OLE, persistence is a property that you can provide to OLE objects by giving them interfaces such as `IPersistStorage` and `IPersistStreamInit`.

When an OLE control has a persistent-storage property, it can automatically store its current state to a disk and load its last known state from a disk without any extra effort on the part of the application that implements it. You can also use persistent storage to create a new instance of an OLE control or to restore an OLE control to a previously stored state.

How OLE Controls are Implemented

OLE controls are implemented as OLE automation components—that is, components that clients access using the `IDispatch` interface. Consequently, OLE controls follow all the rules that must be adhered to by any OLE automation server. Because an OLE control is an OLE automation object, it can be equipped with properties and methods that clients can access to examine property values, set property values, and cause methods to be executed.

Figure 5.19 shows how OLE controls work in an application. At the top of the diagram is an OLE control container. As you can see from the small circles on the diagram, the control container in the illustration implements several OLE interfaces.

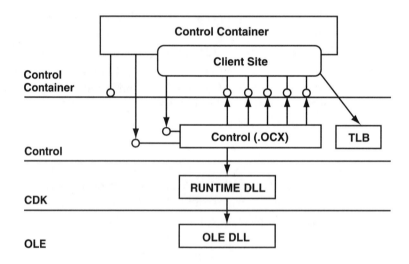

FIGURE 5.19 HOW OLE CONTROLS WORK IN AN APPLICATION.

OLE Control Containers and Container Sites

The rectangle at the top of Figure 5.19 represents an OLE control container. The round-cornered rectangle that is partially embedded in the OLE container represents an OLE container site. When an OLE control is placed in a window, its container site is the part of the window in which the control appears. The container site implements interfaces such as `IOleClientSite`, `IOleInPlaceFrame` (if it supports in-place editing), and `IAdviseSink`.

A server implements interfaces such as IOleObject and IOleInPlaceActiveObject.

Although an OLE control resides inside an OLE container, its immediate owner is its container site. A container site provides a number of interfaces to which an OLE control can connect. A container site can also access the control's container through an OLE interface.

Below the topmost horizontal line in Figure 5.19, is a rectangle that represents an OLE control. As you can see, it is implemented in an .OCX file. (As noted previously, an .OCX file is a type of .DLL that implements an OLE control.) An OLE control can call a number of the interfaces provided by its control site and can also call an interface that accesses its control container.

Type Libraries

On the right-hand side of Figure 5.19, notice the rectangle labeled TLB. It represents a *type library*. In OLE, a type library is a description of a set of interfaces presented by an OLE control. It describes the properties, the methods, and the events that the OLE control implements. If an OLE control is to be accessed from an application, it must have access to a type library. By reading from its type library, an OLE control can determine which properties and methods it can call, and what kinds of events it can implement when it is called upon to do so.

MFC supplies two macros that can provide an OLE control with access to its own type library. To access an OLE control from an application, you must define and declare these macros in the source code that defines and implements the control. DECLARE_OLETYPELIB, must be placed in the control's header (.H) file, and IMPLEMENT_OLETYPELIB must be placed in the control's implementation (.CPP) file. When you create a control using ControlWizard, both macros are automatically created and placed in the proper locations in the control's source files.

The OLE Control Run-Time DLLs

Just below the rectangle labeled Control (.OCX) in Figure 5.19, notice the smaller rectangle labeled RUNTIME DLL. That rectangle represents the OLE control runtime DLLs, a subset of the MFC library that provides all the basic functionality that OLE controls require.

Dynamic link libraries are object-code libraries that are dynamically loaded at runtime. Figure 5.20 illustrates the internal architecture of the OLE control run-time DLLs. As you can see, they supply a number of MFC classes that are specific to OLE controls. The classes provide the following functionalities required by OLE controls:

- ✦ They maintain the .OCX files (the DLLs) in which OLE controls reside.
- ✦ They supply methods that implement stock properties, stock events, and stock methods.
- ✦ They provide stock property pages that you can use in your applications. OLE provides three stock properties you can use to assign properties to OLE controls: one for fonts, one for colors, and one for pictures.
- ✦ They provide a stock property sheet frame in which the three stock property pages can be embedded. This stock frame takes the form of a property sheet—a tabbed dialog box—and the stock pages provided by the run-time DLL take the form of tabbed property pages. (Containers can also provide their own property sheet frames if they so choose.)

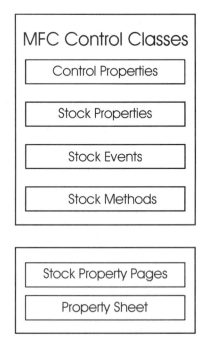

FIGURE 5.20 ARCHITECTURE OF THE OLE RUN-TIME DLLS.

Implementing OLE Controls as In-Process Servers

The mechanism that implements an OLE control is sometimes referred to as an *in-process server*, which is nothing more than a dynamic link library that operates within the context of a single process. (For more about processes, see Chapter 6, "Processes.") An OLE control is typically implemented as an in-process server because an OLE control and the application using it ordinarily reside within the same process. There are exceptions to this rule: In some cases, OLE controls are used by remote processes, such as Web pages accessed over the Internet.

Figure 5.21 is a diagram of an OLE control represented as a classic in-process server. The interfaces are those that are typically implemented by both an OLE control and its server.

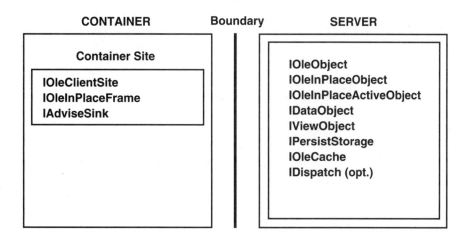

FIGURE 5.21 AN OLE CONTROL IMPLEMENTED AS AN IN-PROCESS SERVER.

Interfaces Implemented by OLE Controls

You can use various kinds of OLE interfaces to expose the methods and data that an OLE control contains. Figure 5.22 shows the kinds of interfaces that can be used to access data and member functions in a typical OLE control.

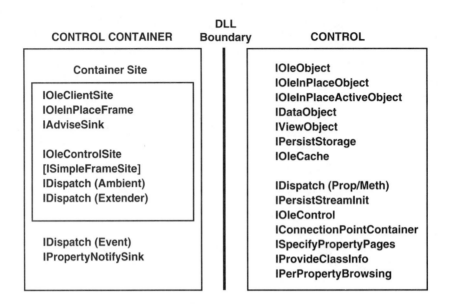

The interface that is used most often to access an OLE control's properties and methods is IDispatch, the primary interface for implementing OLE automation. OLE automation makes it possible for OLE interfaces written in different languages to communicate with each other. The reason that OLE controls usually expose data and member functions through Idispatch is that OLE controls are implemented using OLE automation.

An OLE control container can implement several kinds of IDispatch interfaces, as shown in the left-hand rectangle in Figure 5.22. One IDispatch interface implements ambient properties, which are seen by the OLE control as well as by the control's container sites.

There is also an IDispatch for extended properties, through which an application can communicate with a property of the control or its container without having to know whether the property is owned by the control or its container. In addition, there is an IDispatch for events. When an OLE control implements an event, it tells the container which interface it wants the container to implement. That interface is based on IDispatch, so the container builds an IDispatch interface based on a description in your application's type library.

Another event-related interface is IConnectionPointContainer, shown in the right-hand rectangle in Figure 5.22. IConnectionPointContainer provides an OLE control with connection points, a mechanism that OLE controls use to fire events. Two other important interfaces are `IOleControlSite`, which interfaces a control with its container, and `IOleClientSite`, which interfaces a control with its container site.

Other interfaces that are available to OLE controls include `IPersistStreamInit` and `IPersistStorage`, which implement persistent storage. The `ISimpleFrameSite` interface lets one OLE control contain a group of other controls, such as a group of radio buttons or check boxes. `IPropertyNotifySink` can tell an OLE container that a property value has changed without the container's knowledge. The container can then take appropriate action.

OLE Controls and VBX Controls

One reason OLE controls are such an improvement over VBX controls is that OLE controls are based on MFC classes. In contrast, VBX controls were based on mechanisms provided by Visual Basic. Because OLE controls are MFC-based, they provide all the functionality of C++ classes in general and MFC classes in particular. And, being OLE objects, OLE controls also have all the functionality supplied by the underlying OLE API, such as support for dragging and dropping, support for in-place activation, and a number of other capabilities that were mentioned in the introduction to this chapter.

Creating OLE Controls

The first version of MFC to provide full support for OLE controls was version 4.0. A considerable amount of new functionality was built into the CWnd class in MFC 4.0. As you may recall from Chapter 4, CWnd is the main MFC class for creating and managing windows and other CWnd-derived objects.

Creating OLE Controls in Windows

In MFC 4.0, new code was added to the CWnd class that turned objects into instant containers for OLE controls. Every time you use the Visual C++ AppWizard to generate a framework for a new MFC application, every window, including every child window and every dialog box, is automatically an OLE control container; you don't have to prepare the windows in any special way to equip them with OLE controls. You simply instantiate an OLE control and then initialize it by calling the MFC function CWnd::CreateControl. You can then use your control along all the extra features and capabilities that OLE controls and all other OLE automation objects provide. You'll learn what those features and capabilities are, and how to use them, before you finish this chapter.

Placing OLE Controls in Dialog Boxes

It is even easier to create an OLE control that will be used in a dialog box (or in a window that behaves like a dialog box—for example, a `CFormView` object). That's because Visual C++ has an interactive tool, ControlWizard, that is designed especially for creating OLE controls. ControlWizard is one of the new wizards that were added with the release of Visual C++ 4.0. The Visual C++ ControlWizard is shown in Figure 5.23.

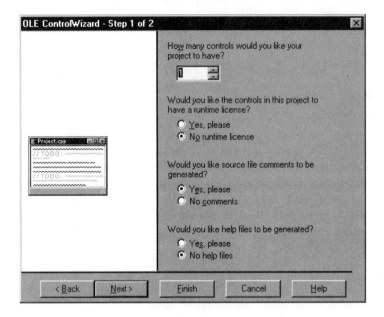

FIGURE 5.23 CONTROLWIZARD.

To add an existing OLE control to a dialog box, you use the Visual C++ utility Component Gallery (demonstrated in "Example: The COMPGAL Program" later in this chapter) to import the control into your application. Then you use the standard tool palette provided by the Visual C++ dialog-box editor to place the control in a dialog box. Then you use ClassWizard to connect your OLE control to a message handler in your application, in the same way you would create a message handler for any dialog-box control.

In some situations—for example, when you need to create an OLE control in a window that is not derived from the `CDialog` class—ControlWizard may lack some of the functionality to you might need. For example, you may need to implement in-place activation—in-place editing of your control inside its container. In such a case, you might have to create the control dynamically, by calling its constructor and then calling the `Create` member function, instead of implementing it interactively using ControlWizard, ClassWizard, and the Developer Studio dialog-box editor. "Implementing OLE Controls," earlier in this chapter, provides more information about implementing an existing OLE control in a Visual C++ application.

OLE CONTROLS AND THE MFC LIBRARY

One reason OLE controls are such an improvement over VBX controls is that OLE controls can be implemented using MFC classes and member functions. In contrast, VBX controls are based on mechanisms provided by Visual Basic and are not very compatible with C++ programs or MFC applications. OLE controls can provide not only the functionality of OLE components but also that of C++ classes in general and MFC classes in particular.

`CObject` is the base class of almost all other classes in MFC, because `CObject` implements the basic MFC run-time object described in Chapter 4. As a result, the `CObject` class and its descendents provide MFC applications with important capabilities, including the ability to obtain run-time type information about classes and support for serialization.

Control Extensions in the MFC Library

MFC 4.0 contains a new set of control extensions designed to support OLE controls. These extensions include a new base class named `COleControl`. In MFC, all OLE controls are derived from `COleControl`.

To support OLE controls, the MFC control extensions do the following:

✦ They implement a standard set of OLE interfaces required for embedded objects.

✦ They implement the `IDispatch` interface to handle the properties and methods of OLE controls.

✦ They expose a set of APIs that make it possible for OLE controls and the container sites to communicate. Figure 5.24 shows the MFC 4.0 OLE class hierarchy.

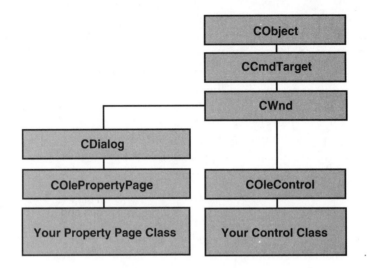

FIGURE 5.24 THE MFC OLE CLASS HIERARCHY.

Another class that isn't OLE-specific but is important in the world of OLE controls is CCmdTarget. As noted in Chapter 4, CCmdTarget is the base MFC class for all classes of objects that can receive and respond to messages. In MFC, CCmdTarget implements message maps, the mechanisms through which functions in Visual C++ applications communicate with each other by sending and receiving messages. OLE controls use a similar kind of map, called a dispatch map.

The COleControl Class

When you want to create an OLE control, you must derive a class from the COleControl class, which is derived from the CWnd class. COleControl implements the standard functionalities required by embedded OLE objects. An embedded object is an OLE interface that is created by one application but can be dragged into a document created by another object and edited there. For example, because Microsoft Excel and Microsoft Word have built-in embedded-object capabilities, you can create a chart in Excel and embed it in a document created by Word. OLE controls require this same kind of support because they can be visually edited.

Figure 5.25 illustrates the process of developing an OLE control.

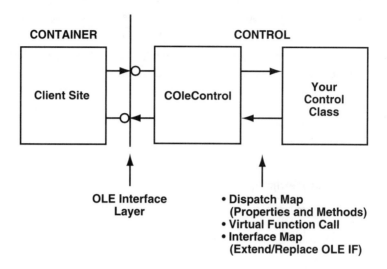

FIGURE 5.25 DEVELOPING AN OLE CONTROL.

COleControl supplies virtual function calls for many of its functionalities so that you can override those functionalities and change them if you need to. Some of the important functionalities supplied by COleControl are as follows:

+ Implementation of any standard OLE interfaces that an OLE control might require. COleControl supports interface maps supplied by MFC, which make it easy to add your own interfaces or other OLE interfaces to your program.

+ Implementation of a dispatch interface that can be used to keep track of the properties and methods of available to OLE interfaces.

+ Exposure of a set of APIs to control container-to-site and site-to-container communication.

DISPATCH MAPS

In a Visual C++ program, when an event takes place in an ordinary Windows custom control the application receives a WM_COMMAND or WM_NOTIFY message. The application then dispatches that message to an appropriate member function of the control's container through a message map. The function to which a message is mapped in this way is often referred to as a *handler* function. By mapping messages to message handlers, a Visual C++ application calls the appropriate member function each time a WM_COMMAND or WM_NOTIFY message is received.

In OLE-aware applications, objects of the `CCmdTarget` class also provide dispatch maps, which OLE automation objects (including OLE controls) use in a similar fashion. In the world of OLE, a dispatch map works much like a message map. When ControlWizard creates an OLE control or adds an existing control to a project, it automatically creates a dispatch map and inserts it into the application's source code. A dispatch map resembles a message map. It looks like this:

```
BEGIN_DISPATCH_MAP(COleCtrlCtrl, COleControl)
    //{{AFX_DISPATCH_MAP(COleCtrlCtrl)
    // NOTE - ClassWizard will add and remove dispatch
    // map entries
    // DO NOT EDIT what you see in these blocks of
    // generated code !
    //}}AFX_DISPATCH_MAP
    DISP_FUNCTION_ID(COleCtrlCtrl, "AboutBox",
    DISPID_ABOUTBOX, AboutBox, VT_EMPTY, VTS_NONE)
END_DISPATCH_MAP()
```

When ControlWizard inserts a message map into a control's source file, the application using the control can track down its properties and methods. Once a dispatch map has been created, ControlWizard uses it to define the properties and methods for the OLE interfaces. Each time a new property or method is defined for an OLE interface, ControlWizard inserts a macro defining that property or method into your application's dispatch map. Subsequently, when an OLE interface with a particular property is needed, your application can use ControlWizard's dispatch maps to track down a `CCmdTarget` object that implements that property.

TESTING AND REGISTERING OLE CONTROLS

When you have created an OLE control, you can test it by running the Test Container application supplied with Visual C++ (Figure 5.26). To use Test Container, just double-click on the **Test Container** icon on the Windows 95 desktop or execute the **Start|Run** taskbar command.

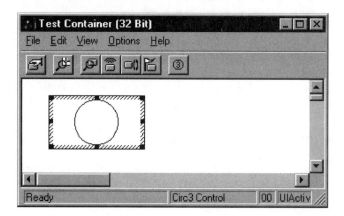

FIGURE 5.26 TESTING AN OLE CONTROL.

When Test Container starts, you can load any OLE control into its window by choosing **Edit|Insert Ole Control.** The control then appears, as shown in Figure 5.26. You can experiment with the control to see whether it does what you want it to do. You can also drag it around the screen by clicking the mouse button in its hatched border and dragging the mouse. You can size it by dragging its sizing handles, and you can flash its color by clicking the mouse in the circle inside the control. You can examine the control's properties by choosing **View|Properties,** and you can view other information about the control and perform other tests on it by choosing other menu commands.

One of the most important features of Test Container is its ability to register OLE controls. Before you can use an OLE control on a particular computer system, you must register it in the system registry (see Chapter 2, "Underneath Windows NT"). When you use an OLE control on the same computer system that was used to create it, registration generally is not a problem. That's because ControlWizard takes care of registering new OLE controls automatically. But before you can use an OLE control that has been created on someone else's computer, it must be registered on your computer system.

If an OLE control is not registered on your system automatically—for example, by an installation program—you can use Test Container to register the control manually.

Example: The OLEDEMO Program

In this section, you'll get a chance to create a simple Windows NT program that displays a dialog box containing an OLE control. You won't create the control; you'll just display it. Later in this chapter, you'll learn how to create your own customized OLE controls and use them in your Windows NT applications.

CREATING THE OLEDEMO PROGRAM

The OLEDEMO sample program lets you register an OLE control manually. To create OLEDEMO, follow these steps:

1. Open Developer Studio if it isn't already open.

2. Use AppWizard to create an application that is an OLE container and supports OLE controls. To generate the application, select the buttons labeled **Container** and **OLE controls** when AppWizard displays the dialog box shown in Figure 5.27.

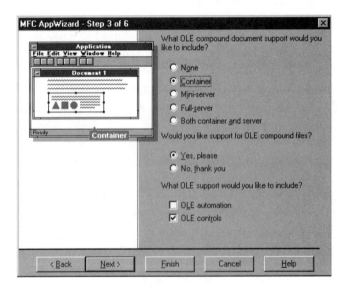

FIGURE 5.27 CREATING A PROGRAM THAT SUPPORTS OLE CONTROLS.

3. When AppWizard finishes creating your application, build the program by choosing Developer Studio's **Build|Build** menu item.

4. Using ControlWizard, create a new OLE control for your application. (For details, see "ControlWizard" later in this chapter.)

5. From Developer Studio's Tools menu, choose **Test Container**. Developer Studio then starts the Test Container application.

6. From the Test Container File menu, choose **Register Controls**. The Controls Registry dialog box then opens (Figure 5.28).

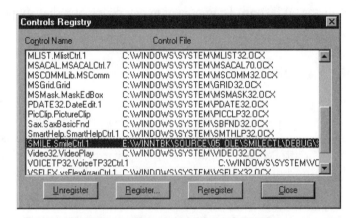

FIGURE 5.28 REGISTERING AN OLE CONTROL.

7. Click the **Register** button. The Register Controls dialog box then opens (Figure 5.29).

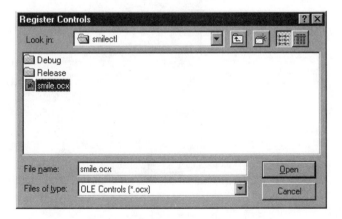

FIGURE 5.29 THE REGISTER CONTROLS DIALOG BOX.

8. Navigate to the directory where you have installed an OLE control and select your OLE control.

9. In the file name list box, double-click your OLE control's **.OCX** filename. Test Container then registers your control and adds it to the list in the Controls Registry dialog box.

10. Close the Controls Registry dialog box by clicking **Close**.

You can now use your OLE control component in any dialog box that supports the use of OLE controls or in any other control container.

ControlWizard

The easiest way (and the recommended way) to create an OLE control is to use Visual C++'s GUI programming tools: ControlWizard, ClassWizard, and the Developer Studio dialog-box editor. ControlWizard is a Visual C++ utility for creating the skeleton of an OLE control DLL. ControlWizard (Figure 5.30) is similar to the Visual C++ AppWizard utility except that instead of generating application frameworks, ControlWizard generates OLE controls.

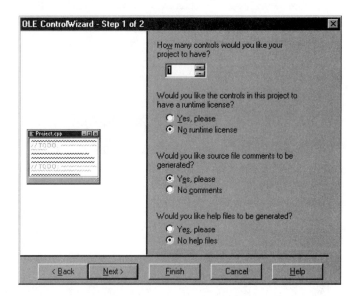

FIGURE 5.30 STARTING CONTROLWIZARD.

In this section, you'll get a chance to open ControlWizard and take a look at how its various features work. In Chapter, you'll get an opportunity to create and implement an OLE control using ControlWizard.

USING CONTROLWIZARD

To open ControlWizard and examine its features, follow these steps:

1. Start Developer Studio if it isn't already running.

2. Open the Developer Studio's **File|New** menu item.

3. When the New dialog box opens (Figure 5.31), select **Project Workspace** from the New list box and click **OK**. Developer Studio then opens a dialog box titled New Project Workspace.

4. Use the **Browse** button to navigate to a folder in which you might want to place an OLE control. Then select the **OLE ControlWizard** icon in the Type list box and click **Create**. Developer Studio opens the first of two ControlWizard dialog boxes.

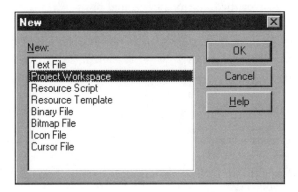

FIGURE 5.31 THE NEW DIALOG BOX.

5. Notice that you can specify how many OLE controls you want to incorporate into your application. You can also click buttons to answer the three other questions in the dialog box. When you click **Next**, Developer Studio displays a second ControlWizard dialog box (Figure 5.32).

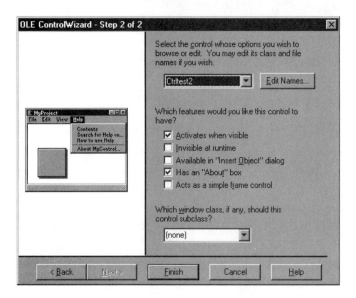

FIGURE 5.32 THE SECOND CONTROLWIZARD DIALOG BOX.

6. When you answer the questions presented in the second ControlWizard dialog box, finish setting up the attributes of your control by clicking **Finish**. Developer Studio then displays an information dialog box. When you click **OK**, ControlWizard creates your OLE control. ControlWizard also adds your new control to your Visual C++ Component Gallery automatically.

WHAT CONTROLWIZARD PROVIDES

These are the functionalities that ControlWizard provides for your OLE control:

✦ An MFC class for your control. When you start ClassWizard, it prompts you for a name for your class. ClassWizard then derives your class from `COleControl`. Your control comes equipped with a set of default methods that you can change to suit your application's requirements.

✦ A set of message maps, dispatch maps, and event maps for your OLE control class. Generally, these maps are empty when ClassWizard first creates your control, although you can have ClassWizard set up a dispatch-map entry for a default About box if you want your control to have one.

✦ A set of stubs that you can fill in with member functions that take care of property access, method access, and other common functionalities. Once your OLE control class is created, you can fill in these empty member functions with executable code. The code you add will give your control's member functions whatever functionality your application requires.

✦ Code to register your OLE control in the system registry. The act of registering a control tells the Windows 95 system that the control exists and where it exists. That's what makes it possible for any OLE-aware applications that may be running on the system to find and use your control.

✦ An object description language (ODL) file for your control. (ODL is a language that Visual C++ uses internally for dealing with OLE controls. If you're interested in learning more about it, refer to *Inside OLE*, which is listed in the Bibliography.)

✦ A property page—that is, a dialog box that you can use to get and set the properties of your OLE control and to set up the code that is called when your control fires events. You can modify this default property page to suit your application's requirements.

ControlWizard generates quite a few files when it creates an .OCX DLL. It also generates a README file that lists each file and explains what it does, so there's no need to provide that information here.

It might be helpful, though, to list some of the most important files and to say a little about them:

✦ **YOURCTL.CPP**. This file implements the class for your OLE control class, which is derived from `COleControl`.

✦ **YOURCTL.H** and **YOURCTL.CPP**. These are your DLL's main source files; they are the files that would be the main application files if you were writing an application instead of a DLL. They implement a class that is derived in turn from `CWinApp`. The **SAMPLE.CPP** file handles such tasks as self registration and initialization.

✦ **YOURCTL.H** and **YOURCTL.PPG**. These files define and implement a default property page that ControlWizard generates for your control.

✦ **YOURCTL.ODL**. Your control's object description language (ODL) file.

Component Gallery

Before you can add an OLE control to a dialog box using the dialog-box editor, you must make the control available to the dialog-box editor's Controls toolbar. The best way to do that is to import the control from the Visual C++ Component Gallery. Before you can import an OLE component from Component Gallery, you must add it to Component Gallery.

When you add an OLE control to Component Gallery, Developer Studio automatically places an icon representing the control on your the dialog-box editor's Controls toolbar. Then you can select the control's icon and place it on a dialog-box template in exactly the same way you would add an ordinary common control to a dialog box using the dialog-box editor.

ADDING AN OLE CONTROL TO A PROJECT STEP BY STEP

To add an OLE control component to a dialog box, these are the general steps to follow:

1. Start Developer Studio if it isn't already started.

2. Open the Visual C++ dialog-box editor and create a new dialog-box template.

3. Choose **Component|Import**. Developer Studio then opens the Component Gallery dialog box.

4. Select the control you want to use and click **Insert** (or just double-click the desired OLE control). An icon representing the control then appears on the dialog-box editor's Controls toolbar, as shown in Figure 5.33.

OLE Control

FIGURE 5.33 PLACING AN OLE CONTROL ON THE CONTROLS TOOLBAR.

5. Select the OLE control you have added to the Controls toolbar and place it in your dialog-box template in the same way you would implement any dialog-box control.

Example: The COMPGAL Program

The COMPGAL example program, in this chapter's folder on the accompanying disk, shows how you can implement an existing OLE control in a Visual C++ application. COMPGAL is an SDI (single document interface) application that was created with AppWizard. When you execute COMPGAL and choose the **Smile Dialog** item from the View menu, the application displays the dialog box shown in Figure 5.34. This dialog box was designed using the Developer Studio dialog box editor. The yellow face is an OLE control. You can toggle back and forth between a smiling face and a frowning face by clicking the button labeled **Demeanor.** Clicking **OK** closes the dialog box.

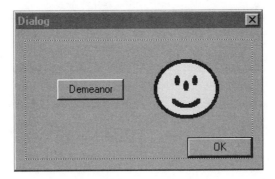

FIGURE 5.34 THE SMILING-FACE DIALOG BOX.

To create a program similar to COMPGAL, these are the steps to follow:

1. Open Developer Studio if it isn't already open.

2. Create an AppWizard application that is a control container and supports OLE controls. Name your application **COMPGAL** and accept AppWizard's defaults for the names of all the program's files.

3. If you haven't done so already, import the smiling-face component named **SMILE.OCX** into Component Gallery.

4. Open the Component Gallery property sheet (Figure 5.35) by selecting the **Insert|Component** menu item, tab to the OLE Controls property page, and click **Import.**

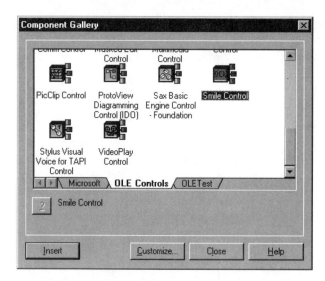

FIGURE 5.35 CREATING AN OLE CONTROL APPLICATION.

5. Select the **SMILE.OCX** icon and click **Insert**.

6. When the Confirm Classes dialog box opens, make sure that only the CSmile click **OK**.

7. When the Component Gallery dialog box regains the focus, close it by clicking **Close**.

8. When the Developer Studio window reclaims the focus, choose the **Insert|Files into project** menu item and add the **SMILE.CPP** and **SMILE.H** files to your project. (They're in the SMILECTL folder inside this chapter's folder on the accompanying disk.)

9. Open the Test Container application and register **SMILE.OCX** by following the steps presented in "Testing and Registering OLE Controls" earlier in this chapter.

10. Using the dialog-box editor, add a dialog box to your application.

11. Using ClassWizard, create a class for your dialog box. Name the dialog-box class CSmileDlg and name the files that define and implement the class **SMILEDLG.CPP** and **SMILEDLG.H**.

12. Add a **SMILE.OCX** control to your dialog-box template and arrange the controls in your dialog box to resemble those shown in Figure 5.36. Notice that the default **Cancel** button has been removed from the dialog-box template and that a button labeled **Demeanor** has been added.

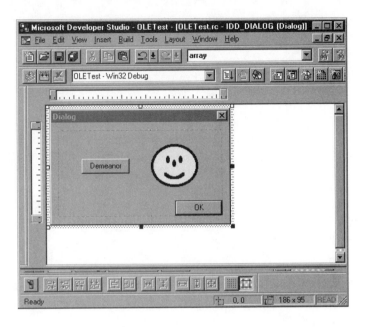

FIGURE 5.36 CREATING THE SMILING-FACE DIALOG BOX.

13. Open ClassWizard and assign a pair of member variables named `m_btnSad` and `m_ctrlSmile` to the `CButton` and `CSmile` classes.

14. Open **COMPGALVIEW.CPP** and insert the following `#include` directive into the appropriate spot in the file (where all the other `#include` directives are):

```
#include "smiledlg.h"
```

15. Using the Visual C++ menu editor, add an item named **Smile Dialog** to your application's main menu.

16. Using ClassWizard, create the following message-handler function for the **Smile Dialog** menu item in **COMPGALVIEW.CPP**:

```
void CCompgalView::OnViewSmiledialog()
{
    // TODO: Add your command handler code here
    CSmileDlg smileDlg;
    smileDlg.DoModal();
}
```

17. Using ClassWizard, create the following BN_CLICKED message handler for the **Demeanor** button in the `CSmileDlg` dialog box.

```
void CSmileDlg::OnButton1()
    {
        if (m_ctrlSmile.GetSad() == TRUE)
            m_ctrlSmile.SetSad(FALSE);
        else m_ctrlSmile.SetSad(TRUE);
    }
```

The preceding procedure is the function that toggles the face in the dialog box between a smile and a frown. The `GetSad` and `SetSad` functions are methods provided in **SMILE.H** and **SMILE.CPP**, which implement the **SMILE.OCX** OLE control.

When you have completed all the preceding steps, you're ready to try out your application. If you have problems with it, open the COMPGAL application in this chapter's folder on the accompanying disk and compare your own work with the example application.

Summary

OLE is such an enormous programming package that isn't possible to cover it in detail in just one chapter. The standard reference on OLE, *Inside OLE*, by Kraig Brockschmidt (see Bibliography) is 1,200 pages long and has been supplemented by many more pages of articles, technical notes, and on-line documentation.

This chapter doesn't try to explain every intricacy covered in *Inside OLE* and the other big books about OLE. Instead, its goal was to give you a head start on the long journey toward mastering OLE by providing simple explanations of a few complicated topics and then presenting a relatively simple example program that shows you how to use OLE controls in your Windows applications. The chapter also presents example programs demonstrating object embedding, in-place editing, the Visual C++ Component Gallery, and OLE controls.

Now that you've read this chapter, you have a fair idea of what OLE can do, and that knowledge can help you decide whether you need to use OLE in your applications. If you do decide to use an OLE feature in your next application—such as object embedding, in-place editing, or OLE controls—you can find more information and examples in your Visual C++ on-line help files, the OLE examples provided on your Visual C++ CD-ROM, and the books about OLE that are listed in the Bibliography.

CHAPTER SIX

PROCESSES

Long ago, in the Dark Ages of DOS, a personal computer could do just one thing at a time. You could load only one application into memory at a time, your computer ran that one application, and that was that. Even in those days, whether we knew it or not, we were working with threads. Because MS-DOS could run only one thread at a time, it was what is now sometimes called a single-threaded operating system. Every application had a single thread, and only one thread could run at a time.

By the time Windows 3.1 came along, PC operating environments had become a little smarter. Windows 3.1 had what is now known as a non-preemptive multitasking environment. Multiple applications could reside in memory at the same time, but only one application could be running. The program being executed still used all the time the CPU had available; although other applications might be memory-resident and might be waiting for a chance to run, they had to wait until the currently executing application terminated.

Windows 3.1 did have certain ways of making it appear that a smarter kind of multitasking was taking place. For example, when Windows 3.1 performed a background task, such as file I/O or a background program, it managed to present the illusion that the background task was being carried out at the same time other operations were being performed. What was really happening was that the foreground task was briefly interrupted many times each second so that the background task could be performed. This kind of CPU time-sharing is called non-preemptive multitasking because the CPU has no direct control over the amount of time allocated to each task.

Windows 3.1 also provided some special interrupt-handing mechanisms that clever programmers could use to switch tasks temporarily. So it was possible, in a manner of speaking, to make a task run in the background while a higher-priority task was executing.

But none of these stopgap measures made Windows 3.1 a true *preemptive multitasking* system, one in which tasks can share CPU time in a way that depends on predetermined priorities and that is managed dynamically by the system. As a result, tasks that Windows 3.1 was trying to run in the background often ran up against active processes that slowed them down, as you may know if you have ever tried background printing under Windows 3.1.

With the introduction of Windows NT, Windows finally entered the era of preemptive multitasking, a task-management system that allows processes (the NT equivalent of tasks) to execute on the same computer at the same time. The operating system divides processes into *threads* and allocates each thread an individual share of CPU time depending on preallocated thread priorities. In Windows NT, a thread is a path of execution within a process. The dividing of processes into threads is called *multithreading*. In this chapter, you'll see how Windows NT creates and manages processes. Chapter 7, "Multithreading," explains in more detail how Windows NT uses multithreading to implement preemptive multitasking.

About This Chapter

To demonstrate how processes are created and used in Windows NT, this chapter presents three sample programs: **MAKEPROC.EXE**, **CONSOLE.EXE**, and **MYCONSOL.EXE**.

Windows NT supports two kinds of applications—graphical user interface (GUI) applications and text-based console applications—and both varieties are covered in this chapter. The first part of the chapter deals with GUI applications, and the second part discusses console applications.

The first sample program, MAKEPROC, creates a standard GUI-style process that displays an ordinary graphical user interface window. The other two sample programs show how processes can be created to display *console-windows*: text windows created using functions in the Win32 API.

Figure 6.1 shows what happens when you run the MAKEPROC program.

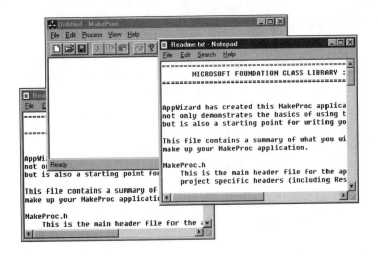

FIGURE 6.1 RUNNING THE MAKEPROC PROGRAM.

MYCONSOL is a simple console application that shows how to display a console window. The CONSOLE program is a little more complicated; it demonstrates how to start and execute a console process from a standard GUI-style window. Console applications such as CONSOLE and MYCONSOL are useful examples, because one of the most common reasons for a Windows program to create a process is to display a console window. (Applications can also create new processes that display standard, non-console document windows; for details, see "Example: Creating a GUI Process" later in this chapter.)

Figure 6.2 shows the output of the MYCONSOL program.

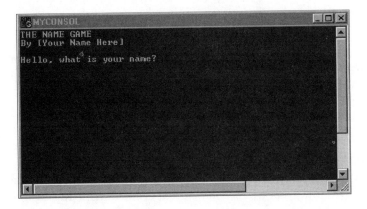

FIGURE 6.2 OUTPUT OF THE MYCONSOL PROGRAM.

Processes and Threads

To understand how Windows NT programs create processes, the first thing you need to know is what a process is. Under Windows 3.x, the smallest entity that was allocated CPU time was a task. Under Windows NT, what used to be called a task is now called a process.

When Windows NT is executing a program, the particular instance of the program that is running is known as a process. For example, when you double-click an application's icon on the Windows NT desktop, Windows NT starts a process that runs the application. If the application supports the simultaneous execution of multiple instances (some applications do and some don't), you can start another instance of the application by double-clicking the application's icon again.

One important difference between Windows 3.x tasks and Windows NT processes is that NT processes are inert; when you create a process under Windows NT, all you get is a 4-GB address space containing code and data for an application's **.EXE** file along with the code and data for any resources the executable owns (such as files, threads, and dynamic memory allocations), as well as the code and data for any dynamic link libraries that the application relies on. All this is loaded into the process's 4GB address space.

But because the process itself is inert, before it can do anything it must start a thread. This thread is the key to the process's coming alive, because the thread is responsible for executing the code that has been loaded into the process's address space. Every process has at least one thread, and any thread can start other threads at any time.

When you start an application under Windows NT, the operating system creates a process and begins executing the primary thread of that process. When this primary thread terminates, so does the process, unless you call the Win32 `ExitThread` function to terminate the primary thread. If you do that, other threads keep running.

Once a process's primary thread has started, other threads can be started. As each thread starts, it gets its own private slice of CPU time, in accordance with a predetermined priority, from a Windows NT software utility called the system scheduler. The system scheduler makes sure that each thread gets its fair share of CPU time without infringing on the time that has been allocated to other threads. You'll learn more about the system scheduler and how it works in Chapter 7, "Multithreading."

In addition to creating new threads, processes can create other processes. When a process spawns another process, the process that does the creating is called a *parent* process, and the process that is created is called a *child* process. You'll see how parent processes create child processes when you experiment with the example programs presented in this chapter.

Creating Processes

A Windows NT application can create a process by calling `CreateProcess`. In Windows NT, the `CreateProcess` call is the key to management of processes. It takes nine parameters, and several of them are pointers to structures. So you can set a very large number of a process's attributes when you create it by calling `CreateProcess`.

This is the syntax of the `CreateProcess` function:

```
BOOL CreateProcess(LPCTSTR lpszImageName,
    LPCTSTR lpszCommandLine,
    LPSECURITY_ATTRIBUTES lpsaProcess,
    LPSECURITY_ATTRIBUTES lpsaThread,
    BOOL fInheritHandles,
    DWORD fdwCreate,
    LPVOID lpvEnvironment,
    LPCSTR lpszCurDir,
    LPSTARTUPINFO lpsiStartInfo,
    LPPROCESS_INFORMATION lppiProcInfo)
```

If `CreateProcess` succeeds, it returns a value of TRUE; if it doesn't succeed, it returns FALSE.

You'll learn much more about `CreateProcess` later in this chapter, and you'll get a firsthand look at how it works in the sample programs. First, though, we'll take an overall look at how processes work in Windows NT and what kinds of things happen when you create processes and set their attributes by calling `CreateProcess`.

Example: Creating a GUI Process

The MAKEPROC sample program, which you can find in this chapter's folder on the accompanying disk, shows how processes create other processes in Windows NT programs. MAKEPROC creates a process by executing the following `CreateProcess` call:

```
BOOL bRetVal = CreateProcess("C:\\WINNT\\NOTEPAD.EXE"
    "WRITE README.TXT", &saProcess, &saThread, FALSE,
    0, NULL, NULL, &si, &piProcess);
```

The new process starts the Windows NT Notepad applet, which displays the README file that's in the MAKEPROC applications directory. Those two things happen because of the first two parameters passed to `CreateProcess`. The first parameter is the full path name of the Notepad applet, and the second parameter is a command line that causes the new process to display the MAKEPROC README file.

PASSING A PATH NAME TO CREATEPROCESS

Notice that the path name of the Notepad applet is hard-coded into the path name parameter C:\\WINNT\\NOTEPAD.EXE. If Notepad has some other path name in your system, you must change this parameter. If MAKEPROC can't find Notepad in the path name that is passed to it, the program displays an error message.

A better way to obtain the path name for CreateProcess would be to call functions such as GetCurrentDirectory, SetCurrentDirectory, and GetFirstDirectory at run time to obtain the file name you need. That way, if the path name changes, CreateFunction still works. You can learn more about GetCurrentDirectory, SetCurrentDirectory, and GetFirstDirectory by consulting your Visual C++ compiler's on-line help files. I'll leave it to you figure out the coding.

LISTING: CREATING A PROCESS

The MAKEPROC program is a framework application written in Visual C++. It executes the CreateFunction call in its view file, PROCVIEW. The call appears in a message handler named OnProcessCreate, and is executed when the user chooses the **Create** item from the program's Process menu. The OnProcessCreate member function is shown in Listing 6.1.

LISTING 6.1 CREATING A PROCESS.

```
void CMakeProcView::OnProcessCreate()
{
    // Structures we need to create processes.
    STARTUPINFO si;
    SECURITY_ATTRIBUTES saProcess, saThread;
    PROCESS_INFORMATION piProcess;

    // Prepare a STARTUPINFO structure for
    // spawning processes.
    ZeroMemory(&si, sizeof(si));
    si.cb = sizeof(si);

    // Prepare to spawn a process. The handle
    // identifying the new process should
```

```
    // be inheritable.
    saProcess.nLength = sizeof(saProcess);
    saProcess.lpSecurityDescriptor = NULL;
    saProcess.bInheritHandle = TRUE;

    // The handle identifying the new thread
    // should not be inheritable.
    saThread.nLength = sizeof(saThread);
    saThread.lpSecurityDescriptor = NULL;
    saThread.bInheritHandle = FALSE;

    BOOL bRetVal = CreateProcess("C:\\WINNT\\NOTEPAD.EXE",
        "WRITE README.TXT", &saProcess, &saThread, FALSE,
        0, NULL, NULL, &si, &piProcess);

    if (!bRetVal)
        MessageBox("Could not create the process.", "Error!");
}
```

MAKEPROC is a straightforward program. `OnProcessCreate` sets up some data structures required by `CreateProcess` and then calls `CreateProcess`. When `CreateProcess` is called, it creates a process and sets up the new process's main thread. The new process then starts. If `CreateProcess` fails to create a new thread, `OnProcessCreate` returns an error message.

You'll learn more about the parameters that are passed to `CreateProcess` as you continue reading this chapter.

Objects and Handles

In the context of the Windows NT operating system, an object is not a C++ object. Instead, it's a lower-level entity that you create by calling various Windows API functions. For example, `CreateProcess` creates a process, and `CreateThread` creates a thread. When an application creates an object, Windows NT allocates a block of memory for the object, initializes the memory with some management information, and returns to the application a handle identifying this object. The application can then manipulate the object by passing the object's handle to other functions.

In Windows NT, anything that you can access using a handle is an object. Thus, windows are objects, and so are Windows controls. You've read about GDI objects and DC objects in previous chapters, and in later chapters you'll read about other kinds of objects such as file objects, event objects, and file-mapping objects. This chapter is about process objects, and Chapter 7 focuses on thread objects. Many other kinds of objects are mentioned in other chapters.

When a thread no longer needs to manipulate an object, it can destroy the object by calling the `CloseHandle` function, which has this syntax:

```
BOOL CloseHandle(HANDLE hObject);
```

When an application calls `CloseHandle` to destroy an object, the system decrements a reference counter for the object. When an object's reference count is decremented to zero, the system frees the memory that has been allocated to manage the object.

VARIETIES OF WIN32 OBJECTS

The many kinds of objects used in Windows NT can be broken down into three categories: kernel objects, graphical device interface (GDI) objects, and user objects. Kernel objects, as you might guess, are objects managed by the Windows NT kernel. GDI objects, as explained in earlier chapters, are graphics-related objects such as pens, brushes, and bitmaps. User objects include many kinds of GUI-related objects such as menus, icons, and cursors that are used to create user-interface devices. These three kinds of objects are implemented in three dynamic link libraries that are supplied with Windows: the USER32, GDI32, and KERNEL32 DLLs.

It is not always easy to identify which of these three categories a particular object belongs to. But generally speaking, user objects support window management, GDI objects support graphics, and kernel objects support memory management. One way to determine whether an object is a kernel, GDI, or user object is to examine the Win32 function that is used to create it. If the object's `Create` function takes a SECURITY_ATTRIBUTES structure as a parameter, it is a kernel object. For example, `CreateProcess` and `CreateThread`, which are kernel objects, expect SECURITY_ATTRIBUTES structures as a parameter. `CreatePen` and `CreateBrush`, which are GDI objects, do not.

COMPARING KERNEL OBJECTS AND OTHER OBJECTS

One special feature of kernel objects is that they are *process-relative*, whereas GDI and user objects are not. This means that a handle to a kernel object is recognized only within the process that created it. Handles to GDI and user objects remain valid when they are passed back and forth by different processes.

As an illustration of this difference between kernel and non-kernel objects, suppose that a process calls `CreateFile` to create a file, which is a kernel object. Also assume that the system responds to this request by returning the handle value 0x87654321. Subsequently, if a thread in another process calls `OpenFile` to open the same file object, the system might return the handle value 0x12345678. Although the two handles are different, they identify the same file-mapping object.

Because handles for kernel objects behave in this way, a thread cannot obtain a handle to an object and pass that handle to a thread in another process using interprocess communication—that is, using file mapping or a pipe, as explained in Chapter 9. If a thread obtains a handle to kernel object and passes it to another thread and if the thread receiving the process then tries to use the handle, the most likely result is an error message.

In contrast, when a project creates a GDI or user object, other processes can access the object using the same handle value among processes. For example, if the system assigns a pen object (which is a GDI object) a handle value of 0x1122334, all processes use this same value to access the pen.

CREATING KERNEL OBJECTS

A process creates a handle to a kernel object by either creating a new kernel object or opening an existing kernel object. Any process can create a new handle to any existing kernel object, provided that the process is aware of the name of the object and has been granted access to it. Processes can inherit or duplicate handles to the following kinds of kernel objects:

+ Process objects
+ Thread objects
+ Event objects
+ Semaphore objects
+ Mutex objects
+ Named and anonymous pipe objects (see Chapter 9)
+ Mailslot objects (pseudo-files used for one-way interprocess communications)
+ File objects
+ Communications devices

All kernel objects except those listed above are private to the process that created them and cannot be duplicated or inherited.

Inheritance of Properties and Resources

A process can inherit the following properties and resources from a parent process:

+ Any inheritable open handle returned by `CreateFile`. This category includes handles to files, console input buffers, console screen buffers, named pipes, serial communication devices, mailslots, and the console of a parent process (unless the process is detached or a new console is created). A child console process also inherits the parent's standard handles as well as access to the input buffer and the active screen buffer.

+ Inheritable open handles to process, thread, mutex, event, semaphore, named pipe, anonymous pipe, and file-mapping objects.

+ Environment variables.

+ The current directory.

A handle that is inherited by a child process refers to the same object as the parent process's handle does. Moreover, the handle has the same value and the same access privileges as the corresponding handle of the parent process.

To use a handle, a child process must retrieve the handle and must have the information that it needs to access the object to which the handle refers. In most cases, the parent process must communicate this information to the child process. This communication can be carried out using various methods, including command lines, pipes, and shared memory.

When a process changes the state of an object whose handle is inherited, the change affects both processes. For example, if a process uses a handle to read from a file whose handle it has inherited, the current file position is moved for all processes using the same handle.

A child process inherits the environment variables and current directory of its parent process by default. However, `CreateProcess` enables the parent process to specify a different current directory or a different block of environment variables. (Environment variables are symbolic variables that represent elements of the operating system. For example, paths and file names are environment variables.)

Using Handles

Applications cannot access kernel, GDI, and user objects directly but must access them indirectly through handles. A handle is usually (but not always) implemented as a pointer to a pointer. Handles are often used to access objects in Windows programs, because a handle is sometimes the only way to keep track of an object as it is moved around in memory by the Windows memory manager.

The Win32 API provides a number of functions for manipulating the handles used to access most kinds of objects. These functions can be used to create object handles, close object handles, and destroy objects.

When a parent process creates a thread or a child process in Windows NT, some kinds of handles can be inherited by the process or thread that's being created. Other kinds of handles are private to the process and cannot be inherited. In other words, handles to some kinds of objects can be duplicated, and handles to other kinds of objects can't be duplicated.

PUBLIC AND PRIVATE HANDLES

Handles to user objects are public. This means that if a process creates a user object, it can share the object's handle with other processes. In contrast, handles to GDI objects are private; only the process that creates a GDI object can use the GDI object's handle. If another process needs to access the same kind of GDI object, it must create a GDI object of its own.

A kernel (memory-management) object can have multiple handles. When a process creates a kernel object, other processes can obtain their own individual handles to the object. Other characteristics of kernel objects vary.

When you create a new process by calling `CreateProcess`, the function's `fInheritHandles` parameter determines whether the child process inherits the parent process's inheritable handles. (The parameters passed to `CreateProcess` are explained in more detail in the section "The *CreateProcess* Function" later in this chapter.)

Table 6.1 lists the three kinds of object handles and shows whether each type of handle can be duplicated or inherited.

TABLE 6.1 CHARACTERISTICS OF OBJECT HANDLES.

	User Objects	GDI Objects	Kernel Objects
Max handles per object	1	1	Multiple
Handles duplicatable?	No	No	Yes
Handles private	No	Yes	Varies
Handles inheritable?	Yes	No	Varies

As Table 6.1 shows, user objects (window-related objects) and GDI objects (graphics-related objects) support only one handle per object. This means that handles to user objects and GDI objects cannot be duplicated by other processes.

How CreateProcess Assigns Handles

As you'll see in the section titled "The CreateProcess Function" later in this chapter, one parameter that you pass to CreateProcess is a PROCESS_INFORMATION structure. When CreateProcess creates a new process, it fills a pair of fields in this structure with handles to both the process being created and its primary thread. These handles can be used as parameters to any function that accepts a thread or process handle. They can also be inherited by child processes, provided that inheritance is granted by the flag that is specified when they are created. The handles are valid until closed, even after the process or thread they represent is terminated.

When an application has created a new process, other processes can call the Win32 function OpenProcess to obtain a handle to the process. OpenProcess can also be called to obtain a process handle's access rights and inheritability properties.

Pseudohandles

The Win32 function GetCurrentProcess returns what is known as a *pseudohandle* to the current process, and GetCurrentThread returns a pseudohandle to the current thread. Pseudohandles can be used just like ordinary handles by the calling process, but they cannot be inherited or duplicated for use by other processes.

Each of the three functions that creates a process or a thread (CreateProcess, CreateThread, and CreateRemoteThread) returns a psuedohandle that uniquely identifies the process or thread being created. A process can obtain its own psuedohandle by calling GetCurrentProcessId. A thread can obtain its own thread identifier by calling GetCurrentThreadId. A thread or process identifier is valid from the time the thread or process is created until it terminates.

DUPLICATING HANDLES

When an object has a handle that can be duplicated by another process, the duplication of a handle works as follows: Suppose that an application creates an event object by calling CreateEvent. The CreateEvent function returns a handle to the event object that it creates, and event objects that are created by CreateEvent can have multiple handles.

Subsequently, if another application needs to open the event that has been created, it can call OpenEvent to obtain its own unique handle to the event object. Alternatively, the second application can call DuplicateHandle to obtain a handle to the event.

When a process makes a copy of a handle by calling DuplicateHandle, the duplicate handle can be used only by the process that created it. DuplicateHandle can be called either by a process that owns a handle or by a child process or a thread of the process that owns the handle.

DuplicateHandle can create a non-inheritable copy of an original handle. It can also make a duplicate handle with access rights that are different from those of the original handle. If a process that owns an original handle makes a copy of the handle by calling DuplicateHandle, the handle that is returned by DuplicateHandle is a non-inheritable copy of the original handle.

If a thread or a child process calls DuplicateHandle to obtain a handle created by a parent process, the handle returned by DuplicateHandle is a non-inheritable handle that can be used only by the child process. If more than one application has a handle to the same event object, each application is responsible for deleting its handle to the object when it finishes using the object. When all handles to an object are closed, the operating system removes the handle from memory.

Using Handles and Pointers in Windows NT Programs

In Windows API (non-Visual C++) applications, it is usually safer to reference a Windows object using a handle than it is to reference the object using a pointer. That's because the operating system manages handles, making sure that an object can always be accessed through its handle even when the object is moved from one location to another in physical memory.

In Visual C++, it's back to pointers again. In Visual C++ applications, it is perfectly safe to use the this and other pointers supported by the Microsoft Foundation Class library. So you'll often see both handles and pointers being used quite liberally in Visual C++ programs written for Windows NT.

ENVIRONMENT VARIABLES

Every process has an environment block that contains a set of environment variables and their values. (From the Windows NT desktop, you can set environment variables by double-clicking the **System** icon in the Control Panel.) By default, a child process inherits its parent process's environment variables. However, an application can specify a different environment for the child process by creating a new environment block and passing a pointer to it as a parameter to CreateProcess.

You can obtain a pointer to a process's environment block by calling the GetEnvironmentStrings. To change an environment variable, call SetEnvironmentVariable. To determine whether a specified variable is defined in the environment of the calling process and, if so, what its value is, call GetEnvironmentVariable.

CLOSING HANDLES

When a process terminates, the operating system automatically closes all handles used by the process and deletes all objects created by the process. However, when a thread terminates, the operating system—with some exceptions—does not automatically close handles that are owned by the thread or delete their associated objects. The exceptions are window, hook, window position, and dynamic data exchange (DDE) conversation objects.

The CreateProcess Function

I've mentioned that Windows NT programs create processes by calling CreateProcess. In this section, you'll learn more about CreateProcess and about what its parameters do. This is the syntax of CreateProcess:

```
BOOL CreateProcess(LPCTSTR lpszImageName,
    LPCTSTR lpszCommandLine,
    LPSECURITY_ATTRIBUTES lpsaProcess,
    LPSECURITY_ATTRIBUTES lpsaThread,
    BOOL fInheritHandles,
    DWORD fdwCreate,
    LPVOID lpvEnvironment,
    LPCSTR lpszCurDir,
    LPSTARTUPINFO lpsiStartInfo,
    LPPROCESS_INFORMATION lppiProcInfo)
```

The parameters passed to `CreateProcess` are as follows:

✦ **lpszImageName.** The path name and file name of the object-code module to execute as a new process. If a partial name is specified, the current drive and current directory are used by default. If the `lpszImageName` parameter is NULL, the module name must be entered in the `lpszCommandLine` string. The specified module can be a Win32 application, or it can be some other type of module (for example, an MS-DOS or OS/2 module) if the appropriate subsystem is available on the local computer.

✦ **lpszCommandLine.** The address of any command line that must be executed to run the new process. If this parameter is NULL, the `lpszImageName` string is recognized as the command line. If neither `lpszImageName` nor `lpszCommandLine` is NULL, `lpszImageName` specifies the module to execute, and `lpszCommandLine` is recognized as the command line.

✦ **lpsaProcess.** Points to a SECURITY_ATTRIBUTES structure that specifies the security attributes for the created process. If `lpsaProcess` is NULL, the process is created with a default security descriptor. For more about security attributes, see "The SECURITY_ATTRIBUTES Structure" later in this chapter.

✦ **lpsaThread.** Points to a SECURITY_ATTRIBUTES structure that specifies the security attributes for the primary thread of the new process. If `lpsaThread` is NULL, the process is created with a default security descriptor.

✦ **fInheritHandles.** Specifies whether the new process inherits handles from the calling process. If `fInheritHandles` is TRUE, each inheritable open handle in the calling process is inherited by the new process. Inherited handles have the same value and access privileges as the original handles.

✦ The **fdwCreate** parameter is used with a set of flags that control the priority of the process and specify certain facts about how the new process is to be created. The flags used with `fdwCreate` are as follows:

  ✦ **CREATE_SUSPENDED:** If this flag is set, the primary thread of the new process is created in a suspended state and does not run until the Win32 function `ResumeThread` is called.

  ✦ **DETACHED_PROCESS:** This flag applies specifically to console processes. If the flag is set, the new process does not have access to the console of the calling process. The new process can create a new console by calling `AllocConsole`, or by jumping to the beginning of a main function that the console uses as an entry point. The DETACHED_PROCESS flag cannot be used with the CREATE_NEW_CONSOLE flag.

✦ **CREATE_NEW_PROCESS_GROUP:** If this flag is set, the new process is the root process of a new process group. A process group, identified by an ID number, includes all processes that are descendents of this root process. The process group ID of the new process group is the same as the process ID, which is returned in the `lppiProcInfo` structure. Process groups enable the Win32 function `GenerateConsoleCtrlEvent` to send the special character signals CTRL+C and CTRL+BREAK to groups of console processes.

✦ **DEBUG_PROCESS:** If set, this flag causes the calling process to be treated as a debugger and causes the new process to be treated as a process being debugged. This means that the system notifies the debugger (the calling process) of all debug events that occur in the process being debugged (the new process).

✦ **DEBUG_ONLY_THIS_PROCESS:** If this flag is set, the calling process is treated as a debugger, and the new process is a process being debugged.

✦ Another set of flags used with the `fdwCreate` parameter controls the new process's priority class, which is used in determining the scheduling priorities of the process's threads. If no priority class is specified, the priority class defaults to NORMAL_PRIORITY_CLASS unless the priority class of the creating process is IDLE_PRIORITY_CLASS. In this case, the default priority class of the child process is also IDLE_PRIORITY_CLASS. Priority flags used with the `fdwCreate` parameter are as follows:

✦ **REALTIME_PRIORITY_CLASS:** the highest possible priority. Preempts the threads of all other processes, including operating system processes that may be performing important tasks—for example, flushing information cached to a disk. If you think you need to assign this priority to a process, think twice; then make it active only for the shortest possible time. Otherwise, the results may be unfortunate. For example, disk caches may not flush and mouse operations may hang.

✦ **HIGH_PRIORITY_CLASS:** a process that performs a time-critical task and must therefore be executed immediately. The threads of a high-priority class process preempt the threads of normal or idle priority class processes. An example of a process that might be given a high priority is Windows Task List, which must respond quickly when called by the user regardless of the load on the operating system. Do not be tempted to use high-priority tasks indiscriminately. In fact, use extreme care in assigning this priority, because a high-priority class CPU-bound application can use nearly all available cycles.

♦ **NORMAL_PRIORITY_CLASS**: an ordinary process with no special scheduling needs.

♦ **IDLE_PRIORITY_CLASS**: a process whose threads run only when the system is idle and are preempted by the threads of any process running in a higher priority class. An example of a process that might have an idle priority class is a screen-saver program.

♦ **lpvEnvironment**. Points to an environment block for the new process. If this parameter is NULL, the new process uses the environment of the calling process. The environment block consists of a null-terminated block of null-terminated strings—that is, two null bytes at the end of the block.

♦ **lpszCurDir**. Points to a null-terminated string that specifies the current drive and directory for the new process. The string must be a full path and file name that includes a drive letter. If this parameter is NULL, the new process is created with the same current drive and directory as the calling process. This option is provided primarily for shells that start applications.

♦ **lpsiStartInfo**. A pointer to a STARTUPINFO structure that defines the characteristics of a window. By passing a pointer to a STARTUPINFO structure when it calls CreateProcess, a parent process can specify the properties of the main window of its child process (see "The STARTUPINFO Structure" later in this chapter).

♦ **lppiProcInfo**. The address of the PROCESS_INFORMATION structure that receives identification information about a new process (see "The SECURITY_ATTRIBUTES Structure," next).

For an example of how CreateProcess can be used in a Windows NT program, see the CONSOLE example program presented in this chapter.

THE SECURITY_ATTRIBUTES STRUCTURE

The lpsaProcess and lpsaThread parameters of the CreateProcess call point to a SECURITY_ATTRIBUTES structure. The structure pointed to by lpsaProcess specifies the security attributes for the created process, and the structure referenced by lpsaThread specifies the security attributes for the primary thread of the new process. If either of these parameters is NULL, then a default security descriptor is used.

This is the architecture of a SECURITY_ATTRIBUTES structure:

```
typedef struct _SECURITY_ATTRIBUTES ( /* sa */
    DWORD nLength;
```

```
    LPVOID lpSecurityDescriptor;
    BOOL bInheritHandle;
} SECURITY_ATTRIBUTES;
```

In a SECURITY_ATTRIBUTES structure, the following things apply:

✦ The nLength element specifies the length of the structure.

✦ The bInheritHandle is a Boolean value that specifies whether the handles associated with the process being created can be inherited.

✦ The lpSecurityDescriptor element points to a SECURITY_DESCRIPTOR structure that contains security information associated with the process being created. A SECURITY_DESCRIPTOR structure includes

  ✦ A pair of security identifier (SID) structures that identify the owner of a process and a primary group to which the process belongs.

  ✦ A pair of access control list (ACL) structures that provide access information about the new process.

For each kind of object associated with a process, there is a creation function (such as CreateProcess or CreateFile) that takes a security attributes argument. This argument always points to a SECURITY_ATTRIBUTES function whose inherit flag determines whether the handle can be inherited.

THE PROCESS_INFORMATION STRUCTURE

The lppiProcInfo parameter of the CreateProcess function is a pointer to a PROCESS_INFORMATION structure, which CreateProcess fills in with information about the console process being created. This is the definition of the PROCESS_INFORMATION structure:

```
typedef struct _PROCESS_INFORMATION { /* pi */
    HANDLE hProcess;
    HANDLE hThread;
    DWORD dwProcessID;
    DWORD dwThreadID;
} PROCESS_INFORMATION;
```

The hProcess member variable is the handle of the process that has been created. The hThread variable is the handle of the new process's main thread. By default, these handles are created with full access rights to the calling process. However, access can be restricted if a security descriptor is specified. The `dwProcessID` variable is a global identifier that identifies the process that has been created. The `dwThreadID` variable is a global identifier that identifies the new process's main thread.

For an example of how a PROCESS_INFORMATION structure can be used with `CreateProcess`, see the CONSOLE example program.

THE **STARTUPINFO** STRUCTURE

The `CreateProcess` function takes a pointer to a STARTUPINFO structure as one of its parameters. Subsequently, a process can call the Win32 function `GetStartupInfo` to retrieve the STARTUPINFO structure that was specified when the process was created.

This is the definition of the STARTUPINFO structure:

```
typedef struct _STARTUPINFO { /* si */
    DWORD cb;
    LPTSTR lpReserved;
    LPTSTR lpDesktop;
    LPTSTR lpTitle;
    DWORD dwX;
    DWORD dwY;
    DWORD dwXSize;
    DWORD dwYSize;
    DWORD dwXCountChars;
    DWORD dwYCountChars;
    DWORD dwFillAttribute;
    DWORD dwFlags;
    WORD wShowWindow;
    WORD cbReserved2;
    LPBYTE lpReserved2;
    HANDLE hStdInput;
    HANDLE hStdOutput;
    HANDLE hStdError;
} STARTUPINFO, *LPSTARTUPINFO;
```

When `CreateProcess` creates a process with a main window, the members of the STARTUPINFO structure specify the window's properties.

When a GUI process is created, the STARTUPINFO parameter affects the first window created by `CreateWindow`. When a console processes is created, STARTUPINFO sets the properties of the process's the console window. Subsequently, the new process can call GetStartupInfo to retrieve the STARTUPINFO structure that was specified when it was created.

These are the members of the STARTUPINFO structure:

+ **cb.** This member specifies the size, in bytes, of the STARTUPINFO structure.

+ **lpReserved.** Set this element to NULL before passing the structure to Create-Process.

+ **lpDesktop.** This field specifies the name of a desktop in which to start the process. If the desktop exists, the new process is associated with this desktop. If the desktop does not exist, a desktop with default attributes is created for the new process.

+ **lpTitle.** If the new process creates a new console window, this element is a pointer to a string to be displayed as a title in the console window's title bar. If the lpTitle parameter is NULL, the name of the process's executable file is used as the window title. This member must be NULL for GUI or console processes that do not create a new console window.

+ **dwX, dwY.** These members are ignored unless dwFlags specifies STARTF_USEPOSITION. If the new process creates a window and if the dwX and dwY parameters are used, they specify the vertical (x) and horizontal (y) offsets, in pixels, of the upper-left corner of the window. The offsets are calculated beginning at the upper-left corner of the screen. For GUI processes, if the x parameter of CreateWindow is CW_USEDEFAULT, the specified position is used the first time CreateWindow is called to create an overlapped window.

+ **dwXSize, dwYSize.** These members are ignored unless dwFlags specifies STARTF_USESIZE. If the new process creates a window, these elements specify the width (dwXSize) and height (dwYSize), in pixels, of the new window. For GUI processes, if the nWidth parameter of CreateWindow is CW_USEDEFAULT, these members apply only the first time CreateWindow is called to create an overlapped window .

+ **dwXCountChars, dwYCountChars.** These elements are ignored unless dwFlags specifies STARTF_USECOUNTCHARS. For console processes that create a new console window, the dwXCountChars and dYCountChars elements specify the screen buffer width (dwXCountChars) and height (dwYCountChars) in character columns and rows. These values are ignored in GUI processes.

+ **dwFillAttribute**. This member is ignored unless the value of dwFlags is STARTF_USEFILLATTRIBUTE. When CreateProcess is used to create a console process, dwFillAttribute specifies the initial text and background colors used by the window.

For an example of a STARTUPINFO structure used with CreateProcess, see the Console program.

HOW CHILD PROCESSES INHERIT PROPERTIES AND RESOURCES

When a process creates a child process by calling CreateProcess, the child process can inherit certain properties and resources from its parent process. In fact, child processes inherit a number of properties and resources from their parents by default. But an application, by overriding certain default settings, can prevent a child process from inheriting any or all properties and resources from its parent.

TERMINATING A PROCESS

A process terminates when any of these conditions occurs:

+ The last thread of the process terminates.
+ Any thread of the process calls the Win32 function ExitProcess.
+ The primary thread of the process returns (this results in an implicit call to ExitProcess).
+ The Win32 function TerminateProcess is called with a handle to the process.

When a process terminates, the following events occur:

+ Open handles to files or other resources associated with the process are closed automatically. Note that the objects referenced by these handles exist until all open handles are closed. This means that an object remains valid after a process closes if another process has a handle to it.

✦ The state of the process object becomes signaled, satisfying any threads that are waiting for the process to terminate. (For more about synchronization and signaled and unsignaled states, see "Signaled and Unsignaled States" later in this chapter.)

✦ The termination status of the process changes from STILL_ACTIVE to the process's exit code.

THE EXITPROCESS FUNCTION

The safest way to terminate a process is to call the ExitProcess, which notifies all DLLs attached to the process that the process is being terminated. (For more information about DLLs, see Chapter 8, "Dynamic Link Libraries.") ExitProcess also ensures that all threads of the process are terminated. This is important, because child processes are not automatically terminated when a parent process terminates.

Surgeon General's Warning

An application can also terminate a process by calling the Win32 function Terminate-Process, but calling TerminateProcess is not recommended except in emergency situations, and Microsoft does not spell out what those situations are. Conclusion: Just say no.

TerminateProcess is not a safe call, because it doesn't notify DLLs that may be attached to the process that the process is being terminated. In contrast, when a function is terminated with a call to ExitProcess, the entry-point function of each attached DLL is invoked with a code warning the DLL of the process's termination.

PROCESS TERMINATION AND EXCEPTION HANDLING

When you call ExitProcess or (watch out!) TerminateProcess, all threads of the process terminate immediately, providing the process with no opportunity to run any more code (one exception: the code that detaches DLLs if ExitProcess is called). Consequently, the Visual C++ version of exception handlers—which are implemented as macros because Visual C++ does not support standard C++ exception handling—may not execute as you expect. That's because ExitProcess forces a process to terminate before it reaches the termination section of any exception-handling code that might be present, such as the FINALLY block of a TRY/FINALLY handler mechanism. For more about how Visual C++ compilers manage instruction handling, see your Visual C++ and Windows NT documentation.

When a process is running, it has a 32-bit termination status that an application can obtain by calling the Win32 function `GetExitCodeProcess`. When a process terminates, its termination status becomes an exit code that can vary depending on what caused the process to terminate. Therefore, an application can call `GetExitCodeProcess` to check to see whether a process has terminated.

While a process is running, its termination status is STILL_ACTIVE. When the process terminates, its termination status becomes an exit code that can be one of the following:

✦   The exit code specified by a call to `ExitProcess` or `TerminateProcess`.

✦   The return value from a process's main or `WinMain` function.

✦   An exception code for an unhandled exception that caused the process to terminate.

The fact that an exit code can have any of the above values may seem confusing. Fortunately, the only process termination status that you usually have to be concerned with is the status STILL_ACTIVE. If a call to `GetExitCodeProcess` reveals that the termination status of a process is STILL_ACTIVE, you'll know that the process is still active. If `GetExitCodeProcess` returns any other value, it means that the process has terminated.

You can terminate a process by passing its exit code to `ExitProcess` or `Terminate-Process`. If a process is terminated in some other way (for example, by a fatal unhandled exception or a **Ctrl+C** signal), the process's termination code is the exception code that caused the termination. The process's exit code is also used as the exit code of any threads of the process that have not yet terminated.

Console Processes

Even though Windows NT is a graphics-oriented system, it supports the creation and management of text-based windows called *console* windows. When Windows NT is running, you can open a console window by choosing the Command promp from the Windows taskbar's Start menu, as shown in Figure 6.3. The methods that you use to create and manage a console window are a little different from the techniques used to create and manage GUI processes.

In the remainder of this chapter, we'll examine console windows, console processes, and the methods used to create and manage console processes.

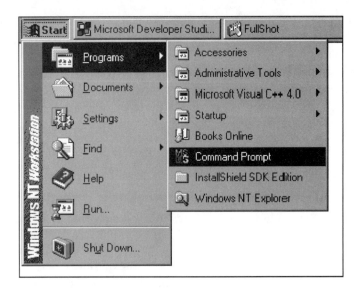

FIGURE 6.3 OPENING A CONSOLE WINDOW.

When a console window opens, you can use it to run MS-DOS applications in the same way DOS programs have always been executed. You can also use console windows under Windows NT to execute MS-DOS commands from command lines and to develop and run text-based applications.

Setting Sizes of Console Windows

In the first part of this chapter, you saw what happens when an application calls `CreateProcess` to start a GUI process. One thing that happens is that the calling process can specify the width and height (in pixels) of the window created by `CreateWindow`, the location (in screen coordinates) of the window created by `CreateWindow`, and the nCmdShow parameter passed to `ShowWindow`. In contrast, when `CreateProcess` is called to start a console process, the values specified in the STARTUPINFO structure are used only when a new console is created.

WHAT'S A CONSOLE WINDOW?

In Windows NT, a console window is a plain vanilla DOS-style window that lacks most of the fancy graphics features of full-fledged GUI windows. For example, you can't equip a console window with dialog boxes, icons, Windows-style pull-down menus, or other GUI-style interface objects. Console windows can come in handy, though, when you want to port a text-based application to Windows NT or when you want to do a special job, such as testing a snippet of code, porting an application from MS-DOS to Windows NT, or communicating with UNIX computers over a network.

Windows NT consoles are implemented in the Win32 console API, a set of functions that were written specifically for the Windows NT SDK and were introduced with the premiere of Windows NT. Today, the Windows console API is also used to create and display console windows under Windows 95. Under Windows NT, the Win32 functions and data structures that are used to create, display, and manipulate console windows are defined in the **WINCON.H** header file.

Consoles are not available in the Windows 3.x environment; they were introduced along with Windows NT and are designed specifically to be used with the Win32 SDK, which is compatible with both Windows NT and Windows 95. To create text-only windows for 16-bit versions of Windows, you can use the QuickWin utility that is supplied with Visual C++.

Using Console Windows

Although console windows don't have all the features of full-fledged GUI-style windows, they do have some of them. For example, you can size a console window, you can close it by selecting the **Close** item from a close-box menu, and you can scroll the text inside a console window using standard scrollbars. The bottom line is that console windows are designed to handle purely text-based input and output; they manage I/O operations using a set of text-based API functions that have capabilities similar to those of the `printf` and `scanf` family of functions familiar to C-language programmers.

Here are some potential uses for console windows:

✦ They can be useful in networking and communications programs. Communications programs are often designed around text windows that accept keyboard input and display characters line-by-line on the screen. A console window can be an ideal way to manage that kind of I/O.

✦ A console window can be a useful device for displaying error messages, particularly when GUI operations are disabled by errors that affect screen graphics.

✦ You can use console windows to create text-based programming tools such as interpreters, compilers, and debuggers. Windows NT can display graphical windows and console windows on the screen simultaneously, so you can use one console window to monitor code that is generating debugging information, while using other console windows to observe such things as memory dumps, error notifications, and event logs.

✦ You'll become particularly fond of the console API if you ever have to port a DOS or UNIX application to Windows NT, especially if you're a DOS or UNIX programmer without much experience writing Windows-style applications. You can simply go through your DOS or UNIX code and convert its I/O functions, such as `printf` and `scanf`, to corresponding functions provided by the console API. Then you can simply compile and execute your Windows NT console application.

CONSOLE WINDOWS AND GUI WINDOWS

Although a console window works only with text-based operations, it does not have to be the only visible window on the Windows NT screen. As Figure 6.4 shows, an application can display multiple console windows and multiple GUI windows on the same screen simultaneously.

FIGURE 6.4 A CONSOLE WINDOW AND A GUI WINDOW.

When a console window is open, it works just like a UNIX or MS-DOS text screen. In fact, one example of a console application is the DOS window application that comes with Windows NT.

When you choose the Command Prompt item from the Start menu on the Windows NT desktop, a console window opens, as shown in Figure 6.5. From that window, you can execute any MS-DOS command in the same way you would from any DOS window: by typing the command and then pressing **Return**.

FIGURE 6.5 A WINDOWS NT CONSOLE WINDOW.

BUILDING A CONSOLE APPLICATION

There are two ways to create a console window: by building an application that uses a console window as its main window, and by opening a console window from a Windows application. When you build a Visual C++ application using AppWizard, it's easy to make your program a console application. Just check the appropriate box when AppWizard displays the dialog box shown in Figure 6.6.

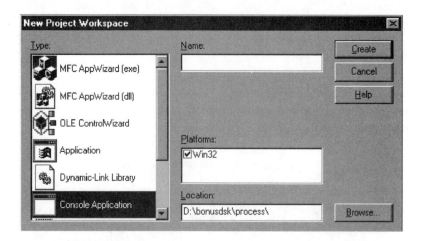

FIGURE 6.6 USING APPWIZARD TO CREATE A CONSOLE APPLICATION.

CREATING CONSOLE WINDOW PROCESSES

Another way to create a console window is to start a special console window process from a Windows application. The Win32 API provides three calls that can be used to create a console window: `AllocConsole`, `CreateProcess`, and `CreateProcessAsUser`. We'll examine all three of those functions in this section. (There are no encapsulations of any of these functions in version 4.0 of the MFC library, the version that was current when this book was written.)

THE ALLOCCONSOLE AND FREECONSOLE FUNCTIONS

The most direct way to open a console window from a Windows application is to call the Windows API function `AllocConsole`. If you ever want to create a console window from an executing application, `AllocConsole` is a good function to know about, because Windows processes are not automatically equipped with console windows. When an application calls `AllocConsole`, a new console window is created and is attached to the currently executing process.

When an application has finished using a console window, it can detach the window from the current process by calling the Win32 function `FreeConsole`.

THE CREATEPROCESS AND CREATEPROCESSASUSER FUNCTIONS

An application can also create a console window by starting a new process and specifically identifying it as a console process. To start a new console process using this method, call `CreateProcess` or `CreateProcessAsUser` with a special flag set.

The flag that sets a new console process is the CREATE_NEW_CONSOLE flag. When `CreateProcess` is called with the CREATE_NEW_CONSOLE flag set, a new console window is created and is attached to the newly created process. If a flag named DETACHED_PROCESS is set when `CreateProcess` is called to create a console process, the new process inherits its console from the calling process.

The CREATE_NEW_CONSOLE flag is described in more detail in the section titled "Using the Win32 Console API" later in this chapter. For more information about creating new console processes by calling `CreateProcess`, see the section titled "Input Buffer and Screen Buffer Handles."

HOW CONSOLE WINDOWS WORK

The mechanism that displays console windows is a special API called the Win32 console, which has two components: an input buffer and a screen buffer. When the user types information that is to be displayed in a console window, the data is stored in the console's input buffer in a queue of input records. Each input record contains information about an input event. When information has been placed in a console's input buffer, it can be transferred to a screen buffer and then displayed on the screen.

LOW-LEVEL AND HIGH-LEVEL FUNCTIONS

The Win32 console provides two kinds of functions for retrieving input information that has been stored in a console's input buffer. When *low-level* functions are used for input-buffer and screen-buffer I/O, the event records stored in a console's input buffer can contain information about keyboard events, mouse events, buffer-resizing events, and menu events. When an application uses *high-level* console I/O functions, the event records stored in the input record contain only character data.

When information that is input by the user has been stored in a console's input buffer, high-level functions filter and process the information before it is displayed on the screen. This filtering action ensures that nonprinting characters behave as expected when they are typed in by the user and sent to the screen. Although high-level functions recognize keyboard information that is typed in by the user, they do not recognize most mouse operations.

Low-level functions provide direct access to a console's input buffer. They do not filter or process information that is input by the user before it is displayed on the screen. Low-level functions track mouse events as well as keyboard events received from the user.

SCREEN BUFFERS

The Win32 console's screen-buffer component is a two-dimensional array of character and color data that can be displayed in a console window. In a console screen buffer, the data for each character to be shown on the screen is stored in a CHAR_INFO structure. This structure contains a code that specifies the ANSI or Unicode character to be displayed (see "The Unicode Character Set") along with the foreground and background colors that are used to display the character.

A console can be equipped with multiple screen buffers, but only one screen buffer can be displayed at a time.

When an application creates a new console, a new input buffer and a new screen buffer are automatically created. A process can call the Win32 function `CreateConsole-ScreenBuffer` to create additional screen buffers for its console. (`CreateConsoleScreenBuffer` is examined more closely in "Using the Win32 Console API" later in this chapter.)

The process associated with the new console can obtain the handles of the new console's input and screen buffers by calling a Win32 function named `GetStdHandle`. The new process can then use those handles to access its console.

The Unicode Character Set

Unicode is an international 16-bit standard for encoding characters. It can encode the complete character sets of languages such as Chinese and Japanese, which have thousands of character symbols. Windows NT supports the use of both ANSI and Unicode characters.

The Win32 SDK is equipped with a set of macros and naming conventions that make it comparatively easy to edit and recompile existing ANSI-compliant applications using the Unicode character set. ANSI and Unicode characters can even be intermixed in the same application.

When a console window is accepting keyboard input or has the keyboard focus, the console API formats each input event—such as a single keystroke, a movement of the mouse, or a mouse-button click—as an input record. That record is kept in the console's input buffer until it is transferred to the screen buffer. Thus, when a console process is running, the console's input buffer contains a queue of input event records.

The screen buffer that is displayed in the console window is considered the active screen buffer. A new screen buffer becomes active when its handle is specified in a call to `SetConsoleActiveScreenBuffer`. (For more information about this function, see "Using the Win32 Console API" later in this chapter.) Even when a screen buffer is inactive, a console process can access it for both reading and writing.

Screen Buffers and Console Windows

There is a difference between a screen buffer and a console window. A screen buffer holds data for each character displayed in a console window. A console window is the rectangular region of a console screen buffer that is displayed on the screen.

SETTING SCREEN BUFFER PROPERTIES

The Win32 API provides a large assortment of functions for changing the size, shape, and appearance of console windows. If a console process has multiple screen buffers, the properties of each console screen can be set independently. The properties associated with a screen buffer include the following:

+ Screen buffer size, usually expressed in character rows and columns.
+ Text attributes, including the foreground and background colors used for displaying text in console windows.
+ The size and location of console windows.
+ The position, appearance, and visibility of the cursor used in a console window.

The Win32 functions that are used to set screen buffer properties are listed and described in "Using the Win32 Console API" later in this chapter.

INPUT BUFFER AND SCREEN BUFFER HANDLES

Earlier in this chapter I mentioned that one way to start a new process is to call `CreateProcess` with the CREATE_NEW_CONSOLE flag set. When an application starts a new console process by using this technique, three new elements are created: a new console window, a new input buffer, and a new screen buffer.

Because the Windows API is used to create console processes, a console's input buffer and screen buffer can be accessed through handles. For instance, to write to an input buffer or to set the attributes of text displayed in a screen buffer, an application must obtain the buffer's handle. To obtain handles that can be used to access a console's input buffer and screen buffer, an application can call the Win32 function `GetStdHandle`.

THE STDIN, STDOUT, AND STDERR HANDLES

When Windows NT creates a console, three handles for controlling the console's I/O operations are also created:

+ The STDIN handle, which can be used to access the console's input buffer.

+ The STDOUT handle, which can access the standard output associated with a process.

+ The STDERR handle, which can access the standard diagnostic (error) handle associated with a process.

A process can obtain these three handles by calling `GetStdHandle`, and can set them by calling `SetStdHandle`. The `SetStdHandle` function can also be called to redirect any or all of these three handles to locations other than a console's I/O functions. This capability makes it possible to pipe data back and forth between a console's I/O functions and other sources and destinations. (For more information on redirecting data using pipes, see Chapter 9, "Interprocess Communications.")

When a process has obtained a standard I/O handle from a console by calling `GetStdHandle`, the process can access the handle by calling any of four console I/O functions provided by the Win32 API. To read from a console's standard output handle, the process can call `ReadFile` or `ReadConsole`. To write to a console's standard input handle, the process can call `WriteFile` or `WriteConsole`. For more details about these four functions, see "Functions that Access Console I/O Buffers" later in this chapter.

INPUT AND OUTPUT I/O FUNCTIONS

As noted earlier, the Win32 console API offers two kinds of functions—high-level functions and low-level functions—for placing information in a console's input buffer and writing information to the console's screen buffer. The I/O functions can also be divided into two other categories: `input` functions and `output` functions. Input functions read information from a console's input buffer, and output functions write information to the screen.

High-level input functions filter and process the data in a console's input buffer and return input as a stream of characters, discarding mouse and buffer-resizing events before the data is written to the screen. High-level output functions write streams of characters to the screen, starting at the current cursor location in the screen buffer. The high-level console I/O functions provided by the Win32 API are `ReadFile`, `WriteFile`, `ReadConsole`, and `WriteConsole`. All these functions are described in this section.

Low-level input functions and low-level output functions provide direct access to a console's input buffer and output buffer but require more programming attention from the software developer. The low-level console I/O functions are `ReadConsoleInput`, `WriteConsoleInput`, `PeekConsoleInput`, `GetNumberOfConsoleInputEvents`, and `FlushConsoleInputBuffer`. All five of these functions are described in this section.

High-level I/O functions provide the easiest way to read a stream of characters from console input or to write a stream of characters to console output. High-level functions are often used in applications, such as networking and communications programs, that use line-by-line input and output.

Low-level console functions can give an application more precise control over a console's operation than high-level functions do. For example, low-level functions can respond to mouse movements and mouse clicks and can handle cut-and-paste operations that involve odd-sized rectangles of text. But low-level functions are more difficult to handle than high-level functions and tend to make a programmer's life more complicated.

An application does not have to use high-level console functions or low-level console functions exclusively; it can use any combination of both.

When a console window is managed using high-level functions, it retrieves data from its input buffer by reading from standard input and writes data to its screen buffer by writing to standard output. A console can also write error messages to standard diagnostic output.

High-level console functions also support redirection of information via pipes (see Chapter 9, "Interprocess Communications"). That capability makes high-level functions useful in networking and communications programs as well as in other kinds of client-server applications.

If a console application requires the use of a mouse as well as a keyboard, low-level functions can be used to track mouse events: events triggered by mouse movements, events caused by the pressing and releasing of mouse buttons, and events caused by mouse actions that affect the size of the active screen buffer. Low-level console functions can be useful when you want to port a character-based application from a text-based environment, such as DOS or UNIX, to Windows NT. Low-level console calls can also be used by applications that rely on mouse input as well as character input from the keyboard.

THE READFILE AND READCONSOLE FUNCTIONS

When an application manages console I/O using high-level console functions, the application reads data from the console's input buffer by executing either `ReadFile` or `ReadConsole`. `ReadFile` supports only the ANSI character set, whereas `ReadConsole` supports both ANSI characters and Unicode.

Another difference is that `ReadFile` can be used to access files, pipes, and serial communications devices, but `ReadConsole` can be used only with console handles. This distinction is important if an application relies on standard handles that may have been redirected.

THE WRITEFILE AND WRITECONSOLE FUNCTIONS

To write data to a console's screen buffer using high-level functions, you can execute `WriteFile` or `WriteConsole`. The `WriteFile` function supports only the ANSI character set, whereas `WriteConsole` supports both ANSI characters and Unicode characters. Also, `WriteFile` can be used to access files, pipes, and serial communications devices, whereas `WriteConsole` can be used only with console handles.

For more information about the syntax and use of `ReadFile`, `ReadConsole`, `WriteFile`, and `WriteConsole`, see "Console Control Handlers" later in this chapter.

OTHER LOW-LEVEL I/O FUNCTIONS

When you manage console I/O using low-level functions, you can read from a console's input buffer by executing `ReadConsoleInput`. To write to a console's screen buffer, you execute `WriteConsoleInput`. Other Win32 functions that are used in low-level console I/O are as follows:

✦ **PeekConsoleInput,** which reads data from a console input buffer without removing any pending input records that the buffer might contain.

✦ **GetNumberOfConsoleInputEvents,** which obtains the number of unread records in a console input buffer.

✦ **FlushNumberOfConsoleInputEvents,** which discards all unread events in a console input buffer.

For more information about `ReadConsoleInput` and `WriteConsoleInput`, see "Console Control Handlers" later in this chapter.

CONSOLE INPUT AND OUTPUT MODES

Every console input buffer is associated with a set of *input modes* that affect input operations. Similarly, every console screen buffer has a set of *output modes* that affect output operations.

The input modes provided by the console API can be divided into two groups: modes that affect high-level input functions and modes that affect low-level input functions. The output modes affect only applications that use the high-level output functions. By setting a console's input and output modes, an application can determine how information from the keyboard is filtered and processed.

By default, high-level console functions filter and process keyboard information to make nonprinting characters behave in ways that many applications expect. For example, the tab character moves the cursor forward (12 spaces by default), and a beep sounds when the bell key is pressed. When the console is in its default low-level mode, mouse input and buffer-resizing events are recognized, along with character input and output operations.

You can obtain and set a console's input and output modes by calling the Win32 functions `GetConsoleMode` and `SetConsoleMode`, which are described in "Using the Win32 Console API" later in this chapter.

HIGH-LEVEL INPUT MODES

The high-level input modes available to console processes are as follows:

+ **Line input mode**, which determines whether line-by-line input from the user is supported. When line input mode is enabled, the `ReadFile` and `ReadConsole` functions return when the **Enter** key is pressed. When line input mode is disabled, `ReadFile` and `ReadConsole` return each time a character becomes available in the console's input buffer.

+ **Processed input mode**, which controls the processing of information received from the backspace, tab, bell, carriage return, and linefeed characters. When processed input mode is enabled, all these characters behave in the same way as when text is being typed on a typewriter.

+ **Echo input mode**, which determines whether keyboard input that is received from the input buffer is echoed to the active screen buffer. The effects of echo input mode depend on the output mode of the active screen buffer.

By default, all three of these high-level input modes are enabled. When that is the case, the console is said to be running in *cooked* mode. If you decide to deactivate one of these modes, it is recommended that you deactivate all three of them, because all three are designed to work together. When all three high-level input modes are deactivated, the console is said to be running in *raw* mode.

HIGH-LEVEL OUTPUT MODES

The console API's high-level output modes are as follows:

✦ **Processed output mode,** which determines whether information in the input buffer is filtered and processed before it is displayed on the screen.

✦ **Wrapping at EOL (end of line) output mode,** which determines whether the cursor moves to the first column in the next screen row when it reaches the end of the current row in the console window.

By default, both of the high-level output modes are enabled, along with the three high-level input modes described under the previous subheading. All five high-level console modes should generally be turned on or off in a group, and not individually, because all five modes are designed to work together.

LOW-LEVEL INPUT MODES

The low-level input modes supported by the Win32 API are as follows:

✦ **Mouse input mode,** which determines whether mouse events sent to the input buffer are recognized.

✦ **Window input mode,** which determines whether buffer-resizing events are recognized.

✦ **Processed input mode,** which controls the filtering and processing of nonprinting characters.

You can obtain information about the current console mode by calling the Win32 function `GetConsoleMode`. To set the current console mode, call `SetConsoleMode`. You can specify which low-level or high-level mode (or combination of modes) you want by setting flag constants that are recognized by `GetConsoleMode` and `SetConsoleMode`. These flags are listed and described in "Using the Win32 Console API" later in this chapter.

CONSOLE CONTROL HANDLERS

As DOS and UNIX programmers know, certain key combinations are often treated in special ways in text-based applications. For example, the **Ctrl+C** key combination is often treated as an interrupt signal, and the **Ctrl+Break** combination is often treated as a break signal.

When a Win32 console process is running, it handles certain key combinations and mouse events with a special kind of function called a *control handler*. In addition to handling the key combinations such as **Ctrl+C** and **Ctrl+Break**, control handlers provide responses to certain mouse events, such as selection of the **Close** menu item. Each console process has a set of control handler functions that are called by the system when the process receives a **Ctrl+C, Ctrl+Break,** or **Ctrl+Close** signal.

Initially, the list of control handlers owned by each process contains only a default handler function that calls the Win32 function `ExitProcess`. An application can provide a console process with additional handler functions—or can remove existing handler functions from a console process—by calling the Win32 procedure `SetConsoleCtrlHandler`.

In the MYCONSOL example program, the following control handler appears in **MYCONSOL.CPP:**

```
BOOL CtrlHandler(DWORD fdwCtrlType)
{
    DWORD exitCode;
    HANDLE hThisProcess = GetCurrentProcess();
    GetExitCodeProcess(hThisProcess, &exitCode);

    switch (fdwCtrlType) {
    case CTRL_C_EVENT:
        ExitProcess(exitCode);
        return TRUE;
    case CTRL_CLOSE_EVENT:
        ExitProcess(exitCode);

    return TRUE;
    case CTRL_BREAK_EVENT:
    case CTRL_LOGOFF_EVENT:
    case CTRL_CLOSE_EVENT:
    default:
        return FALSE;
    }
}
```

In the preceding code fragment, a `switch` statement controls what happens to keyboard and mouse events that are sent to the control handler. If the user presses **Ctrl+C** (a CTRL_C_EVENT), ExitProcess is called and the control handler returns a value of TRUE. The same thing happens when the user activates a CTRL_CLOSE_EVENT by selecting **Close** from the console window's close-box menu. All other events tracked by the control handler return FALSE.

REGISTERING A CONTROL HANDLER

An application invokes a control handler by calling the Win32 function SetConsole-CtrlHandler, passing the function a pointer to the control handler to be used.

SetConsoleCtrlHandler always affects just one process; it does not affect the lists of control handlers for other processes. When a console process receives any of the control signals, it calls the handler functions on a last-registered, first-called basis until it encounters a control handler that returns TRUE. If no handler that returns TRUE is found, the process's default handler is called.

This code fragment, which also appears in **MYCONSOL.CPP**, registers a control handler:

```
// Set console's control handler.
    BOOL bRetVal = SetConsoleCtrlHandler((PHANDLER_ROUTINE)CtrlHandler,
        TRUE);
    if (!bRetVal)
        MyErrMsg("Could not set up control handler.",
            myConsole);
```

USING THE WIN32 CONSOLE API

Console-related functions provided by the Win32 API can be divided into the following categories:

+ Functions that create console windows
+ Functions that release console windows
+ Console I/O
+ Functions that manage I/O handles
+ Functions that manage I/O buffers
+ Console mode functions

Functions that fall into these categories are described in this section.

Functions that Create Console Windows

A process can create a console by calling `AllocConsole`, or by calling `CreateProcess` with certain flags set. `AllocConsole` opens a console window that is attached to the calling process. `CreateProcess` starts a new process and attaches it to a console, either a new console or a console that is attached to the calling process depending on the parameters passed to `CreateProcess`.

Creating a Console with the AllocConsole Function

`AllocConsole` allocates a new console for the calling process. `AllocConsole` does not create a new console process; it merely creates a new console and attaches it to the calling process. To create a new console process, an application must call `CreateProcess`.

Following is the syntax of the `AllocConsole` call:

```
BOOL AllocConsole()
```

If `AllocConsole` succeeds, it returns a value of TRUE; otherwise, it returns FALSE. A process can be associated with only one console window, so `AllocConsole` fails if the calling process already has a console.

When an application allocates a console by calling `AllocConsole`, the new console window is equipped with a set of handles for standard input, standard output, and standard diagnostic output. The new console can then use those handles to manage input, output, and the handling of error messages. A console can obtain its standard I/O handles by calling the Win32 function `GetStdHandle`.

In the CONSOLE program on the accompanying disk, this code fragment in **CONSOLE. CPP** creates a new console by calling `AllocConsole`:

```
void ConsoleAlloc()
{
    AllocConsole();
    while (TRUE)
        /* Do nothing */ ;
    FreeConsole();
}
```

The preceding code fragment does the absolute minimum that is required to display a console window. It merely opens a console window by calling `AllocConsole`, loops until the user closes the console window, and frees the console when the window closes.

As you can observe by executing the CONSOLE program and selecting **Alloc** from the Console menu, this minimal programming effort yields minimal results; the console window doesn't display any text or respond to user input. When the user closes the window, the whole application shuts down. Usually a better way to create and manage a console window is to open a new process with its own console window by calling `CreateProcess`. The new process can then open a console window by making its own `AllocConsole` call.

Creating a Console with the CreateProcess Function

`CreateProcess` creates a new process and the new process's primary thread. The new process then executes a specified file. `CreateProcess` can create and start any kind of Windows NT process; the call is not reserved for use with console processes. However, once an application creates a process, it can open a console for that process by calling `AllocConsole` or by simply jumping to a main function that is used as an entry point by a console associated with the process.

Following is the syntax of `CreateProcess`:

```
BOOL CreateProcess(LPCTSTR lpszImageName,
    LPCTSTR lpszCommandLine,
    LPSECURITY_ATTRIBUTES lpsaProcess,
    LPSECURITY_ATTRIBUTES lpsaThread,
    BOOL fInheritHandles,
    DWORDfdwCreate,
    LPVOID lpvEnvironment,
    LPCSTR lpszCurDir,
    LPSTARTUPINFO lpsiStartInfo,
    LPPROCESS_INFORMATION lppiProcInfo)
```

If `CreateProcess` succeeds, it returns `TRUE`; if not, it returns `FALSE`.

Of the parameters that can be passed to `CreateProcess`, several are particularly applicable to console processes. For example, `lpsiStartInfo` is a pointer to a STARTUPINFO structure that defines the characteristics of a console window. The `lppiProcInfo` parameter is also a pointer to a PROCESS_INFORMATION structure, which contains information about the console process being created.

The STARTUPINFO Structure

When an application calls `CreateProcess` to create a console window, the application can create a STARTUPINFO structure to specify important properties of the new console window. The console process can then pass the address of that structure to the `CreateProcess` call in the `lpsiStartInfo` parameter.

If an application supplies a `NULL` value for the `lpsiStartInfo` parameter, `Create-Process` creates a standard STARTUPINFO structure with default values. Following is the definition of the STARTUPINFO structure:

```
typedef struct _STARTUPINFO {
    DWORD cb;
    LPTSTR lpReserved;
    LPTSTR lpDesktop;
    LPTSTR lpTitle;
    DWORD dwX;
    DWORD dwY;
    DWORD dwXSize;
    DWORD dwYSize;
    DWORD dwXCountChars;
    DWORD dwYCountChars;
    DWORD dwFillAttribute;
    DWORD dwFlags;
    WORD wShowWindow;
    WORD cbReserved2;
    LPBYTE lpReserved2;
    HANDLE hStdInput;
    HANDLE hStdOutput;
    HANDLE hStdError;
} STARTUPINFO, *LPSTARTUPINFO;
```

A process can obtain information about the STARTUPINFO structure currently in use by calling `GetStartupInfo`. Console processes use the following functions to get and set the values of individual member variables of STARTUPINFO structure:

- ✦ **GetConsoleScreenBufferInfo** obtains the window size, the screen buffer size, and the color attributes of a console from a STARTUPINFO structure.
- ✦ **GetConsoleTitle** obtains the title currently displayed in a console window's title bar.
- ✦ **SetConsoleScreenBufferSize** changes the size of a console window's screen buffer.
- ✦ **SetConsoleTextAttribute** sets the color attributes of a console window.

+ **SetConsoleTitle** specifies the title to be displayed in a console window's title bar.
+ **SetConsoleWindowInfo** changes the size of a console window.

Each member variable of the STARTUPINFO structure is described in Chapter 7.

The PROCESS_INFORMATION Structure

The `lpsiStartInfo` parameter of the `CreateProcess` function is a pointer to a PROCESS_INFORMATION structure that provides information about the process being created. When an application calls `CreateProcess`, it creates a PROCESS_INFORMATION structure and returns the address of that structure in `lpsiStartInfo`. Following is the definition of the PROCESS_INFORMATION structure:

```
typedef struct _PROCESS_INFORMATION {
    HANDLE hProcess;
    HANDLE hThread;
    DWORD dwProcessID;
    DWORD dwThreadID;
} PROCESS_INFORMATION;
```

The `hProcess` member variable is the handle of the process that has been created. The `hThread` variable is the handle of the new process's main thread. The `dwProcessID` variable is a global identifier that identifies the process that has been created. The `dwThreadID` variable is a global identifier that identifies the new process's main thread.

Other CreateProcess Parameters

Several other parameters of the `CreateProcess` call have special importance in console processes. The `fInheritHandles` parameter specifies whether the new process inherits handles from the calling process. If `fInheritHandles` is TRUE, each inheritable open handle in the calling process is inherited by the new process. Inherited handles have the same value and access privileges as the original handles.

The `fdwCreate` parameter provides a set of flags that control the priority of the process and specify certain facts about how the new process is to be created. The `fdwCreate` parameter also controls the new process's priority class, which is used in determining the scheduling priorities of the process' threads. Thread priorities are described in more detail in Chapter 7, "Multithreading." The following `fdwCreate` flags are often used with console processes:

✦ **DETACHED_PROCESS**. This flag applies specifically to console processes. If the flag is set, the new process does not have access to the console of the calling process. If the new process wants to create a new console, it can create one by calling `AllocConsole`, or by simply jumping to the beginning of a main function that the console uses as an entry point. The DETACHED_PROCESS flag cannot be used with the CREATE_NEW_CONSOLE flag.

✦ **CREATE_NEW_CONSOLE**. This flag also applies specifically to console processes. If it is set, a new console is created and assigned to the new process. This means that the new process does not inherit the parent process's console. The CREATE_NEW_CONSOLE flag cannot be used with the DETACHED_PROCESS flag. If CREATE_NEW_CONSOLE is set when `CreateProcess` is called, the newly created console is accessible to the child process but not to the parent process. If there is any possibility that console operations managed by the calling process might conflict with console operations managed by the new process, a separate console for the new process should be created.

The `lpsiStartInfo` parameter is a pointer to a STARTUPINFO structure. If `lpsiStartInfo` points to a particular STARTUPINFO structure, the members of that structure control the appearance and behavior of the first new console window displayed by the newly created process. If `lpsiStartInfo` is set to NULL when `CreateProcess` is called, the new process uses a default STARTUPINFO structure.

If the calling process supplies `CreateProcess` with a customized STARTUPINFO structure, the calling process must either set CREATE_NEW_CONSOLE or call `AllocConsole` to create a new console window. A STARTUPINFO structure can set the following characteristics of a console window:

✦ The size (expressed in character cells) and the location (expressed in screen pixel coordinates) of the new console window.

✦ The size (expressed in character cells) of the new console's screen buffer.

✦ The text and background color attributes of the new console's screen buffer.

✦ The name that appears in the title bar of the new console's window.

A child process can call `GetStartupInfo` to determine the values assigned to the member variables of its STARTUPINFO structure. A process cannot change the location of its console window on the screen, but several console functions are available to set or query the other properties specified in the STARTUPINFO structure.

Calling the CreateProcess Function

In the CONSOLE example program, `CreateProcess` is called in **CONSOLE.CPP** to create a new console process. The call is made from the function `ShowConsole`, which looks like this:

```
void ShowConsole()
{
    sui.cb               = sizeof (STARTUPINFO);
    sui.lpReserved       = 0;
    sui.lpDesktop        = NULL;
    sui.lpTitle          = NULL;
    sui.dwX              = 10;
    sui.dwY              = 10;
    sui.dwXSize          = 400;
    sui.dwYSize          = 200;
    sui.dwXCountChars    = 80;
    sui.dwYCountChars    = 42;
    sui.dwFillAttribute  = 0;
    sui.dwFlags          = STARTF_USEPOSITION|STARTF_USESIZE|
                              STARTF_USECOUNTCHARS|
                                  STARTF_USESHOWWINDOW;
    sui.wShowWindow      = SW_SHOWNORMAL;
    sui.cbReserved2      = 0;
    sui.lpReserved2      = 0;

    // Create a new console process.
    CreateProcess("MYCONSOL\\MYCONSOL.EXE", NULL, NULL, NULL,
    TRUE, DETACHED_PROCESS, NULL, NULL, &sui, &pi);

}
```

When `CreateProcess` is called, it is passed the address of a STARTUPINFO structure named `sui`. That structure determines the size, colors, and a few other characteristics of the console window that `ShowConsole` displays. The process that is opened by `CreateProcess` is an executable file named **MYCONSOL.EXE**. This file resides in the MYCONSOL subdirectory.

Functions that Release Console Windows

The following functions release console windows:

- ✦ FreeConsole
- ✦ ExitProcess
- ✦ TerminateProcess

FreeConsole detaches the calling process from its console window (provided one exists) and destroys the console unless it is shared by other processes. If other processes share the console, it is not destroyed until it is released by all processes that share it.

ExitProcess detaches the calling function from its console window (if one exists) and then terminates the function. ExitProcess performs all necessary housekeeping before it terminates a process and is therefore the recommended way to exit a process.

TerminateProcess, like ExitProcess, detaches the calling console from its console window (if there is one) and then closes all threads of the calling function. Then, unlike ExitProcess, it performs a quick-and-dirty exit from the function. When you end a process by calling TerminateProcess, there is no guarantee that the integrity of all data associated with the process will be maintained; specifically, the state of any global data that is being used by any DLLs that are attached to the process may be compromised, and the notification needed to detach a process or detach a thread is not posted to the DLL. If possible, you should avoid shutting down processes by calling TerminateProcess; call ExitProcess instead.

A console process, like any other process, remains in the system until all its threads have terminated and all handles to the process and any of its threads are closed—unless one of them calls ExitProcess, which is what the primary thread should do. You can call CloseHandle to close any handle associated with a process. Alternatively, you can call ExitProcess to perform a clean shutdown of a process, all its threads, and all its handles.

When the last process that is attached to a console terminates or frees the console by calling FreeConsole, the console window is destroyed. When the last thread associated with a process terminates, Windows NT services perform the following steps:

1. All objects opened by the process are implicitly closed.
2. The process's termination status (a value that can be obtained by calling GetExitCodeProcess) changes from its initial value (STILL_ACTIVE) to the termination status of the last thread that terminates.

3. The thread object of the main thread is set to a signaled state, satisfying the needs of any threads that may have been waiting for the object.

4. The process object is set to the signaled state, satisfying the needs of any threads that may have been waiting for the object.

Freeing a Console with the FreeConsole Function

If a process is attached to a console, it can detach itself from its console by calling `FreeConsole`. Following is the syntax of `FreeConsole`:

```
BOOL FreeConsole()
```

If `FreeConsole` succeeds, it returns `TRUE`. If not, it returns `FALSE`.

Freeing a Console with the ExitProcess Function

When you terminate a process by calling `ExitProcess` (the recommended method), `ExitProcess` performs all necessary housekeeping and then informs all DLLs attached to the process that the process is terminating. The DLLs thus have a chance to protect the integrity of their global data and release all necessary resources (such as thread local storage, which is discussed in Chapter 8) before the process ends.

The following syntax is used for calling `ExitProcess`:

```
VOID ExitProcess(UINT uExitCode)
```

`ExitProcess` does not return a value.

The `uExit` parameter shown in the preceding example is an exit code that applies to the process being terminated. This exit code also applies to all threads that are terminated as a result of the call.

An application can obtain the correct exit code for a function by calling the console API function `GetExitCodeProcess`. (As you'll see in Chapter 7, "Multithreading," a similar function—`GetExitCodeThread`—can be used to retrieve a thread's exit code.)

In the CONSOLE example program, the `ExitProcess` function is executed inside a control handler. That takes place in a source-code segment that appears under the heading "Console Control Handlers" earlier in this chapter.

High-Level Console I/O Functions

With the high-level console I/O functions—`ReadFile`, `WriteFile`, `ReadConsole`, and `WriteConsole`—an application can read console input and write console output as a stream of characters. `ReadConsole` and `WriteConsole` behave just like the `ReadFile` and `WriteFile` functions except that they can be used either as wide-character functions (in which text arguments must use Unicode characters) or as ANSI functions (in which text arguments must use characters from the Windows 3.x character set).

Applications that must maintain a single set of sources to support either Unicode or the ANSI character set should use `ReadConsole` and `WriteConsole`.

The ReadConsole Function

The `ReadConsole` function reads character input from the console input buffer and removes it from the buffer. The syntax of this function is as follows:

```
BOOL ReadConsole(HANDLE hConsoleInput, LPVOID lpvBuffer, DWORD cchToRead,
LPDWORD lpcchRead, LPVOID lpReserved)
```

`ReadConsole` returns `TRUE` if it succeeds, and `FALSE` if it does not.

When you call `ReadConsole`, you must provide the function with a handle to a console input buffer (`hConsoleInput`), a pointer to a buffer that receives data from the console input buffer (`lpvBuffer`), and the number of characters that you want the function to read (`cchToRead`). When the call returns, it reports the number of characters that have actually been read in the `lpcchRead` parameter. The `lpReserved` parameter is reserved for future use, so don't touch it.

In the CONSOLE example application, `ReadConsole` is executed from `MConsole::ReadLine`, a member function of the `MConsole` class. The `MConsole::ReadLine` function, which appears **MYCONSOL.H**, looks like this:

```
CString MConsole::ReadLine()
{
    ReadConsole(hConsoleInput, chBuffer, 255, &cRead, NULL);
      CString tempCStr(chBuffer, cRead);
    tempCStr = tempCStr.Left(tempCStr.GetLength()-1);
    nameStr = tempCStr;
    return tempCStr;
}
```

In this code fragment, `ReadLine` retrieves the contents of the console's input buffer, and the retrieved text is converted into a `CString` object (`CString` is an MFC library class that encapsulates strings.) That `CString` object is then returned to the function that called `ReadLine`.

The ReadFile Function

ReadFile reads data from a file or from a console buffer, starting at the position specified by a file pointer. When the read operation is complete, ReadFile adjusts the file pointer by the number of bytes actually read unless the file handle is created with a special attribute called the overlapped attribute. If the file handle is created with the overlapped attribute enabled, ReadFile must be provided with certain information that is used in asynchronous output to adjust the position of the file pointer after the read takes place.

The syntax of ReadFile is identical to the syntax of ReadConsole, with two exceptions: The first parameter of a call to ReadFile can be either a file handle or the handle of an input buffer, and the fifth parameter is the address of an OVERLAPPED structure, which contains information used in asynchronous I/O.

I/O Functions, Console Handles, and File Handles

ReadConsole and WriteConsole can be used only with console handles. In contrast, ReadFile and WriteFile can be used with other kinds of handles, such as handles that access files or pipes. ReadConsole and WriteConsole fail, however, if an application attempts to use them with a standard handle that has been redirected and is no longer a console handle.

If ReadFile or ReadConsole is called with line input mode enabled (the default), there is no return to the calling application until **Enter** is pressed. If line input mode is disabled, ReadFile and ReadConsole do not return until at least one character is available. In either mode, all available characters are read until either no more keys are available or the specified number of characters has been read. Unread characters are buffered until the next read operation.

When ReadFile and ReadConsole return, they report the total number of characters that have been read. If echo input mode is enabled, characters read by ReadFile and ReadConsole are written to the active screen buffer at the current cursor position.

Using the WriteConsole and WriteFile Functions

WriteFile and WriteConsole can write to either an active or an inactive screen buffer. WriteFile can also write to a file or a pipe if the STDOUT handle of the console is redirected.

When processed output mode or wrap at EOL output mode is enabled, the output mode determines the way in which characters are written or echoed to a screen buffer. Characters written by WriteFile or WriteConsole, or echoed by ReadFile or ReadConsole, are inserted in a screen buffer at the current cursor position. As each character is written, the cursor position advances to the next character cell, with one exception: The behavior at the end of a line depends on the screen buffer's wrap at EOL output mode. An application can use `GetConsoleScreenBufferInfo` to determine the current cursor position, and `SetConsoleCursorPosition` to set the cursor position.

Low-Level Console I/O Functions

The low-level console I/O functions provide an application with direct access to a console's input and screen buffers. Thus, they provide the software developer with extensive control over console I/O. With the low-level console I/O functions, an application can do the following:

✦ Obtain information about mouse and buffer-resizing events

✦ Obtain extended information about keyboard input events

✦ Write input records to the input buffer

✦ Read input records without removing them from the input buffer

✦ Determine the number of pending events in the input buffer

✦ Flush the input buffer

✦ Read and write strings of Unicode (16-bit) characters or ANSI characters at a specified location in a screen buffer

✦ Read and write strings of text and background color attributes at specified screen buffer locations

✦ Read and write rectangular blocks of character and color data at a specified screen buffer location

✦ Write single Unicode characters or ANSI characters, or text and background color attribute combinations, to a specified number of consecutive cells beginning at a specified screen buffer location

Functions that Manage I/O Handles

A console process uses object handles to access the input and screen buffers of its console. To help applications manage these handles, the console API provides four functions: `GetStdHandle`, `SetStdHandle`, `CreateFile`, and `CreateConsoleScreenBuffer`.

Console handles returned by `CreateFile` and `CreateConsoleScreenBuffer` can be used in any console functions that require a handle of a console's input buffer or of a console screen buffer. Handles returned by `GetStdHandle` can be used by the console functions if they have not been redirected to refer to something other than console I/O. If a standard handle has been redirected to refer to a file or a pipe, however, the handle can be used only by the ReadFile and WriteFile functions.

When a console process in running, an application can read from the console's standard output handle by calling ReadFile or ReadConsole. To write to a console's standard input handle, a process can call WriteFile or WriteConsole. These four functions are described under the headings that follow.

The GetStdHandle Function

When an application needs to read from or write to a console window, it can obtain the console's I/O handles by calling GetStdHandle. It can then obtain data from the console's input buffer by reading the data from the input handle obtained from GetStdHandle. Conversely, it can send data to the console's screen buffer by writing to the output handle provided by GetStdHandle. GetStdHandle also provides a diagnostic handle that can be used as a destination for error messages.

An application can call GetStdHandle using this syntax:

```
HANDLE GetStdHandle(DWORD fdwDevice)
```

If GetStdHandle is successful, it returns the handle it has obtained. If the call is not successful, it returns NULL.

The fdwDevice parameter is a constant that specifies the kind of handle that the function is being used to obtain. fdwDevice can have one of three values:

+ **STD_INPUT_HANDLE** instructs GetStdHandle to return a standard input handle.
+ **STD_OUTPUT_HANDLE** requests a standard output handle.
+ **STD_ERROR_HANDLE** places an order for a standard error handle.

If GetStdHandle succeeds, it returns the requested handle. If it fails, it returns an INVALID_HANDLE_FLAG. To obtain more information about a failure of the function, an application can call the Win32 GetLastError function.

In the CONSOLE example program, before GetStdHandle is called, a function named MConsole::Open runs a test to see whether the current process has an open console. If there is an open console, the function calls FreeConsole to close it down. Then AllocConsole is called to open a new console. That done, MConsole::Open calls GetStdHandle.

The MConsole::Open member function appears in the file **MYCONSOL.H.** Following is the definition of the function:

```
// Open the console.
BOOL MConsole::Open(BOOL addcrlf)
{
    if(isopen)
        return TRUE;

    if(!::AllocConsole()) {
        ::FreeConsole();
        if(!::AllocConsole())
            return FALSE;
    }

    hConsoleOutput = ::GetStdHandle(STD_OUTPUT_HANDLE);
    hConsoleInput = ::GetStdHandle(STD_INPUT_HANDLE);
    if(addcrlf)
        AddCRLF();
    isopen = TRUE;
    return TRUE;
}
```

Notice that the preceding code fragment calls GetStdHandle twice: once to obtain the current console's output handle and again to obtain its input handle. These two handles are then stowed away for safekeeping in a pair of variables named hConsoleOutput and hConsoleInput. Subsequently, hConsoleOutput and hConsoleInput can be accessed at any time to retrieve the current console process's output and input handles.

The CloseHandle Function

An application can close a console handle by calling CloseHandle. The syntax of CloseHandle is as follows:

```
BOOL CloseHandle(HANDLE hObject)
```

When an application calls CloseHandle, the value of the hHandle parameter should be the handle to be closed. CloseHandle returns TRUE if it succeeds, and FALSE if it does not.

The DuplicateHandle Function

With the DuplicateHandle function, an application can create a duplicate console handle with different access or inheritability characteristics from the original handle.

The CreateFile Function

CreateFile creates, opens, or truncates a file, pipe, communications resource, disk device, or console. CreateFile returns a handle that can be used to access the object.

CreateFile is not solely a console call; it can create any kind of file or file-like object. However, the function has certain parameters and behaviors that apply specifically to consoles.

The syntax of a call to CreateFile is as follows:

```
HANDLE CreateFile(LPCSTR lpszName,
    DWORD fdwAccess,
    DWORD fdwShareMode,
    LPSECURITY_ATTRIBUTES lpsa,
    DWORD fdwCreate,
    DWORD fdwAttrsAndFlags,
    HANDLE hTemplateFile;
```

If CreateFile succeeds, the return value is an open handle that accesses the specified file. If the file already exists when CreateFile is called and if the value of fdwCreate is CREATE_ALWAYS or OPEN_ALWAYS, a subsequent call to GetLastError always returns the constant ERROR_ALREADY_EXISTS even if the function succeeds. If the file does not already exist when CreateFile is called, a subsequent call to GetLastError returns 0.

If CreateFile fails, its return value is INVALID_HANDLE_VALUE.

In the preceding syntax example, the lpszName parameter points to a null-terminated string that specifies the name of the file, pipe, communications resource, disk device, or console that is being created, opened, or truncated. The fdwAccess parameter specifies the kind of access that is granted to the specified file.

When you call CreateFile to create, open, or truncate input or output to a console, you must set lpszName to the value CONIN$ or the value CONOUT$. CONIN$ specifies console input, and CONOUT$ specifies console output.

If the value of lpszName is set to CONIN$ when CreateFile is called, CreateFile can create a handle to console input. If a handle to the process is open as a result of inheritance or duplication, CreateFile can create a handle to the active screen buffer if lpszName is set to CONOUT$. In this case, the calling process must be attached to an inherited console or one allocated by AllocConsole. For console handles, the CreateFile parameters should be set as follows:

✦ If lpszName is set to CONIN$ when CreateFile is called, CreateFile obtains a handle that accesses the specified console's input buffer, even if SetStdHandle has been used to redirect the standard input handle. You can call GetStdHandle to obtain the console's standard input handle.

✦ If lpszName is set to CONOUT$ when CreateFile is called, CreateFile obtains a handle that accesses the specified console's active screen buffer, even if SetStdHandle has been used to redirect the console's standard output handle. In this case, you can call GetStdHandle to obtain the console's standard output handle.

The value of fdwAccess can be set to zero, or it can be set to either one or both of two constants: GENERIC_READ and GENERIC_WRITE. When fdwAccess is set to zero, the application being executed can obtain attributes of a device without actually accessing the device. GENERIC_READ grants read access to the specified file or device, and GENERIC_WRITE grants write access. If both GENERIC_READ and GENERIC_WRITE are set, both read and write access to the file are granted.

If an application calls CreateFile with lpszName set to CON and fwdAccess set to GENERIC_READ, CreateFile opens a console for input. If CreateFile is called with lpszName set to CON and fwdAccess set to GENERIC_WRITE, CreateFile opens a console for output.

If CreateFile is called with lpszName set to CON and fwdAccess set to GENERIC_READ | GENERIC_WRITE, CreateFile fails and returns an ERROR_PATH_NOT_FOUND error.

Other parameters of CreateFile are as follows:

✦ **fdwShareMode**, which specifies how the specified file can be shared.

✦ **lpsa**, which points to a SECURITY_ATTRIBUTES structure that specifies the security attributes for the file.

✦ **fdwAttrsAndFiles**, which specifies the file's attributes and flags.

FUNCTIONS THAT ACCESS CONSOLE I/O BUFFERS

Every console process has one input buffer and at least one screen buffer. The Win32 console API provides many functions for accessing, manipulating, and setting the attributes of console screen buffers and input buffers. These functions are described in this section.

FUNCTIONS FOR MANAGING SCREEN BUFFERS

The Win32 console API provides a number of functions for accessing, managing, and setting the attributes of screen buffers. These functions, and their most important characteristics, are as follows:

+ **CreateConsoleScreenBuffer** creates additional screen buffers for a console process. (The first screen buffer that is attached to the process is created automatically when the process begins.)

+ **SetConsoleActiveScreenBuffer** sets the active screen buffer for a console process. This function is useful only if a console has more than one screen buffer.

+ **GetConsoleScreenBufferInfo** obtains the size of a console window and the size of the screen buffer. This information can then be used to determine how data is displayed on the screen.

+ **GetLargestConsoleWindowSize** returns the maximum possible size of a console's window based on the current font and screen sizes. This function, unlike `GetConsoleScreenBufferInfo`, ignores the screen buffer's size.

+ **SetConsoleWindowInfo** sets the size or location of a screen buffer's window. (Changing the active screen buffer's window size changes the size of the console window displayed on the screen.)

+ **SetConsoleScreenBufferSize** changes the size of a screen buffer.

+ **GetConsoleCursorInfo** returns the size of a console's cursor and tells whether the cursor is visible.

+ **SetConsoleCursorInfo** sets the appearance and visibility of the cursor.

+ **GetConsoleMode** returns the current I/O mode of a console.

+ **SetConsoleCursorPosition** sets a new cursor position. If that position is outside the boundaries of the current window rectangle, the window rectangle shifts automatically to display the cursor.

+ **ScrollConsoleScreenBuffer** scrolls the text displayed in the console window by copying a rectangular block of characters from one screen buffer to another.

Some of the most often used functions in the preceding list are described in detail under the headings that follow.

CALLING THE CREATECONSOLESCREENBUFFER FUNCTION

CreateConsoleScreenBuffer creates a new screen buffer for a console and returns a handle to the buffer. That handle can then be used in any function that needs to access the console's screen buffer. The new screen buffer does not become active, however, until SetConsoleActiveScreenBuffer is called.

As mentioned earlier, when an application changes the active screen buffer by calling SetConsoleActiveScreenBuffer and CreateConsoleScreenBuffer, the handle returned by GetStdHandle is not affected. Similarly, using GetStdHandle to change the STDOUT handle does not affect the active screen buffer.

HOW TEXT IS STORED IN A CONSOLE SCREEN BUFFER

Every character in a console screen buffer is stored in a CHAR_INFO structure, which is defined as follows:

```
typedef struct _CHAR_INFO {
    union {              / * Unicode or ANSI character */
        WCHAR UnicodeChar;
        CHAR AsciiChar;
    } Char;
    WORD Attributes;           /* text and background colors */
} CHAR_INFO, *PCHAR_INFO;
```

The CHAR_INFO data structure contains a union named Char that allows an application to store either Unicode characters or ANSI characters in a console screen buffer. If Unicode characters are used, the application must be compiled as a Unicode-compatible application.

The CHAR_INFO structure also has a WORD member named Attributes, which can be used to set both the foreground color and the background color of each individual character stored in a console screen buffer. When each character in the console's window is displayed, it obtains its foreground (text) color and its background color from its own CHAR_INFO structure.

THE SETCONSOLETEXTATTRIBUTE FUNCTION

An application can set the foreground and background colors of all the characters in a screen buffer by calling `SetConsoleTextAttribute`. The syntax of `SetConsole-TextAttribute` is as follows:

```
BOOL SetConsoleTextAttribute(HANDLE hConsoleOutput, WORD wAttr
```

`SetConsoleTextAttribute` returns `TRUE` if it succeeds, and `FALSE` if it does not.

When an application calls `SetConsoleTextAttribute`, the `hConsoleOutput` parameter is the handle of the console screen buffer being addressed. The `wAttr` parameter can be any combination of the following constants, which are defined in **WINCON.H**:

- ✦ FOREGROUND_BLUE
- ✦ FOREGROUND_GREEN
- ✦ FOREGROUND_RED
- ✦ FOREGROUND_INTENSITY
- ✦ BACKGROUND_BLUE
- ✦ BACKGROUND_GREEN
- ✦ BACKGROUND_RED
- ✦ BACKGROUND_INTENSITY

By the Way

Changing a screen buffer's text attributes by calling `SetConsoleTextAttribute` does not affect the display of characters that have already been written to the screen. Also, the text attributes that are passed to `SetConsoleTextAttribute` do not affect characters written by low-level console I/O functions, such as `WriteConsoleOutput` or `WriteConsoleOutputCharacter`.

When a console process calls `SetConsoleTextAttribute`, the C-language operator | can be used to combine any number of the preceding constants in any order. But sometimes the result of a `wAttr` setting might not be what one might expect, so some experimenting may be necessary. For example, if `wAttr` is set as follows, the result is bright cyan text on a blue background:

```
FOREGROUND_BLUE | FOREGROUND_GREEN | FOREGROUND_INTENSITY | BACKGROUND_BLUE
```

If no background constant is specified in wAttr passed to SetConsoleTextAttribute, the background of the console window is black. If no foreground constant is specified, the text is white. The following wAttr setting produces black text on a white background:

BACKGROUND_BLUE | BACKGROUND_GREEN | BACKGROUND_RED

TEXT ATTRIBUTES IN THE EXAMPLE PROGRAM

In the CONSOLE example application, **MYCONSOL.H** contains three calls to Set-ConsoleTextAttribute. CONSOLE calls just one of these functions—the one named WhiteOnBlack:

```
    // Set screen colors (three choices).
    void WhiteOnBlack(void) {
        SetConsoleTextAttribute(hConsoleOutput, FOREGROUND_RED |
            FOREGROUND_GREEN | FOREGROUND_BLUE);
    }
    void BlackOnWhite(void) {
        SetConsoleTextAttribute(hConsoleOutput,
            BACKGROUND_RED | BACKGROUND_GREEN |
            BACKGROUND_BLUE | BACKGROUND_INTENSITY);
    }
    void RedOnWhite(void) {
        SetConsoleTextAttribute(hConsoleOutput,
            FOREGROUND_RED | FOREGROUND_INTENSITY |
            BACKGROUND_RED | BACKGROUND_GREEN |
            BACKGROUND_BLUE | BACKGROUND_INTENSITY);
    }
```

The WhiteOnBlack function is called from **MCONSOL.CPP** as follows:

```
    // Set console attributes.
    myConsole.WhiteOnBlack();
```

By changing the WhiteOnBlack call in **MYCONSOL.CPP** to a call to BlackOnWhite or RedOnWhite, you can edit the CONSOLE source code to call either of the other two functions—or you can write your own text-color and screen-color functions.

THE GETCONSOLESCREENBUFFERINFO FUNCTION

An application can call `GetConsoleScreenBufferInfo` to obtain the current text attributes of a screen buffer. The syntax of `GetConsoleScreenBufferInfo` is as follows:

```
BOOL GetConsoleScreenBufferInfo(HANDLE hConsoleOutput,
    PCONSOLE_SCREEN_BUFFER_INFO pcsbi
```

`GetConsoleScreenBufferInfo` returns TRUE if it succeeds. If not, it returns FALSE.

The `hConsoleOutput` parameter is the handle of the console screen buffer being accessed. The `pcsbi` parameter is a pointer to a PCONSOLE_SCREEN_BUFFER_INFO structure, which is defined as follows:

```
typedef struct _CONSOLE_SCREEN_BUFFER_INFO {
    COORD dwSize;
    COORD dwCursorPosition;
    WORD wAttributes;
    SMALL_RECT srWindow;
    COORD dwMaximumWindowSize;
} CONSOLE_SCREEN_BUFFER_INFO;
```

The `dwSize` member variable of the CONSOLE_SCREEN_BUFFER_INFO structure specifies the size of the screen buffer, expressed in character columns and rows. The `dwCursorPosition` variable specifies the column and row coordinates occupied by the cursor in the screen buffer. The `wAttributes` variable specifies the foreground and background color attributes that are currently set for the screen buffer.

The `srWindow` variable of the CONSOLE_SCREEN_BUFFER_INFO structure is a SMALL_RECT structure that contains the screen buffer coordinates of the upper-left and lower-right corners of the display window. The `dwMaximumWindowSize` variable specifies the maximum possible size of the console window based on the size of the current screen and of the current screen buffer.

CONSOLE MODE FUNCTIONS

An application can set the input mode of a console by calling the Win32 function `SetConsoleMode`. By calling `GetConsoleMode`, an application can obtain information about a console's current mode. `GetConsoleMode` reports either the current input mode of a console's input buffer or the current output mode of a screen buffer, depending on the parameters passed to it when it is called.

`SetConsoleMode` sets the current mode of either a console input buffer or a screen buffer, depending on the parameters passed to it when it is called. Following is the syntax of a call to `SetConsoleMode`:

```
BOOL SetConsoleMode(HANDLE hConsole, DWORD fdwMode)
```

When an application calls `SetConsoleMode`, the value of `hConsole` should be the handle of a console input buffer or the handle of a console output buffer. The `fdwMode` parameter is a constant that specifies the input or the output mode to set.

CONSTANTS FOR SETTING CONSOLE MODES

The constants listed under the following headings can be passed to `SetConsoleMode` in the `fdwMode` parameter in any combination and in any order. For more details about how they work, see "Console Input and Output Modes" earlier in this chapter.

The constants in the following list can be passed to `SetConsoleMode` to enable high-level console input functions:

+ **ENABLE_PROCESSED_INPUT**. If this constant is passed to `SetConsoleMode` in the `fdwMode` parameter and if a console input handle is passed to the `hConsole` parameter, the specified console's input buffer is set to processed input mode, which supports line-by-line text entry. If line input is also enabled—which should be the case, because processed input mode and line input mode are designed to work together—backspaces and carriage returns are handled in accordance with most typists' expectations; a backspace causes the cursor to move back one space without affecting the character at the cursor position, and carriage return is converted to a carriage return-linefeed character combination. When both line input and processed input are enabled, the **Ctrl+C** key combination is passed to the appropriate control handler whether or not line input is enabled. For more information about control handlers, see "Console Control Handlers" earlier in this chapter.

+ **ENABLE_LINE_INPUT**. When this constant is passed to `SetConsoleMode` along with a console input handle, the `ReadFile` and `ReadConsole` functions return when the **Enter** key is pressed. If line input mode is disabled, both functions return when one or more characters are available in the input buffer.

+ **ENABLE_ECHO_INPUT**. When this constant is passed to `SetConsoleMode` along with a console input handle, keyboard input that is read by `ReadFile` or `ReadConsole` is echoed to the active screen buffer, provided that the process that calls `ReadFile` or `ReadConsole` has an open handle of the active screen buffer. Echo mode cannot be enabled unless line input is also enabled. The output mode of the active screen buffer affects the way echoed input is displayed.

+ **ENABLE_PROCESSED_OUTPUT.** When this constant is used with a console screen buffer handle, the console API performs what are generally considered appropriate actions when nonprinting ANSI control characters are written to a screen buffer. The backspace, tab, bell, carriage return, and linefeed characters are processed; a tab character moves the cursor to the next tab stop (tab stops are set by default in eight-character increments); a bell character produces a nifty beep.

+ **ENABLE_WRAP_AT_EOL_OUTPUT.** When this constant is passed to SetConsoleMode along with a console screen buffer handle, wrap at EOL mode is enabled. If this mode is enabled, the cursor advances to the first column in the next row when it reaches the end of its current row. When the cursor reaches the bottom of the window region, the window's origin is moved down one row, scrolling the contents of the window up one row and keeping the cursor visible on the bottom line of the window. When the cursor reaches the bottom of the screen buffer, the contents of the screen buffer are scrolled up one row, and the top row of the screen buffer is discarded. When wrap at EOL output mode is disabled, the last character in the row is overwritten with any subsequent characters.

The constants in the following list can be passed to the SetConsoleMode call to enable low-level console input functions:

+ **ENABLE_MOUSE_INPUT.** This constant controls whether mouse events are reported in the input buffer. By default, mouse input is enabled and window input is disabled. Changing either of these modes affects only input that occurs after the mode is set; pending mouse or window events in the input buffer are not flushed, and the mouse pointer is displayed regardless of the mouse mode.

+ **ENABLE_WINDOW_INPUT.** This constant controls whether buffer-resizing events are reported in the input buffer. By default, mouse input is enabled and window input is disabled. Changing either of these modes affects only input that occurs after the mode is set; pending mouse or window events in the input buffer are not flushed. The mouse pointer is displayed regardless of the mouse mode.

+ **ENABLE_PROCESSED_INPUT.** This constant controls the processing of input for applications using the high-level console I/O functions. However, if processed input mode is enabled, the **Ctrl+C** key combination is not reported in the console's input buffer. Instead, it is passed to the appropriate control handler function.

Noted in Passing

If a console has multiple screen buffers, the output modes of each buffer can be different. An application can change I/O modes at any time. The output modes of a screen buffer do not affect the behavior of the low-level output functions.

Examples: CONSOLE and MYCONSOL

When you run the CONSOLE program, you can open a console window by choosing either the **Process** item or the **Alloc** item from the program's Console menu. CONSOLE then launches the MYCONSOL application and executes it. If you choose **Process**, CONSOLE starts a new process by calling `CreateProcess`, and runs MYCONSOL under the process that has been created. It you choose **Alloc**, CONSOL does not start a new process but instead opens the CONSOLE window by calling `AllocConsole`.

HOW THE MYCONSOL PROGRAM WORKS

No matter which method you choose to launch the MYCONSOL process, the results are the same. When the process opens its console window, you get an opportunity to play a little game called the Name Game. MYCONSOL starts the Name Game by prompting you to type in your name. If you enter any name except George, the program demands: "Go away, [your Name], bring me George!" When you type the name George, your computer beeps and prints the greeting "Hi, George!"

When the game is finished, MYCONSOL displays a prompt telling you to type **Q** to quit. When you type **Q** and press **Return**, the MYCONSOL window closes and the program terminates. "Hi, George" is not exactly a world-class computer game, but it does demonstrate how console windows can interact with user I/O.

If you want the CONSOLE application to work properly, you must launch it from the Windows NT desktop or the Windows NT Explorer and not from Visual C++. When you launch CONSOLE from Developer Studio's Build menu, the program doesn't have the independence that it needs to open a console process.

THE MCONSOLE CLASS

In the MYCONSOL application, console windows are created using a C++ class called `MConsole`. The `MConsole` class was developed from scratch especially for this book; it does not inherit from classes defined in the MFC library. So it can be used in programs that do not use MFC, and can be incorporated into programs compiled with any Windows NT-compatible compiler.

MConsole is defined in **MYCONSOL.H** and is implemented in **MYCONSOL.EPP**. The program prints the text in its console windows using Windows API functions and the MFC CString class.

Examples: This Chapter's Sample Programs

CONSOLE demonstrates how a console window can be incorporated into a Windows NT program. CONSOLE is a Windows-based MDI application written in Visual C++. It was written using Developer Studio, but it has no need for the document-view structure that the AppWizard utility creates when it generates the framework for a Visual C++ program. Therefore, the CONSOLE project is based on the SLIMMDI program model introduced in Chapter 3 rather than on a framework generated by AppWizard.

The SLIMMDI model does not require files that implement and define document and view classes, so it does not require as much code as a framework-based Visual C++ program.

When you launch the CONSOLE program, it displays a Console Demo window like the one shown in Figure 6.7. The Console Demo window has two menu items—**Process** and **Alloc**—that display console windows. When you choose **Process**, the program displays a console window by starting a new process. This process launches the console application MYCONSOL. When the MYCONSOL process begins, it starts the Name Game, described previously. The source code for the part of the program that executes the Name Game is in **MYCONSOL.CPP** in the accompanying disk. A main function serves as an entry point for the program's console process.

FIGURE 6.7 THE MYCONSOL PROGRAM'S OUTPUT.

Because the program supports multiple console processes, you can play multiple-versions of the Name Game simultaneously, each controlled by its own process.

THE CONSOLE APPLICATION

CONSOLE is an MDI application program that creates and manages multiple processes to display multiple console windows on the screen. The window displayed by CONSOLE is equipped with a main frame window, multiple MDI windows, and a standard menu bar. The program creates console windows that interact with the user in an independent fashion, accepting typed input and displaying messages on the screen.

The main module, **CONSOLE.CPP**, contains the program's WinMain function and its supporting functions.

When a user chooses **Process** from the Console menu, the CONSOLE program creates a console window by calling CreateProcess. The address of the **MYCONSOL.EXE** process is passed to CreateProcess:

```
// Create a new console process.
CreateProcess("MYCONSOL.EXE", NULL, NULL, NULL, TRUE,
    DETACHED_PROCESS, NULL, NULL, &sui, &pi);
```

CreateProcess is called from the ShowConsole function in **CONSOLE.CPP**. When the **CONSOLE.CPP** module executes CreateProcess, **MYCONSOL.EXE** is launched as a new process, displaying a console window.

When you choose a different menu item, **Alloc**, CONSOLE displays a console window not by creating a new process, but by calling the Windows function AllocConsole:

```
void ConsoleAlloc()
{
    AllocConsole();
    while (TRUE);
    FreeConsole();
}
```

The console window that appears when the user selects **Alloc** is a simple window that does nothing but close. When it closes, the application ends.

The **Process** menu item displays a console window in a more elegant—and more useful—manner. Each time the user chooses **Process**, the program starts a new process that creates a new console window. So multiple console windows, each created by a separate process, can appear on the screen at the same time.

THE MYCONSOL APPLICATION

When you launch CONSOLE and choose **Process**, the program starts a new process that executes the MYCONSOL application. MYCONSOL is a console application that can also be executed as a separate program. The MYCONSOL process is an executable (**.EXE**) file that can be run as an independent application.

To build MYCONSOL, you compile a pair of C++ source files named **MYCONSOL.CPP** and **MYSTRING.CPP.** The building of the MYCONSOL program is described in more detail in the next section.

The CONSOLE application launches MYCONSOL by calling `CreateProcess` when the user chooses **Process**. The **MYCONSOL.CPP** file contains the source code that displays a console window when the user selects **Process**. When **MYCONSOL.CPP** and its header file (**MYCONSOL.H**) are compiled, they produce the console application named **MYCONSOL.EXE.**

BUILDING THE EXAMPLE APPLICATIONS

Because CONSOLE and MYCONSOL are constructed from separate executables, you must build them separately. To build MYCONSOL, simply open the MYCONSOL project and execute the MYCONSOL makefile by choosing **Build** from the Project menu. To build CONSOLE, open the CONSOLE project and build it by selecting **Build** from the Project menu.

When you have built both projects, you can place a copy of **CONSOL.EXE** in the same folder as in which **MYCONSOL.EXE** is stored. Then you can execute the program from the Windows NT Program Manager or the Windows NT Explorer application.

Summary

When you want to incorporate a text window into a Windows NT program, you can write a console window: a simple, reliable mechanism for managing text-only I/O. Console windows have a number of different uses in Windows NT applications. For example, they can be useful in networking and communications programs that require terminal-emulation modes and as windows for displaying error messages that affect an application's GUI interface. Console windows might also come in handy if you need to port a text-only program to Windows NT or when you want to test a code module or prototype an application without bothering to write a full-fledged Windows interface.

There are two ways to implement a console window:

✦ By calling the Windows NT function `CreateProcess`, which opens a new process for your console.

♦ By calling the Win32 function `AllocConsole`, which opens a console for the process that is currently running.

Once you have a console up and running, there two ways to manage console I/O: with high-level functions, which support line-by-line input and output, and with low-level functions, which support character-by-character input and output, as well as many kinds of mouse operations. Low-level console I/O functions can be convenient when you want to port a robust text-only application to Windows NT, because you can often convert character-based programs to Windows NT from UNIX, DOS, and other platforms on a call-by-call basis. That's because many I/O functions that are common in UNIX, DOS, and other text-based platforms work much like the I/O functions provided in the Windows console API.

CHAPTER SEVEN

MULTITHREADING

One of the most remarkable capabilities of Windows NT is that it can manage multiple processes so expertly that they appear to be executing at the same time. In fact, if Windows NT is running on a multiprocessor system, it literally can execute multiple processes simultaneously.

Windows NT manages this magic with a feature called *preemptive-multitasking*, which was introduced in Chapter 6, "Processes." Windows NT implements preemptive multitasking using multithreading, a technique for dividing processes into threads and allocating each thread a share of CPU time, based on preallocated priorities. If you're lucky enough to be running Windows NT on a multiprocessor system, the various threads that it allocates can run on different processors.

To make sure that each multithreaded process gets its fair share of CPU time, Windows NT uses a system software component called the *system-scheduler*. A program cannot execute until the system scheduler gives authorization to one of the program's threads. The system scheduler determines which threads should run and when they should run. Lower-priority threads must wait while higher-priority threads complete their tasks. On multiprocessor machines, the system scheduler can move individual threads to different processors to balance the CPU load.

By using preemptive multitasking managed by a system scheduler, Windows NT ensures that a malfunction in one executing application cannot cause unexpected behavior in another application and, even more important, that a malfunctioning application cannot cause a system crash.

This chapter shows how Windows NT implements multithreading and preemptive multitasking and how you can take advantage of these capabilities in your Windows NT applications.

This Chapter's Example Programs

This chapter presents several example applications that illustrate the use of multithreading along with one example program that shows how a timer can be used as an alternative to multithreading. You can find the source code for these programs in this chapter's folder on the accompanying disk. The output of one of the programs, THRDDEMO, is shown in Figure 7.1.

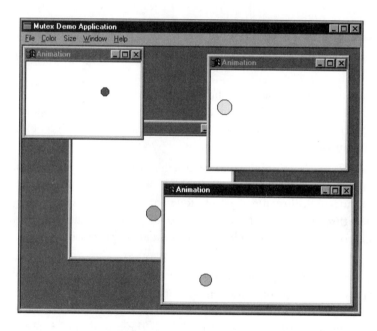

FIGURE 7.1 THRDDEMO PROGRAM DISPLAY.

The sample programs that demonstrate multithreading (and a timer-based alternative) are as follows:

+ **TIMER.** Controls animation with a timer rather than threads.
+ **THRDDEMO.** Demonstrates the operation of threads.

+ **CRITSECT.** Demonstrates critical sections.

+ **MUTEX.** Creates mutex (mutual exclusion) objects, which prevent threads from interfering with each other.

+ **SEMAFORE.** Creates semaphore objects, which limit the number of threads that a process can run at the same time.

+ **EVENT.** Creates event objects to manage threads that run sequentially.

+ **MFCTHRDS.** Shows how to write multithreaded programs using worker threads.

+ **USRTHRD.** Demonstrates how to write multithreaded programs using user-interface threads.

FEATURES OF THE SAMPLE PROGRAMS

All eight of this chapter's sample programs were written in Visual C++. All are equipped with Visual C++ makefiles, so you can build each program separately by choosing the **Build** command from Developer Studio's Build menu. The first six example programs show how you can incorporate multithreading into your Windows NT programs by calling Win32 API functions. All six of the programs in this group are similarly constructed, and all six create a similar screen display that features a bouncing ball.

With the exception of the TIMER program—which demonstrates an alternative to using threads—each application in the bouncing-ball group has a module named **ANIMWND.CPP** that performs thread management. Each program also has a module named **ANIM.CPP** that manages the animation of the bouncing ball.

The six sample programs in the bouncing-ball group also have another feature in common: Although they were all written in Visual C++, they were not generated by AppWizard, because they do not require the document-view architecture that AppWizard creates when it generates application frameworks.

The other two programs—MFCTHRDS and USRTHRD—are full-fledged MFC framework applications that show how MFC supports multithreaded programs. MFC contains two classes for creating threads and several classes for creating thread-synchronization objects such as mutexes, semaphores, and critical sections. But MFC support for multithreading is still fairly limited, and that is why this chapter focuses mainly on demonstrating implementations of multithreading that do not rely on classes implemented in the MFC library. For details on MFC support for mulithreading, see "Multithreading and the MFC Library" later in this chapter.

HOW THE EXAMPLE PROGRAMS WORK

Each of the sample programs that demonstrate non-MFC multithreading displays a bouncing ball that is drawn using a standard Windows bitmap. Each bouncing-ball program is a multiple document interface (MDI) application, so each program can display multiple windows simultaneously. When you run any of the programs in this group, you can display as many windows as you like and each window will contain a merrily bouncing ball. You can change the color, size, and speed of each ball in each window by choosing menu commands.

Because each window in each program is controlled by a separate thread, it appears to the user that all the balls are bouncing around on the screen at the same time. But what's really happening—if you're using a single-processor computer—is that each window containing a bouncing ball has its own slice of CPU time, which is parceled out by the system scheduler. The system scheduler controls the bouncing of the balls in a round-robin fashion, giving each ball the time it needs to move a very small distance and then moving to the next ball. As a result, all the balls appear to be bouncing around in their individual windows at the same time.

A Bouncing-Ball Bug and How We Fix It

There is one potential problem in this method of displaying bouncing balls: All the windows share the same GDI object—a bitmap of a bouncing ball—so there is always a chance that when a thread needs access to the bitmap, another thread might be using it. (As you may recall from Chapter 6, "Processes," a GDI object is not a kernel object, so its handle can be shared by different threads.)

When a thread tries to grab the bouncing-ball bitmap while another thread is already using it, a competition for the bitmap ensues. Sometimes the result is that the thread trying to obtain the bitmap can't get it and displays an ugly black rectangle on the screen instead.

Two of the bouncing-ball programs—CRITSECT and MUTEX—fix this bug by preventing any thread from trying to access the bitmap while another thread is using it. When that kind of competition develops, CRITSECT and MUTEX simply make the waiting thread wait until the other thread is finished with the bitmap and releases it. CRITSECT applies this solution using a mechanism called a critical section object, and MUTEX provides a similar kind of protection using a wait object called a mutex. You'll see how both these programs work later in this chapter.

Animating the Bouncing Ball

In each bouncing-ball program, the code that controls the ball's animation is encapsulated into a simple class named MAnimation. The MAnimation class was designed specifically for this book and does not rely on classes in MFC. This means that the class is compiler-independent, so you can use it in programs that are built using any 32-bit compiler that is compatible with Windows NT.

The bitmap images are drawn in the usual Windows fashion. First, a GDI function is called to create a graphics object (in this case, a bitmap). Then the bitmap object is placed in (or, in Windows jargon, *selected into*) a device context object, or DC. Finally, the bitmap object is drawn to the screen. This process is explained in more detail in Chapter 11, "Windows NT Graphics."

In the constructor of the MAnimation class, which appears in **ANIMWND.CPP** in each example program, the Win32 function GetDC is called to set up a device context. Later in each program, in a member function named MAnimation::MakeNewShape, a bitmap object is created and is drawn into a memory buffer. The Windows API functions that are called to draw the object are CreateCompatibleDC, CreateCompatibleBitmap, and Ellipse.

The animation in each example program is implemented by a member function named MAnimation::AnimateShape. Each time a thread orders an update in the position of the ball, MAnimation::AnimateShape calls the familiar Windows API function BitBlt to copy the bouncing-ball bitmap from memory to the screen.

How Threads Work

The main reason for using multithreading is that it allows processes to perform multiple tasks at the same time. For example, an application might use one thread to handle real-time I/O, such as keyboard and mouse input from the user, while other threads with lower priorities handle tasks that don't have to be carried out in real time—for example, spreadsheet calculations or background printing.

Multiple threads can also be useful in MDI applications. When a multiwindow program has more than one window open, a separate thread can be assigned to handle the action that takes place in each window. You can see how that works by compiling and executing the example programs presented in this chapter.

Multithreading can be especially useful in networking and communications programs. For example, a named pipe server might create a thread to handle communications with each client process that attaches to the pipe. (Pipes are covered in Chapter 9, "Interprocess

Communications.") Threads can also help an application manage input from multiple communications devices.

WHEN SHOULD AN APPLICATION USE THREADS?

You don't need threads to run every application program. (See box, "When Not to Use Multithreading.") But sometimes threads can come in handy when you want an application to perform multiple tasks simultaneously. For example, threads are often used for these purposes:

✦ To apportion tasks efficiently. When a program must perform different tasks simultaneously, it's usually more efficient to implement a thread for each task than it is to launch a separate process for each task.

✦ To assign different priorities to different tasks. Threaded tasks can be assigned different priorities depending on the needs of your application.

✦ For background processing. Threads are ideal mechanisms for the management of background processes, such as background printing. In a well-designed multithreaded program, important time-critical tasks, such as interactive keyboard and mouse I/O, can proceed uninterrupted, in a peppy and responsive manner, while less time-critical processes grind away unnoticed in the background.

✦ To apportion the execution of parallel tasks. Sometimes an application creates several instances that do exactly the same thing. For example, a named pipe server can allocate an identical thread to manage each instance of a pipe. (Pipes are covered in Chapter 9, "Interprocess Communications.")

When Not to Use Multithreading

Multithreading is not the solution to every problem and should not be used in every Windows NT application. When your application has a simple timing-related task to perform—for example, if you want an application to keep an eye on the clock and notify the user when a meeting is about to occur, you might be tempted to create a new thread in your program to do the job. A thread could handle such a task, but that would probably be overkill. Unfortunately, multithreading is not one of the easiest mechanisms to implement in a Windows NT program. It takes a certain amount of time and effort, which may turn out to be wasted when you discover that you could have created a simple timer to do the same job just as effectively. (To see how timers can be used in MFC programs, see the "Timers" section near the end of this chapter.)

On the other hand, there are many situations in which the use of multithreading is justified. For example, multithreading is an ideal mechanism for handling background printing. Multithreading can also come in handy when you want an application to handle disk I/O in the background or to poll a network continually for new connections.

You'll probably think of more uses for multithreading as you read the rest of this chapter and experiment with the example programs.

THE THREAD IS QUICKER THAN THE EYE

Because a computer's CPU divides its processing time into small slices—on the order of 20 milliseconds in an Intel x86 or Pentium processor—multithreading creates the illusion that the activities of all currently active threads are taking place at the same time.

With the example programs, you can use threads to create as many bouncing balls as you like, of varying sizes and colors, and all the balls will seem to be bouncing around completely independently in their windows. That's the magic of threads in action. If you're running Windows NT on a multiprocessor system, the simultaneous movement of the bouncing balls won't be an illusion; the activities of all active threads really will be taking place at the same time. On a multiple-CPU system, Windows NT can distribute threads among processors. This capability speeds processing because each thread has its own private microprocessor.

WHAT THREADS DO AND DON'T DO

On a single-processor system, multiple threads do not necessarily improve execution speed. In fact, a single-CPU computer can slow down if it is forced to keep track of too many threads. You can confirm that for yourself by running this chapter's thread demonstration programs on a single-processor PC; just watch the bouncing ball slow down as you add more threads.

The use of multithreading has other potential drawbacks. For example, if your application needs to synchronize its threads so that they don't conflict with one another, it must create structures and routines that consume memory. You must create those structures and routines, and that requires extra development time. Moreover, keeping track of large numbers of threads consumes CPU time. And if you don't schedule thread operation properly, deadlocks can occur, bringing everything to a halt, when competing threads scramble for CPU time. You should take all these factors into account before committing yourself to using threads in a program.

ALTERNATIVES TO USING THREADS

It isn't always necessary to use threads when you want to execute multiple tasks. Windows NT offers several alternatives to multithreading, including overlapped I/O, multiple processes, and mechanisms that make it possible for the system to wait for multiple events.

Overlapped I/O

Overlapped I/O, sometimes referred to as asynchronous I/O, is a Windows NT mechanism that allows an application to perform separate input-output operations without using threads. Overlapped I/O enables a single thread to initiate multiple, time-consuming I/O requests that can run concurrently.

Overlapped I/O operations make it possible for one pipe to read and write data simultaneously and for a single thread to perform simultaneous I/O operations on multiple pipe handles. For more information about overlapped I/O and an example showing how the technique can be used in a program, see Chapter 9, "Interprocess Communications."

Multiple Processes

Another way a Windows application can carry out multiple tasks simultaneously is to create a separate process (rather than a separate thread) for each task. This technique is widely used as an alternative to threads in 16-bit Windows applications.

Under Windows NT, an application can call `CreateProcess` to start a child process. You saw an example of how this technique works in the CONSOLE program presented in Chapter 6, "Processes." In that program, separate processes display a GUI window and a console window at the same time; the GUI window launches a separate process to display the console window.

In some cases, it's better to split up an application's tasks by using multiple processes than it is to write a separate thread for each task. For example, an application might use multiple processes for functions that require private address spaces and private resources that protect them from the activities of other threads. Generally speaking, though, the multiprocess approach is not the most efficient architecture for applications that carry out multiple tasks simultaneously. It's usually more efficient to use threads, because Windows can create and execute a thread more quickly than it can create and launch a process. The code for the thread has already been mapped into the address space of the process, but the code for a new process must be loaded.

Threads also make more efficient use of processing time and memory because they don't require the startup code that's needed by a process. Moreover, all threads of a process share the same address space and can access the process's global variables. This feature can simplify communications between threads.

Understanding Threads

The Windows API contains two functions that create new threads. `CreateThread` starts a thread that runs in the address space of the calling process. `CreateRemoteThread` starts a new thread that runs in the address space of a different process.

THE CREATETHREAD FUNCTION

`CreateThread` creates a thread that executes within the address space of the calling function. This is the syntax of `CreateThread`:

```
HANDLE CreateThread(LPSECURITY_ATTRIBUTES lpsa, DWORD cbStack,
    LPTHREAD_START_ROUTINE lpStartAddr, LPVOID lpvThreadParm, DWORD
fdwCreate, LPDWORD lpIDTthread);
```

If a call to `CreateThread` succeeds, the function creates a thread and returns a handle to the new thread. If a call to `CreateThread` does not succeed, the function returns NULL. (Similarly, as noted earlier in this chapter, when `CreateProcess` is called to create a new process, handles to the new process and its primary thread are returned.)

THE CREATEREMOTETHREAD FUNCTION

`CreateRemoteThread` is identical to `CreateThread` except that `CreateRemoteThread` has one additional parameter: a handle to the process in which the new thread is created.

Debugger processes call `CreateRemoteThread` to create threads that run in the address spaces of processes other than the processes they are creating.

This is the syntax of `CreateRemoteThread`:

```
HANDLE CreateRemoteThread(HANDLE hProcess,
LPSECURITY_ATTRIBUTES lpsa,
    DWORD cbStack,        LPTHREAD_START_ROUTINE lpStartAddr, LPVOID
lpvThreadParm,
    DWORD fdwCreate, LPDWORD lpIDTthread);
```

The extra parameter that `CreateRemoteThread` expects is the HANDLE variable hProcess.

All information provided in this chapter about `CreateThread` is also applicable to `CreateRemoteThread`.

PARAMETERS OF THE CREATETHREAD FUNCTION

The parameters passed to CreateThread are as follows:

+ **lpsa**. Points to a SECURITY_ATTRIBUTES structure that specifies the security attributes of the thread. If lpsa is NULL, the thread is created with a default security descriptor. The security attributes of a thread include an inheritance flag that determines whether the handle can be inherited by child processes. They also include a security descriptor, which the system uses to perform access checks on all subsequent uses of the thread's handle before access is granted.

+ **cbStack**. Specifies the size, in bytes, of the new thread's stack, which is allocated automatically in the memory space of the current process and is freed when the thread terminates. If a value of zero is passed to cbStack, the stack size of the new thread is the same as that of the stack used by the current process's primary thread. No matter what value is passed, the new thread's stack size grows as needed.

+ **lpStartAddr**. Points to an application-supplied function that the new thread executes as soon as it starts. The pointer passed to lpStartAddr is recognized by the system as the starting address of the new thread. The function referenced by the lpStartAddr pointer takes a single 32-bit argument and returns a 32-bit exit code. For more details on this topic, see "Terminating Threads" later in this chapter.

+ **lpvThreadParm**. Specifies the single 32-bit parameter value passed to the user-supplied function that is the new thread's entry point (see the lpStartAddr parameter).

+ **fdwCreate**. Specifies additional flags that control the creation of the thread. If the CREATE_SUSPENDED flag is specified, the thread is created in a suspended state and will not run until ResumeThread is called. If this value is zero, the thread runs immediately after creation.

+ **lpIDThread**. Points to a 32-bit variable that receives the thread identifier.

The CreateProcess Function Creates Threads, Too

CreateProcess also creates new threads. When an application creates a new process by calling CreateProcess, it returns handles to both the new process and its primary thread.

When an application creates a new thread by calling CreateThread, a handle with full access to the new thread is created. If a security descriptor is not provided in the SECURITY_ATTRIBUTES structure that is passed to CreateThread as a parameter, the handle to the new thread can be used in any function that requires a thread object handle. If a security descriptor is provided, an access check is performed on all subsequent uses of the handle before access to the new thread is granted. If the access check results in the denial of access, the requesting process cannot use the handle to gain access to the thread.

THE ENTRY-POINT FUNCTION OF A NEW THREAD

The lpStartAddr parameter that is passed to CreateThread is the address of a function that is used as the thread's entry point. Typically, the starting address of the new thread is the name of a function that is defined by the application. When the new thread starts running, the executing function is the function that is pointed to by the lpStartAddr parameter. The same function can be specified as the entry point for multiple threads.

SETTING THREAD PRIORITIES

By default, every new thread created by CreateThread has a thread priority of THREAD_PRIORITY_NORMAL. An application can change a thread's priority by calling the Win32 function SetThreadPriority. An application can obtain the current priority of a thread by calling GetThreadPriority.

SIGNALED AND NONSIGNALED STATES

When the application-supplied entry-point function of a thread terminates, the 32-bit value that the function returns is an exit code. The system uses this code to terminate the thread by calling ExitThread. This happens when you return from the thread's entry-point function.

When a thread is active, it is said to be in an nonsignaled state. This means that any other threads that are waiting for the thread to terminate must keep waiting. When a thread terminates, its state changed to signaled. This state alerts any waiting threads that the thread has terminated. Even when a thread has terminated, the thread object (the object referenced by the thread's handle) remains in the system until all handles to the thread have been closed. For more details on thread synchronization and the terminations of threads, see "Synchronizing Threads" and "Terminating Threads" later in this chapter.

WAITING FOR A THREAD TO TERMINATE

Before ThreadFunc terminates, it calls the Win32 function WaitForSingleObject to make sure that the thread controlled by ThreadFunc has terminated. (As explained later, in the section "Synchronizing Threads," WaitForSingleObject halts processing until an object's state is signaled and then moves on.) When WaitForSingleObject confirms that the thread's state is signaled, ThreadFunc calls GetExitCodeThread again to obtain the thread's latest termination status and then returns the thread's exit code to CreateThread. The processing of the thread created by CreateThread is then complete.

THREAD PRIORITIES

Windows NT manages the activities of threads in accordance with priorities that are set when each thread is created. When CreateThread creates a new thread, the thread's priority is set by default to THREAD_PRIORITY_NORMAL. However, an application can change the priority of a thread at any time by calling the Win32 function SetThreadPriority.

The THRDDEMO example program creates a thread with the default priority THREAD_PRIORITY_NORMAL but immediately resets it to THREAD_PRIORITY_BELOW_NORMAL. This happens in Listing 7.1, a code sequence that appears in **ANIMWND.CPP.**

LISTING 7.1 CREATING A THREAD.

```
// Call CreateThread
m_hThread = CreateThread(NULL, 0,
    (LPTHREAD_START_ROUTINE)ThreadFunc,
    this, CREATE_SUSPENDED,
    (LPDWORD) &m_IDThread);

// Set the thread's priority
SetPriority(THREAD_PRIORITY_BELOW_NORMAL);

ResumeThread(m_hThread);
```

To prevent the thread created in Listing 7.1 from starting until its priority is established, the thread is created in a suspended state (with its CREATE_SUSPENDED flag set). Then ResumeThread is called to start the thread.

Every thread has one of these five priorities:

+ THREAD_PRIORITY_HIGHEST

+ THREAD_PRIORITY_ABOVE_NORMAL

+ THREAD_PRIORITY_NORMAL

+ THREAD_PRIORITY_BELOW_NORMAL

+ THREAD_PRIORITY_LOWEST

When an application is running, Windows NT schedules the execution of each thread by going down a list of the application's threads, starting at the highest level and proceeding to the lowest. The first threads that execute are those with a priority of THREAD_PRIORITY_HIGHEST. When no threads of the highest priority are demanding to be executed, Windows NT allocates processing time to threads that have a priority of THREAD_PRIORITY_ABOVE_NORMAL. If no threads with above-normal priority are waiting to be processed, the system schedules threads with a priority of THREAD_PRIORITY_NORMAL. Finally, threads with priorities of THREAD_PRIORITY_NORMAL and THREAD_PRIORITY_LOWEST get their turns.

For most uses, the THREAD_PRIORITY_BELOW_NORMAL and THREAD_PRIORITY_NORMAL settings will probably be adequate. For more time-critical operations, such as managing keyboard I/O or operating communications ports, it might be necessary to schedule threads to run at the above-normal priority or even at the highest priority. But threads with higher priorities should be allowed to run only for very short lengths of time. Otherwise, they can consume all the processing time that a system has available, slowing, or even halting other processes.

At the other end of the scale, threads with the lowest priorities can run only when the system has nothing else to do. Operations such as printing or file indexing can be given low priorities so that they will be carried out only when the CPU has idle time.

Example: The THRDDEMO Program

The THRDDEMO example program, in this chapter's directory on the accompanying disk, demonstrates the use of `CreateThread`. THRDDEMO is a Visual C++ program, but it was not written using AppWizard. The program uses a thread to create and manipulate a bouncing ball. The thread is created in a file named **ANIMWND.CPP**. The animation that makes the ball bounce is implemented in **ANIM.CPP**.

In **ANIMWND.CPP,** this statement calls `CreateThread`:

```
// Call CreateThread
m_hThread = CreateThread(NULL, 0,
        (LPTHREAD_START_ROUTINE)ThreadFunc,
        this, CREATE_SUSPENDED,
        (LPDWORD) &m_IDThread);
```

In this code fragment, a pointer to the entry-point function `ThreadFunc` is passed to `CreateThread` in the `lpStartAddr` parameter. Notice that the pointer to `ThreadFunc` is cast as an LPTHREAD_START_ROUTINE data type. This casting operation ensures that `CreateThread` will recognize `ThreadFunc` as the entry point of a thread. `ThreadFunc` is shown in Listing 7.2.

LISTING 7.2 CREATING A THREAD.

```
// ThreadFunc function
long ThreadFunc(CAnimWnd *pAnimWnd)
{
    long lEndThread = 0;
    pAnimWnd->SetSpeed(TRUE);
    DWORD exitCode;

    while (TRUE) {

        // Introduce a delay if speed is set to slow
        if(pAnimWnd->GetSpeed() == TRUE)
            Sleep(0);
        else
            Sleep(100);

        // When this thread's window closes, the lEndThread
        // variable becomes non-zero (see OnClose function, above).
        lEndThread = GetWindowLong(pAnimWnd->m_hWnd,
// GWL_USERDATA);
        if (lEndThread) {
            // Get this thread's exit code and exit the thread.
            GetExitCodeThread(pAnimWnd->m_hThread, &exitCode);
            ExitThread(exitCode);
```

```
            // Get rid of objects that won't be needed anymore.
            CloseHandle(pAnimWnd->m_hThread);
            delete pAnimWnd->m_pAnimation;
            delete pAnimWnd;      // Created in mainfrm.cpp module.
            break;
        } else {
            // perform tasks.
            if (pAnimWnd != NULL)
                pAnimWnd->Animate();
            else break;
        }
    }

    // Wait for thread to exit.
    DWORD dRetVal = WaitForSingleObject(pAnimWnd->m_hThread, 5000);

    // Message boxes used during debugging (might as well
    // leave them there).
    if (dRetVal == WAIT_FAILED)
        MessageBox(NULL, "Function failed!",
            "ThreadFunc", MB_OK);
    else if (dRetVal == WAIT_TIMEOUT)
        MessageBox(NULL, "Function timed out!",
            "ThreadFunc", MB_OK);

    // Get the thread's exit code again (in case it has
    // changed), and return it as function's return value.
    GetExitCodeThread(pAnimWnd->m_hThread, &exitCode);
    return exitCode;
}
```

In Listing 7.2, the value of a variable named lEndThread is set to 0 (false), and then the line

```
    while (TRUE) {
```

executes an endless loop that calls pAnimWnd->Animate. The pAnimWnd->Animate function, as you may guess from its name, is a member function of an object named pAnimWnd. In THRDDEMO, pAnimWnd is a window object. When pAnimWnd is instantiated, it opens a window that displays a bouncing ball.

The while loop in the ThreadFunc function causes pAnimWnd->Animate to be executed repeatedly until the value of lEndThread is changed to a nonzero value (true).

THE GETWINDOWLONG FUNCTION

During each iteration of the ThreadFunc function's while loop shown in Listing 7.2, the Win32 function GetWindowLong is called to reset the value of lEndThread. For example, this line calls GetWindowLong:

```
lEndThread = GetWindowLong(pAnimWnd->m_hWnd, GWL_USERDATA);
```

Each time a statement such as this calls GetWindowLong, it returns a zero value (false). That continues until the window displayed by pAnimWnd closes. As soon as the pAnimWnd window closes, the Win32 function SetWindowLong resets lEndThread to a nonzero value (true), signaling ThreadFunc that it can now terminate.

The SetWindowLong call appears in **ANIMWND.CPP**, in a function named CAnimWnd::OnClose. This function overrides the MFC class CMDIChildWnd::OnClose. When CAnimWnd::OnClose ends, it calls CMDIChildWnd::OnClose. This permits CMDIChildWnd::OnClose to carry out certain procedures that are necessary to close a window.

This is the CAnimWnd::OnClose function:

```
void CAnimWnd::OnClose()
{
    // TODO: Add your message handler code here and/or call
// default.
    // Pass close message to ThreadFunc by calling
// SetWindowLong.
    long lPrevLong = SetWindowLong(m_hWnd, GWL_USERDATA, 1);

    // Suspend the thread associated with this window.
    // ThreadFunc function will exit the thread.
    SuspendThread(m_hThread);

    CMDIChildWnd::OnClose();
}
```

When SetWindowLong resets lEndThread to a nonzero true, the CAnimWnd::OnClose function returns to its calling function, ThreadFunc. ThreadFunc calls GetExitCode-Thread to obtain the current thread's termination status and then calls ExitThread to terminate the thread. That done, `ThreadFunc` calls `CloseHandle` and the `delete` operator to perform some housekeeping and breaks out of the `while` loop that kept looping until the thread terminated.

SUSPENDING AND RESUMING EXECUTION OF THREADS

No matter what priority a thread has, an application can control when the thread runs or does not run by calling the Win32 functions `SuspendThread` and `ResumeThread`. As you might guess from their names, these two functions suspend and resume the execution of threads.

When you call `CreateThread` to create a new thread, you can create the thread in a suspended state by placing the CREATE_SUSPENDED constant in the `fdwCreate` parameter. You can then start the thread running at any time by calling `ResumeThread`. If you place a zero in `fdwCreate` when you call `CreateThread`, the thread starts running as soon as it is created.

THE SUSPENDTHREAD FUNCTION

When you call `SuspendThread` in an application, Windows NT increments a *suspend count* that is maintained by the system for each thread. When you call `ResumeThread`, the thread's suspend count is decremented. During the execution of an application, whenever a thread's suspend count is greater than zero, execution of the thread is suspended. Subsequently, if the thread's suspend count is decremented to less than 1, the thread resumes execution.

A constant named MAXIMUM_SUSPEND_COUNT specifies the maximum value that any thread's suspend count can have. This constant was created to place a limit on multiple calls to `SuspendThread` that are not balanced by an accompanying `ResumeThread` and vice versa.

THE SLEEP AND SLEEPEX FUNCTIONS

A thread can temporarily suspend its own execution for a specified interval by calling the Win32 functions `Sleep` and `SleepEx`. (The `SleepEx` function causes the current thread to enter a wait state until the specified interval of time has passed or until an I/O completion callback function is called.) With these two functions, an application can specify a specific interval during which a thread is not scheduled for CPU time.

`Sleep` and `SleepEx` can be useful when an application has a thread that responds to user action; they can delay the execution of a thread just long enough for the user to observe the results of an action. The sleep functions have a side benefit, too. When they are used to slow the operation of a thread, other active threads benefit by being allocated more CPU time.

In the THRDDEMO example program, the `Sleep` function is used to control the speed of the bouncing ball. A Boolean member function named m_bFastSpeed keeps track of the ball's speed. If the ball is currently bouncing rapidly, the value of m_bFastSpeed is TRUE. If the ball is bouncing slowly, the value of m_bFastSpeed is FALSE. The `Sleep` function controls the ball's speed by introducing a delay in the ball's animation speed if m_bFastSpeed is set to FALSE. If m_bFastSpeed is set to TRUE, `Sleep` is called with a parameter of zero, which prevents the introduction of any delay.

The behavior of the `Sleep` function in THRDDEMO is determined by a member function named CAnimWnd::GetSpeed, which is defined as follows in **ANIMWND.H**:

```
BOOL GetSpeed() { return m_bFastSpeed; }
```

As you can see, CAnimWnd::GetSpeed merely returns the value of the m_bFastSpeed member function.

The `Sleep` function is called in three places in THRDDEMO. Its first occurrence is in ThreadFunc, which you can find in **ANIMWND.CPP**:

```
// Introduce a delay if speed is set to slow
if(pAnimWnd->GetSpeed() == TRUE)
    Sleep(0);
else
    Sleep(100);
```

In this code fragment, if m_bFastSpeed is set to TRUE, the `Sleep` function introduces a 100-millisecond delay in the thread that is currently executing. If m_bFastSpeed is FALSE, the `Sleep` function introduces no delay.

`Sleep` is called again in two functions that are executed when menu items are selected. Both functions appear in **ANIMWND.CPP**:

```
void CAnimWnd::OnSlow()
{
    m_bFastSpeed = FALSE;
    SetSpeed(FALSE);
    Sleep(100);
}
void CAnimWnd::OnFast()
{
```

```
    m_bFastSpeed = TRUE;
    SetSpeed(TRUE);
    Sleep(0);
}
```

OnSlow is called when the user of THRDDEMO selects the **Slow** item from the Speed menu. OnSlow introduces a 100-millisecond delay in the processing of the currently executing thread. OnFast is called when the user selects **Fast** from the Speed menu. OnFast eliminates any delay that may be in effect and causes the currently executing thread to run at its normal speed.

TERMINATING THREADS

A thread runs until one of the following events occurs:

* ✦ The Win32 function ExitThread is called.
* ✦ The thread function returns. This results in an implicit call to ExitProcess for a primary thread, or to ExitThread for other threads.
* ✦ ExitProcess is invoked explicitly or implicitly by any thread of the process.
* ✦ TerminateThread is called with a handle to the thread.
* ✦ TerminateProcess is called with a handle to the thread's process.

When the application-supplied entry-point function of a thread terminates, the function returns a 32-bit exit code. Windows NT uses this code to terminate the thread by implicitly calling ExitThread. .

If a terminating thread is the primary thread of a process, it terminates in a special way. When a process's primary thread terminates, ExitThread is not called. Instead, ExitProcess is implicitly invoked.

A primary thread can prevent other threads from terminating when it terminates by explicitly calling ExitThread before it exits. In this case, one of the remaining threads can call ExitProcess or ExitThread to ensure that all threads of the process are terminated. An application can use this technique when, for example, an attached DLL is implemented in a thread that does not terminate unless ExitProcess is invoked. (DLLs are covered in Chapter 8, "Dynamic Link Libraries.")

When a thread terminates, the state of the thread object changes from nonsignaled to signaled (see "Synchronizing Threads," next). This action releases any other threads that may have been waiting for the thread to terminate. Then the thread's termination status changes from STILL_ACTIVE to an exit code signaling that the thread has been terminated. If a call to `ExitThread` terminates a thread, the entry-point function of each attached DLL is invoked with a code indicating that the thread is detaching from the DLL.

If a call to `ExitProcess` terminates a thread, the entry-point function of each attached DLL is invoked once to notify the DLL that the process is detaching. DLLs are not notified when a thread is terminated by `TerminateThread` or `TerminateProcess`. An application can call `GetExitCodeThread` to obtain a thread's exit code.

SYNCHRONIZING THREADS

In Windows NT applications, threads often share resources. Consequently, there's always the danger that a thread will modify a resource in a way that another thread does not expect. For example, suppose two threads have write access to the same file or the same block of memory. If one thread writes to the file or memory area that it shares with the other thread and if the other thread doesn't know about it, the result can be a mess of corrupted data.

Things can also get messy when more than one thread attempt to use the same GDI object at the same time. Windows NT doesn't synchronize GDI objects—brushes, bitmaps, and the like—so your application must make sure that threads don't trip on each other's brushes and bitmaps in graphics-oriented programs.

WAITABLE OBJECTS

To prevent these kinds of problems, the Win32 API provides three special synchronization objects called *waitable objects*. Actually, there are more than three kinds of waitable objects, but only three of them are also categorized as synchronization objects. A waitable object is any object that can be in a signaled or nonsignaled state. (If an object is currently in use, it is said to be in a nonsignaled state. If it has terminated, it is said to be in a signaled state.) Waitable objects include processes, thread handles, file handles, named pipe handles (see Chapter 9), console input buffer handles (see Chapter 6), and communication device handles.

To determine whether a waitable object is signaled or nonsignaled, an application can call a Win32 function such as `WaitForSingleObject`, `WaitForMultipleObjects`, or `WaitForDebugEvent`. These wait functions, along with several others provided by the Win32 API, can halt the processing of a thread until the state of the thread changes to nonsignaled or until there is a timeout. To illustrate how wait functions work, this is the syntax of `WaitForSingleObject`:

```
DWORD WaitForSingleObject(HANDLE hObject, DWORD dwTimeout);
```

When you call `WaitForSingleObject`, the `hObject` parameter identifies the object being waited for. The `dwTimeout` parameter is a *timeout interval*, expressed in milliseconds. If the timeout interval elapses before the object's state becomes nonsignaled, the wait function returns. If the `dwTimeout` parameter is `ZERO`, the wait function tests the specified object's state and returns immediately. If `dwTimeout` has a value of `INFINITE`, the timeout interval never elapses. For more details about the wait functions provided by the Windows NT API, see "Wait Functions" later in this chapter.

When an application discovers that a waitable object is in a signaled state, it can call a `WaitFor` function to wait until the object's state switches to nonsignaled. Processing of the program can then resume. One example of a `WaitFor` function is `WaitForInputIdle`, which causes a thread to wait until a specified process is initialized and is waiting for user input. `WaitFor` functions can be useful when you want to synchronize parent and child processes. That's because `CreateProcess` returns without waiting for any child processes to complete their initializations.

Waitable objects can be useful when an application needs to prevent a thread from executing until a specific event occurs. For example, a wait function can be used to block a console input buffer from being read until there is input from the user, such as the pressing of a key or the clicking of a mouse button. Wait functions can also be used to keep a process or thread from starting until a currently executing process or thread terminates. Waitable objects can also come in handy when you want to protect shared resources from being accessed simultaneously by multiple threads or processes—a dangerous condition that can cause program crashes and other disasters.

Synchronization Objects

Four kinds of objects that fall into the category of waitable objects are sometimes referred to as *synchronization objects* because they can be used to synchronize threads. A synchronization object is an object whose handle can be passed to a wait function to coordinate the execution of multiple threads. The state of a synchronization object is always either nonsignaled—a state that means the object is in use and is thus unavailable to other threads—or signaled, which means that the object has completed its work and that other threads can claim it.

More than one process can have a handle to the same synchronization object, making interprocess synchronization possible. The kinds of synchronization objects used in Windows NT are as follows:

+ **Critical section objects,** which protect shared resources by ensuring that only one thread can modify the resource at any given time.

+ **Mutex objects,** which work much like critical section objects and have additional features that enable them to protect resources when multiple threads are used across different processes and different applications.

+ **Semaphore objects,** which limit the number of threads that can be executed simultaneously.

+ **Event objects,** which prevent a thread from starting until the execution of another thread is complete.

CRITICAL SECTION OBJECTS

A critical section object protects resources by allowing only one thread at a time to access a resource or section of code. A critical section object is the simplest kind of synchronization object to use. Critical sections are fast and efficient synchronization objects, but their usefulness has one significant limitation: They work only with threads that are created and accessed within the same process. When a resource is used by threads that span process boundaries, a mutex object (discussed later in this chapter) is the most common alternative to a critical section.

Critical sections can be useful, however, when you want to allow only one thread at a time to modify data or another controlled resource. For example, adding items to a list generally should be carried out by only one thread at a time. By using a critical section object to control access to a linked list, an application can allow the list to be written to by only one thread at a time.

To implement a critical section in a process in a Windows API program, you must create a special kind of Win32 `struct` called a CRITICAL_SECTION structure. (In an MFC program, you can use a `CCriticalSection` object, as explained in "Multithreading and the MFC Library" later in this chapter.) In a Windows API program—or in a program that does not use MFC classes to implement its multithreading capabilities—a CRITICAL_SECTION structure must be allocated as a global or static variable so that all threads in a process can access it. If you want a CRITICAL_SECTION structure to work properly, you must not attempt to access its fields manually. Instead, you must manipulate its fields by calling Win32 API functions.

To initialize a CRITICAL_SECTION structure, an application calls `InitializeCriticalSection`, passing the address of the CRITICAL_SECTION `struct` as a parameter. Then the application can easily protect any section of code in a process from simultaneous access by multiple threads. The application need only execute `EnterCriticalSection` at the beginning of the block of code that is to be protected, and execute `LeaveCriticalSection` at the end of the protected block of code.

EXAMPLE: THE CRITSECT PROGRAM

CRITSECT, a sample program in this chapter's folder on the accompanying disk, shows how a critical section can be used in a Windows program. CRITSECT uses a critical section to fix a bug you may have noticed in the THRDDEMO program.

In THRDDEMO, if you open a large number of windows and then start resizing windows with the mouse, the bouncing ball may become a large black rectangle, or more than one ball may appear in the window. When that happens, it's because the program selects GDI objects (bitmaps) into device contexts, which are objects that can be shared by all processes in the program. (If you aren't familiar with how Windows programs use GDI objects and device contexts, see Chapter 11, "Windows NT Graphics.") When one thread has selected the bouncing-ball bitmap in the device context object being used by the program's view object and another thread attempts to select the same bitmap into same device context, the two operations can interfere with each other and foul up the program's graphics.

In CRITSECT, a critical section prevents that from happening by preventing any thread from accessing the program's view DC object while another thread is using it to draw to the screen. To create a critical section object, the program first defines a CRITICAL_SECTION structure.

```
// Set up a critical section.
CRITICAL_SECTION gCriticalSection;
```

The main window used in CRITSECT is a CWnd-derived object named CAnimWnd. The CRITICAL_SECTION structure that is created in the preceding statement is initialized in the constructor of the program's CAnimWnd object:

```
CAnimWnd::CAnimWnd()
{

    // Initialize critical section before thread starta
    // so it's ready to execute.
    InitializeCriticalSection(&gCriticalSection);

    m_sizeMode = STATIC_SIZE;
    m_bFastSpeed = TRUE;
    m_bSlowSpeed = FALSE;
}
```

CRITSECT implements its bouncing-ball thread in the global function `ThreadFunc`. The `ThreadFunc` function contains a critical section that begins with an `EnterCriticalSection` statement and ends with a `LeaveCriticalSection` function. This is the `ThreadFunc` function in which those two calls appear:

```
// ThreadFunc function
long ThreadFunc(CAnimWnd *pAnimWnd)
{
    long lEndThread = 0;
    pAnimWnd->SetSpeed(TRUE);
    DWORD exitCode;
    LPVOID lpvData;

    lpvData = (LPVOID) LocalAlloc(LPTR,4);
    ASSERT(lpvData != NULL);

    EnterCriticalSection(&gCriticalSection);

    while (TRUE) {

        lpvData = TlsGetValue(dwTlsIndex);

        // Introduce a delay if speed is set to slow
        if (lpvData == &(pAnimWnd->m_bSlowSpeed))
            Sleep(100);
        else
            Sleep(0);

        // When this thread's window closes, the lEndThread
        // variable becomes non-zero (see OnClose function, above).
        lEndThread = GetWindowLong(pAnimWnd->m_hWnd, GWL_USERDATA);
        if (lEndThread) {

            // Get this thread's exit code and exit the thread.
            GetExitCodeThread(pAnimWnd->m_hThread, &exitCode);
            ExitThread(exitCode);

            // Get rid of objects that aren't needed anymore.
            CloseHandle(pAnimWnd->m_hThread);
            delete(pAnimWnd->m_pAnimation);
```

```
            delete(pAnimWnd);
            break;

    } else {
        // perform tasks.
        if (pAnimWnd != NULL) {
            pAnimWnd->Animate();
        } else {
            break;
        }
    }
}

LeaveCriticalSection(&gCriticalSection);

// Get the thread's exit code
// and return it as this function's return value.
GetExitCodeThread(pAnimWnd->m_hThread, &exitCode);
return exitCode;
}
```

MUTEX OBJECTS

A *mutex (mutual exclusion) object* is a synchronization object that can protect shared resources by preventing them from being accessed by multiple threads simultaneously. The state of a mutex object is signaled when it is not owned by any thread, and non-signaled when it is owned by a thread.

To prevent multiple threads from writing to shared memory at the same time, a mutex forces a thread to own a block of code before it is granted access to the code. When a block of code is protected by a mutex, a thread that seeks access to the code must wait for the thread that owns the code to release it. When the code is released, the thread that is seeking access can be granted ownership. After the new owner of the code finishes accessing it, ownership of the code is again released, and so on.

An application creates a mutex object by calling the Win32 function CreateMutex. This is the syntax of CreateMutex:

```
HANDLE CreateMutex(LPSECURITY_ATTRIBUTES lpsa, BOOL fInitialOwner,
    LPCSTR lpszMutexName);
```

If a `CreateMutex` calls succeeds, it returns a handle to the mutex it has created. If unsuccessful, the function returns `NULL`.

The parameters expected by `CreateMutex` are as follows:

+ **lpsa.** A pointer to a SECURITY_ATTRIBUTES structure.

+ **fInitialOwner.** If this flag is `TRUE`, the calling thread requests immediate ownership of the mutex object being created. If this flag is `FALSE`, the mutex is not initially owned.

+ **lpszMutexName.** Points to a string specifying the name of the mutex object. If this parameter is `NULL`, the mutex is created without a name.

Following is a step-by-step overview of how a mutex object works:

1. A thread calls `CreateMutex` to create a mutex object. The creating thread can request immediate ownership of the mutex and can also specify a name for the mutex object.

2. If a thread in another process seeks access to the mutex, it opens a handle to the mutex object by calling the Win32 function `OpenMutex`.

3. Any thread that has obtained a handle to the mutex object can call one of the Win32 wait functions to request ownership of the mutex.

4. If the mutex is owned by another thread (which is the case in this scenario), the wait function that has been called by the thread seeking access withholds access until the thread that owns the mutex releases it.

5. When the thread that owns the mutex is finished with it, the thread releases the mutex by calling `ReleaseMutex`.

6. If `ReleaseMutex` succeeds, the waiting thread is granted access to the released mutex and becomes the mutex's owner.

EXAMPLE: THE MUTEX PROGRAM

The MUTEX sample program, in the MUTEX subdirectory on the accompanying disk, shows how a mutex object can be used in a Windows NT program. MUTEX uses a mutex object to fix the same THRDDEMO bug that was corrected by a critical section in the CRITSECT program.

In MUTEX, a mutex object (rather than a critical section object) prevents corruption of the bouncing-ball bitmap by preventing any thread from accessing the program's view DC object while another thread is using it to draw to the screen. To create a mutex object, the program uses a static member variable named m_hMutex. The m_hMutex variable is declared in **ANIMWND.H** and is defined as follows in **ANIMWND.CPP**:

```
// Initialize m_hMutex, a static member variable.
HANDLE CAnimWnd::m_hMutex = CreateMutex(NULL, TRUE, NULL);
```

Later in **ANIMWND.CPP**, in the member function AnimWnd::OnCreate, the mutex that was initialized in the preceding code fragment is released for use by the first thread that claims it. AnimWnd::OnCreate releases the mutex by calling ReleaseMutex as soon as the program's child thread is created:

```
    // Call CreateThread
    m_hThread = CreateThread(NULL, 0,
        (LPTHREAD_START_ROUTINE)ThreadFunc,
        this, CREATE_SUSPENDED,
        (LPDWORD) &m_IDThread);
    ASSERT(m_hThread != NULL);

    // Release mutex.
    ReleaseMutex(m_hMutex);
```

The first parameter passed to CreateThread is a pointer to a function that will serve as an entry point to the thread being created. In the preceding code fragment, the name of the thread's entry point is ThreadFunc, which appears later in **ANIMWND.CPP**:

```
// ThreadFunc function
long ThreadFunc(CAnimWnd *pAnimWnd)
{
    long lEndThread = 0;
    pAnimWnd->SetSpeed(TRUE);
    DWORD exitCode;
    LPVOID lpvData;

    lpvData = (LPVOID) LocalAlloc(LPTR,4);
    ASSERT(lpvData != NULL);

    while (TRUE) {

        // Wait for mutex.
        WaitForSingleObject(pAnimWnd->m_hMutex, INFINITE);
        lpvData = TlsGetValue(dwTlsIndex);
```

```
        // Introduce a delay if speed is set to slow
        if (lpvData == &(pAnimWnd->m_bSlowSpeed))
            Sleep(100);
        else
            Sleep(0);

        // When this thread's window closes, the lEndThread
        // variable becomes non-zero (see OnClose function, above).
        lEndThread = GetWindowLong(pAnimWnd->m_hWnd, GWL_USERDATA);
        if (lEndThread) {

            // Get this thread's exit code and exit the thread.
            GetExitCodeThread(pAnimWnd->m_hThread, &exitCode);
            ExitThread(exitCode);

            // Get rid of objects that aren't needed anymore.
            CloseHandle(pAnimWnd->m_hThread);
            delete(pAnimWnd->m_pAnimation);
            delete(pAnimWnd);
            ReleaseMutex(pAnimWnd->m_hMutex);
            break;

        } else {
            // perform tasks.
            if (pAnimWnd != NULL) {
                pAnimWnd->Animate();
            } else {
                ReleaseMutex(pAnimWnd->m_hMutex);
                break;
            }
        }
        // Release mutex.
        ReleaseMutex(pAnimWnd->m_hMutex);
    }

    // Get the thread's exit code
    // and return it as this function's return value.
    GetExitCodeThread(pAnimWnd->m_hThread, &exitCode);
```

```
        return exitCode;
}
```

When the program's mutex object has been initialized and released, each thread that is created waits for the mutex to become available before the thread starts processing. This waiting period is established by the following statement, which appears near the beginning of the `ThreadFunc` function:

```
// Wait for thread.
WaitForSingleObject(m_hThread, INFINITE);
```

Each time a thread finishes accessing the mutex in THRDDEMO, it calls `ReleaseMutex`. Because `ReleaseMutex` is called both inside and outside the wait loop that controls the program's threads, calls to `ReleaseMutex` appear several times in the `ThreadFunc` function.

Each time a thread finishes using the mutex, it calls `ReleaseMutex` to free the mutex object:

```
// ...
        // Get rid of objects that aren't needed anymore.
        CloseHandle(pAnimWnd->m_hThread);
        delete(pAnimWnd->m_pAnimation);
        delete(pAnimWnd);
        ReleaseMutex(pAnimWnd->m_hMutex);
        break;

    } else {
        // perform tasks.
        if (pAnimWnd != NULL) {
            pAnimWnd->Animate();
        } else {
            ReleaseMutex(pAnimWnd->m_hMutex);
            break;
        }
    }
    // Release mutex.
    ReleaseMutex(pAnimWnd->m_hMutex);
}
```

SEMAPHORE OBJECTS

A *semaphore object* is a synchronization object that maintains a count between zero and a specified maximum value. When a semaphore is created, it has a specified initial count. Each time a thread uses and releases the semaphore, the semaphore's count is decremented. As long as a semaphore's count is greater than zero, the semaphore's state is signaled. When the semaphore's count is decremented to zero, the semaphore becomes nonsignaled. From that point on, the semaphore can no longer be accessed by any thread.

Semaphore objects can be useful when an application contains a shared resource that supports a limited number of users. Acting as a gate, a semaphore object counts threads as they enter and exit a controlled area and limits the number of threads that share a resource to a specified maximum number.

Suppose, for example, that an application needs to conserve memory by placing a limit on the number of windows that it creates. The SEMAFORE application, which you can find in the SEMAFORE subdirectory on the accompanying disk, shows how an application can use a semaphore object to accomplish that objective.

You create a semaphore object by calling the Win32 function `CreateSemaphore`. Following is the syntax of `CreateSemaphore`:

```
HANDLE CreateSemaphore(LPSECURITY_ATTRIBUTES lpsa, LONG cSemInitial, LONG
cSemMax,
    LPCSTR lpszSemName);
```

`CreateSemaphore` returns a handle to the semaphore that it has created. If the function does not succeed, it returns `NULL`.

`CreateSemaphore` takes the following parameters:

+ **lpsa**. A pointer to a SECURITY_ATTRIBUTES structure.

+ **cSemInitial**. The semaphore's initial count.

+ **cSemMax**. The semaphore's maximum count, usually the same value as `cSemInitial`. If this is the case, the semaphore can no longer be accessed when `cSemInitial` threads are running.

+ **lpszSemName**. The semaphore's name, if any. If this value is `NULL`, the semaphore is created without a name.

EXAMPLE: THE SEMAFORE PROGRAM

The use of semaphore objects is demonstrated in the SEMAFORE sample program provided in the SEMAFORE subdirectory on the accompanying disk. The semaphore object is implemented as a static member variable named m_hSemaphore. This variable is declared in **ANIMWND.H** and is initialized as follows in **ANIMWND.CPP**:

```
// Initialize m_hSemaphore, a static member variable.
HANDLE CAnimWnd::m_hSemaphore = CreateSemaphore(NULL, MAX_THREADS,
MAX_THREADS, NULL);
```

The initial count of the m_hSemaphore object is declared to be a constant named MAX_THREADS. Later in **ANIMWND.H**, MAX_THREADS is initialized with a value of 4. Thus, when the program is executed, m_hSemaphore allows a maximum number of four windows to be created.

When m_hSemaphore has been initialized, OnCreate uses the object by calling WaitForSingleObject every time it is about to create a thread:

```
DWORD dRetVal = WaitForSingleObject(CAnimWnd::m_hSemaphore, 0);
```

When the preceding statement is executed, if the m_hSemaphore object's countdown has not yet reached zero, a new thread is created. If the thread's count has been decremented to zero, a new thread is not created. Instead, the program displays an explanatory message box like the one shown in Figure 7.2.

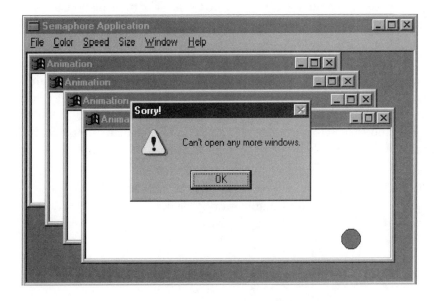

FIGURE 7.2 MESSAGE DISPLAYED WHEN NO MORE WINDOWS CAN BE OPENED.

In the `ThreadFunc` function, each thread that is created releases m_hSemaphore before it terminates. To release m_hSemaphore, each thread calls `ReleaseSemaphore`:

```
ReleaseSemaphore(CAnimWnd::m_hSemaphore, 1, NULL);
```

The parameter 1 specifies that the semaphore object's count is to be decremented by 1 when the semaphore is released. A NULL value is passed in the last parameter in lieu of an address that will receive the semaphore's previous (current) count. A NULL value means that no storage of a previous count is required.

EVENT OBJECTS

An *event object* is a synchronization object that can delay the start of a thread until another thread has terminated. Event objects can be useful when an application contains a thread that should not start until another thread has terminated.

To illustrate the use of event objects, suppose you want to write a compiler that builds programs in three stages: preprocessing, compilation, and linking. You can design the program to do its work by running three threads sequentially: first a preprocessing thread, then a compilation thread, and finally a linking thread. Sequential threads might also be useful in a program that manages serial communications. By using sequential threads, the program could wait for a client to finish a transmission before allowing another client (or a server) to start another transmission.

Event objects can manage sequential threads because an event object can be set to a signaled state either with an explicit call to a Win32 function or by simply releasing a waiting thread. To set an event object to a signaled state, an application can call either `SetEvent` or `PulseEvent`. The `SetEvent` function sets the state of a nonsignaled event object to signaled. `PulseEvent` releases all threads that may be waiting for an event object and then sets the event object's state to signaled. Alternatively, an event object can be set to a signaled state by merely releasing a waiting thread.

There are two kinds of event objects: auto-reset event objects and manual-reset event objects. When an auto-reset event object that is in a signaled state releases a waiting thread, the release of the thread automatically toggles the state of the event object to nonsignaled. If no threads are waiting, the event object's state remains signaled.

Manual-reset event objects work differently. When a manual-reset event object that is in a signaled state releases a waiting thread, the release of the thread does not toggle the state of the event object to nonsignaled. When the state of a manual-reset event object is signaled, the only thing that can put the object into a nonsignaled state is an explicit call to `SetEvent` or `ResetEvent`. Until `SetEvent` or `ResetEvent` is explicitly called, a manual-reset object that is signaled remains signaled no matter how many waiting threads it releases.

THE CREATEEVENT FUNCTION

To create an event object, an application calls the Win32 function `CreateEvent`, which has this syntax:

```
HANDLE CreateEvent(LPSECURITY_ATTRIBUTES lpsa, BOOL fManualReset,
    BOOL fInitialState, LPCTSTR lpszEventName);
```

A successful call to `CreateEvent` returns a handle to the event that has been created; an unsuccessful call returns `NULL`. `CreateEvent` takes these parameters:

✦ **lpsa.** A pointer to a SECURITY_ATTRIBUTES structure.

✦ **fManualReset.** `TRUE` if the object to be created is a manual-reset object; otherwise, `FALSE`.

✦ **fInitialState.** `TRUE` if the initial state of the object to be created is signaled; otherwise, `FALSE`.

✦ **lpszEventName.** A pointer to a name string if the object to be created is to have a name; otherwise, `NULL`.

EXAMPLE: THE EVENTS PROGRAM

The EVENTS application, in the EVENTS subdirectory on the accompanying disk, demonstrates the use of event objects. In EVENTS, two threads are created. One thread displays a window containing a bouncing ball, and the other thread displays a dialog box that contains the message "Thread 2 won't start until you click OK."

Figure 7.3 shows the pause message box that is displayed by the EVENTS program.

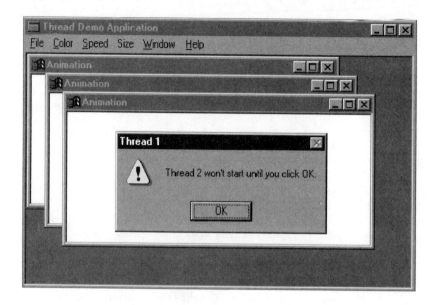

FIGURE 7.3 OUTPUT OF THE EVENTS PROGRAM.

The event object used in EVENTS is implemented as a member variable named m_hEvent, which is initialized near the top of the ANIMWND.CPP file:

```
// Initialize m_hEvent static member variable
HANDLE CAnimWnd::m_hEvent = CreateEvent(NULL, FALSE, FALSE, NULL);
```

When the user selects **New** from the File menu, the program starts a thread that displays the dialog box containing the pause message. The program then calls the Win32 function WaitForMultipleObjects, which causes the pause message box to remain on the screen until the user closes it by clicking **OK**.

The code that starts the message-box thread and then waits until it terminates appears in the OnCreate function in **ANIMWND.CPP**:

```
// Create Thread 1
m_hThread = CreateThread(NULL, 0,
    (LPTHREAD_START_ROUTINE)MsgFunc,
    this, 0,
    (LPDWORD) &m_IDThread);
ASSERT(m_hThread != NULL);
```

```
WaitForMultipleObjects(2, m_hTHREADS, TRUE, INFINITE);

return 0;
}
```

The event object used in the EVENTS program is an auto-reset object, so the thread that creates the pause message box does not have to call ResetEvent before it closes. As soon as the thread terminates, the message-box thread is set to a nonsignaled state, and the thread that displays the bouncing-ball window is free to begin.

When the dialog box closes, the second thread starts, displaying the bouncing-ball window. The bouncing-ball thread is created in this section of the OnCreate function:

```
// Create Thread 2
m_hThread = CreateThread(NULL, 0,
    (LPTHREAD_START_ROUTINE)ThreadFunc,
    this, CREATE_SUSPENDED,
    (LPDWORD) &m_IDThread);
ASSERT(m_hThread != NULL);

// Set the thread's priority.
SetPriority(THREAD_PRIORITY_BELOW_NORMAL);

// Call ResumeThread to start the thread.
Resume();

OnSizeStatic();
```

WAIT FUNCTIONS

When an application calls a wait function, the function checks the state of the synchronization object (or objects) specified in its parameter list and also checks for any other conditions that could cause it to return. If the wait function discovers no conditions that mandate a return and if the function's timeout interval has not elapsed, the calling thread enters an efficient wait state, consuming very little CPU time while waiting for the conditions that can cause it to return to be satisfied.

When a program calls WaitForSingleObject or WaitForSingleObjectEx, it passes the wait function a handle to a synchronization object. WaitForSingleObject and WaitForSingleObjectEx return when the state of the specified object is signaled or when the specified timeout interval elapses.

Three Win32 functions—WaitForMultipleObjects, WaitForMultipleObjectsEx, and MsgWaitForMultipleObjects—fall into the category of multiple-object functions. They allow the calling thread to specify an array containing one or more synchronization object handles. Multiple-object functions accept parameters that can cause them to return when the state of any one of the specified objects is signaled. In such a case, the value returned by the wait function specifies the array index of the object that caused the function to return. Alternatively, a multiple-object function can be set to return only when the state of all objects is signaled at the same time. In this case, the return value simply indicates that the specified conditions were satisfied.

When a multiple-object function is waiting for all objects that it controls to be signaled, the function does not modify the state of the specified objects until all the objects are signaled simultaneously. For example, a mutex object can be signaled, but the calling thread does not become the owner of the mutex until the other objects are also signaled. In the meantime, some other thread may obtain ownership of the mutex, delaying satisfaction of all specified conditions.

MsgWaitForMultipleObjects is identical to WaitForMultipleObjects except that it can also return when a specified type of input is available in the calling thread's input queue. For example, a thread could call MsgWaitForMultipleObjects to block its execution until either the state of a specified object is signaled or there is mouse input available in the thread's input queue. When input is available, the thread can call GetMessage or PeekMessage to retrieve it.

WaitForSingleObjectEx and WaitForMultipleObjectsEx have a special characteristic: They can optionally perform an alertable wait. During an alertable wait, a wait function can return when the specified conditions are satisfied, but it can also return if the system queues a completion routine for execution by the waiting thread.

Multithreading and the MFC Library

Version 4.0 of the MFC library was the first MFC release to contain support for mulithreading. Until MFC 4.0 was introduced, the only way to implement the multithreading capabilities of Windows NT was to call C-language functions or Win32 API functions.

With the double-barreled release of Visual C++ 4.0 and MFC 4.0, Microsoft introduced two new MFC classes to support multithreading and changed the hierarchy of the CWnd class to make it support multithreading. But overall, MFC support for multithreading was still minimal at best.

THE MFC LIBRARY'S SUPPORT FOR MULTITHREADING

MFC 4.1, which was current when this book was written, offers several classes that can be used to create synchronization objects such as mutexes and semaphores (which are described under separate headings later in this chapter). Still, MFC support for multithreading is not yet perfect.

One example of the shortcomings of MFC support for multithreading is that MFC objects are not thread-safe at the object level, but only at the class level. This means that your application cannot contain two separate threads that manipulate the same CString object unless you protect the object with an appropriate synchronization mechanism such as a critical section or mutex (both described under separate headings in this chapter). If you don't use a synchronization object, one thread can change the contents of the CString object without the other thread's knowing about the change. When the second thread wants to access the string, it will find a string whose contents have suddenly and unexpectedly changed.

Because MFC support for multithreading has this shortcoming, five of the sample programs presented in this chapter ignore MFC and implement their support for multithreading by calling Windows API functions. However, two of the example programs—MFCTHRDS and USRTHRD—show how you can use MFC thread-related classes in your own applications.

I haven't bothered to demonstrate the MFC synchronization-object classes in this chapter because they are only thin wrappers around their associated Windows API functions. As long as I was using Windows API functions to implement multithreading, it seemed logical and consistent to use the Windows API function for the synchronization objects in the programs.

THE MFC LIBRARY'S THREAD-RELATED CLASSES

One of the MFC library's new thread-support classes is CWinThread. The other MFC thread class is called CWinApp. In version 4.0 and later of the MFC library, CWinThread is the class that is used to create the main thread of execution in an application.

CWinApp is derived from CWinThread. After an MFC application has instantiated its main thread from CWinApp, the application can create additional threads by instantiating CWinThread-derived objects. (Or, if you prefer, you can do as I've done in most of the example programs in this chapter; you can simply use the Windows API to create additional threads without bothering to instantiate any new CWinThread objects.)

Thread objects of the CWinThread class typically exist for the duration of the thread. You can modify this behavior by setting a CWinThread member variable named m_bAutoDelete to FALSE.

According to the on-line help files supplied with Visual C++, using the CWinThread class uses thread local storage (see the "Thread Local Storage" section in Chapter 8) to make your code and MFC "fully thread-safe." However, this guarantee is not ironclad, as I noted earlier in discussing MFC multithreading and the CString class. If you take reasonable precautions, though, you can use CWinThread to implement multithreading in an MFC program, as I've done in the MFCTHRDS and USRTHRD example programs presented in this chapter. In fact, any thread that contains MFC must be instantiated from the CWinThread class.

Evolution of the CWinApp Class

The CWinApp class is the base class from which Windows application objects are derived. In a Visual C++ program based on the AppWizard framework, an application object provides member functions for initializing and running the program. In early versions of MFC, CWinApp was derived from a class named CCmdTarget. The CCmdTarget class, which is still used in MFC programs, is derived from the mother of all MFC classes: CObject.

In MFC 4.0 and later, the CWinApp class is derived from CWinThread. Now it is the CWinThread class, and not the CWinApp class, that is derived from CCmdTarget. Figure 7.4 shows this new class hierarchy.

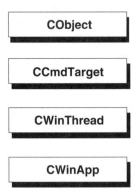

FIGURE 7.4 HIERARCHY OF THE CWINTHREAD CLASS.

In an application based on the Visual C++ AppWizard framework, you must create one and only one object derived from CWinApp. A Visual C++ program constructs its CWinApp-derived object when other C++ global objects have been constructed, so the program's CWinApp object is already available by the time Windows calls the WinMain function, the main function of a Visual C++ program.

When you derive an application class from CWinApp, you must override the Visual C++ InitInstance member function to create your application's main window object.

Accessing CWinApp Objects

In addition to the CWinApp member functions, MFC provides the following global functions to access your CWinApp object and other global information:

+ **AfxGetApp**. Obtains a pointer to the CWinApp object.

+ **AfxGetInstanceHandle**. Obtains a handle to the current application instance.

+ **AfxGetResourceHandle**. Obtains a handle to the application's resources.

+ **AfxGetAppName**. Obtains a pointer to a string containing the application's name. Alternately, if you have a pointer to the CWinApp object, use m_pszExeName to get the application's name.

VARIETIES OF MFC THREADS

MFC provides support for two kinds of threads. *Worker* threads are typically used to perform operations that do not require user input, operations such as calculations, screen updating, and background printing. *User-interface* threads are designed to handle user input and to respond to user events without affecting other threads that may be running in an application.

The main difference between user-interface threads and worker threads is that user-interface threads have a *message pump*. That means they can receive and process messages and can therefore interact with the user of your application. In contrast, worker threads have no message pump, so they cannot process messages. When you need to create a thread that does not require any input from the user, the easiest thing to do is to create a worker thread. For example, if you wanted to create a thread to perform background calculations in a spreadsheet program or to create a window display without requiring any input from the user, your easiest choice might be to write a worker thread. But if you wanted to use MFC to create a thread that relied on keyboard input from the user, you would have to make it a user-interface thread.

One advantage of using user-interface threads is that the Visual C++ ClassWizard utility supports them. You can create a user-interface thread automatically with ClassWizard, and you can then use ClassWizard to add member functions to the class and to integrate the class with your program and with other MFC classes it contains.

The CWinApp class, and classes derived from it are examples of user interface threads. Your applications can also derive user-interface threads directly from CWinThread.

Although the MFC library provides separate tools for writing worker threads and user-interface threads and supplies thread-related functions that make distinctions between worker threads and user-interface threads, the Win32 API makes no such distinctions. The Win32 API does not know anything about the differences between worker threads and user-interface threads. All it needs to execute a thread is the thread's starting address.

CREATING THREADS USING MFC

To create a thread using CWinThread, call the MFC function AfxBeginThread. There are two forms of this function to choose from, depending on whether you want to create a worker or a user-interface thread. To create a user-interface thread, pass AfxBeginThread a pointer to the CRuntimeClass of your CWinThread-derived class. To create a worker thread, pass to AfxBeginThread a pointer to your thread's controlling function. For both kinds of threads, you can use optional AfxBeginThread parameters to specify your thread's priority, stack size, creation flags, and security attributes. AfxBeginThread returns a pointer to your new CWinThread object.

A statement that creates a thread by calling AfxBeginThread is usually implemented as a member function of a class. When a Visual C++ application creates a thread by calling AfxBeginThread, the thread is created as soon as the calling function is executed. The MFCTHRDS program, one of the sample applications presented in this chapter, shows how AfxBeginThread can be used to create a worker thread in a Visual C++ program.

There is another way to create a thread using a CWinThread object. Instead of calling AfxBeginThread, you construct your own CWinThread-derived object and then call CreateThread to initialize it. This two-stage method can be useful when you want to create a CWinThread object that does not have to be repeatedly destroyed and reconstructed as successive and threads are created, executed, and terminated.

The main advantage of using AfxBeginThread is that it returns a pointer to a CWinThread object, whereas a thread-creating function in a Win32 program returns a handle to a thread. In a Visual C++ program, a CWinThread object is more useful than a handle to a thread, because CWinThread is an MFC class and therefore enjoys all the usual benefits of MFC classes, such as smooth interaction with the Visual C++ framework and with other classes in MFC.

When a program contains an `AfxBeginThread` function that creates a thread, the entry-point function executes as soon as `AfxBeginThread` is executed. When the entry-point function executes, the thread starts. When the entry-point function terminates, so does the thread.

When a process uses `AfxBeginThread` to start a thread, the thread's entry-point procedure must have the following prototype:

```
UINT MyControllingFunction(LPVOID pParam);
```

As you can see, a thread entry-point function called by `AfxBeginThread` takes one parameter: a single 32-bit value. The value that is provided to the thread's entry-point function is the value of the `AfxBeginThread` function's `pParam` variable. If `pParam` refers to a structure, the entry-point function can use the structure not only to pass data from the calling function to the thread but also to pass data back from the thread to the caller. If an entry-point function uses `pParam` to pass the address of such a structure back to its caller, the thread must notify the caller when the results are ready.

When a thread entry-point function terminates, it returns a `DWORD` value indicating the reason the function has terminated. Typically, an entry-point function returns an exit code of zero if it has successfully created a thread. It can return other values to specify different types of errors.

WORKER THREADS

Creating a worker thread in an MFC application is very similar to creating a thread using the Win32 API. To create a worker thread in an MFC program, you must write a C-style function (not a member function) that serves as an entry point to your thread. Then, at the point in your program where you want the thread to be created, you provide a pointer to the function that serves as the thread's entry point.

In an MFC application, an entry-point function for a worker thread has this syntax:

```
UINT ThreadFunc(LPVOID pParam)
{
    // ...
}
```

Notice that the preceding statement is a definition of a C-style global function and not a definition of a member function. In a Visual C++ program, you cannot use a member function of a class as the entry-point function of a worker thread. If you try, the Visual C++ compiler returns an error message.

Starting a Thread

Once you write a thread entry-point function using the syntax shown under the preceding heading, you start the thread by calling `AfxBeginThread`, as in this example:

```
CWinThread *pThread = AfxBeginThread(ThreadFunc,
    (LPVOID) this,
    THREAD_PRIORITY_BELOW_NORMAL,
    0,
    CREATE_SUSPENDED);
```

The procedure for calling an MFC worker thread in a Visual C++ program is much like the procedure for calling a thread in a Win32 (non-MFC) program. But there are some important differences. One difference is that a Visual C++ program can use `AfxBeginThread`, as shown in the preceding example, whereas a non-MFC program creates a thread by calling the Win32 `CreateThread` function:

```
m_hThread = CreateThread(NULL, 0,
    (LPTHREAD_START_ROUTINE)ThreadFunc,
    this, CREATE_SUSPENDED,
    (LPDWORD) &m_IDThread);
```

Another difference is that `AfxBeginThread` creates and initializes a `CWinThread` object and returns a pointer to that object. From that point on, you can use the pointer returned by `AfxBeginThread` to access the thread object that `AfxBeginThread` has created.

In contrast, the MFC `CreateThread` function creates a handle to a thread and returns that handle. Subsequently, you access the thread through the handle returned by `CreateThread`.

There are similarities, as well as differences, between `AfxBeginThread` and `CreateThread`. Both functions, for example, accept the address of a thread entry point as a parameter. But for Visual C++ users, there is a second version of the `AfxBeginThread` function. As you have seen, one overridden version of `AfxBeginThread` takes a thread entry-point address as a parameter. The other overridden version of the function accepts the address of a `CWinThread` object as a parameter. When you create a thread by passing `AfxBeginThread` a pointer to a `CWinThread` object, the thread you wind up creating is a user-interface thread.

This is the syntax of the version of `AfxBeginThread` that creates a worker thread:

```
CWinThread* AfxBeginThread(
    AFX_THREADPROC pfnThreadProc,
```

```
LPVOID pParam,
int nPriority = THREAD_PRIORITY_NORMAL,
UINT nStackSize = 0,
DWORD dwCreateFlags = 0,
LPSECURITY_ATTRIBUTES lpSecurityAttrs = NULL );
```

To create an MFC worker thread, you pass the following parameters to `AfxBeginThread`:

+ **pfnThreadProc.** A pointer to the address of the thread's entry-point function.

+ **pParam.** The parameter to be passed to the controlling function.

+ **nPriority** (optional). The priority of the thread. The default is normal priority. For more information on the available priority levels, see `::SetThreadPriority` in the *Win32 Programmer's Reference*.

+ **nStackSize** (optional). The stack size for the thread. Default is the same size stack as the creating thread.

+ **dwCreateFlags** (optional). CREATE_SUSPENDED if you want the thread to be created in a suspended state. The default is 0, or start the thread normally.

+ **lpSecurityAttrs** (optional). The desired security attributes. The default is the same access as the parent thread. For more information on the format of this security information, see SECURITY_ATTRIBUTES in the *Win32 Programmer's Reference*.

`AfxBeginThread` creates and initializes a `CWinThread` object for you, starts it, and returns its address so that you can refer to it later. Checks are made throughout the procedure to make sure that all objects are deallocated properly should any part of the creation fail. To see how you can call `AfxBeginThread` to create a worker thread, see "The MFCTHRDS Program" later in this chapter.

When an entry-point function is executed to create a worker thread, the `pParam` variable passed to the entry-point function by `AfxBeginThread` must be the constructor that instantiated the thread object when it was created. The entry-point function can interpret the `AfxBeginThread` function's `pParam` variable in any manner it chooses. It can treat `pParam` as a scalar value, for example, or as a pointer to a structure containing multiple parameters. The entry-point function can even ignore the `pParam` parameter.

USER-INTERFACE THREADS

A user-interface thread is an MFC thread that can handle user input and can respond to user events without affecting other threads that may be running in an application.

Although user-interface threads have capabilities that worker threads do not have, there is nothing to prevent an application from creating and using a user-interface thread without taking advantage of all the thread's capabilities. In other words, an application can always use a user-interface thread instead of a worker thread—but the opposite is not true. You can never use a worker thread in situations that require interaction between the thread and the user. User-interface threads are more smoothly integrated into the MFC environment than worker threads are. My preference is to use only user-interface threads in MFC programs, avoiding the use of worker threads completely.

There are at least two reasons for using user-interface threads rather than worker threads in MFC applications whenever possible. When you use a worker thread in an application, its entry point is always a global C-style function and not a member function of a C++ class. So, when you use a worker thread in a C++ program, you wind up with a global C-style function floating around in your application, not directly tied to any object and not encapsulated in any class. That is not a desirable feature in a C++ program, because it is not consistent with the object-oriented design requirements of code encapsulation and limited access to data. Generally speaking, well-designed C++ programs avoid the use of global, nonmember functions, because free-floating functions have no means of encapsulating their code or data inside objects and cannot be transported from one application to another as readily as member functions are.

When you build an application using the Visual C++ framework, you can use ClassWizard to create user-interface threads automatically and your thread class becomes an integral part of your application's C++ framework. ClassWizard creates an implementation file (.**CPP** file) and a header file (.**H** file) for your thread class, and you can use ClassWizard to create and maintain thread-related member variables, member functions, and events.

Creating a User-Interface Thread

To create a user-interface thread, the first thing step is to derive a class from `CWinThread`. You must declare this class using the `DECLARE_DYNCREATE` macro, and you must implement it by invoking the `IMPLEMENT_DYNCREATE` macro. If you create your thread class using the ClassWizard, it automatically constructs an object that invokes both macros in accordance with the requirements of Visual C++ and MFC.

When you create a user-interface thread by calling `AfxBeginThread`, you must override some functions, and you can override others if you wish to. Table 7.1 summarizes these functions.

TABLE 7.1 FUNCTIONS OVERRIDDEN BY USER-INTERFACE THREADS.

Function Name	Purpose
`ExitInstance`	Performs cleanup when a thread terminates. Usually overridden.
`InitInstance`	Performs thread instance initialization. Must be overridden.
`OnIdle`	Performs thread-specific idle-time processing. Not usually overridden.
`PreTranslateMessage`	Filters messages before they are dispatched to `TranslateMessage` and `DispatchMessage`. Not usually overridden
`ProcessWndProcException`	Intercepts unhandled exceptions thrown by the thread's message and command handlers. Not usually overridden.
`Run`	Controlling function for a thread. Contains the message pump. Rarely overridden.

Instantiating a User-Interface Thread

When you have derived a user-interface thread class from `CWinThread`, you must instantiate an object of your `CWinThread`-derived class. You can construct your thread object either on the stack or on the heap, using either of these standard styles:

```
CMyWinThread myThread;
```

or

```
CMyWinThread *pMyThread = CMyWinThread;
```

When you have instantiated a `CWinThread`-derived object, call `AfxBeginThread` to initialize your thread. To provide your thread's entry-point function with a pointer to the thread object you have instantiated, place the RUNTIME_CLASS of your thread object in the `AfxBeginThread` function's `pThreadClass` parameter. You can obtain your thread object's runtime class by calling the `CObject` member function `GetRuntimeClass`. (To see how `AfxBeginThread` and `GetRuntimeClass` can be called to create a user-interface thread, see "The USRTHRDS Program" later in this chapter.)

Constructing a User-Interface Thread

There are two ways to construct a user-interface thread. One way is to create an object derived from `CWinThread`, as explained previously, and then to initialize the object by calling `CreateThread`. This two-stage construction method is useful if you want to create a `CWinThread`-derived object that you can start and terminate at will—for example, between successive creations and terminations of thread executions.

The other way to create a user-interface thread is to execute the version of AfxBeginThread that is specifically designed to create objects derived from CWinThread. This is the format of the version of AfxBeginThread that creates user-interface threads:

```
CWinThread* AfxBeginThread(
    CRuntimeClass* pThreadClass,
    int nPriority = THREAD_PRIORITY_NORMAL,
    UINT nStackSize = 0,
    DWORD dwCreateFlags = 0,
    LPSECURITY_ATTRIBUTES lpSecurityAttrs = NULL );
```

To create a user-interface thread, pass the following parameters to AfxBeginThread:

+ **pThreadClass**. The RUNTIME_CLASS of an object you have derived from CWinThread.

+ **nPriority** (optional). The priority of the thread. The default is normal priority. For more information on the available priority levels, see ::SetThreadPriority in the *Win32 Programmer's Reference*, Volume 4.

+ **nStackSize** (optional). The stack size for the thread. Default is the same size stack as the creating thread.

+ **dwCreateFlags** (optional). CREATE_SUSPENDED if you want the thread to be created in a suspended state. The default is 0, or start the thread normally.

+ **lpSecurityAttrs** (optional). The desired security attributes. The default is the same access as the parent thread. For more information on the format of this security information, see SECURITY_ATTRIBUTES in the *Win32 Programmer's Reference*.

How AfxBeginThread Handles User-Interface Threads

With two exceptions, the user-interface version of AfxBeginThread works just like the worker-thread version; it creates and initializes a CWinThread object for you, starts it, and returns its address so that you can refer to it later. Checks are made throughout the procedure to make sure that all objects are deallocated properly if any part of the creation fails.

One difference between the worker version and the user-interface version of AfxBeginThread is that the first parameter passed to the user-interface version is the RUNTIME_CLASS of the object being derived from CWinThread. In a framework-based Visual C++ program, the RUNTIME_CLASS of an object is a data structure that contains information needed by an application framework to create an object of a class at run time. You can obtain the RUNTIME_CLASS of an object by executing the CObject member function GetRuntimeClass. (For more information about creating user-interface threads, see the "The USRTHRDS Program" later in this chapter; for more details about run-time classes, see your Visual C++ documentation.)

There is one other difference between an AfxBeginThread function that creates a worker thread and one that creates a worker thread: The version of AfxBeginThread that creates a user-interface thread has no pParam parameter.

THE MFC LIBRARY'S THREAD-SYNCHRONIZATION CLASSES

MFC provides seven classes that are designed to be used in thread-synchronization operations. These classes include five *synchronization-object* classes and two *synchronization-access* classes. The five synchronization objects are CSyncObject, CCriticalSection, CMutex, CSemaphore, and CEvent. The synchronization-access objects are CMultiLock and CSingleLock.

CSyncObject is a pure virtual class that provides functionality common to the synchronization objects in Win32. CCriticalSection, CMutex, CSemaphore, and CEvent are all derived from CSyncObject. The CSingleLock and CMultilock classes are MFC encapsulations of the Win32 API functions WaitForSingleObject and WaitForMultipleObjects.

The CCriticalSection Class

CCriticalSection is an MFC class that you can use to create critical section objects. To use a CCriticalSection-derived object, you construct the critical section object when it is needed. You can then access the critical section when the constructor returns. When you are finished accessing the critical section, you call the CCriticalSection::Unlock member function to free the critical section.

An alternative is to use a variable of the CCriticalSection type as a data member of the class to which you want to control access. During construction of the controlled object, call the constructor of the CCriticalSection data member, specifying whether the critical section is initially owned and specifying the object's security attributes.

To access a resource controlled by a CCriticalSection object, you construct a variable of the CSingleLock or CMultiLock in your resource's access member function. Then you call the lock object's Lock member function (for example, CSingleLock::Lock). At this point, one of three things happens:

+ Your thread is allowed access to the resource.

✦ Your thread must wait for the resource to be released. Then it is allowed access to the resource.

✦ Your thread is forced to wait for the resource to be released and must time out while waiting for access.

All three of these possibilities have one thing in common: In each case, your resource has been protected.

To release a resource from protection by a CCriticalSection object, you call your lock object's Unlock member function (for example, CSingleLock::Unlock) or allow the lock object to fall out of scope.

For an example of how to use the CCriticalObject class, see the MTGDI application in the Samples folder on the Visual C++ CD-ROM.

The CMutex Class

CMutex is the MFC encapsulation of a mutex object—that is, a synchronization object that prevents simultaneous access to a resource by multiple threads. To use the CMutex object in a Windows NT program, you can either construct and initialize a CMutex object in a single step or use a variable of the CMutex type in the class that uses the object. To construct and initialize a mutex object in a single step, you pass the CMutex constructor the name of the mutex you want to create. You can then access the mutex when the constructor returns. When you have finished using a mutex object, you free it by calling the CSyncObject::Unlock member function.

To use a CMutex object as a member variable of a class, you call the constructor of the CMutex member variable during construction of the object you want to protect. Before an application accesses a resource protected by a CMutex variable, it must create another member variable of either the CSingleLock type or the CMultiLock type. Then the application calls the lock object's Lock member function (for example, CSingleLock::Lock). To release the resource, the application calls the lock object's Unlock member function (for example, CSingleLock::Unlock) or allows the lock object to fall out of scope.

To see how a CMutex object can be used in a Windows application, examine the MTGDI and MUTEXES applications in the Samples folder on the Visual C++ CD-ROM.

The CSemaphore Class

CSemaphore is the MFC class that lets you create synchronization objects—that is, objects that allow a limited number of threads in one or more processes to access a resource. A CSemaphore object maintains a count of the number of threads currently accessing a specified resource.

Semaphores, as you have seen, can be useful when an application needs to control access to a shared resource that can support only a limited number of users. The current count of a CSemaphore object is always the number of additional users allowed. When the count reaches zero, all attempts to use the resource are inserted into a system queue and wait until they either time out or the count rises above 0. The maximum number of users who can access the controlled resource at one time is specified during construction of the CSemaphore object.

To use a CSemaphore object, you can either construct the object when it is needed or use a variable of the CSemaphore type as a data member of the class you want to protect. To use the second alternative, call the constructor of your CSemaphore data member during the construction of the object you want to protect, specifying the initial access count, the maximum access count, the name of the semaphore (if it will be used across process boundaries), and the security attributes of the semaphore.

To lock and free resources protected by CSemaphore objects, use the CSingleLock, CMultiLock, and Lock member functions in the same way that you use them for CMutex and CCriticalSection objects.

The MTGDI example program, which you can find in the Samples folder on the Visual C++ CD-ROM, demonstrates how CSemaphore objects can be used in Windows NT programs.

The CEvent Class

CEvent is used to instantiate events—that is, synchronization objects that allow one thread to notify another that an event has occurred. Events can be useful when you need to notify a thread that it's time to perform its assigned task. For example, an application may need to notify a thread that copies data that new data is available. By using a CEvent object to notify the copy thread when new data is available, the thread can perform its task as soon as a chance arises.

MFC provides two kinds of CEvent objects: manual objects and automatic objects. To set or reset a manual CEvent object, you call the CEvent::SetEvent or CEvent::ResetEvent member function. An automatic CEvent object automatically returns to a nonsignaled (unavailable) state after at least one thread is released.

To use a CEvent object, you can either construct it when it is needed or create a CEvent member variable when you construct the class you want to protect. You can lock and free a resource controlled by a CEvent object by using the CSingleLock and CMultiLock classes.

For an example of how `CEvent` objects can be used in Windows NT programs, see the MTGDI example program in the Samples folder on the Visual C++ CD-ROM.

EXAMPLES: USRTHRDS AND MFCTHRDS

As explained in "Multithreading and the MFC Library" earlier in this chapter, MFC provides support for two kinds of threads: worker threads and user-interface threads. Worker threads are typically used to perform operations that do not require user input—operations such as calculations, screen updating, and background printing. User-interface threads are designed to handle user input and to respond to user events without affecting other threads that may be running in an application.

Two applications on the accompanying disk—MFCTHRDS and USRTHRDS—show how worker threads and user-interface threads can be used in Visual C++ programs.

The USRTHRDS Program

USRTHRDS is similar to the MFCTHRDS program described under the next heading. USRTHRDS creates a user-interface thread by calling `AfxBeginThread` from inside the `CAnimWnd::OnCreate` member function in **ANIMWND.CPP**. The difference is that USRTHRDS uses the overridden version of `AfxBeginThread` that creates user-interface threads.

The user-interface version of `AfxBeginThread` does not take a variable that points to an entry-point function. Instead, it expects a variable that contains the RUNTIME_CLASS of a thread object derived from `CWinThread`. In USRTHRDS, the `CObject` member function `GetRuntimeClass` is called to retrieve the RUNTIME_CLASS of the program's `CWinThread`-derived thread object:

```
CMyWinThread *pMyThread = AfxBeginThread(
    m_myThread->GetRuntimeClass(),
    THREAD_PRIORITY_BELOW_NORMAL,
    0,
    CREATE_SUSPENDED);
ASSERT_VALID(pThread);
```

The thread entry-point function is called by `AfxBeginThread`.

The MFCTHRDS Program

MFCTHRDS creates a worker thread by calling `AfxBeginThread` from **ANIMWND.CPP**. The program calls `AfxBeginThread` from inside the `CAnimWnd::-OnCreate` member function:

```
CWinThread *pThread = AfxBeginThread(ThreadFunc,
        (LPVOID) this,
        THREAD_PRIORITY_BELOW_NORMAL,
        0,
        CREATE_SUSPENDED);
    ASSERT_VALID(pThread);
```

The thread entry-point function called by `AfxBeginThread` creates a thread synchronized by a mutex object (see "Mutex Objects" earlier in this chapter). This is the entry-point function called by `AfxBeginThread`:

```
// ThreadFunc function
UINT ThreadFunc(LPVOID pParam)
{
    CAnimWnd *pAnimWnd = (CAnimWnd*) pParam;
    long lEndThread = 0;
    pAnimWnd->SetFastSpeed(TRUE);
    DWORD exitCode;
    LPVOID lpvData;
    lpvData = (LPVOID) LocalAlloc(LPTR,4);
    ASSERT(lpvData != NULL);

    while (TRUE) {
        // Wait for mutex.
        WaitForSingleObject(pAnimWnd->m_hMutex, INFINITE);
        lpvData = TlsGetValue(pAnimWnd->m_dwTlsIndex);

        // Introduce a delay if speed is set to slow
        if (lpvData == &(pAnimWnd->m_bSlowSpeed))
            Sleep(100);
        else
            Sleep(0);
        // When this thread's window closes, the lEndThread
        // variable becomes non-zero (see OnClose function, above).
        lEndThread = GetWindowLong(pAnimWnd->m_hWnd, GWL_USERDATA);
        if (lEndThread) {
            // Get this thread's exit code and exit the thread.
            GetExitCodeThread(pAnimWnd->m_hThread, &exitCode);
            ExitThread(exitCode);
```

```
                    // Get rid of objects that aren't needed anymore.
                    CloseHandle(pAnimWnd->m_hThread);
                    delete(pAnimWnd->m_pAnimation);
                    delete(pAnimWnd);
                    ReleaseMutex(pAnimWnd->m_hMutex);
                    break;
                } else {
                    // perform tasks.
                    if (pAnimWnd != NULL) {
                        pAnimWnd->Animate();
                    } else {
                        ReleaseMutex(pAnimWnd->m_hMutex);
                        break;
                    }
                }
                // Release mutex.
                ReleaseMutex(pAnimWnd->m_hMutex);
            }
            // Get the thread's exit code
            // and return it as this function's return value.
            GetExitCodeThread(pAnimWnd->m_hThread, &exitCode);
            return exitCode;
}
```

Timers

Windows NT, like Windows 3.x, comes equipped with a set of timers that can divide CPU time among various tasks. In some circumstances, you can use timers to schedule events instead of using threads.

There are differences, however, between the behaviors of events scheduled by timers and those of tasks scheduled by threads. When you allocate CPU time to a task by using a timer, the task always receives the amount of time that it is allotted, regardless of the amount of CPU time that may be available. When you use threads to allocate time slices to multiple tasks, Windows NT determines how much time to give to each thread depending on how much CPU time is available.

The TIMER Program

In the first of this chapter's example programs—the TIMER program on the accompanying disk—the Win32 function SetTimer is called to initialize a timer. That happens in the member function named CAnimWnd::OnCreate, which appears in the file ANIMWND.CPP. This is the code sequence in which SetTimer is called:

```
// Set up the shape parameters.
int CAnimWnd::OnCreate(LPCREATESTRUCT /* p */)
{
    if (!SetTimer(1, 0 /* start fast */, NULL)) {
        MessageBox("Not enough timers available.",
                    "CAnimWnd", MB_ICONEXCLAMATION | MB_OK);

        // If creation failed...
        return -1;

    } else {

        // Instantiate an animation object.
        m_pAnimation = new MAnimation(m_hWnd);
        ASSERT(m_pAnimation != NULL);
    }

    OnSizeStatic();

    return 0;
}
```

Later in **ANIMWND.CPP,** in a member function named CAnimWnd::SetSpeed, SetTimer is called to set the timer's speed:

```
// Change the shape's speed
void CAnimWnd::SetSpeed()
{
    // Re-create the timer.
    KillTimer(1);
    if (!SetTimer(1, m_bFastSpeed ? 0 : 100, NULL)) {
```

```
        MessageBox("Not enough timers available.",
            "CAnimWnd", MB ICONEXCLAMATION | MB_OK);
        DestroyWindow();
    }
}
```

Finally, in a member function `CAnimWnd::OnTimer`, the Win32 function `OnTimer` is called to synchronize the animation of an object with the speed of the timer. The animation function's name is `m_pAnimation->AnimateShape`. This is the code sequence in which the animation function is synchronized with the timer:

```
void CAnimWnd::OnTimer(UINT nIDEvent)
{
    // TODO: Add your message handler code here and/or call default

    RECT rcClient;

    GetClientRect(&rcClient);
    m_pAnimation->AnimateShape(rcClient);

    CMDIChildWnd::OnTimer(nIDEvent);
}
```

Although timers can be useful in Windows programs, their usefulness is sometimes limited by the fact that they do not support preemptive multitasking. Timers control the execution of processes in a clockwork fashion; a timer receives control of the CPU each time a certain number of clock ticks has elapsed and relinquishes control when a predetermined operation is complete. If an application requires a form of time management that's more sophisticated than that, threads are required.

Summary

One of the most important new features of Windows NT is support for preemptive multi-tasking—the ability to run multiple processes simultaneously by allocating each process a slice of CPU time. Windows NT supports preemptive multitasking by using multi-threading, a technique for dividing processes into threads and allocating each thread a share of CPU time, depending on preallocated thread priorities.

In this chapter, you learned two techniques for building multithreading capabilities into Windows NT programs: by using the thread-related classes provided by MFC, and by making direct calls to Win32 API functions. When a process has been divided into multiple threads, these threads must be synchronized if they are to operate properly. In Windows NT, several kinds of synchronization objects are provided to synchronize thread operations. These objects are mutexes (mutual exclusion objects), semaphores, and event objects.

This chapter explains how threads and synchronization objects are used in Windows NT applications. Example applications demonstrate the use of timers, threads, mutex objects, semaphores, and event objects in Windows NT programs. The example programs contain a thread class (`MThread`) and an animation class (`MAnimation`) that you can use in your own applications.

CHAPTER EIGHT

DYNAMIC LINK LIBRARIES

If you've ever written a program for Windows—either 16-bit Windows or Windows NT—you've used dynamic link libraries. DLLs are object-code libraries that let multiple programs share code, data, and resources. They are so important in the world of personal computing that Microsoft Windows owes its very existence to them; most of the functions and features of the Windows API (both the 16-bit and the 32-bit versions) are implemented as a giant collection of DLLs.

DLLs are also used extensively by Windows applications. In fact, many large, complex applications are made up mostly of DLLs.

Why are DLLs so important in Windows programming? Because they let programs that are loaded into memory at the same time share code and resources, speeding processing and conserving memory. DLLs can also be automatically loaded into memory when they are needed and automatically purged from memory when they are no longer needed, freeing even more memory for other needs.

Still another reason that DLLs are important is that some Windows mechanisms, such as device drivers, must be implemented as DLLs to meet the demands of Windows NT. For example, device drivers must be implemented as dynamic link libraries because DLLs are the only executables that are always loaded and are callable from any executing application or library. OLE controls, Microsoft's 32-bit successors to VBX controls, are also implemented as DLLs.

From a developer's point of view, DLLs are useful for storing large numbers of resources—such as icons, dialog boxes, and bitmaps—that must be instantly accessible to applications and libraries. DLLs can also come in handy when you want to write code

423

that registers and implements systemwide window classes. DDLs are ideal for this purpose because the Windows messaging system gives them preferential treatment over applications. In fact, the operating system virtually guarantees the availability of DLLs to any executing application or library any time the DLL is needed.

Dynamic link libraries have many other uses. For example, DLLs are often used to store code that supports global window classes, implement interrupt-driven code, and implement code for systemwide mouse, keyboard, and message filtering

In a nutshell, whenever you need an instantly usable library of functions or resources that can be called at any time by one or more executing applications, you should consider creating a DLL. When you get accustomed to writing DLLs, you're sure to find many uses for them in your applications.

Varieties of Windows DLLs

Procedures for creating and linking DLLs have been overhauled several times since the initial release of Microsoft C/C++ (the predecessor to Microsoft Visual C++). Many rules for writing DLLs that were enforced in earlier versions of Visual C++ and the MFC library no longer apply to Visual C++ programs written for Windows NT. Also, some newer DLLs that work with Windows NT balk at being used with version 2.0 or earlier of MFC. And DLLs written for 16-bit Visual C++ follow a different set of rules than DLLs written for version 1.1 of Visual C++ for Windows NT.

All told, this sounds like a confusing state of affairs for developers who want their DLLs to work across all platforms. To help you sort things out, this chapter divides Windows DLLs into three major categories. Once you know what those categories are and how to use them, you can write DLLs that work on any Windows platform. The three categories are as follows:

+ Windows 3.x DLLs, which were designed for 16-bit versions of Windows.

+ VCPP 1.0 DLLs, which were introduced with the premiere of version 1.0 of Visual C++, were the favored variety of 32-bit DLLs until the introduction of Visual C++ 4.0 and MFC 4.0.

+ MFC 4.0 DLLs, which made their debut with the introduction of Visual C++ 4.0 and MFC 4.0, are designed to be used with those versions and later versions of Visual C++ and MFC. You can create MFC 4.0 DLLs using AppWizard. MFC 4.0 DLLs come in several flavors designed to meet specific requirements and demands.

This chapter covers all three of these varieties, because many older DLLs are likely to be around for some time. Developers of Windows NT and Windows 95 software could encounter any of the three varieties of DLLs at any time.

In this chapter, each DLL category is described under a separate major heading, and an example program demonstrating the use of each kind of DLL is provided. MFC 4.0 DLLs receive the lion's share of the attention because they are the newest kind and are the type recommended for use in new Windows NT (and Windows 95) programs. The example program that demonstrates the use of MFC 4.0 DLLs is named DLLTESTAPP. It is presented in the section titled "Example: The DLLTESTAPP Program."

When you execute the DLLTESTAPP program, it calls functions implemented in an MFC 4.0 DLL to create dialog boxes in which messages are displayed. Figure 8.1 shows one of the dialog boxes created by DLLTESTAPP.

FIGURE 8.1 DIALOG BOX CREATED BY THE DLL TESTAPP PROGRAM.

This chapter also presents one sample program, named SHAREMEM, that demonstrates a thread-related mechanism called *thread local storage*, or TLS. For more information about this sample program, see the "Thread Local Storage" section later in this chapter.

About DLLs

Dynamic link libraries derive their name from the fact that they are dynamically linked with functions in an application when the application is executed—and not statically linked during the build process, when the application is being linked.

When a library is statically linked with an application, all references to functions and data in the library must be resolved at link time and cannot be modified when the application is run. When references to functions and data in a DLL are dynamically linked, they do not have to be resolved until run time, when the functions or data are about to be used. That is what makes it possible for applications to share code and data stored in DLLs. Dynamic linking also makes it possible for an application to delay the loading of a DLL until it is needed and to unload the DLL once it is no longer needed. That can help an application use memory more efficiently.

Although a dynamic link library can be an executable file, a DLL is never a full-fledged application. That's because a DLL is controlled by the task (or, in Windows NT, the process) of its calling function. A DLL does not have its own stack but instead shares the stack that is owned by its caller's process. Also, a DLL has neither a message-processing loop nor a message queue, so it can't stand on its own as a full-fledged application. Static and dynamic linking are examined in more detail in "Dynamic Linking" later in this chapter.

UPDATING DLL-EQUIPPED APPLICATIONS

One big benefit of DLLs is that they let you modify and enhance applications without having to rebuild them. You can create an updated version of an application that uses DLLs by simply substituting new and improved DLLs for the ones that were shipped with the original application. In contrast, when an application is linked with functions in a statically linked library, the application must be relinked if there is any change to any function in the application's supporting libraries.

Suppose, for example, that your company wanted to design a text editor, a telecommunications program, and a fax-modem driver. Text-editing routines designed for use by both the text editor and the telecommunications program might be placed in the same DLL. Communications routines for both the telecommunications program and the fax-modem program could be placed in another DLL. Still another DLL could contain code for menus, dialog boxes, and window-manipulation routines common to all three programs.

By accessing these three DLLs from your applications, you could save time in program development. Because routines implemented in the DLLs can be shared by all three programs, customers running your applications would save disk space and memory. And your programs would load faster, because they would share object code.

Code modules that are implemented as DLLs can be modified easily because they can be updated individually. DLLs are linked with their clients at run time and not at link time. So when you update an application by modifying a DLL, you don't have to recompile, or even relink, your application. To modify code that is implemented in a DLL stored on a disk, all you have to do is overwrite the old DLL with the new one. The next time you run a client that references the DLL, the client simply uses the new DLL instead of the old one.

Using DLLs in C++ and Other Languages

No matter what language you program in, if you write programs for Windows you can use DLLs. Dynamic link libraries work with all Windows-compatible languages—object-oriented languages and non-object-oriented languages as well.

Software developers who write C++ programs can develop libraries of classes and objects that can be exported by DLLs. And programmers that work in all languages can write DLLs that export functions, data, and resources. Furthermore, DLLs are not language-sensitive. If you use conditional compilation to apply the extern "C" attribute to functions when it is required, you can use the same DLL in C and C++ programs.

When DLLs Aren't Optional

In many cases, DLLs aren't an optional convenience but instead are a necessity. Some functions and features provided by the Windows API are accessible only from DLLs. For instance, the functions SetWindowsHook and SetWindowsHookEx can be called only from DLLs. Also, installable drivers for Windows, known as DRVs, must be implemented as DLLs.

Even when you don't incorporate your own DLLs into a Windows application, you can rest assured that your application makes calls to DLLs. Most of the files in the Windows API are either program files or DLLs. Every time an application makes a Windows call such as CreateWindow, TextOut, MessageBox, or GetParent, it is calling a DLL. For instance, this call—even though it looks like any other function call—is actually a call to a dynamic link library:

```
HWND hWnd;
hwndParent = GetParent(hWnd);
```

Windows NT recognizes this code fragment as a call to a DLL, because GetParent is implemented as a DLL in **USER32.DLL**, which is found in the \WINNT\SYSTEM32 (or \WINDOWS\SYSTEM32) directory.

EXECUTABLE AND NON-EXECUTABLE DLLs

A DLL can be an executable file, but it doesn't have to be. For example, font libraries, which contain no executable code, can be stored as DLLs. DLLs can also be used to store other kinds of resource libraries, such as libraries that contain icons, bitmaps, and strings. With the exception of font libraries, however, every resource library created by a developer must contain at least one code segment. Font-library DLLs are the only kind of DLLs you can implement that contain no executable code.

DLLs can have various file name extensions, depending on their uses. For example, DLLs used as font resources have the extension **.FON**; device-driver DLLs have the extension **.DRV**; and executable DLLs used by the operating system have the extension **.EXE**.

Three system DLLs—**GDI32.DDL**, **USER32.DDL**, and **KERNEL32.DDL**—are loaded when Windows NT starts up. They are three of the Win32 system's most important DLLs. The GDI32 (graphics device interface) DLL is responsible for exporting the painting, drawing, plotting, printing, and color functions of Windows. The USER32 DLL controls almost everything in Windows involving window creation, communications, hardware, and messaging. The KERNEL32 DLL handles Windows functions involving memory management, multitasking, and resources.

These three DLLs contain most of the Windows NT functions called by applications and by user-written libraries. They also pass communications among applications and subsystems that make up the Windows NT operating system.

DLL CLIENTS

Although a DLL can be an executable file, functions that a DLL contains cannot be executed independently. A function implemented in a DLL must be called by an application or by a library, which can be another DLL. An application or library that calls a DLL is often referred to as a *client*. (There are other kinds of clients in Windows NT, too, but when the word *client* is used in this chapter, it refers to a DLL client.)

When a DLL has been loaded into memory, any function that the DLL exports can be used by any executing client. If a client calls a function in the DLL, the client's call is directed to the correct DLL and then to the called function. As long as any client continues to use any function in a loaded DLL, the DLL remains in memory. But if the operating system discovers that the DLL is no longer being used by any client and if the memory occupied by that DLL is needed for another purpose, Windows NT unloads the DLL.

In both 16-bit Windows and Windows NT, DLLs and their clients are stored in separate areas of memory. A DLL can (and usually does) contain multiple functions, and any client that references the DLL can call any function in the DLL just as if the function were part of the client's executable code.

DLLs and Windows NT

One significant difference between Win16 DLLs and Windows NT DLLs results from Windows NT being a 32-bit operating system. In 16-bit versions of Windows, when a DLL is loaded into memory, multiple applications can share the code and the data in that DLL. That's because every client of a loaded DLL has access to the same copy of the DLL. In the 16-bit Windows environment, a single copy of a DLL can be accessed by multiple processes simultaneously, because each DLL has its own data segment, which contains all the static and global variables needed by the DLL as well as the DLL's own private local heap. A DLL's local heap is available to any process running under Windows 3.x, regardless of which process called the function contained in the DLL.

In Windows NT, the situation is very different, for two reasons. In Windows NT, a DLL does not have a local heap. When a Windows NT process loads a DLL, the system maps the DLL's code and data into the address space of the process. When a function in a DLL requests memory from the system, the memory must be allocated from the process's address space because no other process has access to this allocated memory.

The other reason is that in Windows NT, global and static variables allocated by a DLL are not shared among multiple mappings of the DLL. If two processes use the same DLL, the code for the DLL is loaded into memory once but is mapped into the address space of both processes. However, each process has a separate set of the DLL's global and static variables. The system gives each mapping of a DLL its own set of variables by taking advantage of a Win32 mechanism called file mapping. File mapping, and another interprocess-communication mechanism called pipes, is the topic of Chapter 9.

When a DLL is loaded into memory in Windows NT, it is placed in the system heap, sometimes known as the global heap (also described in Chapter 9). Then the address range of the DLL is mapped into the address space of the process that loaded it. Later, if another process attempts to load the DLL, the operating system finds the DLL and maps the address range of the DLL into the address space of that process. Then both processes can access the DLL. This process is illustrated in Figure 8.2.

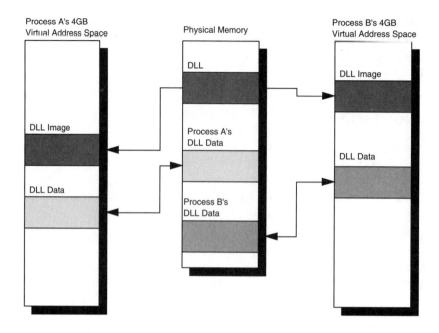

FIGURE 8.2 HOW DLLs ARE MAPPED INTO MEMORY.

Memory Moving and Memory Mapping

When you refer to Figure 8.2, it is important to note that mapping information into a process's virtual memory space is not the same thing as copying the file from one block of memory to another. When information is mapped into a process's memory, nothing moves; the information remains where it is, but it appears to the process that the information has been moved into its address space. For more information on memory mapping, see Chapter 9, "Interprocess Communications."

Static and Dynamic Linking

A client can call a function that is stored in a DLL in the same way that it would call any other function. But DLLs are not compiled and linked in the same way that applications and standard libraries are compiled and linked. Applications and conventional libraries are statically linked, and DLLs are dynamically linked.

STATIC LINKING

When an application calls a function that is stored in a conventional library, the application must link with the library while the application is being built—specifically, during the linking process. In this kind of linking, called *static* linking, a copy of the called library function is placed in the application's executable file at link time. As a result, a separate copy of the library function is placed in the executable file of each application that uses the function.

Figure 8.3 illustrates static linking. When an application that uses static linking is compiled, the compiler generates references to the addresses of library functions that the program calls. When the program is linked, the linker resolves those references.

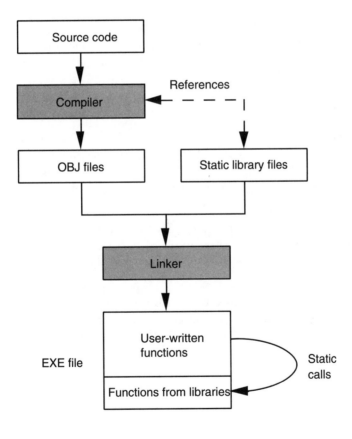

FIGURE 8.3 STATIC LINKING.

During static linking, the linker copies all object code from each object-code file and each library—including routines that are not called into the executable file that it is compiling. Then the linker incorporates all the object code that it has found into the executable application (the **.EXE** file).

To perform this task, the linker searches each library file used in the compilation, resolves the remaining function references, and retrieves the code of each required function into the **.EXE** file it is building. Thus, the linker replaces the addresses left unresolved by the compiler with real addresses and ensures that the code of every called function is included in the program.

If the linker cannot find the code of a function that it needs, it generates an error message. If it finds the code it needs, it builds the application's **.EXE** file; the role of the static library used in the compilation and linking process is then over. The code that the library has provided is now incorporated into the executable application that needed it, so the code that the static library contains is no longer required.

Dynamic Linking

Dynamic linking is very different from static linking. When an application calls a function that is stored in a dynamic link library, the linker does not provide the application with its own copy of the function. Instead, at link time, a reference to the function is placed in a file that will be accessible to the application's executable file at run time.

References to DLL functions can be stored in three kinds of files depending on the category of the DLL. These three kinds of files are import libraries, module definition (.DEF) files, and header files; for details, see "Three Categories of DLLs" later in this chapter.

No matter where the reference to a DLL function is stored, the reference tells the application where it can find the object code of the function at run time. At run time, the application uses its reference to locate the function stored in the DLL. Dynamic linking is illustrated in Figure 8.4.

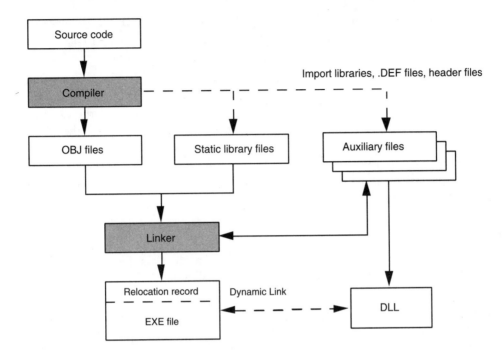

FIGURE 8.4 DYNAMIC LINKING.

LINKING A CLIENT WITH A DLL

When the Visual C++ linker links a client with a DLL, the linker searches the program's source files and statically linked library files for each external function in the program each time the function is called. If the linker finds the function in a library or object module that is statically linked with the application, the linker copies the function's code into the .EXE file that it is creating.

If the linker cannot find the function's code, it searches any available auxiliary files (such as import libraries) that may contain references to functions that are implemented in DLLs. Each time such a reference is found, information specifying where the reference can be found is stored in a relocation record in the application's .EXE file. A relocation record contains information that the Windows NT operating system uses to access and execute the function's code dynamically. This record includes the name of the function and the name of the DLL from which the function came.

At run time, when the client calls a function exported by a DLL, the client looks through its relocation records for the information that it needs to find the exported function. When it obtains the name of the DLL that implements the function, the Win32 operating system automatically loads the DLL that contains the function into memory (if it is not already in memory), and then calls the function. Windows NT also adds a patch to the image of the program's code in memory so that the program can access functions in the DLL whenever they are needed.

LOADING AND EXECUTING DLLS

Figure 8.4 shows how DLLs are dynamically linked. Now let's take a look at how DLLs are loaded into memory and see how the processes of linking and loading are related. There are two ways to load a dynamic link library into memory:

+ An application can link to a DLL at the same time the application is loaded, just as if the DLL were a statically linked library, such as the C run time library. This method is sometimes called *implicit loading*. (A longer and more confusing name for this technique is *load-time dynamic linking*.)

+ A process can load a DLL only when the DLL is needed and unload the DLL when it is no longer needed. This technique is sometimes referred to as *explicit loading*. (A longer and less user-friendly name for this method is *run-time dynamic linking*.)

No matter which method a process uses to load a DLL, the DLL attaches to the process when the process starts or when one of its threads calls the LoadLibrary function. When a DLL attaches to a process, the operating system maps the DLL module into the address space of the process, making the DLL's executable code available to the process. When a DLL detaches from a process (because the process terminates or because FreeLibrary is called), the DLL module is unmapped from the address space of the process.

Implicitly Loading a DLL

When a Windows NT process loads a DLL by implicit loading, the operating system must know where to find the DLL. Therefore, when you create an application that will load a DLL implicitly, you must link your application's executable module with an import library associated with the DLL.

An *import library* is a statically linked library that provides information about a DLL. When the operating system needs to locate functions or data stored in an implicitly loaded DLL, it consults the DLL's import library. In pre-NT versions of Windows, developers had to write import libraries when they wanted to use implicitly loaded DLLs. However, the 32-bit Visual C++ compiler that comes with Windows NT generates an import library automatically when it compiles a DLL. Later, at run time, the system uses the DLL's import library to access functions implemented in the DLL.

Implicit loading works in the following way: At link time, when an application is preparing a process for the implicit loading of a DLL, the application performs two important operations. First, it maps the DLL's code into the process's virtual address space. Then it creates an import library using the virtual address of each function implemented in the DLL as an entry function and recording that function in the DLL's import library. (For more information on import libraries, see "Import Libraries" later in this chapter.)

Although an implicitly loaded DLL is mapped into an application's memory when the application is linked, it is important to note that the DLL's code is not actually loaded into memory until the DLL is needed. If a DLL is not being used and its memory is needed for another purpose, the system can unload the DLL until it is needed again. Thus, implicitly loaded DLLs do not require any more memory space than explicitly loaded DLLs. However, they do require a little extra baggage: a range of dedicated virtual memory and an import library.

Explicitly Loading a DLL

When a process does not load a DLL until it is needed, that is called explicit loading. Explicit loading is a slightly more efficient method of loading DLLs than implicit loading, because it doesn't require a dedicated range of virtual memory or an import library. A process explicitly loads a DLL by calling LoadLibrary. When the DLL is no longer needed, it can be freed with a call to FreeLibrary. If a DLL does not have any other clients when FreeLibrary is called, the DLL is unloaded from memory. If the DLL has other clients, it is not unloaded until all its clients have called FreeLibrary.

When an application has explicitly loaded a DLL, it can call the Win32 function GetProcAddress to obtain the starting addresses of any functions implemented in the DLL. When the DLL is no longer needed, the process can explicitly unload it by calling FreeLibrary. This method eliminates the need to link with an import library.

When a process calls LoadLibrary to load a DLL, it calls GetProcAddress to obtain the starting address of any function that is implemented in the DLL. Run-time dynamic linking eliminates the need to link the process with an import library. The process does not explicitly call the DLL's functions, so it does not generate the external references.

If a process calls `LoadLibrary` to access a DLL module that is already mapped into the address space of the calling process, `LoadLibrary` simply returns a handle to the DLL and increments the reference count that the process maintains. If the DLL is not already loaded into memory, `LoadLibrary` checks to see whether the DLL has a `DllEntryPoint` function. If it does, the operating system calls the function in the context of the thread that called `LoadLibrary`.

If `LoadLibrary` succeeds in finding and loading a DLL, it returns a handle to the DLL that it has loaded. The calling process then uses this handle to identify the DLL in calls to other functions, such as `GetProcAddress` or `FreeLibrary`.

DLL Entry and Exit Points

There are differences between the way DLLs are loaded and accessed in Windows 3.x programs and the way they are loaded and accessed in Windows NT. In the Windows 3.x environment, the initialization function for DLLs is named `LibMain`. Usually, when a 16-bit Windows application creates a DLL, it calls `LibMain` to handle most of the DLL's initialization. When `LibMain` completes its job, it returns control to the `LibEntry` function. `LibEntry`, in turn, returns control to Windows. Then the DLL can be accessed.

When it is time for a DLL to be unloaded in a Win16 program, a function named `WEP` (which stands for Windows exit procedure) is called. If any cleanup procedures are needed before the DLL is unloaded, they are managed by the `WEP` function. `WEP` performs a number of standard DLL cleanup operations before the DLL is unloaded.

DLL Entry Points in Windows NT

`LibMain` can serve as a DLL entry point in a Win32 program, just as in Windows 3.x. However, Win32 provides an alternative DLL entry-point function named `DllEntryPoint`. Windows NT applications can use either `LibMain` or `DllEntryPoint` as an entry point for DLLs.

In Windows NT, `DllEntryPoint` is not an actual function but instead is a template that can be assigned any legal function name. (You can assign a function name to `DllEntryPoint` by using the `-entry` option on the link command.) When you create a `DllEntryPoint` function, you can give it any name you like—including `LibMain`, as illustrated in the following example:

```
link -entry:LibMain out:mydll.dll mydll.exp mydll.obj $(mylibs)
```

DllEntryPoint Is Optional

Now for more complexities: Although the Win32 API provides a new `DllEntryPoint` function for Windows NT applications to use, an application does not have to specify it in order to access a DLL. In fact, as you will see in "Varieties of Windows NT DLLs" later in this chapter, applications that use `DllEntryPoint` functions are out of favor, because newer, easier ways are now available for writing Windows NT DLLs.

If you create a `DllEntryPoint` function when you link a Windows NT application, the operating system calls it whenever any one of the following events occurs:

+ Your DLL attaches to a process.

+ Your DLL detaches from a process.

+ Your DLL attaches to a thread.

+ Your DLL detaches from a thread.

When you write a Windows NT program using Visual C++, there are easier ways to ensure that DLLs are handled properly when these kinds of events occur. For details, see "Varieties of Windows NT DLLs" later in this chapter.

IMPORT LIBRARIES

An import library, as you have seen, provides a client with the information it needs to store information about the DLL and the functions implemented in the DLL. When you build a client that implicitly references a DLL (see "Implicitly Loading a DLL" earlier in this chapter), you must link the client with the DLL's import library. The linker uses the import library to build any executable module that requires access to the DLL.

When you write a program using 32-bit Visual C++, the compiler generates an import library automatically when it compiles a DLL. (Other versions of Visual C++ provide a utility that you must use to write your own import libraries; see the box titled "IMPLIB Bites the Dust" later in this chapter.)

Import Libraries Have New Rules in Windows NT

In versions of Microsoft C and C++ that preceded the release of Visual C++, there was an alternative to using import libraries. In version 7 of Microsoft C/C++ and its predecessors, instead of instructing the compiler to generate an import library, you could write a module definition (**.DEF**) file for a client and include import information in a section of that file labeled `IMPORTS`. In Windows NT Visual C++, this is not an option; the Win32 Visual

C++ compiler does not recognize IMPORTS sections in .DEF files. However, .DEF files used by Windows NT do have EXPORTS sections (explained in the next section, "Module Definition Files").

Rules that govern the importing and exporting of functions have also changed in other ways with the advent of Windows NT. First, when you write a .DEF file for a DLL client in 32-bit Visual C++, the file should not contain an IMPORTS section. If it does, the compiler doesn't return an error, but you can expect a warning message.

If the .DEF file that you are compiling has an IMPORTS section (for example, if it is from an old, pre-Windows NT program), you can simply remove that section. This has no adverse effects because .DEF files used in Visual C++ Windows NT compilations do not need IMPORTS sections. When you compile a DLL in Visual C++ for Windows NT, the compiler automatically generates an import library, eliminating the need for IMPORTS sections in .DEF files. For more information about how import libraries are generated and used, see "Loading and Executing DLLs" earlier in this chapter.

Another important change is that Visual C++ for Windows NT does not recognize the _export attribute in the headers of the definitions of functions. In 16-bit versions of Visual C++, when you wanted to export a function from a DLL, you could place the _export attribute in the header of the function's definition. That served the same purpose as listing the name of the function in the EXPORTS section of a .DEF file linked with the DLL. In Visual C++ for Windows NT, this option is not permitted; Win32 Visual C++ does not recognize the name _export. Instead, the Win32 API recognizes an attribute named dllexport, which is described in the section "Exporting Functions from VCPP 1.0 DLLs" later in this chapter.

MODULE DEFINITION FILES

Another kind of file you may encounter in writing DLLs is a module definition file, or .DEF file. A module definition file is a text file containing one or more module statements that describe various attributes of a dynamic link library. .DEF files provide the Visual C++ linker with the information it needs to make the functions in the DLL accessible to the DLL's client. Listing 8.1 shows the format of a module definition file.

LISTING 8.1 EXAMPLE OF A MODULE DEFINITION FILE.

```
; Example of a module definition file.

LIBRARY Select
```

```
CODE MOVEABLE DISCARDABLE
DATA SINGLE
EXPORTS
    WEP                 @1  RESIDENTNAME
    StartSelection      @2
    UpdateSelection     @3
    EndSelection        @4
    ClearSelection      @5
```

Every module definition file for a DLL begins with a LIBRARY statement and also contains an EXPORTS statement. The LIBRARY statement identifies the .DEF file as a module definition file that is associated with a DLL and specifies the name of the DLL's import library.

The EXPORTS statement lists the names of the functions exported by the DLL. Each EXPORTS statement can also contain an ordinal number written in the form @n. In source files that access functions exported by DLLs, any exported function that has been assigned an ordinal number in a .DEF file can be accessed using either its name or its ordinal number.

The .DEF file shown in Listing 8.1—named **DLLMSG.DEF**—has an EXPORTS section that expresses a function as the ordinal number @1, as follows:

```
EXPORTS
    _ShowDLLDlg@4           @1      NONAME
```

As you can see, the EXPORTS section file is preceded by the word EXPORTS and is divided into three columns. The names of functions exported by the DLL appear in the first column. The ordinal numbers assigned to those functions appear in the second column. An alternative name, or alias, for the function can be placed in the third column. If the function has no alias, the word NONAME can appear in the third column.

In the preceding example, the function ShowDLLDlg is identified by its full C++ name, or, in Microsoft jargon, its *decorated* name. When a member function of a C++ class is used in a .DEF file, the class must be referred to by its decorated name. To obtain a list of decorated names, you can link the application using the /MAP option. (For details, see Books Online or your Visual C++ documentation.) In this case, the name of the ShowDLLDlg function provided in the EXPORTS section is _ShowDLLDlg@4.

Only one function is exported, so it is assigned the ordinal number @1. In a .DEF file, the ordinal number assigned to a function is always preceded by the character @. If more functions were exported, they could be assigned the numbers @2, @3, and so on.

If a function in a DLL is expressed as an ordinal number, clients of the DLL can then use that number, instead of the function's name, to refer to the DLL's functions. Rules for referring to exported functions by the ordinal numbers specified in a .DEF file are spelled out in more detail in the Microsoft *Win32 Programmer's Reference*.

In 16-bit versions of Visual C++—but not in 32-bit versions of Visual C++—there is an alternative method for exporting functions from DLLs. In a 16-bit Visual C++ program, you can export a function from a DLL by placing the _export attribute in the header of the function's definition. This technique does not work with 32-bit versions of Visual C++; beginning with version 2.0 of Visual C++, the `dllexport` attribute replaced the _export attribute.

A module definition file can also contain statements that determine other attributes of a DLL. For example, a .DEF file can contain SECTIONS statements that change the default scope of global and static variables.

IMPLIB Bites the Dust

In 16-bit versions of Visual C++, Microsoft provides a utility for creating import libraries. This tool, called IMPLIB, is an .EXE file that you must run manually from a command line every time you compile a DLL. IMPLIB then creates an import file, which you must link with every client that references your DLL.

In 32-bit Visual C++, the IMPLIB tool is not supplied. It is no longer needed, because an import library is generated automatically each time a DLL is compiled. It is still your responsibility, however, to link an import file with each client of your DLL. For more information on how import libraries work, see "Loading and Executing DLLs" earlier in this chapter.

Building Clients and DLLs

When you build a DLL, you use three tools: the Visual C++ compiler (CL386), the Visual C++ Library Manager (LIB32), and the linker (LINK32). Compiling a DLL involves the same procedures as compiling any executable file, but there are some extra steps that use some different compiler and linker switches.

Figure 8.5 shows how a DLL is compiled and linked in Win32 C++. Figure 8.6 illustrates the compiling and linking of a DLL client.

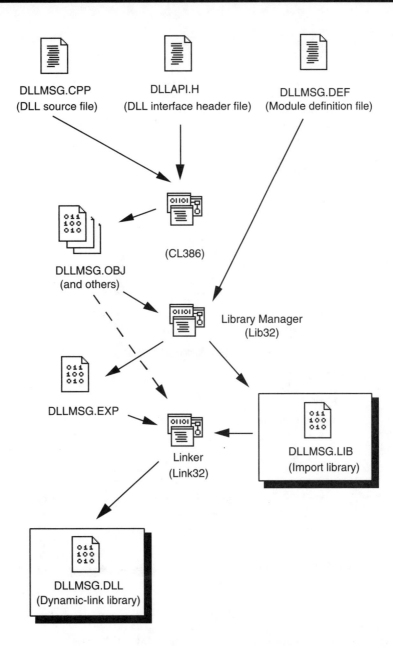

FIGURE 8.5 BUILDING A DLL.

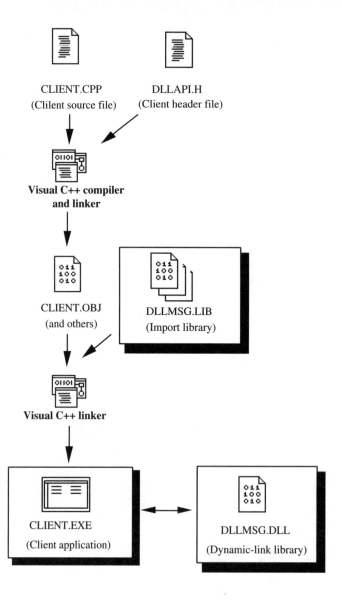

CLIENT.CPP
(Clilent source file)

DLLAPI.H
(Client header file)

**Visual C++ compiler
and linker**

CLIENT.OBJ
(and others)

DLLMSG.LIB
(Import library)

Visual C++ linker

CLIENT.EXE
(Client application)

DLLMSG.DLL
(Dynamic-link library)

FIGURE **8.6** BUILDING A CLIENT.

The DLL that is built in Figure 8.5 is named **DLLMSG.DLL**. The client that is built in Figure 8.6 is named **CLIENT.CPP**. The two figures illustrate the complete build of a sample program named DLLMsg, which is discussed later in this chapter.

BUILDING A DLL

To compile and link a dynamic link library, you need one or more source-code files. In the build shown in Figure 8.5, the source file used to build the DLL's main module is named **DLLMSG.CPP**. The main module of a DLL's source file can include one or more header (.H) files. The DLL that is built in Figure 8.5 exports just one function, which is declared in a header file named **DLLAPI.H**. This same header file is included in the compilation of the DLL's client, as shown in Figure 8.6. To build a DLL using this method, you need a module definition file. **DLLMSG.DEF** is used in the build shown in Figure 8.5. When you build a DLL, the compiler uses the DLL's .C, .CPP, and .H files to create an object-code (.OBJ) file. In Figure 8.5, the object file generated by the compiler is named **DLLMSG.OBJ**.

The compiler also creates several other interim files that are used internally during the compiling and linking process—files with extensions such as **.RES** and **.RBJ**. Once a DLL file and an accompanying import library are produced, the **.OBJ** file and the other interim files are no longer needed except as makefile targets to inhibit unnecessary recompiling.

If a DLL has a module definition file, it is not passed to the compiler; instead, it goes directly to the Library Manager (Lib32). The Library Manager uses this .DEF file, along with the **.OBJ** file and other interim files produced by the compiler, to generate an export library file and an import library file. In Figure 8.5, these two files are named **DLLMSG.EXP** and **DLLMSG.LIB**.

Later, when it is time to build a client for the DLL, the DLL's import library file is supplied to the client to help the client locate and obtain functions and data exported by the DLL. However, once the DLL has been built, there is no further need for the DLL's export library file.

When the Library Manager has created an **.EXP** file and an import library (.LIB) file, the linker uses those files, along with the **.OBJ** file and other interim files, to build the final object file for the DLL. In Figure 8.5, this file is named **DLLMSG.DLL**.

Later, when the DLL's client is built, the **.LIB** file that was generated during the DLL's build is linked to the client. That happens because the client needs the information that the **.LIB** file contains to resolve the external references to DLL functions. When the client is linked with the **.LIB** file, the client obtains the information that it needs to locate the DLL and the functions and data that the DLL exports at run time.

BUILDING A CLIENT

To execute a DLL, you need a DLL-aware client—that is, an application or a library that is equipped with an import library. That's because a DLL cannot be executed independently; it can be executed only indirectly, by a client.

Figure 8.6 illustrates the compiling and linking of a client for a DLL. Specifically, the diagram shows the procedures used to build the client application for the sample program DLLMsg. The client has one .CPP file (**CLIENT.CPP**) and one header file (**DLLAPI.H**). The **DLLAPI.H** header file is also included in the compilation of the program's DLL.

The procedures that are used to build a client are similar to those used to build a DLL, but they are simpler. When you build a client, the Visual C++ compiler uses the client's source files to compile an .OBJ file and several other interim object files. These files then go to the linker, along with the import library (**.LIB**) file that the client needs to reference functions and data exported by a DLL. In Figure 8.6, the .OBJ file produced by the compiler is named **CLIENT.OBJ**.

Another file used in the build shown in Figure 8.6 is an import library file named **DLLMSG.LIB**. This file was generated earlier during the build of the DLL file **DLLMSG.DLL**.

In the linking stage, the linker uses the .OBJ file generated by the compiler and the .LIB file provided by the client to generate the program's executable (.EXE) file. The executable produced by the build in Figure 8.6 is named **CLIENT.EXE**.

Once **CLIENT.EXE** has been built, it can access functions, data, classes, and objects that are exported by the DLL named **DLLMSG.DLL**, which was generated earlier in the build shown in Figure 8.5. At run time, when the client needs to access functions or data exported by the DLL, the client uses the information that it obtained from its import library at link time to locate the functions or data that it needs from the DLL.

DLLs and MFC Class Libraries

If a DLL uses classes in the Microsoft Foundation Class (MFC) library, the DLL must be linked with a special, DLL-specific version of MFC . When you compile a debug version of a Win32 DLL, you must link it to an MFC library named **NAFXDWD.LIB**. When you compile a release version of a Win32 DLL, it must be linked with another special MFC library named **NAFXCWD.LIB**.

Although it's good to be aware of this, you will rarely, if ever, have to worry about it. When you compile a DLL using the Developer Studio, a list box in the Project Options dialog box tells the Visual C++ compiler that you are compiling a DLL. If you select the **Dynamic-link library** entry, the compiler automatically links your DLL with the NAFXDWD library, depending on whether you're building a debug version or a release version of your DLL.

USING DEVELOPER STUDIO TO BUILD DLL PROJECTS

Although you can build DLLs and clients by writing makefiles and executing DOS-style command lines, the recommended way to compile and link DLL projects with Visual C++ is to use AppWizard.

With AppWizard, you can build DLLs in the same way that you build other executables: by choosing the **File|New|Project Workspace** item under the Options menu and then selecting **MFC AppWizard (dll)** when AppWizard displays the New Project Workspace dialog box (Figure 8.7).

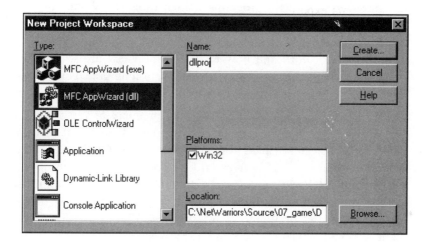

FIGURE 8.7 THE PROJECT OPTIONS DIALOG BOX.

To build an application that is the client for a DLL, you follow the same procedures you would follow to build any other application. Then you provide your application with a module definition file that gives the application the information it needs to access functions, data, or both provided by a DLL. To learn how to create module definition files and make them accessible to applications and DLLs, see "Module Definition Files" earlier in this chapter.

Varieties of Windows NT DLLs

Many kinds of DLLs work with Windows NT programs, and there are many options for accessing and linking DLLs that can be called from Windows NT programs. Rules for writing and accessing different varieties of Windows DLLs overlap in many ways, and, unless you have some background on how DLLs work, the whole topic of Windows DLLs can get confusing.

As mentioned at the beginning of this chapter, I have divided the many combinations of DLLs and DLL linkages used in Windows programs into three major categories:

✦ **Windows 3.x DLLs.** These DLLs can be compiled as 16-bit or 32-bit DLLs and can be called from any program written for any version of Windows. Windows 3.x DLLs are not written using the Visual C++ application framework, and they do not rely on the MFC library or on routines in the Win32 API. They are not guaranteed to work with programs written using the Visual C++ application framework or classes implemented in MFC. But they are the only variety of DLLs that work as written with 16-bit versions of Windows, and you should know how they work and how to use them. There are still many of them around, and they probably will be around for a long time. For a closer look at Windows 3.x DLLs, see "Windows 3.x DLLs," next.

✦ **VCPP 1.0 DLLs** were introduced with the premiere of version 1.0 of Visual C++. In their day, they were the most streamlined variety of DLLs available. VCPP 1.0 DLLs can be called from any Windows or Windows NT application, including Visual C++ and non-Visual C++ programs written using MFC. That means VCPP 1.0 DLLs can be used with applications written with Visual C++, Borland C++, Delphi, or any other development environment that generates code for Windows or Windows NT. VCPP 1.0 DLLs are described in more detail in "VCPP 1.0 DLLs" later in this chapter.

✦ **MFC 4.0 DLLs** made their debut with the introduction of Visual C++ 4.0 and MFC 4.0. One of the most important features of MFC 4.0 DLLs is that AppWizard can generate them for you automatically when you write applications using Visual C++ 4.0. Another major feature of MFC 4.0 DLLs is that you can link them to MFC in different ways, depending on your preferences and the requirements of your application. To make this versatility possible, Visual C++ divides MFC 4.0 DLLs into three subcategories. Each of these subcategories is described under a separate heading in the section titled "MFC 4.0 DLLs."

Each of these main categories of DLLs is described under a separate section heading. At the end of each major section, an example program shows you how each kind of DLL work, and how to use it in your Windows NT applications. Another sample program, **SHAREMEM.CPP**, demonstrates how DLLs can share data using a Win32 mechanism called thread local storage.

Windows 3.x DLLs

If you're an experienced Windows 3.1 programmer, you'll recognize the Windows 3.x DLL as the variety most commonly used in 16-bit Windows programs. A Windows 3.x DLL has the explicit entry-point function `LibMain` and an explicit termination function `WEP`. (As you'll see in later sections, VCPP 1.0 DLLs also have entry-point and WEP functions, but you don't have to write `LibMain` or `WEP` functions in framework-based Visual C++ programs; they are managed automatically by the compiler.)

Until Windows NT made its debut, DLLs—specifically, Windows 3.x DLLs—were generally compiled and linked using non-GUI-based compilers such as Version 7 of Microsoft C/C++. Windows 3.x DLLs are now considered obsolete and are in the process of fading away. So they are not fully documented in the manuals that come with Windows NT or the newest versions of 16-bit or 32-bit Visual C++.

The MFC library did not exist when Windows 3.x DLLs were invented, so they do not use MFC classes, and they are not guaranteed to work with MFC applications.

You'll see how Windows 3.x DLLs work under Windows NT in the example program named DLLMSG later in this chapter.

How Windows 3.x DLLs Work

In a Windows 3.x DLL, the `LibMain` function performs all initialization, and the `WEP` function performs all cleanup operations.

This is the format of a `LibMain` function:

```
extern "C"
int FAR PASCAL LibMain(HINSTANCE hInstance, WORD
     segAddr, WORD heapize, LPSTR commandLine)
{
     return TRUE;
}
```

As the preceding example shows, a `LibMain` function takes four parameters:

+ An **instance handle** (the instance handle of the DLL).
+ **segAddr**. In 16-bit Windows programs, this is the DLL's data segment address.
+ **heapSize**. The size of the DLL's heap.
+ **commandLine**. A command line (specified only when the DLL is manually loaded); otherwise, this parameter is NULL.

The parameters that are passed to LibMain can have different meanings depending on what LibMain is designed to do. For example, if you're creating a DLL that registers a window class and creates a window or if you want a DLL to load a resource, you can supply the required instance handle in the hInstance parameter.

If LibMain is successful, it returns a nonzero value. If a zero value is returned, Windows NT unloads the DLL.

Before Windows unloads a Windows 3.x DLL, the Windows API calls the DLL's WEP function. The WEP then performs any housekeeping that may be needed before the DLL is unloaded.

The syntax of a WEP function is as follows:

```
extern "C" int FAR PASCAL _WEP(int param)
{
    return TRUE;
}
```

A WEP function requires one parameter: an int data type (called param in the preceding example). If you call a WEP from an application, you can pass any value you like in the param argument. But when Windows calls a WEP function, it passes one of two specific constants to the function. When a DLL that has a WEP is unloaded, Windows passes the constant _FREE_DLL to the WEP function. Just before Windows unloads a DLL, it calls WEP and passes it the constant WEP_SYSTEMEXIT.

As the preceding example illustrates, you must use the name _WEP when you refer to a WEP in source code. The specific cleanup functions that a DLL's WEP performs depend on the needs of the DLL. If a call to WEP is successful, a nonzero value is returned.

Example Windows 3.x DLL: The DLLMSG Program

DLLMSG is an example of a Windows 3.x DLL. It is a straightforward program: The client call a DLL, and the DLL displays a dialog box like the one shown in Figure 8.8.

FIGURE 8.8 THE DLLMSG DIALOG BOX.

Listing 8.2 (**DLLMSG.CPP**) is the source file for a DLL referenced in the program. Listing 8.3 (**CLIENT.CPP**) presents the source code for the DLLMSG program's client application. Listing 8.4 (**DLLAPI.H**) is the DLL's header file, and Listing 8.5 (**DLLMSG.DEF**) is the DLL's module definition file. Listing 8.6 (**CLIENT.DEF**) is the client's .DEF file.

LISTING **8.2** DLLMSG.CPP

```
DLLMSG.CPP
// dllmsg.cpp
// A simple DLL
// Copyright 1994, 1995, Mark Andrews

#include <windows.h>
#include "dllapi.h"

extern "C"
int FAR PASCAL LibMain(HINSTANCE hInstance, WORD segAddr,
    WORD heapize, LPSTR commandLine)
0.{
    return TRUE;
}

extern "C"
int FAR PASCAL _WEP(int param)
{
    return TRUE;
}

////////////////////////////////////////////////////////////////////////
// Public DLL interface

LPSTR theMsg = "Your message goes here.";

extern "C"
BOOL FAR PASCAL ShowDLLDlg(LPSTR wintitle)
{

    MessageBox(NULL, theMsg, wintitle, MB_OK);
    return TRUE;
}
```

Listing 8.3 CLIENT.CPP

```cpp
// client.cpp
// Client module for a DLL demonstration
// modified to demonstrate the use of DLLs
// Copyright 1994, 1995, Mark Andrews

#include <windows.h>
#include "dllapi.h"

int PASCAL WinMain(HINSTANCE, HINSTANCE, LPSTR, int)
{
    LPSTR msg = "Your Message Here";

    ShowDLLDlg(msg);
    return 0;
}
```

Listing 8.4 DLLAPI.H

```c
// dllapi.h
// Interface definition file for a demonstration DLL
// Copyright 1994, 1995, Mark Andrews

extern "C"
BOOL FAR PASCAL ShowDLLDlg(LPSTR wintitle);
```

Listing 8.5 DLLMSG.DEF

```
; dllmsg.def: Declares the module parameters for
; the DLL demo program.
;

LIBRARY             DLLMSG

DESCRIPTION         'DLL Demo'
CODE                MOVEABLE PRELOAD
DATA                SINGLE MOVEABLE PRELOAD
HEAPSIZE            8192

EXPORTS
```

```
_ShowDLLDlg@4            @1           NONAME
```

LISTING **8.6** CLIENT.DEF

```
; client.def: Declares the module parameters
; for the application.

NAME               CLIENT
DESCRIPTION        'DLL Demo'

STUB               'winstub.exe'
EXETYPE            WINDOWS

HEAPSIZE           8192
STACKSIZE          8192
```

RUNNING THE **DLLMSG** PROGRAM

When you launch the DLLMSG application, it executes a simple `WinMain` function. This tiny `WinMain` function registers a window (which is never displayed) and calls a function named `ShowDLLDlg`, which is implemented as a DLL. This is a complete listing of the DLLMSG `WinMain` function:

```
int PASCAL WinMain(HINSTANCE, HINSTANCE, LPSTR, int)
{
    LPSTR msg = "Your Message Here";

    ShowDLLDlg(msg);
    return 0;
}
```

The `ShowDLLDlg` function shown in the preceding example is declared in a header file named **DLLAPI.H**. This file is included in the compilations of both the client's implementation file (**CLIENT.CPP**) and the DLL's implementation file (**DLLMSG.CPP**). **DLLAPI.H** contains one definition:

```
extern "C"
BOOL FAR PASCAL ShowDLLDlg(LPSTR wintitle);
```

Most of the work is done by **DLLMSG.CPP**, the implementation file for the program's DLL. This file contains a `LibMain` function that returns TRUE if there are no errors, a

WEP function that returns TRUE if there are no errors, and the function that displays the program's message box:

```
extern "C"
BOOL FAR PASCAL ShowDLLDlg(LPSTR wintitle)
{

    MessageBox(NULL, theMsg, wintitle, MB_OK);
    return TRUE;
}
```

VCPP 1.0 DLLs

With the release of version 1.0 of Visual C++, Microsoft introduced a new and improved way to write DLLs. In this chapter, DLLs that fall into this new category are referred to as VCPP 1.0 DLLs. VCPP 1.0 DLLs were designed for use by applications written and compiled using Visual C++ 1.0 and version 2.0 of MFC.

VCPP 1.0 DLLs had a short lifetime; they became obsolete with the double-barreled release of Visual C++ 4.0 and MFC 4.0. But they still work fine with programs written for Windows 95 or Windows NT, and they are still useful because they support the C++ classes implemented in MFC. If you ever encounter a need to access a VCPP 1.0 DLL from an application, you can build the DLL using Developer Studio in the same way you would build any other dynamic link library.

One important characteristic of VCPP 1.0 DLLs is that they don't require entry or exit procedures, and .DEF files are optional. VCPP 1.0 DLLs support the single-threading, multithreading, and preemptive multitasking capabilities of Windows NT.

Even though VCPP 1.0 DLLs don't require module definition files, supplying a **.DEF** file can provide certain advantages—for example, clients can refer to exported functions by their ordinal numbers rather than by their names. See your compiler's on-line documentation for more details.

LINKING VCPP 1.0 DLLS WITH THE MFC LIBRARY

To understand how VCPP 1.0 DLLs work, it helps to know how Microsoft has implemented the MFC library. (Knowing how MFC is implemented can also help you understand how MFC 4.0 DLLs work. MFC 4.0 DLLs are described under the heading "MFC 4.0 DLLs" later in this chapter.)

The Two Versions of the MFC Library

Microsoft ships two different versions of MFC with Visual C++. When you build an application (or a DLL) using Visual C++, you specify which version of MFC you want your customers to use when you ship the release version of your application.

When your application relies on the statically linked version, the MFC classes you use are dynamically linked with your application at design time, so you don't have to distribute a copy of MFC with your application. In contrast, when your application uses the dynamically linked version of MFC, you must distribute a copy of that version along with your application.

When you create a Visual C++ DLL using AppWizard, you can specify which MFC version you want your application or DLL to access when AppWizard prompts you for that information.

MFC Pluses and Minuses

Each version of MFC—the dynamically linked version and the statically linked version—has its own advantages and disadvantages. Applications built with the dynamically linked version require considerably less memory and disk space and may also run faster than applications that use the statically linked MFC library. However, if your application uses the dynamically linked version, you must supply a copy of the MFC DLL to each user of your program, and you must make sure that the MFC library DLL is installed in each user's system along with your application.

Fortunately, the dynamically linked version of MFC is redistributable: When you create and build an application that uses it, you are free to distribute a copy along with each copy of your application. In fact, if you use MFC classes in an application, you must link your application with the dynamically linked versions of the MFC library.

VCPP 1.0 DLLs AND THE USRDLL LIBRARY

When Visual C++ 1.0 was introduced and the VCPP 1.0 DLL made its debut, the statically linked version of MFC was named USRDLL. (With the introduction of MFC 4.0, the term USRDLL became obsolete. What used to be called the USRDLL library is now called the static link version of the "regular" MFC DLL; for details, see "MFC 4.0 DLLs" later in this chapter.) As a result, VCPP 1.0 DLLs accessed the statically linked version of MFC by defining the preprocessor symbol _USRDLL when they were compiled. (In MFC 4.0 DLLs, even though the name of the USRDLL library has changed, you still access the statically linked MFC by defining the preprocessor symbol _USRDLL.)

LINKING WITH THE MFC LIBRARY DLL

The MFC library that is implemented as a shared DLL is named AFXDLL. That name has not changed with the introduction of version 4.0 of the MFC library. So MFC 4.0 DLLs, as well as VCPP 1.0 DLLs, can access functions implemented in version 4.0 MFC. To link a VCPP 1.0 DLL (or an MFC 4.0 DLL) with the statically linked version, define the preprocessor symbol _AFXDLL in your DLL's source code.

If you ship an application with a VCPP 1.0 DLL that accesses the AFXDLL version of MFC, you must distribute a copy of the AFXDLL library with your application, and you must make sure that AFXDLL is installed in your customers' computer systems along with your program. If you ship your application with any MFC 4.0 DLLs that use classes implemented in MFC, those DLLs can access the same copy of the MFC DLL.

If you ship your application with a VCPP 1.0 DLL that supports OLE, you must also supply each user of your program with a run-time MFC library named **MFCO30.DLL**. Furthermore, if you ship your application with a VCPP 1.0 DLL that uses any of the database classes implemented in MFC, you must provide each of your application's users with still another run-time library, **MFCD30.DLL**. And if you ship your program with any VCPP 1.0 DLLs that require Unicode support, there are other run-time DLLs you must supply. For more details on the various dynamically linked MFC libraries that are available, see Books Online or your Visual C++ 4.0 documentation.

_export Is Obsolete in Win32

In the Win32 SDK—and, consequently, in 32-bit Windows NT DLLs—the _export keyword is obsolete. In Win32, the `dllexport` attribute replaces _export in DLLs and clients that call DLLs. If you use _export in a Win32 or in a 32-bit Visual C++ program, you'll get an error message.

EXPORTING FUNCTIONS FROM VCPP 1.0 DLLs

One of the most noteworthy features of VCPP 1.0 DLLs is that they export functions, data, classes, and objects by using the keywords `dllexport` and `dllimport`. These two keywords are storage-class modifiers that are specific to Microsoft C and C++. They are handy for DLL writers to have around, because they eliminate the need for module definition files.

When you use a VCPP 1.0 DLL, you can identify any function in the DLL as an exportable function by simply declaring it using the `dllexport` modifier. Then you can access the function from a client by declaring the same function using the dllimport modifier.

When a VCPP 1.0 DLL uses dllexport and dllimport attributes to identify a function, the DLL does not require a module definition file. However, clients of a VCPP 1.0 DLL—like clients of any other kind of DLL—must still be linked with an import library to obtain access to the function.

USING VCPP 1.0 DLLs

To identify a function in a VCPP 1.0 DLL as an exported function, you place the dllexport attribute in a function definition similar to this in your DLL's header file:

```
#define DLLExport __declspec(dllexport)
DLLExport void DLLMessage(LPSTR dlltitle);
To reference this function from a client, you place a function definition like
this in the client's header file:
#define DLLImport __declspec(dllexport)
extern DLLImport void DLLMessage(LPSTR dlltitle);
```

When you have written a pair of definitions such as those in the preceding example and have provided the DLL's client with an import library file, you can access the function from the DLL's client.

In the two preceding code fragments, you may notice that dllexport and dllimport are used in conjunction with the keyword __declspec. That's because dllexport and dllimport are attributes and not keywords and therefore cannot be used alone. The required syntax is as follows:

```
__declspec(dllAttribute)
```

In the preceding examples, the keyword and attribute constructs __declspec(dllexport) and _declspec(dllimport) are defined as preprocessor macros and are assigned the names DLLImport and DLLExport. These macros are defined merely for the sake of convenience; they make it easier to refer to the unwieldy constructs __declspec(dllexport) and __declspec(dllimport) in source code.

To export functions, VCPP 1.0 DLLs generally use the standard "C" interface. In other words, the declaration of a function exported from a VCPP 1.0 is written in this format:

```
extern "C" EXPORT ExportedFunction();
Example VCPP 1.0 DLL: The WINHOST Program
```

The WINHOST sample application shows how a VCPP 1.0 DLL can be accessed from a Windows NT program. It also shows how a C++ object can be exported by a VCPP 1.0 DLL. When you execute WINHOST, it displays a console window that contains two messages, as shown in Figure 8.9. (A console window is a text window that an application can display using Win32 functions. Console windows are described in detail in Chapter 6, "Processes.")

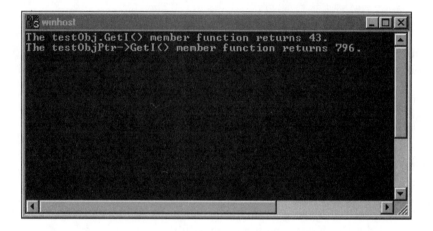

FIGURE **8.9** THE WINHOST DISPLAY.

Listings 8.7–8.10 present some of the source code of the WINHOST program. For complete source code, refer to this chapter's folder on the accompanying disk.

LISTING **8.7** WINHOST.CPP

```
WINHOST.CPP
// WINHOST.cpp

#include <iostream.h>
#include <afx.h>
#include "dlllib.h"
#include "WINHOST.h"

int main()
{
    testObj.SetI(43);
    testObjPtr->SetI(796);
```

```
    cout << "The testObj.GetI() member function returns "
        << testObj.GetI() << '.' << endl;
    cout << "The testObjPtr->GetI() member function returns "
        << testObjPtr->GetI() << '.' << endl;

    while (TRUE);

    return 0;
}
```

LISTING 8.8 WINHOST.H

```
// WINHOST.h

#define DLLImport _declspec(dllimport)

DLLImport TestClass testObj;
DLLImport TestClass *testObjPtr;
```

LISTING 8.9 DLLLIB.CPP

```
// dlllib.cpp

#define DEFINING
#include "dlllib.h"

INTERFACE TestClass testObj;
INTERFACE TestClass *testObjPtr = new TestClass;
```

LISTING 8.10 DLLAPI.H

```
// dlllib.h

#ifdef DEFINING
#define INTERFACE _declspec(dllexport)
#else
#define INTERFACE _declspec(dllimport)
#endif

class INTERFACE TestClass
{
```

```
private:
    int i;
public:
    TestClass() {}
    ~TestClass() {}
    void SetI(int mi){ i = mi; }
    int GetI( void ){ return i; }
};
```

RUNNING THE **WINHOST** PROGRAM

As noted in Chapter 6, "Processes," the entry point for a console window is a `main` function. The `main` function of the WINHOST program is defined as follows:

```
int main()
{
    testObj.SetI(43);
    testObjPtr->SetI(796);

    cout << "The testObj.GetI() member function returns "
        << testObj.GetI() << '.' << endl;
    cout << "The testObjPtr->GetI() function returns "
        << testObjPtr->GetI() << '.' << endl;

    while (TRUE) ;

    return 0;
}
```

This `main` function uses the C++ string operator `cout` to print two messages in a console window. It obtains the two numbers that are printed in the message by calling the function `SetI`, which is a member function of a class named `TestClass`. This class and its member functions are defined in **DLLLIB.H**. `TestClass::SetI` is called twice: first by value and then by reference. This demonstration shows that a function exported by a DLL can be called either way. This is the definition of `TestClass`:

```
class INTERFACE TestClass
{
private:
```

```
    int i;
public:
    TestClass() {}
    ~TestClass() {}
    void SetI(int mi){ i = mi; }
    int GetI( void ){ return i; }
};
```

DLLLIB.H also contains the definition of a preprocessor macro that is used to access the attributes `dllexport` and `dllimport`. This macro, named `INTERFACE`, is defined as follows:

```
#ifdef DEFINING
#define INTERFACE _declspec(dllexport)
#else
#define INTERFACE _declspec(dllimport)
#endif
```

In the preceding code fragment, the `INTERFACE` macro is conditionally defined in two ways. If the macro is defined in a module that exports an object or a function—as in the DLLLIB.H code module—the macro is expanded as follows:

```
_declspec(dllexport)
```

If the macro appears in a module that imports a function—for example, the DLL `Import` function defined in Listing 8.8—it is expanded as follows:

```
_declspec(dllimport)
```

In Listing 8.9, **DLLLIB.CPP**, the macro `DEFINING` is defined, so the `INTERFACE` macro is expanded as `_declspec(dllexport)`. The class `TestClass` is then exported in two ways: on the heap, so that it can be called by value, and on the stack, so that it can be called by reference.

```
#define DEFINING
#include "dlllib.h"

INTERFACE TestClass testObj;
INTERFACE TestClass *testObjPtr = new TestClass;
```

In Listing 8.8, **WINHOST.H,** a macro named `DLLImport` is defined as `_declspec` `(dllimport)`. `TestClass` is then imported in two ways: by value, as an object named `testObj`, and by reference, as an object pointer named `testObjPtr`.

```
DLLImport TestClass testObj;
DLLImport TestClass *testObjPtr;
```

WINHOST does not require a module definition file, because it references VCPP 1.0 DLLs using the attributes `dllimport` and `dllexport`. Although the program exports an object that is a member of a class, the object class is not derived from any class defined in MFC, so the program works with Win32 Visual C++, which shipped with version 2.0 of MFC.

MFC 4.0 DLLs

With the twin releases of Visual C++ 4.0 and MFC 4.0, Microsoft unveiled a new AppWizard with some interesting new features. One new feature lets you use AppWizard to build dynamic link libraries.

One important feature of MFC 4.0 DLLs is that you can link them to MFC in different ways, depending on your preferences and the requirements of your application. To create a DLL using AppWizard, you simply choose the **MFC AppWizard (dll)** option in AppWizard's New Project Workspace dialog box. (For a step-by-step demonstration of how AppWizard can be used to generate a DLL automatically, see "Defining `_doserrmsg`" later in this chapter.)

How MFC 4.0 DLLs Work

To understand how MFC 4.0 DLLs work, it helps to be familiar with some new terminology that Microsoft has begun to use in its DLL documentation. Microsoft still ships two versions of MFC with Visual C++. When you buy Visual C++, you still get a statically linked version and a dynamically linked version of the MFC library. But new terminology—and new levels of complexity—have been added.

Microsoft now refers to the statically linked version of MFC as the *static-link version.* And the dynamically linked version is now referred to as the *shared version.* You should get used to hearing these terms from now on.

The Static-Link MFC Library

In MFC 4.0, the static-link MFC library has the same characteristics as the familiar statically linked MFC library that was used in earlier versions of Visual C++. In other words, the static-link version is the MFC 4.0 equivalent of what used to be called the USRDLL library before the advent of MFC 4.0.

As noted earlier, the name USRDLL is obsolete in MFC 4.0. However, when AppWizard creates a DLL that links dynamically with the shared version of MFC, AppWizard still sets up the link by defining the _USRDLL preprocessor symbol in the DLL's source code.

The Shared MFC Library

In MFC 4.0, the shared MFC library has the same characteristics as the library that was called the dynamically linked MFC library, or the AFXDLL library, before the advent of MFC 4.0.

In MFC 4.0, as in previous versions of MFC, the shared version is named AFXDLL. When you use AppWizard to create a DLL that links dynamically with the shared version of the MFC library, AppWizard defines the _AFXDLL preprocessor symbol when it builds your DLL.

REGULAR AND EXTENSION DLLs

Along with new terms, Microsoft has created some new levels of detail that affect the creation and implementation of DLLs. In MFC 4.0, there are now two different kinds of shared (dynamically linked) MFC libraries: the regular shared MFC library and the extended shared MFC library.

The regular shared MFC library has the same characteristics as the version of MFC that used to be called the statically linked version. When you equip an MFC 4.0 application with DLLs that access MFC classes, you can save memory and disk space by writing DLLs that access the regular shared MFC library. But you must ship a copy of the regular shared MFC library with your application.

When you link a DLL with the extended shared MFC library, you can create MFC-derived classes that actually become extensions to the hundreds of Microsoft classes implemented in MFC 4.0. You can then make your own derived classes available to other applications that access the MFC-derived classes or functions implemented in your DLL.

Creating Extension DLLs

The extension version of the shared MFC library is a new kind of MFC library that made its premiere along with MFC 4.0. When you create a DLL that accesses the extended version of the shared MFC library, any new classes that you implement in your DLL become integral parts of the shared MFC library that you ship with your application. Other applications that are loaded into the user's computer system can then access your new classes without loading another DLL into memory.

When you create a DLL that links with the extension version of the shared MFC library, your DLL is called an extension DLL. You can create extension DLLs almost automatically using AppWizard. You click the radio button labeled **MFC Extension DLL (using shared MFC DLL)** when AppWizard displays the dialog box shown in Figure 8.10 (The process of creating a DLL with AppWizard is described in more detail in "Defining _doserrmsg" later in this chapter.)

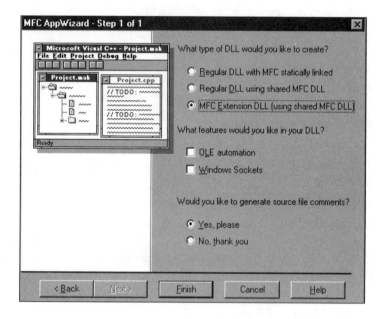

FIGURE 8.10 CREATING AN EXTENSION DLL.

Creating Regular DLLs

In previous releases of MFC, USRDLL was the name of the statically linked version of MFC. To access MFC classes from one of your own DLLs, all you had to do was statically link your DLL to the statically linked version of MFC. In MFC 4.0, you can obtain this same functionality by statically linking your DLL with the static-link version of what is now called the regular version of MFC. Such a DLL is called a regular DLL. Functions exported by a regular DLL can be called by any Win32 application as well as by programs that also use MFC.

In MFC 4.0, you can easily create regular DLLs using AppWizard. When AppWizard displays its first DLL-generation dialog box (shown in Figure 8.11), you link your DLL to the regular version of MFC by clicking the radio button labeled **Regular DLL with MFC statically linked.** AppWizard generates a regular DLL and statically links it with the static-link version of the MFC DLL by defining the _USRDLL preprocessor symbol when it builds your DLL.

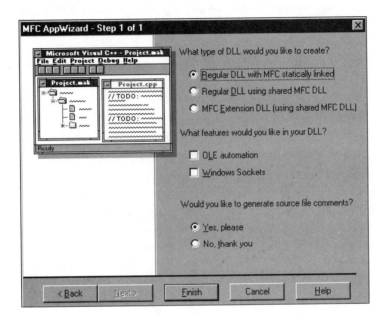

FIGURE 8.11 CHOOSING THE KIND OF DLL YOU WANT TO CREATE.

LINKING WITH A SHARED MFC LIBRARY

In MFC 4.0, as in earlier versions of MFC, you can save memory and disk space by dynamically linking your application's DLLs to a shared version of the regular MFC library. In that way, multiple applications can access the same copy of the MFC library, saving disk and memory space.

When you want to create a DLL that dynamically links with the shared MFC library, you can easily create your DLL using AppWizard. When AppWizard displays its first DLL-generation dialog box (Figure 8.11), you link your DLL to the regular version of MFC by clicking the radio button labeled **Regular DLL with MFC dynamically linked.** In this way, functions in your DLL can be called only by MFC applications that are also dynamically linked to the shared version of MFC.

When you use AppWizard to link a DLL dynamically with the shared version of the regular MFC library, AppWizard simply refrains from defining the _USRDLL preprocessor symbol when it builds your DLL. Instead, AppWizard defines the _AFXDLL preprocessor symbol. (If AppWizard were to define the _USRDLL preprocessor symbol in your DLL's source code, you would obtain a static link to the static-link version of the regular version of the MFC library.)

When you dynamically link a DLL to the regular shared version of the MFC library, functions in your DLL can be called by any Win32 application, whether or not the program uses MFC classes.

DEFINING _DOSERRMSG

If you try to build a DLL and get a link error complaining that something called _doserrmsg is not defined, select **Options/Project/Linker** from the Developer Studio menu bar and then select **Input** from the Category text box. When the libraries that are being used in the link appear in the Object/Library Modules text box, make sure that the name of the library **libc.lib** appears at the end of the list, right after the name of the **nafxdwd** library. If it doesn't, type it in. Then close the Linker Options dialog box and the Project Options dialog box by clicking their **OK** buttons. After you have done all that, rebuild your DLL by selecting **Build** or **Rebuild All** from the Project menu. That should solve your problem.

CREATING DLLS WITH APPWIZARD

When you use AppWizard to generate an MFC 4.0 DLL, AppWizard lets you choose the kind of DLL you want to create (Figure 8.11). These are the options that AppWizard offers:

✦ **Regular DLL with MFC statically linked.** This choice creates a regular DLL that links with the static-link MFC 4.0 library. When you choose this option, the Visual C++ linker accesses functions in the static-link version of MFC and links your application to MFC at build time. Win32 applications and MFC applications can call functions exported from this kind of DLL.

✦ **Regular DLL using shared MFC DLL.** When you make this selection, the Visual C++ linker links your application to the dynamically linked (shared) version of MFC at run time. Using this kind of DLL can reduce the disk and memory requirements of your application if your program has multiple executable files that access MFC. This variety of DLL can be used by both Win32 applications and MFC applications.

✦ **MFC Extension DLL (using shared MFC).** If you make this choice, your application is linked to the shared version of MFC at run time. This option can reduce your application's disk and memory requirements if your program has multiple executable files that access MFC. Only MFC applications can call functions implemented in this kind of DLL.

CREATING AN MFC 4.0 DLL STEP BY STEP

To generate an MFC 4.0 DLL using AppWizard, follow these steps:

1. Choose the **File|New** menu item.

2. When the New dialog box opens, choose **Project Workspace** from the New list box.

3. Close the New list box by clicking **OK**.

4. When the New Project Workspace list box opens, you can build a DLL with App-Wizard by simply selecting the **Dynamic-Link Library** item from the Type list box.

5. Type a name for your DLL project in the Name text box.

6. Click the **Create** button.

7. When the first AppWizard dialog box opens, you can decide which kind of MFC 4.0 DLL you want AppWizard to generate: a regular DLL with MFC statically linked, or a regular DLL that uses a shared MFC DLL. When you have specified the kind of DLL you want to create, click **Finish**. AppWizard then builds your DLL in the same way it builds any executable, creating both an object library (an **.OBJ** file) and a DLL (a **.DLL** file).

Later, when you develop an application that accesses your DLL, you must link the application with the .OBJ file that is created during Step 7. When you ship an application that accesses your DLL, you must also provide your customers with the .DLL file that is generated in Step 7.

BUILDING A DLL CLIENT STEP BY STEP

Building a DLL client is just like building an ordinary application except for a few extra steps that involve linking with libraries. To build a Windows-based client application using version 4.0 of Visual C++, these are the general steps to follow:

1. Build your client project, with or without AppWizard, in the same way you would build any other Visual C++ project. To use a shared version of MFC, an application must be built as an MFC application.

2. Using Developer Studio, add your dynamic link library's **.DLL** and **.LIB** files to your project.

3. Build and execute your client application.

For a more comprehensive guide to building a DLL client, see "Building a Program that Accesses an Extension DLL" later in this chapter.

EXAMPLE: THE DLLTESTAPP PROGRAM

This chapter's main example program, DLLTESTAPP, has two parts: an MFC 4.0 DLL named WINNTDLL and an application that calls the DLL; the application is named DLLTESTAPP. Figure 8.12 shows the custom dialog box displayed by DLLTESTAPP.

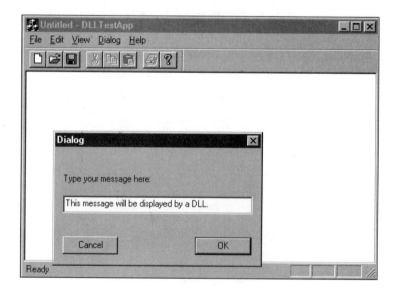

FIGURE 8.12 OUTPUT OF THE DLLTESTAPP PROGRAM.

The DLL that is implemented in the WINNTDLL file implements an MFC-derived class named CTestClass. CTestClass has several member functions, including one that displays a message box and one that displays a custom message box designed using Studio App. The custom message box contains an edit box in which the user can type text. The text that the user has entered can subsequently be displayed in the application's message box.

How the **DLLTESTAPP** Program Works

Both the DLLTESTAPP program and the WINNTDLL dynamic link library were created using AppWizard. WINNTDLL is an extension DLL that was built using the second AppWizard option: **MFC Extension DLL (using shared MFC DLL)**. For an explanation of this option, see "Linking with a Shared MFC Library" earlier in this chapter.

When you execute DLLTESTAPP, it calls member functions that are implemented in WINNTDLL. DLLTESTAPP is a document-view application that calls WINNTDLL from its `CView` class, `DLLTestAppView`. The application's `DLLTestAppView` object calls WINNTDLL using two menu commands: **Dialog|Send** and **Dialog|Recieve**.

When the user executes DLLTESTAPP and chooses the **Dialog|Send** menu item, DLL-TESTAPP executes a member function named `DLLTestAppView::OnDialogSend`. This member function displays a custom dialog box titled Send a Message (shown in Figure 8.12). The user then types a message inside the edit box labeled **Type your message here**. When the user clicks **OK**, DLLTESTAPP calls a member function implemented in WINNTDLL. That member function, `CTestClass::SetMessage`, stores the user's message in the member variable `CTestClass::m_msg`.

When the user chooses **Dialog|Receive**, DLLTESTAPP calls another WINNTDLL member function named `GetMessage`. The `GetMessage` function retrieves the text stored in the `m_msg` member variable and returns the text to DLLTESTAPP. DLLTESTAPP then displays the user's message in a standard message box, as shown in Figure 8.13.

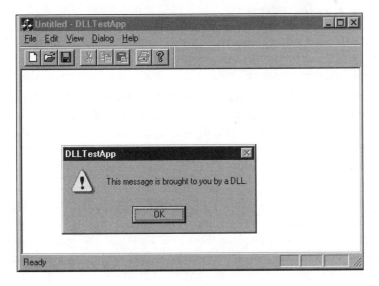

FIGURE 8.13 THE DLLTESTAPP MESSAGE BOX.

ARCHITECTURE OF THE **DLLTESTAPP** PROGRAM

Although AppWizard makes creation of MFC 4.0 DLLs almost automatic, there is still some work you must do yourself. The source code shows how AppWizard helped create the DLL-TESTAPP and WINNTDLL programs. It also shows the extra work that had to be done to make the two projects work together.

CHARACTERISTICS OF EXTENSION DLLS

WINNTDLL is an extension DLL that was built using the shared version of MFC. In MFC 4.0, an MFC extension DLL typically implements reusable classes derived from existing MFC classes. Extension DLLs can also be used for passing MFC-derived objects to and from applications.

An MFC extension DLL uses a shared version of MFC in the same way that an application uses the shared AFXDLL version, with a few additional considerations. An extension DLL, unlike an MFC application, does not have a CWinApp-derived object. An extension DLL calls the MFC function AfxInitExtensionModule in its DllMain function. Your application should check the return value of this function. If AfxInitExtensionModule returns a zero value, your application's DllMain function should return 0 also. If an extension DLL is designed to export CRuntimeClass objects or resources to an application, it creates a CDynLinkLibrary object during the initialization process.

BUILDING AN EXTENSION DLL

To create an extension DLL using AppWizard, you select **MFC Extension DLL (using shared MFC DLL)** when AppWizard prompts you. In an application that has already been compiled, you can change this option using the Project Settings dialog box.

When you create an extension DLL, you must also provide a header (.H) file. AppWizard generates a module definition (.DEF) file when it generates your DLL, but you don't have to do anything with AppWizard's .DEF file unless you want to access the functions in your DLL using ordinal numbers. In that case, you must place the names of the functions in your DLL's .DEF file, and you must assign ordinal numbers to the functions listed in the .DEF file.

There are two methods for exporting functions from an extension DLL created by AppWizard. The first technique can export whole classes without requiring you to track down their decorated names and place them in a .DEF file. The second strategy requires you to place decorated names in a .DEF file. The second method is more efficient, because it provides you with a way to export the names of symbols using their ordinal numbers. But you may prefer the first method because it doesn't require the use of ordinal numbers.

EXPORTING CLASSES WITHOUT USING DECORATED NAMES

If you want to export a class from an extension DLL without using decorated names, you must use the extern "C" construct to initialize your DLL and register its classes with Windows NT. In the **WINNTDLL.H** file, this is the line that initializes **WINNTDLL.H**:

```
extern "C" AFX_EXT_API void WINAPI InitWINNTDLL();
```

You must also insert the AFX_EXT_CLASS keyword into the heading of your class's definition. For example, in **WINNTDLL.H**, CTestClass is defined this way:

```
class AFX_EXT_CLASS CTestClass : public CObject
{
private:
    CString m_msg;
public:
    CTestClass();
    ~CTestClass();
    void ShowMessage(CString msg);
    void SetMessage(CString s);
    CString GetMessage();
};
```

This technique allows you to export entire classes without placing the decorated names for all the symbols of that class in the .DEF file.

EXPORTING SYMBOLS USING THEIR ORDINAL NUMBERS

There is another method you can use if you prefer to place the decorated names for all external symbols in your .DEF file. This method is most useful if you don't need to export many symbols from your DLL. If you have many symbols to export, you might not want to use this method, because it requires the use of a large number of decorated names.

To use the decorated-names method, place the following code at the beginning and end of your header file:

```
#undef AFX_DATA
#define AFX_DATA AFX_EXT_DATA
    // <body of your header file>
#undef AFX_DATA
#define AFX_DATA
```

The preceding code ensures that your DLL is compiled correctly for an extension DLL. Leaving out these four lines may cause your DLL to either compile incorrectly or link incorrectly.

When you have inserted the necessary code in your file, you must obtain the decorated names of all the classes you want to export (you can do that by linking your application using the /MAP option), and then you must place those names in your application's **.DEF** file.

BUILDING A PROGRAM THAT ACCESSES AN EXTENSION DLL

A program that accesses functions in an MFC extension DLL must be an MFC application—that is, an application that contains a CWinApp-derived object. One such program is the WINNTDLL sample program, which appears in Listings 8.11 through 8.14.

The easiest way to create such an application is to generate a framework for it using AppWizard. When AppWizard displays the dialog box shown in Figure 8.14, select the **As A Shared DLL** option. Then AppWizard creates an application that can access functions in an MFC extension DLL.

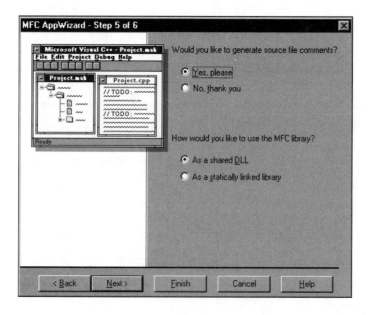

FIGURE 8.14 BUILDING A PROGRAM THAT ACCESSES AN EXTENSION DLL.

In an application that has already been compiled, you can select this option by tabbing to the General property page in the Project Settings property sheet and selecting the shared-DLL option from the Microsoft Foundation Classes list box.

When you create an application that is designed to access your extension DLL, you must add your DLL's import library to your application's project. To do that, follow these steps:

1. From the Developer Studio editor, choose the **Build|Settings** menu item.
2. When the Project Settings property sheet (Figure 8.15) opens, tab to the Link property page.
3. Select **Input** from the Category drop-down combo box.
4. Type the name of your DLL's import library in the text box labeled **Output file name**.
5. Close the Project Settings dialog box by clicking **OK**.
6. Include the name of your DLL's header (.H) file in the file that implements your client application. The following line includes **WINNTDLL.H** in the **DLLTESTAPP-VIEW.CPP** file:

```
#include "WINNTDLL.h"
```

7. Build your application by choosing Developer Studio's **Build|Build** menu item.

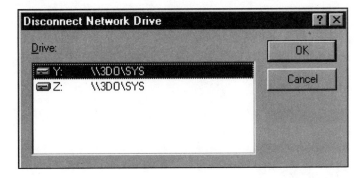

FIGURE 8.15 LINKING AN APPLICATION WITH A DLL'S .OBJ FILE.

LISTING 8.11 WINNTDLL.H

```
// WINNTDLL.h

// Initialize the DLL, register the classes, etc.
extern "C" AFX_EXT_API void WINAPI InitWINNTDLL();

class AFX_EXT_CLASS CTestClass : public CObject
```

```
{
private:
    CString m_msg;
public:
    CTestClass();
    ~CTestClass();
    void ShowMessage(CString msg);
    void SetMessage(CString s);
    CString GetMessage();
};
```

LISTING **8.12** WINNTDLL.H

```
// WINNTDLL.cpp : Defines the initialization routines
// for the DLL.
//
#include "stdafx.h"
#include "WINNTDLL.h"
#include <afxdllx.h>
#ifdef _DEBUG
#define new DEBUG_NEW
#undef THIS_FILE
static char THIS_FILE[] = __FILE__;
#endif
/////////////////////////////////////////////////////////////////////////////
// Initialization of MFC Extension DLL
static AFX_EXTENSION_MODULE WINNTDLL = { NULL, NULL };

extern "C" int APIENTRY
DllMain(HINSTANCE hInstance, DWORD dwReason, LPVOID lpReserved)
{
    if (dwReason == DLL_PROCESS_ATTACH)
    {
        TRACE0("WINNTDLL.DLL Initializing!\n");

        // Extension DLL one-time initialization
        AfxInitExtensionModule(WINNTDLL, hInstance);

        // Insert this DLL into the resource chain
```

```
            new CDynLinkLibrary(WINNTDLL);
    }
    else if (dwReason == DLL_PROCESS_DETACH)
    {
            TRACE0("WINNTDLL.DLL Terminating!\n");
    }
    return 1;    // ok
}
// Exported DLL initialization is run in context of
// running application
extern "C" void WINAPI InitWINNTDLL()
{
    // create a new CDynLinkLibrary for this app
    new CDynLinkLibrary(WINNTDLL);
    // nothing more to do
}
/////////////////////////////////////////////////////
// CTestClass functions
//
CTestClass::CTestClass() {}
CTestClass::~CTestClass() {}
void CTestClass::ShowMessage(CString msg)
{
    AfxMessageBox(msg);
}
void CTestClass::SetMessage(CString s)
{
    m_msg = s;
}
CString CTestClass::GetMessage()
{
    return m_msg;
}
```

LISTING 8.13 DLLTESTAPPVIEW.H

```
// DLLTestAppView.h : interface of the CDLLTestAppView
// class
```

```
//
#define VAR2CTRL FALSE  // These defines make DDX
                                        // a little clearer.
#define CTRL2VAR TRUE

class CDLLTestAppView : public CView
{
protected: // create from serialization only
    CDLLTestAppView();
    DECLARE_DYNCREATE(CDLLTestAppView)
    void OnInitialUpdate();

// Attributes
public:
    class CDLLTestAppDoc* GetDocument();

// Operations
public:
// Overrides
    // ClassWizard generated virtual function overrides
    //{{AFX_VIRTUAL(CDLLTestAppView)
    public:
    virtual void OnDraw(CDC* pDC);   // overridden to draw
                                                    //this view
    virtual BOOL PreCreateWindow(CREATESTRUCT& cs);
    protected:
    //}}AFX_VIRTUAL

// Implementation
public:
    virtual ~CDLLTestAppView();

#ifdef _DEBUG
    virtual void AssertValid() const;
    virtual void Dump(CDumpContext& dc) const;
#endif

private:
    CString m_msg;
public:
```

```
        void SetMessageString(CString s)
            { m_msg = s; }
protected:
// Generated message map functions
protected:
        //{{AFX_MSG(CDLLTestAppView)
        afx_msg void OnDialogReceive();
        afx_msg void OnDialogSend();
        //}}AFX_MSG
        DECLARE_MESSAGE_MAP()
};
#ifndef _DEBUG  // debug version in DLLTestAppView.cpp
inline CDLLTestAppDoc* CDLLTestAppView::GetDocument()
    { return (CDLLTestAppDoc*)m_pDocument; }
#endif
/////////////////////////////////////////////////////////////////////////////
```

LISTING 8.14 DLLTESTAPPVIEW.CPP

```
// DLLTestAppView.cpp : implementation of the
//CDLLTestAppView class
//
#include "stdafx.h"
#include "DLLTestApp.h"
#include "DLLTestAppDoc.h"
#include "DLLTestAppView.h"
#include "WINNTDLL.h"
#include "DlgGetMsg.h"

#ifdef _DEBUG
#define new DEBUG_NEW
#undef THIS_FILE
static char THIS_FILE[] = __FILE__;
#endif

/////////////////////////////////////////////////////////////////////////////
// CDLLTestAppView
IMPLEMENT_DYNCREATE(CDLLTestAppView, CView)
BEGIN_MESSAGE_MAP(CDLLTestAppView, CView)
```

```
    //{{AFX_MSG_MAP(CDLLTestAppView)
    ON_COMMAND(ID_DIALOG_RECEIVE, OnDialogReceive)
    ON_COMMAND(ID_DIALOG_SEND, OnDialogSend)
    //}}AFX_MSG_MAP
END_MESSAGE_MAP()
/////////////////////////////////////////////////////////////////////////////

// CDLLTestAppView construction/destruction
CDLLTestAppView::CDLLTestAppView()
{
    // TODO: add construction code here
}

CDLLTestAppView::~CDLLTestAppView()
{
}

void CDLLTestAppView::OnInitialUpdate()
{
    // An initial message to start off with.
    m_msg = "This message is brought to you by a DLL.";
}

BOOL CDLLTestAppView::PreCreateWindow(CREATESTRUCT& cs)
{
    // TODO: Modify the Window class or styles here by modifying
    //   the CREATESTRUCT cs
    return CView::PreCreateWindow(cs);
}

/////////////////////////////////////////////////////////////////////////////
// CDLLTestAppView drawing
void CDLLTestAppView::OnDraw(CDC* pDC)
{
    CDLLTestAppDoc* pDoc = GetDocument();
    ASSERT_VALID(pDoc);
    // TODO: add draw code for native data here
}

/////////////////////////////////////////////////////////////////////////////
```

```
// CDLLTestAppView diagnostics
#ifdef _DEBUG
void CDLLTestAppView::AssertValid() const
{
    CView::AssertValid();
}

void CDLLTestAppView::Dump(CDumpContext& dc) const
{
    CView::Dump(dc);
}

CDLLTestAppDoc* CDLLTestAppView::GetDocument() // non-debug version is inline
{
    ASSERT(m_pDocument->IsKindOf(RUNTIME_CLASS(CDLLTestAppDoc)));
    return (CDLLTestAppDoc*)m_pDocument;
}
#endif //_DEBUG
/////////////////////////////////////////////////////////////////////////
// CDLLTestAppView message handlers
void CDLLTestAppView::OnDialogReceive()
{
    // Show the last message that was
    // input by the user.
    CTestClass myTestObj;
    myTestObj.ShowMessage(m_msg);
}

void CDLLTestAppView::OnDialogSend()
{
    // Instantiate the get-message dialog box.
    CDlgGetMsg dlgGetMsg;
    // m_msg = dlgGetMsg.m_editMsg;
    // Display the get-message dialog box.
    dlgGetMsg.DoModal();
    // Copy the user's entry into this class's
    // local m_msg variable.
    m_msg = dlgGetMsg.m_editMsg;
}
```

Thread Local Storage

Thread local storage, often abbreviated TLS, is a mechanism that individual threads running under a multithreaded process use to allocate for storing private, thread-specific data. (Multithreading is the topic of Chapter 7.) With thread local storage, you can associate data with a specific thread of execution. For example, if you were designing a computer game, you might want to associate data with each combatant in a battle as combat started. Then, as each thread terminated, you could save in a database the changes in the data collected about each fighter, such as each foe's wounds and the like. In this way, you could keep a running record of the state of each player in the game.

In Windows NT programs, thread local storage is often a good alternative to the use of global and static variables. Global and static variables can come in handy in a program but can also be dangerous. Global variables are often inadvertently changed in strange and mysterious ways as functions seemingly pop out of nowhere, zap the value of a variable, and then disappear. When you don't know which function changed a global variable, or when or why, the result can be an immediate program crash or an even more insidious disaster.

Thread local storage is one mechanism provided by the Windows API to help you solve such problems. By using thread local storage, you can give each thread in an application a private area where it can store the values of global variables. When a thread keeps the values of these variables in thread local storage, they can be used as global variables by the thread that owns them but not by any other threads.

TLS AND THE C RUN-TIME LIBRARY

A good example of the use of thread local storage, as explained by Jeffrey Richter in his excellent book *Advanced Windows* (see Bibliography), is the way in which the C run-time library avoids global-variable problems when it executes the strtok function. In C, strtok finds the next token in a string. The first time an application calls the run-time library's strtok function, it returns the address of the token being sought and also saves the address of the string in its own static variable. Later, each time the application makes another call to strtok passing NULL as a parameter, strtok refers to the string address that it has saved.

It isn't necessary for a function such as strtok to use thread local storage in a single-threaded application, because there are no other threads that can change the value of the string the function has saved without the original function knowing about the change. But in a multithreaded environment, it's possible for one thread to call strtok, and for another thread to make another call to strtok before the first thread calls strtok again. In that kind of situation, the second thread could cause strtok to overwrite its static variable with a new address without the first thread knowing anything about it. The first thread might then call strtok and get a value back that's based on the address of the second thread's string. You can figure out for yourself what kind of havoc that kind of scenario could cause in a program.

To prevent such disasters, the C run-time library uses thread local store in C implementations that are designed to run in multithreaded environments. You can use TLS in your multithreaded applications, too.

USING THREAD LOCAL STORAGE

Any kind of Windows NT executable can use thread local storage, but TLS is most commonly used in dynamic link libraries. When a DLL stows data for safekeeping in thread local storage, the DLL can access the data whenever it is called, requiring the calling thread to keep track of where the data is stored and without any danger of any other threads corrupting the data.

There are two kinds of thread local storage that DLLs (or other executables) use: static TLS and dynamic TLS. Static TLS is easier to use than dynamic TLS, because it does not require any function calls; it simply sets up a data-storage area for a thread to use and then lets the thread use it. Dynamic TLS is more complicated but more versatile. It allows you to allocate thread local storage when you need it and to deallocate your TLS space when you finish using it.

USING STATIC THREAD LOCAL STORAGE

To use static thread local storage, all you have to do is to use the __declspec keyword (described in "Using VCPP 1.0 DLLs" earlier in this chapter) to declare a TLS variable. For example, the following statement declares a TLS integer variable named tls_i and initializes it with the value 1:

```
__declspec(thread) int tls_i = 1;
```

In this statement, the __declspec(thread) prefix tells your Visual C++ compiler that the tls_i variable being declared should be placed in its own private storage area of the DLL or other executable being processed. To make this operation work properly, you must make sure that the variable following __declspec (thread)—in this case, the variable tls_i—is declared as either a global variable or a static variable, either inside or outside the function being executed. You can't declare a local variable to be of type __declspec(thread), but there is no reason to do that anyway, because it makes no sense to use thread local storage with local variables.

When you compile a DLL or other executable in which you have used static TLS, your Visual C++ compiler puts all the declared TLS variables into their own private code section. This file is named, logically enough, **.tls.** Then, when you link your executable, the Visual C++ linker combines all the individual **.tls** sections and generates a single **.tls** section in the resulting **.EXE** or **.DLL** file.

When you have finished building an executable that uses TLS and your executable is loaded into memory, Windows NT looks for a **.tls** section in your **.DLL** or **.EXE** file. If Windows finds a **.tls** section, it dynamically allocates a block of memory that's large enough to hold all your static TLS variables. Subsequently, each time a function in your executable refers to a static TLS variable, your application goes to the block of memory that has been allocated to TLS storage and tracks down the variable.

If the process using static thread local storage has more than one thread, Windows automatically allocates another block of memory for each additional thread's static TLS variables. Windows makes sure that each thread has access only to its own static TLS variables and isn't able to access the TLS variables belonging to any other thread.

Thread local storage is easier to use than dynamic thread local storage, but it isn't as versatile. Static TLS can run into trouble when an application calls `LoadLibrary` to link to a DLL that also contains static TLS variables, or calls `FreeLibrary` to unload a DLL that contains static TLS variables. When that happens, your TLS data is not properly initialized, and any attempt to access it can result in an access violation. That is the only disadvantage of using static TLS; as long as you don't use `LoadLibrary` or `FreeLibrary` with DLLs that contain TLS areas, static thread local storage is safe. But if your application calls `LoadLibrary` or `FreeLibrary` to load and unload DLLs, you should use dynamic thread local storage, which is described next.

Using Dynamic Thread Local Storage

When your application (or DLL) needs to allocate thread local storage space dynamically, use dynamic TLS instead of static TLS, which was described under the previous heading. The Win32 API provides four functions for allocating and managing dynamic thread local storage: `TlsAlloc, TlsGetValue, TlsSetValue,` and `TlsFree.`

When a thread calls the `TlsAlloc` function, it creates a global variable called a TLS index. `TlsAlloc` then allocates a block of memory for thread local storage and places a pointer to the memory block it has created in the TLS index.

Internally, Windows NT stores TLS variables in an array inside a memory block called the *thread control block*. The `TlsAlloc` function allocates thread local storage areas in the thread control block.

When a TLS memory area has been allocated and a TLS index has been created, every client that is authorized to access the stored data is provided with the address to the data that is stored in the TLS index. Then, when a client requires access to the DLL's data, the client attaches to the data, preventing other clients from accessing the data. When the client has finished accessing the data, it detaches from the data, freeing the data for access by other clients. This system provides multiple clients with access to a DLL's data, while preventing multiple processes from attempting to modify the data at the same time.

When a DLL or other executable stores variables using thread local storage, the DLL is required to keep track of just one TLS index. The system can use that index to determine which thread is calling the DLL.

Windows NT can store as many as 64 TLS indexes for each process that uses thread local storage. This limit guarantees that if enough memory is available, any single process can store as many as 64 different DLLs using TLS in memory at the same time.

For as long as a thread is active, the FS segment register in the 386, 486, or Pentium processor points to the data block that holds the thread's TLS variables. Each time a process that uses TLS switches threads, Windows NT updates the FS register to point at the appropriate TLS memory block.

Calling Win32's TLS Functions

Internally, Windows NT stores information about TLS data-storage areas in a set of data structures made up of bit flags. Figure 8.16 shows the internal data structures that Windows NT uses for managing TLS.

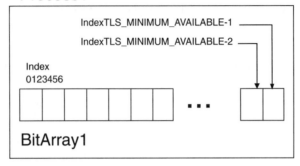

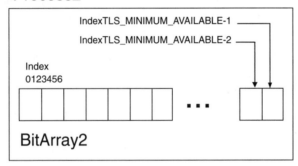

FIGURE 8.16 HOW WINDOWS NT STORES TLS FLAGS.

The data structures illustrated in Figure 8.16 show how Windows NT stores TLS information about a single process. An additional set of structures must be used for each additional process that uses or accesses thread local storage. In Figure 8.16, each flag shown can be set to the constant FREE or to the constant INUSE, depending on whether a thread local storage area associated with the flag is in use.

CALLING THE TLSALLOC FUNCTION

When a set of structures such as those shown in Figure 8.16 have been set up, you can start using them by calling the Win32 function TlsAlloc. This is the syntax of the TlsAlloc function:

```
DWORD TlsAlloc(VOID);
```

When a process executes `TlsAlloc`, it scans the bit flags in the set of internal structures used by the process and locates a FREE flag. When a flag is found and allocated, the flag's setting is changed from FREE to INUSE, and `TlsAlloc` allocates an `LPVOID` array of 64 addresses. `TlsAlloc` then returns the index of the flag in the bit array, which is a value of 0 the first time `TlsAlloc` is called. If `TlsAlloc` fails to locate a FREE flag in the structures it is searching, it returns the constant TLS _OUT_OF_INDEXES.

If `TlsAlloc` returns successfully, what usually happens next is that the DLL or other executable that is using thread local storage saves the index in a global variable. Each time you call `TlsAlloc`, it increments the index value that it returns. If `TlsAlloc` returns an index value of, say, 5, it means that the `LPVOID` pointer at index 5 is reserved for you in every thread currently executing in your process as well as in any threads that might be created later.

Now that you know the `TlsAlloc` function, we can take a look at the other three Win32 functions that are used in TLS operations.

CALLING THE TLSSETVALUE FUNCTION

`TlsSetValue` places an `LPVOID` value (or any other 32-bit value) in a thread that has been set up by `TlsAlloc`. This is the syntax of the `TlsSetValue` function:

```
BOOL TlsSetValue(DWORD dwTlsIndex, LPVOID lpvTlsValue);
```

The value that `TlsSetValue` places in a thread's array is specified in the `lpvTlsValue` argument passed to `TlsSetValue`. The location where the value is placed in the array is specified by `dwTlsIndex`. The value of `lpvTlsValue` is associated with the thread making the call to `TlsSetValue`. If a call to `TlsSetValue` is successful, its return value is TRUE.

When a thread calls `TlsSetValue`, it changes the layout of its own array. A thread cannot set a TLS value for another thread. The only way to pass initialization data from one thread to another is to pass a single 32-bit value to the `CreateThread` function. `CreateThread` then passes this value to the thread function as its only parameter.

When you call `TlsSetValue`, make sure that you pass it a valid index value—that is, an index value that has been returned from an earlier call to `TlsAlloc`. If you pass an invalid index value, `TlsSetValue` happily stores the value in the specified thread array without making any validity checks. Beware.

CALLING THE TLSGETVALUE FUNCTION

You can retrieve a value from a thread's array by calling the `TlsGetValue` function:

```
LPVOID TlsGetValue(DWORD dwTlsIndex);
```

`TlsGetValue` returns the value that was associated with the TLS slot at index `dwTlsIndex`. The `TlsGetValue` function sees only the array that belongs to the calling thread and, like `TlsSetValue`, performs no validity check on the index that you pass it. Again, beware.

CALLING THE TLSFREE FUNCTION

The `TlsFree` function, as its name implies, frees a slot in a TLS index when the slot is no longer needed. This is the syntax of `TlsFree`:

```
BOOL TlsFree(DWORD dwTlsIndex);
```

`TlsFree` simply informs the system that this slot no longer needs to be reserved. The result is that the INUSE flag in your process's bit flags array is reset to FREE and can be allocated in the future if a thread later calls `TlsAlloc`. If a call to `TlsFree` succeeds, the function returns TRUE. Trying to free a slot that has not been allocated returns an error.

THREAD LOCAL STORAGE STEP BY STEP

These steps summarize how a DLL sets up and uses thread local storage:

1. The DLL calls `TlsAlloc` to allocate a TLS index.
2. The DLL dynamically allocates a block of memory for a thread and calls `TlsSetValue` to store the starting address of the memory allocated to the thread.
3. Each time a subsequent thread is initialized, the DLL calls `TlsSetValue` to allocate an additional block of dynamic memory and calls `TlsSetValue` to store the starting address of each additional memory block. Windows 95 automatically resolves the process's TLS index and the thread's internal ID to return a memory location that is different from the locations used by previous threads.
4. Each time the DLL needs to access the dynamic memory associated with a thread, the DLL retrieves the address of the appropriate block of memory by calling `TlsGetValue`. Again, the system uses the thread's ID to determine which thread's memory address to return. As each thread detaches from its calling process, it retrieves its TLS memory address and then explicitly releases

the dynamic memory that it uses for thread local storage. If a thread fails to take this step, the system does not clean up the memory until the process exits, leaving unavailable resources hanging around.

5. When the process detaches from the DLL, it releases the TLS index by calling the `TlsFree` function.

EXAMPLE: THE **SHAREMEM** PROGRAM

Listing 8.15, **SHAREMEM.CPP,** is a source-code listing for a sample DLL that uses shared memory. To use the DLL, you call it from a client application—for example, one of the client applications presented in this chapter.

LISTING 8.15 A DLL THAT USES SHARED MEMORY.

```
// sharedll.cpp
// A DLL entry-point function sets up shared memory using
// named file mapping.

#include <windows.h>
#include <memory.h>

#define SHMEMSIZE 4096

static LPVOID lpvMem = NULL; // Shared-memory address.

// LibMain() is the DllEntryPoint function for this DLL.

BOOL LibMain(HINSTANCE hinstDLL,    // DLL module handle.
      DWORD fdwReason,              // Reason called.
      LPVOID lpvReserved) {         // Reserved.

   HANDLE hMapObject = NULL;        // Handle to file mapping.
   BOOL fInit, fIgnore;

   switch (fdwReason) {

// Here the DLL attaches to a process, either when the
// process initializes or the client calls LoadLibrary.

      case DLL_PROCESS_ATTACH:
```

```
        // Create a named file mapping object.

        hMapObject = CreateFileMapping(
            (HANDLE) 0xFFFFFFFF, // Use paging file.
            NULL,                     // No security attributes.
            PAGE_READWRITE, // Read/write access.
            0,            // Size: High 32 bits
            SHMEMSIZE, // Size: Low 32 bits.

            "dllmemfilemap");     // Map-object name
        if (hMapObject == NULL)
            return FALSE;

// The first process to attach initializes memory.

        fInit = (GetLastError() !=
                        ERROR_ALREADY_EXISTS);

// Get a pointer to the file-mapped shared memory.

        lpvMem = MapViewOfFile(
            hMapObject,      // Mapped object.
            FILE_MAP_WRITE, // Read/write access.
            0,               // High offset.

            0,               // Low offset.
            0);              // Map entire file.
        if (lpvMem == NULL)
            return FALSE;

// Initialize memory if this is the first process.

        if (fInit)
            memset(lpvMem, '\0', SHMEMSIZE);

        break;

// The attached process creates a new thread.

    case DLL_THREAD_ATTACH:
        break;
```

```
// The thread of the attached process terminates.

        case DLL_THREAD_DETACH:
            break;

// The DLL now detatches from a process, either when the
// process terminates or when FreeLibrary is called.

        case DLL_PROCESS_DETACH:

// Unmap shared memory from the process's address space.

            fIgnore = UnmapViewOfFile(lpvMem);

// Close process's handle to the file-mapping object.

            fIgnore = CloseHandle(hMapObject);

            break;

        default:
            break;

    }

    return TRUE;
    UNREFERENCED_PARAMETER(hinstDLL);
    UNREFERENCED_PARAMETER(lpvReserved);

}
// This function sets the contents of shared memory.
VOID SetSharedMem(LPTSTR lpszBuf) {
    LPTSTR lpszTmp;

    // Get the address of the shared memory block.

    lpszTmp = (LPTSTR) lpvMem;

    // Copy the null-terminated string into shared memory.

    while (*lpszBuf)
        *lpszTmp++ = *lpszBuf++;
    *lpszTmp = '\0';
```

```
}

// This function gets the contents of shared memory.
VOID GetSharedMem(LPTSTR lpszBuf, DWORD cchSize) {
    LPTSTR lpszTmp;

    // Get the address of the shared memory block.

    lpszTmp = (LPTSTR) lpvMem;

    // Copy from shared memory into the caller's buffer.

    while (*lpszTmp && --cchSize)

        *lpszBuf++ = *lpszTmp++;
                *lpszBuf = '\0';
}
```

HOW THE **SHAREMEM** PROGRAM WORKS

The DLL presented in Listing 8.15 has an entry-point function named `LibMain`. The module definition file for the DLL is named **MYPUTS.DEF**. It contains the following information:

```
LIBRARY myputs
EXPORTS
    myPuts
```

The DLL uses file mapping to map a block of named shared memory into the address space of each process to which the DLL is attached. Each time the DLL attaches to a new process, its entry-point routine calls `CreateFileMapping` to create a file-mapping object. `CreateFileMapping` either creates or opens a named file-mapping object, depending on whether a file-mapping object is already open.

The first process to which the DLL attaches creates the file-mapping object. Subsequent processes open a handle of the existing object. `GetLastError` triggers initialization of the shared memory, because it returns NO_ERROR to the first process and ERROR_ALREADY_EXISTS to subsequent processes.

The Win32 function `MapViewOfFile` maps the file-mapping object into the address space of each process, returning a pointer to the memory. But shared memory is not always mapped to the same address; it can be mapped to a different address in each process. Because the location of shared memory can be different for each process, each process has its own instance of a global variable named `lpvMem`.

The `lpvMem` variable is declared as a global variable to make it available to each function implemented in the DLL. The assumption is that the DLL's global data is not shared. Therefore, each attaching process has its own instance of `lpvMem`.

Shared Data and Module Definition Files

By default, DLL data is not shared. But you can change this default behavior by modifying the DLL's .DEF file. When you execute the DLL, any memory it shares persists only as long as the DLL is attached to a process. In this example, the shared memory is released when the last handle of the file-mapping object is closed.

To create persistent shared memory, a DLL can create a detached process when the DLL attaches to the first process. If this detached process uses the DLL and does not terminate, it has a handle of the file-mapping object that prevents the shared memory from being released.

Summary

There are three ways to write a DLL for a Windows NT program: the Windows 3.x way (for Windows 3.x applications), the Visual C++ 1.0 way (for programs written after the introduction of Visual C++ 1.0 but before the premiere of Visual C++ 4.0), and the MFC 4.0 way (for Windows 95 and Windows NT programs written using Visual C++ 4.0 and version 4.0 of the Microsoft Foundation Class library).

Window 3.x DLLs are clunky but are likely to be around for a long time, so you never know when you'll encounter the need to use one. Similarly, if you ever encounter a Visual C++ 1.0 DLL, a knowledge of how it works will come in handy.

This chapter focuses mainly on MFC 4.0 DLLs, which come in several varieties, and showed you how to use them in your applications. MFC 4.0 DLLs can be generated automatically by AppWizard and can be used to create and export MFC extension classes (classes that automatically become extensions to Microsoft's MFC library). When you create a Microsoft extension class in an extension DLL, any MFC-compatible application loaded into a computer system's memory can use your class.

This chapter concludes with an example application that shows how to create an MFC extension DLL using AppWizard and how to access that class from a Visual C++ program.

CHAPTER NINE

INTERPROCESS COMMUNICATIONS

Two of the most important features of Windows NT are buried so deeply within Microsoft's on-line documentation that many programmers scarcely know of their existence and have no idea how to use them. Two such features—file mapping and pipes—are extremely important, because they allow processes to communicate and to share data. In other words, they provide Windows NT with a capability called *interprocess communications*.

File mapping allows multiple processes to map virtual pages to the same physical memory so that the processes can share data. The shared memory is backed up either by a user-specified file or by a system *swap file*, a special file maintained by the system to ensure file coherence during file-mapping operations.

Pipes are another mechanism that Windows NT processes can use to share data. When an application has set up a pipe, processes send information through the pipe by writing to it in the same way they would write to a file. Similarly, processes retrieve information from the pipe by reading from it in the same way they would read from a file. The sending and receiving processes can be running on the same machine or on different computer systems.

Pipes allow threads and processes to share data. In fact, because Windows NT does not give processes direct access to each other's data, pipes and file mapping are the only data-sharing mechanisms that are available to Windows NT processes.

There are two general categories of pipes: *named* pipes and *anonymous* pipes. As you might guess, the difference is that named pipes have names, and anonymous pipes do not. When a process needs to connect to a named pipe, it executes a function that uses the name of the pipe as a parameter. To connect to an anonymous pipe, a process uses a handle.

This Chapter's Example Programs

To illustrate the use of file mapping, this chapter presents a pair of example programs named MAPFILE and MAPSHARE. The MAPFILE program shows how file mapping can simplify the manipulation of long disk files. MAPSHARE shows how processes can use file mapping to share files stored on a disk.

To demonstrate the use of pipes, three sample programs are included. ANON is a console application that demonstrates the use of anonymous pipes. CLIENT and SERVER let users chat with each other in real time using named pipes, either on a single computer or on a pair of workstations connected across a network.

Figure 9.1 shows the output of the CLIENT program.

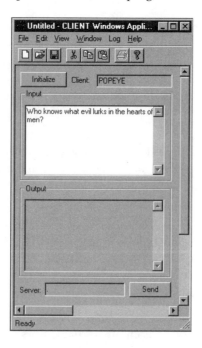

FIGURE 9.1 THE CLIENT PROGRAM'S SCREEN DISPLAY.

File Mapping

File mapping is an elegant and ingenious mechanism for solving a problem that often arises in applications that create and manipulate files. In such applications, it's sometimes difficult to decide whether you should access a file in the traditional way—by opening it, reading it, and closing it—or in a more complex but more efficient way. One alternative that can conserve memory and provide more control over a file is to open the file and use a buffering algorithm to read from and write to different parts of the file.

When you can't decide between the direct approach and the buffering approach, Windows NT doesn't restrict you to either one. Instead, it offers the best of both worlds by providing memory-mapped files. In an application that uses memory-mapped files, you can allocate a memory address to a file that is stored on a disk as if the file were stored in memory. Then you can access data in the file using the file's assigned address in the same way you access data that is actually stored in RAM. In other words, once a file on a disk has been mapped into memory, you can access it as if it were sitting in memory, at the precise address it has been mapped to.

File mapping is so simple that the first time you hear about it, you may feel that you've missed something. Rest assured that you haven't. To use file mapping, an application need not buffer any data or perform any file I/O whatsoever. You just assign an address to a disk file and start using the data in the file in your program. It's that easy. Moreover, Windows NT places few restrictions on the use of memory-mapped files except for limiting the size of any individual memory-mapped file to 2 GB.

How to Use File Mapping

To use file mapping in an application, follow three basic steps:

1. Open a file by calling `CreateFile`. When you call `CreateFile`, you create a kernel object called a *file object*. Kernel objects—as explained in Chapter 6, "Processes"—are objects managed by the Windows NT kernel. In file-mapping operations, a file object represents an open instance of a file, device, directory, or volume.

2. If a file-mapping object for the file being mapped does not yet exist, create one by calling `CreateFileMapping`. If a file-mapping object for the file does exist, call `OpenFileMapping` to open it. A *file-mapping object* is a kernel object that describes the full size of the file being mapped as well as its access rights. When a file-mapping object has been created, other processes can pass its name to `OpenFileMapping` to obtain a handle to the mapped object.

3. Create a *file view* of your mapped file in an address space by calling `MapViewOfFile`. A file view is a block of virtual address space that a process uses to access a mapped file's contents.

These three steps are described in more detail in "Using File Mapping" later in this chapter.

Quicker than the Eye

Although it appears that file mapping takes place instantaneously, data in a memory-mapped file is not actually mapped into memory at the same time memory-mapping instructions are issued. Instead, much of the file input and output necessary to implement memory mapping is cached to improve system performance. You can override this behavior and force the system to perform disk transactions immediately by calling the Win32 function `FlushViewOfFile`.

WAYS TO USE FILE MAPPING

There are three basic ways to use memory-mapped files in a Windows NT application:

✦ The most common use for memory-mapped files is to access data stored on disk using a memory address in the same way the data would be accessed if it were actually in memory.

✦ You can also use memory-mapped files in the same way Windows NT uses them: as an easy-to-manage method for loading and executing applications and DLLs.

✦ Finally, memory-mapped files can be used to share blocks of data in memory between multiple processes. Windows NT uses this technique internally when a user tries to run a second instance of an application.

Memory-mapped files shouldn't be used to share writeable files over a network, because Windows NT cannot guarantee coherent views of the data. If someone's computer updates the contents of the file, someone else's computer might have the original data in memory and will not see that the information has changed.

MANAGING LONG FILES WITH FILE MAPPING

Memory-mapped files are especially useful when the files being mapped are very large. That's because a process can open a file for memory mapping but delay the mapping until later. Subsequently, when the process needs to access information in the file, the process does not have to map the entire file into memory at one time. Instead, it can map in a smaller portion of the file, called a *view*.

It takes few physical resources simply to open a file for memory mapping, even if the file is extremely large. Therefore, opening a large file for memory mapping requires almost no overhead. Once a file is opened for memory mapping, smaller views of the file can be mapped into the process's address space just before I/O is performed. Then the process can access locations in the views that have been opened without loading the entire file into memory.

Another advantage of using memory-mapped files is that the system performs all data transfers needed for memory-mapping operations using pages of data. (A page of data is system-specific; it consumes 4KB on a 386/Pentium-based computer.) The virtual memory manager bases all its operations on memory pages, so it can perform memory-mapping operations very efficiently. In memory-mapped file operations, disk read and write instructions are limited to sequences of pages. When small reads or writes are needed, they are effectively cached into one larger operation, reducing the number of times a hard-disk read-write head has to move.

As an illustration of how file mapping can make the management of long files more memory-efficient, suppose you were writing an application that had to reverse the order of the bytes in an extremely long file (not a practical example, perhaps, but one that is useful for illustration). If you wanted to carry out this task in a traditional way, you could simply allocate enough memory to hold a copy of the complete file and then copy the entire file into that memory space in reverse order. That would be a fairly efficient way of doing things, but it would require a large amount of memory, because both files would have to reside in memory at the same time.

To perform this task in a more memory-efficient way, there are several file-buffering schemes you should use. Some require more memory than others, and some are more efficient than others. But the simplest, most efficient, and most elegant technique of all is file mapping.

To reverse the contents of a file using file mapping, all you have to do is to open the file and then tell Windows NT to reserve a region of virtual address space for it. Essentially, Windows NT then pretends that the first byte of the file is mapped to the first byte of the address space that has been allocated. That means you can access the region of virtual memory as if it were actually the first byte of the file. In fact, if there happens to be a single zero byte at the end of the file, you can simply call the C run-time function `strrev` to reverse the data in the file.

The most remarkable advantage of this kind of operation is that Windows NT manages all the file caching for you. You don't have to allocate any memory, load file data into memory, write data back to the file, or free any memory blocks at all. Unfortunately, the possibility that an interruption, such as a power failure, might corrupt data still exists with memory-mapped files.

A sample program named MAPFILE, presented later in this chapter, shows how Windows NT applications can use file mapping to simplify the management of long files.

SHARING DATA THROUGH FILE MAPPING

In Windows NT, memory-mapped files are more than just an easy method for managing memory. They are also the only mechanism that multiple Windows NT processes can use to share data stored in memory. As you may recall from Chapter 2, "Underneath Windows NT," every Windows NT process runs in its own protected area of memory and cannot directly access data stored in memory areas owned by other processes. However, if a process is granted access to a disk file, it can map that file (or a portion of it) into its own address space. This technique preserves the integrity of the private address spaces that are allocated to processes, while providing processes with access to shared files.

Figure 9.2 shows how memory-mapped files are used in Windows NT.

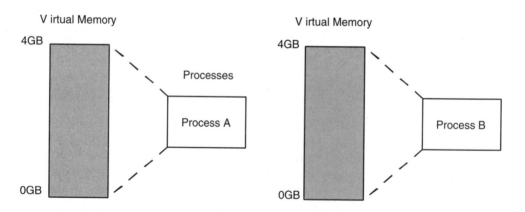

FIGURE 9.2 USING MEMORY-MAPPED FILES.

Windows NT provides a good example of how file mapping can be used to share data. To understand this example, consider what happens when you start an application under Windows NT. As soon as the application starts, Windows NT calls `CreateFile` to open the application's **.EXE** file. The system then calls `CreateMappingFile` to create a file-mapping object, a kernel object that describes the full size of the file being mapped as well as its access rights. Next, the system calls `MapViewOfFile` to create a file view of the newly created process. The result is that the application's .EXE file is mapped into the process's address space.

When this file-mapping operation is complete, Windows NT sets the instruction register of the user's CPU to point to the first byte of executable code in the mapped view of the file. Only then does the CPU start executing the code.

If the user runs a second instance of the same application, Windows NT checks to see whether a file-mapping object already exists for the desired application. If a file-mapping object does exist, the system doesn't create a new file object or file-mapping object. Instead, Windows NT maps a view of the file a second time, this time in the context of the newly created process's address space. The system accomplishes this trick by mapping the same disk file into two address spaces simultaneously. This scheme saves memory, because both processes share the same pages in physical memory that contain code to be executed.

SHAREMEM, the second sample program presented in this chapter, demonstrates how Windows NT applications use file mapping to share data.

USING FILE MAPPING TO SHARE MEMORY

Still another use for file mapping is to let multiple processes share memory. When you want to use file mapping for this purpose, you create a file-mapping object by calling `CreateFileMapping`, which has this syntax:

```
HANDLE CreateFileMapping(HANDLE hFile, LPSECURITY_ATTRIBUTES lpsa,
    DWORD fdwProtect, DWORD dwMaximumSizeHigh,
    DWORD dwMaximumSizeLow, LPSTR lpName);
```

If you call `CreateFileMapping` to create a file-mapping object and the system discovers that a file-mapping object with the same parameters already exists, the function does not create a new object. Instead, it returns a process-relative handle that identifies the file-mapping object that already exists. To determine whether `CreateFileMapping` has created a new file-mapping object, call `GetLastError`, a function that is normally called to determine why a Windows API function call has failed. But sometimes, as in the case of `CreateFileMapping`, you can call `GetLastError` if a function call has succeeded. If `GetLastError` returns ERROR_ALREADY_EXISTS after `CreateFileMapping` has been called, it means that `CreateFileMapping` has returned a handle to an existing file-mapping object. If you don't want to use this existing object, you can close its handle.

In-Memory File Mapping

CreateFileMapping has several parameters that can be used in special ways for particular purposes. For example, if you want to let two processes share data that is not already stored in a disk file, you can pass the value (HANDLE) 0xFFFFFFFF as the hFile parameter to CreateFileMapping. That argument tells Windows NT that you want to perform in-memory file mapping—that is, that you want the system to treat a region of memory as though it were a file. Windows NT responds by setting aside a region of bytes in the disk's paging file to accommodate your request. The amount of memory is determined by the dwMaximumSizeHigh and dwMaximumSizeLow parameters of CreateFileMapping.

When you have created an in-memory file-mapping object and have mapped a view of it into a process's address space, you can use it as you would any region of memory. If other processes want to share the same memory, they can't call CreateFileMapping in the hope that Windows NT will find the handle of the existing file-mapping object and return it. If another process calls CreateFileMapping, passing (HANDLE) 0xFFFFFFFF as the hFile parameter, Windows NT assumes that the process wants to create an in-memory file mapping.

One technique for sharing an in-memory file mapping is for the process creating the in-memory file-mapping object to assign it a name. Then the process wanting to share the object can call OpenFileMapping using the same name. This is the same procedure that was discussed earlier.

When each process sharing the file-mapping object no longer needs to access it, CloseHandle is called. Only after all the processes have closed their handles to the file-mapping object does Windows NT delete the object from its memory. In the case of in-memory mapped files, the committed pages in the paging file are also decommitted at this time.

Reading and Writing Mapped Files

It is important to remember that when multiple processes map the same file-mapping object into their respective address spaces, all the processes are accessing the same data. This must be the case, because only one physical page of memory is involved; it has simply been mapped to different address spaces for each process accessing it.

But because the file-mapping mechanism is based on the use of ordinary files, it is possible for a process to call CreateFile to open the same file that another process has mapped and then read from and write to the file using ReadFile and WriteFile. The ReadFile and WriteFile functions use memory buffers, and this situation has the potential for causing problems.

Suppose, for example, that a process calls `ReadFile` to read part of a file into a buffer. Then suppose that the process modifies the data and writes it back by calling `WriteFile`. Finally, suppose that the file-mapping object that is being used is not aware of any of this. If all those things happened, the coherency of the file could be destroyed.

To prevent this kind of disaster, `CreateFile` has an `fdwShareMode` parameter that you can set to zero for files that are to be memory-mapped. By placing a zero value in `fdwShareMode`, you can tell `CreateFile` that your process should have exclusive access to the file and that no other process should be allowed to open it.

FILE MAPPING AND VIRTUAL MEMORY

To understand how Windows NT uses file mapping, it helps to have an overall understanding of how Windows NT manages virtual memory. That topic was covered briefly in Chapter 2, "Underneath Windows NT," but we'll go into a little more detail here.

It is important to understand that in Windows NT, there is no relationship between the amount of physical memory that is available on the user's system and the memory addresses that the operating system assigns. In fact, Windows NT routinely allocates memory addresses that don't even exist on the user's system.

Under Windows NT, this is not a dangerous practice at all, because the memory addresses that the operating system allocates are not physical memory addresses, but virtual memory addresses. These virtual memory addresses are managed by a system service called the virtual memory manager, or VMM.

How Windows NT Allocates Virtual Memory

No matter how much physical memory is available in a system, the Windows NT virtual memory manager provides each executing process with access to four gigabytes of virtual-memory address space by caching files to and from disk. Within the 4 GB of virtual memory locations that Windows NT allocates to each process residing in RAM, Windows NT reserves the upper 2 GB of virtual memory for itself. The lower 2 GB of virtual memory space in the block is allocated to the process.

Figure 9.3 shows how each process uses the 4 GB of addresses that it receives from the Win32 operating system.

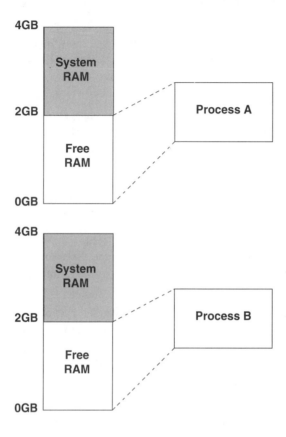

FIGURE 9.3 HOW PROCESSES USE VIRTUAL-MEMORY ADDRESSES.

Chips Ahoy

....

The Win32 paging system works especially well with Intel X86 and Pentium processors because X86/Pentium page directories and page tables fit neatly into 4KB pages, with space for exactly 1,024 (1KB) entries on each page. This means that a single page table can reference 4MB (1,024 x 4,096 bytes) of data. In turn, a single page directory can reference 4GB (1,024 x 4MB) of data. So page tables and page directories can be easily paged to and from disk to obtain additional physical memory or to make more physical memory available when it is needed by other processes. Conversions are a little more complex for systems that use larger pages—for example, 8KB pages—but they're still not very difficult to figure out.

Using Virtual Memory

The Win32 API provides six functions for managing virtual memory. The most common use for these functions is to allocate, deallocate, and protect large blocks of memory. For the most part, the Win32 virtual-memory system operates transparently, working quietly in the background to handle your application's memory needs. However, the Win32 API does provide the following functions to give you more direct control over virtual-memory operations:

✦ The `VirtualAlloc` and `VirtualFree` functions allocate and deallocate virtual memory.

✦ The `VirtualLock` and `VirtualUnlock` functions lock and unlock virtual memory.

✦ The `VirtualProtect` and `VirtualProtectEx` functions set the level of protection of a block of virtual memory (see "Page Table Entries" later in this chapter). The special feature of `VirtualProtectEx` is that can be used on processes other than the calling process.

✦ To obtain information about the virtual memory available to a process, an application can call `VirtualQuery` or `VirtualQueryEx`. The `VirtualQueryEx` function can retrieve information about virtual memory owned by processes other than the calling process.

Page Maps

To implement file mapping, the virtual memory manager uses a mechanism called *page maps*. When a thread accesses a virtual address that has been paged to disk, the VMM loads the information back into memory from disk. Then the VMM—with the help of the host hardware—translates, or *maps*, the virtual addresses of the executing processes into physical addresses where data is stored. Paging data to disk frees RAM that is not currently being accessed, enabling applications and the NT system to use it for more immediate needs.

When a page is moved into or out of physical memory, the VMM records the operation by updating page maps that are associated with all executing processes. By using this paged memory-management system, Windows NT creates a flat 32-bit address space that can be freely accessed without any need to distinguish between near and far pointers. Furthermore, the Win32 disk-caching mechanism is built into the system, so every application in memory automatically has access to as much as 4 GB of virtual memory space, with the addition of any special disk-caching software.

Memory mapping also ensures that individual processes do not corrupt each others' memory or (even worse!) overwrite memory used by the operating system.

How Win32 Translates Virtual Addresses

To the Win32 operating system, a virtual address is just a placeholder for information that is used to find an actual physical address. Windows NT divides every 32-bit virtual address into three parts, as shown in Figure 9.4.

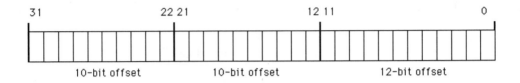

FIGURE 9.4 WINDOWS NT 32-BIT VIRTUAL ADDRESS.

As Figure 9.4 illustrates, the lowest-order part of a virtual address is 12 bits long; each of the other parts contains 10 bits. Each of the three parts is used independently as an offset into a page of memory. When a virtual address has been retrieved, it can be used to locate any address on any page that is being used by any process (application or task) stored in memory.

Page Directories, Page Tables, and Page Frames

Virtual addressing works in Windows NT in the following way: Each process has a single, unique page of memory called a *page directory*. A page directory, like any other page in memory, is simply a one-page block of RAM (4 KB on a 386/Pentium-based system). On a Pentium computer, a page directory holds exactly 1,024 four-byte values called *page-directory entries*, or PDEs.

Each PDE is used to locate another page of memory called a page table. Every page table contains exactly 1,024 four-byte values called *page table entries*, or PTEs. Finally, each PTE points to a page of memory called a *page frame*.

When Win32 has retrieved a virtual address, it uses the highest-order 10 bits in that virtual address to locate a page directory. Next, the second-highest 10-bit offset is used to locate a page table. Then the low-order 12 bits of the virtual address are used as an index to a page frame.

Using these three layers of indirection, Win32 can locate any page of memory owned by any process. Every page in the system is either a page directory, a page table, or a page frame.

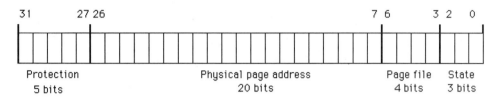

FIGURE 9.5 PAGE TABLE ENTRY.

Page Table Entries

As shown in Figure 9.5, a page table entry is divided into four parts:

+ The five highest-order bits are used as a flag that specifies a level of protection for the page. This flag can be one of three constants: PAGE_NOACCESS, PAGE_READONLY, or PAGE_READWRITE.

+ If the page associated with the page table entry is stored in memory, the 20 next highest bits specify the page's physical address. A 20-bit address can access 4 GB of memory, so a page table entry can be used to locate any address within the virtual 4 GB address range that Windows NT assigns to each process.

+ Windows NT uses 16 disk-based page files to cache memory. The second-highest four bits in a page table entry specify the page file that can be used to cache the page of memory referenced by the page table entry.

+ The lowest-order three bits in a page table entry are used to specify the protection level of the page that is referenced. A page can be in one of three states: present in memory (P), written to but not saved (D), and in transition (T). Win32 sets the value of these three bits automatically as pages are moved into and out of memory. You can also set these values manually.

Figure 9.6 shows what the memory in a Windows NT computer looks like to an executing application.

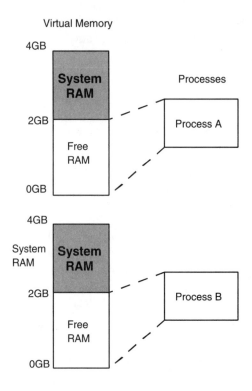

Virtual Memory

FIGURE 9.6 HOW PROCESSES SEE VIRTUAL MEMORY.

Another important fact about Windows NT memory management is that when you start an NT application, the operating system doesn't actually load the program's complete executable file into memory. Instead, it reserves a portion of the application's 2GB address space for it's executable and maps the executable file into that reserved space. Once this file-mapping process is complete, NT takes care of all the paging, buffering, and caching that is needed to run the application.

To illustrate how all this works, suppose that when your application starts executing, it tries to jump to the address of an instruction that hasn't yet been loaded into memory. Windows NT immediately recognizes that the page of code containing the target of the jump has not yet been read into RAM. This isn't satisfactory at all, so the operating system does what it needs to do to make your code work. It finds an available page of physical memory, discarding or paging out other code or data if necessary, and loads the page of code containing your application's jump target into RAM. Then the OS maps that page into your application's virtual address space and jumps to the specified instruction.

The OS repeats this operation each time your application tries to access code or data that has not yet been loaded into physical memory.

Sir Speedy

To make the strategy shown in Figure 9.2 work as fast and as efficiently as possible, Windows does not allocate physical memory when it is requested, but only when it is accessed. As a result, a large amount of physical memory can be allocated almost as quickly as a small amount. In fact, it takes about the same amount of time to allocate 5MB of memory as it takes to allocate 500KB.

To make this kind of speed possible, Windows NT uses asynchronous threads (see Chapter 7, "Multithreading") to allocate, free, and swap memory as needed.

USING FILE MAPPING

Now that you have an overall picture of how Windows NT uses virtual memory, we can return to the topic of file mapping and take a closer look at `CreateFile` and other Win32 file-mapping functions used in Windows NT.

As mentioned earlier in this chapter, a file mapping operation can be broken down into three basic steps:

1. Open a file by calling `CreateFile`.
2. Create a file-mapping object by calling `CreateFileMapping`.
3. Map your file into an address space by calling `MapViewOfFile`.

To unmap a view of a file, call `UnmapViewOfFile`. To flush a mapped file view, call `FlushViewOfFile`. To close a file that has been used for memory mapping, call `CloseHandle`. Each of these calls is discussed separately under the headings that follow.

Calling the CreateFile Function

You have seen that the first step in mapping a file is to open the file by calling `CreateFile`:

```
HANDLE CreateFile(LPCSTR lpFileName, DWORD dwDesiredAccess,
    DWORD dwShareMode, LPSECURITY_ATTRIBUTES lpSecurityAttributes,
    DWORD dwCreationDisposition, DWORD dwFlagsAndAttributes,
    HANDLE hTemplateFile);
```

We examined the syntax of `CreateFile` in considerable detail in Chapter 6, "Processes," so there is no need to repeat here everything we said. But `CreateFile` has two parameters—`dwDesiredAccess` and `dwShareMode`—that are particularly important in file-mapping operations, so we'll take a closer look at them.

The `dwDesiredAccess` parameter specifies what kind of access other processes should have to the file being created. You can specify read access, write access, or both read and write access. To specify both read and write access, set the `dwDesiredAccess` parameter to both GENERIC_READ and GENERIC_WRITE, ORing the two values together.

If you set `dwDesiredAccess` to zero, Windows NT does not allow other processes to share the file you are creating. If a process tries to open the file, the system returns the constant value INVALID_HANDLE_VALUE.

The `dwSharedMode` parameter to `CreateFile` specifies how the file being created can be shared. Setting `dwSharedMode` to the constant FILE_SHARE_READ flag instructs the system to allow other processes to open the file for reading only. Later, if any other process tries to open the file for writing, Windows NT returns a file handle of INVALID_HANDLE_VALUE. If you set `dwShareMode` to FILE_SHARE_WRITE, the system allows the file to be opened for writing only. To allow both reading and writing, specify both FILE_SHARE_READ and FILE_SHARE_WRITE, ORing the two values together.

When a call to `CreateFile` is successful, the function returns a file handle. Otherwise, the constant INVALID_ HANDLE_VALUE is returned.

CALLING THE CREATEFILEMAPPING FUNCTION

To create a file-mapping object, use the handle returned by `CreateFile` to call `CreateFileMapping`. This is the syntax of the `CreateFileMapping` function:

```
HANDLE CreateFileMapping(HANDLE hFile, LPSECURITY_ATTRIBUTES
lpFileMappingAttributes, DWORD flProtect, DWORD dwMaximumSizeHigh, DWORD
dwMaximumSizeLow, LPSTR lpszMapName);
```

`CreateFileMapping` expects the following parameters:

+ **hFile**. A file handle that has been returned by an earlier call to `CreateFile`.

+ **lpFileMappingAttributes**. A pointer to a SECURITY_ATTRIBUTES structure. (See Chapter 6, "Processes," for a description of the SECURITY_ATTRIBUTES structure.) If `lpFileMappingAttributes` is NULL, your file-mapping object is created with a default security descriptor, and the resulting handle is not inherited.

+ **flProtect**. Specifies the kind of protection desired for the file view when the file is mapped. This parameter can have three values: PAGE_READONLY, PAGE_ READWRITE, or PAGE_WRITECOPY. PAGE_READONLY provides read-only access to the committed region of pages. PAGE_READWRITE provides read-write access to the committed region of pages. PAGE_WRITECOPY provides copy-on-write access to the committed number of pages. This means that the Windows NT memory manager uses the CPU's paging feature to share memory wherever possible and duplicates a page of memory in RAM only when absolutely necessary.

+ **dwMaximumSizeHigh** and **dwMaximumSizeLow**. These two parameters specify the size of the mapped file in bytes. Because files used under Windows NT can be larger than 4 GB and because 32 bits can't specify anything larger than 4 GB, CreateFileMapping concatenates these two parameters to calculate the mapped file's size. The dwMaximumSizeHigh parameter specifies the high-order 32 bits, and dwMaximumSizeLow specifies the low-order 32 bits. For files that are 4 GB or less, dwMaximumSizeHigh will always be 0 (zero). By using these two parameters together, Windows NT can process files as large as 18 billion gigabytes.

+ **lpszMapName**. This parameter is a zero-terminated string that assigns a name to the file-mapping object that is being created. This name can be used to share the object with another process.

When a call to CreateFileMapping is successful, the function returns a handle to a file-mapping object. If CreateFileMapping fails, its return value is NULL.

CALLING THE MAPVIEWOFFILE FUNCTION

When you have created a file-mapping object, you call MapViewOfFile to map the file into an address space. This is the syntax of the MapViewOfFile function:

```
LPVOID MapViewOfFile(HANDLE hFileMappingObject,
    DWORD dwDesiredAccess, DWORD dwFileOffsetHigh,
    DWORD dwFileOffsetLow, DWORD dwNumberOfBytesToMap);
```

The parameters that you pass to MapViewOfFile are as follows:

+ **hFileMappingObject**. Identifies the handle of a file-mapping object. This can be a handle returned by an earlier call to either CreateFileMapping or OpenFileMapping (discussed later).

✦ **dwDesiredAccess.** Specifies the type of access to the file view that will be allowed and, by extension, the protection of the pages mapped by the file. FILE_MAP_WRITE provides both read and write access; FILE_MAP_READ provides read-only access. FILE_MAP_COPY provides copy-on-write access, which means that the memory manager uses the CPU's paging capability to share memory wherever possible.

✦ **dwFileOffsetHigh** and **dwFileOffsetLow.** These two parameters specify the high-order 32 bits and the low-order 32 bits of the file offset where mapping is to begin. The combination of the high and low offsets must specify an offset within the file that matches the system's memory allocation granularity, or the function fails. The offset must be a multiple of the allocation granularity. Use the `GetSystemInfo` function, which fills in the members of a SYSTEM_INFO structure, to obtain the system's memory allocation granularity.

✦ **dwNumberOfBytesToMap.** Specifies the number of bytes of the file to map. If `dwNumberOfBytesToMap` is zero, the entire file is mapped.

CALLING THE OPENFILEMAPPING FUNCTION

If a file-mapping object for the file being mapped has already been created, you can open it by calling `OpenFileMapping`. (If a file-mapping object for the file does not yet exist, you must call `CreateFileMapping` instead of `OpenFileMapping` to create a new file-mapping object.)

The syntax of the `OpenFileMapping` function is as follows:

```
HANDLE OpenFileMapping(DWORD dwDesiredAccess, BOOL bInheritHandle, LPCTSTR lpName);
```

The following parameters are expected by `OpenFileMapping`:

✦ **dwDesiredAccess.** Specifies the access that will be allowed to the file-mapping object being opened. The value passed in this argument can be FILE_MAP_WRITE (read-write access), FILE_MAP_READ (read-only access), FILE_MAP_ALL_ACCESS (same as FILE_MAP_WRITE), and FILE_MAP_COPY (copy-on-write access).

✦ **bInheritHandle.** Specifies whether the returned handle is to be inherited by a new process during process creation. A value of TRUE means that the new process inherits the handle.

✦ **lpName.** Points to a string that names the file-mapping object to be opened. If there is an open handle to a file-mapping object by this name and if the security descriptor on the mapping object does not conflict with the **dwDesiredAccess** parameter, the open operation succeeds.

UNMAPPING A VIEW OF A FILE

You can unmap a view of a file by calling UnmapViewOfFile, which has this syntax:

```
BOOL UnmapViewOfFile(LPVOID lpBaseAddress);
```

The only parameter expected by UnmapViewOfFile is lpBaseAddress, which must hold a value returned by an earlier call to MapViewOfFile.

```
LPBYTE lpByte = (LPBYTE) MapViewOfFile(hFileMapping,
   FILE_MAP_WRITE,            // Desired access
   0, 1 * 1024 * 1024 * 1024, // Starting byte in file
   1 * 1024 * 1024 * 1024);   // NumBytes to map
```

Windows NT provides the UnmapViewOfFile function because things can get messy when multiple processes share files. UnmapViewOfFile frees the address space reserved for file views and flushes any changes back to disk.

FLUSHING A VIEW OF A FILE

The UnmapViewOfFile function forces all the modified data in memory to be written back to the disk image. If you want to make sure that your updates have been written to disk, you can force Windows NT to write all the modified data back to the disk image by calling FlushViewOfFile, which has this syntax:

```
BOOL FlushViewOfFile(LPVOID lpBaseAddress,
   DWORD dwNumberOfBytesToFlush);
```

The FlushViewOfFile function expects the address of a mapped view (returned by the previous call to MapViewOfFile) as a parameter. FlushViewOfFile also expects the number of bytes to write to disk. If you call FlushViewOfFile and none of the data has been changed, the function simply returns without writing anything to the disk.

CLOSING A FILE

You close a file-mapping object by calling CloseHandle. You also call CloseHandle to close the file-mapping object's corresponding file handle.

```
CloseHandle(hFileMapping);
CloseHandle(hFile);
```

In each of these cases, `CloseHandle` is an ordinary Windows API `CloseHandle` function that takes a handle as a parameter. The handle passed to the first of the two preceding calls is a handle to a file-mapping object, and the handle passed to the second call is a file handle.

THE MAPVIEWOFFILEEX FUNCTION

In the same way that the `VirtualAlloc` function allows you to suggest an initial address to reserve address space, the `MapViewOfFileEx` function suggests that a file be mapped into a particular address. `MapViewOfFileEx` can be useful when you are using memory-mapped files to share data with other processes. The syntax of `MapViewOfFileEx` is the same as that of `MapViewOfFile`:

```
LPVOID MapViewOfFileEx(HANDLE hFileMappingObject,
    DWORD dwDesiredAccess, DWORD dwFileOffsetHigh,
    DWORD dwFileOffsetLow, DWORD dwNumberOfBytesToMap,
    LPVOID lpBaseAddress);
```

All the parameters expected by `MapViewOfFileEx` are identical to those required by `MapViewOfFile`, with the single exception of the last parameter, `lpBaseAddress`. In the `lpBaseAddress` parameter, you specify a target address for the file being mapped. The address must be on an even allocation granularity boundary (usually 64 KB); otherwise, `MapViewOfFileEx` returns `NULL`, indicating an error.

If Windows NT cannot map your file at the location you specify—usually because the file is too large and would overlap another reserved address space—the `MapViewOfFileEx` function fails and returns `NULL`. `MapViewOfFileEx` does not attempt to locate another address space that can accommodate the file. If you specify `NULL` as the `lpBaseAddress` parameter, `MapViewOfFileEx` behaves exactly the same as `MapViewOfFile`.

EXAMPLE: REVERSING THE BYTES IN A FILE

This chapter's first sample program, MAPFILE, shows how file mapping can simplify the management of large files, conserving memory in the process. More specifically, MAPFILE shows how a Windows NT application can use memory-mapped files to reverse the contents of an ANSI text file.

MAPFILE is a Visual C++ adaptation of a C-language program named FILEREV that was written by Jeffrey Richter and published in an article in Microsoft Systems Journal.

MAPSHARE, the second sample program you'll encounter in this chapter, is a Visual C++ adaptation of a second C-language program (named MMFSHARE), also by Richter, from the same article.

MAPFILE lets you specify the name of an existing file by typing the name in a dialog box. The program then makes a copy of the file so that the original file won't be rendered unusable by a reversal of its contents. MAPFILE then opens the duplicate file by calling `CreateFile`.

To reverse the contents of the file it has copied, MAPFILE calls the C run time function `strrev`. Because `strrev` is written to work with C-style strings, which end with a zero byte, MAPFILE increases the length of the file by one character and appends a zero byte to the file. Finally, the program reverses the order of the string with a call to `strrev`:

```
strrev(lpvFile);
```

MAPFILE also takes an extra step that is required when the order of a text file is reversed. In a text file, each line is terminated by a return character (`'\r'`) followed by a newline character (`'\n'`). But when MAPFILE calls `strrev` to reverse the order of the characters in the file, the file's newline characters also are reversed. To make it possible for the modified text file to be opened in a text editor, MAPFILE converts every occurrence of the `'\n\r'` character sequence back to its original `'\r\n'` order. This operation is accomplished in a segment of code that reads as follows:

```
lpch = strchr(lpvFile, '\n');

while (lpch != NULL) {
    *lpch++ = '\r';    // Change the '\n' to '\r'.
    *lpch++ = '\n';    // Change the '\r' to '\n'.

    // Find the next occurrence.
    lpch = strchr(lpch, '\n');
}
```

When MAPFILE has modified the file, the program's final task is to remove the zero byte that it added earlier. This job requires the repositioning of a file pointer and a call to the `SetEndOfFile` function:

```
SetFilePointer(hFile, dwFileSize, NULL, FILE_BEGIN);
SetEndOfFile(hFile);
```

EXAMPLE: SHARING MEMORY WITH FILE MAPPING

The MAPSHARE sample program shows how multiple Windows NT processes can use file mapping to exchange data. Because the program requires the running of two separate processes, you must start two instances of the program. When each instance is invoked, it creates a dialog box that contains an edit box in which you can type a message.

To copy data from one instance of MAPSHARE to another instance using file mapping, type a message in the text box that appears in any dialog box. Then click on the button labeled **Map Data**. MAPSHARE calls `CreateFileMapping` to create a 4-KB in-memory file. It names the file object it has created MAPSHAREDATA. The program then puts a view of the file into the process's address space and copies the data from the Edit control into the memory-mapped file.

After MAPFILE has copied its data from one process to another, the program unmaps the view of the file, disables the **Map Data** button, and enables the **Close Data Mapping** button. This button closes your file-mapping object by destroying the data contained within it.

Understanding Pipes

As noted at the beginning of this chapter, a pipe is a conduit through which information travels from one process to another. On local computers using Windows NT, processes and threads can transmit information to each other and retrieve information from each other through pipes. On Windows NT workstations connected on a network, pipes can transmit information across the network and retrieve information from remote machines.

Because Windows NT processes are not designed to share data even when they are running on the same machine, pipes can be a handy mechanism for threads and processes when they need to share data. In fact, because the NT operating system does not give processes access to each other's data, pipes are the only data-sharing mechanism that is available to Windows NT processes.

Pipes are easy to use for this purpose because they work much like files. When an application has set up a pipe, processes can send information through the pipe by writing to it, in the same way they would write to a file. Similarly, processes can retrieve information from the pipe by reading from it, in the same way they would read from a file. Pipes work the same way when they send information across a network. And they are as easy to use on networked computers as they are on a local machine.

One benefit of using pipes for network communications is that they are protocol-independent. When an application sends information across a network through a pipe, the pipe does not know or care what network protocol is being used. To an application using pipes, it does not matter whether a pair of computers that need to share information are using NetBEUI, TCP/IP, or some other protocol. This means that the application does not have to be written with any particular variety of networking in mind; all the application has to do is to set up a pipe and start using it in the same way it would use the pipe to exchange information between threads or processes on a single machine.

Another advantage of using pipes is that they are compatible with LAN Manager applications and installations.

A Windows NT pipe, like a physical pipe that a plumber installs, has two ends; information goes in one end and comes out the other. Information can flow through an electronic pipe in only one direction at a time. But the flow of information can be quickly reversed, so it can appear that the pipe is moving data in both directions simultaneously.

Because information can flow through a pipe in either direction, pipes can be divided into two categories: one-way pipes and two-way pipes. A one-way pipe has one end that is read-only and one end that is write-only. In contrast, both ends of a two-way pipe can be either read from or written to.

Pipes can also be categorized in another way. You will often hear pipes referred to as either anonymous pipes or named pipes. As you might guess, the difference between named pipes and anonymous pipes is that named pipes have names, whereas anonymous pipes do not. Processes can access anonymous pipes by name. To access an anonymous pipe, a process needs to use a process handle.

To create a pipe, a process calls the Win32 function `CreatePipe`. Because anonymous pipes can be accessed using handles, they are convenient mechanisms for transferring data between related processes—that is, between a parent process and a child process or between two child processes of the same parent process.

A process creates a child process by calling `CreateProcess`. In Chapter 6, "Processes," `CreateProcess` was called to create a console process. As you'll see in this chapter, `CreateProcess` can also create GUI-style Windows processes.

Every anonymous pipe has at least two handles: one that can be used to transmit data, and one that can be used to receive data. A process with a handle to one end of an anonymous pipe can communicate with a process that has a handle to the other end. Because handles are used to access anonymous pipes, processes on both ends of an anonymous pipe must be running on the same computer. Anonymous pipes cannot be used for network communications. To use the pipe mechanism for network communications, you must use a named pipe.

A named pipe has a name assigned by a process. To create a named pipe, a process calls the Win32 function `CreateNamedPipe`, passing the name of the pipe as a parameter. Once a named pipe is created, it can be accessed by any process running on the same computer, or by a process running on any computer that is connected over a network (security permitting). To access a named pipe, a process must provide the name of the pipe to the process that created the pipe. This requirement adds an extra measure of security to information that is shared through pipes.

ANONYMOUS PIPES

Because of complexities that can arise in managing handles, anonymous pipes are not as useful for transferring data between unrelated process, and they cannot be used for communications over a network.

The `CreatePipe` function creates an anonymous pipe and returns two handles: one to the read end of the pipe and a second one to the write end. The process that creates the pipe can provide other processes with the handles they need to access the pipe. Communications through the pipe can then begin.

To write to an anonymous pipe, a process calls the Win32 function `WriteFile`. To read from an anonymous pipe, a process calls `ReadFile`. An anonymous pipe exists until the ends of the pipe are closed.

Following is the syntax of the `CreatePipe` function:

```
BOOL CreatePipe(PHANDLE phRead, PHANDLE phWrite,
    LPSECURITY_ATTRIBUTES lpsa, DWORD cbPipe);
```

If the `CreatePipe` call succeeds, it returns `TRUE`; otherwise, it returns `FALSE`.

When you call `CreatePipe`, you pass the function four variables:

+ **phRead**. A pointer to a handle. In this parameter, `CreatePipe` supplies the address of a handle to the read end of an anonymous pipe.

+ **phWrite**. A pointer to a handle. In this field, `CreatePipe` supplies an address of a handle to the write end of an anonymous pipe.

+ **lpsa**. A pointer to the SECURITY_ATTRIBUTES structure that provides a security descriptor for the pipe and tells whether the pipe's handles are inherited. If this parameter is NULL, the pipe has a default security descriptor and its handles are not inherited.

+ **cbPipe**. Specifies the number of bytes reserved for the pipe. This value is just a suggestion; the system uses it to calculate an appropriate buffer size. If you pass a zero value in this parameter, the system uses a default value.

In addition to providing security-related information, the SECURITY_ATTRIBUTES structure referenced by `lpsa` specifies whether the handles of the pipe are to be inherited. If the `bInheritHandle` member of the structure is TRUE, the handles are inherited. (As noted under the next heading, "How Anonymous Pipes Work," you can call `DuplicateHandle` to override this behavior.)

When an application has created an anonymous pipe by calling `CreatePipe`, the application can retrieve the read and write handles through the pointers that it has placed in the `phRead` and `phWrite` parameters. Subsequently, the process that called `CreatePipe` can write to the new pipe by calling `WriteFile` and can read from it by calling `ReadFile`.

For examples of how these functions are used, see "Calling the `ReadFile` Function" later in this chapter.

How Anonymous Pipes Work

Anonymous pipes are most often used to transmit information between a parent process and a child process. The parent process can set up communications with a child process by creating a pair of one-way anonymous pipes: one to carry information from the parent process to the child process, and a second pipe to carry information from the child process to the parent process.

When a parent process needs to set up communications with a child process using anonymous pipes, the parent process typically redirects the standard input and output handles of the child process by calling `GetStdHandle` and `SetStdHandle`. To understand how this works, it is necessary to have an understanding of standard input and output handles.

In a Windows NT application, as in most applications, a process normally accepts what is known as standard input (STDIN) from the keyboard and writes standard output (STDOUT) to the screen. However, an application can direct a process to accept input from a source other than STDIN or to write its output to a destination other than STDOUT. To determine the source of its standard input and the destination of its standard output, every process maintains a pair of handles: a standard input handle and a standard output handle. An application can determine what a process's current standard input handle is by calling `GetStdHandle`. A process can set a process's standard input or standard output handle by calling `SetStdHandle`.

The GetStdHandle Function

`GetStdHandle` takes the constant value STD_INPUT_HANDLE or the constant value STD_OUTPUT_HANDLE as a parameter.

Following is the syntax of the `GetStdHandle` function:

```
HANDLE GetStdHandle(DWORD nStdHandle)
```

`GetStdHandle` returns a handle specified by the `fdwDevice` parameter. Possible values for `fdwDevice` are as follows:

+ STD_INPUT_HANDLE. A standard input handle.
+ STD_OUTPUT_HANDLE. A standard output handle.
+ STD_ERROR_HANDLE. A standard error handle.

The SetStdHandle Function

To redirect a process's standard input handle, an application can call `SetStdHandle` with a STD_INPUT_HANDLE parameter. To redirect a process's standard output handle, an application can call the `SetStdHandle` function with a STD_OUTPUT_HANDLE parameter.

The syntax of the `SetStdHandle` function is as follows:

```
BOOL SetStdHandle(DWORD IDStdHandle, HANDLE hHandle)
```

`SetStdHandle` returns a Boolean value: TRUE if the function succeeds, and FALSE if it does not.

Parameters passed to `SetStdHandle` are as follows:

+ **IDStdHandle.** Specifies the handle to be set. Possible values are the same as those listed for the `GetStdHandle` function's `fdwDevice` parameter under the previous heading.
+ **hHandle.** Supplies the handle to be used as the standard input, standard input, or standard error handle.

Using the GetStdHandle and SetStdHandle Functions

An application can obtain the current input and output handles of a process by calling `GetStdHandle`. With the `SetStdHandle` function, an application can force a process to accept input from an anonymous pipe instead of from the keyboard and to write its output to an anonymous pipe rather than to the screen.

When a pair of anonymous pipes is created and configured, the parent process can communicate with the child process through the pipes, as shown in Figure 9.7.

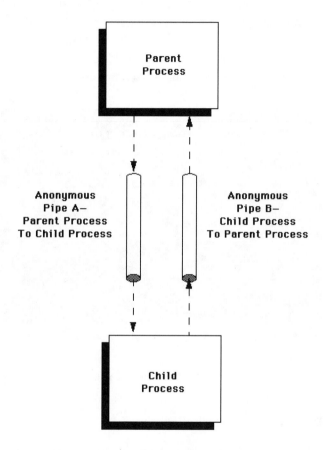

FIGURE 9.7 ANONYMOUS PIPES.

The ANON program in this chapter's directory on the accompanying disk demonstrates how processes communicate with each other through anonymous pipes. The ANON program creates a parent process and a child process and then redirects the child process's standard input and standard output to a pair of anonymous pipes.

When you execute the ANON program, a parent process reads a short text file from a disk. Then the parent process writes the file to a child process through an anonymous pipe. When the child process receives the file, it writes the file to an output pipe using redirected STDOUT. The parent process then uses its own standard output, which has not been redirected, to write the file to the screen. By reading and writing a file in this roundabout fashion, ANON shows how anonymous pipes can be used in a Windows NT program.

Figure 9.8 shows the ANON program's screen display.

FIGURE 9.8 THE ANON PROGRAM'S SCREEN DISPLAY.

CREATING A PAIR OF ANONYMOUS PIPES

The source code of the ANON program, listed in the **PARENT.CPP** and **CHILD.CPP** files on the accompanying disk, sets up a pair of anonymous pipes that can be used to transfer information between a parent process and a child process.

Redirecting the Output of a Child Process

Figure 9.9 shows how an anonymous pipe can be created to carry information from a child process to a parent process.

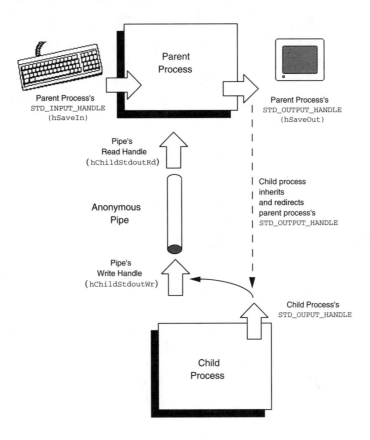

Parent
Process

Parent Process's
STD_INPUT_HANDLE
(hSaveIn)

Parent Process's
STD_OUTPUT_HANDLE
(hSaveOut)

Pipe's
Read Handle
(hChildStdoutRd)

Child process
inherits
and redirects
parent process's
STD_OUTPUT_HANDLE

Anonymous
Pipe

Pipe's
Write Handle
(hChildStdoutWr)

Child Process's
STD_OUPUT_HANDLE

Child
Process

FIGURE 9.9 ANONYMOUS PIPE FROM A CHILD PROCESS TO A PARENT PROCESS.

In the ANON program, an anonymous pipe is created in **PARENT.CPP**. These are the steps carried out in that file to create an anonymous pipe:

1. The parent process's current standard output handle is stored in a HANDLE variable named hSaveStdout. This step is taken because the procedure shown in Figure 9.9 requires the temporary use of the parent process's STD_OUTPUT_HANDLE. When the child process and its anonymous pipe link have been created, the parent process's original STD_OUTPUT_HANDLE is restored.

    ```
    hSaveStdout = GetStdHandle(STD_OUTPUT_HANDLE);
    ```

2. When the parent process's STD_OUTPUT_HANDLE has been saved, CreatePipe is called to create an anonymous pipe that will transmit the child process's standard output to the parent process. Note that the child

process has not yet been created. Every anonymous pipe has a read handle and a write handle. When the child process used in ANON is created, the program writes its standard output to hChildStdoutWr, the write handle of the anonymous pipe that is created in this step. The parent process can then read the information from hChildStdoutRd, the pipe's read handle. This is the call that creates an anonymous pipe:

```
if (! CreatePipe(&hChildStdoutRd, &hChildStdoutWr, &saAttr, 0))
    ErrorExit("CreatePipe function failed\n");
```

3. SetStdHandle is called to redirect the STD_OUTPUT_HANDLE of the child process to hChildStdoutWr, the write handle of the newly created anonymous pipe. Actually, the standard output handle that is redirected in this step is the parent process's STD_OUTPUT_HANDLE. However, this handle is temporarily being used to redirect the standard output of the child process that is being created. Specifically, it is being used to create a unique standard output handle that can be inherited by a child process—which still has not yet been created.

   Recall that in Step 1, the parent process's original STD_OUTPUT_HANDLE was saved in hSaveOut. After a child process has been created and its standard input and output handles redirected to a pair of anonymous pipes, the parent process can still access its original STD_OUTPUT_HANDLE through the hSaveOut handle. When the child process is created, the parent process and the child process will have different standard output handles.

   This is the statement that calls SetStdHandle to redirect the child process's standard output to the write handle of the anonymous pipe:

```
if (! SetStdHandle(STD_OUTPUT_HANDLE, hChildStdoutWr))
    ErrorExit("Redirecting STDOUT failed");
```

In the three preceding steps, an anonymous pipe was created to carry information from a child process to a parent process. In the next set of steps, you will learn how to create another anonymous pipe that can carry information from a parent process to a child process, moving the information in the opposite direction. When this second pipe is set up, you will be ready to create the child process that uses both pipes.

Redirecting the Input of a Child Process

You've seen how the ANON program creates an anonymous pipe that carries information from a child process to a parent process. In the next set of steps, you'll see how to create another anonymous pipe that carries information from a parent process to a child process.

In the previous set of steps, a parent process's STD_OUTPUT_HANDLE was redirected so that a unique standard output handle could be inherited by a child process. The same technique is used to redirect the standard input handle of a child process to a different anonymous pipe. (Remember, anonymous pipes are one-way pipes, so it takes two of them to make a two-way communication link.)

The procedures for redirecting a child process's standard input are exactly the reverse of those listed under the preceding heading. In the next set of steps, the child process's standard input handle is redirected to the pipe's read handle rather than the other way around. The anonymous pipe that will be created next works like the one shown in Figure 9.10.

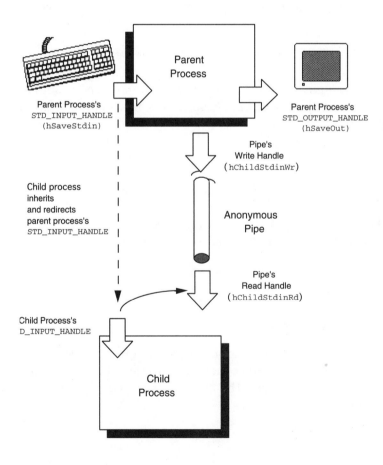

FIGURE 9.10 ANONYMOUS PIPE FROM A PARENT PROCESS TO A CHILD PROCESS.

Creating a Second Anonymous Pipe

To create an anonymous pipe like the one shown in Figure 9.10, the child process borrows its parent process' STD_INPUT_HANDLE. Then this handle is redirected to the read handle of an anonymous pipe. Next, the child process is created, inheriting its parent process's standard input and output handles, which have been redirected. When all these operations are complete, the parent process and the child process can communicate with each other in both directions through a pair of anonymous pipes.

These are the steps for creating an anonymous pipe that carries information from a parent process to a child process:

1. The parent process calls `GetStdHandle` to save its current standard input handle in a variable named `hSaveStdin`:

   ```
   hSaveStdin = GetStdHandle(STD_INPUT_HANDLE);
   ```

2. The parent process calls `CreatePipe` to create an anonymous pipe. As in the previous set of steps, `CreatePipe` returns handles to the read and write ends of the pipe:

   ```
   if (! CreatePipe(&hChildStdinRd, &hChildStdinWr,
   &saAttr, 0))
       ErrorExit("Stdin pipe creation failed\n");
   ```

3. The parent process calls `SetStdHandle` to redirect the child process's standard input to the read handle of the anonymous pipe:

   ```
   if (! SetStdHandle(STD_INPUT_HANDLE, hChildStdinRd))
   ErrorExit("Redirecting Stdin failed");
   ```

A PROBLEM OF INHERITANCE

When an application has created a pair of anonymous pipes and has redirected their input and output handles, one more operation must be carried out before the application creates the child process that uses the pipes. This operation is necessary because of the inheritance characteristics of Win32 objects.

As you have seen, a parent process creates a child process by calling CreateProcess. But first, the parent process calls GetStdHandle and SetStdHandle to redirect the child process's standard input and output handles to the pipe's read and write handles.

This procedure works because CreateProcess creates processes that inherit their parent processes' standard input and output handles. However, a problem arises when a child process inherits its parent process's handle to the write end of an anonymous pipe. In the ANON program, the handle that is affected by this problem is the hChildStdinWr handle shown in Figure 9.10.

The problem arises because data is written to an anonymous pipe as a stream of bytes. The recipient reads the information by calling ReadFile. Normally, in communications transmitted through anonymous pipes, no protocol is used to let the reading and writing processes know how many bytes are read. Reading simply continues until all write handles to the pipe are closed. Then ReadFile terminates and returns FALSE.

When a child process's standard input and output are redirected to create an anonymous pipe, the parent process must ensure that the child process does not inherit the parent process's handle to the write end of the pipe. When a child process inherits a handle to the write end of an anonymous pipe, both processes wind up with an open write handle to the pipe. Then, when ReadFile is called to read from the pipe, the function cannot terminate because both processes have an open handle to the write end of the pipe. That prevents the read operation from terminating and brings communications to a halt.

To ensure that this does not happen, you must provide the child process with a noninheritable copy of the parent process's write handle. You create a noninheritable copy of a parent process's standard output handle by calling DuplicateHandle, which creates noninheritable copies of handles. Then the parent process calls CloseHandle to close its original, inheritable handle. This technique leaves the parent process with a pipe handle that it can use, but that the child's process does not inherit.

To provide a child process with a noninheritable handle to the write end of an anonymous pipe, follow these steps:

1. When you have created an anonymous pipe from a parent process to a child process and you have the child process's standard input, call DuplicateHandle. In the following code sequence, which appears in **PARENT.CPP**, DuplicateHandle is called to create a noninheritable handle named

hChildStdinWrDup. When the call is complete, hChildStdinWrDup is a noninheritable copy of hChildStdinWr:

```
fSuccess = DuplicateHandle(GetCurrentProcess(), hChildStdinWr,
    GetCurrentProcess(), &hChildStdinWrDup, 0,
    FALSE, // not inherited
    DUPLICATE_SAME_ACCESS);
if (! fSuccess)
    ErrorExit("DuplicateHandle failed");
```

2. The parent process closes the inheritable write handle:

```
CloseHandle(hChildStdinWr);
```

3. The parent process creates the child process that it will communicate with through its new anonymous pipes:

```
if (! CreateChildProcess())
    ErrorExit("Create process failed");
```

4. The parent process's original standard input and output handles are restored:

```
if (! SetStdHandle(STD_INPUT_HANDLE, hSaveStdin))
    ErrorExit("Re-redirection of Stdin failed.\n");
if (! SetStdHandle(STD_OUTPUT_HANDLE, hSaveStdout))
    ErrorExit("Re-redirection of Stdout failed.\n");
```

When this procedure is complete, the parent process calls ReadFile to read from the pipe. This enables the parent process to read the data written to standard output by the child process.

When a child process is created and its anonymous pipes are configured, the anonymous pipes work like the pipes shown in Figure 9.11. Then the pipes can be used for communication between the parent process and the child process, as shown in the diagram.

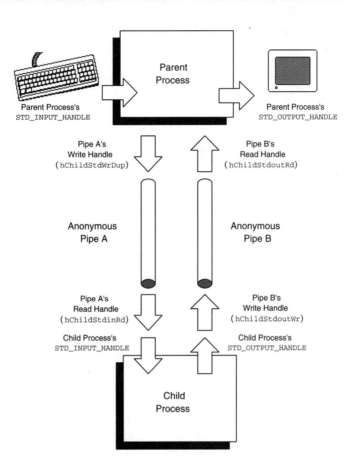

FIGURE 9.11 ANONYMOUS PIPES WHEN CONFIGURATION IS COMPLETE.

The receiving process continues to read from the pipe until all write handles to the pipe are closed. This ordinarily occurs when the child process calls `CloseHandle` or terminates, which automatically closes all handles.

USING ANONYMOUS PIPES

In the ANON program, as you have seen, this statement calls `CreatePipe` to create an anonymous pipe:

```
if (! CreatePipe(&hChildStdoutRd, &hChildStdoutWr, &saAttr, 0))
    ErrorExit("CreatePipe function failed\n");
```

When this statement is executed in **PARENT.CPP,** `CreatePipe` places in `hChildStdoutRd` a handle to the child process's standard output. The `saAttr` parameter is a pointer to a SECURITY_ATTRIBUTES structure, and the zero parameter at the end of the function's parameter list requests the system to assign a default length to the pipe created by the call.

When `CreatePipe` has redirected the child process's standard input and standard output in this fashion, the child's parent process starts communicating with the child process through the pipe.

Calling the ReadFile Function

Following is the syntax of the `ReadFile` function:

```
BOOL ReadFile(HANDLE hFile, LPCVOID lpBuffer,
    DWORD nNumberOfBytesToRead, LPDWORD lpNumberOfBytesRead,
    LPOVERLAPPED lpOverlapped);
```

`ReadFile` can read data from any object, including a pipe, that has Windows NT handles just as if the object were a file. `ReadFile` starts reading data at the position specified by the file pointer `lpBuffer`. When the read operation is complete, `ReadFile` advances the file pointer to point to the byte in the file that will be the first byte of the next read operation—unless the file handle was created with the overlapped attribute (see "Handling Multiple CLIENT Processes" later in this chapter). If the file handle was created for overlapped I/O (see "Named Pipe Modes" later in this chapter), the application is responsible for adjusting the position of the file pointer after the read.

If `ReadFile` is successful, it returns TRUE. Otherwise, it returns FALSE.

These are the parameters that are passed to `ReadFile`:

+ **hFile.** Identifies the file to be read. The file handle must have been created with the GENERIC_READ flag set.

+ **lpBuffer.** Points to the buffer that receives the data that is read from the file.

+ **nNumberOfBytesToRead.** Specifies the number of bytes to be read from the file.

+ **lpNumberOfBytesRead.** Points to the number of bytes read when the call returns.

+ **lpOverlapped.** Points to an OVERLAPPED structure that specifies values needed for overlapped read and write operations. Overlapped operations are supported by named pipes but not by anonymous pipes. In a `ReadFile` call that is made to read an anonymous pipe, a `NULL` value should be passed to this argument. For more information on overlapped I/O operations, see "Named Pipe Modes" later in this chapter.

Calling the WriteFile Function

To write to an anonymous pipe, a process passes the pipe's write handle to `WriteFile`, which returns when it has written a specified number of bytes to the pipe. If the pipe's buffer is full and bytes remain to be written, `WriteFile` does not return until some other process or thread reads from the pipe, freeing more buffer space.

Following is the syntax of the `WriteFile` function:

```
BOOL WriteFile(HANDLE hFile, CONST VOID *lpBuffer,
    DWORD nNumberOfBytesToWrite, LPDWORD lpNumberOfBytesWritten,
    LPOVERLAPPED lpOverlapped);
```

`WriteFile` can write data from any object, including a pipe, that can be handled like a file. `WriteFile` starts writing data at the position specified by the file pointer `lpBuffer`. When the write operation is complete, `WriteFile` advances the file pointer to point to the byte in the file that will be the first byte of the next write operation—unless the file handle was created with the overlapped attribute (see "Named Pipe Modes" later in this chapter). If the file handle was created for overlapped I/O, the application is responsible for adjusting the position of the file pointer after the write.

If `WriteFile` is successful, it returns TRUE. Otherwise, it returns FALSE.

These are the parameters that are passed to the `WriteFile` function:

+ **hFile.** Identifies the file to be written to. The file handle must have been created with the GENERIC_READ flag set.

+ **lpBuffer.** Points to the buffer containing the data to be written to the file.

+ **nNumberOfBytesToWrite.** Specifies the number of bytes to be written to the file.

+ **lpNumberOfBytesWritten.** Points to the number of bytes written when the call returns.

+ **lpOverlapped.** Points to an OVERLAPPED structure that specifies values needed for overlapped read and write operations. Overlapped operations are supported by named pipes but not by anonymous pipes. In a `WriteFile` call that is made to read an anonymous pipe, a `NULL` value should be passed to this argument.

How a Parent Process Calls ReadFile and WriteFile

In the ANON example program, the parent process calls `ReadFile` to read the contents of a text file stored on a disk. Then the parent process calls `WriteFile` to write the file to an anonymous pipe. The code sequence that calls both functions is in **PARENT.CPP**:

```
// Read from a file and write its contents to a pipe.

for (;;) {
    if (! ReadFile(hInputFile, chBuf, BUFSIZE, &dwRead, NULL) ||
        dwRead == 0) break;
    if (! WriteFile(hChildStdinWrDup, chBuf, dwRead,
        &dwWritten, NULL)) break;
}
```

How a Child Process Calls ReadFile and WriteFile

When the parent process in the ANON program has written a message to a file, the child process calls `ReadFile` to read the message. The child process then calls `WriteFile` to return the same message to its parent process. The code sequence in which the child process calls `ReadFile` and `WriteFile` is in **CHILD.CPP**:

```
for (;;) {
        // Read from standard input.
        fSuccess = ReadFile(hStdinRd, chBuf, BUF_SIZE, &dwRead,
            NULL);

        if (! fSuccess || dwRead == 0)
            break;

        // Write to standard output.
        fSuccess = WriteFile(hStdoutWr, chBuf, dwRead,
            &dwWritten, NULL);
        if (! fSuccess)
            break;
}
```

Other Examples

In the SERVER example program on the accompanying disk (examined in more detail in the next section, "Named Pipes"), the `WriteFile` function is called in the following code sequence:

```
if (clients[i].live) {
    retCode = WriteFile (clients[i].hPipe, buffer, strlen(buffer),
        &bytesWritten, &clients[i].overlap);
...
```

The SERVER program appears in a loop that checks to see whether any clients are connected (the clients are listed in an array named clients[n]). If a connected client is found, the program calls WriteFile to transmit the client a message through a named pipe.

In the CLIENT program, which is also examined in the "Named Pipes" section, WriteFile is called to write to a named pipe:

```
// Write the string to the pipe.
if (hPipe == NULL)
    MessageBox("Is the server started?", "Can't find server!",
        MB_OK | MB_ICONQUESTION);
else {
    retCode = WriteFile (hPipe, cOutputString, BUF_SIZE,
        &bytesWritten, &OverlapWrt);
    if (!retCode) {
        lastError = GetLastError();

        // If there is an IO_PENDING error, wait until
        // the event completes successfully.
        if (lastError == ERROR_IO_PENDING)
            WaitForSingleObject (hEventWrt, (DWORD)-1);
}
```

Named Pipes

A named pipe is a one-way or two-way pipe that has a name assigned by a process. Processes can address a named pipe by its name rather than through a handle. For this reason, unrelated processes, which cannot easily access each other's handles, can communicate more easily through named pipes than through anonymous pipes.

Named pipes can perform both one-way and two-way communications, and, unlike anonymous pipes, they can be used for network communications.

THE CREATEPIPE AND CREATENAMEDPIPE FUNCTIONS

In applications that use named pipes, there are two kinds of processes: server processes and client processes. As noted in Chapter 10, "Networking Windows NT," Windows NT processes communicate over a network using the Windows NT protocol suite. Figure 9.12 shows how network communications can take place through named pipes. Notice the named pipe at the bottom of the diagram.

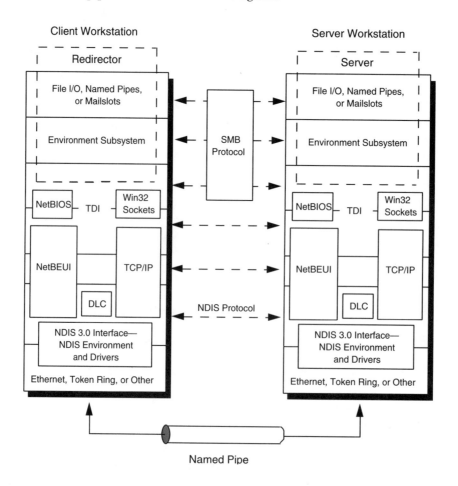

FIGURE 9.12 NETWORK COMMUNICATIONS THROUGH A NAMED PIPE.

Processes running on the same computer can also communicate through named pipes. On a local machine, a server process creates a named pipe by calling `CreateNamedPipe`. A client process on a local machine can create a named pipe by calling `CreateFile` or can connect to an existing named pipe by calling `ConnectNamedPipe`.

Figure 9.13 shows how local server and client processes can communicate through named pipes.

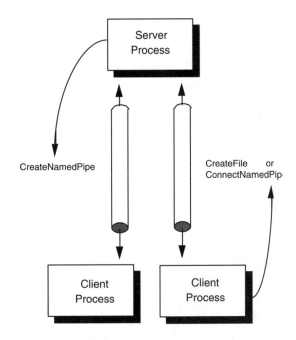

FIGURE 9.13 LOCAL COMMUNICATIONS THROUGH NAMED PIPES.

When a server process creates a named pipe by calling `CreateNamedPipe`, the server process supplies a name for the pipe. Other processes, both local and remote, can then use the pipe to communicate with the process that has created the pipe. However, they can refer to the pipe only by its name, so they must be supplied with the name of the pipe before they can access it.

A server process can create any number of instances of the same named pipe. All instances of a named pipe share the same pipe name, but each instance has its own supply of named-pipe buffers and handles, and each instance provides a separate pipeline for client-server communications. When a client process calls `CreateFile` or `CallNamedPipe`, supplying the name of an existing pipe, the client process is connected to an instance of the pipe. Thus, multiple client processes—local or remote—can use different instances of the same named pipe simultaneously.

Any client process (subject to security checks) can access a named pipe. In fact, it is easy for client processes to communicate locally or across a network through named pipes. A server process can quickly and easily create a named pipe by calling `CreateNamedPipe`. Client processes can then simply call `CreateFile` or `ConnectNamedPipe` to connect to an instance of the named pipe.

CREATING NAMED PIPES

`CreateNamedPipe` creates an instance of a named pipe and returns a handle that can be used to access the pipe. A named pipe server can call `CreateNamedPipe` to create the first instance of a new pipe and to establish the pipe's attributes. A server can also call `CreateNamedPipe` to create a new instance of an existing named pipe. An instance of a named pipe is always deleted when the last handle to the instance of the named pipe is closed.

Client processes do not create named pipes by calling `CreateNamedPipe`. When a client process needs to create a named pipe, or needs to connect to an existing named pipe, it calls `CreateFile` or `CallNamedPipe`. These two functions are described later in this chapter.

Synchronous and Asynchronous I/O

When you create a named pipe by calling `CreateNamedPipe`, you specify a number of modes that affect the use and behavior of the pipe. Some of these modes can be set differently for each handle to a pipe, and others must be the same for all handles to a pipe. For example, in the `fdwOpenMode` parameter to `CreateNamedPipe`, a process can specify whether overlapped mode or write-through mode is enabled for the pipe. Overlapped mode is often referred to as asynchronous mode; another name for write-through mode is synchronous mode.

When write-through mode is enabled, functions that write data to a named pipe do not return until the data has been transmitted across the network and has been placed in the pipe's buffer on the remote computer. When write-through mode is not enabled, the system enhances the efficiency of network operations by buffering data until a minimum number of bytes accumulate or until a maximum time elapses.

Only named pipes support asynchronous, or overlapped, operations. Anonymous pipes do not. By overlapping pipe transmission, an application can speed processing through named pipes by allowing background processing during transmission of data. For more details about the overlapped and synchronous I/O modes, see "Handling Multiple Client Processes" later in this chapter.

Because anonymous pipes do not support overlapped read and write operations, the `ReadFileEx` and `WriteFileEx` functions—which are reserved for use with overlapped operations—cannot be used with anonymous pipes. When you use `ReadFile` or `WriteFile` with an anonymous pipe, the `lpOverLapped` parameter is ignored.

Syntax of the CreateNamedPipe Function

Following is the syntax of the `CreateNamedPipe` function:

```
HANDLE CreateNamedPipe(LPCSTR lpszPipeName, DWORD fdwOpenMode,
    DWORD fdwPipeMode, DWORD nMaxInstances, DWORD cbOutBuf,
    DWORD cbInBuf, DWORD dsTimeout, LPSECURITY_ATTRIBUTES
lpsa);
```

If a call to `CreateNamedPipe` succeeds, the function returns a handle to the server end of the named pipe that it creates. If the call does not succeed, it returns the constant INVALID_HANDLE_VALUE. If the `nMaxInstances` parameter is greater than the constant PIPE_UNLIMITED_INSTANCES, the return value is ERROR_INVALID_PARAMETER. If a call to `CreateNamedPipe` returns an error, you can obtain more detailed error information by calling `GetLastError`.

The following parameters are passed to `CreateNamedPipe`:

+ **lpszPipeName**. A pointer to a null-terminated string that uniquely identifies the pipe being created. (Note that if you pass a path name in this parameter, you don't have to be concerned with case, because Windows path names are not case-sensitive.)

+ **fdwOpenMode**. A 32-bit word that specifies the directions in which data can flow through the pipe and specifies the access rights that the client and server have to the pipe. This parameter also tells whether write-through mode is enabled, specifies whether overlapped mode is enabled, and provides security-related properties. (For more about overlapped mode and write-through mode, see "Handling Multiple Client Processes" later in this chapter.)

+ **fdwPipeMode**. Flags that specify the type, read mode, and wait mode of the pipe handle.

+ **nMaxInstances**. Specifies the maximum number of instances that can be created for a pipe.

+ **cbOutBuf.** Specifies the number of bytes to reserve for the pipe's output buffer.

+ **cbInBuf.** Specifies the number of bytes to reserve for the pipe's input buffer.

+ **dsTimeout.** Specifies the pipe's default timeout value, expressed in milliseconds.

+ **lpsa.** Points to the pipe's SECURITY_ATTRIBUTES structure.

Calling CreateNamedPipe in the Example Programs

The SERVER program provided on the accompanying disk demonstrates how a server can communicate with multiple clients via named pipes. The following code sequence, which appears in **SERVER.H**, creates a named pipe by calling CreateNamedPipe:

```
// Create a local named pipe named '\\.\pipe\demo'. The
// period (\.\\) means that it's a local pipe.
hPipe = CreateNamedPipe ("\\\\.\\pipe\\demo",
// Pipe name = 'demo'.
    PIPE_ACCESS_DUPLEX // Two-way pipe.
    | FILE_FLAG_OVERLAPPED, // Use overlapped structure.
    PIPE_WAIT // Wait for messages.
    | PIPE_READMODE_MESSAGE // Specify message mode pipe.
    | PIPE_TYPE_MESSAGE,
    MAX_PIPE_INSTANCES, // Maximum instance limit.
    BUF_SIZE, // Buffer sizes.
    BUF_SIZE,
    TIME_OUT, // Specify time out.
    &sa); // Security attributes.
// ...
```

The parameters passed to CreateNamedPipe in the preceding code fragment are described in the paragraphs that follow.

Pipe Names

Every named pipe must have a name that uniquely distinguishes it from other named pipes. Applications use the names of pipes in calls to the Win32 functions CreateNamedPipe, CreateFile, and CallNamedPipe, which create named pipes, and to the WaitNamedPipe function, which waits for a pipe to become available for connection.

You name a pipe by placing a name of your choice in the `lpszPipeName` parameter of the `CreateNamedPipe` call. The `lpszPipeName` parameter is a string that has this form:

```
\\.\pipe\pipename
```

The `pipename` part of a pipe's name is a full path name that can contain letters, numbers and special characters, but cannot include the backslash character. The maximum length of the `pipename` string is 256 characters. Pipe names are not case-sensitive.

In Windows NT, the path name of a remote computer on a network always begins with a pair of backslashes (\\). A path name that begins with two backslashes and a period (\\.) is interpreted as a local path name rather than a network path name. Thus, if you passed this path name to the `CreateNamedPipe` function:

```
\\.\solar_system\saturn
```

Win32 would look for a directory named **\solar_system** and a file named **\saturn** on your local workstation. In contrast, this path name:

```
\\galaxy\solar_system\saturn
```

would be interpreted as the name of a directory named **\solar_system** and a file named **\saturn** on a remote computer named **\\galaxy**.

In the CLIENT and SERVER programs described in this chapter, the pipe used for communications between the server and its clients is named **demo**. For the sake of simplicity, the name of the pipe is hard-coded into the text of both programs.

In **CLIENTVW.CPP**, the pipe name **demo** is passed to the `CreateNamedPipe` function that creates the pipe:

```cpp
    // Create a local named pipe named '\\.\PIPE\demo'. The
    // period (\.\\) means that it's a local pipe.
    hPipe = CreateNamedPipe ("\\\\.\\PIPE\\demo",
    // Pipe name = 'demo'.
        PIPE_ACCESS_DUPLEX // Two-way pipe.
        | FILE_FLAG_OVERLAPPED, // Use overlapped structure.
        PIPE_WAIT // Wait for messages.
        | PIPE_READMODE_MESSAGE // Specify message mode pipe.
        | PIPE_TYPE_MESSAGE,
```

```
        MAX_PIPE_INSTANCES, // Maximum instance limit.
        BUF_SIZE, // Buffer sizes.
        BUF_SIZE,
        TIME_OUT, // Specify time out.
        &sa); // Security attributes.
// ...
```

When the pipe named **demo** has been read, the client program calls `CreateFile` to connect to the file that the server has created. The name of the pipe is also passed to `CreateFile`, as shown in **CLIENTVW.CPP**:

```
    CString fileString = "\\\\" + m_serverName + "\\PIPE\\demo";
    strcpy(fileName, fileString.GetBuffer(LINE_LEN+NAME_SIZE+2));
    // Call CreateFile() to connect to the named pipe.
    hPipe = CreateFile (fileName, // Pipe name.
        GENERIC_WRITE // Generic access, read/write.
        | GENERIC_READ,
        FILE_SHARE_READ // Read and write access.
        | FILE_SHARE_WRITE ,
        NULL, // No security.
        OPEN_EXISTING, // Fail if not existing.
        FILE_FLAG_OVERLAPPED, // Use overlap.
        NULL); // No template.
// ...
```

In the preceding example, the name of the pipe being accessed is the first parameter that is passed to `CreateFile`. For more information about `CreateFile`, see "The CreateFile Function" later in this chapter.

Named Pipe Modes

When you create a named pipe by calling `CreateNamedPipe`, you specify a number of modes that affect the use and behavior of the pipe. Some of these modes can be set differently for each handle to a pipe, and others are the same for all handles to a pipe.

In the `fdwOpenMode` parameter to `CreateNamedPipe`, a process that can specify overlapped mode or write-through mode is enabled for the pipe that is being created. When write-through mode is enabled, functions that write data to a named pipe do not return until the data has been transmitted across the network and has been placed in the pipe's buffer on the remote computer. When write-through mode is not enabled, the system maximizes the efficiency of network operations by buffering data until a minimum number of bytes accumulate or until a maximum time elapses.

The `ReadFile`, `WriteFile`, `ConnectNamedPipe`, and `TransactNamedPipe` functions can execute either synchronously or as overlapped operations. `ReadFileEx` and `WriteFileEx` can be used only with pipes that have overlapped mode enabled. Anonymous pipes cannot be placed in overlapped mode; if you want your application to use overlapped mode, you must use named pipes.

The flags that enable write-through mode or overlapped mode are as follows:

+ **FILE_FLAG_WRITE_THROUGH.** This flag enables write-through mode. It affects only write operations on byte-type pipes, and only when the client and server processes reside on different computers.

+ **FILE_FLAG_OVERLAPPED.** When this flag is set, overlapped mode is enabled.

When `CreateNamedPipe` is called in the CLIENT program (in **CLIENTVW.CPP**), a FILE_FLAG_OVERLAPPED flag is passed to `CreateNamedPipe`:

```
// Create a local named pipe named '\\.\PIPE\demo'. The
// period (\.\\) means that it's a local pipe.
hPipe = CreateNamedPipe ("\\\\.\\PIPE\\demo",
// Pipe name = 'demo'.
    PIPE_ACCESS_DUPLEX // Two-way pipe.
    | FILE_FLAG_OVERLAPPED, // Use overlapped structure.
    PIPE_WAIT // Wait for messages.
    | PIPE_READMODE_MESSAGE // Specify message mode pipe.
    | PIPE_TYPE_MESSAGE,
    MAX_PIPE_INSTANCES, // Maximum instance limit.
    BUF_SIZE, // Buffer sizes.
    BUF_SIZE,
    TIME_OUT, // Specify time out.
    &sa); // Security attributes.
// ...
```

The write-through mode of a named pipe handle affects the behavior of byte-type pipes (see "Writing Data Using Byte Mode and Message Mode" later in this chapter) when data is transmitted across a network. To enable write-through mode for a named pipe handle, a process sets the FILE_FLAG_WRITE_THROUGH flag when it calls `CreateNamedPipe` to create a server process or calls CreateFile to create a client process. If this flag is not set when `CreateNamedPipe` or `CreateFile` is called, write-through mode is disabled.

When write-through mode is not enabled, efficiency of network operations is increased because data is buffered until a minimum number of bytes have been transmitted or until a maximum time period has elapsed. This increased efficiency makes it possible for multiple write operations to be combined into a single network transmission. It also means that a write operation can be completed successfully when the data is in the outbound buffer but has not been transmitted across the network. A client process can call `SetNamedPipe-HandleState` (see "Other Functions" later in this chapter) to control the number of bytes and the timeout period before transmission for a pipe on which write-through mode is disabled.

When write-through mode is enabled, the transmission across the network is not delayed, and the write operation is not completed until the data is in the pipe buffer on the remote machine. Write-through mode can be useful in applications that require synchronization with every write operation. The system always performs write operations on message-type pipes as if write-through mode were enabled.

Access Modes

There are three access-mode flags that can be used in the `fdwOpenMode` parameter. The same access-mode flag must be specified for each instance of the pipe. The access-mode flags recognized by `fdwOpenMode` are as follows:

+ **PIPE_ACCESS_DUPLEX.** When this flag is enabled, the pipe is bidirectional; both server and client processes can read from and write to the pipe. Thus, the server has the equivalent of GENERIC_READ | GENERIC_WRITE access to the pipe. The client can specify GENERIC_READ, or GENERIC_WRITE, or both, when it connects to the pipe using `CreateFile`.

+ **PIPE_ACCESS_INBOUND.** This flag sets the flow of data in a pipe to go from client to server only. This setting gives the server the equivalent of GENERIC_READ access to the pipe. When this flag is set, the client must specify GENERIC_WRITE access when connecting to the pipe.

+ **PIPE_ACCESS_OUTBOUND.** This flag sets the flow of data in a pipe to go from server to client only. This setting gives the server the equivalent of GENERIC_WRITE access to the pipe. When the PIPE_ACCESS_OUTBOUND flag is set, the client must specify GENERIC_READ access when connecting to the pipe.

The `fdwOpenMode` parameter can also include any combination of three security access mode flags. These flags can be different for different instances of the same pipe. They can be specified without concern for what other `fdwOpenMode` flags have been specified. These three flags are as follows:

✦ **WRITE_DAC.** When this flag is set, the caller has write access to the named pipe's discretionary ACL (access-control list). A discretionary ACL is controlled by the owner of an object and specifies the access of particular users or groups to an object. For example, the owner of a file can use a discretionary ACL to control which users can have access to a file.

✦ **WRITE_OWNER.** Setting this flag gives the caller write access to the named pipe's owner.

✦ **ACCESS_SYSTEM_SECURITY.** This flag grants the caller write access to the named pipe's system ACL. System ACLs are controlled by system administrators. With a system ACL, a system administrator can audit any attempts to gain access to an object.

When `CreateNamedPipe` is called (in **CLIENTVW.CPP**), a PIPE_ACCESS_DUPLEX flag is passed to `CreateNamedPipe`:

```
// Create a local named pipe named '\\.\PIPE\demo'. The
// period (\.\\) means that it's a local pipe.
hPipe = CreateNamedPipe ("\\\\.\\PIPE\\demo",
// Pipe name = 'demo'.
    PIPE_ACCESS_DUPLEX // Two-way pipe.
    | FILE_FLAG_OVERLAPPED, // Use overlapped structure.
    PIPE_WAIT // Wait for messages.
    | PIPE_READMODE_MESSAGE // Specify message mode pipe.
    | PIPE_TYPE_MESSAGE,
    MAX_PIPE_INSTANCES, // Maximum instance limit.
    BUF_SIZE, // Buffer sizes.
    BUF_SIZE,
    TIME_OUT, // Specify time out.
    &sa); // Security attributes.
// ...
```

Writing Data Using Byte Mode and Message Mode

In the `fdwPipeMode` parameter to `CreateNamedPipe`, you can specify how you want data written to the pipe you are creating: as a stream of bytes or as a stream of messages. When you create a PIPE_TYPE_MESSAGE pipe, the system treats each write operation to the pipe as a message unit. When you create a PIPE_TYPE_BYTE pipe, information is transmitted as streams of bytes.

These flags are used only to determine how data is written to a named pipe. Two other flags are used to determine whether data is read from a pipe in message or byte mode. Those flags are described later in this chapter.

If you pass the PIPE_TYPE_BYTE flag to `CreateNamedPipe` or if you do not provide any byte-type or message-type specification, a byte-type pipe is created. If you specify PIPE_TYPE_MESSAGE in the fdwPipeMode parameter, a message-type pipe is created. If you specify zero in `fdwPipeMode` the pipe defaults to byte-type mode. You cannot set the PIPE_TYPE_BYTE when the PIPE_READMODE_MESSAGE flag is set.

The message-mode and byte-mode flags that determine how information is received from a pipe in the read direction are PIPE_TYPE_MESSAGE and PIPE_READMODE_ MESSAGE. The PIPE_TYPE_MESSAGE flag can be used with the PIPE_READMODE_ MESSAGE flag or the PIPE_READMODE_BYTE flag.

Reading Data Using Byte Mode and Message Mode

In the `fdwPipeMode` parameter of `CreateNamedPipe`, you can specify how you want data read from the pipe you are creating: as a stream of bytes or as a stream of messages. When you create a PIPE_READMODE_MESSAGE pipe, the system treats each read operation from the pipe as a message unit. When you create a PIPE_READMODE_BYTE pipe, data is received from the pipe as streams of bytes.

The PIPE_READMODE_MESSAGE and PIPE_READMODE_BYTE flags are used only to determine how information is read from a named pipe. Two other flags (PIPE_TYPE_MESSAGE and PIPE_TYPE_BYTE) are used to determine whether information is written to a pipe in message or byte mode.

When you create a named pipe by calling `CreateNamedPipe`, you specify either PIPE_READMODE_BYTE or PIPE_READMODE_MESSAGE mode, but not both. If you specify zero, the parameter defaults to byte-read mode. PIPE_READMODE_BYTE can be used with either PIPE_TYPE_MESSAGE or PIPE_TYPE_BYTE. PIPE_READMODE_ MESSAGE can be used only if PIPE_TYPE_MESSAGE is also specified.

When a byte-mode pipe handle has been created, a read operation is completed successfully when all available bytes in the pipe are read or when the specified number of bytes is read. For a pipe handle in message-read mode, a `ReadFile` or `ReadFileEx` operation is completed successfully only when the entire message is read. If the specified number of bytes to read is less than the size of the next message, the function reads as much of the message as possible before returning FALSE. In this case, you can read the remainder of the message by making additional calls to `ReadFile` or by calling

ReadFileEx or PeekNamedPipe. PeekNamedPipe returns TRUE after reading a complete or partial message and reports the number of bytes remaining in a partially read message.

When a message-type pipe has multiple unread messages, a read operation using a message-read pipe handle returns after reading one message. An operation using a byte-read handle does not recognize messages; it reads all available bytes up to the specified number.

In the CLIENT program, the PIPE_TYPE_MESSAGE flag is passed to the Create-NamedPipe function:

```
// Create a local named pipe named '\\.\PIPE\demo'. The
// period (\.\\) means that it's a local pipe.
hPipe = CreateNamedPipe ("\\\\.\\PIPE\\demo",
// Pipe name = 'demo'.
    PIPE_ACCESS_DUPLEX // Two-way pipe.
    | FILE_FLAG_OVERLAPPED, // Use overlapped structure.
    PIPE_WAIT // Wait for messages.
    | PIPE_READMODE_MESSAGE // Specify message mode pipe.
    | PIPE_TYPE_MESSAGE,
    MAX_PIPE_INSTANCES, // Maximum instance limit.
    BUF_SIZE, // Buffer sizes.
    BUF_SIZE,
    TIME_OUT, // Specify time out.
    &sa); // Security attributes.
// ...
```

Blocking Mode and Nonblocking Mode

The fdwPipeMode parameter to CreateNamedPipe recognizes a pair of flags that can be used to specify blocking or nonblocking mode. When a pipe with blocking mode enabled is used with the ReadFile, WriteFile, or ConnectNamedPipe function, the function does not return until its operation is completed. Completion occurs when there is no more data to read, when all data is written, or when a client is connected.

When the PIPE_WAIT flag is passed to CreateNamedPipe, blocking mode is enabled. The PIPE_NOWAIT flag enables nonblocking mode.

Although the Win32 API supports nonblocking mode, Microsoft explains that this mode is supported for compatibility with the Microsoft LAN Manager version 2.0 and suggests that it not be used to implement overlapped I/O with named pipes. Instead,

Microsoft suggests that you use overlapped I/O, which enables applications to execute time-consuming `ReadFile`, `WriteFile`, and `ConnectNamedPipe` operations in the background while other operations continue uninterrupted. For more information about overlapped I/O, see "Handling Multiple Client Processes" later in this chapter.

By default, all named pipe handles returned by `CreateNamedPipe` or `CreateFile` are created with blocking mode enabled. A process can enable nonblocking mode for a server's pipe handle by specifying PIPE_NOWAIT when it calls `CreateNamedPipe`. Server and client processes can change a pipe handle's wait mode by specifying either PIPE_WAIT or PIPE_NOWAIT when they call `SetNamedPipeHandleState`. (For more information about `CreateFile` and `SetNamedPipeHandleState`, see "Other Functions" later in this chapter).

The nMaxInstances Parameter

The nMaxInstances parameter specifies the maximum number of instances that can be created for this pipe. The same number must be specified for all instances. Acceptable values range from 1 through the value defined as PIPE_UNLIMITED_INSTANCES. If this parameter is PIPE_UNLIMITED_INSTANCES, the number of pipe instances that can be created is limited only by the availability of system resources.

The first time a process calls `CreateNamedPipe`, the process specifies the maximum number of instances of the pipe that can exist simultaneously. As long as this maximum number is not reached, the server can call `CreateNamedPipe` repeatedly to create additional instances of the pipe.

In the CLIENT program, the nMaxInstances parameter is set to the constant MAX_PIPE_INSTANCES, which is hard-coded to a value of 100:

```
// Create a local named pipe named '\\.\PIPE\demo'. The
// period (\.\\) means that it's a local pipe.
hPipe = CreateNamedPipe ("\\\\.\\PIPE\\demo",
// Pipe name = 'demo'.
    PIPE_ACCESS_DUPLEX // Two-way pipe.
    | FILE_FLAG_OVERLAPPED, // Use overlapped structure.
    PIPE_WAIT // Wait for messages.
    | PIPE_READMODE_MESSAGE // Specify message mode pipe.
    | PIPE_TYPE_MESSAGE,
    MAX_PIPE_INSTANCES, // Maximum instance limit.
    BUF_SIZE, // Buffer sizes.
    BUF_SIZE,
```

```
        TIME_OUT, // Specify time out.
        &sa); // Security attributes.
// ...
```

The cbOutBuf and cbInBuf Parameters

The `cbOutBuf` parameter, set to the constant BUF_SIZE in the CLIENT program, specifies the number of bytes to reserve for the output buffer. The `cbInBuf` parameter, also set to BUF_SIZE in the CLIENT application, specifies the number of bytes to reserve for the input buffer.

These are advisory only. The actual buffer size reserved for each end of a named pipe is either the system default, the system minimum or maximum, or the specified size rounded up to the next allocation boundary.

The dwTimeout Parameter

The `dwTimeout` parameter specifies the default timeout value, in milliseconds, if `WaitNamedPipe` specifies NMPWAIT_USE_DEFAULT_WAIT. Each instance of a named pipe must specify the same value.

The lpsa Parameter

The `lpsa` parameter points to a SECURITY_ATTRIBUTES structure that specifies the security attributes for the pipe. Because named pipes are implemented as a file system and because that file system supports the `lpsa` parameter, `lpsa` will always have an effect when specified.

If `lpsa` is NULL, the pipe is created with a default security descriptor, and the resulting handle is not inherited. Note that access to some security attributes can be granted by setting particular flags in the `fdwOpenMode` parameter.

HANDLING MULTIPLE CLIENT PROCESSES

If you were to describe the simplest of all possible I/O operations using pipes, it would be a sequential scenario: A server process would call `CreateNamedPipe` to create a single instance of a pipe. The server would then connect to a single client, communicate with the client, disconnect the pipe, close the pipe handle, and terminate. If other clients were waiting to be served, the server would connect the sole instance of its pipe to each client, in sequence, connecting and disconnecting the pipe as needed.

With a single-threaded server that operates in this fashion, it is easy to coordinate operations that affect multiple clients, and it is easy to protect shared resources—for example, a database file—from being accessed simultaneously by multiple clients. However, a single-threaded server requires close coordination of overlapped operations so that the application being executed can allocate processor time for handling the simultaneous needs of the clients. More important, a single-threaded server offers poor performance. A better way to communicate with multiple clients simultaneously is to create multiple pipe instances, and that is how pipes operate in most implementations.

In Windows NT programs, there are two basic techniques for servicing multiple pipe instances. A server process can use one of the following strategies:

+ Create multiple threads (or processes) and use a separate thread or process for each instance of the pipe.

+ Overlap operations by providing an OVERLAPPED structure and enabling overlapped I/O in calls to `ReadFile`, `WriteFile`, and `ConnectNamedPipe`. (An application can also overlap operations by calling `ReadFileEx` and `WriteFileEx`, which require a completion routine to be executed when an operation is complete; for details, see "Overlapped I/O" later in this section.)

The Multiple-Thread Approach

Multithreaded servers are easier to implement than single-threaded servers, because, in a multithreaded server, each thread that is created handles communications for only a single client. The system allocates processor time to each thread as needed. But each thread uses system resources, a potential disadvantage for a server that handles a large number of clients.

Other problems can occur if the actions of one client necessitate communications with other clients (as with a network game program, where a move by one player must be communicated to the other players).

Overlapped I/O

When functions run asynchronously—using overlapped I/O—each function that is called can return immediately, even before its operations are finished. This means that time-consuming operations can be executed in the background while the calling thread is free to perform other tasks.

Overlapped operations make it possible for a single process to read and write data to and from other processes simultaneously, and for a single thread to perform simultaneous I/O operations on multiple pipe handles. This makes it possible, in turn, for a single-threaded server process to handle communications with multiple client processes efficiently.

When a named pipe is created with overlapped mode enabled, a thread that performs time-consuming read, write, and connect operations can return immediately, while its I/O operations continue to be processed in the background. This arrangement enables the thread that started the operation to perform other operations while its I/O operations are still being processed. For example, in overlapped mode, a thread can handle simultaneous I/O operations on multiple instances of a pipe or perform simultaneous read and write operations on the same pipe handle. If overlapped mode is not enabled, functions that perform read, write, and connect operations on the pipe handle do not return until the operation is finished.

A minor disadvantage of using overlapped I/O is that the process using the structure must update a file pointer in the buffer (or in a file) manually each time a read or a write operation is performed. The technique for doing this is to modify the offset field of the overlapped structure manually after each read. The offset is obtained from the GetOverlappedResult call.

Enabling Overlapped Operations

A process can enable overlapped operations on a named pipe by setting the FILE_FLAG_OVERLAPPED flag when it creates the pipe's handle. The process can set this flag when it calls CreateNamedPipe to create a server process or when it calls CreateFile to create a client process.

A process that uses overlapped I/O must also provide a pointer to an OVERLAPPED structure when it calls CreateNamedPipe or CreateFile. An OVERLAPPED structure contains information used in asynchronous input and output. It has the following form:

```
typedef struct _OVERLAPPED {
    DWORD Internal;
    DWORD InternalHigh;
    DWORD Offset;
    DWORD OffsetHigh;
    HANDLE hEvent;
} OVERLAPPED;
```

An OVERLAPPED structure has the following members

- ✦ **Internal** and **InternalHigh**. Reserved for use by the operating system.

- ✦ **Offset**. Specifies a file position at which the transfer starts. This position is a byte offset from the start of the file. The calling process sets this member before calling `ReadFile` or `WriteFile`. It is ignored when `ReadFile` or `WriteFile` reads from or writes to named pipes and communication devices.

✦ **OffsetHigh.** Specifies the high word of the byte offset at which to start the transfer. This member is ignored when the functions read from and write to named pipes and communication devices.

✦ **hEvent.** Identifies an event set to the signaled state when the transfer has been completed. The calling process sets this member before calling `ReadFile`, `WriteFile`, `ConnectNamedPipe`, or `TransactNamedPipe`.

If a process does not set the FILE_FLAG_OVERLAPPED flag when it creates a handle, overlapped mode is disabled. After a pipe handle has been created, its overlapped mode cannot be changed. However, the overlapped mode can be different for server and client handles to the same pipe instance.

The `ReadFile`, `WriteFile`, `TransactNamedPipe`, and `ConnectNamedPipe` functions can operate asynchronously only if the specified pipe handle has been created with overlapped mode enabled and if a pointer to an OVERLAPPED structure is specified. If the pipe's OVERLAPPED pointer is NULL, the operation is performed synchronously even if the pipe handle has overlapped mode enabled.

The overlapped-structure approach should be used whenever a pipe is expected to block a read or a write for any significant length of time. In such a case, overlapped I/O allows the thread to return immediately from a read or write to service any other part of the application that is being executed. An overlapped structure should also be used with a named pipe whenever an application expects to perform simultaneous reads and writes.

The CLIENT and SERVER programs provided on the accompanying disk show how an OVERLAPPED structure creates separate threads for each instance of a pipe. If a server process needs to use write-through operations to communicate with more than one client, it must create a separate thread for each client process. This makes it possible for one or more threads to run while other threads are waiting.

CLIENT and SERVER use overlapped I/O to communicate with each other through named pipes. SERVER sets the OVERLAPPED flag when it calls `CreateNamedPipe`, and CLIENT calls `ReadFile` with overlapped I/O enabled when it reads from the pipe. In this code fragment, which appears in **CLIENTVW.CPP**, CLIENT reads asynchronously from a named pipe:

```
// The following do/while loop reads the named pipe until it is
// broken. The ReadFile function uses an overlapped structure.
// When the event handle reports a completed read, this loop
// writes the message to the client dialog's edit panel.
```

```
    do {
        // Read data from the pipe.
        retCode = ReadFile(pClientView->hPipe, inputBuf, BUF_SIZE,
            &bytesRead, &OverlapRd);
// ...
```

For a more detailed explanation of how overlapped I/O works in CLIENT and SERVER, see "The CLIENT and SERVER Programs" later in this chapter.

THE CREATEFILE FUNCTION

As you have seen, a server process creates a named pipe by calling `CreateNamedPipe`. A client process creates a named pipe or connects to an existing instance of a named pipe by calling the Win32 function `CreateFile`. (Alternatively, a client process can call the `CallNamedPipe` function, as explained later in this chapter.)

`CreateFile` can create, truncate, or open a pipe or any other file-type object. If a pipe instance is available when `CreateFile` is called, the function returns a handle to the client end of the pipe instance. If no instances of the pipe are available, a client process can call `WaitNamedPipe` to wait for an instance to become available. Then the process calls `CreateFile` to open the pipe.

Following is the syntax of the `CreateFile` function:

```
HANDLE CreateFile(LPCSTR lpszName, DWORD fdwAccess, DWORD fdwShareMode,
    LPSECURITY_ATTRIBUTES lpsa, DWORD fdwCreate,
    DWORD fdwAttrsAndFlags, HANDLE hTemplateFile);
```

If `CreateFile` succeeds, the return value is an open handle of the specified pipe or file. If the specified pipe or file exists before `CreateFile` is called and if the `fdwCreate` parameter is CREATE_ALWAYS or OPEN_ALWAYS, a subsequent call to `GetLastError` returns the value ERROR_ALREADY_EXISTS, even if `CreateFile` has succeeded. If the file does not exist before `CreateFile` is called, `GetLastError` returns 0. If `CreateFile` fails, its return value is INVALID_HANDLE_VALUE.

Pipe Dreams

Because `CreateFile` can be used to create or open files and other file-like devices as well as to create or open pipes, some of its parameter settings would make little or no sense when used with pipes. They should be considered undefined when pipes are being opened or created. Experiment if you like, but let common sense be your guide.

The CreateFile Function: An Example

The CLIENT example program calls CreateFile to connect to a named pipe that the SERVER program has created. In CLIENT, the call to CreateFile appears on the accompanying disk in **CLIENTVW.CPP**:

```
CString fileString = "\\\\" + m_serverName + "\\PIPE\\demo";
strcpy(fileName, fileString.GetBuffer(LINE_LEN+NAME_SIZE+2));
// Call CreateFile() to connect to the named pipe.
hPipe = CreateFile (fileName, // Pipe name.
        GENERIC_WRITE // Generic access, read/write.
        | GENERIC_READ,
        FILE_SHARE_READ // Read and write access.
        | FILE_SHARE_WRITE ,
        NULL, // No security.
        OPEN_EXISTING, // Fail if not existing.
        FILE_FLAG_OVERLAPPED, // Use overlap.
        NULL); // No template.
```

Parameters Accepted by the CreateFile Function

These are the parameters accepted by CreateFile:

✦ **filename.** A pointer to a null-terminated string that specifies the name of the file, pipe, communications resource, disk device, or console that is being created, opened, or truncated.

✦ **fdwAccess.** A double word that specifies the access mode of the specified file or pipe. The available access modes are read access, write access, read/write access, and device query access. The Win32 API supplies a collection of constants that you can use to build a value for this parameter. These constants are as follows:

    ✦ **0.** Allows an application to query file or pipe attributes without actually accessing the specified file or pipe.

    ✦ **GENERIC_READ.** Specifies read access to the file or pipe. When this constant is applied, data can be read from the file or pipe, and a file pointer can be moved.

    ✦ **GENERIC_WRITE.** Specifies write access to the file or pipe. This setting allows data to be written to the file or pipe and allows a file pointer to be moved.

+ **GENERIC_READ | GENERIC_WRITE.** Both flags must be set to obtain both read and write access to a file or pipe.

+ **dwShareMode.** Specifies how the file or pipe can be shared. This parameter can be a combination of the following values:

    + **0.** Prevents the file or pipe from being shared.

    + **FILE_SHARE_READ.** Permits other clients to have read access to the file or pipe.

    + **FILE_SHARE_WRITE.** Permits other clients to have write access to the file or pipe.

+ **lpsa.** Points to a SECURITY_ATTRIBUTES structure that specifies the security attributes for the file or pipe. The file system must support this parameter for it to have an effect.

+ **fdwCreate.** Specifies whether a pipe (or file) is being opened or created and provides the system with other information about the pipe or file. This parameter must be one of the following values:

    + **CREATE_NEW.** Creates a new pipe or file. Fails if the specified pipe or file already exists.

    + **CREATE_ALWAYS.** Creates a new or file pipe, overwriting any existing file that has the same name.

    + **OPEN_EXISTING.** Opens the specified file or pipe. Fails if a file or pipe with the specified name does not exist.

    + **OPEN_ALWAYS.** Opens the specified pipe or file if it exists. If a pipe or file with the specified name does not exist, the function creates the file as if the `fdwCreate` parameter were CREATE_NEW.

    + **TRUNCATE_EXISTING.** Opens the pipe or file. Once opened, the pipe or file is truncated so that its size is zero bytes. The calling process must open the file with at least GENERIC_WRITE access. Fails if the file does not exist.

+ **fdwAttrsAndFlags.** Specifies attributes and flags for the pipe or file being opened or created. If `CreateFile` opens the client side of a named pipe, `fdwAttrsAndFlags` can also contain Security Quality of Service (SQOS) information. When a calling application specifies the SECURITY_SQOS_ PRESENT flag, the `fdwAttrsAndFlags` parameter can contain one or more security-related values. For more information on this topic, see your compiler's on-line help files. Any combination of the following flags and attributes can be placed in the `fdwAttrsAndFlags` parameter except when the FILE_

ATTRIBUTE_NORMAL setting is specified (the FILE_ATTRIBUTE_NORMAL setting must be used alone):

✦ **FILE_ATTRIBUTE_ARCHIVE.** Make a file an archive file. Applications use this flag to mark files for backup or removal.

✦ **FILE_ATTRIBUTE_NORMAL.** This setting means that the pipe or file being opened or created has no other attributes set. This attribute is valid only if used alone.

✦ **FILE_ATTRIBUTE_HIDDEN.** A file is hidden; the file is not to be included in ordinary directory listings.

✦ **FILE_ATTRIBUTE_READONLY.** A file is read-only. Applications can read the file but cannot write to it or delete it.

✦ **FILE_ATTRIBUTE_SYSTEM.** A file is part of, or is used exclusively by, the operating system.

✦ **FILE_ATTRIBUTE_TEMPORARY.** A file is being used for temporary storage. The systems attempts to keep all its data in memory for quicker access rather than flush the data back to mass storage. Your application should delete temporary files when they are no longer needed.

✦ **FILE_ATTRIBUTE_ATOMIC_WRITE.** Reserved for future use by Microsoft.

✦ **FILE_ATTRIBUTE_XACTION_WRITE.** Reserved for future use by Microsoft.

✦ **FILE_FLAG_WRITE_THROUGH.** Instructs the operating system to write through any intermediate cache and go directly to a file. The operating system can still cache writes but cannot lazily flush the writes.

✦ **FILE_FLAG_OVERLAPPED.** Enables overlapped communications. (See "Handling Multiple Client Processes" earlier in this chapter.) This setting instructs the operating system to initialize a pipe or file so that the functions `ReadFile`, `WriteFile`, `ConnectNamedPipe`, and `TransactNamedPipe` return the constant ERROR_IO_PENDING if they take a significant amount of time to complete. When the operation is finished, the associated event object is set to the signaled state. When the FILE_FLAG_OVERLAPPED attribute is set, `ReadFile` and `WriteFile` must be provided with an OVERLAPPED structure (a structure required for overlapped communications; see "Named Pipe Modes" earlier in this chapter). The FILE_FLAG_OVERLAPPED attribute requires OVERLAPPED reading and writing.

✦ **FILE_FLAG_NO_BUFFERING.** Specifies that a file is to be opened with no intermediate buffering or caching to be performed by the system. Reads and writes to the file must begin on sector boundaries.

✦ **FILE_FLAG_RANDOM_ACCESS.** Specifies that a file is accessed randomly. Windows NT uses this flag to optimize file caching.

✦ **FILE_FLAG_SEQUENTIAL_SCAN.** Specifies that the file is to be accessed sequentially from beginning to end. Specifying this flag can increase performance for applications that read potentially large files using sequential access.

✦ **FILE_FLAG_DELETE_ON_CLOSE.** Specifies that the operating system is to delete the file immediately after all its handles have been closed.

✦ **FILE_FLAG_BACKUP_SEMANTICS.** Specifies that a file is being opened or created for a backup or restore operation. The operating system ensures that the calling process overrides file security checks, provided it has permission. The relevant permissions are SE_BACKUP_NAME and SE_RESTORE_NAME.

✦ **FILE_FLAG_POSIX_SEMANTICS.** Specifies that a file is to be accessed according to POSIX rules. This setting permits the use of multiple files with names that differ only in case. It should be used only with systems that support such naming. Files created with this flag set may not be accessible by applications written for MS-DOS, Windows 3.x, or Windows NT.

✦ **hTemplateFile.** Specifies a handle with GENERIC_READ access to a template file. The template file supplies extended attributes for the file being created.

How the CreateFile Function Works

When a client process calls `CreateFile` to open a handle to a named pipe, `CreateFile` returns FALSE if the pipe exists but all its instances are busy. If `GetLastError` is then called to obtain more information and returns ERROR_PIPE_BUSY, the client process calls `WaitNamedPipe` to wait for an instance of the pipe to become available. `CreateFile` fails if the access specified by the calling program (duplex, outbound, or inbound) is incompatible with the access that was specified when the server created the pipe.

The handle that `CreateFile` returns defaults to byte-read mode and blocking-wait mode, with overlapped mode and write-through mode disabled. The client process calling `CreateFile` can enable overlapped mode by setting the FILE_FLAG_OVERLAPPED flag or can enable write-through mode by setting the FILE_FLAG_WRITE_THROUGH flag. The client can call `SetNamedPipeHandleState` to enable nonblocking mode by setting the PIPE_WAIT flag or can enable message-read mode by setting PIPE_READMODE_MESSAGE.

`CreateFile`, like the `CreateNamedPipe` function described earlier, accepts advisory input-buffer and output-buffer parameters. The actual buffer size reserved for each end of a named pipe is either the system default, the system minimum or maximum, or the specified size rounded up to the next memory allocation boundary.

THE CALLNAMEDPIPE FUNCTION

Rather than call `CreateFile`, a client process can call the Win32 function `CallNamedPipe`, which combines several I/O operations. `CallNamedPipe` connects to a pipe instance (after waiting for one to become available, if necessary). Then `CallNamedPipe` writes a message, reads a message, and closes its pipe handle.

`CallNamedPipe` can be used only by a client process and only with a message-type pipe (which is described in "Access Modes" earlier in this chapter). `CallNamedPipe` connects to a message-type pipe if one is available. If no pipe is available, `CallNamedPipe` waits for an instance of the pipe. Then it reads from the pipe and closes it.

A server process can call `ConnectNamedPipe` to determine when a client process is connected to a specified handle. If the pipe handle is in blocking mode, `ConnectNamedPipe` does not return until a client is connected. Calling `CallNamedPipe` is equivalent to calling `CreateFile` (or calling `WaitNamedPipe`, if `CreateFile` cannot open the pipe immediately) and then calling `TransactNamedPipe` (see "Other Functions") and `CloseHandle`.

Return Values

If the `CallNamedPipe` function succeeds, it returns TRUE; otherwise, the return value is FALSE.

If the message written to the pipe by the server process is longer than `cbReadBuf`, `CallNamedPipe` returns FALSE, and a subsequent call to `GetLastError` returns ERROR_MORE_DATA. The remainder of the message is discarded, because `CallNamedPipe` closes the handle to the pipe before returning. `CallNamedPipe` fails if the pipe is a byte-type pipe.

Syntax of the CallNamedPipe Function

Following is the syntax of the `CallNamedPipe` function:

```
BOOL CallNamedPipe(LPCSTR lpszPipeName, LPVOID lpvWriteBuf,
    DWORD cbWriteBuf, LPVOID lpvReadBuf, DWORD cbReadBuf,
    LPDWORD lpcbRead, DWORD dwTimeout);
```

`CallNamedPipe` accepts the following parameters:

+ **lpszPipeName.** Points to a null-terminated string specifying the pipe's name.
+ **lpvWriteBuf.** Points to the buffer containing the data written to the pipe.
+ **cbWriteBuf.** Specifies the size, in bytes, of the write buffer.
+ `lpvReadBuf`. Points to the buffer that receives the data read from he pipe.
+ **cbReadBuf.** Specifies the size, in bytes, of the read buffer.
+ **lpcbRead.** Points to a 32-bit variable that receives the number of bytes read from the pipe.
+ **dwTimeout.** Specifies the number of milliseconds to wait for the named pipe to be available. The `dwTimeout` parameter accepts either numeric values or the following constants:
  + **NMPWAIT_NOWAIT.** This value instructs `CallNamedPipe` not to wait for the named pipe. If the pipe is not available, `CallNamedPipe` returns an error.
  + **NMPWAIT_WAIT_FOREVER.** Causes `CallNamedPipe` to wait indefinitely.
  + **NMPWAIT_USE_DEFAULT_WAIT.** Instructs `CallNamedPipe` to use the timeout specified in `CreateNamedPipe` as a default.

OTHER FUNCTIONS

There are several miscellaneous functions that client and server processes can call to read from and write to a named pipe. For example, the `PeekNamedPipe` function reads data transmitted through a pipe without removing the contents of either a byte-type or a message-type pipe. `PeekNamedPipe` also returns additional information about the pipe instance. The `TransactNamedPipe` function writes a request message and reads a reply message in a single operation, speeding network performance. You can use this function with message-type pipes if the pipe handle of the calling process is set to message-read mode.

When a client and server finish using a pipe instance, the server calls `Disconnect-NamedPipe` to close the connection to the client process. This function makes the client's handle invalid (if it has not already been closed). Any unread data in the pipe is discarded.

To ensure that all bytes or messages written to the pipe are read by the client, the server calls `FlushFileBuffers`, which does not return until the client has read all data from the pipe. After the client is disconnected, the server calls `CloseHandle` to close its handle to the pipe instance. Alternatively, the server can use `ConnectNamedPipe` to enable a new client to connect to this instance of the pipe.

A process can retrieve information about a named pipe by calling `GetNamedPipeInfo`, which returns the type of the pipe, the size of the input and output buffers, and the maximum number of pipe instances that can be created. The `GetNamedPipeHandleState` function provides several facts about a pipe handle, including the read and wait modes of the pipe, the current number of pipe instances, and additional relevant information for pipes that communicate over a network. `SetNamedPipeHandleState` sets the read and wait mode of a pipe handle. For client processes communicating with a remote server, the function also controls the maximum number of bytes to collect or the maximum time to wait before transmitting a message (assuming that the client's handle was not opened with write-through mode enabled).

The `ReadFile` and `WriteFile` functions can be used with either byte-type or message-type pipes. `ReadFileEx` and `WriteFileEx` can be used with either byte-type or message-type pipes if the pipe handle was opened for overlapped operations. Unlike `ReadFile` and `WriteFile`, which use an event object to signal completion, `ReadFileEx` and `WriteFileEx` specify a completion routine—a function that is queued for execution when a read or write operation is finished. `ReadFileEx` and `WriteFileEx` provide applications with an alternate method for managing overlapped file I/O.

As you can see, the behaviors of these functions vary depending on the kinds of pipes they access and the modes of the specified pipe handles.

The CLIENT and SERVER Programs

To illustrate the use of named pipes, this chapter introduces a pair of example programs named SERVER and CLIENT. You launch the SERVER program first. Then you can create multiple clients and connect them to the server. You can create your clients on multiple computers connected on a network or on a single computer running Windows NT.

SERVER is a bare-bones SDI application. It is not based on a framework created by AppWizard and does not use the document-view architecture that framework-based programs have. It doesn't need that much sophistication, because its only job is to provide file-server support for its companion CLIENT program; so the amount of code that it requires is kept as small as possible. CLIENT is a full-scale Windows application incorporating the document-view architecture provided by Visual C++.

Together, CLIENT and SERVER make up a simple communications application that can be used either locally or over a network. The program provides individual text windows for as many as 100 clients. Clients can send messages by typing messages in their text windows.

Figure 9.14 shows the screen display of the CLIENT program.

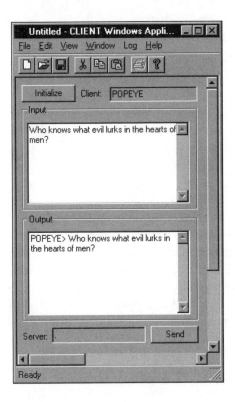

FIGURE 9.14 THE CLIENT PROGRAM'S SCREEN DISPLAY.

Before you launch the CLIENT program, you must start SERVER, the windowless application that implements the server end of the pipe. When SERVER is running, you can launch CLIENT. When CLIENT starts, it displays a window like the one shown in Figure 9.1. The CLIENT window contains two large text boxes. Outgoing messages are typed in the uppermost text box; the lower text box echoes outgoing messages and displays incoming messages. The CLIENT window also contains an assortment of controls that you can use to set up communications and send messages.

If you are running the CLIENT demonstration on a single machine, you can display two CLIENT windows on the same screen by launching two instances of CLIENT. If you are running the demonstration on two Windows NT workstations, you can start the server on either computer. Then you can launch one instance (or more) of CLIENT on the other machine.

When two CLIENT windows are displayed, either on one computer or on a pair of computers connected on a network, the **Initialize** button in each window can be pressed to set up communications. The windows can then be used for exchanging messages. When a user types a message in the top text panel and presses **Return,** the message appears in the bottom text panel in both windows.

While CLIENT is running, the local user of the program can type text in the output panel and click **Send** to send the text to all connected clients. Each time the local user clicks **Send,** the main thread reads any text that has been typed into the output panel of the user's view window and writes the text to the server. When the server echoes the text, it appears in the local user's input panel as well as in the view windows of all other connected users.

The CLIENT program also illustrates several features of Visual C++ that are not related to pipes or networking:

+ **Serialization.** Serialization allows objects derived from the CObject class to save information to files and retrieve information from files automatically. When you open a client window and start sending messages, CLIENT keeps a log of them. Any time you like, you can save the log by choosing **Save** from the File menu. You can also load old logs by choosing **Load** from the File menu. The serialization support built into CObject makes it easy to incorporate these capabilities into Visual C++ programs. The serialization feature of the CLIENT program is described in more detail in "Serialization" later in this chapter.

+ **The CFormView class.** The windows in the CLIENT program are derived from CFormView, an MFC class that is a cross between a window class and a dialog-box class. Essentially, a CFormView window is a modeless dialog that supports serialization, document objects, and other features of views. For more about the CFormView window, see "CFormView Windows" later in this chapter.

+ **Dialog data exchange.** DDX is a mechanism for placing values in dialog controls automatically and for automatically retrieving data from dialog-box controls. This feature of the MFC library is described in more detail in "Dialog Data Exchange" later in this chapter.

+ **The CTime class.** MFC also provides a CTime class that makes it easy to build time-related features into Visual C++ programs. In the CLIENT program, CTime is used to include a time stamp in every message log that is created; for details, see "The CTime Class" at the end of this chapter.

RUNNING THE **SERVER** PROGRAM

To launch and run the SERVER program, follow these steps:

1. Start the SERVER application from the Windows NT desktop or from the File Manager. When SERVER starts, it displays a message box (Figure 9.15) informing you that the server is running.

FIGURE 9.15 THE SERVER PROGRAM'S STARTUP MESSAGE BOX.

2. Close the message box by clicking **OK**.
3. The server creates a named pipe on your Windows NT workstation by calling `CreateNamedPipe`. This operation is described in "Creating Named Pipes" earlier in this chapter.
4. The server's main window stays active but becomes minimized, collapsing to an icon that remains on the Windows NT desktop. You can then launch one or more client programs. Each client you create connects to the server automatically.

RUNNING THE **CLIENT** PROGRAM

Once the SERVER program has set up a named pipe on your local computer, you can create and connect as many clients to the pipe as you like, subject only to a limit that is hard-coded in the program. (As written, the program has a client limit of 100; for details, see "How the CLIENT and SERVER Programs Work" later in this section.) You can create clients on the same computer that is running SERVER, or on remote computers connected to the server on a network.

To run one or more instances of the CLIENT program, follow these steps:

1. Launch the CLIENT application from the Windows NT desktop or the Windows NT File Manager.

2. CLIENT opens its main window, shown in Figure 9.16. This window is an object derived from the MFC CFormView class (see "CFormView Windows" near the end of this chapter).

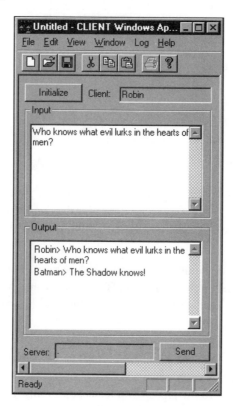

FIGURE 9.16 THE CLIENT WINDOW.

3. When the CLIENT program opens its CFormView window, click the button labeled **Initialize**. The application then displays a modeless dialog box labeled Create Client, shown in Figure 9.17.

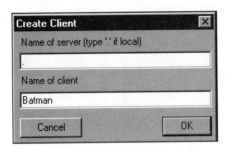

FIGURE 9.17 THE CREATE CLIENT DIALOG BOX.

4. In the Create Client dialog box, type in a client name of your choice and the path name and name of your client's server. If you want to connect to a server that is running locally on your workstation, simply type a period (.) in the path name text box. (For more information about client and server path names, see "Pipe Names" earlier in this chapter.)

5. When you have created a client, its name appears in the text box labeled **CLIENT** in the upper-right corner of the CLIENT program's main window. The name and path name of the server to which the client is connected appear in the text box labeled SERVER in the window's lower-right corner.

6. Close the Create Client dialog box by clicking **OK**.

7. You can create a second client by repeating steps 1 through 6. You must create at least two clients—either across a network or on the same computer— to execute the CLIENT and SERVER example programs. If you supply the correct information in the Create Client dialog box each time you create a client, the new client connects automatically to the server program and can then communicate with all other connected clients through an instance of a named pipe.

8. When you have created as many clients as you like, the users of the workstations running your clients can communicate by typing messages in the client windows displayed on their workstations. If you have only one workstation, you can open two clients and display their windows side by side on the same monitor, as shown in Figure 9.18. You can then pretend that you are several users sitting at individual workstations.

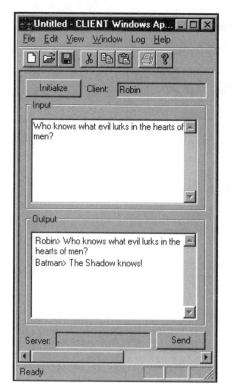 

FIGURE 9.18 RUNNING TWO **CLIENT** PROGRAMS ON THE SAME WORKSTATION.

9. To send a message, enter it in the text box labeled **Input** and then click **Send**. That sends your message to the server connected to your client. The server then transmits the message to all connected clients, including the client that sent it. When the message is received from the server, it appears in the text box labeled **Output** in each client's window.

10. All connected clients can send messages to one another in this way. Each time any client sends a message, all clients receive the message in the input panels of their client windows.

11. When you have finished experimenting with the CLIENT program, you can exit the program by selecting **Quit** from the File menu. The program asks you whether you would like to save your test file to a disk. If you answer **Yes**, the application saves your message to a log file.

How the CLIENT and SERVER Programs Work

In its `InitInstance` function, the SERVER program instantiates its main window class and then displays a dialog box informing you that the server is running. Then the application collapses its main window into an icon that appears on the Windows NT desktop. That keeps the server window out of your way but active and able to serve any clients that you and other users may create.

The SERVER program's `InitInstance` function is in **SERVER.CPP**. It looks like this:

```
BOOL CTheApp::InitInstance()
{
    // Standard initialization of a main window.
    SetDialogBkColor();

    m_pMainWnd = new CMainWindow;
    m_nCmdShow = m_nCmdShow;
    m_pMainWnd->UpdateWindow();
    // Display message confirming that the server is running.
    MessageBox(m_pMainWnd->m_hWnd, "The server is running.",
        "Ready!", MB_OK | MB_ICONEXCLAMATION);
    // Display window as an icon.
    ShowWindow(m_pMainWnd->m_hWnd, SW_SHOWMINIMIZED);
    m_pMainWnd->UpdateWindow();
    return TRUE;
}
```

The SERVER program's main window class is named `CMainWindow`. The constructor of the `CMainWindow` class starts a server thread automatically. This thread creates an instance of the server side of a named pipe. Then the program waits for a client to connect.

The following code fragment is the constructor of the `CMainWindow` class. It also appears in the **SERVER.CPP** file:

```
CMainWindow::CMainWindow()
{
    LONG lpServerThreadID;

    VERIFY(Create(NULL, "SERVER Demo",
        WS_OVERLAPPEDWINDOW, rectDefault, NULL,
        MAKEINTRESOURCE(IDR_MAINMENU)));
```

```
    // Create the first instance of a server side of the pipe.
    CreateThread ((LPSECURITY_ATTRIBUTES)NULL, // No security.
        (DWORD)0, // Same stack size.
        (LPTHREAD_START_ROUTINE)ServerProc, // Thread procedure.
        (LPVOID)this, // Parameter.
        (DWORD)0, // Start immediately.
        (LPDWORD)&lpServerThreadID); // Thread ID.
}

void CMainWindow::OnAbout()
{
    CDialog(IDD_ABOUTBOX).DoModal();
}
```

In the preceding code fragment, the CMainWindow constructor calls CreateThread to start the first server thread. Notice that a pointer to a procedure named ServerProc is passed to CreateThread. The ServerProc procedure is the entry point of the thread.

How the SERVER Program Creates SERVER Threads

The SERVER application can create multiple threads, one for each client. Every time a client connects to the server, it creates a new thread. Each new thread, in turn, creates and services a new instance of the server side of a named pipe. The SERVER program creates named pipes by calling CreateNamedPipe. As many as 100 instances of the CLIENT program can then be launched. Each client can communicate with the SERVER program, and with other clients, through its individual instance of the named pipe.

The server and all its clients use overlapped communications to keep their I/O operations as fast and efficient as possible. CreateNamedPipe is called in the ServerProc function, the entry-point function for threads. The following code sequence appears in ServerProc, which you can find in **SERVER.CPP**. It is the sequence that calls CreateNamedPipe each time SERVER needs to create a pipe:

```
    // Create a local named pipe named '\\.\PIPE\demo'. The
    // period (\.\\) means that it's a local pipe.
    hPipe = CreateNamedPipe ("\\\\.\\PIPE\\demo",
    // Pipe name = 'test'.
        PIPE_ACCESS_DUPLEX // Two-way pipe.
        | FILE_FLAG_OVERLAPPED, // Use overlapped structure.
        PIPE_WAIT // Wait for messages.
```

```
        | PIPE_READMODE_MESSAGE // Specify message mode pipe.
        | PIPE_TYPE_MESSAGE,
        MAX_PIPE_INSTANCES, // Maximum instance limit.
        BUF_SIZE, // Buffer sizes.
        BUF_SIZE,
        TIME_OUT, // Specify time out.
        &sa); // Security attributes.
// ...
```

A limit of 100 clients is hard-coded into the SERVER program. You can increase that limit if you like. The limit is set by a global variable named `clientCount`. In a line near the top of **SERVER.CPP**, `clientCount` is defined as follows:

```
DWORD clientCount = 0;
```

Each time a client connects to the server, the server creates another thread. This thread also waits for a client. As you have seen, the first server thread is created in the `CMainWindow` constructor. Subsequent threads are created in the `ServerProc` function, which is the entry-point function for each thread. Each time `ServerProc` executes, it starts a new thread. This is the code sequence that `ServerProc` executes each time it creates a thread:

```
CreateThread ((LPSECURITY_ATTRIBUTES)NULL, // No security
                                          // attributes.
        (DWORD)0, // Use same stack size.
        (LPTHREAD_START_ROUTINE)ServerProc.
        (LPVOID)hWnd, // Parameter to pass.
        (DWORD)0, // Run immediately.
        (LPDWORD)&ServerThreadID); // Thread identifier.
// ...
```

Each time `ServerProc` creates a thread, the function calls a `CMainWindow` member function named `Broadcast`, which is in **SERVER.CPP**. By cycling through an array, `Broadcast` sends each message typed by each user to all clients that are connected to the server. Following is the `Broadcast` function:

```
// The Broadcast member function
void CMainWindow::Broadcast(char *buffer)
{
    DWORD i; // Index through array.
    DWORD bytesWritten; // Used in WriteFile().
```

```
DWORD retCode; // Traps return codes.
char Buf[LINE_LEN]; // Message Buffer.
DWORD lastError; // Traps returns from GetLastError().

for(i=0; i < clientCount; i++) {

    // If client isn't alive, don't bother to write to it.
    if (clients[i].live) {
        retCode = WriteFile (clients[i].hPipe, buffer,
        strlen(buffer),
        &bytesWritten, &clients[i].overlap);

        // Check for three kinds of errors: IO_PENDING,
        // NO_DATA, and
        // other. If there's an IO_PENDING error, wait for
        // the event.
        // If it's anything else, other than NO_DATA (pipe client
        // disconnected), notify the user.

        if (!retCode) {
            lastError = GetLastError();

            // It's an IO_PENDING error; wait for the event.
            if (lastError == ERROR_IO_PENDING) {
                WaitForSingleObject (clients[i].hEvent, (DWORD)-1);
            } else {
                if (lastError != ERROR_NO_DATA) {
                    wsprintf (Buf, "%s = %d", buffer,
                    GetLastError());
                    MessageBox(Buf, "Debug,Broadcast:",
                    MB_OK);
                }
                clients[i].live = FALSE;
            }
        }

    } //if client.live
} // for loop
}
```

The ServerProc Module

The SERVER program does most of its work in the function `ServerProc`, a thread entry-point function that appears in **SERVER.CPP**. The `ServerProc` function module creates an instance of the server side of the named pipe and then waits for a client to connect. Once the client connects, the global array named `Clients` is updated to include information about the new client. Then `ServerProc` launches another server thread that will wait for the next client. After this new thread is launched, the original `ServerProc` thread starts a read loop, reading data from the named pipe with each iteration.

As you have seen, SERVER stores information about all its clients in the global array named `Clients`. The `Broadcast` function, also implemented in **SERVER.CPP**, transmits messages to the clients in the `Clients` array. When a message arrives from a procedure's client, `ServerProc` calls `Broadcast` to transmit the message to all the other clients in the array.

When `ServerProc` calls `Broadcast`, it steps through the `Clients` array, transmitting to each client each message that is sent.

Starting the CLIENT Program

When SERVER starts, users can launch as many as 100 instances of CLIENT, either on the server machine or on remote computers. To start a client, you can launch the CLIENT application from the Windows NT desktop while the server is running.

The CLIENT application calls `CreateFile` to connect to a named pipe. If the connection succeeds, CLIENT creates a thread that contains a read loop. This loop reads any messages that are received from the server. Once a message is read, it is printed in the input panel of the CLIENT program's view window.

CLIENT calls `CreateFile` from a code sequence in **CLIENTVW.CPP**. The call to `CreateFile` is in a member function named `CClientVwSetUpPipe`, which is called when CLIENT's view object is initialized. Following is the part of the `CClientVw::SetUpPipe` function that calls `CreateFile`:

```
void CClientVw::SetUpPipe()
{
    HANDLE hThread;

    CString fileString = "\\\\" + m_serverName + "\\PIPE\\demo";
    strcpy(fileName, fileString.GetBuffer(LINE_LEN+NAME_SIZE+2));

    // Call CreateFile() to connect to the named pipe.
```

```
hPipe = CreateFile (fileName, // Pipe name.
    GENERIC_WRITE // Generic access, read/write.
    | GENERIC_READ,
    FILE_SHARE_READ // Read and write access.
    | FILE_SHARE_WRITE ,
    NULL, // No security.
    OPEN_EXISTING, // Fail if not existing.
    FILE_FLAG_OVERLAPPED, // Use overlap.
    NULL); // No template.
// ...
```

While CLIENT is running, the user can type text in the program's main window and then click **Send** to send the text to all connect clients. Each time the local user clicks **Send**, the main thread reads any text that has been typed into the output panel of the user's view window and writes the text to the server. When the server echoes the text back, it appears in the local user's input panel as well as in the view windows of all other connected users.

In the `CClientVw::SetUpPipe` member function, CLIENT sets up an overlapped structure for reading user input. Then the program reads user input by calling `ReadFile` in a do-while loop in a function named `ReadPipe`. The loop that reads data from the pipe is in **CLIENTVW.CPP**. It is reproduced here:

```
do {
    // Read data from the pipe.
    retCode = ReadFile(pClientView->hPipe, inputBuf, BUF_SIZE,
        &bytesRead, &OverlapRd);

    if (!retCode) { // Error checking.
        lastError = GetLastError();

        // Check for three kinds of errors: IO_PENDING,
        // BROKEN_PIPE, or other. If there is an IO_PENDING
        // error, wait for the event handle to complete
        // successfully.

        if (lastError == ERROR_IO_PENDING) {
            WaitForSingleObject (hEventRd, (DWORD)-1);

        } else {       // If pipe is broken, tell user ...
            if (lastError == (DWORD)ERROR_BROKEN_PIPE)
```

```
        MessageBox (pClientView->m_hWnd,
            "Connection to this client has been broken.",
            "", MB_OK);
    else {      // ... or flag unknown errors and break.

        #ifdef _DEBUG      // This works only in debugging
        char Buf[80]; // compilations.
        wsprintf (Buf,
            "ReadFile failed; see winerror.h error #%d",
            GetLastError());
        MessageBox (pClientView->m_hWnd, Buf,
            "CLIENT: Debug", MB_OK);
        #endif

    }
    break;

    }

}

// Send message to CClientVw object, which displays the message.
pClientView->WriteMessage(inputBuf);
} while (1);
```

Near the end of this code fragment, notice that a member function named pClient-View->WriteMessage is called. This member function writes messages to the CLIENT window's output panel. The pClientView->WriteMessage member function is in **CLIENTVW.CPP:**

```
void CClientVw::WriteMessage(char *inputBuf)
{
    // Write message to output edit panel. Note that this text
    // has been read from the pipe, so if this works, the pipe
    // is working.

    // Place the new message in the output panel.
    CString tempStrObj = inputBuf;
    if (tempStrObj != "") {
        tempStrObj = tempStrObj.SpanExcluding("\n\r");
        m_editRead == "";
        UpdateData(FALSE);
        m_editRead = tempStrObj;
```

```
        UpdateData(FALSE);
    }    // inputBuf = "";

    // Select all text in output panel.
    CWnd *pWnd = GetDlgItem(IDD_EDITWRITE);
    ASSERT_VALID(pWnd);
    CEdit *pControl = (CEdit *)pWnd;
    pControl->SetSel(0, -1);
}
```

To send a message, the user of the CLIENT program clicks **Send** in the application's CFormView window. The program then executes a member function named CClient-View::OnSend. The OnSend member function uses the MFC dialog data exchange (DDX) feature to transfer data typed by the user to the program's document object. The DDX mechanism is described in "Dialog Data Exchange" later in this chapter. This is the ClientVw::OnSend function, which you can find in **CLIENTVW.CPP:**

```
// This function executes when the user clicks the
// Send button.
void CClientVw::OnSend()
{
    CString outputString;
    char *cOutputString;

    // Transfer data from view object's controls to
    // the current document.
    UpdateData();
    m_pDoc->m_editRead = m_editRead;
    m_pDoc->m_editWrite = m_editWrite;
    m_pDoc->m_clientName = m_clientName;
    m_pDoc->m_serverName = m_serverName;

    // Construct a string to send through the pipe.
    outputString = m_clientName + "> " + m_editWrite + "\r\n";
    cOutputString = outputString.GetBuffer(BUF_SIZE);
```

```
    // Write the string to the pipe.
    if (hPipe == NULL)
        MessageBox("Is the server started?",
      "Can't find server!",
            MB_OK | MB_ICONQUESTION);
    else {
        retCode = WriteFile (hPipe, cOutputString, BUF_SIZE,
            &bytesWritten, &OverlapWrt);
        if (!retCode) {
            lastError = GetLastError();

            // If there is an IO_PENDING error, wait until
            // the event completes successfully.
            if (lastError == ERROR_IO_PENDING)
                WaitForSingleObject (hEventWrt, (DWORD)-1);
        }
    }
}
```

SPECIAL FEATURES OF THE CLIENT PROGRAM

Along with its pipes-related features, the CLIENT program introduces four useful features of Visual C++ that are not related to pipes or networking. Those features are serialization, the CFormView class, dialog data exchange, and the CTime class. In the sections that follow, we'll discuss each of these features.

Serialization

When you start the CLIENT program, it automatically opens a log file that records all messages that are sent and received. At any time, you can save your message log file by choosing **Save** from the File menu. You can also load any saved log file by choosing **Open** from the File menu.

You can read the currently open message log file by choosing **Display** from the Log menu. The CLIENT program then displays the message log in a dialog window like the one shown in Figure 9.19.

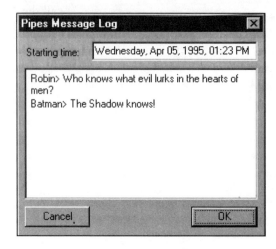

FIGURE 9.19 THE CLIENT PROGRAM'S MESSAGE LOG FILE.

If you quit the program without saving your message log, the program displays a dialog box (Figure 9.20) asking whether you want to save the log file before the program terminates.

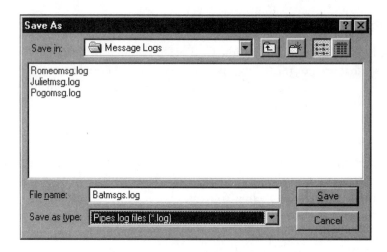

FIGURE 9.20 DIALOG BOX FOR SAVING THE MESSAGE LOG FILE.

In a Visual C++ application, the first step in implementing serialization is to derive a class from the CObject class. Then you place a call to the DECLARE_SERIAL macro in the header file of the class that you want to serialize, and you call the IMPLEMENT_SERIAL macro in the class's implementation (**.CPP**) file.

In addition, if you have added new data members to the class you want to serialize, you override a CObject member function named Serialize with your own Serialize function.

The DECLARE_SERIAL and DECLARE_DYNCREATE macros generate all the header and implementation code that is needed to create a serializable CObject subclass. DECLARE_SERIAL contains all the functionality of the DECLARE_DYNAMIC and DECLARE_DYNCREATE macros, so if you place a DECLARE_SERIAL call in a class definition, you don't have to call DECLARE_DYNAMIC or DECLARE_DYNCREATE.

The syntax of the DECLARE_SERIAL macro is as follows:

```
DECLARE_SERIAL(className)
```

In this syntax example, className is the name of the class that is to have serialization capability.

Following is the syntax of the IMPLEMENT_SERIAL macro:

```
IMPLEMENT_SERIAL(className, baseClassName, schemaNumber)
```

The className parameter passed to IMPLEMENT_SERIAL is the name of the class being serialized. The baseClassName parameter is the name of that class's base class, and schemaNumber is a version number that you assign to objects in the class being serialized. You use schema numbers to keep track of changes in class modifications. Each time you modify a class, you assign it a higher schema number. Schema numbers must be 0 or greater.

When you are serializing a class from storage to memory, if the schema number of the object on the disk does not match the version number of the class in memory, an exception is thrown. This arrangement can help prevent the serialization to disk of an incorrect version of an object.

Using the Serialization Macros

To implement serialization in the CLIENT program, several changes were made in the program's document and view files. In the definition of the CClientDoc class—which appears in **CLIENTDC.CPP**—this DECLARE_SERIAL statement was added:

```
DECLARE_SERIAL(CPlayer)
```

This declaration statement has a corresponding `IMPLEMENT_SERIAL` statement that appears at the beginning of **CLIENTDC.H** (the header file in which the `CClientDoc` class is defined):

```
IMPLEMENT_SERIAL(CPlayer, CObject, 1)
```

When these changes were made, the `Serialize` member function of the `CClientDoc` class had to be overridden. When AppWizard builds a framework for a Visual C++ program, it places the source code for an empty `Serialize` function in the `.CPP` file that it builds for the application's document class. To provide the application with the ability to serialize documents, AppWizard's `Serialize` function must be overridden.

This is how the `Serialize` function is modified in the CLIENT program:

```
// Serialization function
void CClientDoc::Serialize(CArchive& archive)
{
    if (ar.IsStoring()) {
        TRACE( "Serializing a CPlayer out.\n" );
        ar << m_time_t;
        m_msgList.Serialize();
    }
    else
    {
        ar >> m_time_t;
        m_msgList.Serialize();
    )
}
```

There are two formats that you can use to serialize data, and both are illustrated in the preceding example. In the code fragment, `m_time_t` is a `time_t` structure (defined in the Win32 header file **TIME.H**), and `m_msgList` is a `CStringList` object (defined and implemented in MFC).

The `time_t` structure has an overloaded << operator that can be used for archiving in much the same way that the << operator can be used for stream I/O in Visual C++. (For more about the CLIENT program's timestamp feature, see "The `CTime` Class" near the end of this chapter.) You also use the << operator in Visual C++ to serialize the primitive data types `BYTE`, `WORD`, `DWORD`, and `DLONG`.

In `Serialize` functions, the << and >> operators are overloaded in a special way by the `CArchive` class. The overloaded `CArchive::archive` << operator is called the archive insertion operator; it reads archived data from a disk archive. The `CArchive::archive >>` operator is the archive extraction operator; it writes data to a disk archive.

Many MFC objects—including `CStringList` objects, such as the `m_msgList` object in the preceding example—can manage serialization on their own without requiring the `>>` and `<<` operators. To serialize such objects, you simply let them call the `Serialize` member function inside your document class's `Serialize` function. That's how the `m_msgList` object serializes itself in the preceding example.

Serialization Tips

When you write a `Serialize` function that saves a class's member variables to disk, you should write them in the same order in which they appear in the object's definition when the object is defined. Conversely, when your function serializes a class's member variables from disk, they should be extracted in the same order that they were inserted. That way, you can ensure that each member variable that is written to disk is correctly matched with each member variable that is read from disk when the data is deserialized.

The Insertion and Extraction Operators

When you override the `CObject` class's `Serialize` member function, your `Serialize` function—like the one shown in the preceding example—must call a member function for the `CArchive` class called `Archive::IsStoring`. The `Archive::IsStoring` function evaluates to `TRUE` when information is to be written to disk, and evaluates to `FALSE` when information is being read from disk. In a serialization function, you typically call `IsStoring` to determine whether you should use the `<<` or `>>` operator. You can see how this test works by examining the code in the preceding example.

Restrictions on Data Types in Archiving Operations

Although the `archive <<` and `archive >>` constructs work much like the C++ constructs `cout <<` and `cin >>`, they are much more sensitive about the kinds of data they can handle. The only primitive data types that `archive <<` and `archive >>` can serialize are BYTE, WORD, DWORD, and DLONG. This means that if you try to serialize even such a common data type as an `int`, the compiler returns an error.

If a program is writing to disk—storing data to an archive—the archive insertion operator (`<<`) is used to write data about the object being serialized to the file associated with the archive. If the program is reading data from an archive, the archive extraction operator (>>) is used to read each member variable of the object being serialized.

When you use the insertion and extraction operators in a `Serialize` function, they perform all the operations necessary to make sure that the member variables are correctly written or read.

Reading and Writing Files

An object of class `CArchive` always encapsulates one disk file. Thus, the `archive <<` construct writes data to a disk file (represented as a `CArchive` object), and the `archive >>` construct reads data from a file (represented as another `CArchive` object).

When you create a `CArchive` object, you can use it for either reading from a disk file or writing to a disk file; you can't use it for both purposes. If you want to read data from a file and write data to the same file, you must create two `CArchive` objects—one for reading and one for writing.

Here's how to create a `CArchive` object that reads a disk file:

```
CArchive archive( pFile, CArchive::load );
```

To create a `CArchive` object that writes data to a disk, execute this kind of statement:

```
CArchive archive( pFile, CArchive::store );
```

Serializing a Complete Object

When you have made an object serializable—when you have written a `Serialize` function that can manage the serialization of the object's member functions—you can serialize the entire object by invoking just one `archive <<` or `archive >>` construct.

In a nutshell, this is how to implement serialization in your programs:

1. Derive a class from `CObject`.
2. Place a call to the DECLARE_SERIAL macro in the class's declaration.
3. Define a default constructor for the class (a constructor with no arguments).
4. Call the IMPLEMENT_SERIAL macro in the class's implementation file.
5. Write a `Serialize` member function for your class that overrides the `CObject` class' `Serialize` member function.

CFormView Windows

The CLIENT program creates its screen display by creating a form view window, a window that belongs to a class named `CFormView`. `CFormView` is a subclass of the MFC `CView` class, which provides view objects for GUI windows. (Windows and views are described in Chapter 4, "Programming Windows NT with Visual C++.")

The `CFormView` class combines features of a modeless dialog box with features of an ordinary document window. The main window of the CLIENT program was implemented using a `CFormView` window, because windows derived from `CFormView` are more versatile and more attractive than modeless dialog boxes and are also easier to write and implement. `CFormView` windows can be sized and equipped with scrollbars, and they support the DDX data exchange system, which offers an easy method for updating window controls and retrieving their current values. The `CFormView` window used in the CLIENT program is defined in **CCLIENTVW.H** and is implemented in **CLIENTVW.CPP**.

The CFormView Class

Objects created from the `CView` class draw the client areas of frame windows and provide input and output for information stored in documents. View classes include `CView`, `CScrollView` `CEditView`, and `CFormView`.

`CFormView` was used to create the interface for two of the example programs in this book: the CLIENT application in this chapter, and the Socks application in Chapter 10, "Networking Windows NT."

The `CFormView` class is useful, but it's a little tricky to implement. That's because AppWizard does not provide a mechanism for creating a form-view object in a new application. To create a framework for a program that uses a form-view window, you run AppWizard in the usual way. But you must then replace the view class that AppWizard creates with a special kind of view object instantiated from the `CFormView` class.

You create this object as if it were a dialog box, using the Developer Studio's dialog box editor. To create a `CFormView` object and incorporate it into your application, follow these steps:

1. Using the Developer Studio dialog box editor, design a dialog box.
2. Right-click over the dialog editor's default dialog box template and choose **Properties** from the pop-up menu. The dialog editor then displays a Dialog Properties property sheet (Figure 9.21).

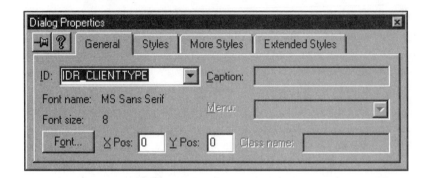

FIGURE 9.21 THE DIALOG PROPERTIES DIALOG BOX.

3. Tab to the Styles property page (Figure 9.22).

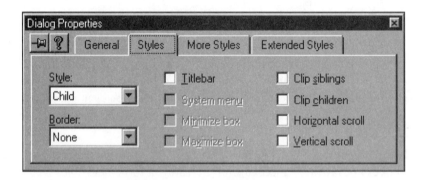

FIGURE 9.22 THE STYLES PROPERTY PAGE.

4. When the Styles property sheet opens, make the following selections:

    ✦ From the Style list box, select **Child**.

    ✦ From the Border list box, select **None**.

    ✦ If the Titlebar box is checked, remove the check mark.

5. If you want your form view to handle commands from menus and accelerators, tab to the General property page and do the following: In the ID list box, enter the same ID that is assigned to the menu or accelerator resource whose commands you want your view object to handle. If you are writing a single

document interface application, select **IDR_MAINFRAME** as the dialog ID for your `CFormView` object. If you are writing a multiple document interface application, select the MDI child's ID (**IDR_yourappTYPE**) as the dialog's ID.

6. Create a view class derived from `CFormView`. In your application, this class replaces the `CView`-derived view class supplied by AppWizard. With the form view dialog template still open, select the **ClassWizard** command from the Resource menu. Developer Studio then opens the ClassWizard property sheet.

7. From the Class name list box, select **CFormView**.

8. Click **Add Class** and choose the **New** item from the pop-up menu. ClassWizard opens a dialog box named Create New Class, as shown in Figure 9.23.

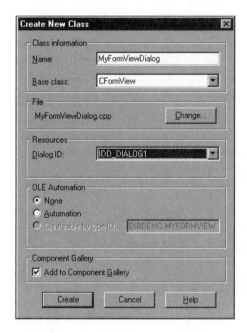

FIGURE 9.23 THE CREATE NEW CLASS DIALOG BOX.

9. In the Name text box, enter a name for your `CFormView`-derived class, and name the implementation and header files that you want ClassWizard to create for your class.

10. In the Base class list box, select the `CFormView` class. Then close the Create New Class dialog box and create your form-view dialog box by clicking the **Create** button.

11. If you want to automate the controls in your form-view window, use ClassWizard to associate any member variables that you want to automate with corresponding form-view controls. You can then take advantage of DDX and dialog exchange validation (DDV) to transfer data automatically to and from your form-view window. This procedure is discussed in more detail later in this chapter.

12. Associate your form-view window with your application's document and frame-window classes. From the Developer Studio editor, open your application's main implementation file (the **.CPP** file that bears only the name of your application).

13. Locate your application's `InitInstance` member function.

14. In that function, modify the call to `AddDocTemplate` by replacing the name of your application's original view class with the name of the new class you have derived from `CFormView`.

15. From the Developer Studio editor, remove from your project the original file that AppWizard created for your application's view class. Select the original file's icon in Developer Studio's left window pane and then choose **Cut** from the Edit menu.

16. From the Windows NT desktop, delete the ClassWizard (**.CLW**) file from your project directory.

17. Open ClassWizard and build an updated ClassWizard (**.CLW**) file.

Dialog Data Exchange

In the MFC library, the `CDialog` class is the base class for creating dialog boxes. Descendents of `CDialog` include `CFileDialog`, `CPrintDialog`, `CFontDialog`, `CColorDialog`, and `CFindReplaceDialog`, which provides a standard dialog for search-and-replace file operations. Another descendent of the `CDialog` class is `CDataExchange`, an interesting class that automates the retrieval of data from dialog box controls.

CDialog has two mechanisms for automating the operation of dialog boxes: dialog data exchange and dialog exchange validation. In a Visual C++ program, the AppWizard and ClassWizard utilities use DDX and DDV to generate code that automatically initializes the values of the controls in a dialog box before it opens. The same mechanisms can automatically retrieve the values of the dialog box's controls when the user closes the dialog box by clicking **OK**.

AppWizard and Class Wizard can implement DDX and DDV automatically in framework-generated programs. As a Visual C++ programmer, you have to know just two things: how to instruct ClassWizard to implement the system for you, and how to use the MFC member function UpdateData.

The UpdateData member function takes one parameter: a Boolean value. The source code that implements a dialog box can call UpdateData in either of the following ways (both forms have the same meaning):

```
UpdateData()
```

or

```
UpdateData(TRUE)
```

If an application executes either of these two statements, the value of each variable associated with an automated control in a dialog box is transferred to the control associated with the variable.

Conversely, if an application executes the statement

```
UpdateData(FALSE)
```

the value of each control that is associated with a variable is transferred to that variable.

To use Visual C++'s DDX and DDV tools to automate your dialog box controls, follow these steps:

1. Create a new dialog box using Developer Studio's dialog box editor.
2. Choose **ClassWizard** from Developer Studio's View menu.
3. When the ClassWizard property sheet opens, tab to the Member Variables property page (Figure 9.24).

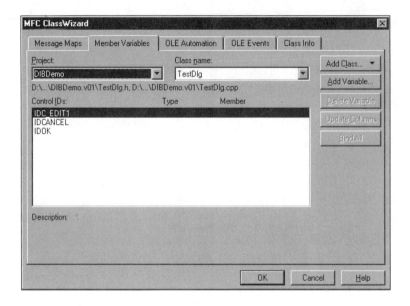

FIGURE 9.24 THE MEMBER VARIABLES PROPERTY PAGE.

4. From the Control IDs edit box, select the edit control that you want to automate, as shown in Figure 9.24.

5. Click the **Add Variable** button. ClassWizard opens a dialog box titled Add Member Variable (Figure 9.25).

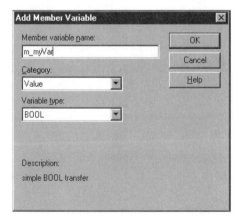

FIGURE 9.25 THE ADD MEMBER VARIABLE DIALOG BOX.

6. In the Member Variable Name edit box, enter a name for the edit control that you want to automate, as shown in Figure 9.25.

7. In the Category edit box, choose **Control** if the control that you are automating is a check box or a button. If the control is an edit control, choose the **Value** item.

8. In the Variable type edit box, specify the type of data you want to associate with your control.

9. Close the Add Member Variable dialog box by clicking **OK**.

10. When the ClassWizard property page regains the focus, notice that the name you have entered for your variable now appears in the list box labeled Control IDs.

11. If the control that you are automating is an edit box, specify the maximum length of the string shown in the edit box in the list box titled Maximum Characters.

12. Close the ClassWizard property page by clicking **OK**.

The AFX_DATA_INIT and AFX_DATA Structures

As you complete the procedures outlined under the preceding heading, ClassWizard automatically creates two data structures and places them in your source code. One of these structures, called an AFX_DATA_INIT map, is placed in the class's implementation (.CPP) file. The other structure, called an AFX_DATA definition structure, is placed in the .H file that defines the dialog box's class.

The AFX_DATA_INT structure resembles the message-map declarations that ClassWizard places in header files. This is an example from the SOCKS program in Chapter 10, "Networking Windows NT:"

```
CClientVw::CClientVw()
    : CFormView(CClientVw::IDD)
{
    //{{AFX_DATA_INIT(CClientVw)
    m_editRead = "";
    m_editWrite = "";
    m_serverName = "";
    m_clientName = "";
    //}}AFX_DATA_INIT
}
```

Not surprisingly, the AFX_DATA structure that ClassWizard creates for a particular class looks very much like the class's message map. Following is the AFX_DATA implementation that corresponds to the AFX_DATA_INIT definition shown in the preceding example:

```
//{{AFX_DATA(CClientVw)
enum { IDD = IDR_CLIENTTYPE };
CStringm_editRead;
CStringm_editWrite;
CStringm_serverName;
CStringm_clientName;
//}}AFX_DATA
```

AFX_DATA_INIT and AFX_DATA structures resemble message-map definitions and message maps for a good reason: They operate in much the same way. By checking AFX_DATA_INIT and AFX_DATA structures, the system looks for dialog box controls with values that should be retrieved or updated, and retrieves or updates those controls automatically.

In Visual C++, you usually open a modal dialog box by calling a member function named DoModal. Once you have automated a dialog box's controls using the DDX mechanism, you can initialize any control inside the dialog box by simply setting the variable that is associated with the control before you open the dialog box. When the user closes a dialog box containing automated controls, the application automatically retrieves the values of those variables and places them in the variables that correspond to the automated controls. This happens before the dialog box closes. By overriding the view's OnUpdate function, an application can update the controls in a view object automatically each time the view needs updating.

In the CLIENT example program, the UpdateData function is used extensively in **CLIENTVW.CPP**. That's because many controls in the application's main window change dynamically as the user sends and receives messages. For example, in the OnInit function, a pair of variables named m_clientName and m_serverName are set to the client and server names that the user has specified:

```
// Get client and server names from init dialog box.
m_clientName = m_dlgInit->m_clientName;
m_serverName = m_dlgInit->m_serverName;
```

In **CLIENTVW.CPP**, the following code sequence transfers data from the CLIENT window to the CLIENT program's document object:

```
UpdateData();
m_pDoc->m_editRead = m_editRead;
```

```
m_pDoc->m_editWrite = m_editWrite;
m_pDoc->m_clientName = m_clientName;
m_pDoc->m_serverName = m_serverName;
```

The CTime Class

The CLIENT program instantiates the MFC library's CTime class to create a message-log time stamp. The program then calls the CTime member function Format to create a string that can be used to print the current date and time. This string is then stored in a CString object named m_timeStr.

All this takes place in the following code sequence, which you can find in the **CLIENTDC.CPP** file on the accompanying disk:

```
CString CClientDoc::SetStartTime()
{
    CTime theTime = CTime::GetCurrentTime();
    CString m_timeStr = theTime.Format("%A, %b %d, %Y, %I:%M %p");
    return m_timeStr;
}
```

For more detailed information about the CTime class and the CTime::Format member function, see the on-line help files and the Visual C++ documentation.

Summary

This chapter addresses two major topics. First, it explains file mapping, a mechanism that Windows NT uses to map data stored on disk into the 4GB virtual address space owned by a process. Then the chapter explains how processes and threads exchange information using anonymous pipes and named pipes:

✦ Processes use anonymous pipes to exchange information on local machines. Named pipes can be used either on local machines or on computers connected across a network.

✦ Because Windows NT processes do not share memory even when they are running on the same machine, pipes can be a handy mechanism for threads and processes to use when they need to share data. Pipes work much like files, so processes transmit and retrieve information using pipes in much the same way that they write to and read from disk files.

✦   Named pipes are useful when an application needs to transmit information across a network or obtain information from a remote computer. Named pipes are easy to use for this purpose, because they are protocol-independent and have file-like characteristics.

This chapter introduces three example programs: ANON, which demonstrates the use of anonymous pipes, and a pair of programs named CLIENT and SERVER. The latter programs demonstrate how named pipes can be used to exchange data between processes running on the same computer or between a local computer and remote computers connected across a network.

CHAPTER TEN

NETWORKING WINDOWS NT

The Internet has been such a hot topic over the past year or two that you may have wondered whether Windows NT is Internet-ready. Well, Windows NT is not just Internet-ready—it was Internet-ready before the Internet was cool. Windows NT has had the Internet's native communications protocol, TCP/IP, built in since the first Windows NT software package rolled off the Microsoft assembly language.

Windows NT is compatible with many other communications protocols, too. Many companies use Windows NT (and Windows 95) workstations on networks that are controlled by UNIX servers and communicate with each other over Novell networks. Windows NT servers and workstations also fit nicely into local area networks (LANs) made up of Windows 3.1 and Windows for Workgroups workstations. Computers running the Windows NT Server operating system—a special high-end version of Windows—can even control networked networks made up of a mixture of Windows and Macintosh workstations.

With the release of version 4.0, Windows NT has become more network-savvy than ever. Now, when you install Windows NT, the NT installation wizard automatically displays a property sheet that lets you specify many different attributes of the network you are using, including the communications protocol that you want to use (Figure 10.1). If you say you're using the Internet protocol TCP/IP, the installer walks you through the TCP/IP installation process. When the installer prompts you type in your IP address, you simply comply. (You'll learn more about TCP/IP and how Windows NT uses it in the section headed "The TCP/IP Protocol" later in this chapter.)

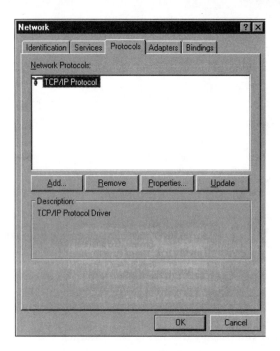

FIGURE 10.1 INSTALLING TCP/IP.

The installer then prompts you for a few other specifics about your network setup and installs the rest of Windows NT. And that's all there is to it. When the installation is complete, you're ready to log on to the Internet.

If you want to connect your Windows NT computer to a network using some other protocol, that's easy, too. Windows NT supports protocols from many different vendors, including Banyan, Digital Equipment (DEC), SunSoft, and others. You can put your Windows NT computer online using any of those protocols at any time you like, during the installation of Windows NT or later.

Customizing the HOSTS and SYSTEM Files

When you have installed TCP/IP, you should customize a pair of Windows system files that are designed to help your workstation find other computers on the TCP/IP network. You can customize your HOSTS and SYSTEM files by following these steps:

1. Open a DOS-style console window or some other text editor, such as the Notepad applet that's accessible from the Windows NT Start menu.

2. Using DOS commands, navigate to the \WINNT\SYSTEM32\DRIVERS\ETC directory that your TCP/IP software created (most likely in your WINDOWS directory) when you installed TCP/IP.

3. When you have made the \WINNT\SYSTEM32\DRIVERS\ETC directory the current directory, open the HOSTS file in that directory by typing **EDIT HOSTS**.

4. When Windows NT's DOS-style text editor appears, modify the HOSTS file by adding the IP addresses, domains, and names of your NT server and your Windows NT client (or clients) along with the IP addresses of any other machines that your network administrator suggests. For the format and examples of entries in the HOSTS file, see the comments at the beginning of the file or contact your network administrator.

5. Save your modified HOSTS file by choosing **Save** from the File menu. (For more details about HOSTS files, see the heading "Host Tables" later in this chapter.)

When you develop a Windows NT application using Visual C++, it's just as easy to build TCP/IP support into your program. If you use AppWizard to build your application framework, one of the first questions AppWizard asks you is whether you want your program to support TCP/IP networking. If you answer yes, as shown in Figure 10.1, AppWizard automatically builds TCP/IP support into your program.

About This Chapter

In this chapter, you'll learn some important facts about how the Internet's TCP/IP protocol works, and you'll learn how to create Windows NT programs with Internet support built in. This chapter also introduces the MFC classes CAsyncSocket and CSocket, which make it easier to use the TCP/IP protocol.

To give you hands-on experience developing Internet-ready applications, this chapter presents two sample programs. The first program, NETWORK, demonstrates basic principles of computer networking. SOCKS lets you create a Windows NT application that has TCP/IP support—and a miniterminal—built in. If your Windows NT system is connected to a TCP/IP network, you'll be able to use SOCKS to connect your system to another TCP/IP user's system and then chat with that person in real time using the miniterminal that the program provides. If your Windows NT computer does not have access to a TCP/IP network, you can start two instances of SOCKS and watch their miniterminals interact on the same screen.

Figure 10.2 shows the SOCKS screen display. The output of the NETWORK program is shown in Figure 10.3.

FIGURE 10.2 THE SOCKS SCREEN DISPLAY.

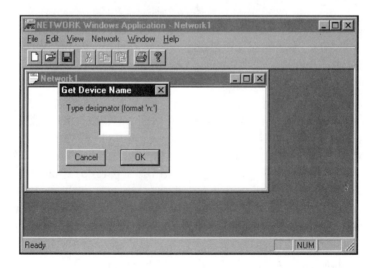

FIGURE 10.3 OUTPUT OF THE NETWORK PROGRAM.

The SOCKS program derives its name from the fact that it manages its network connections using the Windows sockets API. Support for this API is built into Windows NT and is supported by two classes that are implemented in the MFC library. You'll be introduced to the sockets API in this chapter, and the SOCKS program will show you how to use it in your own Windows NT applications.

When you execute the SOCKS program, it opens a form-view window like the one shown in Figure 10.4. You listen for incoming transmissions by clicking the **Listen** toolbar button (the ear) or selecting **Listen** from the Sockets menu. By clicking the **Connect** toolbar button (the fingers) or selecting the **Connect** menu item, you can connect your workstation to another computer running the SOCKS program.

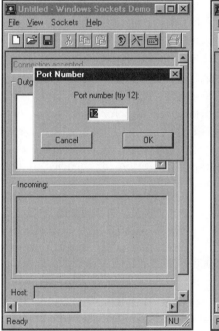 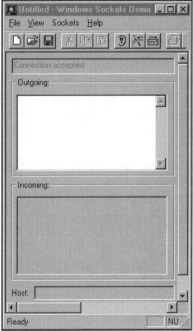

FIGURE 10.4 CONNECTING TO ANOTHER WORKSTATION USING THE SOCKS PROGRAM.

When the two machines connect, you and the user at the other end can send messages back and forth by typing them in the **Input** window and clicking **Transmit** (the envelope below an arrow). Whenever you send or receive a message it is displayed in the output window.

For more details on how SOCKS works, see "Example Program: SOCKS" later in this chapter.

Understanding Windows NT Networking

What's most significant about Windows NT networking is that support for many kinds of networking is built in. Before the advent of Windows NT, support for networking was not ordinarily built into the operating systems used by personal computers. Instead, networking software was added as needed to supply interconnections among groups, or *workgroups*, of PCs.

The first kind of networking that was introduced for DOS-based PCs was LAN. When a need arose for LAN communications among PC workgroups, Microsoft introduced a communications software package called LAN Manager. It supplied peer-to-peer communications—communications not based on a client-server model—to locally networked DOS machines. Later, as PC workgroups moved from DOS to Windows, Microsoft introduced a special edition of Windows called Windows for Workgroups, a standard Windows package with built-in peer-to-peer networking for locally connected computers running Windows.

Windows NT, with its built-in support for TCP/IP and other networking protocols, adds a new chapter to the story of Windows networking. Windows NT has built-in support not only for peer-to-peer networking but also for client-server networking. And the networking features of Windows NT are suitable both for local area networking and for the kind of wide area networking—primarily TCP/IP-based networking—that is now commonly used by large corporations, government agencies, and educational institutions.

DATACOM STACKS

In Chapter 2, "Underneath Windows NT," I mentioned that the Win32 operating system is a cross between a layered operating system and a client-server operating system. Similarly, Windows NT has characteristics of both a layered system and a client-server system. In the Windows NT networking environment, any computer running Windows NT can operate as either a client or a server. Any networked computer running Windows NT, whether it is being used as a server or as a workstation, manages its network operations using a layered mechanism called a *protocol suite*, or telecommunications *stack*.

Many different kinds of data communications stacks, or *datacom* stacks, are used in computer communications. The best-known such stack is the open systems interconnection (OSI) protocol stack, illustrated in Figure 10.5.

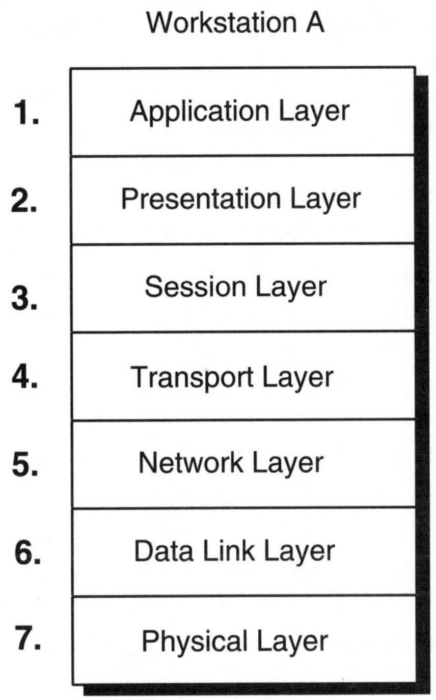

Workstation A

1.	Application Layer
2.	Presentation Layer
3.	Session Layer
4.	Transport Layer
5.	Network Layer
6.	Data Link Layer
7.	Physical Layer

FIGURE 10.5 THE OSI REFERENCE MODEL.

To communicate across networks, Windows NT uses a special kind of protocol stack that's loosely modeled after the OSI stack shown in Figure 10.5. (You'll learn much more about the Windows NT datacom stack in the second half of this chapter.) The OSI stack is also used as a model, at least to some degree, by most other varieties of computer networking systems. For this reason, the OSI stack is sometimes called the *OSI reference model.*

As Figure 10.5 illustrates, the OSI stack is based on an architecture that divides networking protocols into seven levels of functionality. For this reason, it is sometimes referred to as the OSI seven-layer protocol suite, or the OSI seven-level stack.

What connection does the diagram shown in Figure 10.5 have to the topic of computer networking? There is a connection, but it requires a little explanation. So let's turn our attention away from Figure 10.5 for a moment and take a look at how two computers might communicate with each other in a client-server environment. When we've done that, we'll return to Figure 10.5.

Establishing a Network Connection

From a client-server point of view, the Windows NT networking system operates in much the same way that most other client-server operating systems do. Windows NT takes a request (usually an I/O request) from an application running on a local workstation and passes the request to a remote workstation. The request is executed on the remote workstation, and the networking system returns the results to the local workstation.

As an illustration of this process, suppose you are working at a computer running Windows NT and want to read information from a file stored on a hard drive connected to a remote Windows NT workstation. To retrieve the information, you send an I/O request over the network. The request might be something like, "Read x number of bytes from file y on machine z."

To send this request, the networking software must be able to find machine z and then determine what kind of communications software machine z understands. In addition, machine z must have access to networking software that can understand your request, must retrieve the requested information, and must transmit the requested information back to you (provided that network security restrictions permit this operation to take place).

There are many protocols that networked computers use to carry out I/O operations such as the one just described. For example, before information is transmitted over a network, many protocols divide the information into small blocks called *packets*. When information is transmitted in packets, the computer that receives the information must reassemble it, perform parity checks to ensure that it is not garbled or incomplete, decode it if necessary, and finally send it to whatever operating system component can provide the requested service. (In this case, a request for information stored on a disk would be carried out by the File Manager.)

Once these operations have taken place, the requested information can be retrieved from disk by the remote computer and can be sent back to you across the network. The recipient must decode the packets of information it has received, formulate its reply, and inform the remote computer that it has received the requested information satisfactorily.

Windows NT and the OSI Protocol Stack

When you attempt to carry out an operation such as the one just described, there is one potential problem (barring hardware or software malfunctions) that can make the attempt fail: The two computers attempting to communicate across the net may be using incompatible hardware or software. To avoid this pitfall, many manufacturers have tried to adopt compatibility standards for the hardware and software packages used for network communications. As a result, many hardware and software vendors have adopted a model for computer networking drawn up by the International Standards Organization (ISO), an international standards-setting body. The networking standard is the OSI reference model. As noted previously, it is also referred to as the OSI protocol suite, or as simply the OSI stack.

The OSI stack serves mainly as a model, and not as a rigid standard, for network communications suites. Many different networking systems are based on the OSI suite, but few, if any, comply with it exactly. The Windows NT networking system adheres to the OSI model closely enough to be compatible with several other networking systems—which are also based, more or less, on the OSI reference model.

More details about the Windows NT protocol suite are provided later in this chapter.

The OSI Seven-Level Stack

The OSI stack is based on a design that divides networking protocols into seven levels of functionality. For this reason, it is often referred to as the OSI seven-layer protocol suite, or the OSI seven-level stack.

By Any Other Name...

If you're beginning to think that the OSI stack has many different names, you're right. But don't worry—the name OSI stack will be enough for you to remember once you're finished with this chapter. As soon as you say "OSI stack," people in the know will understand what you mean.

Now we're ready to refer again to the diagram of the OSI stack that was presented in Figure 10.5.

The OSI reference model assumes that every workstation on a network is equipped with seven levels of APIs and that these seven levels are arranged inside each workstation in a seven-layer stack. As Figure 10.5 illustrates, the layers are numbered consecutively from the bottom of the stack to the top. Each layer manages one aspect of network communications.

Layer 1, known as the physical layer, is where network communications takes place. For example, if your computer is connected to a LAN with an Ethernet card, the API at layer 1 is the software that interfaces your computer with its Ethernet card. The top layer in the OSI stack—layer 7, or the application layer—is where your computer's application software resides.

The layers that lie between layer 1 and layer 7 provide services that must be performed before your application software can communicate with similar software running on other computers on the network. The work performed by layers 2 through 6 is described later in this chapter.

For protocol suites such as the OSI suite to work properly, the arrangement of the layers in the suite must be the same on every computer in the network. In the OSI model, if the third level of machine x's datacom stack performs a certain function, the third level of software in machine z's datacom stack must perform the same function. This is always true, even if machines using the OSI stack are different brands running different kinds of processors and running applications written in different languages.

One of the most important features of the software layers in the OSI stack is this: Although each layer of the stack communicates only with the layers immediately above and below it, it does not appear this way to the APIs in each layer. Instead, when your computer is communicating with another computer across a network, each layer of software in your computer's OSI stack appears to be communicating directly with the corresponding layer of software in the other computer's stack. This illusion, a result of the design of the OSI stack, is sometimes referred to as *virtual communication*. In Figure 10.5, dotted lines between workstation A and workstation B represent virtual communication.

THE APPLICATION LAYER AND THE PHYSICAL LAYER

The two layers of the stack that benefit most from virtual communication are layer 7, the application layer, and layer 1, the physical layer. At layer 7, when an application running on your computer needs to communicate with an application running on a remote computer, the local application sends out a message that appears to go directly to the application running on the remote computer. The remote application then receives what it perceives to be a message coming directly from your application. The remote application responds by sending a reply that appears to go directly to your application.

When your application receives what looks like a reply coming directly from the remote application, it sends an acknowledgment, and the round of communications is complete. Because of the way the OSI stack works, neither application is aware that its messages to and from the other application are making their way through many layers of network protocols. Neither application needs to be aware of the existence of a network. As far as the two applications are concerned, there is no way for them to tell whether they are communicating across a network or with another instance of the same application running on the same machine.

When you compile and execute the example programs presented in this chapter, you'll see that this is true. The SOCKS program can be used to exchange messages across a network—or between processes running on the same computer.

The physical layer of the OSI protocol suite also benefits from the model's stack-based architecture. By the time a message from an application reaches layer 1 of the stack, and is therefore ready to go out over the net, it has been reduced to packets of raw data that are ready to be transmitted. Similarly, when the API at layer 1 receives a message, the message can be treated as just so much raw data to be passed to the next layer of the stack. Layer 1 is concerned only with sending and receiving data and neither knows nor cares what kind of information the data might contain.

This seven-layer solution to network problems is a win-win situation for software designers and network engineers. It makes life easier for the software engineers who design a particular kind of networking software, because their software module must communicate with only two other kinds of modules and not with every kind of module in the stack. It also simplifies the job of the networking administrator, because the administrator is concerned with only one layer of the stack (the physical layer). The result is that all the computers on the network can use the same kinds of protocols, even though the machines may be supplied by different vendors.

Because the functions in the Win32 API use stack-based communications procedures, they are independent of any particular protocol; when you implement them in an application, your application can communicate with any other application running on any other Windows NT system, no matter what kinds of communications systems the two machines are using.

THE SEVEN LAYERS IN THE OSI STACK

The lower four layers (layers 1 through 4) of the OSI model are often seen as a group of APIs that manage communications. These four layers enable users to set up connections through which data in different formats can move from its source to its destination.

The upper three layers (layers 5 through 7) are often viewed as a group of APIs that interface applications with local network hardware. Their role is to make sure that the local computer can understand what the remote computer is transmitting and that the local computer packages information to be transmitted in a form that remote computers can understand.

For users, the application layer is the key layer of the OSI model. This layer is where the standards for important services such as file transfer, electronic mail, and terminal access are placed. The application layer is where data becomes information that can be used.

The seven layers of the OSI reference model are as follows:

✦ **Layer 1 (the physical layer).** This is the layer where the physical connection between the network and the computer equipment is established. Protocols at the physical layer are rules for the transmission of raw bits across the physical medium as well as rules for connectors and wiring.

✦ **Layer 2 (the data link layer).** Where the data is packaged to be transmitted when it is received. (A link is the logical connection between systems that have access to the same physical medium.) The data link layer is also responsible for ensuring that data arrives at the next layer without errors.

✦ **Layer 3 (the network layer).** The layer that routes data, deciding which path it will take through the network. At the transmitting end, the network layer accepts packets (units of data) from the data link layer. Then the network layer routes the packets over as many links and through as many intermediate systems as necessary to reach their destination. At the destination, the packets are delivered to the transport layer of the receiving system.

✦ **Layer 4 (the transport layer).** The layer responsible for providing reliable data flow between sender and receiver. This job is important, because some network layer implementations deliver data with high reliability, others with less. The transport layer also makes sure that data arrives at the correct destination.

✦ **Layer 5 (the session layer).** Manages the setup and termination of a communications path. It establishes connections between systems in much the same way that an automatic dialer does between two telephone systems.

✦ **Layer 6 (the presentation layer).** Converts messages to an internationally standardized format so that they can be understood by both the sending and the receiving systems. This process is symmetrical; local formats are converted for sending, and received data is converted to local formats.

✦ **Layer 7 (the application layer).** Provides the interface between user programs and the network.

The Windows NT Protocol Stack

As noted earlier, the OSI reference model is not a strict networking specification that all hardware and software vendors must follow. Instead, it is a general framework for network protocols that few, if any, systems implement precisely. Furthermore, the seven layers in the

OSI stack do not necessarily correspond to actual software modules. Transport software, for example, frequently crosses several boundaries.

Figure 10.6 shows how the networking components used by Windows NT correspond to the specifications laid down by OSI for its seven-level protocol suite. The two systems do not exactly match, but the Windows NT system corresponds more closely to the OSI model than many proprietary protocol suites do.

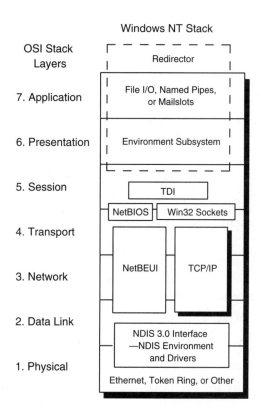

FIGURE 10.6 THE WINDOWS NT PROTOCOL SUITE.

HOW THE WINDOWS NT STACK WORKS

In Figure 10.6, notice that four of the layers in the Windows NT protocol suite are associated with products or services that are specific to the NT networking system. For example, in the Windows NT suite, layer 7—called the application layer in the OSI model—is occupied by three NT-specific APIs: the file I/O API, the named pipes API, and the mailslots API.

The file I/O API is, as you might guess, an interface that manages file I/O. Named pipes, an API that implements communications between threads and processes, is described in Chapter 9. The mailslots API handles broadcast-style transmissions from one machine to multiple machines on a network. For more information about mailslots, refer to your compiler's online help files.

Layer 6 of the Windows NT stack—called the presentation layer in the OSI model—is occupied by Windows NT's environment subsystems, which were introduced in Chapter 2, "Underneath Windows NT." An environment subsystem, as explained in Chapter 2, is a user-mode server that provides an API specific to an operating system. When an application calls an API routine, the call is delivered through an NT local procedure call (LPC) to an environment subsystem. The environment subsystem executes the API routine and returns the result to the application process through another LPC.

Layer 5 of the NT protocol suite, called the session level in the OSI model, is occupied in Windows NT by a component called the redirector. The redirector, described in more detail in "The Redirector" later in this chapter, passes I/O requests back and forth between the presentation layer (environment subsystems) and the transport layer (the transport driver interface) in the Windows NT protocol stack.

Layers 2, 3, and 4 in the Windows NT stack include the following components:

✦ The NetBIOS and NetBEUI protocols. The NetBIOS protocol provides networking compatibility with computers running MS-DOS and older versions of Windows and with stream-based communications systems such as the NetWare Link (NWLink) protocol. NetBEUI provides compatibility with existing LAN Manager, LAN server, and MS-NET installations (MS-NET is an aging protocol for networking MS-DOS machines).

✦ Windows sockets and the TCP/IP protocol, which provide Windows NT with wide area networking capability.

✦ The NDIS 3.0 interface, which provides compatibility with OS/2 network drivers.

NetBEUI is the protocol most often used for connecting Windows NT workstations connected through Ethernet interfaces over local area networks. TCP/IP is a popular protocol for wide area communications over large networks, such as the Internet. TCP/IP is examined in some detail in the section headed "The TCP/IP Protocol" later in this chapter.

Windows NT comes with NetBIOS and NDIS protocol software. You can also install these two protocols from Control Panel, following the same steps for installing TCP/IP that AppWizard prompts you for when you install Windows NT.

Stack-Based and Client-Server Networking

The Win32 networking structure has some features of a client-server networking system and some features of a layered networking system. Figure 10.7 is a simplified illustration of client-server networking in Windows NT.

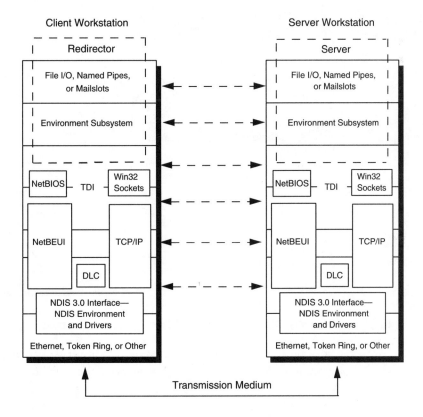

FIGURE 10.7 WIN32 CLIENT-SERVER COMMUNICATIONS.

Notice that in Figure 10.7, one Win32 stack is labeled Client Workstation, and the other stack is labeled Server Workstation. Also note that the redirector spans layers 5 through 7 in the client workstation, whereas a component named the server spans the same layers in the server machine. The redirector and server components are described in "Networking Windows NT" later in this section.

From the point of view of operating system architecture, layers 5 through 7 of the Windows NT networking stack are implemented in the I/O manager component of the NT executive (which is described in Chapter 2, "Underneath Windows NT"). This arrangement is illustrated in 10.8.

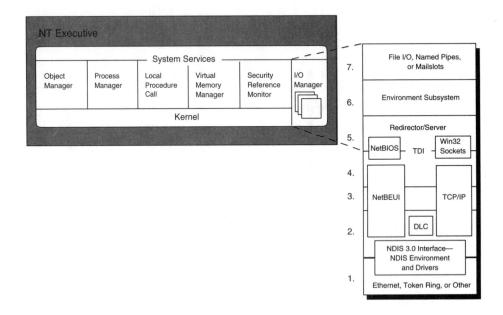

FIGURE 10.8 HOW WIN32'S LAYERED AND CLIENT-SERVER FEATURES FIT TOGETHER.

Because the Win32 networking system has characteristics of a client-server system as well as features of a layered system, the networking components in the Win32 I/O system work differently in client and server workstations. When a Windows NT workstation is being used as a client, making an I/O request to a server, the I/O subsystem works as shown in Figure 10.9.

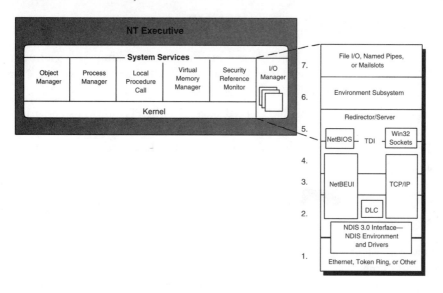

FIGURE 10.9 CLIENT-SIDE VIEW OF NETWORK I/O.

Figure 10.10 shows how the I/O subsystem works when a Windows NT workstation is being used as a server, responding to clients' I/O requests.

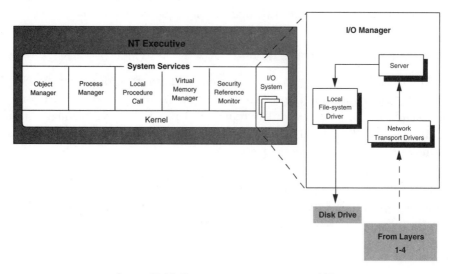

FIGURE 10.10 SERVER-SIDE VIEW OF NETWORK I/O.

Networking Windows NT

Windows NT networking is implemented in Win32 networking API. The networking API is a descendent of a networking product for MS-DOS named Microsoft Networks. Introduced in 1984, Microsoft Networks is sometimes referred to as MS-NET.

Although quite a bit of time has elapsed since 1984 by PC industry standards, some of the features of MS-NET are still alive and well in Windows NT. Two of these features—the redirector and the server—are still important. They have been rewritten a number of times and bear little resemblance to their MS-NET ancestors, but the tasks they perform today are similar to what they did in 1984.

THE REDIRECTOR

The Windows NT network redirector is part of the NT executive—specifically, it's part of the kernel's I/O manager. The redirector is what makes it possible for a Windows NT-based machine to access resources on other machines across a network. The redirector can access remote files, named pipes, and printers from a client machine.

The redirector is implemented as a file system driver (a software utility that accepts I/O requests from applications and passes them to physical device drivers.) It derives its name from the fact that it takes I/O requests from applications and redirects them to a network driver. The network driver then sends the requests to a remote server.

THE NETWORK TRANSPORT DRIVER

When an application seeks I/O access to a remote file, directory, or printer, Win32 passes the request to the redirector. The redirector then passes the request to a network driver called a *network transport driver*. The transport driver is accessed through a transport driver interface (TDI). The TDI communicates across the network to a remote server, which fulfills the application's I/O request.

When the redirector needs to communicate with the network transport driver through the TDI, the redirector passes I/O requests to the transport driver in the form of I/O request packets, or IRPs. An IRP is a data structure that controls how I/O information is processed at each stage of I/O operations. Every I/O request is represented by an IRP as it travels from one component of the I/O system to another. This process is illustrated in Figure 10.11.

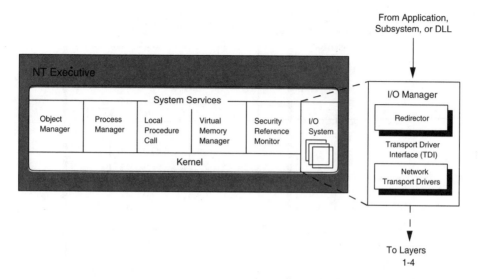

FIGURE 10.11 THE REDIRECTOR AND THE TDI.

THE SMB PROTOCOL

The redirector transmits data to the TDI using the server message block (SMB) protocol, a communications specification for formatting messages to be sent across a network.

The SMB protocol, like the redirector and the network server, dates to the days of MS-NET, so it is compatible with older MS-NET and LAN Manager servers. This compatibility provides Windows NT with network access to systems running MS-DOS, older versions of Windows, and OS/2. Windows NT is equipped with security protection to ensure that shared data is protected from unauthorized access when it is transmitted over networks that use these older systems.

Figure 10.12 shows how the SMB protocol is used in Windows NT network communications. The illustration also shows the NDIS protocol, which provides compatibility with OS/2 network drivers.

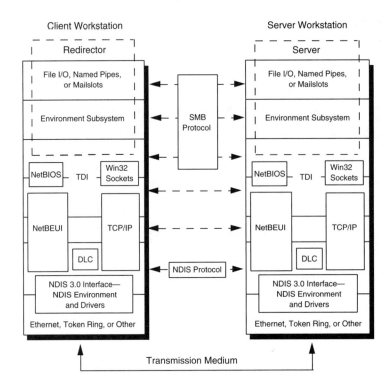

FIGURE 10.12 THE SMB AND NDIS PROTOCOLS.

HOW THE REDIRECTOR WORKS

When the redirector receives an I/O request from its host machine, it opens a channel called a virtual circuit to the remote machine; then it sends its data over that virtual circuit. The redirector maintains one virtual circuit for each server to which its host system is connected, and it multiplexes requests that are destined for all servers across the same virtual circuit. The network transport driver determines how to implement the virtual circuit and send the data across the network connection.

Between the time an NT workstation sends a request and the time it receives a reply, the redirector provides a pseudo-file system that behaves like a local file system even though it operates across a network. If the physical link from one computer to another fails, the redirector must recover the connection, if possible. If that is not possible, the redirector must at least make sure that failure occurs gracefully enough for an application to try to restore the connection.

How Windows NT Server Works

The Windows NT network server, like the redirector, is part of the NT executive. Like the redirector, the network server is implemented as a file system driver; it can cache network files directly to disk when it determines that disk caching would save time. That provides the network server with an efficient method for handling file operations that involve large amounts of data. Because the network server is part of the NT executive, it can directly call the NT cache manager—which handles disk-caching operations—to optimize data transfers.

If the server receives a request to read a large amount of data, it calls the cache manager to locate the data in the cache (or to load the data into the cache if it isn't already there) and to lock the data in memory. The server then transfers the data directly from the cache to the network, avoiding unnecessary disk access or data copying.

The network server, like the redirector, uses the SMB protocol and therefore is compatible with MS-NET and LAN Manager. This compatibility allows the server to process requests that originate not only from other Windows NT systems but also from systems running LAN Manager software.

Windows NT Protocols

Back in the days of MS-NET system, the NetBIOS interface was used to pass streams of data structured in the SMB format directly across the network. Software implementing the NetBIOS interface resides in layer 4 (the transport layer) of the Windows NT stack.

The NetBIOS protocol gives Windows NT the ability to communicate with computers running MS-DOS and older versions of Windows. It also provides compatibility with other stream-based communications systems, such as the NetWare Link protocol.

The NetBEUI Protocol

Although Windows NT supports NetBIOS, a faster and more efficient choice for local area NT networking is the NetBEUI (NetBIOS extended user interface) protocol. NetBEUI is a small, efficient protocol that is tuned for very fast operation on small LANs.

Developed by IBM to operate underneath the NetBIOS network interface, NetBEUI spans layers 2 through 4 in the Windows NT stack.

When you install Windows NT, you can click a check box to install NetBEUI automatically.

(described in Chapter 9, "Interprocess Communications"), and the Win32 mailslots API. (The latter is of interest to you only if the network you are connected to uses it; see your Visual C++ online help utility for details.)

The outstanding feature of the networking API functions is that they are network-independent; no matter what kind of protocol a Windows NT workstation is using and no matter what kind of network the workstation is connected to, the functions supplied in the networking API always work the same way. For example, the NETWORK program presented later in this chapter works on a pair of workstations connected using NetBEUI in exactly the same way that it works on a pair of workstations that are connected using TCP/IP.

Linking with the mpr.lib Library

To call the functions implemented in the network API, you must link your application with the Win32 API library **MPR.LIB** as follows:

1. From the Development Studio's Build menu, select **Settings** .

2. When the Project Settings property sheet appears, tab to the Link property page.

3. From the Category list box, select **Input**.

4. Type **mpr.lib** in the Object/Library Modules text box, as shown in Figure 10.13.

5. Close the Project Settings property shot by clicking the **Close** button.

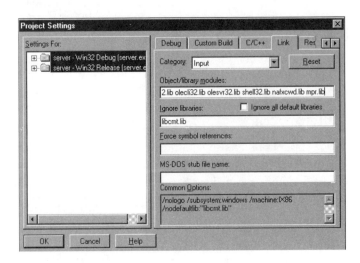

FIGURE 10.13 LINKING WITH THE **MPR.LIB** LIBRARY.

DLC AND TCP/IP

Another protocol supported by Windows NT is the data link control (DLC) protocol. It is used primarily to access IBM mainframe computers or printers connected directly to the network rather than through a port. You can install DLC by selecting the **Network** option in the Windows NT Control Panel.

Finally, Windows NT supports TCP/IP (transmission control protocol/Internet protocol), a popular protocol that supports data communications across wide area networks. TCP/IP compatibility allows Windows NT users to communicate with the Internet and with popular UNIX-based bulletin board, news, and electronic mail services. TCP/IP is examined in more detail in the section headed "The TCP/IP Protocol" later in this chapter. TCP/IP, like NetBEUI, can be installed automatically along with Windows NT.

NDIS

The network driver interface specification (NDIS) interface, which spans the physical and data link layers in the Windows NT stack, connects network card drivers with Windows NT's transport drivers. It allows designers of network cards and transport drivers to interface their products with the Windows NT stack without having to worry about the many specifications and requirements of various transport protocols. Conversely, it allows software engineers to design networking APIs without having to be concerned with the various specifications and requirements of particular network cards or transport drivers.

Software developers write device drivers for Windows NT using the Windows NT DDK, which is available as a stand-alone product from Microsoft. The DDK provides functions and data structures for writing NDIS interfaces, transport driver interfaces, and other interfaces to support specific transport drivers and network card drivers.

The Win32 Networking API

The Win32 networking API provides a set of API functions that are independent of communications systems and protocols. With these functions, Windows NT applications can communicate with other applications across networks without being concerned with the rules or specifications of specific network providers or physical network implementations.

Applications can use the Win32 API functions to make and cancel network connections and to retrieve information about the current configuration of networks. In addition, the Win32 API implements a version of NetBIOS for applications that require it.

The functions implemented in the networking API are not the only Win32 functions that can be used by networking applications. Applications can also communicate over networks using the Windows sockets API (described later in this chapter); named pipes

The **NETRESOURCE** Structure

Some of the functions in the networking API take a pointer to a NETRESOURCE structure as a parameter. A NETRESOURCE structure provides a list of facts about a network resource. Pointers to NETRESOURCE structures are passed to functions that enumerate resources on a network and to functions that enumerate currently connected resources. A NETRESOURCE structure looks like the following:

```
typedef struct _NETRESOURCE {   /* nr */
    DWORD   dwScope;
    DWORD   dwType;
    DWORD   dwDisplayType;
    DWORD   dwUsage;
    LPTSTR  lpLocalName;
    LPTSTR  lpRemoteName;
    LPTSTR  lpComment;
    LPTSTR  lpProvider;
} NETRESOURCE;
```

A NETRESOURCE structure has the following elements:

* **dwScope.** Some functions enumerate network resources; they list the names of various network resources and network connections in various ways. When network resources are being enumerated, this element specifies the scope of the enumeration. Set the value of `dwScope` to the constant RESOURCE_CONNECTED when you want to enumerate resources that are connected. Set the value of `dwScope` to RESOURCE_GLOBALNET when you want to enumerate all resources on the network, whether are not they are currently connected to your workstation. Use the value RESOURCE_REMEMBERED when you want to enumerate persistent resources—resources that are automatically restored when the user logs on.

* **dwType.** This member is a bitmap that specifies the kind of resources to be enumerated. Set `dwType` to a value of RESOURCETYPE_ANY when you want all resources enumerated, to RESOURCETYPE_DISK when you want disk resources enumerated, and to RESOURCETYPE_PRINT when you want print resources enumerated.

* **dwDisplayType.** The `dwDisplayType` element specifies how objects should be displayed in a network browsing user interface. The value of this element can be one of the following:

✦ RESOURCEDISPLAYTYPE_DOMAIN, which means that the object should be displayed as a domain.

✦ RESOURCEDISPLAYTYPE_GENERIC, which means that the method used to display the object does not matter.

✦ RESOURCEDISPLAYTYPE_SERVER, which means that the object should be displayed as a server.

✦ RESOURCEDISPLAYTYPE_SHARE, which means that the object should be displayed as a *sharepoint* (an object, such as printer, a directory, or a file, that is not a container).

✦ **dwUsage.** This element is a bitmap that specifies what kind of resources are to be enumerated from the standpoint of their usage. It is defined only if dwScope is set to RESOURCE_GLOBALNET. If the value of dwUsage is RESOURCEUSAGE_ CONNECTABLE, the name pointed to by lpRemoteName can be passed to the WNetAddConnection function to make a network connection. If the value of dwUsage is RESOURCEUSAGE_CONTAINER, it is assumed to be a container, and the name pointed to by lpRemoteName can be passed to the WNetOpenEnum function to enumerate the resources in the container.

✦ **lpLocalName.** This member points to the name of a local device if the dwScope member is RESOURCE_CONNECTED or RESOURCE_REMEMBERED. The value of lpLocalName is NULL if the connection does not use a device. Otherwise, it is undefined.

✦ **lpRemoteName.** The lpRemoteName element points to a remote network name if the entry is a network resource. If the entry is a current or persistent connection, lpRemoteName points to the network name associated with the name pointed to by lpLocalName.

✦ **lpComment.** Points to a provider-supplied comment.

✦ **lpProvider.** Points to the name of the provider owning this resource. The value of this member can be NULL if the name of the provider is not known.

CONNECTING TO A NETWORK

You connect a Windows NT workstation to a remote computer by calling the Win32 function WNetAddConnection2. (There is also a WNetAddConnection function, but it is provided for backward compatibility with older Windows systems. For new applications, you should call WNetAddConnection2.)

The syntax of WNetAddConnection2 is as follows:

```
DWORD WNetAddConnection2(LPNETRESOURCE lpNetResource,
    LPSTR lpszPassword, LPSTR lpszUserName, DWORD fdwConnection)
```

If WNetAddConnection2 succeeds, the return value is the constant NO_ERROR. Otherwise, the return value is an error code, which can be retrieved by calling the network API function WNetGetLastError.

WNetAddConnection2 takes four parameters:

- ✦ A pointer to a NETRESOURCE structure that specifies the network resource to connect to.
- ✦ A pointer to the password being used to make the connection, expressed as a C-style string.
- ✦ A pointer to the user name being used to make the connection, also expressed as a C-style string.
- ✦ **fdwConnection.** A bitmap that describes the kind of connection being made. The value of fdwConnection can be either zero or the constant CONNECT_UPDATE_PROFILE. If fdwConnection is set to CONNECT_UPDATE_PROFILE, information about the connection is stored in the user's profile. If a value of zero is used, the user's profile is not updated.

With the WNetAddConnection2 and WNetCancelConnection2 functions, an application can control whether a network connection is persistent from one session to the next.

DISCONNECTING FROM A NETWORK

The Win32 function WNetCancelConnection2 disconnects a Windows NT workstation from a network. (There is also a WNetCancelConnection function, but it is provided for backward compatibility with older Windows systems. For new applications, you should call WNetCancelConnection2.) The syntax of WNetCancelConnection2 is as follows:

```
DWORD WNetCancelConnection2(LPSTR lpszUserName, DWORD fdwConnection, BOOL fForce)
```

If WNetCancelConnection2 succeeds, the return value is the constant NO_ERROR. Otherwise, the return value is an error code, which can be retrieved by calling WNetGet-LastError.

WNetCancelConnection2 takes three parameters:

+ **lpszUserName.** Points to a null-terminated string that specifies the name of either the redirected local device or the remote network resource to disconnect from. If lpszName specifies a redirected local resource, only the specified redirection is broken; otherwise, all connections to the remote network resource are broken.

+ **fdwConnection.** A bitmap that describes the kind of connection being made. The value of fdwConnection can be either zero or the constant CON-NECT_UPDATE_PROFILE. If fdwConnection is set to CONNECT_UPDATE_PROFILE, information about the connection is stored in the user's profile. If a value of zero is used, the user's profile is not updated.

+ **fForce.** Specifies whether the requested disconnection should take place if there are open files or open jobs on the connection that would be affected. If fForce is FALSE, the function fails if there are open files or jobs.

CONNECTING WITH NETWORK RESOURCES

The WNetConnectionDialog function creates a dialog box that lets you browse through network resources and connect with a resource if desired. This is the syntax of WNetConnectionDialog:

```
DWORD WNetConnectionDialog(HWND hwnd, DWORD fdwResourceType)
```

If WNetConnectionDialog succeeds, the return value is the constant NO_ERROR. If the user cancels out of the dialog, the return value is 0xFFFFFFFF. In all other cases, the function returns the same error code that can be obtained by calling the network function WNetGetLastError.

WNetConnectionDialog takes two parameters: a handle to the currently open window, and a double word that specifies the kind of resource to open. At present, the constant RESOURCETYPE_DISK must be passed in the second parameter.

In the NETWORK example program, the WNetConnectionDialog function is called in **NETWORK.CPP,** as follows:

```
DWORD retVal;
HWND hwnd = pView->m_hWnd;

retVal = WNetConnectionDialog(hwnd, RESOURCETYPE_DISK);
```

When `WNetConnectionDialog` is called in the preceding code sequence, the program displays a network connection dialog box like the one shown in Figure 10.14.

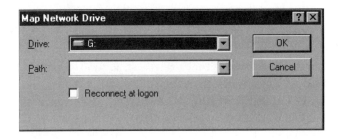

FIGURE 10.14 CONNECTING WITH A NETWORK RESOURCE.

DISCONNECTING FROM NETWORK RESOURCES

`WNetDisconnectionDialog` creates and displays a dialog box that allows you to disconnect from network resources. Following is the syntax of `WNetDisconnectDialog`:

```
DWORD WNetDisconnectDialog(HWND hwnd, DWORD fdwResourceType)
```

If `WNetDisconnectDialog` returns successfully, the return value is the constant NO_ERROR. If the user cancels out of the dialog, the return value is 0xFFFFFFFF. In all other cases, the function returns the same error code that can be obtained by calling `WNetGetLastError`.

`WNetDisconnectDialog` takes two parameters: a handle to the currently open window, and a double word that specifies the kind of resource to open. The value of the second parameter can be RESOURCETYPE_DISK or RESOURCETYPE_PRINT.

In the NETWORK program, this code sequence in **NETWORK.CPP** calls `WNetDisconnectDialog`:

```
DWORD retVal;
HWND hwnd = pView->m_hWnd;

retVal = WNetDisconnectDialog(hwnd,
 RESOURCETYPE_DISK);
```

When `WNetDisconnectDialog` is called, the program displays a network disconnect dialog box resembling the one in Figure 10.15.

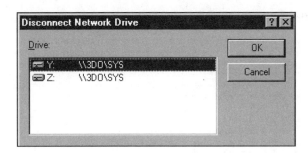

FIGURE 10.15 DISCONNECTING FROM A NETWORK RESOURCE.

ENUMERATING NETWORK RESOURCES

You can enumerate the resources on a network—list the names of various network resources and network connections in various ways—by calling the functions WNetOpenEnum, WNetEnumResource, and WNetCloseEnum. The WNetOpenEnum function starts an enumeration of network resources or connections. WNetEnumResource continues the enumeration, and WNetCloseEnum ends it.

To enumerate a network container resource, an application passes to WNetOpenEnum the address of a NETRESOURCE structure. WNetOpenEnum then creates a handle to the resource described by the NETRESOURCE structure.

When WNetOpenEnum returns, the application passes to WNetEnumResource the handle returned by WNetOpenEnum. WNetEnumResource returns information about the resource in the form of an array of NETRESOURCE structures. When the handle created by WNetOpenEnum is no longer needed, your application can close it by calling WNetCloseEnum.

In the NETWORK example program on the accompanying disk, WNetOpenEnum is called in this code sequence in **NETWORK.CPP:**

```
dwResult = WNetOpenEnum(RESOURCE_CONNECTED,
    RESOURCETYPE_DISK,
    0,      // enumerate all resources.
    lpnr,   // NULL first time this function is called.
    &hEnum); // handle to resource.
```

Next, the following sequence calls `WNetEnumResource`:

```
dwResultEnum = WNetEnumResource(hEnum, // Resource handle.
    &cEntries,  // Defined locally as 0xFFFFFFFF.
    lpnrLocal,  // LPNETRESOURCE.
    &cbBuffer); // Buffer size.
```

Finally, `WNetCloseEnum` is called:

```
    dwResult = WNetCloseEnum(hEnum);
```

To display the results of the preceding enumeration functions, the NETWORK program opens a dialog window containing a list box, as shown in Figure 10.16.

FIGURE 10.16 ENUMERATING NETWORK RESOURCES.

THE WNETOPENENUM FUNCTION

The `WNetOpenEnum` function starts an enumeration of network resources or network connections. The syntax of the function is as follows:

```
DWORD WNetOpenEnum(DWORD fdwScope, DWORD fdwType, DWORD fdwUsage,
    LPNETRESROUCE lpNetResource, LPHANDLE lphEnum)
```

The parameters passed to `WNetOpenEnum` include a pointer to a NETRESOURCE structure (`lpNetResource`) and a handle to a text buffer (`lphEnum`). `WNetOpenEnum` stores information about the resources or network connections that it enumerates in the buffer referenced by the `lphEnum` handle.

If `WNetOpenEnum` returns successfully, its return value is the constant NO_ERROR and the buffer contains the requested data. The calling application can continue to call

WNetEnumResource to complete the enumeration. If WNetDisconnectDialog returns a value of ERROR_NO_MORE_ITEMS, there are no more entries and the buffer contents are undefined. If the return value is not NO_ERROR or ERROR_NO_MORE_ITEMS, it is an error code that can be retrieved by calling WNetGetLastError.

THE WNetEnumResource FUNCTION

The WNetEnumResource function continues a network-resource enumeration started by WNetOpenEnum:

```
DWORD WNetEnumResource(HANDLE hEnum, LPDWORD lpcEntries, LPVOID
    lpvBuffer, LPDWORD lpcbBuffer)
```

The parameters that must be passed to the WNetEnumResource function are:

+ **hEnum**. Identifies an enumeration instance. This is the same handle that is returned by WNetOpenEnum.

+ **lpcEntries**. Points to a variable specifying the number of entries requested. If the number requested is 0xFFFFFFFF, the function returns as many entries as possible. If the function returns successfully, the variable pointed to by the lpcEntries parameter contains the number of entries actually read.

+ **lpvBuffer**. Points to a buffer to receive the enumeration results. This array is an array of NETRESOURCE structures. Your application is responsible for allocating enough memory to store the array of NETRESOURCE structures that the WNetEnumResource call retrieves. You should allocate a buffer of adequate size (16KB is typical) and then pass a pointer to that buffer to WNetEnumResources in the lpvBuffer parameter. When you have allocated space for lpvBuffer, you provide the size of the buffer to the lpcbBuffer parameter (the next item in this list). WNetEnumResources uses the value of lpcbBuffer to truncate the array of NETRESOURCE structures that it returns if buffer space is exhausted.

+ **lpcbBuffer**. Points to a variable that specifies the size, in bytes, of the lpvBuffer parameter.

THE WNetCloseEnum FUNCTION

The WNetCloseEnum function ends a network-resource enumeration started by WNetOpen-Enum. The syntax of WNetCloseEnum is as follows:

```
DWORD WNetCloseEnum(HANDLE hEnum)
```

WNetCloseEnum takes one parameter: a handle to an enumeration instance. This is the same handle that is returned by WNetOpenEnum when the enumeration begins.

THE WNETGETCONNECTION FUNCTION

The WNetGetConnection function retrieves the name of the network resource that is associated with a local device. For example, if a remote CD-ROM drive named \\SATURN\CDROM2$ is connected to your NT workstation as drive H:, you might pass the H: designator to WNetGetConnection, which would then return the string \\SATURN\CDROM2$.

This is the syntax of WNetGetConnection:

```
DWORD WNetGetConnection(LPTSTR lpszLocalName, LPSTR lpszRemoteName,
    LPDWORD lpcchBuffer)
```

WNetGetConnection takes three parameters: a pointer to a local name expressed as a C-style string, a pointer to a remote network-resource name expressed as a C-style string, and a pointer to a variable that specifies the size, in characters, of the buffer pointed to by the lpszRemoteName parameter when the function returns.

If WNetGetConnection succeeds, it returns the value NO_ERROR. If it fails, it returns an error code that you can retrieve by calling GetLastError. If the function fails because the buffer is not big enough, the lpszRemoteName parameter returns the required buffer size.

CALLING THE WNETGETCONNECTION FUNCTION

The example program NETWORK calls the WNetGetConnection function in this statement in **MNTETWORK.CPP**:

```
dwResult = WNetGetConnection((LPTSTR) tempStr, (LPSTR)szDeviceName,&cchBuff);
```

When WNetGetConnection is called, NETWORK prompts the user for the local name of a remote disk drive by displaying a dialog box like the one shown in Figure 10.17. When the user types in the name of a disk drive (followed by a colon) and closes the dialog box, the program displays another dialog box showing the path name of the specified remote drive.

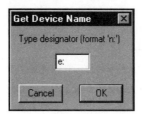

FIGURE 10.17 GETTING THE NAME OF A CONNECTION.

THE WNETGETUSER FUNCTION

WNetGetUser retrieves the current default user name or the user name used to establish a network connection.

```
DWORD WNetGetUser(LPSTR lpszLocalName, LPTSTR lpszUserName,
    LPDWORD lpcchBuffer)
```

WNetGetUser takes three parameters: a pointer to a local name expressed as a C-style string, a pointer to a buffer that is to receive a user name expressed as a C-style string, and a pointer to a variable that specifies the size, in characters, of the buffer pointed to by the lpszUserName parameter when the function returns.

If WNetGetUser succeeds, it returns the value NO_ERROR. If it fails, it returns an error code that you can retrieve by calling GetLastError. If the function fails because the buffer is not big enough, the lpszRemoteName parameter returns the required buffer size.

If you pass a NULL value to WNetGetUser in the lpszLocalName parameter, the function returns the name of the current user. If lpszLocalName is a network name and the user is connected to that resource using a different name, Windows NT may not be able to resolve the user name to return. In this case, Windows NT may make an arbitrary choice from possible user names.

THE WNETGETLASTERROR FUNCTION

The WNetGetLastError function retrieves the most recent extended error code set by a Windows network function. Following is the syntax of WNetGetLastError:

```
DWORD WNetGetLastError(LPDWORD lpdwErrorCode, LPTSTR lpszDescription,
    DWORD cchDescription, LPTSTR lpszName, DWORD cchName)
```

If WNetGetLastError successfully obtains the last networking error reported, its return value is NO_ERROR. If the caller supplies an invalid buffer, the function's return value is ERROR_INVALID_ADDRESS.

The parameters to WNetGetLastError are as follows:

✦ **lpdwErrorCode.** Points to a variable that receives the error code reported by the network provider. This error code is specific to the network provider. (A network provider is a central computer system running server software that provides network services; an example of a network provider is the Windows NT Advanced Server.)

✦ **lpszDescription.** Points to a buffer that receives a C-style string describing the error.

✦ **cchDescription.** Specifies the size, in characters, of the buffer pointed to by the lpszDescription parameter. If the buffer is too small for the error string, the string is truncated but still null-terminated. A buffer at least 256 characters long is recommended.

✦ **lpszName.** Points to a buffer that receives the null-terminated string, identifying the network provider that caused the error.

✦ **cchName.** Specifies the size, in characters, of the buffer pointed to by the lpszName parameter. If the buffer is too small for the error string, the string is truncated but still null-terminated.

The NETWORK example program calls WNetGetLastError in a member function (in **NETWORK.CPP**) named MNetwork::NetErrorHandler. Figure 10.18 shows an error message displayed by the MNetwork::NetErrorHandler function.

FIGURE 10.18 WNETGETLASTERROR ERROR MESSAGE.

THE NETBIOS FUNCTION

The network function `Netbios` is provided primarily for applications that were written for the NetBIOS protocol and are being ported to Windows. Applications that don't require compatibility with NetBIOS can usually use other interfaces, such as mailslots and named pipes (see Chapter 9), to accomplish tasks similar to those supported by `Netbios`.

Following is the syntax of `Netbios`:

```
UCHAR WNetBios(PNCB pncp)
```

The `Netbios` function takes one parameter, a pointer to a network control block (NCB) structure. A network control block is a structure defined by the Win32 operating system. An NCB structure contains information about a network's environment and a pointer to a buffer that is used for messages or for additional data about the network.

For synchronous requests (see Chapter 9, "Interprocess Communications"), the return value of `Netbios` is the completion code of the NCB specified in the `pncb` parameter. There are two possible return values for asynchronous requests that are accepted. If an asynchronous command is completed when `Netbios` returns to its caller, the return value is the completion code of the NCB, just as if it were a synchronous NCB. If the asynchronous command is still pending when the `Netbios` call returns, the return value is 0. If the NCB address specified by the `pncb` parameter is invalid, the function's return value is NRC_BADNCB.

Example: The NETWORK Program

This chapter's first example program, NETWORK, shows how you can connect to and disconnect from a remote network resource. It also illustrates how you can retrieve the names of network resources connected to your Windows NT workstation. Figure 10.19 shows the NETWORK screen display.

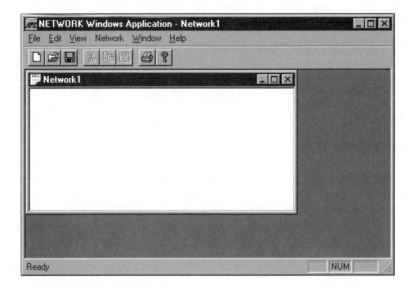

FIGURE 10.19 THE NETWORK SCREEN DISPLAY.

NETWORK demonstrates some of the networking fundamentals covered so far in this chapter. In this chapter's second sample program—the SOCKS application presented near the end of the chapter—you'll find practical uses for the networking operations demonstrated in NETWORK.

In the NETWORK program, a pair of source files named **DEVICES.CPP** and **GETDEV.CPP** display dialog boxes that let you connect and disconnect from network resources. **NETWORK.CPP** implements the MNetwork class—a simple networking class written for this book—and **NETWORK.H** defines the class. The member functions in the MNetwork class are called from the file **NETVIEW.CPP**. Information is stored in a CDocument object implemented in **NETDOC.CPP**.

RUNNING THE NETWORK PROGRAM

The NETWORK program demonstrates how you can use functions that are provided in the Win32 network API to set up and maintain communications across a network. The program, written in Visual C++, is an MDI application equipped with a standard pull-down menu bar and a set of dialog boxes. It shows how you can connect and disconnect remote disk drives and how you can obtain information about disk drives on remote machines.

Figure 10.20 illustrates the NETWORK program's menu.

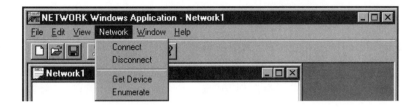

FIGURE 10.20 THE NETWORK PROGRAM'S MENU.

Using the dialog boxes provided by NETWORK, you can do the following:

✦ Connect your Windows NT workstation to remote disk drives.

✦ Disconnect your workstation from remote disk drives.

✦ Obtain the path name of a remote disk drive by typing in the disk drive's local name. (For example, if you enter **H:**, the NETWORK program might respond \\SATURN\CDROM2.)

✦ List, in various formats, the kinds of resources that are available on your network.

When you connect to a remote disk drive using the NETWORK program, the program's File menu treats the remote drive in the same way that it treats local drives. The program lets you load files, save files, and browse through files on remote drives in the same way that you perform these operations using local drives.

All the network-related operations in NETWORK are implemented using functions provided in the Win32 networking API. However, the program encapsulates the Win32 networking functions that it uses in the C++ class `MNetwork`. `MNetwork` does not rely on any MFC classes, so you can use the source code that defines and implements the class in any C++ program written for Windows NT, and you can compile the code using any NT-compatible compiler.

TCP/IP and the Windows Sockets API

The first half of this chapter introduced some general principles of computer networking and presented a sample program named NETWORK that showed how a pair of computers can connect across a network in a client-server environment.

Now that we have all that behind us, we can turn our attention to the more specific topic of Windows NT networking. The rest of this chapter will focus on three main topics:

- ✦ The TCP/IP protocol, which lets computers access each other over the Internet.
- ✦ The Windows sockets API, which provides TCP/IP support to Windows NT.
- ✦ The CSocket and CAsyncSocket classes, which let you access the Windows Sockets API using the MFC library.

THE TCP/IP PROTOCOL

Before you can use the Windows sockets API, you must have a basic understanding of TCP/IP. Once you've installed the TCP/IP API on your Windows NT workstation, you can start writing TCP/IP-related applications for Windows NT.

TCP/IP is not just a communications protocol, and it is not just an API. It's a suite made up of many data communications protocols. The suite derives its name from two of those protocols: the transmission control protocol (TCP) and the Internet protocol (IP). There are many other protocols in the suite, but TCP and IP are two of the most important.

In 1969, the Defense Advanced Research Projects Agency—sometimes referred to as DARPA—funded a project to create an experimental packet-switching network (one that moves data grouped into packets). As part of its project, DARPA set up a computer network called ARPANET to study techniques for providing reliable, vendor-independent communications that could interface with a variety of client and host machines. ARPANET was so successful that many other organizations inside and outside the government were soon using it for day-to-day computer communications.

In 1975, ARPANET was promoted from experimental to operational status, and the Defense Communications Agency took over the job of administering it. ARPANET kept growing, and in 1983 it was split into two parts. Most of the network became MILNET, a military network used for unclassified communications. ARPANET remained on the network but was slimmed down. Together, MILNET and ARPANET were referred to as the Internet. ARPANET formally passed out of existence in 1990, but the Internet continued to grow, eventually becoming the monster it is today.

In 1983, the year the Internet was born, the first TCP/IP specifications were published as part of a set of standards called the Military Standards (MIL STD). The government decreed that all host machines connected to the Internet were required to convert to the MIL STD protocols. To make the conversion easier, DARPA bankrolled an effort by the firm of Bolt, Beranek, and Newman to implement TCP/IP in the Berkeley version of UNIX. Since then, UNIX and TCP/IP have gone together like a horse and carriage. It's possible to have one without the other, as Windows NT is proving, but UNIX and TCP/IP are so closely bonded that separating them successfully has never been a trivial operation.

How TCP/IP Handles Data

Different kinds of networking APIs send out data in different forms—that is, using different types of data structures. Different networking APIs also use different kinds of terminology to describe the structures they use for header encapsulation.

APIs that use TCP/IP send out data in two different kinds of formats. Some TCP/IP APIs send data in uninterrupted streams that work like file streams. When data is sent in a stream, it goes to only one destination, and that destination cannot be changed without stopping the stream and then starting it up again.

Other APIs, sometimes called *packet-driven* APIs, divide data into small packets before they send it. By splitting a transmission into packets, an API can send a transmission to any number of destinations by simply changing the destination address.

The most commonly used packet-based API for TCP/IP communications is the user datagram protocol, or UDP. The most widely used stream-based API is the Berkeley Software Distribution (BSD) sockets API, which was developed at the University of California at Berkeley.

Packet-based protocols, such as UDC, have a couple of advantages over stream-based protocols in applications that need a convenient way to send short amounts of data over reliable transmission lines. UDC transmissions move fast and are easy to manage, but they are not as reliable as stream-based transmissions, especially when large amounts of data must be transmitted over facilities whose reliability is not guaranteed.

When you want to transmit considerable amounts of data over a network with guaranteed reliability, your best choice is a stream-based protocol, such as Windows sockets, which you will learn more about later in this chapter.

Other Features of TCP/IP

TCP/IP did not achieve the fame it has today just because the government sponsored it, although that certainly helped. The main reason TCP/IP became popular is that the TCP/IP protocols met an important need for worldwide computer communication, and they happened to have some features that made them especially suitable for fulfilling that need. Following are three important features of the TCP/IP protocols:

✦ TCP/IP does not depend on any specific physical network hardware. The TCP/IP protocols can integrate many different kinds of networks and can be run equally well using many different kinds of hardware. You can use TCP/IP on Ethernet, a Token Ring network, a dial-up line, an X.25 network, or almost any other kind of transmission hardware.

✦ The TCP/IP protocols provide open protocol standards, freely available and developed independently from any specific computer hardware or operating system. The Internet aside, TCP/IP is so widely supported that it has proven to be a useful system for uniting different hardware and software.

✦ TCP/IP workstations and networks use a homogeneous and universally accepted addressing system that provides every TCP/IP network worldwide with a unique address. That makes every user's address accessible to every other user, regardless of any user's location.

The Windows Sockets API

The Windows sockets API defines a network programming interface for Microsoft Windows. This interface is based on the BSD programming model, which is the de facto standard for TCP/IP networking. The Windows sockets API contains all the functionality of BSD Sockets—often referred to as Berkeley Sockets—along with a set of extensions that provide extra features for Windows programmers.

The Windows sockets API was originally engineered to work with the 16-bit Windows operating system. It was designed to appeal to software designers who were familiar with writing sockets applications for UNIX and other non-Windows environments and to simplify the task of porting existing sockets-based source code to Windows. The 16-bit Windows sockets API contains all the familiar Berkeley Sockets-style routines as well as a set of Windows-specific extensions designed to allow programmers to take advantage of the message-driven design of Window programs.

The Windows sockets API for Windows NT, a 32-bit version of the original, is designed to be compatible within all implementations and versions of Microsoft Windows beginning with version 3.0. It supports Windows sockets implementations and Windows sockets applications in both 16-bit and 32-bit operating environments. Windows sockets for Windows NT also supports multithreaded Windows processes.

BSD SOCKETS AND WINDOWS SOCKETS

The Windows sockets API contains two sets of functions: One set corresponds to the functions defined in the BSD Sockets API, and the other set contains Windows-specific extensions.

It's easy to tell the difference between the BSD-style functions and the Windows-specific extensions. The BSD-style functions are typed in all-lowercase letters. All the Windows-specific functions are typed in a mixture of uppercase and lowercase letters. Also, they all begin with the letters WSA, which stands for Windows sockets API.

BSD-STYLE FUNCTIONS IN THE WINDOWS SOCKETS API

Table 10.1 lists and describes the BSD-style socket functions in the Windows sockets API

TABLE 10.1 BSD-STYLE SOCKET FUNCTIONS IN THE WINDOWS SOCKETS API.

Function	Description
accept( )	Acknowledges an incoming connection is and associates it with an immediately created socket. The original socket is returned to the listening state.
bind( )	Assigns a local name to an unnamed socket.
closesocket ( )	Removes a socket description from the per-process object reference table. Only blocks if SO_LINGER is set.
connect( )	Initiates a connection on the specified socket.
getpeername ( )	Retrieves the name of the peer connected to the sdpecified socket descriptor.
getsockname ( )	Retrieves the current name for the specified socket.
getsockopt ( )	Retrieves options associated with the specified socket descriptor.
htonl ( )	Converts a 32-bit quantity from host byte order to network byte order.
htons ( )	Converts a 16-bit quantity from host byte order to network byte order.
inet_addr ( )	Converts a character string representing a number in the internet standard "." notation to an internet address value.
inet_ntoa ( )	Converts an Internet address value to an ASCII string in "." notaion; i.e. "a.b.c.d."
ioctlsocket ( )	Provides control for descriptors.
listen ( )	Listens for incoming connections on a specified socket.
ntohl ( )	Converts a 32-bit quantity from network byte order to host byte order.
ntohs ( )	Converts a 16-bit quantity from a network byte order to a host byte order
recv ( )*	Receives data from a connected socket.
recfrom ( )*	Receives data from either a connected or unconnected socket.*
select ( )*	Performs synchronous I/O multiplexing.
send ( )*	Sends data to a connected socket.

continued

TABLE 10.1 CONTINUED

Function	Description
sendto ( )*	Sends data to either a connected or unconnected socket.
setsockopt ( )	Stores options associated the specified socket descriptor.
shutdown ( )	Shuts down part of a full-duplex connection.
socket ( )	Creates an endpoint for communication and return a socket descriptor.

*This routine can block if it is acting on a blocking socket.

WINDOWS EXTENSION FUNCTIONS IN THE WINDOWS SOCKETS API

Table 10.2 lists and describes the Windows extension functions in the Windows sockets API.

TABLE 10.2 WINDOWS EXTENSION FUNCTIONS IN THE WINDOWS SOCKETS API.

Function	Description
WSAAsyncGetHostByAddr ( )	Nonblocking version of gethostbyaddr ( )
WSAAsyncGetHostByName ( )	Nonblocking version of gethostbyname ( )
WSAAsyncGetProtoByName ( )	Nonblocking version of getprotobyname ( )
WSAAsyncGetProtoByNumber ( )	Nonblocking version of getprotobynumber ( )
WSAAsyncGetServByName ( )	Nonblocking version of getservbyname ( )
WSAAsyncGetservByPort ( )	Nonblocking version of getservbyport ( )
WSACancelAsyncRequest ( )	Cancels an outstanding instance of a WSAAsyncGetXByY function
WSACancelBlockingCall ( )	Cancels an outstanding blocking API call
WSACleanup ( )	Signs off from the underlying Windows Sockets DLL
WSAGetLastError ( )	Obtains details of last Windows Sockets API error
WSAIsBlocking ( )	Determines if the underlying Windows Sockets DLL is already blocking an exisiting call for this thread
WSABlockingHook( )	"Hooks" the blocking method used by the underlying Windows Sockets implementation
WSASetLastError( )	Sets the error to be returned by a subsequent call to SAWGetLastError
WSAGetLastError ( )	Obtains details of the last Windows Sockets API error
WSAStartup ( )	Initializes the underlying Windows Sockets DLL
WSAUnhookBlockingHook ( )	Restores the original blocking function

BLOCKING AND NONBLOCKING FUNCTIONS

A more important difference between the BSD and Windows function sets is that the Windows set contains a group of functions that solve a common problem in TCP/IP programming. *Blocking* occurs when a function starts an operation and does not return until the operation is complete. Blocking generally causes no problem when a function carries out a fast operation and returns immediately. But blocking can become a serious problem when a function takes a long time to finish and return.

Blocking can become an extremely serious problem when a function has the task of sitting and waiting to receive a transmission from a remote system. When a blocking function is assigned this kind of role, it simply stops the program until it receives the transmission it is waiting for. If the transmission never arrives, the system hangs up forever.

Windows sockets has addressed this problem by adding a group of nonblocking functions to the function set provided by the BSD Sockets API. All these functions begin with the letters WSAAsync. For example, WSAAsyncSelect instructs Windows sockets to send a message to a specified window when it detects a specified event. WSAAsyncSelect is a nonblocking function, so it can wait for an incoming transmission without blocking other functions. That makes it an ideal alternative to the BSD function recv, which is a blocking function.

When you write applications that use Windows sockets, you should always use the nonblocking functions provided by the Windows sockets extensions rather than the BSD-style blocking functions.

MFC AND THE WINDOWS SOCKETS API

The Microsoft Foundation Class library now includes two classes that are designed to simplify the use of the Windows sockets API. These two new functions are CAsyncSocket and CSocket.

A CAsyncSocket object encapsulates the Windows sockets API, providing an object-oriented abstraction that makes it much easier to use Windows sockets in an MFC program. If you are working solely on the Win32 platform, you can take advantage of additional socket functionality built into those two operating systems.

USING THREADS TO WRITE NONBLOCKING FUNCTIONS

In a Windows NT application, there is an alternative to using nonblocking Windows sockets functions to overcome the blocking limitations of BSD functions. The alternative is to write a multithreaded application that can prevent blocking functions from hanging the system by implementing blocking functions in threads.

Although you may find it interesting to experiment with this approach, remember that multithreaded applications can't be ported to Windows environments that don't support threading, so an application that uses multiple threads is not as portable as one that doesn't. Also, threads are more difficult to manage than the nonblocking functions in the Windows sockets API. So I consider the Windows sockets nonblocking functions to be the better alternative.

USING THE CASYNCSOCKET CLASS

To use a CAsyncSocket object, you must include the **AFXSOCK.H** header file in your application. To instantiate a CAsyncSocket object, call its constructor and then call the CAsyncSocket::Create member function. This function creates the a socket handle (type SOCKET) that provides the CAsyncSocket class with its underlying functionality.

When you have instantiated a CAsyncSocket object, you can create a server socket by calling the Listen member function, or you can create a client socket by calling the Connect member function. When the server socket receives a connection request, it calls the Accept function. Other CAsyncSocket member functions can be used to carry out communications between sockets.

When it's time to terminate your TC/IP communications, you must destroy your CAsyncSocket object if it was created on the heap by calling its destructor. The CAsyncSocket class's destructor automatically cleans everything up by calling a Close function.

USING THE CSOCKET CLASS

The CSocket class is derived from the CAsyncSocket class, from which it inherits an encapsulation of the Windows sockets API. CSocket, like CAsyncSocket, requires you to include **AFXSOCK.H** in your application. A CSocket object represents a higher level of abstraction of the Windows sockets API than that of a CAsyncSocket object. CSocket works with classes CSocketFile and CArchive to manage the sending and receiving of data.

A CSocket object also provides blocking (see "Blocking and Nonblocking Functions" earlier in this chapter), which is essential to the synchronous operation of the CArchive class. (You'll need to use the CArchive class if you want your application to support the serialization, or automatic saving and loading, of files.)

When you use CSocket, blocking functions—such as Receive, Send, ReceiveFrom, SendTo, and Accept (all inherited from CAsyncSocket)—do not return a an error when communications are blocked. (In contrast, a CAsyncSocket object does return an error message.) Instead, CSocket's blocking member functions wait until the operation completes. (An exception: the original call terminates with the error WSAEINTR if the CancelBlockingCall is called while a CSocket blocking function is blocking.)

To create a CSocket object, follow the same procedure used to create a CAsyncSocket object: Call the object's constructor and then call Create to create the underlying socket handle (type SOCKET). The default parameters of the Create member function create a stream socket, but, if you are not using the socket with a CArchive object, you can specify a parameter to create a datagram socket instead or bind to a specific port to create a server socket.

When you have created a CSocket object, you can connect to a client socket using Connect on the client side and Accept on the server side. Next, you create a CSocketFile object and associate it with the CSocket object in the CSocketFile constructor.

After you have done all that, you can create a CArchive object for sending and one for receiving data, as needed. Then you can associate each of these archive objects with the CSocketFile object in the CArchive constructor.

When communications are complete, you must destroy the CArchive, CSocketFile, and CSocket objects.

Networking Protocols

In the first half of this chapter, you learned how important protocols are in computer communications. In the world of international politics, diplomatic protocols can smooth the relations between nations separated by cultural and historical differences. Similarly, in the world of computer communications, protocols make it possible for different kinds of hardware and software to get along even though they might have different native languages.

Earlier sections of this chapter also introduced the OSI reference model, a seven-layer communications stack developed by the International Standards Organization. This architectural model has rarely (if ever) been implemented in its purest form by any hardware or software manufacturer. But it does serve as a universally recognized model for communications systems.

Windows NT communications use a communications stack modeled after the OSI stack. As you'll see, the TCP/IP protocols can also be arranged in a kind of stack that reflects some of the features of the OSI model.

As you may recall, the OSI reference model is made up of seven layers of protocols that define the functions of data communications. Each layer represents a function that is performed when applications or other software modules send messages to each other across a network. When two software modules on the same layer communicate with each other across a network, it appears to them as if they are communicating directly. In fact, all their transmissions are being processed through the lower layers of the stack, moving down the stack on the transmitting end and moving up the stack on the receiving end.

This is a simplified explanation of how a data communications (datacom) stack works. In a real stack, a layer is not necessarily occupied by a single protocol. In reality, as you saw when the Windows NT stack was described earlier in this chapter, a layer of a protocol stack defines a general kind of data communications function that can be performed by two, three, or more protocols. Moreover, a single service may span two or more layers of a stack. For example, in the Windows NT stack, the redirector spans layers 5, 6, and 7 of the OSI stack. Figure 10.21 illustrates the Windows NT protocol stack.

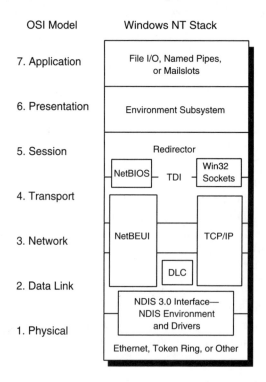

FIGURE 10.21 THE WINDOWS NT PROTOCOL SUITE.

As Figure 10.21 shows, a layer in a stack can contain multiple protocols, with each providing a service suitable to the function of that layer. For example, an electronic mail protocol and a file transfer protocol might occupy the same layer of the stack. Both protocols provide user services, so both of them could be considered part of the application layer (layer 7) of the OSI.

THE WINDOWS NT PROTOCOL SUITE

As you saw in Chapter 7, Windows NT uses a protocol stack, but it does not exactly match the OSI reference model. Similarly, the TCP/IP protocols can also be grouped into a stack-like arrangement, and that stack also differs from the OSI version. In fact, the TCP/IP stack departs more from the OSI model than the Windows NT protocol suite does. One reason is that TCP/IP occupies only a portion of the OSI stack and is therefore—well, you could call it a short stack.

Experts disagree on how the TCP/IP protocol stack should be represented in diagrams. In fact, they even disagree on how many layers it has. Most descriptions of the TCP/IP stack assert that it has three to five functional layers. The Department of Defense says there are four layers, and because the DOD set the original standard, that's the model used in this chapter.

Figure 10.22 shows how the TCP/IP protocol suite compares with the OSI reference model and the Windows NT reference model.

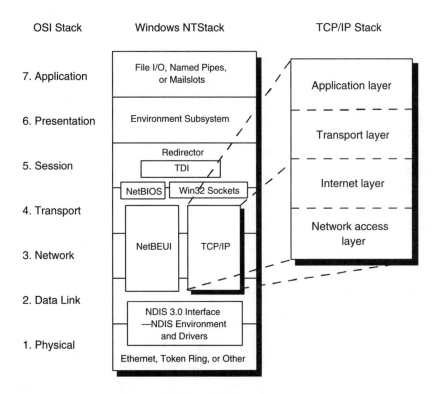

FIGURE 10.22 THE TCP/IP PROTOCOL SUITE.

In the TCP/IP stack, as in the OSI reference model, data is passed down the stack when it is being sent to the network, and it is passed up the stack when it is being received from the network. In the TCP/IP model, to ensure proper delivery, each layer in the stack adds control information to the data that it handles. This control information is placed at the beginning of the data being transmitted and is therefore called a header. This addition of delivery information at every layer of the stack is called *encapsulation.*

When a computer using TCP/IP protocols receives data, it handles the data in the opposite fashion: Each layer strips off the header that was added by its corresponding layer on the transmission stack. The receiving layer then passes the data to the layer above it.

Let's look more closely at the function of each layer, working our way up from the network access layer to the application layer.

THE NETWORK ACCESS LAYER

The network access layer is the lowest layer in the TCP/IP stack. It can be seen as encompassing the functions of the three lowest layers of the OSI reference model: the network, data link, and physical layers. The protocols in the network access layer make it possible for the system to deliver data to the other devices on a directly attached network.

The TCP/IP network access layer defines how the network transmits IP datagrams. APIs that reside at the network layer encapsulate IP datagrams into frames that can be transmitted by the network and convert IP addresses into addresses appropriate for the physical network over which the datagram is transmitted. The protocols in the network layer are often implemented as combinations of device drivers and related programs. Some network-layer modules encapsulate and deliver the data to the network, whereas others perform related functions, such as address mapping.

THE INTERNET LAYER

The layer above the network access layer in the TCP/IP stack is the Internet layer. The Internet protocol, the basic building block of TCP/IP, is situated in the Internet layer. IP provides the basic packet delivery service on which TCP/IP networks are built. All other protocols—in the layers above and below IP—use the Internet protocol to deliver data. All TCP/IP data, both incoming and outgoing, passes through the Internet protocol regardless of its final destination.

Responsibilities of the Internet protocol include the following:

+ Defining the datagram, which is the basic unit of transmission on the Internet.

✦ Defining the Internet addressing system.

✦ Breaking down datagrams and reassembling them into structures that can be transmitted across the network.

✦ Moving data between the network access layer and the transport layer.

✦ Routing datagrams to remote hosts.

THE TRANSPORT LAYER

The transport layer, also known as the host-to-host transport layer, lies just above the Internet layer in the TCP/IP stack. The two most important protocols in the transport layer are the transmission control protocol and the user datagram protocol. Both protocols deliver data between the application layer and the Internet layer. When you write a network application, you can choose between TCP and UDP, picking the one you feel is best for your application.

If your application demands very reliable data delivery service with comprehensive error detection and correction, the protocol to pick is TCP. The TCP protocol verifies that data is delivered across the network accurately and in the proper sequence. It is a reliable, connection-oriented, byte-stream protocol.

The UDP protocol provides low-overhead datagram delivery service without error checking. If your application does not require a great deal of error checking—which may be the case if it provides its own error checking—you might decide to use the user data protocol. UDP is a less complex protocol that can send and receive messages with very little overhead. UDP can come in handy in applications that transmit small amounts of data, when the overhead required for extensive error-checking may be greater than the work of simply retransmitting the data.

Addresses and Port Numbers

TCP/IP transmits data in two steps. First, the data is transmitted over the network from a local machine to a remote machine. Then, within the machine that receives the data, the data is carried to the correct process.

To perform these two tasks, TCP/IP uses three mechanisms:

✦ **Gateways** that deliver data to the correct network.

✦ **IP addresses** that uniquely identify every network on the Internet, delivering data to the correct host.

♦   **Protocol addresses** and **port numbers.** When a transmission arrives at the destination workstation, protocol addresses and port numbers deliver data to the correct software module within the host.

Network administrators are generally responsible for managing gateways; other Windows NT users are more likely to be concerned with IP addresses and protocol and port numbers. The following paragraphs focus on those topics.

IP ADDRESSES

Every network on the Internet has a unique IP address. When you have an IP address and you're an Internet user, any other Internet user can contact you.

Every IP address is written as four decimal numbers separated by periods, in this format:

```
156.151.128.21
```

Each of the four numbers in an IP address has a range of zero to 255, or 0x00 to 0xFF in hexadecimal notation. In hexadecimal notation, this is the range of possible values for one byte. Therefore, an Internet address is made up of four single-byte numbers, each one separated by a period.

IP and E-Mail Addresses

All Internet users have both a four-number IP address and an E-mail address, and both addresses mean the same thing. The E-mail address is written in the form userName@ipName.extension. For example, the IP address 156.151.128.21 is the same as this E-mail address: marka@parvati.com.

People usually put their E-mail addresses instead of their IP addresses on their business cards, because they find it easier to remember words than to remember numbers. Most commercial E-mail software allows users to send and receive electronic mail using the character-based E-mail address system. When the user types in an E-mail address, the software converts the address to IP format automatically.

Even though E-mail addresses are used extensively in corporate and interoffice communications, on-line Internet directories almost always store user addresses in the IP format, so dedicated TCP/IP fans also use IP addresses extensively.

CLASSES AND CATEGORIES OF INTERNET ADDRESSES

IP addresses are divided into four classes. The Internet maintains a limited number of addresses (called Class A addresses) for very large networks—networks having large numbers of computers. There is a larger set of addresses (Class B) for medium-size networks, and there is a still larger number of addresses (Class c) for small networks. Figure 10.23 shows the differences in Class A, B, and C addresses.

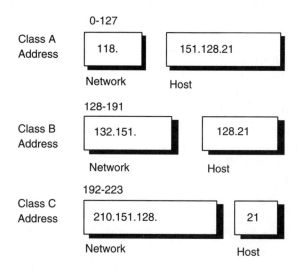

FIGURE 10.23 IP ADDRESSES.

As Figure 10.23 illustrates, the first byte of an IP address determines the class of the address. Here is how the three classes are divided:

+ The first byte of a Class A address is always less than 128, or less than 0x80 in hexadecimal notation. The first byte is the number of a network, and the last three bytes are used to designate the host computers on the network. The first address in Figure 10.23 is a Class A address.

+ The first byte of a Class B address can range from 128 to 191, or from 0x80 to 0xBF in hexadecimal notation. The second byte can have any value. The first two bytes identify the network, and the last two bytes identify the host computers on the network. Because two bytes are used to designate the network, that leaves only the last two bytes to designate host machines. A Class B address cannot accommodate nearly as many computers as a Class A address can, but a class B network can still include more than 65,000 computers. The second address in Figure 10.23 is a Class B address.

+ The first byte of a Class C address can range from 192 to 223, or from 0xC0 to 0xDF in hexadecimal notation. The second and third bytes can have any values. The first three bytes identify the network and the last byte identifies the host. This arrangement of numbers restricts the number of computers in a Class C network to around 250. (Some addresses use the 256 individual integers, but others are reserved and not available for use in addresses.) The third address in Figure 10.23 is a Class C address.

+ If the first byte of an IP address is greater than 223 (0xDF), the address is reserved. You can ignore reserved addresses.

Figure 10.23 illustrates how the address structure varies with address class. The Class A address is 26.104.0.19. The first bit of this address is 0, so the address is interpreted as host 104.0.19 on network 26. One byte specifies the network and three bytes specify the host. In the address 128.66.12.1, the two high-order bits are 1 and 0, so the address refers to host 12.1 on network 128.66. Two bytes identify the network and two identify the host. Finally, in the Class C example, 192.178.16.1, the three high-order bits are 1 1 0, so this is the address of host 1 on network 192.178.16—three network bytes and one host byte.

Some IP addresses are not available for general use. It has been noted that addresses with a first byte greater than 223 are reserved. There are also two Class A addresses, 0 and 127, that are reserved for special uses. Network 0 designates what is known as a default route, and network 127 is known as a loopback address.

Default route 0 is used to simplify the routing information that IP must handle. Loopback address 27 simplifies network applications by allowing the local host to be addressed in the same manner as a remote host. You use these special network addresses when configuring a host.

Some host addresses are also reserved for special uses. In all network classes, host numbers 0 and 255 are reserved. An IP address with all host bits set to zero identifies the network itself. For example, 26.0.0.0 refers to network 26, and 128.66.0.0 refers to network 128.66. Addresses in this form are used in routing table listings to refer to entire networks. An IP address with all bits set to one is a broadcast address, that is used to simultaneously address every host on a network. The broadcast address for network 128.66 is 128.66.255.255. A datagram sent to this address is delivered to every individual host on network 128.66.

Subnet Masks

A network manager can break a network into subnetworks by applying *subnet masks* to the network's IP address. Subnet masks are recognized only by the networks that they apply to and not by the Internet.

When you apply a subnet mask to an Internet address, you shift the dividing line between the network portion of the address bits and the host portion of the address. This shift divides the network portion of the address into subnetworks. Some of the host workstations on the network can then belong to one subnetwork while other workstations belong to another subnetwork.

Networks are split into subnets for many reasons, often because subnetting permits the decentralized management of host addressing. Without subnetting, a single administrator is usually responsible for managing the host addresses on an entire network. By subnetting, the administrator can let subnet administrators handle portions of the network.

Geographical divisions and router allocation can also be reasons for subnetting. Routers and gateways can connect geographically separated subnets if each physical network has a unique network address. Portions of networks that use different kinds of hardware can also be grouped in subnets.

CREATING A SUBNET

To create a subnet, you apply a subnet mask to an IP address, as shown in Figure 10.24. If a bit in the mask is set, the equivalent bit in the IP address is interpreted as a network bit. If a bit in the mask is clear, the bit belongs to the host part of the address. Remember that this arrangement is recognized only within the affected network; to the rest of the Internet, the address is still interpreted as a standard Class A, B, or C IP address. Figure 10.24 illustrates the most commonly used kind of subnet mask, which extends the network portion of a class B address by an additional byte. The subnet mask that accomplishes this is 255.255.255.0.

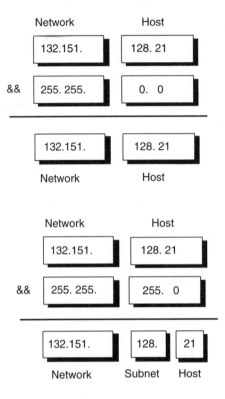

FIGURE 10.24 A SUBNET MASK.

In the address 255.255.255.0, all bits are on in the first three bytes, and all bits are off in the last byte. In Figure 10.24, two different subnet masks are applied to a Class B IP address.

In a Class B address, as noted earlier, the first two bytes define the network that the address belongs to, and the third and fourth bytes are used to identify the host machines on the network. Ordinarily, the subnet mask that is applied to a Class B address is 255.255.0.0, as shown in the top diagram in Figure 10.24. That results in a standard Class B address, in which two bytes represent the user's network and two bytes represent the user's address.

When a different subnet mask is applied to a Class B address, the mask changes this arrangement, as shown in the lower drawing in Figure 10.24. When a subnet mask of 255.255.255.0 is applied to the same Class B address, only the first byte of the user's address identifies the user's network. The second byte now identifies the user's subnet within the network, and the last byte identifies each workstation on that subnet.

Remember, though, that this change is visible only to workstations within the affected network. To the rest of the Internet, the address to which the subnet mask has been added is still a standard Class B address and still looks like the top drawing in Figure 10.24.

Subnet masks are often made up of only the numbers 0 and 255. However, that is not a requirement; other numbers can also be used. For example, you could divide a Class C address into four subnets by applying the subnet mask 255.255.255.192 (the number 192 is 0xC0 in hexadecimal notation). Applying this mask to a Class C address defines the two high-order bits of the fourth byte as the subnet part of the address, creating 16 subnets. Then the two low-order bits can be used to designate 16 host workstations on each subnet. If you apply the mask 255.255.255.192 to a Class B address, you create more than a thousand subnets, each of which can accommodate as many as 16 workstations.

If you don't want to bother with all this hexadecimal math, you can probably meet most of your networking needs by simply using a subnet mask of 255.255.255.0. If you have a Class C address, it usually means that you can connect more than 200 computers to your network without having to worry about subnetting.

Protocols, Ports, and Sockets

To find a computer on the Internet, all you need is a four-byte IP address. But when two computers start exchanging information, they need additional numbers to specify the kind of information that is being sent and received. These extra identifiers are called *protocol numbers* and *port numbers*. The combination of an Internet address and a port number is called a *socket*.

When an API that resides on one computer needs to send data to an API on another computer, the transmitting API identifies itself to the receiving API by inserting a protocol number into the header of the datagram it is sending. To specify the kind of message it is sending, the transmitting API also sends the receiving API a second identifier, the port number. This port number is also placed in the header of the datagram being sent.

When your Windows NT workstation receives a datagram from a remote computer, it interprets the protocol and port numbers in the datagram's header by consulting two text files that are kept in the \SYSTEM32\DRIVERS\ETC directory. The file in which protocol numbers are stored is called PROTOCOL. The file that contains port numbers is called SERVICES.

Protocol Numbers

The PROTOCOL file is stored in the form of a table. This table contains the name of each protocol that your TCP/IP software recognizes, along with a number that represents each protocol name. Widely used protocols, often referred to as well-known services, have numbers that are recognized throughout the Internet. For instance, protocol 0 is always the Internet protocol, which is officially named ip. And protocol 20 is always the user datagram protocol, or udp.

There are many other well-known services on the Internet. They include standard network protocols such as FTP, which is used for file transfers, and TELNET, which is used to set up communications with IP addresses.

A protocol table has a single entry on each line. Each line is made up of the official name of a protocol, an associated protocol number, and—optionally—a private alias for the protocol name. An *alias* is a name that can be privately used on the host workstation in place of the official service name. Comments in a protocol table begin with the symbol #.

Your Windows NT system comes with a default PROTOCOL file that is automatically placed in your \SYSTEM32\DRIVERS\ETC directory when you install your TCP/IP software. The PROTOCOL file supplied with Windows NT has the format shown in Table 10.3.

TABLE 10.3 FORMAT OF THE WINDOWS NT PROTOCOL FILE.

Protocol Name	Assigned Number	Alias	Comment
ip	0	IP	Internet protocol
icmp	1	ICMP	Internet control message protocol
ggp	3	GGP	Gateway-gateway protocol
tcp	6	TCP	Transmission control protocol
egp	8	EGP	Exterior gateway protocol
pup	12	PUP	PARC universal packet protocol
udp	17	UDP	User datagram protocol
hmp	20	HMP	Host monitoring protocol
xns-idp	22	XNS-IDP	Xerox NS IDP
rdp	27	RDP	"Reliable datagram" protocol
rvd	66	RVD	MIT remote visual disk

As Table 10.3 illustrates, the official name of the IP protocol is ip. Its protocol number is 0, and you can refer to it on your Windows NT system as IP.

The protocol table that Windows NT installs by default is far from complete. There are several commercial applications for connecting Windows operating systems to the Internet. When you install those applications, they provide much longer lists of widely used port names and numbers.

Summing it all up, this is how protocol numbers work:

1. When a datagram arrives at the correct IP address, the IP layer knows that the datagram must be delivered to one of the transport protocols situated above it in the TCP/IP stack. To determine which protocol should receive the datagram, the IP API checks the datagram's protocol number.

2. The IP API then delivers the datagram to the protocol that matches its protocol number. For example, if the protocol number is 6, IP delivers the datagram to TCP. If the protocol number is 17, the datagram goes to UDP.

PORT NUMBERS

After the Internet protocol passes incoming data to the transport protocol, the transport protocol passes the data to the correct application process. Application processes, also referred to as network services, are identified by 16-bit port numbers. Every datagram header contains two port numbers: a source port number, which identifies the process that sent the data, and a destination port number, which identifies the process that is to receive the data.

Port numbers, like protocol numbers, are kept in a special text file. In a Windows NT system, the text file that defines port numbers is named SERVICES and resides in the directory \SYSTEM32\DRIVERS\ETC. When you install TCP/IP software on a Windows NT system, a default SERVICES file is automatically placed in your \SYSTEM32\DRIVERS\ETC directory. Entries in the SERVICES file have this format:

```
echo 7/tcp
discard 9/tcp sink null
discard 9/udp sink null
systat 11/tcp
systat 11/tcp users
daytime 13/tcp
```

```
daytime 13/udp
netstat 15/tcp
qotd 17/tcp quote
chargen 19/tcp ttytst source
chargen 19/udp ttytst source
ftp-data 20/tcp
ftp 21/tcp
telnet 23/tcp
// ...
```

The preceding example is only a part of the default Windows NT SERVICES file. You can read the complete file by installing TCP/IP and then loading your SERVICES file into a text editor.

The format of the SERVICES file is similar to the format of the PROTOCOLS file. The file is formatted as a table in which each line contains three entries:

+ The official name of the service.

+ An entry that combines a port number and a protocol number, with a slash mark separating the two numbers.

+ An optional list of aliases that can be privately used on the host workstation in place of the official service name. Multiple aliases may be entered for each port name. If multiple aliases are used, they are separated by white spaces.

As the example shows, port numbers are not unique between transport layer protocols; they are unique only within a specific transport protocol. Both TCP and UDP can, and do, assign the same port numbers to different services. This system works because each protocol listed in the SERVICES file is assigned two numbers: one specifying its protocol number, and the other specifying its port number. Together, these two numbers uniquely identify a specific process that data should be delivered to.

All port numbers below 256 are reserved for well-known services. Port numbers that range from 256 to 1024 are used for services such as rlogin (a remote login service) that were originally developed for UNIX systems. However, most of these services, including rlogin, are no longer UNIX- specific.

SOCKETS

When a computer on the Internet sends a datagram to another computer, the header of the datagram includes not only the recipient's IP address; but also a second identifier that is made up of a protocol number and a port number. With this protocol/port identifier, the recipient's TCP/IP API can route the datagram to the appropriate protocol and to the correct port.

The protocol/port identifier that a TCP/IP workstation creates has no accepted name that I know of. But when you add a protocol/port identifier to the end of an IP address, what you wind up with is a socket. A socket, then, is a combination of an IP address and a combination protocol/port number.

A conventional way to express a socket number is to follow the conventional three-byte IP address with an additional dot, followed by an additional number. For example, an IP address and a socket number could be expressed as 156.151.128.21.3382. The first four numbers make up an IP address. The fifth number, 3382, is a socket number.

As you can see, a socket is a number that uniquely identifies a single network process within a single IP address. Thus, a socket uniquely identifies a single network process throughout the Internet.

A Note on Terminology

Sometimes the terms *socket* and *port number* are used interchangeably. In fact, well-known services are frequently referred to as well-known sockets. In this chapter, the word *socket* is used to identify the combination of an IP address and a port number.

DYNAMICALLY ASSIGNED SOCKETS

When a workstation sends a datagram to another workstation, two different socket identifiers are needed: one for the transmitting workstation and another for the recipient. If only one socket number were used, it would identify the protocol and port at only one end of the transmission. Two socket numbers are needed because every transmission has two ends.

To distinguish between the protocol and port identifier used by a transmitting workstation and the protocol and port identifier used by the recipient, the transmitting workstation dynamically allocates its own socket identifier and uses well-known protocol and port numbers to specify the identifier of the destination socket.

To allocate its own socket identifier dynamically, the transmitting station simply assigns its originating socket an arbitrary number. It then places that socket number in the header of the datagram. To identify the socket that it is transmitting to, the originator of the datagram uses a well-known socket identifier. To identify its own socket, the originating workstation uses the socket identifier that it has dynamically assigned. This procedure is illustrated in Figure 10.25.

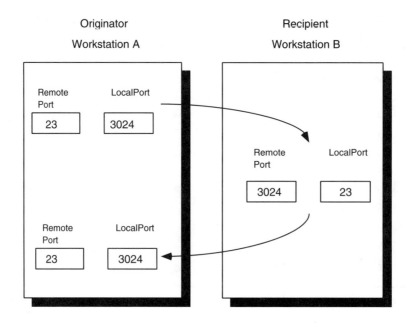

FIGURE 10.25 SENDING AND RECEIVING A DATAGRAM.

Workstation A, the originator of a datagram, is dispatching a message to a recipient, Workstation B. Workstation A is sending its message to Port 23. Port 23 is the port number of TELNET, a well-known API. The job of the TELNET API is to send and receive messages.

You can see from the diagram that Machine A has addressed its message to Port 23 on Workstation B. But you can't tell which port the message is originating from on Workstation A. It looks as if it is originating from Port 3024, but that can't be a real port, because it lies outside the range of well-known port numbers.

Let's assume, though, that the message coming from Workstation A is being transmitted by Port 23, the TELNET port number. Messages being transmitted from a particular port on one machine to the same port on another machine use identical port numbers, so Workstation A cannot use Port 23 to identify the origin of the datagram it is sending—even though the datagram is originating from Port 23. Therefore, Workstation A uses an arbitrary number—3024—as a return address for this particular datagram.

In the header of its datagram, Workstation A identifies the return address of its datagram as 3024. Workstation B has no way of knowing that this number is an alias for Port 23. However, Workstation B knows all it needs to know to send the datagram to its proper port, and, as we shall see, Workstation B also knows all it needs to know to address its reply to the correct port when it sends its reply back to Workstation A.

Workstation B knows that the datagram should go to Port 23, because Workstation B has addressed its datagram to Port 23, and Port 23 is a well-known port number. Workstation B also knows that when it replies to Workstation A's datagram, it should send its reply to Port 3024.

Workstation B has never heard of Port 3024—it's a number that Workstation A made up—but that's OK. When Workstation B replies to the message, it simply sends its reply to Port 3024, even though it knows that's a phony port number.

When Workstation B's reply gets back to Workstation A, addressed to a port number that doesn't exist, Workstation A knows that the reply is intended for Port 23, because Workstation A made up the number 3024 in the first place. So Workstation B's reply finally makes it back to Port 23 on Workstation A, the port that sent the original datagram.

Figure 10.25 illustrates this scenario. The operation is made possible by the fact that socket numbers don't always have to identify well-known sockets; when a workstation transmits a datagram to another workstation, TCP/IP rules allow the transmitter of the message to use a socket number that is dynamically assigned.

The TCP/IP API has built-in mechanisms for ensuring that it does not dynamically assign duplicate port numbers to multiple processes and that the numbers that it assigns fall outside the range of standard port numbers.

TCP/IP Name Services

As you have seen, every network interface attached to a TCP/IP network is identified by a unique 32-bit IP address. But the numbers that make up IP addresses are difficult to remember, type correctly, and pronounce. So most people use pronounceable names rather than IP addresses to communicate over the Internet.

To make Internet communications easier, an alphabetical, pronounceable host name can be added to any IP address. E-mail addresses and aliases can also be assigned to IP addresses. When an IP address has been assigned a host name, an E-mail address, or an alias, your TCP/IP software can retrieve the corresponding IP address.

There are two common mechanisms for translating host names into IP addresses. One, the host table, is a text file stored in your \SYSTEM32\DRIVERS\ETC directory along with your PROTOCOL and SERVICES files. The other mechanism, called the domain name service (DNS), is a database maintained by the Internet's administrators. There are various software utilities that you can use to access the DNS on the Internet.

HOST TABLES

A host table, stored in your system as a HOSTS file, lists all the IP address that you're interested in along with their host names and, optionally, any aliases that you have assigned.

When you install your TCP/IP software, a default host file is stored automatically in your \SYSTEM32\DRIVERS\ETC directory. This file is almost empty when it is installed, but you can easily add addresses to it. Addresses in a HOSTS file look like this:

```
127.0.0.1 localhost
156.151.128.21 shiva mark
156.151.128.22 shakti tanya
156.151.254.1 portal
156.151.254.3 dns
```

A HOSTS file is formatted as a table, with two or more entries on each line. The first entry is always an IP address. The second entry is a host name that corresponds to that address. If you wish, you can add aliases to the end of each line. You can use multiple aliases separated by white spaces. Comments in HOSTS files are preceded by the symbol #.

When you have equated an IP address with a host name (and possibly some aliases) in a HOSTS file, you can use that host name (or any aliases you have defined) in any TCP/IP command in place of its corresponding IP address. When the TCP/IP API encounters the host name or alias you have supplied, it looks up the name or alias in your system's host table.

Commercial TCP/IP software packages come with utilities you can use to build host tables automatically, using data available from the Network Information Center (NIC). If you own a TCP/IP package for your Windows NT workstation, you can learn to build host tables by referring to the documentation that came with your software.

DOMAIN NAME SERVICE

Host tables can be useful, particularly on small networks, because they can be kept concise and can be easily maintained. But if you communicate with many networks and workstations, constantly updating a local host table can become time-consuming. So the Internet provides the automated alternative, the domain name service. DNS is a centralized, automated database of IP and host names that is maintained on the Internet.

Commercial TCP/IP software packages come with tools that you can use to access the Internet's domain name services. For details, see the manuals that document such packages.

Obtaining an IP Address

If you want to become a TCP/IP user, you must obtain an IP address. There are four common ways to do that:

✦ Get your own Internet address directly from Internet's administrators.

✦ Work for an organization or be affiliated with an organization or institution that has an Internet address.

✦ Rent an Internet connection from a commercial provider.

✦ Connect to the Internet through a commercial information system such as CompuServe, America Online, or Prodigy.

CONNECTING DIRECTLY TO THE INTERNET

The most direct way is to obtain forms from the Internet's DDN Network Information Center, fill them out, and send them in. That will get you a permanent Internet address that you can carry with you forever, like your Social Security number. But it won't connect you to the Internet. To do that, you'll have to go to a commercial provider or, at considerable expense, obtain the hardware that it takes to set up a direct connection.

Obtaining a network address from the NIC is simple and costs little or nothing, and you can do it by either postal mail or electronic mail. The mailing address is:

DDN Network Information Center
14200 PARK Meadow Drive
Suite 200
Chantilly, VA 22021

DDN's E-mail address is hostmaster@nic.ddn.mil. The organization's telephone numbers are 1-800-365-3642 and 1-703-802-4535.

OBTAINING AN IP ADDRESS THROUGH AN ORGANIZATION

An easy way to obtain an Internet address is to work for or be affiliated with a company or organization that has an Internet address. In this case, you can see your network or Internet administrator and request an E-mail address. Then you can use that to connect to the Internet.

This approach is simple and doesn't cost anything, but if you ever leave the company, organization, or institution that provides you with your E-mail address, you will lose it.

FINDING A COMMERCIAL PROVIDER

There are several telecommunications companies that can provide you with your own connection to the Internet—and your own private Internet address—for a monthly fee. Although this method of getting an IP address costs money, it is usually less expensive than signing up with a commercial (and more limited) network such as CompuServe, America Online, or Prodigy.

Most companies that provide Internet connections offer at least two different kinds of services. You can choose what is known as a shell account, which offers a limited kind of access to the Internet, or you can select an IP account, which costs more but lets you take advantage of all Internet services.

If you have an ordinary (non-TCP/IP) telecommunications program such as CrossTalk or ProComm Plus, a shell service is what you need. With a shell service, you can browse through files on the Internet, chat with other users, and read news items and bulletin boards. But you can't execute TCP/IP commands from your Windows NT workstation.

If you own a real TCP/IP software package, such as Chameleon from NetManage or PC/TCP from FTP Software, you'll need an IP account to tap the power within your telecommunications software. With a full-service IP connection, you can execute TCP/IP commands such as ftp (for file transfers) and even run remote applications from your NT-equipped PC, just as if you were sitting at a UNIX workstation. (If you're communicating through a modem instead of over a direct wire, things will run slower, but that is a limitation on your end of the system and not a limitation of your Internet connection.)

Companies that can provide you with an Internet connection include Netcom of San Jose, CA (408-554-8649 or info@netcom.com), Performance Systems International (PSInet) of Reston, VA (703-620-6551 or info@psi.com), Portal Communications of Cupertino, CA (408-973-9111 or cs@cup.portal.com), Whole Earth 'Lectronic Link (the WELL), Sausalito, CA (415-332-4335 or info@well.sf.ca.us), and UUNET of Falls Church, VA (703-206-5600 or 1-800-4-UUNET-4 or help@uunet.uu.net).

These are not the only companies that provide Internet connections for a fee. There are dozens of others. To obtain an up-to-date list, contact

NSF Network Service Center (NNSC)
BBN Laboratories Inc.
10 Moulton St.
Cambridge, MA 02138

NFC's telephone number is 617-873-3361. The organization's E-mail address is nnsc@nnsc.nsf.net.

Example Program: SOCKS

This chapter's second sample program, SOCKS, demonstrates how you can use the functions provided in the Windows sockets API to write your own TCP/IP-based applications.

The SOCKS program was written before Microsoft added the CSocket and CAsyncSocket classes. When these classes were introduced, I made a valiant attempt to update the program to use the CAsyncSocket class. (I didn't try to write a version of the program that would use CSocket because it was immediately apparent that its functionality was too limited to meet the SOCKS program's needs.) I soon discovered that CAsyncSocket also fell a little short of offering the required functionality. As it turned out, I decided that neither class had anything to offer the program that it couldn't do already, so I wound up leaving SOCKS the way it was.

I will admit that SOCKS is a little more complicated and difficult to understand than it would have been if I had modified it to use AsyncSocket. Because there were no MFC classes to rely on when the program was written, the program uses a complex callback architecture to access functions provided in the sockets API. If you know how callbacks work in Windows programs, you can easily figure out the architecture of the SOCKS program. But if you don't, you may have some difficulty puzzling out its architecture.

Briefly, this is how SOCKS works: When the program creates its main window, the OnCreate message handler in **SOCKSVW.CPP** calls the Windows sockets function WSAStartup. (WSAStartup is not used in programs that rely on CSocket or AsyncSocket. But in a program that directly accesses Windows sockets, WSAStartup initializes Windows sockets and consequently is always the first socket function that you call.)

When SOCKS finishes using Windows sockets, it calls the WSACleanup function—a requirement for applications that directly access the Windows sockets API but not for programs that rely on CSocket or CAsyncSocket.

BUILDING THE SOCKS PROGRAM

To compile and link the SOCKS program, simply launch Visual C++, navigate to the directory where the program is stored, and build the program by choosing **Build** from the Options menu. Then you can execute the program from the Windows 95 desktop.

Because SOCKS has a prewritten makefile (generated by AppWizard), you don't have to build a makefile to compile and link SOCKS. However, to write your own programs with the Windows sockets API, there are two essential procedures that you must carry out. First, you must include **WINSOCK.H** in your compilation. (This header file defines the functions in the Windows sockets API.) Second, you must link your application with **WSOCK32.LIB**.

To carry out these two operations, follow these steps:

1. Choose the **Settings** item from Developer Studio's Build menu.
2. Tab to the Link property page in the Project Settings dialog box.
3. Select **Input** in the Category drop-down combo box.
4. In the Object/library modules text box, type **wsock32.lib**.
5. Close the Project Settings list box by clicking **OK**.
6. Build the SOCKS application by choosing **Build** from the Build menu.

RUNNING THE SOCKS PROGRAM

To execute the SOCKS program, follow these steps:

1. If possible, connect two Windows NT workstations using TCP/IP.
2. On one Windows NT workstation, launch the SOCKS application from the Program Manager, the File Manager, or the Visual Workbench editor. We'll call this machine Workstation A.
3. On the second Windows NT workstation (or on the same workstation if you don't have access to a network), launch a second instance of the SOCKS program. We'll call this machine (or this instance of the SOCKS application) Workstation B.
4. When TCP/IP starts, it displays a dialog box like the one shown in Figure 10.26. On both workstations, close this dialog box by clicking **OK**.

FIGURE 10.26 TCP/IP STARTUP DIALOG BOX.

5. When the SOCKS application window appears on Workstation A, choose the **Listen** command from the menu or click the **Listen** button (the ear icon) on the toolbar.

6. The SOCKS program responds by displaying the Port Number dialog box, as shown in Figure 10.27. In the edit box labeled **Port number (try 12)**, enter either a port number or the name of a service listed in your SERVICES file. (For information about the SERVICES file, see "Protocols, Ports, and Sockets" earlier in this chapter.) Experiment with various port numbers and names.

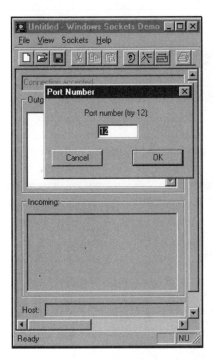 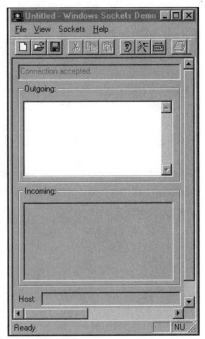

FIGURE 10.27 PORT NUMBER DIALOG BOX.

7. Close the Port Number dialog box by clicking **OK**.

8. When the SOCKS window opens on Workstation B, click the **Connect** toolbar button (the fingers icon) or select the **Connect** command from the menu. The application responds by displaying a dialog box prompting you for a host name, as shown in Figure 10.28, that prompts you for the name of a remote host.

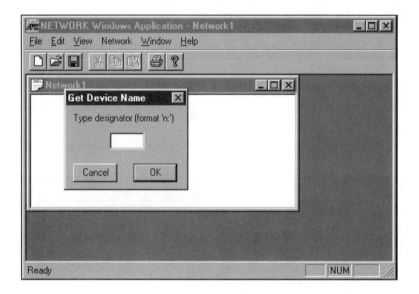

FIGURE 10.28 HOST NAME DIALOG BOX.

9. If you are running the SOCKS program on two Windows NT workstations, enter the name of the remote computer that you are connected to. If you are running the program on just one workstation, enter the name of your computer.

10. Close the Host Name dialog box by clicking **OK**.

11. The Port Number dialog box now appears on the machine making the connection. The user of this machine now types in a port number or the name of a service, as explained in Step 6.

12. When a TCP/IP connection is made, each workstation displays a "Connection accepted" announcement in the one-line message window just above the outgoing message panel. When the connect message appears in the windows of both workstations, you can start sending and receiving messages.

13. To send a message, type it in the outgoing panel and click the **Transmit** button (the envelope beneath the arrow). Read the replies to your messages in the window's incoming panel.

14. When you are finished sending and receiving messages, cancel your connection by selecting the **Cancel Connection** command from the Sockets menu.

How the SOCKS Program Works

The SOCKS program implements the Windows sockets API, which imposes a host of special requirements. Some formidable challenges arose in the process of writing the SOCKS application.

For example, some Windows sockets calls, such as `WSASyncSelect` and `WSAGet` require an application to respond to specific messages that are sent to a specified window. And messages sent to windows are more difficult to track down in framework-based Visual C++ programs than they are in programs written in C.

In a traditional API-style (non-MFC) Windows application, it is easy to respond to a message that is dispatched to a program's main window, because the application's main window procedure handles messages in its main event loop. Things are trickier in programs with frameworks generated by AppWizard, because an AppWizard framework handles your application's main window procedure for you and hides your program's main event loop in a place that's difficult to find—unless you know where to look for it.

When you want to trap a message in a Visual C++ program, you must write a message handler and tell your application where your message handler is by placing an entry in a message map. SOCKS relies extensively on custom-designed message handlers and message maps. Message handlers and message maps are introduced in Chapter 4, "Programming Windows NT with Visual C++."

Starting the SOCKS Program

When you launch the SOCKS program, the `OnCreate` member function of the application's view object starts Windows sockets by calling a function named `SOCKStartup`. `SOCKStartup` is called from **SOCKSVW.CPP**, which implements the program's view object. `SOCKStartup` is implemented in the following way in **WSOCK.CPP**:

```
// SOCKStartup member function.
void CSocket::SOCKStartup(CView *pView)
{
    WSADATA WSAData;
    char szTemp[80];
    int status;

    if ((status = WSAStartup(MAKEWORD(1,1), &WSAData)) == 0) {
        MessageBox(pView->m_hWnd, WSAData.szDescription,
            WSAData.szSystemStatus, MB_OK);
```

```
    } else {
        sprintf(szTemp, "%d is the err", status);
        MessageBox(pView->m_hWnd, szTemp, "Error:", MB_OK);
    }
}
```

As you can see, SOCKStartup starts Windows sockets by calling WSAStartup. When a client tries to connect, a member function named CSocket::FillAddr is called. This function retrieves the client's IP address, gets the host's name, and locates the service to which the client is trying to connect. If the FillAddr member function returns successfully, the client is allowed to connect.

Following is the CSocket::FillAddr function:

```
BOOL CSocket::FillAddr(HWND hWnd, PSOCKADDR_IN psin, BOOL bConnect)
{
    DWORD dwSize;
    PHOSTENT phe;
    PSERVENT pse;
    char szTemp[200];
    int status;

    psin->sin_family = AF_INET;

 if (!bConnect) {

        // Retrieve user's IP address. We assume that the hosts
        // file in %systemroot%\system\drivers\etc\hosts
        // contains your computer name.

        dwSize = sizeof(m_szBuf);
        gethostname(m_szBuf, dwSize);
    }

    phe = gethostbyname(m_szBuf);
    if (phe == NULL) {
        sprintf(szTemp,
            "Error %d. Make sure '%s' is in the hosts file.",
                WSAGetLastError(), m_szBuf);

        MessageBox(hWnd, szTemp, "gethostbyname function failed.",
            MB_OK);
```

```
        return FALSE;
    }
    memcpy((char *)&(psin->sin_addr), phe->h_addr,
        phe->h_length);

// Retrieve the Port number

    /*
    status = DialogBox(hInst,
        "TCPPORTNUM",
        hWnd,
        GetTcpPort);
    */

    CDlgPort dlgPort;
    dlgPort.m_editPort = "12";      // Put suggested port number
                                    // in edit box.
    status = dlgPort.DoModal();
    if (status == IDOK) {
        CString tempStr = dlgPort.m_editPort;
        char *cTempStr = tempStr.GetBuffer(BUF_LEN);
        strcpy(m_szBuf, cTempStr);

        if ((portno = atoi(m_szBuf)) == 0)
            status = 2;
        else
            status = 1;
    }

    switch(status) {
        case 0: // User canceled request.
            return FALSE;

        case 1: // actual port number entered
            psin->sin_port = htons(portno);
            break;

        case 2: // Service name entered

            // Find the service name, m_szBuf, which is a
            // type-tcp protocol in the SERVICES file.
```

```
        pse = getservbyname(m_szBuf, "tcp");
        if (pse == NULL) {
            sprintf(m_szBuf,
                "Error %d. This must be a valid TCP service.",
                WSAGetLastError());
            MessageBox(hWnd, m_szBuf,
                "getservbyname function failed",
                MB_OK);
            return FALSE;
        }
    psin->sin_port = pse->s_port;
    break;

    // Save port number.
    m_portNum = psin->sin_port;

    default:
        return FALSE;
    }
    return TRUE;
}
```

THE CSOCKET CLASS AND THE SOCKPROC FUNCTION

The SOCKS program does its job by instantiating a C++ class named CSocket. The CSocket class, derived from the MFC class CObject, encapsulates a number of the functions implemented in the Windows sockets API.

The SockProc function is a member function of CSocket. SockProc, implemented in **WSOCK.CPP**, is structured much like a standard C-language Windows procedure. SockProc expects the same parameters that a standard Windows procedure expects, and it handles them in the same way a standard window procedure would handle them: with a switch statement that detects messages and dispatches them to message handlers.

The SOCKS program implements WSA functions by calling the SockProc function and passing it parameters that cause it to perform specified tasks. Messages are passed to SockProc in a parameter named message. SockProc handles the message parameter by examining it in a series of case tests and taking whatever action the appropriate message requires.

ARCHITECTURE OF THE SOCKS PROGRAM

Most of the functions that implement the client side of the application are implemented in **SOCKSVW.CPP**. A message map in **SOCKSVW.CPP** links client functions with a switch statement in **WSOCK.CPP**. The message map in **SOCKSVW.CPP** looks like this:

```
BEGIN_MESSAGE_MAP(CSOCKSVw, CFormView)
    //{{AFX_MSG_MAP(CSOCKSVw)
    ON_WM_CREATE()
    ON_COMMAND(ID_SOCKETS_CONNECT, OnSocketsConnect)
    ON_COMMAND(ID_SOCKETS_LISTEN, OnSocketsListen)
    ON_COMMAND(ID_SOCKETS_TRANSMIT, OnSocketsTransmit)
    ON_COMMAND(ID_SOCKETS_CANCELCONNECTION, OnSocketsCancel)
    ON_WM_DESTROY()
    ON_UPDATE_COMMAND_UI(ID_SOCKETS_TRANSMIT, OnUpdateSocketsTransmit)
    ON_UPDATE_COMMAND_UI(ID_SOCKETS_CONNECT, OnUpdateSocketsConnect)
    ON_UPDATE_COMMAND_UI(ID_SOCKETS_LISTEN, OnUpdateSocketsListen)
    //}}AFX_MSG_MAP
    ON_MESSAGE(WSA_READ, OnWSARead)
    ON_MESSAGE(WSA_ACCEPT, OnWSAAccept)
    ON_MESSAGE(WM_ONSOCKLISTEN, OnSockListen)
    ON_MESSAGE(WM_ONSOCKCONNECT, OnSockConnect)
    ON_MESSAGE(WM_ONSOCKGETHOSTNAME, OnSockGetHostName)
    ON_MESSAGE(WM_ONSOCKSENDTCP, OnSOCKSendTCP)
    ON_MESSAGE(WM_ONSOCKDESTROY, OnSockDestroy)
    ON_MESSAGE(WM_ONSOCKCANCEL, OnSockCancel)
END_MESSAGE_MAP()
```

Each time a message implemented in this message map is dispatched, a member function associated with the message is executed. For example, when the user chooses the **Connect** menu command or the **Connect** toolbar button, the message map in **SOCKSVW.CPP** detects an ON_SOCKETS_CONNECT message. As a result, a member function named OnSocketsConnect (also in **SOCKSVW.CPP**) is called:

```
void CSOCKSVw::OnSocketsConnect()
{
    // TODO: Add your command handler code here
    SendMessage(WM_ONSOCKCONNECT);
    m_tcpMsg = m_socket->m_msgString;
```

```
    UpdateData(FALSE);
}
```

As the preceding code fragment shows, OnSocketsConnect executes a SendMessage function with a WM_ONSOCKCONNECT argument. That argument causes another member function, OnSockConnect, to be executed. Following is the OnSockConnect function:

```
LRESULT CSOCKSVw::OnSockConnect(WPARAM wParam, LPARAM lParam)
{
    m_listenActive = FALSE;
    m_connectActive = FALSE;
    m_transmitActive = TRUE;

    (SockProc(m_hWnd, WM_COMMAND, IDM_CONNECT, lParam));

    m_tcpMsg = m_socket->m_tempCString;
    m_hostName = m_socket->m_tempCString2;
    UpdateData(FALSE);

    return TRUE;
}
```

Because OnSockConnect is executed as a result of a SendMessage function, the system passes a wParam parameter and an lParam parameter to OnSockConnect. The OnSockConnect function then passes the lParam to SockProc, along with an IDM_CONNECTwParam, a WM_COMMAND message identifier, and a handle to the SOCKS application's window. When the SockProc function executes, the IDM_CONNECT argument directs SockProc to the following case statement:

```
case IDM_CONNECT: {

    SOCKADDR_IN dest_sin; // DESTination Socket INternet

    // Get the name of the remote host and
    // STORE THE STRING IN m_szBuf.

    // Display dialog box that gets host's name.
    CDlgHostName dlgHostName;
    status = dlgHostName.DoModal();
    m_tempCString = dlgHostName.m_editName;
    m_tempStr = m_tempCString.GetBuffer(BUF_LEN);
```

```
strcpy(m_szBuf, m_tempStr);
m_tempCString = "Host name is: " + m_tempCString;
m_tempCString2 = m_szBuf;     // Host's name
m_remoteHost = m_szBuf;          // Save host name.

// m_szBuf = tempStr.GetBuffer(BUF_LEN);

if (!status) // User cancelled request from ...
    break;     // ... previous dialog box.

sock = socket( AF_INET, SOCK_STREAM, 0);
if (sock == INVALID_SOCKET) {
    MessageBox(hWnd, "socket function failed",
        "Error:", MB_OK);
    break;
                }

// Retrieve the IP address and TCP Port number.
// (Global variable m_szBuf contains the remote
// host's name).

if (!FillAddr( hWnd, &dest_sin, TRUE)) {
    closesocket( sock );
    break;
}

if (connect( sock, (PSOCKADDR) &dest_sin,
    sizeof(dest_sin)) < 0) {
    closesocket( sock );
    MessageBox(hWnd, "connect function failed",
        "Error:", MB_OK);
    break;
}
// Now we have a connection —

m_msgString = "Connection established.";

// Send main window a WSA_READ when either data is
// pending on the socket (FD_READ) or the connection is
// closed (FD_CLOSE)
```

```
     if ((status = WSAAsyncSelect( sock, hWnd, WSA_READ,
        FD_READ | FD_CLOSE )) > 0) {
        wsprintf(m_szBuf, "%d (0x%x)");
        MessageBox( hWnd, "Error on WSAAsyncSelect()",
            m_szBuf, MB_OK);
        closesocket( sock );
     }
}
break; // IDM_CONNECT
```

When the preceding case statement is executed, it displays a dialog box that obtains the host's name. Most of the other sockets-related operations in the SOCKS program operate in a similar fashion. To see the `SockProc` function, refer to **WSOCK.CPP**.

Summary

This chapter covers two main topics related to Windows NT networking: the general principles of computer networking and the Windows Sockets API and the TCP/IP communications protocol. You've learned how to write TCP/IP applications and how to use your applications to communicate with other Windows NT workstations running TCP/IP.

A sample program, SOCKS, shows how you can connect with other computer users and chat with them in real time using TCP/IP. SOCKS is a Visual C++ application that has two parts: a server application that manages communications, and a client program that you can launch once the server is running. The client program's main window is an interactive text window that was created using the MFC `CFormView` class.

The SOCKS application also shows how serialization—the automatic loading and saving of disk files—can be built into Visual C++ programs. When you run SOCKS, it automatically generates a log of all messages that are sent and received, and you can use serialization to load and save message logs that have been generated in TCP/IP sessions.

CHAPTER ELEVEN

WINDOWS NT GRAPHICS

Microsoft Windows has never been regarded as a particularly friendly environment for graphics programming, and it isn't hard to understand why. The graphics mechanisms in the Windows API have always been slow and unwieldy, particularly in applications designed to be run on 16-bit systems, and most 16-bit drivers for Windows video cards have been notoriously slow.

With the advent of Windows NT, this unfortunate situation began to change. Windows NT didn't come with any advanced new mechanisms for speeding graphics programming, but with the operating system zooming along at a 32-bit clip, Windows graphics got faster automatically. Then came a series of other innovations that began to add real speed to Windows graphics.

With the help of ever-faster Pentium processors (not to mention 300-MHz DEC Alphas) and a growing supply of supercharged video cards, the speed of Windows started to improve even more. By the time Windows 95 and Windows NT 4.0 appeared, Microsoft and other software publishers had introduced a new crop of programming tools that were especially designed to boost the speed of Windows graphics:

- ✦ The WinG (pronounced "Win-Gee") software development kit, a programmer's package designed to help developers create ultra-high-speed 32-bit and 16-bit games.

- ✦ A set of new function calls, such as StretchDIBits and CreateDIBSection, that have added WinG-style graphics capabilities to the Win32 API. These calls are designed for developers who want to create high-speed graphics for the 32-bit Windows NT and Windows and don't need the 16-bit graphics capabilities provided by WinG.

✦ The Windows Game SDK, an even newer developer's package that speeds up Windows graphics by writing directly to the video hardware built into modern graphics cards.

Thanks to these innovations, and to others that you'll learn about in this chapter, the speed of Windows graphics has improved so dramatically that even game manufacturers—whose speed requirements are among the highest in the computer industry—are gearing up to start moving away from MS-DOS and toward Windows as a platform for action games.

This chapter will introduce you to the fundamentals of computer graphics and will show you how to incorporate some simple but impressive animated graphics routines into your Windows NT programs. Two example applications on the accompanying disk demonstrate topics covered in this chapter. SPRTDEMO illustrates the use of traditional graphics-related techniques that Windows programmers are familiar with. The other program, CREATION, demonstrates some newer graphics techniques that are available for use in Windows NT applications.

Figure 11.1 shows the output of the SPRTDEMO program.

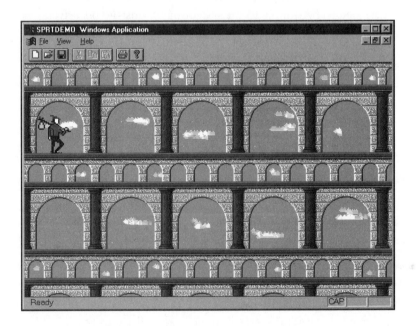

FIGURE 11.1 OUTPUT OF THE **SPRTDEMO** PROGRAM.

SPRTDEMO demonstrates sprite animation; it is a flicker-free animation program that moves an irregularly shaped bitmap over a complex background. SPRTDEMO uses conventional Windows objects such as GDI (graphics device interface) objects, DC (device context) objects, and conventional bitmaps. These graphics mechanisms are familiar to Windows programmers. What's special about SPRTDEMO is that it demonstrates how MFC graphics classes can be used for animation in Visual C++ programs.

The CREATION program demonstrates some newer graphics-related features of Windows NT, primarily involving the use of device-independent bitmaps, or DIBs.

Features of Windows NT Graphics

This chapter starts with an overview of some of the graphics features of Windows NT. Then the chapter shows how you can incorporate many of the old and new features of Windows NT into your Windows programs.

Some of the most important new (or relatively new) graphics-related features of Windows NT are as follows:

+ **Device-independent bitmaps (DIBs).** DIBs are slowly replacing traditional device-dependent bitmaps (DDBs) in graphics-intensive applications. Ordinary DDBs are easier to create and use than DIBs are, so DDBs are still widely used when ultra-precise color rendering is not an issue and when lightning-fast animation is not required. But DIBs can produce truer colors on a wider variety of output devices than ordinary DDBs can, and the colors that DIBs produce can be controlled more precisely. Both DIBs and DDBs are demonstrated in the sample programs in this chapter.

+ **32-bit coordinates.** All coordinates and object sizes used in Windows NT graphics have been widened from 16 bits to 32 bits, and handles to graphics objects are now 32 bits wide. If you use MFC classes in your programs, this change to 32-bit graphics should not be a serious problem; the data structures used in Visual C++ should take care of most conversions for you. However, if you have some old applications lying around that store graphics data in 16-bit structures, watch out!

+ **Matrix transforms.** The Win32 API contains more than a dozen graphics functions that can change the shapes of images by performing offsetting, scaling, skewing, and rotation operations. With these new functions, you can turn rectangles into parallelograms, draw ellipses with oblique axes, and perform all kinds of tricks with 3-D graphics.

✦ **Bezier curves.** In the new world of Win32 graphics, a Bezier spline is a curved line defined by four points: the two endpoints and another pair of control points that define the curvature of the line. The control points affect the line's curve by exerting a pull, much like a pair of magnets. The result is an eye-pleasing curve that can be precisely controlled, provided that you grasp the math.

✦ **Paths.** A *path* is a collection of lines (straight, curved, or both) that can be stored in a device-context object. When a path has been assembled, an application needs only a single command to draw or fill the shape that it describes. You can also use paths to draw outlined text using TrueType fonts. The outlines of the text can be empty or can be filled using floods or stroking, a procedure that creates a pattern made up of straight lines.

✦ **New BitBlt-style functions.** `BitBlt` is a familiar Windows API function that copies bitmaps from one block of memory to another. (The MFC library's version of `BitBlt` is the `CDC::BitBlt` member function.) `StretchBlt`, another familiar Windows API function, combines `BitBlt` with scaling. (The MFC version of `StretchBlt` is `CDC::StretchBlt`.) The Win32 API and MFC 4.0 have added two functions to this family: `MaskBlt` (or `CDC::MaskBlt`), which can copy a bitmap onto a complex background through a mask, and `PlgBlt` (or `CDC::PageBlt`), which copies a bitmap with a rectangular shape into a parallelogram-shaped destination, skewing the original bitmap as required.

Using Graphics Objects in Windows Programs

In non-Visual C++ programs written using the Windows API, graphics objects such as pens and brushes are known as GDI objects, whereas objects that interface graphics objects with devices such as monitor screens and printed pages are called DC objects. Figure 11.2 shows the graphics classes provided in Visual C++.

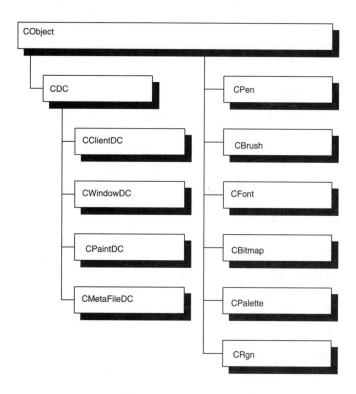

FIGURE 11.2 GRAPHICS CLASSES IN THE MFC LIBRARY.

In Windows API-style (non-Visual C++) programs, GDI and DC objects are accessed using handles. Examples of GDI handles are HBRUSH (for accessing brushes), HPEN (for pens), HBITMAP (for bitmaps), and so on. Windows API-style functions that return handles to GDI objects include such procedures as CreateCompatibleBitmap, CreatePen, and CreatePatternBrush.

Handles of DC objects have always had the HDC data type. Functions that manipulate HDC handles include GetDC, CreateCompatibleDC, BeginPaint, and EndPaint.

In Visual C++, the CGdiObject class encapsulates the functionality of GDI structures. CGdiObject is an abstract class, so an application can't directly instantiate objects of this class. But a number of concrete classes, such as CPen, CBrush, and CBitmap, are derived from CGdiObject. And classes that are derived from CGdiObject provide many graphics-related data structures and member functions.

The CDC class encapsulates the functionality of the device context objects used in Windows API-style applications. In Visual C++, DC objects are members of the CDC class, and the GetDC, CreateCompatibleDC, BeginPaint, and EndPaint functions are CDC member functions.

The example programs show how the CGdiObject and CDC classes can be used in Windows NT applications. The features of both programs are described at the end of this chapter.

The CGdiObject Class

Windows NT supports many kinds of graphics devices, such as monitor screens and printers, using the GDI function library. Implemented as a dynamic link library, GDI is one of the three main DLLs that implement Windows NT. (The DLLs are **KERNEL32.DLL**, **USER32.DLL**, and **GDI32.DLL**; for details, see Chapter 2, "Underneath Windows NT.")

The GDI library provides the Win32 API with functions that create various kinds of objects. For example, the GDI function CreatePen creates a pen, the CreateCompatibleBitmap function creates a bitmap that is compatible with the current graphics device driver, and CreateSolidBrush creates a brush that draws in a solid color. (To create a brush that draws in a pattern, there is a CreatePatternBrush call.)

When a Visual C++ function needs to use a graphics object such as a pen or a brush, it instantiates the object from a class derived from CGdiObject, such as the CPen or CBrush class. (As noted previously, CGdiObject is an abstract class and therefore cannot be instantiated directly.) In MFC, six classes of drawing objects are derived from CGdiObject:

+ **CPen.** A tool for drawing lines and borders or shapes. Your application can specify a pen's thickness and color and whether it draws plain or dashed lines.

+ **CBrush.** A bitmapped block of pixels that can fill an area with a color or a pattern.

+ **CBitmap.** An array of bits in which one or more bits correspond to a pixel on the display device.

✦ **CFont.** A collection of characters of a particular typeface and a particular size. A font is usually stored as a resource and is device-specific.

✦ **CPalette.** An array of colors that an application can use to draw with graphics objects.

✦ **CRgn.** A shape that can be filled, painted, inverted, framed, and used to perform hit testing (testing for the cursor's location). A CRgn object is made up of one or more rectangles, polygons, or ellipses, mixed or matched in any combination.

The CGdiObject classes are shown in Figure 11.3.

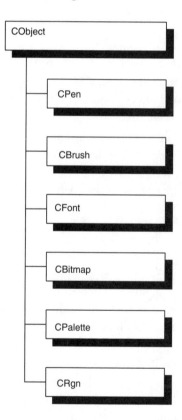

FIGURE 11.3 CGDIOBJECT CLASSES.

CGdiObject and its descendents contain many functions for creating and manipulating graphics devices such as brushes, pens, and bitmaps. GDI member functions work in conjunction with device drivers. When an application has a drawing operation to perform, it makes a call to a GDI member function to obtain a graphics object. The GDI member function then processes the call and passes it to a device driver.

In Windows NT graphics, a device driver is a DLL that receives input from GDI procedures, converts them to device commands, and passes those commands to the appropriate device.

CREATING A GRAPHICS OBJECT

Member functions of CGdiObject and its descendents can interface an application with various kinds of device drivers, depending on what kind of device an application is drawing to. For example, GDI member functions can communicate with one device driver to get a screen-drawing object, and with an different device driver to create an object that draws to a printer. In this way, a GDI member function can use the same user input to write information to graphics devices that require different kinds of inputs because they use different output technologies.

The GDI member function CreateCompatibleBitmap creates a bitmap that is compatible with the current graphics device driver. The SPRTDEMO example program uses CreateCompatibleBitmap several times. In this statement, CreateCompatibleBitmap creates a bitmap that is compatible with the current device context:

```
myBitmap.CreateCompatibleBitmap(pDC, m_bkgWidth, m_bkgHeight);
```

USING GRAPHICS OBJECTS

When an application calls a member function of the CGdiObject class, the program passes the function the parameters that are needed to create the desired graphics object. The member function creates the desired object by loading an appropriate device driver. Once the specified graphics object is created, the application can call another function to set the object's attributes in preparation for a drawing operation.

For example, an application might call a function that selects a brush pattern and a color, chooses a line color and a line width, or a selects a font, depending on what kind of graphics operation is about to be performed. Then the application could select the object into a CDC object (a procedure explained later in this chapter) and call a function to draw the object.

Two Ways to Create Graphics Objects

In Visual C++, there are two ways to create a graphics object. The first way is to write a constructor that instantiates and initializes the object in a single step. The second technique is to write a constructor that creates the object and to initialize the object with a separate function.

The one-step procedure is concise and easy to use, but it can throw an exception (it can result in a situation that requires an exception handler) if an illegal parameter is passed to the constructor being invoked or if there is a problem in allocating memory. The two-step method is more complicated but generally safer.

One-Step Creation of a Graphics object

Every graphics object defined in MFC has a constructor that can create and initialize the object in a single step. For example, you can instantiate and initialize a CPen object by invoking a constructor written in the following format:

```
CPen myPen(PS_SOLID, 4, RGB(0,0,0));
```

In this example, the arguments passed to the CPen constructor specify the style, the width, and the color that are to be used to create the pen. Constructors for other kinds of graphics arguments take different kinds of parameters.

There are other one-step ways to create and object and set its attributes, depending on the kind of object you are creating. For example, instead of calling CreatePen as shown in the preceding example, you can call CreatePenIndirect (which lets you specify pen attributes by passing a pointer to a structure). Alternatively, you can call CreateStockObject (a CGdiObject member function that lets you specify attributes by passing a predefined constant).

Other calls to create graphics objects include CBitmap::CreateCompatibleBitmap, CBrush::CreateSolidBrush, and CBrush::CreatePatternBrush. The MFC library contains many other member functions for creating objects derived from CGdiObject.

Two-Step Creation of a Graphics object

To instantiate any graphics object in two steps, you invoke a default constructor that takes no arguments. This method creates a graphics object without initializing it. You can then initialize the object, immediately or at a later point in your application.

For example, you can create a CPen object without initializing it by invoking a default constructor that instantiates the object either on the current function's stack frame or on the heap, as follows:

```
CPen myPen;
```

or

```
CPen *pMyPen = new CPen;
```

You can then call other functions to set the attributes of the object you have created.

The following code fragment shows how you can construct a CPen object with a default constructor and then initialize it using CreatePen (the function's Boolean return value tells you whether your pen object is successfully initialized):

```
CPen aPen;
if (pPen.CreatePen(PS_SOLID, 4, RGB( 0, 0, 0 ));
    // Your code goes here.
```

SELECTING A GRAPHICS OBJECT INTO A CDC OBJECT

When you have constructed a graphics object using either the one-step or the two-step approach, you must select the device into the current device context before you can use it. To select a graphics object into a device context, call the Win32 function SelectObject (see "Selecting Graphics objects" later in this chapter).

The CDC Class

The CDC class is an MFC class that interfaces graphics objects such as pens, brushes, bitmaps, and fonts with devices that display or print images. Whereas a GDI object is always associated with a graphics object such a pen or a brush, a CDC object is always associated with a specific device, such as a particular kind of Hewlett-Packard printer or a VGA display.

In Windows NT, CDC objects and GDI objects are implemented in different ways. Functions that create and implement CDC objects are provided in the GDI32 library, which is implemented as a single DLL. In contrast, every CDC object is implemented as a device driver, and every CDC device driver is implemented as an individual DLL. For example, the CDC device driver that displays images on a VGA monitor is named **VGA.DLL**.

Visual C++ implements device contexts as objects derived from the CDC class. With CDC objects, you can paint and draw images and text on a wide range of devices such as monitor screens, printed pages, and fax modems.

The CDC class implements so many kinds of DLLs that it is the second largest class in the MFC library. It contains more than 100 member variables and member functions. Only the CWnd class, which encapsulates window classes and member functions, is larger.

Figure 11.4 shows the CDC classes in the MFC library.

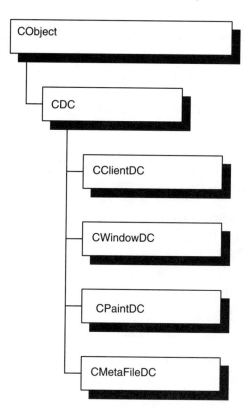

FIGURE 11.4 CDC CLASSES IN THE MFC LIBRARY.

SELECTING GRAPHICS OBJECTS

Life would be simpler without CDC objects. If there were no such thing as a device context, you would be able to create a graphics object such as a pen, set its attributes, and then use it immediately to draw an object.

In Windows NT, as in earlier versions of Windows, CDC objects add an extra layer of complexity to drawing operations. When you want to draw a shape in a Windows program, you can't just pick up a drawing object, such as a pen, and then draw the shape in a window. Instead, you have to associate a pen with a device context object—that is, an object of the CDC class—and then use the CDC object to draw the image. In Windows jargon, associating a graphics object such as a pen or a brush with a CDC object is known as *selecting* the graphics object into the CDC object.

Windows programs require the use of DC objects because graphics objects such as pens and brushes must use different kinds of algorithms to display or print images on different kinds of devices. Because of this requirement, a Windows application cannot draw images by manipulating a GDI object directly; instead, it must manipulate the GDI object indirectly by calling member functions of the CDC class. For example, an application never draws a line on a video screen by simply calling a member function of the CPen class. Instead, it selects a CPen object into a CDC object and then draws the line by calling the CDC member function LineTo, which draws a straight line on an output device such as screen or a printed page.

Several kinds of device contexts can be used in Windows programs. For example, every window has its own private DC, which can be used for drawing operations that take place in that particular window. Other kinds of DCs are described in "Kinds of Device Contexts" later in this chapter.

The following code sequence shows how you can select a CPen object into a window's private DC and then use that pen to draw a line. In this case, LineTo is called to draw a line from point m_x to point m_y (m_x and m_y are member variables that are assumed to be predefined):

```
void CMyView::DrawALine()
{
    // (1) Retrieve this view's private DC.
    CDC *pDC = GetDC();

    // (2) construct a GDI object—in this case, a pen.
    CPen myPen;

    // (3) Select &myPen into this view's private DC. Notice
    // that a pointer to the previous contents of the DC
    // is transferred to *pOldPen for safekeeping.
    // When we are finished with the DC we have
    // obtained, we will restore it to its original state
```

```
    // by calling Select Object again.
    CPen *pOldPen = pDC->SelectObject(&myPen);

    // (4) Call LineTo to draw a line from m_x to m_y.
    pDC->LineTo(m_x, m_y);

    // (5) Restore the DC we have obtained to its original // state.
    pDC->SelectObject(pOldPen);
}
```

The preceding code fragment defines a member function of a CView object named CMyView. The statements in the example are divided into steps. This is what happens in each step:

1. In a Visual C++ program generated by AppWizard, every CView object has a private device context with a pointer that can be retrieved by calling the member function Cwnd::GetDC. Step 1 obtains a pointer to the current view's private device context by calling Cwnd::GetDC. (In Visual C++ programs, as in this example, a pointer to the current view's private DC is conventionally named pDC.)

2. An MFC constructor is invoked to instantiate a graphics object of the CPen class. CPen is derived from the CGdiObject class. In the preceding example, the CPen object that is constructed is named myPen.

3. This step calls CDC::SelectObject to select myPen into the current view's private device context. The SelectObject member function selects a specified object into a specified DC structure and transfers a pointer to the object that was previously associated with the DC structure to another DC pointer. SelectObject then returns a pointer to the CDC object that the graphics object has been selected into.

4. The CDC::LineTo member function is called to draw a line from point m_x to point m_y.

5. SelectObject is called again to restore the DC to its original state.

NT Lifts Five-Per-Customer Limit on DCs

The Windows 3.x operating system allowed only five common DCs to be in use at the same time. This limitation was not imposed on each application, but on the entire system! The reason was that the window manager stored common DCs in a special cache in each application's heap, and space in that cache was limited. Failing to deallocate unneeded device contexts, particularly when a new device context was assigned with each iteration of a loop, could quickly consume all the available space on an application's heap. If another application needed a DC and couldn't get one, the second application could misbehave or even crash.

In Windows NT, every application has four gigabytes of virtual address space, so DC objects are no longer stored in a special cache with limited space, and the Windows 3.x limit of five DCs has been lifted. However, if you want your application to be portable to Windows 3.x systems, you should make sure that it uses no more than five common DCs simultaneously. And you should release common DCs when they are no longer needed (see "Releasing Device Contexts.").

RELEASING DEVICE CONTEXTS

When a device context has been restored to its original state, one more step must be taken before the system can free the DC for other uses. This step is known as *releasing* the DC.

In a non-Visual C++ (Windows API) application, every device context that is created must eventually be released. Some DCs, called private device contexts (see "Kinds of Device Contexts" later in this chapter), belong to particular windows and are released automatically when their windows are destroyed. Other DCs, called common device contexts, must be explicitly released when they are no longer needed. A non-MFC application can release a common DC by calling `ReleaseDC` or `EndPaint`.

In a Visual C++ application, when you create a CDC object using a constructor, it is not necessary to release the object by calling `ReleaseDC` or `EndPaint`. When you invoke the object's constructor, the DC is released automatically.

The MFC library provides a `CDC::ReleaseDC` function, but applications ordinarily do not use it; instead, an application that uses MFC classes usually lets a common DC's destructor release the DC.

Using CDC Objects

In all, six kinds of graphics objects can be selected into a CDC object:

+ Pens (for line drawing)
+ Brushes (for painting and filling)

✦ Bitmaps (for displaying graphics stored in memory and for copying or scrolling parts of the screen)

✦ Palettes (for defining the set of available colors)

✦ Regions (for clipping and other operations)

✦ Paths (for painting and drawing operations)

The MFC library supplies CDC member functions for performing the following kinds of graphics operations:

✦ Drawing and painting many kinds of shapes, such as lines, rectangles, ellipses, polygons, and regions (irregularly shaped objects)

✦ Printing text in color or black-and-white

✦ Getting and setting the colors of objects and text and the background colors of windows

✦ Scrolling screen and text displays

✦ Telling a program what parts of the screen should be updated because their contents have been changed

✦ Providing important data, such as start-of-page and end-of-page information, to printers

✦ Playing metafiles (files that can display assorted bitmaps, shapes, text, and other objects on a screen or a printed page)

BITMAPS: DDBs AND DIBs

The CDC functions that have changed most in recent versions of Windows are those used for creating and managing bitmaps. In computer graphics, a *bitmap* is a data structure in which pixels are stored. *Pixels* are the colored dots that produce the images on a monitor. Because of the direct one-to-one relationship between pixels stored in a bitmap and pixels displayed in a window, bit-copying functions such as BitBlt can be used to copy bitmaps stored in memory directly into windows displayed on a screen.

Ever since the Windows operating environment was introduced, Windows programmers have used DDBs to display images in Windows. The device-dependent bitmap was the only kind of bitmap available to Windows programmers until about 1989. Since then, DDBs have been falling out of favor, replaced by DIBs in graphics-intensive applications.

A DIB, as its name suggests, can be used on any DIB-compatible device. A DDB, in contrast, is guaranteed to be compatible only with the device for which it was designed.

(See "Architecture of the DIB Structure" later in this chapter.) Consequently, a DIB can display more accurate colors on a wider variety of output devices than a DDB can. To implement this feature, a DIB structure contains a data table in which values that equate to colors can be stored. A DDB structure does not contain such a table.

Another advantage of DIBs is that a number of super-fast bit-copying mechanisms are now available for use with DIBs. Applications that use turbocharged DIB-based graphics are now beginning to replace DIBs in high-performance Windows programs.

Using BitBlt and StretchBlt with DIBs

One fast bit-copying procedure that can be used with DIBs but not with DDBs is the Windows API function `StretchDIBits`. (As of MFC 4.0, `StretchDIBits` was not available as an MFC library member function.) Another DIB-specific Windows API function is `CreateDIBSection`, which reserves a block of memory for DIB storage and then ensures that when a DIB is loaded into that area of RAM, it can be treated just like an ordinary DDB. When you allocate a block of memory for DIB storage by calling `CreateDIBSection`, the block of memory you have allocated is known as a DIB section.

`CreateDIBSection` is a useful function for dealing with DIBs, because it combines the advantages of using DIBs with the developer friendliness of using DDBs. Once you have allocated a DIB section by calling `CreateDIBSection`, and have loaded a DIB into the reserved DIB section, you can treat it just like an ordinary DDB. This means that all the old-style bitmap functions, such as `CDC::BitBlt` and `CDC::StretchBlt`, work just as well with DIBs that have been stored in DIB sections as they do with DDBs.

Copying Bitmaps in Windows Programs

In this section, you'll see how you can use the MFC `CDC::BitBlt` and `CDC::StretchBlt` functions in your Windows NT applications. The operations described in this section are based on the SPTRDEMO example program.

SPRTDEMO is designed to work with device-dependent bitmaps. However, because `CDC::BitBlt` and `CDC::StretchBlt` work in exactly the same way with DDBs and with DIBs stored in DIB sections, what you'll learn in this section also applies to DIBs that have been stored in memory using `CreateDIBSection`.

Using the CDC::BitBlt Member Function

To execute a `CDC::BitBlt` member function, you must use two device contexts: a *private device context* and a *common device context*. (A private DC belongs to a particular view;

a common DC can be obtained when a drawing operation requires more than one DC. For more information about these and other types of DCs, see "Common Device Contexts" later in this chapter.)

The following list outlines the steps for using CDC::BitBlt. The steps are taken from the SPRTDEMO program:

1. Retrieve a pointer to the current view's private device context. In some cases, Visual C++ supplies a DC pointer (conventionally named pDC). For example, the OnDraw message handler—which AppWizard supplies as a member function of every view class—provides a pDC pointer as an argument. If the framework doesn't supply you with a pDC pointer in the function definition you are using, you can obtain one by calling CWnd::GetDC.

2. Create a common DC object that is compatible with the current device context. You can create such a DC object by calling CreateCompatibleDC, as in the following example:

   ```
   CDC *m_dcBackdrop;
   m_dcBackdrop.CreateCompatibleDC(pDC);
   ```

3. Call CreateCompatibleBitmap to create a bitmap that is compatible with the graphics device you are using. In Visual C++, a bitmap is an object of the CBitmap class, which is a subclass of CGdiObject. The following code fragment constructs a CBitmap object named m_bmBkg and then calls CreateCompatibleBitmap. The second and third arguments to CreateCompatibleBitmap specify the size of the bitmap that is being created. In this case, the new bitmap is the size of a predefined rectangle named m_bmRect:

   ```
   CBitmap m_bmBackdrop;
   m_bmBkg.CreateCompatibleBitmap(pDC, m_bigRect.right,
       m_bigRect.bottom);
   ```

4. Select the bitmap into a common device context. In the following code fragment, SelectObject selects the m_bmBkg bitmap that was created in Step 3 into a common DC object named m_dcBackdrop (which was obtained in Step 1) and returns a bitmap pointer. In case there is a GDI object that was previously associated with m_dcBackdrop, its pointer is placed in m_pOldMapMem for safekeeping. This operation makes it possible to restore m_dcBackdrop to its previous state when it is no longer needed.

   ```
   CBitmap *m_pOldMapMem;
   pOldMapMem = m_dcBackdrop.SelectObject(&m_bmBkg);
   ```

5. When Steps 1 through 4 are complete, `BitBlt` is called to copy the bitmap associated with `m_dcMem` to the bitmap that has been selected into `m_dcBackdrop`. Notice that when `BitBlt` is called, the boundary rectangle of the source bitmap is named `m_invalidRect`. The boundary rectangle of the destination bitmap is named `m_bmRect`.

```
// Copy portion of background to m_dcBackdrop, inverting

// colors.
m_dcBackdrop.BitBlt(0, 0, m_bigRect.right, m_bigRect.bottom,
    &m_dcMem, m_invalidRect.left, m_invalidRect.top, NOTSRCCOPY);
```

6. When the copying operation is finished, `SelectObject` is called again to restore `m_dcBackdrop` to its original state:

```
m_dcBackdrop.SelectObject(m_pOldMapMem);
```

USING THE CDC::STRETCHBLT MEMBER FUNCTION

The `CDC::StretchBlt` member function is identical to `CDC::BitBlt`, except that `StretchBlt` has two extra parameters (the two next to the end) that specify the width and height of the origin rectangle. The following `StretchBlt` member function copies a bitmap selected into a device context named `dcMem` into a device context named `dcBkg`. The boundary rectangles of the source bitmap are stored in a pair of `int` variables named `m_bmWidth` and `m_bmHeight`. The boundary rectangle of the destination bitmap is named `m_invalidRect`:

```
dcBkg.StretchBlt(m_invalidRect.left, m_invalidRect.top,
    m_invalidRect.right, m_invalidRect.bottom, &dcMem,
    0, 0, m_bmWidth, m_bmHeight, SRCINVERT);
```

NEW BIT-COPYING FUNCTIONS

Along with familiar member functions such as `BitBlt` and `StretchBlt`, some newer bitmap-moving functions have been added to the Win32 API. Some of these new functions, such as `SetDIBits` and `StretchDIBits`, work only with DIBs. But one new function, `MaskBlt`, works with DDBs as well as with DIBs that have been stored in DIB sections.

`StretchDIBits` copies and scales a DIB in a single operation. `SetDIBits` and a related function, `SetDIBitsToDevice`, initialize the pixel array that contains the image of a DIB. The CREATION sample program uses `StretchDIBits` for its screen-drawing operations.

The `MaskBlt` function copies a bitmap through a mask in one operation. It is designed to stencil irregularly shaped bitmaps onto complex backgrounds.

Kinds of Device Contexts

Windows applications use several kinds of device contexts, and different procedures are used to create DCs of different kinds. The device contexts used in Windows programs are as follows:

+ **Private device contexts.** These DCs belong to a particular window. A private DC is created when its window is created and is destroyed when its window is destroyed. Private DCs supply all the functionality that is needed for certain simple drawing operations, such as `MoveTo` and `LineTo`. More-complex drawing functions, such as `BitBlt` and `StretchBlt`, require additional DCs.

+ **Common device contexts** provide drawing capabilities. A window can have only one private DC, so common DCs can be created when a window needs additional DCs.

+ **Memory device contexts** store bitmapped images in memory. Applications can use memory DCs to move bitmaps from one memory location to another or between memory storage and the screen.

+ **Printer device contexts** support graphics operations on laser printers, dot-matrix printers, ink-jet printers, and plotters.

+ **Class device contexts** are associated with specific classes of windows. Class DCs are now considered obsolete; new applications should use common DCs instead.

PRIVATE DEVICE CONTEXTS

A private DC is always associated with a particular window. When a private DC is no longer needed, no special measures have to be taken to destroy it because it is destroyed automatically when its window closes. Win32 creates a private DC each time a window of a particular class is created, provided that the window style CS_OWNDC is specified in the window's WNDCLASS structure when the window is registered.

When AppWizard generates a Visual C++ application, Visual C++ automatically creates a private DC for each view that the program uses. Some message handlers provided by MFC, such as `OnDraw`, provide applications with pointers to the private DCs used by views. When a pointer to a private DC is not provided, a Visual C++ application can obtain one by calling `GetDC` or `GetDCEx`.

COMMON DEVICE CONTEXTS

If a window displays only text or simple line graphics, it may be able to handle all the required graphics using its built-in private DC. However, if a window requires more-complex drawing operations, such as the sprite animation procedures demonstrated in this chapter's graphics programs, common DCs must be allocated.

MEMORY DEVICE CONTEXTS

A memory DC is a device context that can store a bitmap in memory. Different kinds of display devices use different formats to display bitmaps, so a memory DC is always compatible with a specific kind of bitmap, one that is associated with a specific kind of display device.

An application creates a memory-class device context by calling the MFC `CreateCompatibleDC` member function. The application supplies the function with a DC pointer that has already been associated with a specific display device. The system responds by creating a bitmap with a compatible color format. When an application has created a bitmap in memory by calling `CreateCompatibleDC`, the application can select a bitmap into the device context by calling `SelectObject`. The application can then store a bitmap of the specified size in the device context.

An application can create smooth, flicker-free graphics by calling `CreateCompatibleDC` to store a bitmap in memory instead of drawing the bitmap directly on the screen. The application can then copy the bitmap from memory to the screen rather than from the disk to the screen. Because moving a bitmap from memory to the screen is faster, it prevents flickers and flashes in animated screen displays.

SPRTDEMO and CREATION use this technique to create screen animation. SPRTDEMO calls the MFC member function `CDC::BitBlt` to copy bitmaps into memory and then move them to the screen. CREATION uses the same technique with the Windows API function `StretchDIBits`.

PRINTER DEVICE CONTEXTS

A printer device context is a DC that you can use to draw images on a dot-matrix printer, an ink-jet printer, a laser printer, or a plotter. To create a printer device context, you call the MFC `CreateDC` member function.

CLASS DEVICE CONTEXTS

Class DCs work like common device contexts but are provided only for backward compatibility with older Windows systems. Microsoft advises that Class DCs not be used in new applications.

The Two Faces of DIB

There are two kinds of DIBs: Windows DIBs, which are used by Windows NT, and Presentation Manager DIBs, which were designed for the OS/2 Presentation Manager and are considered obsolete. The DIBs referred to in this chapter are Windows DIBs.

Architecture of the DIB Structure

A device-independent bitmap is made up of two parts: a header and a bit array. The header contains data structures that provide information about the bitmap. The bit array, as its name suggests, is a map of the pixels in the bitmap.

Figure 11.5 shows the structure of a DIB.

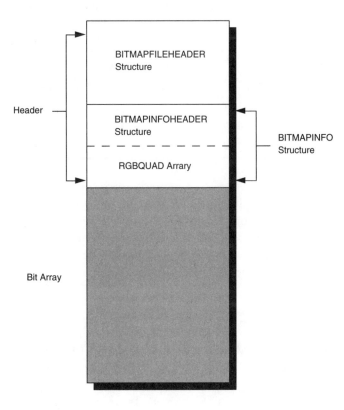

FIGURE 11.5 STRUCTURE OF A DIB.

SCAN LINES IN A DIB BIT ARRAY

The scan lines in the bit array are arranged upside down with respect to the address of each bit in the DIB file. The bits that make up the last scan line in the file appear first in the bit array, and the bits that make up the first scan line appear last. This anomaly requires some thought when you manipulate bits in your code.

Figure 11.6 illustrates the arrangement of the bit array section of a DIB structure.

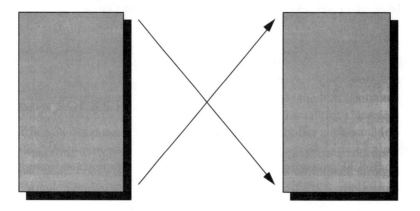

FIGURE 11.6 BIT ARRAY SECTION OF A DIB STRUCTURE.

'Til DIB Do You Part

Oddly, there is no requirement for the header part of a DIB and the bit array part of the DIB to be in contiguous memory blocks. So the area of memory that lies between the header section and the bit-array section of a DIB is, theoretically, undefined. In practice, most developers combine the two parts of a DIB into a single memory block. That way, you don't fragment memory, and you have only one block of memory to worry about.

FORMAT OF A DIB HEADER

The header part of a DIB is subdivided into two parts: a BITMAPFILEHEADER structure and a BITMAPINFO structure. The BITMAPFILEHEADER structure contains information about the file that contains the DIB. The BITMAPINFO structure defines the dimensions of the bitmap and provides information about the DIB's colors. Figure 11.5, presented earlier, shows how a BITMAPFILEHEADER structure and a BITMAPINFOHEADER structure are combined to form the header of a device-independent bitmap.

The BITMAPFILEHEADER structure in a DIB's header holds information about the type, size, and layout of the file that contains the DIB. Table 11.1 lists the contents of a BITMAPFILEHEADER data structure.

TABLE 11.1 CONTENTS OF A **BITMAPFILEHEADER** STRUCTURE.

Field	Data Type	Contents
bfType	WORD	Type of file. Must be BM.
bfSize	DWORD	Specifies the size of the file, in bytes. (Volume 5 of the Microsoft *Win32 Programmer's Reference* provides different description of this field but is incorrect.)
bfReserved1, bfReserved2	WORDS	Reserved; each word must be set to O.
bfOffBits	DWORD	Specifies the offset from the beginning of the BITMAPFILEHEADER structure to the start of the structure's bit array.

PARTS OF A **BITMAPINFO** STRUCTURE

The BITMAPINFO part of a DIB's header has two parts: a BITMAPINFOHEADER and an RGBQUAD array. The BITMAPINFOHEADER structure contains information about the dimensions and color format of a DIB. The RGBQUAD array contains information about the colors used in the DIB. Table 11.2 lists the contents of a BITMAPINFOHEADER data structure.

TABLE 11.2 CONTENTS OF A **BITMAPINFOHEADER** STRUCTURE.

Field	Data Type	Contents
bSize	DWORD	Size of the BITMAPINFOHEADER structure.
biWidth, biHeight	LONGs	The width and height of the bitmap pixels.
biPlanes	WORD	Specifies thenumber of planes used by the target device. Must be set to 1.

continued

TABLE 11.2 CONTINUED

biBitCount	WORD	Defines the color resolution of the DIB, in bits per pixel. Only four values are valid: 1, 4, 8, and 24. Meanings of these values are: 1 = 2 colors, 4 = 16 colors, 8 = 258 colors, 24 = no color table.
biCompression	DWORD	Specifies the type of compression used to store the bitmap. Three values are valid: BI_RLE4, BI_RLE_8, and bSize. The most common choice is BI_RGB, which decodes rapidly and is most widely suported.
biSizeImage	DWORD	Specifies the acutal size of the bitmap's byte array. A DIB's byte array is DWORD-aligned at the end of each scan line, so the formula for calculating the value in this field (should you ever have to do it) is: biSizeImage = (((biWidth * biBitCount) +31) & ~31) >> 3) * biHeight
biXPelsPerMeter, biYPelsPerMeter	LONGs	These two long words specify application-defined values for desirable dimensions of the bitmap. This file is for use by your application; GDI doesn't touch it. If you don't use this field, enter a 0 value for each word.
biClrUsed	DWORD	Provides a method for using smaller color tables. A 0 in this field means that number of colors in the color table is specified in the biBitCount field. A non-zero value in this field specifies the exact number of colors in the table.
biClrImportant	DWORD	Specifies that the first n colors of the table are most important to the DIB. If other colors are not available, this field asks GDI to try to make at least these colors as accurate as possible. A 0 value in this field means that all colors are important.

The RGBQUAD portion of a BITMAPINFO structure is an array of RGBQUAD data types that define the colors in a DIB. The RGBQUAD data types provide information about the DIB's color palette. (A palette is an array of colors that an application can use when drawing graphics to a particular display device. For details, see the "Palettes" section later in this chapter.)

An RGBQUAD structure describes a color in terms of relative intensities of red, green, and blue. An RGBQUAD array is stored in memory as an array of color indices. Each color index maps to a specific pixel in the rectangular region that encloses the bitmap. The size of the array, expressed in bits, is equivalent to the width of the DIB's enclosing rectangle (expressed in pixels) times the height of the rectangle (also expressed in pixels) times the number of color bits associated with the current display device.

This is the Windows `typedef` that defines an RGBQUAD structure:

```
typedef struct tagRGBQUAD {
    BYTE rgbBlue;
    BYTE rgbGreen;
    BYTE rgbRed;
    BYTE rgbReserved;
} RGBQUAD;
```

In an RGBQUAD structure, the `rgbBlue`, `rgbGreen`, and `rgbRed` bytes define the intensities of the blue, green, and red colors in each pixel of the DIB being displayed.

An application can retrieve the size of a device's palette by calling `GetDeviceCaps`, specifying the NUMCOLORS constant as the second parameter. To retrieve the horizontal and vertical resolution of a video display or a printer (expressed in pixels per meter), an application can call `GetDeviceCaps` and specify HORZSIZE or VERTSIZE as the call's second parameter.

An application creates a DIB by initializing the required structures and calling the Win32 function `CreateDIBitmap`. Then it initializes its RGBQUAD structure by calling `SetDIBits`. To display a DIB that already exists, an application copies the DIB from memory to a display device by calling `StretchDIBits`, `SetDIBitsToDevice`, `BitBlt`, or `StretchBlt`. To set the pixels in a particular display device, an application calls either `SetDIBitsToDevice` or `BitBlt`.

Palettes

When you create a device-dependent bitmap, its colors are supplied by the device for which the DDB is created and cannot be changed later to match the requirements of a different output device.

Device-independent bitmaps handle colors very differently. The colors used by a DIB are determined by an array of color codes called a *color palette*, or simply a *palette*. There are four kinds of palettes that determine the colors used by Windows applications:

+ **The hardware palette.** A color lookup table that is built into a video display card. When you use a palette-based display adapters (which is what most video cards are) and specify the DIB_PAL_COLORS display mode in your application, the pixels you see on the screen are indices into the colors that have been placed in your video card's hardware palette.

+ **The system palette.** A copy of the hardware palette maintained by a system software mechanism called the Palette Manager. The system palette provides all the colors that can appear on a particular output device at a particular time. Because the number of colors that a video system can display at one time is limited, the system palette is designed to hold a maximum of 256 colors. (The term *system palette* can be confusing, because it is sometimes used instead of the term *hardware palette* to refer to the hardware palette provide by the system's video display hardware.)

✦ **Logical palettes.** Palette objects created by applications. A logical palette is implemented as an array of colors that an application can use for drawing graphics using a particular device context. When an application has created a logical palette, it can pass those colors to the Palette Manager for use in the system palette.

✦ **The default logical palette.** The DEFAULT_PALETTE stock object provided by the graphics device interface. The default logical palette contains the VGA colors and is used for supporting applications that do not explicitly use palettes.

✦ **Identity palettes.** A logical palette that contains a set of colors laid out in exactly the same order as the colors in the system palette. By setting up an identity palette, an application can avoid time-consuming index lookups, significantly increasing processing speed.

To set the colors of the system palette and make them available to Windows programs, Windows uses the Palette Manager. The only way your application can access the system palette is through the Palette Manager.

THE SYSTEM PALETTE

The system palette is divided into two parts: one for 20 colors that are fixed, or *static*, and one for a collection of colors that applications can modify. The total number of colors provided by the system palette can vary depending on the kind of display device being used. However, every system palette has exactly 20 fixed colors that applications cannot change. Applications can set the remaining 236 colors in the system palette using the Palette Manager.

Sixteen of the 20 static colors correspond to the 16 standard colors used by a standard 16-color VGA display. The other four static colors were chosen for their visual appeal and are used by Windows.

Obtaining the Size of the Hardware Palette

An application can retrieve the size of a device's hardware palette by calling `GetDeviceCaps`, specifying the NUMCOLORS constant as the second parameter. To retrieve the horizontal and vertical resolution of a video display or a printer (expressed in pixels per meter), an application can call `GetDeviceCaps` and specify HORZSIZE or VERTSIZE as the call's second parameter.

THE DEFAULT LOGICAL PALETTE

For applications that need to use only the 16 standard VGA colors, Windows maintains the 16-color default logical palette. If you want to use it in an application, you can access it by selecting the DEFAULT_PALETTE stock object into a device context. Then you can use any of the 16 colors without being concerned with color tables.

The 20 static colors provided by the system palette have several uses. Their most important function is to provide VGA color functionality for any application that does not explicitly use palettes; in such applications, a color that is not derived from a palette is mapped to the 16 standard VGA colors just as it would be on a VGA device driver, so there are no color-table or color-palette concerns.

The Windows window manager is an example of an application that uses the standard default palette. It uses the default palette's 20 static colors in the default logical palette to draw window borders and other standard Windows objects. The static colors also provide a standard set of colors for drawing background windows that have run out of custom colors to choose from and must somehow find colors that match the 20 standard colors. (This situation is described in more detail under the next heading.)

Most computers running Windows have video cards that can generate at least 256 colors. In the rema

inder of this section, for the sake of consistency, I'll take the liberty of pretending that every Windows system has a 256-color display. Remember, though, that not every Windows system uses a 256-color display; some systems can display only 16 screen colors, and other systems can display millions of colors at a time.

CUSTOMIZING THE SYSTEM PALETTE

In computer systems with 256-color displays, an application can place as many as 236 nonstatic colors in the system palette by providing those colors to the Palette

Manager. The application can then generate its screen display using the system palette that it has customized.

To set up a system palette that can be used to display the colors in a particular device-independent bitmap, an application must use the colors in the DIB's color table to set up a logical palette. The application can then pass these colors to the Palette Manager for incorporation into the system palette.

To create a logical palette, an application calls `CreatePalette`. Then it selects the palette into a device context by calling `SelectPalette`. (The `SelectObject` function does not work with palettes.) Then the application calls another Windows API function named `RealizePalette` to transfer the colors in its logical palette to the system palette. Only then can the colors specified by the application be used to create screen displays. Here is the syntax of `CreatePalette`:

```
HPALETTE CreatePalette(const LOGPALETTE* lplgpl);
```

The `lplgpl` argument points to a LOGPALETTE (logical palette) structure that contains information about the colors in the logical palette being created.

The syntax of `SelectPalette` is as follows:

```
HPALETTE SelectPalette(HDC hdc, PALETTE hpal, BOOL fPalBak);
```

In a call to `SelectPalette`, the `hdc` parameter is a handle to the device context into which the logical palette is to be selected, and the `hpal` parameter is a handle to the logical palette. The `fPalBak` parameter specifies whether the palette is a background palette. When a window is associated with a background palette, the setting of the `fPalBak` flag determines whether the window's palette becomes a foreground palette when the window gains the input focus.

The syntax of `RealizePalette` is as follows:

```
UINT RealizePalette(HDC hdc);
```

The `hdc` parameter is the handle of the palette being realized.

`SelectPalette` and `RealizePalette` are usually called in succession:

```
HPALETTE SelectPalette(hDC, hBluePal, FALSE);
UINT RealizePalette(hDC);
```

Figure 11.7 illustrates the process of obtaining a logical palette for a DIB from the Palette Manager.

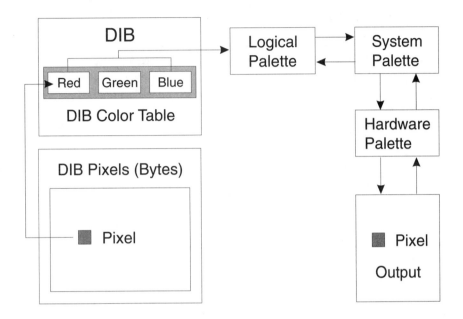

FIGURE 11.7 OBTAINING A LOGICAL PALETTE.

Palette objects follow most of the same rules as other graphics objects. They should be deleted when no longer needed by using DeleteObject, and they must be deselected from all DCs before being deleted (by using SelectPalette to select a different palette into the DC). One notable difference is that an application can select a palette object into more than one DC (belonging to a single device) at a time, but the palette's realization remains constant for all of the DCs.

USING PALETTES IN MULTIPLE WINDOWS

When multiple windows are displayed on the screen, the active, or topmost, window has the highest priority in obtaining the colors it needs for its display from the Palette Manager. If the topmost window does not use all 236 of the nonstatic colors that are available, any colors that it does not need can be claimed by the other windows on the screen. Those other windows are sometimes referred to as background windows.

If the topmost window has laid claim to all 236 of the nonstatic colors in the system palette, none of the windows in the background can set any system palette colors to suit their own requirements. Instead, they must try to come as close as they can to the colors they are designed to use by picking the nearest color they can find from the 236 colors that the topmost window has placed in its logical palette.

When multiple windows request colors from the Palette Manager, it considers each window's request using a priority that is based on the window's Z order. As the requests of various windows are granted, the number of colors available from the system palette decreases. When all 236 colors are used up, any remaining windows must settle for using colors that have already been set by higher-priority windows or, in the worst case, using the 20 static colors that are always available.

How the DIBDEMO Program Uses Palettes

In the DIBDEMO application on the accompanying disk, both `RealizePalette` and `SelectPalette` are called to display the colors in the background DIB's color array. Both procedures are called from a member function named `CCreationView::OnDoRealize`, which is called whenever a window is activated.

Before either `RealizePalette` or `SelectPalette` is called, `OnDoRealize` retrieves a pointer to the background DIB's palette by executing the following statement:

```
m_pBkgPal = pDoc->GetDocPalette();
```

The preceding statement stores a pointer the background DIB's palette in a variable named `pPal`. Then `OnDoRealize` executes the following statement:

```
CClientDC appDC(pAppFrame);
```

This statement constructs an object of an MFC class named `CClientDC`, which is a subclass of `CDC`. A `CClientDC` object is a special kind of DC object that is associated with the client area of a window. It takes care of calling `GetDC` when a window object is constructed and calling `ReleaseDC` when the window is destroyed.

In the preceding statement, a `CClientDC` object named `appDC` is created and associated with a window referred to as `*pAppFrame`. This window is defined earlier in the `OnDoRealize` function as the application's main frame window. Thus, the device context named `appDC` is associated with the application's main frame window.

When `appDC` has been constructed, the following statement is executed. It selects the `pPal` palette—that is, the background DIB's palette—into the application's main frame window. This makes the background DIB's palette the default palette for the DIBDEMO program.

```
m_pBkgOldPal = appDC.SelectPalette(m_pBkgPal,
    ((HWND)wParam) != m_hWnd);
```

MAPPING SYSTEM PALETTE COLORS TO A LOGICAL PALETTE

When a window displayed by an application is on the desktop, the application can map the colors in a logical palette to the system palette by calling `RealizePalette`. Then the colors on the logical palette are displayed.

To map a set of colors to a logical palette without any delay, an application can call `AnimatePalette`. Alternatively, an application can call `SetPaletteEntries`, which sets up a set of colors for a logical palette but does not display them until `RealizePalette` is called.

`AnimatePalette` can be useful when you want an application to display a window and a set of new colors simultaneously. When you want to delay the display of a new set of colors until a particular window opens, call `SetPaletteEntries` to set up your new colors and then call `RealizePalette` when the window associated with those colors becomes active.

CREATING AND USING LOGICAL PALETTES

When an application has created and realized a logical palette that matches a DIB's color table, the application calls `StretchDIBits` to copy the DIB to the screen using the proper colors. When an application calls `StretchDIBits`, Windows performs the requested DIB-copying operation using a process like the one shown in Figure 11.8.

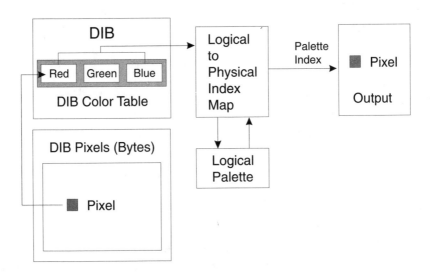

FIGURE 11.8 CALLING THE STRETCHDIBITS FUNCTION.

The `StretchBlt` call shown in Figure 11.8 is a roundabout operation that requires many index lookups and consumes a considerable amount of processing time. Every time an application calls `StretchBlt`, Windows retrieves a color value for each pixel in the DIB and converts that color to an RGB value by looking it up in the DIB's color table. When the system has obtained the RGB value of each pixel, it tries to match that color to a color that is defined in the currently selected logical palette. Each logical palette index value the system finds is then translated to an index into the physical palette index values. The resulting value is then passed to the device driver that handles the current output device so that the pixel that has been looked up can be written to the display video memory.

Every time an application calls `StretchBlt` to copy a DIB to the screen, the system performs this entire operation on *every pixel* in the DIB.

There must be a better way. Fortunately, there is one. It's the procedure shown in Figure 11.9.

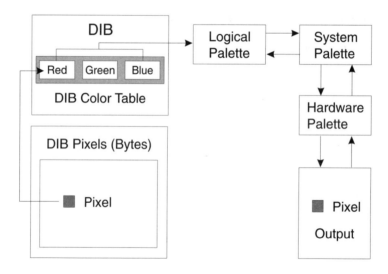

FIGURE 11.9 WRITING DIB PIXEL VALUES DIRECTLY TO VIDEO MEMORY.

STREAMLINING DIB COPYING WITH IDENTITY PALETTES

The operation shown in Figure 11.9 dispenses with the logical-to-physical index translation table shown in Figure 11.8 and lets the system write all the necessary DIB pixel values directly to video memory. The secret formula for this shortcut is simple: All that is required is that the logical and physical palettes that are identical. In other words, what is needed is an identity palette.

An identity palette is a logical palette that contains a set of colors laid out in exactly the same order as the colors in the system palette. By setting up an identity palette, an application can avoid time-consuming index lookups, significantly increasing processing speed.

CREATING AN IDENTITY PALETTE

There are a couple of ways to create an identity palette, but the only one that is guaranteed to work all the time (more or less) is a two-step operation. First, you create a logical palette for the entire color table of the DIB you want to copy, and then you select that logical palette into the screen DC and realize it. Windows then takes your set of colors and maps them or inserts them into the system palette as it sees fit. This process requires a bit of fancy color shuffling, but it's worth it, because in the long run it speeds your application's DIB-copying operations considerably.

To perform the color shuffling that the process depends on, these are the steps to follow:

1. Create a logical palette.

2. Call the Windows API function GetSystemPaletteEntries to grab all 256 system color codes from the system palette.

3. Stuff these values into your logical palette by calling SetPaletteEntries. If this call is successful, your new logical palette exactly matches the system palette when the call returns. But there is now one problem: The colors in the DIB that you're copying are now shuffled around, because the DIB's pixel values no longer index the correct colors in the logical palette.

4. To repair this damage, walk through each color in your DIB's color table; for each one, call GetNearestPaletteColor. This function finds an entry in your new logical palette that matches (or is at least close to) the color in your DIB's color table.

5. Use this information to create a translation table for the DIB pixel values.

6. Next, walk through each pixel in your DIB, looking up the new index value of each pixel in your translation table and writing it back to your DIB. If this operation is successful, your DIB's pixels now map correctly to your logical palette. The only possible problem is that some color information might be lost if the original logical palette does not map well to the system palette, but this outcome is unlikely.

7. The final step is to reshuffle your DIB's color table so that it contains exactly the same RGB values as your new logical palette, arranged in exactly the same order. This final step is not essential unless you want to use the new RGB values in your DIB's header later, and this is not often the case in animation programs. Usually, it's sufficient to wind up with the palette you want. If your DIB never gets saved, you probably don't care whether its color table winds up arranged differently from when you started. But be aware that if you ever to want to save your DIB back to its original file, the colors in its color table will have a different arrangement from the one they had when you first loaded the DIB.

The SPRTDEMO Program

To illustrate how conventional (device-dependent) bitmaps work in a real program, a sample Windows NT application named SPRTDEMO is provided in this chapter's directory on the accompanying disk. SPRTDEMO is an animation program that draws a cartoon-like character on the screen and lets you move the character around by pressing keys on your keyboard. Figure 11.10 shows the SPRTDEMO program's screen display.

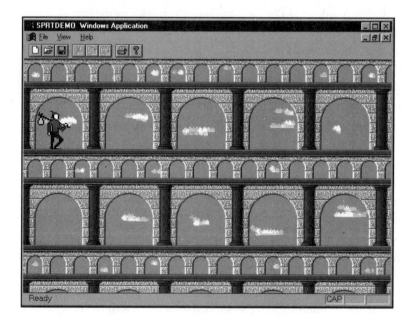

FIGURE 11.10 THE SPRTDEMO SCREEN DISPLAY.

When you start SPRTDEMO and select **New** from the File menu, the program draws a character on the screen as shown in Figure 11.10. You can then move the character to the left, to the right, up, or down, by pressing the arrow keys.

DEVELOPMENT OF THE **SPRTDEMO** PROGRAM

SPRTDEMO is a Visual C++ application based on a framework generated by AppWizard. It implements a view object in **SPRITVW.CPP**, and it implements a document object in **SPRITDOC.CPP**.

SPRTDEMO was originally part of a computer game written for the Windows 3.x environment. The program implements animation by calling the CDC member functions BitBlt and StretchBlt. As you have seen, BitBlt can copy a bitmap from one memory location to another when no resizing is needed. StretchBlt can copy and resize a bitmap simultaneously.

To copy a bitmap through a mask using BitBlt or StretchBlt, you need to perform two operations. First, the mask must be copied to the bitmap's destination. Then the bitmap must be copied to its destination through the mask. The new Windows API function MaskBlt which combines a mask-copying operation and a bitmap-copying operation into a single step. When this book was written, however, this function had not yet been incorporated into Visual C++. It is not used in the SPRTDEMO program.

HOW THE **SPRTDEMO** PROGRAM WORKS

SPRTDEMO uses AppWizard's conventional document-view architecture. The program's view class, CSpriteView, is implemented in **SPRITVW.CPP**; the document class, CSpriteDoc, is implemented in **SPRITDOC.CPP**.

The constructor of CSpriteView initializes two arrays of bitmaps using the C++ new operator. One set of bitmaps shows a figure of a player in an adventure game. The other array is set of black masks that outline the player so that the figure can be displayed properly against a complex background. The bitmaps are stored in arrays so that the program can cycle through the two arrays simultaneously, creating step animation. The program also uses a third bitmap: a full-screen background against which the figure of the character is displayed.

Following is the constructor that creates the three bitmaps used in SPRTDEMO:

```
//////////////////////////////////////////////////////////////////////////
// CSpriteView construction/destruction

CSpriteView::CSpriteView()
{
```

```
    // TODO: add construction code here
    // Create player and player mask bitmaps
    for (int n = 0; n < 5; n++) {
        m_bmRtBoy[n] = new CBitmap;
        ASSERT_VALID(m_bmRtBoy[n]);
    }
    for (n = 0; n < 5; n++) {
        m_bmRtBoyM[n] = new CBitmap;
        ASSERT_VALID(m_bmRtBoyM[n]);
    }

    m_bmRiseBoy = new CBitmap;
    ASSERT_VALID(m_bmRiseBoy);

    m_bmRiseBoyM = new CBitmap;
    ASSERT_VALID(m_bmRiseBoyM);

    // Create a bitmap for the background.
    m_bmMem = new CBitmap;
    ASSERT_VALID(m_bmMem);
}
```

The m_bmRiseBoy bitmap is a figure of a player holding a balloon. The balloon transports the player from one floor of a structure to the next. The bitmaps were created using App Studio. The player bitmap is illustrated in Figure 11.11.

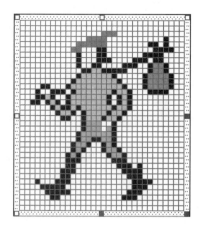

FIGURE 11.11 FIGURE USED IN THE SPRTDEMO PROGRAM.

The second bitmap is a black mask shaped like the figure. Figure 11.12 shows what the App Studio bitmap editor looked like when the mask was being created.

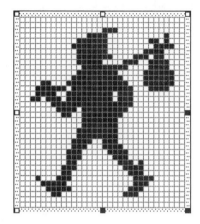

FIGURE 11.12 MASK USED IN THE SPRTDEMO PROGRAM.

The third bitmap, the background, is illustrated in Figure 11.13.

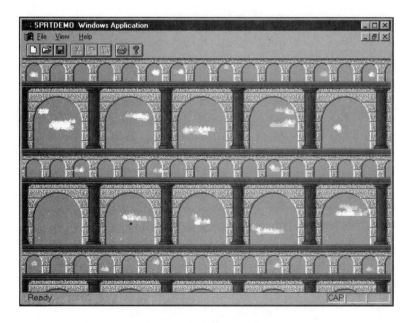

FIGURE 11.13 THE SPRTDEMO SCREEN BACKGROUND.

THE SPRTDEMO BITMAPS

When SPRTDEMO has created the three bitmaps, a function named PrepareAnimation loads them into memory and sets their sizes and screen locations. This is a fragment of the PrepareAnimation function:

```
void CSpriteView::PrepareAnimation(CDC *pDC)
{
    // This is the floor the player starts on.
    m_currentFloor = m_startY;

    // He starts walking to the right.
    m_moveDir = RIGHT;

    // stepCount controls step animation.
    m_stepCount = 3;

    m_fFirstKeyPress = TRUE;

    int retVal = m_bmRtBoy[0]->LoadBitmap(IDB_RTBOY1);
    ASSERT (retVal != 0);
    retVal = m_bmRtBoy[1]->LoadBitmap(IDB_RTBOY2);
    ASSERT (retVal != 0);
    retVal = m_bmRtBoy[2]->LoadBitmap(IDB_RTBOY3);
    ASSERT (retVal != 0);
    retVal = m_bmRtBoy[3]->LoadBitmap(IDB_RTBOY4);
    ASSERT (retVal != 0);
    retVal = m_bmRtBoy[4]->LoadBitmap(IDB_RTBOY5);

    retVal = m_bmRtBoyM[0]->LoadBitmap(IDB_RTBOYM1);
    ASSERT (retVal != 0);

    // ...

    retVal = m_bmRiseBoyM->LoadBitmap(IDB_RTUPBOYM1);
    ASSERT (retVal != 0);

    retVal = m_bmMem->LoadBitmap(IDB_ARCHES);
    ASSERT (retVal != 0);

    // Create a rect the size of the player bitmap.
    m_bmRect.SetRect(0, 0, m_bmWidth, m_bmHeight);
```

```
    // Create a rect the size of the zoomed bitmap.
    m_zoomRect.SetRect(0, 0, m_zoomWidth, m_zoomHeight);

    // Create a background bitmap of the player's size.
    m_bmPlayer.CreateCompatibleBitmap(pDC, m_zoomRect.right,
        m_zoomRect.bottom);

    // Create some device contexts that are
    // compatible with the current device context.
    m_dcPlayer.CreateCompatibleDC(pDC);
    m_dcMask.CreateCompatibleDC(pDC);
    m_dcMem.CreateCompatibleDC(pDC);
    m_dcBackdrop.CreateCompatibleDC(pDC);
    m_dcTemp.CreateCompatibleDC(pDC);

    // Create a screen-size background bitmap.
    m_bmBackdrop.CreateCompatibleBitmap(pDC,
        pDC->GetDeviceCaps(HORZRES),
        pDC->GetDeviceCaps(VERTRES));

    // Select bitmaps into current device context,
    // and save previous bitmaps.
    m_pOldMapMem = m_dcMem.SelectObject(m_bmMem);
    m_dcBackdrop.SelectObject(&m_bmBackdrop);
}
```

In the preceding code fragment, the bitmaps that draw the player and the mask are loaded into memory as bitmaps that measure 32 pixels wide by 32 pixels high—the standard size for an icon. Later in the program, StretchBlt doubles the player's size to 64 by 64 pixels when the figure is drawn on the screen.

In the following code fragment, the OnDraw member function of the CSpriteView class draws the background and the character on the screen. To draw the background, OnDraw calls another CSpriteView member function named DrawBackdrop. To draw the player, OnDraw calls a member function named DrawPlayer:

```
void CSpriteView::OnDraw(CDC* pDC)
{
    CSpriteDoc* pDoc = GetDocument();

    // TODO: add draw code here
```

```
    if (m_needsRedraw) {

        // Paint background DIB to the screen.
        DrawBackdrop(pDC);

        // Copy player bitmap from memory to screen.
        DrawPlayer(pDC);

        // Reset redraw flag.
        m_needsRedraw = FALSE;
    }
}
```

`DrawBackdrop` calls `CDC::BitBlt` to draw its view window's background:

```
// Paint bitmap to screen.
void CSpriteView::DrawBackdrop(CDC* pDC)
{
    int screenWidth = pDC->GetDeviceCaps(HORZRES);
    int screenHeight = pDC->GetDeviceCaps(HORZRES);

    pDC->BitBlt(0, 0, screenWidth, screenHeight, &m_dcMem,
        0, 0, SRCCOPY);
        m_needsRedraw = FALSE;
}
```

Animation in the Example Programs

Animation techniques used in computer graphics fall into two main categories. One variety of animation, called *frame* animation, repeatedly redraws an entire window (or screen) to provide an illusion of movement on the screen. The other kind of animation is called sprite animation. In *sprite* animation, the shape to be animated is enclosed in the smallest rectangle possible, and only that rectangle is redrawn when the character moves.

The most difficult kind of sprite animation to implement is step animation, which creates motion within a bitmap as the bitmap moves across (or up or down) the screen. In SPRTDEMO, a cartoon-like character moves his legs and his arms as he walks across the screen. That's step animation.

Sprite animation is more difficult to implement than frame animation because of the necessity to calculate the boundary rectangles of shapes in real time. But sprite animation often results in smoother and speedier movement, particularly on computers with processors that perform at less than lightning speeds. SPRTDEMO and CREATION use sprite animation to create motion on the screen.

MOVING IN DIFFERENT DIRECTIONS

The SPRTDEMO and CREATION applications use similar techniques to implement animation, although SPRTDEMO is a little fancier. Each program executes a function named MoveLeft when the user presses the left arrow key and executes a function named MoveRight when the user presses the right arrow key. For up and down movement, MoveUp and MoveDown are provided. In SPRTDEMO, a balloon lifts the character from floor to floor when the user presses the up arrow key.

This is the source code of the MoveLeft and MoveRight functions used in SPRTDEMO:

```
void CSpriteView::MoveLeft(CRect clientRect)
{
    // TODO: Add your command handler code here
    CRect oldRect, newRect, tempRect;

    m_moveDir = LEFT;

    // Reducing X to less than 0 doesn't work.
    if (m_startX <= 0) {
        m_startX = 0;
        return;
    }

    oldRect.SetRect(m_startX, m_startY, m_startX + m_zoomWidth,
        m_startY + m_zoomHeight);

    m_startX-;

    newRect.SetRect(m_startX, m_startY, m_startX + m_zoomWidth-2,
        m_startY + m_zoomHeight);

    // Invalidate changed area.
    tempRect.UnionRect(oldRect, newRect);
    m_invalidRect.IntersectRect(tempRect, clientRect);
    InvalidateRect(m_invalidRect, FALSE);

    if (m_fFirstKeyPress == TRUE) {
```

```
        m_needsRedraw = FALSE;
        m_fFirstKeyPress = FALSE;
    }

    // Now draw the player and update the window.
    DrawPlayer(GetDC());
    UpdateWindow();
}

void CSpriteView::MoveRight(CRect clientRect)
{
    // TODO: Add your command handler code here
    CRect oldRect, newRect, tempRect;
    int rightCoord = m_startX + m_zoomWidth;
    int bottomCoord = m_startY + m_zoomHeight;

    m_moveDir = RIGHT;

    // oldRect is the player's current bounds rect.
    oldRect.SetRect(m_startX, m_startY, rightCoord, bottomCoord);

    // Move X coords 1 pixel to the right.
    m_startX++;
    rightCoord++;

    // newRect is the player's bounds rect after moving.
    newRect.SetRect(m_startX, m_startY, rightCoord, bottomCoord);

    // Invalidate the whole changed area (oldRect + newRect).
    tempRect.UnionRect(oldRect, newRect);
    m_invalidRect.IntersectRect(tempRect, clientRect);
    InvalidateRect(m_invalidRect, FALSE);

    // This keeps the action smooth the first time a key is pressed.
    if (m_fFirstKeyPress == TRUE) {
        m_needsRedraw = FALSE;
        m_fFirstKeyPress = FALSE;
    }

    // Now draw the player and update the window.
    DrawPlayer(GetDC());
```

```
    UpdateWindow();
}
```

In the `MoveLeft` and `MoveRight` functions, rectangles surrounding the old and new locations of the animated character are combined into a single rectangle called `m_invalidRect`. The `InvalidateRect` member function is called to invalidate the rectangle named `m_invalidRect`. In Windows programs, invalidating a particular rectangle in a window causes the rectangle to be redrawn the next time the window is updated.

When `InvalidateRect` returns, a drawing sequence named `DrawPlayer` is called to redraw the portion of the screen that needs to be updated. `DrawPlayer` uses the rectangle `m_invalidateRect` to ensure that it redraws only the portion of the screen that contains changes.

To keep the animation flicker-free, `DrawPlayer` performs all drawing operations in memory and then copies the redrawn areas to the screen. That prevents the flickering and flashing that can take place when screen refreshes occur during drawing operations.

When `DrawPlayer` draws a shape, it stencils the shape through a mask that prevents the background from being disturbed. Many graphics programs do that, but SPRTDEMO does it a little differently.

When you want to copy an irregularly shaped bitmap onto a complex background without disturbing the background, there is an easy way and a harder way. The easy way is to draw the bitmap on a black background and stencil it onto the screen through a white-on-black mask. Figure 11.14 shows a bitmap and a mask constructed in that fashion.

FIGURE 11.14 HOW MASKS ARE USED IN THE EXAMPLE PROGRAMS.

To use such a mask, you paint in onto the screen using a logical AND operation (see "Copying Modes"). The white area of the mask paints its area of the screen white, whereas the black background of the mask leaves the rest of the screen background undisturbed.

When you have copied a white mask onto the screen, you can use another AND operation to paint a bitmap with a black background onto the area that has been painted white by the mask. This is a simple procedure, and the results look fine.

The problem with this approach is that you cannot use it to paint a bitmap that has a black border. That's because the black border bleeds into the black background and becomes invisible, as shown in Figure 11.15.

FIGURE 11.15 WHAT TO WATCH OUT FOR IN BITMAP COPYING.

Because the animated figure in SPRTDEMO has a black border, a slightly more complex operation is used to copy the figure to the screen. First, the bitmap is drawn on a white background and not a black one. That prevents the figure's black border from disappearing into a black background. Next, the mask used in the program is black-on-white and not the reverse. As you'll see momentarily, when a bitmap has a white background, its mask should have a white background, too.

To paint this bitmap-mask combination onto the screen, SPRTDEMO uses some fancy tricks involving the inversions of colors. To understand how these tricks work, you must understand the copying modes that are used in bitmap-copying functions.

COPYING MODES

All Windows NT bit-copying functions—such as BitBlt, StretchBlt, MaskBlt, and StretchDIBits—use copying modes that determine how bitmaps are copied from their original locations to their destinations. When you execute a bit-copying function, you must pass it an argument that specifies which copying mode should be used. For example, this `BitBlt` function uses a copying mode named SRCCOPY:

```
m_dcBackdrop.BitBlt(0, 0,
    m_bmRect.right, m_bmRect.bottom, &m_dcMem,
    m_invalidRect.left, m_invalidRect.top, SRCCOPY);
```

The SPRTDEMO program uses the SRCCOPY mode as well as the SRCCOPY, NOT-SRCCOPY, SRCINVERT, and SRCAND copying modes.

SPRTDEMO creates its screen display by executing a member function named `DrawPlayer`. In `DrawPlayer`, several graphics modes are used to draw a background and a figure on the screen:

```
///////////////////////////////////////////////////////
// Function to draw a character
//
void CSpriteView::DrawPlayer(CDC *pDC)
{
    CRect rect, winRect, updateRect, tempRect;
    CBitmap *pOldMapMem;

    //m_stepCount controls the step animation.
    if (m_stepCount == 4)
        m_stepCount = 0;
    else m_stepCount++;

    // Select bitmaps into current device context,
    // and save previous bitmaps.

    switch (m_moveDir) {
        case RIGHT:
        case LEFT: {
            m_pOldMapZ =
m_dcPlayer.SelectObject(m_bmRtBoy[m_stepCount]);
            m_pOldMapMask =
m_dcMask.SelectObject(m_bmRtBoyM[m_stepCount]);
            break;
        }
```

```
    case UP: {
        m_pOldMapZ =
            m_dcPlayer.SelectObject(m_bmRiseBoy);
        m_pOldMapMask =
            m_dcMask.SelectObject(m_bmRiseBoyM);
        break;
    }
    case DOWN: {
        m_pOldMapZ =
m_dcPlayer.SelectObject(m_bmRtBoy[4]);
        m_pOldMapMask =
m_dcMask.SelectObject(m_bmRtBoyM[4]);
        break;
    }
}

// m_bmPlayer is a player-size bitmap defined earlier.
pOldMapMem = m_dcTemp.SelectObject(&m_bmPlayer);

// Set smallest clipping rect. (m_invalidRect is player's
// old bounds rect + player's new bounds rect. It was set
// by the MoveLeft/Right/Up/Down function.)

pDC->IntersectClipRect(&m_invalidRect);

// Copy part of background to m_dcTemp, inverting colors.
m_dcTemp.BitBlt(0, 0,
    m_zoomRect.right, m_zoomRect.bottom, &m_dcMem,
    m_invalidRect.left, m_invalidRect.top,
    NOTSRCCOPY);

// Draw mask to m_dcTemp.
m_dcTemp.StretchBlt(0, 0,
    m_zoomRect.right, m_zoomRect.bottom, &m_dcMask,
    0, 0, m_bmRect.right, m_bmRect.bottom,
    SRCAND);

// Draw player to m_dcTemp and invert destination.
m_dcTemp.StretchBlt(0, 0,
```

```
        m_zoomRect.right, m_zoomRect.bottom, &m_dcPlayer,
        0, 0, m_bmRect.right, m_bmRect.bottom,
        SRCINVERT);

    // Copy changed portion of m_dcTemp to screen.
    pDC->BitBlt(m_invalidRect.left, m_invalidRect.top,
        m_invalidRect.right, m_invalidRect.bottom, &m_dcTemp,
        0, 0, SRCCOPY);

    if (m_fFirstKeyPress == TRUE) {
        m_needsRedraw = FALSE;
        m_fFirstKeyPress = FALSE;
    }

    // Restore m_dcTemp to its previous use.
    m_dcTemp.SelectObject(pOldMapMem);
}
```

These are the copying modes in the preceding code example:

+ SRCCOPY copies a source rectangle directly to a destination rectangle.

+ NOTSRCCOPY copies a bitmap directly into a destination rectangle, inverting the source bitmap's pixels.

+ SRCINVERT combines the colors of the source and destination rectangles using the logical XOR operator. When you copy a colored image to a destination rectangle using the XOR operator, the colors in the image are reversed. That makes the destination rectangle look like a color negative of the original image.

+ SRCAND copies a bitmap to a destination rectangle using the logical AND operator. Black areas of the source bitmap have no effect on the destination rectangle. If a source bitmap has a black background (or a white background that has been inverted to black), that area of the destination bitmap is left undisturbed. If a portion of the destination bitmap has been painted white and if the corresponding area of the source bitmap is colored, the colors in that area are copied directly onto the white area of the destination bitmap.

To see how these copying modes work in SPRTDEMO, examine the preceding code example. The comment lines explain how copying modes are used in each step of the character-drawing process.

The CREATION Program

This chapter's second example program, CREATION, is similar to the SPRTDEMO program described in the previous section. However, there are two major differences between the two applications.

The most obvious difference is that the two programs have different screen displays and use different bitmaps for the backgrounds and sprites. A more important difference, from a programming point of view, is that the programs use different kinds of bitmaps to create their screen displays. SPRTDEMO implements screen animation using traditional device-dependent bitmaps; CREATION uses DIBs to create its screen display.

Figure 11.16 shows the screen display of the CREATION program.

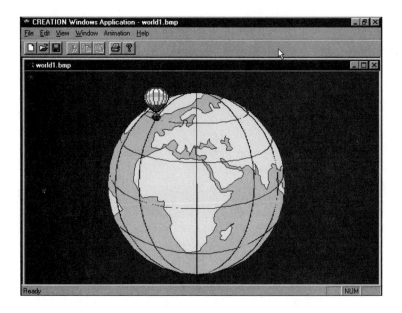

FIGURE 11.16 THE CREATION PROGRAM'S SCREEN DISPLAY.

HOW THE CREATION PROGRAM WORKS

CREATION, like SPRTDEMO, is a Visual C++ application built on a framework generated by AppWizard. CREATION uses AppWizard's conventional document-view architecture. Most of the CREATION application's drawing operations take place in the **CREATVW.CPP** and **CREATDOC.CPP** files. **CREATEVW.CPP** file implements the program's view object, and **CREATDOC.CPP** implements the program's document object.

CREATDOC.CPP contains some of the procedures for loading, initializing, and manipulating DIB files. The rest of the program's DIB-related functions are defined and implemented in **MDIB.H** and **MDIB.CPP**.

LOADING DIBs INTO MEMORY

In a Visual C++ program, you load conventional DDBs into memory by calling `CBitmap::LoadBitmap`. Loading a device-independent bitmap into memory is a bit more complicated; you must first initialize a BITMAPINFO structure and create a file to store the DIB. Then you open the file, compute the size of the file, copy the file into memory by calling `WriteFile`, and close the file.

CREATION loads DIBs into memory by executing three functions in **CREATVW.CPP**. `LoadBkgDIB` loads the program's background bitmap. `LoadImage` loads a sprite into memory, and `LoadMaskDIB` loads a bitmap mask:

```
void CCreationView::LoadBkgDIB(CDC *pDC)
{
    CCreationDoc* pDoc = GetDocument();

    // Copy background DIB from disk.
    BOOL bRetVal = pDoc->LoadBkgDIB(m_pDIBBkg, "res\\world1.bmp");
    ASSERT(bRetVal);
    ASSERT_VALID(m_pDIBBkg);

    // Set background DIB's attributes.
    m_pDIBBkg->SetDIBInfo();

    // Get some of those attributes.
    m_bkgScanLines = m_pDIBBkg->GetNrScanLines();
    m_lpBkgBits = m_pDIBBkg->GetPVBits();
    m_lpBkgBitsInfo = m_pDIBBkg->GetBitsInfo();
    m_bkgDIBWidth = m_pDIBBkg->GetDIBWidth();
    m_bkgDIBHeight = m_pDIBBkg->GetDIBHeight();
}

void CCreationView::LoadImageDIB(CDC *pDC)
{
    CCreationDoc* pDoc = GetDocument();

    // Copy background DIB from disk.
```

```
    BOOL bRetVal = pDoc->LoadImageDIB(m_pDIBImage,
        "res\\balloons.bmp");
    ASSERT(bRetVal);
    ASSERT_VALID(m_pDIBImage);

    // Set background DIB's attributes.
    m_pDIBImage->SetDIBInfo();

    // Get some of those attributes.
    m_imageScanLines = m_pDIBImage->GetNrScanLines();
    m_lpImageBits = m_pDIBImage->GetPVBits();
    m_lpImageBitsInfo = m_pDIBImage->GetBitsInfo();
    m_imageDIBWidth = m_pDIBImage->GetDIBWidth();
    m_imageDIBHeight = m_pDIBImage->GetDIBHeight();

    m_bmWidth = m_imageDIBWidth;
    m_bmHeight = m_imageDIBHeight;
}

void CCreationView::LoadMaskDIB(CDC *pDC)
{
    CCreationDoc* pDoc = GetDocument();

    // Copy background DIB from disk.
    BOOL bRetVal = pDoc->LoadMaskDIB(m_pDIBMask, "res
\\balloon.bmp");
    ASSERT(bRetVal);
    ASSERT_VALID(m_pDIBMask);

    // Set background DIB's attributes.
    m_pDIBMask->SetDIBInfo();

    // Get some of those attributes.
    m_maskScanLines = m_pDIBMask->GetNrScanLines();
    m_lpMaskBits = m_pDIBMask->GetPVBits();
    m_lpMaskBitsInfo = m_pDIBMask->GetBitsInfo();
    m_maskDIBWidth = m_pDIBMask->GetDIBWidth();
    m_maskDIBHeight = m_pDIBMask->GetDIBHeight();
}
```

Each of the three functions shown in the preceding example loads a DIB by calling another function. All three functions called in the example are implemented in **MDIB.CPP**. The three **MDIB.CPP** functions are named `CCreationDoc::LoadBkgDIB`, `CCreationDoc::LoadImageDIB`, and `CCreationDoc::LoadMaskDIB`.

SELECTING A PALETTE

When you use a DIB in a Windows NT program, you must copy its palette to the system palette in order to display the colors stored in the DIB's color array. An application can use only one system palette at a time, so the sprites and the background in CREATION use the same colors for their displays.

When a window displayed by an application is on the desktop, the application can map the colors stored in a logical palette to the system palette by calling `RealizePalette`. The colors on the logical palette are then mapped to the system palette so they can be displayed. Another Win32 function, `SelectPalette`, is used to select a specified logical palette into a specified device context.

In CREATION, both `RealizePalette` and `SelectPalette` are called to display the colors in the background DIB's color array. Both procedures are called from a member function named `CCreationView::OnDoRealize`. The `OnDoRealize` member function is called whenever a window is activated.

Before either `RealizePalette` or `SelectPalette` is called, `OnDoRealize` retrieves a pointer to the background DIB's palette by executing the following statement:

```
m_pBkgPal = pDoc->GetDocPalette();
```

The preceding statement stores a pointer to the background DIB's palette in a variable named `pPal`. Then `OnDoRealize` executes the following statement:

```
CClientDC appDC(pAppFrame);
```

This statement constructs an object of an MFC class named `CClientDC`, which is a subclass of `CDC`. A `CClientDC` object is a special kind of DC object that is associated with the client area of a window. It takes care of calling `GetDC` when a window object is constructed and calling `ReleaseDC` when the window is destroyed.

In the preceding statement, a `CClientDC` object named `appDC` is created and associated with a window referred to as `*pAppFrame`. This window is defined earlier in the `OnDoRealize` function as the CREATION application's main frame window. Thus, `appDC` is associated with the application's main frame window.

When `appDC` has been constructed, the following statement is executed. It selects the pPal palette—that is, the background DIB's palette—into the CREATION application's main frame window. This makes the background DIB's palette the default palette for the CREATION program:

```
m_pBkgOldPal = appDC.SelectPalette(m_pBkgPal,
    ((HWND)wParam) != m_hWnd);
```

FUNCTIONS FOR COPYING AND DISPLAYING DIBs

To display the DIBs that it loads, CREATION executes a `DrawPlayer` member function similar to the function of the same name that is used in SPRTDEMO. The big difference, of course, is that CREATION copies its bitmaps to and from memory, and then displays them, by calling DIB-related functions.

THE STRETCHDIBITS FUNCTION

In each document window that it creates, CREATION draws a background bitmap by calling `StretchDIBits`. Then it uses a mask-copying operation to draw an animated figure over the background bitmap. Finally, it animates the character using an animation sequence similar to the one employed in SPRTDEMO.

This is the format of the `StretchDIBits` function:

```
int StretchDIBits(HDC hDC, int XDest, int YDest,
    int nDestWidth, in nDestHeight, int XSrc, int YSrc,
    int nSrcWidth, int nSrcHeight, CONST VOID *lpBits,
    LPBITMAPINFO lpBitsInfo, UINT iUsage, DWORD dwRop;
```

Parameters expected by the `StretchDIBits` function are as follows:

+ **hdc.** A handle to the device context associated with the destination DIB.
+ **XDest.** The x-coordinate, in logical units, of the upper-left corner of the destination rectangle.
+ **YDest.** The y-coordinate, in logical units, of the upper-left corner of the destination rectangle.
+ **nDestWidth.** The width, in logical units, of the destination rectangle.
+ **nDestHeight.** The height, in logical units, of the destination rectangle.
+ **XSrc.** The x-coordinate, in pixels, of the source DIB's boundary rectangle.

✦ **YSrc.** The y-coordinate, in pixels, of the source DIB's boundary rectangle.

✦ **nSrcWidth.** The width, in pixels, of the source DIB's boundary rectangle.

✦ **nSrcHeight.** The height, in pixels, of the source DIB's boundary rectangle.

✦ **lpBits.** A pointer to the source DIB's bits, which are stored as a byte array.

✦ **lpBitsInfo.** A pointer to the source DIB's BITMAPINFO structure.

✦ **iUsage.** An integer that specifies whether the `bmiColors` member of the DIB's BITMAPINFO structure is provided and, if so, whether `bmiColors` contains explicit RGB values or indices. This field must be one of the following values:

   ✦ **DIB_PAL_COLORS.** The array contains 16-bit indices into the logical palette of the source DC.

   ✦ **DIB_RGB_COLORS.** The color table contains literal RGB values.

   ✦ **DIB_PAL_INDICES.** There is not color table for the bitmap; instead, the DIB itself contains indices into the system palette. In this case, no color translation occurs.

✦ **dwRop.** Specifies how the source pixels, the destination DC's current brush, and the destination pixels are to be combined to form the new image.

In the CREATION program's `DrawPlayer` member function, `StretchDIBits` is called several times. This `StretchDIBits` function moves a sprite into a memory bitmap, reversing the sprite's colors:

```
StretchDIBits(m_dcBackdrop.m_hDC,
    0, 0, m_bigRect.right, m_bigRect.bottom,
    0, 0, m_imageDIBWidth, m_imageDIBHeight,
    m_lpImageBits, m_lpImageBitsInfo, DIB_RGB_COLORS, SRCINVERT);
```

The `DrawPlayer` member function also uses the standard bitmap-copying function `BitBlt`. When a sprite has moved, `BitBlt` copies the changed portion of a memory bitmap to the screen.

You can find the CREATION program's `DrawPlayer` member function in **CREATVW.CPP.** This is the complete function:

```
/////////////////////////////////////////////////////
// Function to draw a character
//
void CCreationView::DrawPlayer(CDC *pDC)
{
```

```
CRect rect, winRect, updateRect, tempRect;
CBitmap *pOldMapMem;

CCreationDoc* pDoc = GetDocument();

// Select bitmaps into current device context,
// and save previous bitmaps.
m_pOldMapZ = m_dcPlayer.SelectObject(m_bmImage);
m_pOldMapMask = m_dcMask.SelectObject(m_bmMask);
m_pOldMapBkg = m_dcBkg.SelectObject(m_bmBackground);

// m_bmBkg is a player-size bitmap defined earlier.
pOldMapMem = m_dcBackdrop.SelectObject(&m_bmBkg);

// Set smallest clipping rect.
pDC->IntersectClipRect(m_invalidRect.left, m_invalidRect.top,
    m_invalidRect.right, m_invalidRect.bottom);

// (1) Copy portion of background to m_dcBackdrop.
SetDIBitsToDevice(m_dcBackdrop.m_hDC,
    0, 0, m_bigRect.right, m_bigRect.bottom, m_invalidRect.left,
    480-(m_invalidRect.top)-m_zoomHeight, 0, m_bkgScanLines,
    m_lpBkgBits, m_lpBkgBitsInfo, DIB_RGB_COLORS);

// (1 1/2) Invert colors in bitmap.
m_dcBackdrop.BitBlt(0, 0, m_bigRect.right,
m_bigRect.bottom,
    NULL, 0, 0, DSTINVERT);

// (2) Draw mask to m_dcBackdrop.
StretchDIBits(m_dcBackdrop.m_hDC,
    0, 0, m_bigRect.right, m_bigRect.bottom,
    0, 0, m_maskDIBWidth, m_maskDIBHeight,
    m_lpMaskBits, m_lpMaskBitsInfo, DIB_RGB_COLORS, SRCAND);

// (3) Draw player to m_dcBackdrop and invert destination.
StretchDIBits(m_dcBackdrop.m_hDC,
    0, 0, m_bigRect.right, m_bigRect.bottom,
    0, 0, m_imageDIBWidth, m_imageDIBHeight,
    m_lpImageBits, m_lpImageBitsInfo, DIB_RGB_COLORS, SRCINVERT);
```

```
    // (4) Copy changed portion of m_dcBackdrop to screen.
    pDC->BitBlt(m_invalidRect.left, m_invalidRect.top,
        m_invalidRect.right, 480-(m_invalidRect.top)
-m_zoomHeight,
        &m_dcBackdrop, 0, 0, SRCCOPY);

    // (4) Copy changed portion of m_dcBackdrop to screen.
    // ::GetDIBits(pDC->m_hDC, (HBITMAP)m_bmBkg.m_hObject, 0,
    //    m_screenHeight, NULL, m_lpBkgBitsInfo, DIB_RGB_COLORS);

    // Restore m_dcBackdrop to its previous use.
    m_dcBackdrop.SelectObject(pOldMapMem);

    // Return old bitmaps to current device contexts.
    m_dcPlayer.SelectObject(m_pOldMapZ);
    m_dcMask.SelectObject(m_pOldMapMask);
    m_dcBkg.SelectObject(m_pOldMapBkg);
}
```

Summary

This completes our exploration of some of the charted and previously uncharted regions of Windows NT. The journey is finished, so there is little more to say. I hope you have learned some things about Windows NT and that you are as interested as I am in learning more. Happy programming!

BIBLIOGRAPHY

Andrews, Mark. *Learn Visual C++ Now*. Redmond, WA: Microsoft Press, 1996.

Andrews, Mark. *Migrating to Windows 95*. New York: AP Professional, 1996.

Andrews, Mark. *Visual C++ Object-Oriented Programming*. Carmel, IN: Sams, 1993.

App Studio User's Guide. Redmond, WA: Microsoft Press, 1993.

Atkinson, Lee, Mark Atkinson, and Ed Mitchell. *Using Microsoft C/C++ 7*. Carmel, IN: Que Corporation, 1992.

Barkakati, Nabajyoti. *Microsoft C/C++ 7 Developer's Guide*. Carmel, IN: Sams, 1992.

Barkakati, Nabajyoti. *Object-Oriented Programming in C++*. Carmel, IN: Sams, 1989.

Booch, Grady. *Object Oriented Design*. Redwood City, CA: Benjamin/Cummings, 1991.

Brockschmidt, Kraig. *Inside OLE*. Redmond, WA: Microsoft Press, 1996

C Language Reference (for Visual C++). Redmond, WA: Microsoft Press, 1993.

C++ Language Reference (for Visual C++). Redmond, WA: Microsoft Press, 1993.

C++ Tutorial (for Visual C++). Redmond, WA: Microsoft Press, 1993.

Christian, Kaare. *The Microsoft Guide to C++ Programming*. Redmond, WA: Microsoft Press, 1992.

Class Library User's Guide (for Visual C++). Redmond, WA: Microsoft Press, 1993.

Custer, Helen. *Inside Windows NT*. Redmond, WA: Microsoft Press, 1992.

Ellis, Margaret A., and Bjarne Stroustrup. *The Annotated C++ Reference Manual.* Reading, MA: Addison-Wesley, 1990.

Faison, Ted. *Borland C++ 3 Object-Oriented Programming.* Carmel, IN: Sams, 1989.

Hansen, Augie. *C Programming: A Complete Guide to Mastering the C Language.* Reading, MA: Addison-Wesley, 1989.

Hansen, Tony L. *The C++ Answer Book.* Reading, MA: Addison-Wesley, 1990.

Hunt, Craig. *TCP/IP Network Administration.* Sebastopol, CA: O'Reilly and Associates, 1992/1993.

Hunter, Bruce H. *Understanding C.* Berkeley: Sybex, 1984.

Kernighan, Brian W., and Dennis M. Ritchie. *The C Programming Language*, Second Edition. Englewood Cliffs, NJ: Prentice-Hall, 1985.

Klein, Mike. *DLLs and Memory Management.* Carmel, IN: Sams, 1992.

Kochmer, Jonathan. *NorthWestNet's Guide to Our World Online*, Fourth Edition. Bellevue, WA: NorthWestNet and Northwest Academic Compu ting Consortium, Inc., 1993.

Kruglinski, David J. *Inside Visual C++.* Redmond, WA: Microsoft Press, 1993.

LaFore, Robert. *Object-Oriented Programming in Microsoft C++.* Corta Madera, CA: Waite Group Press, 1991.

Lippman, Stanley B. *C++ Primer*, Second Edition. Reading, MA: Addison-Wesley, 1992.

Miller, Mark A. *Troubleshooting TCP/IP.* San Mateo, CA: M&T Books, 1992.

Murray, William H. III, and Chris H. Pappas. *Microsoft C/C++ 7: The Complete Reference.* Berkeley: Osborne McGraw-Hill, 1992.

Nemeth, Evi, Garth Snyder, and Scott Seebass. *UNIX System Administration Handbook.* Englewood Cliffs, NJ: PTR Prentice Hall, 1989.

Petzold, Charles. *Programming Windows.* Redmond, WA: Microsoft Press, 1990.

Petzold, Charles. *Programming Windows 3.1.* Redmond, WA: Microsoft Press, 1992.

Petzold, Charles. *Programming Windows 95.* Redmond, WA: Microsoft Press, 1996.

Prata, Stephen. *C++ Primer Plus.* Corta Madera, CA: Waite Group Press, 1991.

Rector, Brent E. *Developing Windows 3.1 Applications* with Microsoft C/C++, Second Edition. Carmel, IN: Sams, 1992.

Richter, Jeffrey. *Advanced Windows*. Redmond, WA: Microsoft Press, 1995.

Schildt, Herbert. *C: The Complete Reference*, Second Edition. Berkeley: Osborne McGraw-Hill, 1987.

Stevens, Al. *Teach Yourself C++*. New York: Management Information Source, Inc., 1991.

Stroustrup, Bjarne. *The C++ Programming Language*, Second Edition. Reading, MA: Addison-Wesley, 1990.

System Guide (for Windows NT). Redmond, WA: Microsoft Press, 1993.

Tondo, Clovis L., and Scott E. Gimpel. *The C Answer Book*. Englewood Cliffs, NJ: Prentice-Hall, 1985.

Visual C++ Class Library Reference. Redmond, WA: Microsoft Press, 1993.

Visual Workbench User's Guide. Redmond, WA: Microsoft Press, 1993.

Wiener, Richard S., and Lewis J. Pinson. *An Introduction to Object-Oriented Programming and C++*. Reading, MA: Addison-Wesley, 1988.

Wiener, Richard S., and Lewis J. Pinson. *The C++ Workbook*. Reading, MA: Addison-Wesley, 1990.

Win32 Programmer's Reference, Vols. 1 through 5. Redmond, WA: Microsoft Press, 1993.

Win32 Tools User's Guides. Redmond, WA: Microsoft Press, 1993.

Winblad, Ann L., Samuel D. Edward, and David R. King. *Object-Oriented Software*. Reading, MA: Addison-Wesley, 1990.

INDEX